DAYS OF RAGE

ALSO BY BRYAN BURROUGH

The Big Rich: The Rise and Fall of the Greatest Texas Oil Fortunes

Public Enemies: America's Greatest Crime Wave and the Birth of the FBI, 1933–34

Barbarians at the Gate: The Fall of RJR Nabisco (with John Helyar)

Dragonfly: NASA and the Crisis Aboard Mir

Vendetta: American Express and the Smearing of Edmond Safra

DAYS OF RAGE

America's Radical Underground,
the FBI, and the Forgotten Age
of Revolutionary Violence

BRYAN BURROUGH

PENGUIN PRESS | NEW YORK | 2015

PENGUIN PRESS
Published by the Penguin Publishing Group
Penguin Random House LLC
375 Hudson Street
New York, New York 10014

USA • Canada • UK • Ireland • Australia
New Zealand • India • South Africa • China

penguin.com
A Penguin Random House Company

First published by Penguin Press, an imprint of Penguin Publishing Group,
a division of Penguin Random House LLC, 2015

ISBN 978-1-59420-429-6

Printed in the United States of America
10 9 8 7 6 5 4 3 2 1

DESIGNED BY LAUREN KOLM

For my mother

There's a group of youngsters cropping up who is getting tired of this brutality against our people. They are going to take some action; it might be misguided; it might be disorganized; it might be unintelligent; but they're going to get a little action. And there are going to be some whites who are going to join in along with them.

—MALCOLM X, 1964

At the end of the sixties or the beginning of the seventies, it seemed like people were going underground left and right. Every other week I was hearing about somebody disappearing.

—JOANNE CHESIMARD, AKA ASSATA SHAKUR, BLACK LIBERATION ARMY

And there's some rumors going 'round, someone's underground . . .

—THE EAGLES, "WITCHY WOMAN," 1972

AUTHOR'S NOTE

Without a doubt, this book is the single most difficult project I have ever attempted. During more than five years of research, I thought of quitting any number of times. When I began work in 2009, I had no idea of the challenges involved, or the complexities of dealing with veterans of the radical left. If you said I was naïve, well, I couldn't argue with you.

Eleven years ago I wrote a book called *Public Enemies*, in which I employed a million or so pages of newly released FBI files to tell the story of the Bureau's pursuit of John Dillinger, Pretty Boy Floyd, and a half dozen other Depression-era criminals. In approaching this book, I assumed I would be able to draw on similar resources to document the rise and fall of the 1970s-era underground groups. Big mistake. FBI files, those the Bureau has made publicly available, are almost useless to a historian. Only a fraction of the paperwork these investigations generated has been issued, and almost all of it is dreck, either highly redacted headquarters summaries or page after page of highly redacted, and highly repetitive, "airtels" and telegrams. One could learn far more about the underground from newspapers.

The existing literature was helpful, but contained gaping holes. Of the ten or so books and films dealing with the Weather Underground, few contain much detailed information on what interested me most: how the group actually operated underground. There are two good books about the Symbionese Liberation Army from the 1970s, but none on the Black Liberation Army, the FALN, or the United Freedom Front. John Castellucci's 1986 book about the Family, *The Big Dance*, is packed with good information but so loosely structured it is often hard to follow.

In the absence of fresh documentation, I was obliged to fall back on the basic skills I learned as a young newspaper reporter many years ago: pounding the pavement, hitting the phones. Veterans of the underground were easy enough to track down. The problem was getting them to talk candidly about decades-old crimes they had rarely if ever spoken of publicly, and which in some cases might still be the subject of law enforcement interest.

During my first year of research, I cold-called any number of aging underground figures. The conversation usually went something like this:

"Hello, my name is Bryan Burrough. You don't know me from Adam, and I don't share your politics. Would you be willing to tell me about that building you bombed in 1972?"

Click.

This became somewhat frustrating. A turning point came when, during the course of people's deflecting my questions, I was directed to their attorneys. The group of radical lawyers who handled underground cases turned out to be surprisingly small; maybe fifteen attorneys, almost all in New York, Chicago, and San Francisco, handled just about every major case. A handful worked on dozens of cases spanning multiple underground groups. With the help of several of these attorneys—people motivated simply by a wish to accurately recapture a piece of little-remembered American history—I was able to begin building bridges to their clients, many of whom remain distrustful of anyone associated with the mainstream media. Some interviews took months to negotiate. Even once a veteran of the underground agreed to speak with me, it sometimes took four or five meetings to begin earning something like the trust that is necessary for someone to share secrets with a complete stranger. I am deeply grateful to all those who did.

CONTENTS

CAST OF CHARACTERS

WEATHER UNDERGROUND, AKA WEATHERMAN, 1969 TO 1977

BERNARDINE DOHRN: beautiful, brainy, first among equals, "la Pasionaria of the Lunatic Left"

JEFF JONES: California-raised "surfer dude," co-leader, Dohrn's onetime lover, principal instigator of 1975–76 "inversion strategy"

BILL AYERS: effusive child of wealth, enthusiastic writer, named to national leadership after the Townhouse bombing

ELEANOR STEIN: New York cell, national leadership, later married Jeff Jones

ROBBIE ROTH: thoughtful Columbia University SDSer, New York cell, named to national leadership after Townhouse

MARK RUDD: hero of 1968 Columbia protests, early Weatherman leader, eventually marginalized

JOHN JACOBS, AKA "JJ": Columbia organizer, Weatherman's intellectual pioneer, principal author of founding Weatherman paper

TERRY ROBBINS: SDS organizer, Bill Ayers's best friend, intense and dedicated, leader of Townhouse cell

CATHY WILKERSON: Townhouse survivor, later West Coast bomb maker

KATHY BOUDIN: Townhouse survivor, longtime Weatherman

HOWARD MACHTINGER: University of Chicago PhD candidate and intellectual, led first West Coast "actions"

"PAUL BRADLEY": pseudonym for San Francisco cadre active in California bombings

"MARVIN DOYLE": pseudonym for Bay Area radical who worked closely with national leadership circa 1971–72

RON FLIEGELMAN: New York cell, explosives expert

RICK AYERS: Bill Ayers's brother, organized West Coast logistics

ANNIE STEIN: Eleanor Stein's mother, political adviser

CLAYTON VAN LYDEGRAF: aging Seattle radical, Weatherman cadre, later led purge of Weather Underground and Prairie Fire Organizing Committee

BLACK LIBERATION ARMY, AKA BLA, 1971 TO 1973

ELDRIDGE CLEAVER: famed radical writer, BLA's intellectual leader

DONALD COX, AKA "D.C.": BLA's military strategist

SEKOU ODINGA, AKA NATHANIEL BURNS: Cleaver's number three in Algiers, most important black militant of underground era

LUMUMBA SHAKUR: Odinga's boyhood friend, BLA adviser

ZAYD SHAKUR: Lumumba's brother, BLA intellectual

RICHARD "DHORUBA" MOORE, AKA DHORUBA BIN-WAHAD: rangy, motor-mouthed street intellectual, instrumental in BLA's formation

JOHN THOMAS: Army veteran, leader of Georgia training camp

THOMAS "BLOOD" McCREARY: Brooklyn soldier

TWYMON MEYERS: trigger-happy soldier, probably most violent revolutionary of the underground era

RONALD CARTER: Army veteran, leader of Cleveland cell, prime suspect in Foster-Laurie murders, January 1972

JOANNE CHESIMARD, AKA ASSATA SHAKUR: last BLA leader

SYMBIONESE LIBERATION ARMY, 1973 TO 1975

DONALD DeFREEZE, AKA CINQUE: escaped California convict, Berkeley radical, founder and first leader of the SLA

MIZMOON SOLTYSIK: DeFreeze's lover and aide-de-camp

BILL AND EMILY HARRIS: strident SLA members

KATHLEEN SOLIAH: SLA supporter turned recruit

PATTY HEARST: California heiress, SLA member

FALN, 1974 TO 1980

OSCAR LÓPEZ: leader, onetime Chicago community organizer

CARLOS TORRES: López's number two

MARIE HAYDEE TORRES: Torres's wife, convicted of 1977 Mobil Oil bombing

GUILLERMO "WILLIE" MORALES: FALN soldier, bomb maker

DYLCIA PAGAN: FALN member, mother of Morales's child

DON WOFFORD AND LOU VIZI: FBI pursuers

SAM MELVILLE JONATHAN JACKSON UNIT, AKA UNITED FREEDOM FRONT, 1976 TO 1984

RAY LUC LEVASSEUR: charismatic leader, noted Maine radical

TOM MANNING: Levasseur's number two man, convicted in 1981 murder of New Jersey State Trooper Philip Lamonaco

PAT GROS LEVASSEUR: mother of Levasseur's three daughters

CAROL MANNING: Tom's wife

JAAN LAAMAN: onetime SDS radical, late recruit

RICHARD WILLIAMS: recruit, convicted in Lamonaco murder

KAZI TOURE: recruit

LEN CROSS: FBI pursuer

MUTULU SHAKUR GROUP, AKA "THE FAMILY," 1977 TO 1981

MUTULU SHAKUR: leader, longtime New York radical, acupuncturist, stepfather of the late rapper Tupac Shakur

SEKOU ODINGA: co-leader, governor on Shakur's engine

TYRONE RISON, AKA "LB": Army veteran, subleader

MARILYN BUCK: leader of white-radical contingent, among most determined white radicals of the underground era

SILVIA BARALDINI: intense Italian-born radical, moved from Prairie Fire Organizing Committee to May 19 Community Organization to Shakur's group

ALSO . . .

SAM MELVILLE AND JANE ALPERT: underground pioneers

GEORGE JACKSON: California convict, would-be underground messiah

PROLOGUE

The woman sitting across from me in a bustling Brooklyn diner is a sixty-eight-year-old grandmother now, freckled and still very attractive. She has warm eyes and short silver hair combed over her ears. She wears a long-sleeved pink blouse. At her side her five-month-old grandson burbles in his stroller. By training she is a math teacher. She has taught almost thirty years in the New York schools. This was what she decided to do when she got out of jail.

Her name is Cathy Wilkerson, and many years ago she was briefly famous. In her twenties she belonged to the Weather Underground, the militant group that famously declared war on the United States in 1970. Its favored weapons were bombs, which it spent six long years detonating in New York, San Francisco, Chicago, Boston, Pittsburgh, and Washington. It was Wilkerson's family townhouse in Greenwich Village that was destroyed in the group's most infamous bombing, on March 6, 1970. The accidental explosion killed three of her closest friends, including her lover. She was one of two survivors who crawled from the rubble and made their way underground.

Years ago Wilkerson wrote a memoir of her radical youth, called *Flying Close to the Sun*. But as several of her peers did in their own books, she left out almost all details of her underground career. There is page after page about being lonely and penniless and adrift, but she has never explained what she actually did underground. There is almost nothing about her clandestine work, about her role in the bombings. This is our sixth meeting, and while she is happy to discuss old friends and old politics, she has sweetly resisted my entreaties to discuss her involvement in what are euphemistically known as the Weather Underground's "political actions."

Another Weatherman alumnus, however, has told me. He is the father of Wilkerson's adult daughter, in fact, and though they rarely speak, he happens to live four blocks away. Even though he perfected the group's bomb design and served for years as its explosives guru, he—unlike Wilkerson—has never been publicly identified. A grandfather with a patchy white beard, he can be seen most mornings walking a tiny white poodle through the streets of his neighborhood, which is called Park Slope.

"So," I say, "I've been told what your role was."

Her eyelids flutter. She reaches down and begins to rock the stroller. "You think you know?" she says.

"Yes," I say. "You were the West Coast bomb maker."

There is a long pause. She glances down at her grandson. He begins to spit up. She reaches down, wipes off his chin, and takes him into her arms, gently sliding a bottle between his lips.

"Look," she finally says. "I felt I had a responsibility to make the design safe after the Townhouse." The bomb design, she means. "I didn't want any more people to die."

And then she begins to talk about that secret life, about the bombs she built and detonated, mostly in the San Francisco area, all those years ago. The story she tells is like many I heard from those who joined Weather and other radical underground groups of the 1970s, who mistakenly believed the country was on the brink of a genuine political revolution, who thought that violence would speed the change. It is elusive and impressionistic, a mixture of pride and embarrassment, marked with memory lapses that may or may not be convenient.

Interviews for this book, many of which took months to negotiate and arrange, played out across the country and beyond, at a Mexican restaurant in Berkeley, a remote farmhouse in Maine, a North Carolina hotel, a series of cafés in Rome, a Senegalese buffet in Harlem, a taco joint in Albuquerque, a tenement beside the Brooklyn Bridge, the homes of retired FBI agents in New Jersey, California, and elsewhere, as well as a prison or two. Like many of those I saw, Wilkerson is angry at some of her old friends and, forty-odd years later, still grappling to make sense of what she did.

"It's all so fantastic to me now," she says as we rise to leave. "It's just so absurd I participated in all this."

"The challenge for me," I say on the sidewalk outside, "is to explain to people today why this all didn't seem as insane then as it does now."

"Yes," she says, stepping into a morning rain. "That's it exactly."

Imagine if this happened today: Hundreds of young Americans—white, black, and Hispanic—disappear from their everyday lives and secretly form urban guerrilla groups. Dedicated to confronting the government and righting society's wrongs, they smuggle bombs into skyscrapers and federal buildings and detonate them from coast to coast. They strike inside the Pentagon, inside the U.S. Capitol, at a courthouse in Boston, at dozens of multinational corporations, at a Wall Street restaurant packed with lunchtime diners. People die. They rob banks, dozens of them, launch raids on National Guard arsenals, and assassinate policemen, in New York, in San Francisco, in Atlanta. There are deadly shoot-outs and daring jailbreaks, illegal government break-ins and a scandal in Washington.

This was a slice of America during the tumultuous 1970s, a decade when self-styled radical "revolutionaries" formed something unique in postcolonial U.S. history: an underground resistance movement. Given little credibility by the press, all but ignored by historians, their bombings and robberies and shoot-outs stretched from Seattle to Miami, from Los Angeles to Maine. And even if the movement's goals were patently unachievable and its members little more than onetime student leftists who clung to utopian dreams of the 1960s, this in no way diminished the intensity of the shadowy conflict that few in America understood at the time and even fewer remember clearly today.

In fact, the most startling thing about the 1970s-era underground is how thoroughly it has been forgotten. "People always ask why I did what I did, and I tell them I was a soldier in a war," recalls a heralded black militant named Sekou Odinga, who remained underground from 1969 until his capture in 1981. "And they always say, 'What war?'"

Call it war or something else, but it was real, and it was deadly. Arrayed against the government were a half-dozen significant underground groups—and many more that yearned to be—which, while notionally independent of one another, often shared members, tactics, and attorneys. Of these, only the Weather Underground, the first and by far the largest, has earned any real analysis. The Symbionese Liberation Army, a ragtag collection of California ex-cons and radicals who pulled off the underground's most infamous action, the kidnapping of newspaper heiress Patricia Hearst in 1974, was widely dismissed as a pack of loonies. Many doubted that the Black Liberation Army, a murderous offspring of the Black Panthers, even existed. A Puerto Rican independence group known as the FALN, the most determined bombers in U.S. history, remains cloaked in secrecy to this day; not one of its members has ever spoken a meaningful word about its operations. The United Freedom Front, a revolutionary cell consisting of three blue-collar couples and their nine children, robbed banks and bombed buildings well into the 1980s. An interracial group of radicals called the Family did much the same, yet remained so obscure that no one even knew it existed until a fateful afternoon in 1981 when an armored-car robbery went badly awry, three people died, and America was reintroduced to a movement it had assumed dead years before.*

This was strange, even at the time. Because radical violence was so deeply

---

*These six organizations are the most significant of the modern underground era in terms of their longevity and the impact of their "political actions." But they were not, by any means, the only radical groups that committed violent acts on U.S. soil during the 1970s and early 1980s. Probably the most important underground group not chronicled in this book is the George Jackson Brigade, which robbed at least seven banks and detonated twenty pipe bombs in the Pacific Northwest between March 1975 and December 1977. There are other groups that committed even greater mayhem but can't easily be defined as underground organizations. One is the band of four Black Muslim men who carried out the so-called Zebra Murders, fourteen execution-style killings of white people in San Francisco during a six-month period in 1973 and 1974. Another was a squad of Croatian nationalists responsible for what at the time was the deadliest terrorist attack in the United States since 1920, a bombing at New York's LaGuardia Airport in 1975 that killed eleven people.

woven into the fabric of 1970s America that many citizens, especially in New York and other hard-hit cities, accepted it as part of daily life. As one New Yorker sniffed to the *New York Post* after an FALN attack in 1977, "Oh, another bombing? Who is it this time?" It's a difficult attitude to comprehend in a post-9/11 world, when even the smallest pipe bomb draws the attention of hundreds of federal agents and journalists.

"People have completely forgotten that in 1972 we had over nineteen hundred domestic bombings in the United States," notes a retired FBI agent, Max Noel. "People don't want to listen to that. They can't believe it. One bombing now and everyone gets excited. In 1972? It was every day. Buildings getting bombed, policemen getting killed. It was commonplace."

There are crucial distinctions, however, between public attitudes toward bombings during the 1970s and those today. In the past twenty-five years terrorist bombs have claimed thousands of American lives, over three thousand on 9/11 alone. Bombings today often mean someone dies. The underground bombings of the 1970s were far more widespread and far less lethal. During an eighteen-month period in 1971 and 1972, the FBI reported more than 2,500 bombings on U.S. soil, nearly 5 a day. Yet less than 1 percent of the 1970s-era bombings led to a fatality; the single deadliest radical-underground attack of the decade killed four people. Most bombings were followed by communiqués denouncing some aspect of the American condition; bombs basically functioned as exploding press releases. The sheer number of attacks led to a grudging public resignation. Unless someone was killed, press accounts rarely carried any expression of outrage. In fact, as hard as it may be to comprehend today, there was a moment during the early 1970s when bombings were viewed by many Americans as a semilegitimate means of protest. In the minds of others, they amounted to little more than a public nuisance.

Consider what happened when an obscure Puerto Rican group, MIRA, detonated bombs in two Bronx theaters in New York on May 1, 1970. Eleven people suffered minor injuries when one device went off at the Dale Theater during a showing of *Cactus Flower*. The second exploded beneath a seat at the cavernous Loew's Paradise while a rapt audience watched *The Liberation of L.B. Jones*; when police ordered everyone to leave, the audience angrily refused, demanding to see the rest of the movie. When the theater was forcibly cleared, an NYPD official said later, the audience "about tore the place apart."[1] Neither the bombings nor the Paradise audience's reaction was deemed especially newsworthy; the incident drew barely six paragraphs in the *New York Times*.

The public, by and large, dismissed the radical underground as a lunatic fringe, and in time that's what it became. But before that day, before so many fell victim to despair or drugs or the FBI, there was a moment when the radical underground seemed to pose a legitimate threat to national security, when its political "actions" merited the front page of the *New York Times* and the cover of *Time* magazine and drew constant attention from the White House, the FBI, and the CIA. To the extreme reaches of the radical left, to those who dared to believe that some sort of second American Revolution was actually imminent, these years constituted a brief shining moment, perhaps its last. To others, the bombings were nothing more than homegrown terrorism; the excesses of the radical left during the 1970s helped nudge America toward the right end of the political spectrum and into the arms of Ronald Reagan and the conservatives. But in the eyes of much of mainstream America, to ordinary working people in Iowa and Nevada and Arkansas who hadn't the time or the inclination to study the communiqués of bomb-throwing Marxists, who wanted only to return to normalcy after long years of disorienting change, it was insanity.

In the end, the untold story of the underground era, stretching from 1970 until the last diehards were captured in 1985, is one of misplaced idealism, naïveté, and stunning arrogance. Depending on one's point of view, its protagonists can be seen as either deluded dreamers or heartless terrorists, though a third possibility might be closer to the truth: young people who fatally misjudged America's political winds and found themselves trapped in an unwinnable struggle they were too proud or stubborn to give up. This book is intended to be a straightforward narrative history of the period and its people. Any writer makes judgments, but I have tried to keep mine to a minimum, especially where politics is concerned.

It is ultimately a tragic tale, defined by one unavoidable irony: that so many idealistic young Americans, passionately committed to creating a better world for themselves and those less fortunate, believed they had to kill people to do it. The story is long and labyrinthine, alternately exciting and sad, and it all begins, in a way, with a tortured couple living in New York's East Village in the summer of 1969. They were like so many in the faltering protest movement at that restive decade's end: long-haired, free-spirited, and mired in gloom. The one thing that set them apart from friends who raised their fists and chanted antiwar slogans in demonstrations of the day was that late one night, after removing a carton of cottage cheese, a quart of yogurt, and some leftover salad from their refrigerator, they replaced it all with a hundred bright red sticks of dynamite.

01

"THE REVOLUTION AIN'T TOMORROW. IT'S NOW. YOU DIG?"

Sam Melville and the Birth of the American Underground

NEW YORK CITY | AUGUST 1969

On a drizzly Friday afternoon they drove north out of the city in a battered station wagon, six more shaggy radicals, a baby, and two dogs, heading toward a moment unlike any they had seen. *Jimi. Janis. The Who. The Dead.* They were like hundreds of thousands of young Americans that season, one part aimless, druggy, and hedonistic, two parts angry, idealistic, and determined to right all the wrongs they saw in 1969 America: racism, repression, police brutality, the war.

Traffic on the New York State Thruway was slow, but a pipeful of hashish and a few beers left everyone feeling fine. Ten miles from their destination, the car sagged into a traffic jam. One couple got out to walk. The girl, who was twenty-two that day, was Jane Alpert, a petite, bookish honors graduate of Swarthmore College with brunette bangs. She wrote for the *Rat Subterranean News*, the kind of East Village radical newspaper that published recipes for Molotov cocktails. Later, friends would describe her as "sweet" and "gentle." As she stepped from the car Alpert lifted a copy of *Rat* to ward off the raindrops.

Beside her trudged her thirty-five-year-old lover, Sam Melville, a rangy, broad-chested activist who wore his thinning hair dangling around his shoulders. Melville was a troubled soul, a brooder with a dash of charisma, a man determined to make his mark. Only Jane and a handful of their friends knew how he intended to do it. Only they knew about the dynamite in the refrigerator.

Slogging through the rain, they didn't reach the Woodstock festival until almost midnight. Ducking into a large tent, Jane curled up beside a stranger's air mattress and managed an hour of sleep. She found Melville the next morning wandering through the movement booths, manned by Yippies and Crazies and Black Panthers and many more. After a long day listening to music, she glimpsed him deep in conversation with one of the Crazies, a thirty-something character named George Demmerle, who could usually be found at New York demonstrations in a crash helmet and purple cape. "That George," Melville said as they left. "He really is crazy. I offered to spell him at the booth, but he said only bona fide Crazies ought to work the official booth."

"That's because he's old," Jane said. "He wants to be a twenty-year-old freak." When Melville dropped his head, Jane realized she had offended him. He and Demmerle were almost the same age.

The echoes of Jimi Hendrix's last solo could still be heard at Woodstock on Monday morning when Jane left the East Village apartment she shared with Melville and walked to work. They had been squabbling all summer and had decided to see other people. That night, though, she canceled a date and returned to the apartment to find him glumly sitting on the bed. "I thought you had a date," he said.

"I changed my mind."

"Why?"

"Because I'd rather be with you."

He said nothing, which was unusual. She lay beside him.

"What's wrong, Sam?" she asked.

It took a moment before he said, "I planted a bomb this afternoon."

The first bombs had already exploded in America, scores of them, and self-styled "revolutionaries" were already as thick as the air that sweltering August night, but the man who really started it all—who became a kind of Patient Zero for the underground groups of the 1970s—was Sam Melville. Until he and his friends began planting bombs around Manhattan in the summer of 1969, protest bombings had been mostly limited to college campuses, typically Molotov cocktails heaved toward ROTC buildings late at night. All but forgotten today, Melville was the first to take antigovernment violence to a new level, building large bombs and using them to attack symbols of American power. While later groups would augment his tactics with bank robbery, kidnapping, and murder, Melville's remained the essential blueprint for almost every radical organization of the next decade.

He was born Samuel Grossman in the Bronx in 1934, making him a decade older than many of his revolutionary peers. In his teens he adopted the surname Melville, after the author of his favorite book, *Moby-Dick*. He had a difficult upbringing; his parents separated before he was five, and he grew up poor in Buffalo. He drifted through his twenties, working as a draftsman. By the time he turned thirty-one, he had married and separated and was teaching plumbing at a trade school, aimless and unsatisfied, searching for a purpose to his life.

He found it during the Columbia University unrest in 1968, when angry students were occupying campus buildings in protest of discriminatory policies and the Vietnam War. Their cause enthralled Melville, who quit his job on an impulse and took one delivering copies of a radical newspaper, the *Guardian*. He began dating Jane after selling her a subscription. Jane had grown up in Forest Hills, Queens, and knew next to nothing about Melville's two specialties, radical politics and sex, both of which she found she liked quite a bit. Under his guidance she became intoxicated by life in "the Movement": the demonstrations, the sit-ins, the meetings, the sense that the world was changing and she was helping make it happen. "This country's about to go through a revolution," Melville told her. "I expect it to happen before the decade is over. And I intend to be a part of it."

Jane threw herself into the brave new world of radical politics with a convert's zeal, taking the job at *Rat Subterranean News*. She and Melville moved in together, renting an apartment on East Eleventh Street. It was there, amid a hazy tableau of marijuana and Movement politics, that she realized

Melville's talk of revolution wasn't abstract. He wasn't satisfied with placards and slogans; he wanted to *do something*, something to bring on the revolution.

It was in the fall of 1968 that Melville began to talk about bombs. New York City, he knew, had a long history of bombings. There was the anarchist bombing on Wall Street in 1920, which killed thirty-eight people, and another that killed two policemen at the World's Fair in 1940. But the bomber who obsessed Melville was one he knew from boyhood: George Metesky, the original Mad Bomber. A disgruntled employee of Consolidated Edison, Metesky planted thirty-three bombs around Manhattan between 1940 and his arrest in 1957. Twenty-two of them exploded—at Grand Central Terminal, at Pennsylvania Station, at Radio City Music Hall—and a dozen or more people were injured. After Columbia Melville began spray-painting buildings with the graffito GEORGE METESKY WAS HERE.

For the moment, bombing was still just an idea. But that winter, as 1968 gave way to 1969, Melville began planning some kind of bombing campaign with his friends. They were all angry. Times were changing, and not for the better. The Movement—the great swelling of young Americans that had thronged the streets in protest over the past three years—was crumbling. Everyone sensed it. A new president, Richard Nixon, was entering the White House, pledging to crack down on student radicals. What that meant had become clear at the Democratic National Convention in August, when Chicago police used truncheons to beat down demonstrators, leaving them bloodied, bowed, and defeated.

Repression: It was all anyone in the Movement was talking about that winter. Many were giving up hope. But others, Melville included, began talking about fighting back, about a genuine revolution, about guns, about bombs, about guerrilla warfare. Jane privately thought it all ridiculous, brave speechifying fueled by too much free time and too many drugs. And in time Melville appeared to drop the subject. It was clear, however, that he wanted to do *something*, and to Jane's amazement, "something" arrived unannounced that February. In fact, there were two of them, "Jean" and "Jacques." Melville took Jane aside and told her they were genuine revolutionaries—Canadian revolutionaries, dedicated to the freedom of their native Quebec. Their real names were Alain Allard and Jean-Pierre Charette, and their terrorist group, Front de libération du Québec, known as the FLQ, was responsible for more than 160 acts of violence in Canada—killing at least eight people—since 1963, including the bombing of the Montreal Stock Exchange just days before. They were on the run.

Melville had not only met the two Canadian terrorists through mutual acquaintances but had agreed to hide them in a friend's apartment. They wanted to get to Cuba. Melville had promised to take care of everything, and for the next few weeks he did. He arranged for a post office box, retrieved their mail, brought them newspapers, even bought their food. In turn he spent hours closeted with the two, quizzing them on the minutiae of revolutionary work: the ins and outs of safe houses, false papers, and, most of all, bombs. Jean and Jacques drew Melville diagrams and showed him how to insert bombs into briefcases. They even tutored him on how to cover his mouth when telephoning in bomb threats.

One night Jane returned to the apartment and found Melville pacing nervously. "They've come up with a plan," he said.

Jane stared.

"They want to hijack a plane to Cuba."

"You're not serious."

They were. He was. Even though every nerve in her body told Jane not to, she agreed to help. She did it, she told herself, out of love. The real reason, though she couldn't admit it for years, was the excitement. She was involved in something bigger than herself. They were changing the world. This was justified. This was important.

Over the next two weeks, everything came together quickly. Melville managed to buy a gun. Jane selected a Miami-bound plane to hijack. On Monday, May 5, they followed the two Canadians to LaGuardia Airport and said goodbye. "How can we ever thank you?" one asked.

"We are all fighting for the same cause," Jane replied.

That night Jane and Melville hunched over a radio until the announcer on WBAI read a news bulletin: "National Airlines flight number ninety-one has been diverted from Miami to Cuba, where it has now landed."

Melville and Jane shouted for joy, hopping like rabbits, they were so excited. "Those little bastards," Melville crowed over and over. "They did it. They did it!"*

After the hijacking, Melville's confidence soared. Finally, after months of talk, he began laying concrete plans for the bombing campaign he envisioned. He started practicing with disguises. Jane was startled one day when, lying in the bathtub, she saw a strange man enter the apartment. He looked like a businessman, clean-shaven, wearing a suit and a fedora. It took a moment before she realized it was Melville. "We can't afford to look like hippies anymore," he explained. "The revolution ain't tomorrow. It's now. You dig?"[1]

Jane saw her lover's bombing plans as just another of his fantasies. Talk of bombing she dismissed as a "silly scheme" intended "to win my attention and boost his self-esteem." Yet Jane's skepticism only seemed to propel Melville forward. One night that June, she found him hunched over a hand-drawn map. That day, he announced, he and a friend had staked out a building site and followed a truck carrying dynamite all the way to the Major Deegan Expressway. Following the truck, he said, would lead to the source of its dynamite.

Jane looked at him balefully. Maybe, she suggested, he should try looking in the Yellow Pages under "explosives." When he did, Melville was startled to find three listings, including one in the Bronx. All were for a company called Explo Industries. Soon he began talking excitedly about plans to rob the Explo warehouse. Jane rolled her eyes. She might have laughed out loud had she known what Melville also didn't: A short drive north, in much of New England, dynamite could be purchased simply by walking into any construction-supplies retailer.

After staking out the warehouse, Melville and two pals made their move on the night of Monday, July 7, 1969. They left at eleven. Jane waited. Midnight came and went. Another hour ticked by. She watched the clock.

At 1:20 a.m., Sam and his pals burst into the apartment, wide smiles on

---

*Allard and Charette remained in Cuba for ten years. Upon their return to Canada in 1979, both were arrested and served jail terms on old bombing charges. A U.S. effort to extradite the pair was denied in 1991.

their faces. They plunked down four boxes on the kitchen floor. The robbery had gone smoothly; once the night watchman saw their gun, he offered no resistance. They left him tied up. Jane gingerly opened the top of one box. Inside was row upon row of red dynamite sticks, each wrapped in paper. The words NITRO-GLYCERINE—HIGHLY FLAMMABLE were printed on each. They took the yogurt and the salad out of the refrigerator and slid the boxes in. Sam was as happy as Jane had ever seen him. Once everyone left, they made love, Alpert wrote later, "the most tender and passionate in a long time."

The dynamite in the couple's refrigerator quickly became the focus of discussion among their dozen or so radical friends, all of whom, like Melville, were eager to put it to use. A few days after the robbery, Melville rented a $60-a-month apartment on East Second Street, where they moved the dynamite. The new flat became his clandestine workshop, where he began experimenting with bomb designs. On Saturday, July 26, the sixteenth anniversary of Fidel Castro's disastrous raid on a Cuban army barracks, he told Jane he was ready to mark the date with their first "action."

Their target would be a United Fruit warehouse on a Hudson River pier in lower Manhattan; United Fruit, best known for its Chiquita bananas, had been a major investor in Cuba. Melville had already built two bombs and slid them into large vinyl pocketbooks. At dusk he and Alpert and a friend strolled down to the Hudson, where the warehouse, with the words UNITED FRUIT emblazoned on one side, lay in darkness. Standing at the end of the dock, they could see no security, no watchmen. The only sound, other than the whiz of cars on the nearby West Side Highway, was the lapping of water below. While the women stood guard, Melville took one of the bombs and disappeared into the gloom. He returned a minute later, took the second bomb, then left again. He hurried back and herded the women away, saying, "Let's go."

They rushed back to their apartment and turned on the radio, eagerly awaiting the news. None came. In the morning Jane pored over the *Times*: nothing. They began to suspect that police had covered up the news. That afternoon they made an anonymous call to WBAI, the radical radio station, and an hour later it finally carried the news. The two bombs, set beside the warehouse, had blown a hole in an outer wall and wrecked a door. Unfortunately, they learned, United Fruit no longer used the facility. It was being used instead by a tugboat company. Melville was crestfallen. "I used up forty sticks of dynamite on that job," he complained. "That's one quarter of what we've got."

Their friends were furious at being left out of the plan. But that wasn't what delayed their new bombing campaign. Alpert came home from work one evening and found Melville in bed with one of her friends. Afterward he wanted to break up. Then he changed his mind. They began to fight, then they agreed to try sleeping with other people. Melville was morose. And then came that rainy weekend they all went up to Woodstock and then sullenly drove back to New York and Alpert came home from a long day at work and Melville confessed he had planted a new bomb without her.

"Where did you plant the bomb?" Alpert asked.

"At the Marine Midland Bank."

The name meant nothing to Alpert. It wasn't a target they had discussed. It stood at 140 Broadway, a few blocks up from Wall Street.

"Why Marine Midland?" Alpert asked.

"No particular reason," Melville said. "I just walked around Wall Street till I found a likely-looking place. It's one of those big new skyscrapers, millions of tons of glass and steel, some fucking phony sculpture in the front. You just look at the building and the people going in and out of it, and you know."

"What time did you set the bomb for?" Alpert asked.

"Eleven o'clock."

Alpert stared at the clock. Barely an hour away.

"Sam, you never even cased that building," she said, worried. "Do you know what the Wall Street area is like at eleven o'clock on a weeknight? People work there until after midnight. Cleaning women. File clerks. Keypunch operators. Did you make a warning call or anything?"

Melville shifted.

Alpert all but dragged him to a pay phone up the street. She made the call, reaching a security guard. She told him about the bomb and pleaded with him to evacuate the building. The guard seemed annoyed.

"I'd like to help you, lady, really, I would," he said. "But I don't leave this post until midnight when I make rounds."

"But the bomb's going to go off at eleven."

"I see your point." The guard sighed. "I'll do what I can."

Back in the apartment, Alpert and Melville sat by the radio, waiting. The news came a few minutes after eleven.

Melville had simply wandered into the building and left the bomb next to an elevator on the eighth floor. That night about fifty people, almost all women, were working on the floor, inputting data into bookkeeping machines. When the bomb went off at 10:45 p.m., the explosion destroyed several walls, blowing an eight-foot hole in the floor and dumping a ton of debris down into the seventh floor, where more people were working. Windows shattered, generating a blizzard of flying glass; several women's dresses were cut to shreds. Sirens echoed through lower Manhattan. Ambulances carted away twenty people who had been injured, none of them seriously.

Alpert was apoplectic—not because of the injuries but because of Melville's motivation. The bombing, she saw, had nothing to do with the war or Nixon or racism. She knew Melville better than anyone, and she knew this was about her. As she wrote years later, "Because I had threatened to abandon him, for even one night, by sleeping with another man, he had taken revenge on a skyscraperful of people."

Afterward they drafted a communiqué, which called the bombing an act of "political sabotage." Jane typed up three copies and sent them to *Rat*, the *Guardian*, and the Liberation News Service. Alpert was actually at *Rat* when the paper's editor, Jeff Shero, slit open the envelope and read it.

"Far fuckin' out!" he yelped.

For their next bombing, a group of their friends pitched in. On September 18, 1969, as President Nixon delivered a speech at the United Nations, two miles north, Alpert and the others gathered around Melville as he assembled a bomb. He used fifteen sticks of dynamite, a blasting cap, and a Westclox alarm clock. When he finished, he lowered the device into a handbag Jane had stolen. Wearing a white A-line dress and kid gloves, she slid the bag's strap over her shoulder, gave the group a salute, and left. She took the bus downtown, cushioning the bag on her lap, and got off at Foley Square, home to the U.S. Courthouse, with its vast, colonnaded façade; the New York County Courthouse; and Alpert's destination: the two-year-old Federal Building, a forty-two-story rectangle of glass and steel. At the elevator bank, Alpert pressed the button for the fortieth floor. Reaching it, she stepped into an empty hallway. She left the bomb in an electrical-equipment closet.

Around 1 a.m. the conspirators gathered on the roof of an apartment house in the East Village. They had trained a telescope on the upper floors of the Federal Building. All the skyscraper's lights remained ablaze. High atop the building, an airplane beacon blinked its orange eye. They waited, taking turns at the telescope. The minutes ticked by like hours. Then, suddenly, a few minutes before two, every light in the Federal Building silently winked out.

"Holy shit," someone breathed.

"An explosion of undetermined origin," the *Times* called it the next morning, by which time Melville had already learned they had bombed not the Army Department, as planned, but an office suite belonging to the Department of Commerce. The blast had blown a six-foot hole in a wall and a twenty-five-by-forty-foot hole in the ceiling, mangling furniture and file cabinets on the floor above. No one had been injured.

A few days later Alpert was walking into the *Rat* offices when she saw police cruisers outside. She stopped at a pay phone and called in. An editor said the cops wanted the Marine Midland communiqué. Alpert killed time in a diner before returning. The cops were gone. But she knew that she and her friends had been sloppy. Too many people were too chatty. Still, she allowed herself to relax when Melville left for a radical gathering in North Dakota.

Melville was still away when some of the others, led by a young militant named Jim Duncan, decided they wanted to bomb something, too.* Duncan targeted the Selective Service induction center on Whitehall Street in lower Manhattan, the building where every man of age in the borough had to

---

*"Jim Duncan" is a pseudonym.

register for the draft. On the night of October 7, Duncan left his bomb in a fifth-floor bathroom. When it detonated, at 11:20 p.m., the explosion wrecked the entire floor, scattering debris throughout the building and blowing out windows. No one was injured. The communiqué, which Duncan wrote himself, was mailed to media outlets across the city. It said the bombing was in support of the North Vietnamese, "legalized marijuana, love, Cuba, legalized abortion and all the American revolutionaries and G.I.'s who are winning the war against the Pentagon [and] Nixon. [S]urrender now." The reaction at *Rat*, and among everyone they knew in the Movement, was joyful.

Afterward, Jane and the others planned their most ambitious attack to date: a triple bombing, aimed squarely at centers of American corporate power. They planned to strike on Monday, November 10, 1969. The day before, Melville returned, having run out of money; once he got some, he said, he was going back to North Dakota. He spent the day talking with his pal George Demmerle of the Crazies, excitedly telling him everything. The two agreed to bomb something together that week. Jane was beside herself. None of them much cared for Demmerle.

Still, they decided to go ahead. Jane typed up the communiqué in advance, mailing it to the newspapers. On Monday they built the bombs. That night they left them at their targets: the RCA Building at Rockefeller Center, the General Motors Building at Fifth Avenue and Fifty-ninth Street, and the headquarters of Chase Manhattan Bank. Everything went smoothly. By midnight everyone had returned to the apartment. Then they phoned in their warnings and waited.

The bombs began detonating at 1:00 a.m. The first exploded on the empty sixteenth floor of the Chase Manhattan building just as police, reacting to the warning call, finished a fruitless search; the blast ripped through an elevator shaft, sending debris cascading all the way to the street. The bomb on the twentieth floor of the RCA Building detonated in a vacant office suite, panicking dozens of guests in the Rainbow Room restaurant, forty-five floors above; men in tuxedos and women in gowns scurried down a freight elevator and stairwells to the street. The office suite was demolished; dozens of windows were blown out. The bomb at the General Motors Building accomplished much the same.

Once again the sound of sirens echoed through the streets of Manhattan. Alpert and the others were thrilled. For the police, however, the bombings represented an escalation they could not ignore. This was simply unprecedented, three bombings in one night; the city had never seen anything like it. The next morning the NYPD's cigar-chomping chief of detectives, Albert Seedman, tromped through the wreckage, shaking his head and muttering under his breath. His men had been investigating the bombings since the first one, at United Fruit, and had made no headway whatsoever. He decided to form a special squad of twenty-five handpicked detectives to find the perpetrators.

Seedman considered calling the FBI, who he suspected knew more than he did; after the Federal Building bombing, the head of the Bureau's New York office, a square-jawed veteran named John Malone, had called to say they were working an informant in the case. That morning, as Seedman was establishing his command center at the RCA Building, Malone called again. "It took a while," Malone said, "but the informant finally gave up our man."

"Who is it?" Seedman asked.

"His name is Sam Melville."

The three explosions ignited a new kind of civic tumult that would become all but commonplace in New York and other cities in the next decade: a rash of bombings followed by a wave of copycat threats, followed by the mass evacuations of skyscraper after skyscraper, leaving thousands of office workers milling about on sidewalks, wondering what had happened. That Tuesday the NYPD was obliged to check out three hundred separate bomb threats. The next day, November 12, the Associated Press counted thirty just between the hours of 8 a.m. and 1 p.m. A dozen buildings had to be emptied, including the Pan Am Building, on Forty-fifth Street, the Columbia Broadcasting building, on Fifty-first Street, and a library in Queens. Afterward the *Times* editorialized that "periodic evacuation of buildings [may become] a new life style for the New York office worker." The columnist Sidney Zion, noting how powerless the city appeared during a string of bombings now entering its fourth month, said New York "was rapidly becoming Scare City."[2]

Even as Melville and his friends rejoiced that Tuesday, teams of undercover FBI and NYPD men began filtering into their neighborhood. The next day Albert Seedman heard from the FBI's John Malone. "Our informant says Melville is ready to do another job tonight," Malone said. "This time they plan to place bombs in U.S. Army trucks parked outside a National Guard armory. The trucks will be driven inside late at night, and the bombs will go off a few hours later."

"Which armory?"

"He didn't say."

There were three: two in Manhattan, one in Queens. "We can cover them all," Malone said. "In fact, we can ask the army to park plenty of trucks outside each armory. He can have his pick."

All that day Malone and Seedman took reports from the surveillance teams. By midafternoon they believed that Melville was working in his workshop on East Second Street. Not until it was too late would anyone realize that he wasn't.

Melville had left the apartment that morning at eight, ducking out to meet his friend Robin Palmer, who had planned a bombing of his own. It was to be a busy day, Melville's last before returning to North Dakota the next morning. He was determined to go out with a bang—literally—with two separate actions: one with Palmer that evening, the other with George Demmerle later that night. Palmer's target, which he had scouted himself, was the Criminal Courts Building, at 100 Centre Street, where a group of Black Panthers, the so-called Panther 21, was on trial for an alleged conspiracy to kill New York policemen. That morning Melville built at least five dynamite bombs. Afterward they took the subway downtown to the courthouse and slid one behind a plumbing-access panel in a fifth-floor men's room. They were careful. No one noticed.

The bomb exploded at 8:35 p.m., demolishing the men's room, leveling a seventy-foot terra-cotta wall, and shattering windows. Pipes burst, spilling a river of water down through the stairwells. Other than those at a night-court trial three floors above, few people were in the building; one woman sitting on a toilet a floor below the explosion was blown fifteen feet through the air but was unhurt. Albert Seedman took the call while at dinner in Midtown. Roaring downtown in his limousine, he toured the wreckage, broken glass crunching beneath his shoes, so angry he could spit. Melville had done this under their very noses. However, they had all three New York armories under surveillance now, and one last chance to stop him before he struck again.

As Seedman simmered, Jane Alpert returned home from work. She found Melville standing in the dark, peering through the window blinds. He put a finger to his lips. "They're back," he murmured.

"You're sure?" she asked.

"Same white car. Same guys."

"Sam, if you know it's the bomb squad, then don't go out. Stay here until they leave."

He gave her a long, lingering hug. "I can't stay," he said. "I promised George I'd meet him."

Then he kissed her once more, picked up his knapsack, slung it over his shoulder, and left. Inside the bag were four ticking bombs.

This time they saw him. An FBI agent atop a neighboring building watched as Melville and George Demmerle emerged onto the roof and scrambled across six adjacent rooftops before sliding out a doorway onto East Third Street. Melville was wearing an olive-drab air force uniform, Demmerle work pants and a denim jacket. Once on the street, they split up.

FBI agents trailed Melville as he trotted down into the subway. Taking the No. 6 train north, he emerged onto the platform at Twenty-third Street. Above, two FBI agents and an NYPD detective named Sandy Tice were waiting in a battered blue Chevrolet. They watched as Melville popped out of the subway entrance and strolled east on Twenty-third. The Chevrolet slowly followed, fifty yards back. At the end of the block, Melville turned left, onto Lexington Avenue. Tice got out and followed on foot.

It was 9:45 p.m. Keeping well back, Tice followed Melville almost all the way to Twenty-sixth Street, when he spotted George Demmerle lingering on the corner at Twenty-fifth, presumably serving as a lookout. Tice stepped to one side, studying the menu outside an Armenian restaurant, as Melville disappeared around the corner onto Twenty-sixth, heading straight toward the armory, where three army trucks were lined up along the curb.

A minute ticked by. Demmerle remained moored in place. Tice meandered back south a block, fearing he would be seen. After another minute or so, Melville reappeared on the corner of Twenty-sixth and Lexington. To Tice's relief, he still had the knapsack slung over his shoulder.

A moment later Demmerle followed Melville back down Twenty-sixth Street. This time Tice ran forward to follow. When he turned left onto Twenty-sixth, he was startled to see the two barely twenty feet in front of him. Ahead, on the south side, loomed the enormous redbrick armory. The block was nearly empty; certain he was about to be spotted, Tice looked for cover. Just then a man in a tight suede suit walking a tiny Pekinese strode by. Thinking fast, Tice winked at the man and asked, "Sir, can you tell me where a man might find a little action around here?"

Ahead, Tice could see Melville squatting down beside one of the trucks, digging for something in his knapsack. Before the man with the Pekinese could answer, Tice spotted his two FBI partners, guns drawn, sprinting toward Melville from the far end of the block.

"Drop it!" one yelled as Melville hefted the knapsack.

Tice broke into a run.

"No! No!" he shouted. "Don't drop it, for Christ's sake!"

Melville froze. The two FBI agents shoved him and Demmerle against one of the trucks as Tice ran up and snatched the canvas bag. He put his ear to it. He heard ticking.

"Where's the bomb squad?" Tice shouted.

The FBI men began searching Melville, who made a face. "Relax," he said. "They're not set to go off until two o'clock."

News coverage of Melville's arrest spawned another wave of bomb threats across the New York area the next day, with more than three hundred that Friday alone. Dozens of buildings had to be evacuated, including the New York Stock Exchange, Lincoln Center, the General Post Office, the Union Carbide Building, both the *New York Times* and the *Daily News* buildings, the *Newsweek* building, the Queens Criminal Court, the U.S. Army Military Ocean Terminal in Brooklyn, the Susan Wagner High School on Staten Island, and three schools in Great Neck, Long Island.

By then police had already arrested Jane, who joined Melville and George Demmerle in jail. All but Melville made bail. Not long after, Demmerle was revealed to be the FBI's informant; he had been working for the Bureau since 1966. Melville and Jane's friends in the Movement, meanwhile, hailed the couple as heroes. As Jane was led out of court, a crowd of supporters raised fists and shouted, "Right on!" which the *Times* identified as "a new left, black revolutionary phrase of support." The applause continued two weeks later during a rally at a Times Square hotel, where 350 supporters listened as Allen Ginsberg read his poetry and the actress Ultra Violet, Andy Warhol's muse, sang.

Six months later Jane and Melville pled guilty to conspiracy charges. Melville was sentenced to thirteen years on a federal complaint and eighteen on state charges. He was sent to the Attica Correctional Facility, outside Buffalo, where he wrote a series of letters that were published as a book, *Letters from Attica*. After the prison erupted in a massive rebellion in September 1971, police characterized Melville as one of the inmate leaders. On September 13, as state troopers stormed the prison, he was killed in Attica's D Yard. State officials claimed he was shot as he prepared to throw a Molotov cocktail. Later, lawyers for the inmates insisted he had been murdered. Even before his death Melville had been an inspiration to many young revolutionaries who dreamed of a war against the U.S. government. He was the first, the trailblazer. In death he became perhaps their greatest martyr.

Jane Alpert, meanwhile, didn't go to prison. Instead, like dozens of other young radicals that spring, she went underground.

02

"NEGROES WITH GUNS"

Black Rage and the Road to Revolution

The United States has a long history of political violence, from its birth in revolutionary battles to a bloody civil war to two centuries of occasional race riots, draft riots, and labor riots. Acts of political terrorism, at least until the past twenty-five years, have been comparatively rare; before the modern era, the most significant was a series of bombings by an anarchist group that climaxed in the September 1920 attack on Wall Street. With the possible exception of the Ku Klux Klan, the United States until 1970 had never spawned any kind of true underground movement committed to terrorist acts.

There are so many myths about the 1970s-era underground. Mention today that an armed resistance movement sprang up in the months after My Lai, the Manson family, and Woodstock, and the most common response is something along the lines of "Oh, wasn't that a bunch of hippies protesting the Vietnam War during the sixties?" This couldn't be more wrong. The radicals of this new underground weren't hippies, they weren't primarily interested in the war, and it wasn't the 1960s. The last years of that decade did see a rise in campus violence, it's true, but the first true protest-bombing campaign, by Sam Melville's group, didn't arrive until mid-1969, and headline bombings didn't become widespread until 1970. And while Melville and his peers certainly embraced the counterculture, they were the furthest thing from hippies, who tended toward hedonism and pacifism. The young radicals who engaged in bombings and the assassination of policemen during the 1970s and early 1980s were, for the most part, deadly serious, hard-core leftists. Members of the Black Liberation Army read Mao as part of their mandatory daily political-education classes.

An even more prevalent myth, however, is that the radical violence that commenced in 1970 was a protest against the Vietnam War. In fact, while members of this new underground were vehemently antiwar, the war itself was seldom their primary focus. "We related to the war in a purely opportunistic way," recalls Howard Machtinger, one of the Weather Underground's early leaders. "We were happy to draw new members who were antiwar. But this was never about the war."

What the underground movement was truly about—what it was always about—was the plight of black Americans. Every single underground group of the 1970s, with the notable exception of the Puerto Rican FALN, was concerned first and foremost with the struggle of blacks against police brutality, racism, and government repression. While late in the decade several groups expanded their worldview to protest events in South Africa and Central America, the black cause remained the core motivation of almost every significant radical who engaged in violent activities during the 1970s. "Helping out the blacks, fighting alongside them, that was the whole kit and caboodle," says Machtinger. "That was all we were about."

"Race comes first, always first," says Elizabeth Fink, a radical attorney in Brooklyn who represented scores of underground figures. "Everything started with the Black Panthers. The whole thrill of being with them. When you heard Huey Newton, you were blown away. The civil rights movement had turned bad, and these people were ready to fight. And yeah, the war. The country was turning into Nazi Germany, that's how we saw it. Do you have the guts to stand up? The underground did. And oh, the glamour of it. The glamour of dealing with the underground. They were my heroes. Stupid me. It was the revolution, baby. We were gonna make a revolution. We were so, so, so deluded."

The underground groups of the 1970s were a product of—a kind of grungy bell-bottomed coda to—the raucous protest marches and demonstrations of the 1960s. If the story of the civil rights and antiwar movements is an inspiring tale of American empowerment and moral conviction, the underground years represent a final dark chapter that can seem easier to ignore. To begin to understand it, one needs to understand the voices of black anger, which began to be noticed during the 1950s. All of it, from the first marches in Alabama and Mississippi all the way to the arrest of the last underground radical in 1985, began with the civil rights movement, a cause led by black Americans. And what was true at its inception remained true through the '60s and into the '70s-era underground: Blacks, for the most part, led, and whites followed. It was black leaders who initiated the first Southern boycotts; black leaders who led the sit-ins and gave the great speeches; black leaders who, when other avenues appeared blocked, first called for violence and open rebellion. At the end of the '60s, it was violent black rhetoric that galvanized the people who went underground.

It started in 1954. By that point American blacks, especially those laboring under Jim Crow in the South, had been subjected to almost a century of oppression, police brutality, discrimination, disenfranchisement, and lynching. They were, by and large, second-class citizens living in poverty, denied access to the best jobs and schools and subjected to intermittent atrocities, from the murder of fourteen-year-old Emmett Till in 1955 to that of the activist Medgar Evers eight years later. While groups like the NAACP had been campaigning for equal rights for decades, the modern civil rights movement gained momentum with 1954's *Brown v. Board of Education*, the landmark Supreme Court decision that overturned school segregation.

A year later came the boycott of public buses in Montgomery, Alabama, a protest that vaulted a minister named Martin Luther King Jr. to national prominence. A group he formed with other ministers, the Southern Christian Leadership Conference, emerged as an umbrella organization for black protests. King's movement gained momentum during the fight to desegregate schools in Little Rock, Arkansas, in 1957, and then burst into international consciousness with a series of "sit-ins" that began in Greensboro, North Carolina, in 1960. A new medium, television, broadcast images of enraged Southern sheriffs dragging away black protesters that mobilized an entire generation of white people, many of them college students, who would come to define the 1960s. Then came the Freedom Riders, Bull Connor's snapping German shepherds in Birmingham, Alabama, the March on Washington, Selma. Along the way "the Movement" was born.

Through it all, King famously counseled a Gandhian policy of nonviolent resistance as the surest way to overcome ingrained Southern racism. From the beginning, however, his hymns of peace were accompanied by a deeper, angrier, little-noticed bass line throbbing ominously in the background of the civil rights symphony. This was the siren song of what many blacks termed "self-defense" but which a generation of wary whites saw simply as a call to violence, to shotgun blasts in the night, to rioting, to black men rampaging through streets of burning white homes and businesses. This music began softly, barely audible, in the late 1950s, then rose in volume through the early 1960s until becoming a full-throated chorus in 1966 and 1967. By 1968 it was a battle song. "Self-defense" became "struggle," then "resistance," then "Black Power," then revolution and guerrilla warfare and death.

In some ways, it was a very old song. Calls for black uprisings date at least to the slave revolts of Nat Turner and Denmark Vesey, and cries for black militancy and separatism surfaced as early as the late 1800s. Modern black militarism dates to the years before World War I, when shadowy groups such as the African Blood Brotherhood and later Marcus Garvey's Universal Negro Improvement Association advocated the formation of paramilitary "self-defense units." Garvey's Universal African Legions were rifle-toting pseudo-soldiers in navy uniforms who marched through Harlem in the 1920s. These were fringe movements at best, barely noticed outside the black community.

The notion of a violent struggle against White America received little currency during the 1950s; King's message was the only one most Americans, black and white alike, were able to hear. But the specter of racial violence was always there, and as the years wore on with little sign of the seismic changes many blacks demanded, the voices of militancy grew louder. Between 1959 and 1972, the torch of "self-defense" was passed between five consecutive black men and their acolytes.

The first, and least remembered, was Robert F. Williams, head of the NAACP chapter in the Ku Klux Klan stronghold of Monroe, North Carolina. A grandson of slaves, Williams spent his early years working in Detroit factories, where he became a labor organizer. Returning home in 1955, he wasted little time confronting Monroe's white power structure, boycotting whites-only lunch counters and demanding in vain that black children be allowed to use the town pool. After watching a Klansman force a black girl to dance at gunpoint, Williams formed the Black Armed Guard, arguing that "armed self-reliance" was necessary in the face of Klan "terrorism." Its members were mostly NAACP men who started carrying guns. "If the 14th Amendment to the United States Constitution cannot be enforced in this social jungle called Dixie at this time, then Negroes must defend themselves, even if it is necessary to resort to violence," he once told reporters.

Williams became an international figure during 1958's infamous "Kissing Case." Two black boys, aged seven and nine, had participated in a schoolyard kissing game in which a white Monroe girl gave one of the boys a peck on the cheek; the boys were arrested for molestation, jailed, beaten, and sent to a reform school. Williams led a defense effort that eventually included Eleanor Roosevelt and, after a British newspaper exposé, demonstrations in Paris, Rome, and Vienna; in Rotterdam the U.S. embassy was stoned. Soon after, the boys were released. Williams, in turn, emerged as a minor celebrity, feted by Northern progressives in Harlem and other black strongholds.

During and after the case, Williams gave newspaper interviews in which he openly advocated black self-defense; if the Klan attacked a black man in Monroe, he swore, there would be retribution. "We must be willing to kill if necessary," he told one reporter. Alarmed, the NAACP suspended him. Williams was unrepentant. Then, in 1961, when Freedom Riders came to the area to register black voters, a white couple drove into an angry black crowd. Williams took the couple into his home, then briefly refused to let them leave, saying it would be unsafe. Afterward, prosecutors charged him with kidnapping. When Williams fled, the FBI issued a warrant charging him with unlawful interstate flight. With the help of radical friends in Harlem, he made his way to Canada and then to Cuba, becoming among the first, but far from the last, U.S. radical to be warmly welcomed by Fidel Castro.

In Cuba Williams became a one-man factory of anti-Americanism. It was there he wrote the book that became his legacy, *Negroes with Guns*, in which he argued that North Carolina authorities began protecting blacks only after they armed themselves. Between 1962 and 1965 Williams churned out a stream of bellicose writings, many in a self-published newspaper, the *Crusader*. Castro even gave him a radio show broadcast into Southern states, called *Radio Free Dixie*. During the Cuban Missile Crisis of 1962, Williams called on black servicemen to engage in armed insurrection. Even at the height of his notoriety, however, he remained a marginal figure, familiar mostly to other radicals and the FBI. He all but disappeared after moving to China in 1965.

The second, and vastly more influential, messenger of black militancy was a charismatic Harlem preacher named Malcolm Little, better known to history as Malcolm X. Unlike Williams and King and most other black leaders seen on American television, Malcolm was a native of cold Northern slums, where blacks faced conditions every bit as daunting as those in the Jim Crow South: poverty, widespread unemployment, poor housing, and rampant police brutality. A black man arrested in Harlem in the 1960s could routinely expect a beating; when policemen killed a black citizen, there was rarely a successful prosecution. It was no accident that when underground groups began forming in 1970 and 1971, their targets were rarely slumlords or army barracks or politicians. They were almost always policemen.

Focusing on these issues, Malcolm X had an exponentially greater influence on blacks than on whites. This was in large part because he never seriously engaged with the Southern civil rights movement (always the primary focus of white interest). He spent much of his career performing in a rhetorical theater that few whites even knew was open.

Malcolm was born in Omaha in 1925, one of eight children. His father, Earl, was a Baptist lay preacher and an ardent member of Marcus Garvey's Universal Negro Improvement Association; from an early age, Earl's sense of black pride and self-reliance was instilled in Malcolm. Legend holds that the

Klan harassed Earl Little for his views and forced the family to flee Omaha; they settled in Lansing, Michigan, in 1928.

As Malcolm later told his story, he was among the better students at his junior high school but became withdrawn after a teacher told him that his idea of becoming a lawyer was not a "realistic goal for a nigger." After eighth grade he moved to a half sister's home in Boston; at seventeen he fled to Harlem, where he became a street hustler, dealing drugs, robbing stores, and working as a pimp. Back in Boston, he began burglarizing the homes of wealthy whites; arrested in 1946, he was sentenced to eight to ten years at the Charlestown State Prison.

Like many blacks who would go underground in the 1970s, Malcolm was radicalized behind bars, poring over nationalist texts recommended by older inmates. It was his brother, Reginald, who drew him into an obscure sect called the Nation of Islam. The Nation had been founded in 1930 by a Detroit clothing salesman named Wallace D. Fard, who preached that blacks had ruled the earth six thousand years ago, until their destruction by a renegade black wizard named Yakub, who then created the white man—the "white devil," in the Nation's mythos; blacks, Fard prophesied, would destroy the white devil in a future apocalypse. Until his disappearance and presumed death in 1934, Fard imbued his disciples with a message of racial pride, economic equality, and personal discipline. Over the next twenty years his protégé, Elijah Muhammad, quietly built the Nation into a small but vocal group of clean-cut, impeccably dressed black separatists, including a paramilitary wing called the Fruit of Islam. Still, by 1952, when Malcolm emerged from prison, Muhammad had only a few hundred followers.

Malcolm changed everything. Six-foot-three, handsome, intense, and bursting with charisma, he immediately became Muhammad's protégé. At a storefront mosque in Detroit, on street corners, and later in Chicago and Boston, Malcolm mesmerized black crowds. His sermons, while ostensibly religious, were ringing anthems of black empowerment, pride, and self-defense, concepts many blacks had never heard aired in public. The Muslims dressed neatly and forbade drugs and alcohol. A mosque typically featured a blackboard Islamic flag with the words FREEDOM, JUSTICE AND EQUALITY beneath, alongside an American flag with the words CHRISTIANITY, SLAVERY,

SUFFERING, AND DEATH. Men and women sat separately. There were typically no hymns, only an occasional soloist singing a Nation song, such as one written by Louis X (later Louis Farrakhan), "A White Man's Heaven Is the Black Man's Hell."[1]

Malcolm's fame grew when he took command of Harlem's 116th Street Mosque No. 7 in 1954. A whirlwind in a camelhair overcoat, he spent hours on stepladders outside the Broadway Bar, the African National Memorial Bookstore, and the Optimal Cigar Store, repeating his personal story of petty crime and drug abuse, outlining the Nation's path toward redemption, prophesying the apocalypse, and denouncing White America as a racist, doomed land. The congressman who ran Harlem, Adam Clayton Powell Jr., recognized his talent and invited him to speak at the landmark Abyssinian Baptist Church. Elijah Muhammad saw it, too, and named Malcolm his personal representative in 1957. Malcolm, in turn, put the Black Muslims on the map, building bridges to black newspapers and black intellectuals such as novelist James Baldwin and the actor Ossie Davis. He began writing a syndicated column called God's Angry Men.

The incident that made Malcolm a Harlem legend occurred in April 1957, when a Black Muslim named Johnson X Hinton interrupted the police beating of a black man and was himself beaten, handcuffed, and taken to the 28th Precinct house. A crowd of two thousand gathered outside the station; a newspaperman summoned Malcolm in hopes he could stop a riot in the making. As a row of sharply dressed members of the Fruit of Islam lined up outside the station, Malcolm was allowed inside to inspect Johnson's wounds; Johnson was badly hurt and was taken to a hospital. With a single whispered word to an aide, Malcolm then dispersed the angry crowd. "That," one police official was overheard to mutter, "is too much power for one man to have."

This and similar incidents drew hundreds of young blacks into the Nation of Islam at a time when "black nationalism," a growing sense of black pride, was taking hold in Harlem, the cultural capital of Black America. The rise of Malcolm and the Nation of Islam, in fact, paralleled the gradual radicalization of many Northern black elites, especially in Harlem. The avenues above 125th Street had long been home to writers and artists inclined to leftist and even communist causes. In the late 1950s, lacking sources of inspiration in the United States, they began looking overseas. Black pride, as well as a developing sense of African heritage, was stoked by the birth of postcolonial African states and their new black leaders, especially Ghana's radical, U.S.-educated Kwame Nkrumah, whose 1958 open-car tour of Harlem drew cheering crowds. The Cuban Revolution, bringing with it Castro's rise to power, along with his outspoken support of the U.S. civil rights movement, was wildly popular in Harlem. Dozens of black intellectuals, from Baldwin to Julian Mayfield, joined the Fair Play for Cuba Committee. Even before his exile, Robert Williams visited Cuba and toured the streets of Havana, a straw hat on his head and a pistol strapped to his hip. The Cuban leader's popularity among blacks soared after his visit to Harlem in September 1960; the first black leader he met was Malcolm, who afterward termed Castro "the only white person I ever liked."

Malcolm, Robert Williams, and the Cuban Revolution "helped create a new generation of black nationalists who studied local organizing, the politics of armed self-defense, and global upheavals with equal fervor," Peniel E. Joseph writes in his history of black militancy, *Waiting 'til the Midnight Hour*, but it was "the 1961 assassination of Congo leader Patrice Lumumba [that] transformed them into radicals." Coming four months after Castro's visit, Lumumba's death at the hands of a white Belgian firing squad prompted unprecedented outrage among New York's new black nationalists. Harlem's *Amsterdam News* termed it an "international lynching" carried out "on the altar of white supremacy." On February 15, 1961, crowds of angry black nationalists stormed the United Nations, igniting melees with guards and days of protests. One group of demonstrators told reporters that Negroes were henceforth to be called "Afro-Americans."

"Who died for the black man?" someone yelled.

"Lumumba!"

"Who died for freedom?"

"Lumumba!"

This was something altogether new in America, the image of furious Northern blacks standing in sharp contrast to their stoic Southern brethren marching behind Martin Luther King. Malcolm rode this wave of discontent to national prominence, earning profiles and interviews in *Life* and the *New York Times* in which he unleashed verbal thunderbolts like a vengeful Zeus. He attacked moderate black leaders as race traitors, excoriating King as "a chump, not a champ," and the baseball great Jackie Robinson as an Uncle Tom. As violence spread in the South—the assassination of Medgar Evers in 1963, fire hoses and snapping dogs in Birmingham—Malcolm's rhetoric grew steadily more violent, climaxing in perhaps his best-known speech, delivered to a group of black leaders in Detroit in November 1963. It was there, drawing the distinction between moderates and militants, that he famously conjured the image of two types of slaves: docile "house Negroes," who cared for their sick white masters, and hardened "field Negroes," who wished them dead. In doing so, he foresaw the only logical conclusion to any campaign for black equality in America: a revolution. A violent revolution. He proclaimed:

> You don't have a peaceful revolution. You don't have a turn-the-other-cheek revolution. There's no such thing as a nonviolent revolution. . . . Revolution is bloody, revolution is hostile, revolution knows no compromise, revolution overturns and destroys everything that gets in its way. And you, sitting around here like a knot on the wall, saying, "I'm going to love these folks no matter how much they hate me." No, you need a revolution. Whoever heard of a revolution where they lock arms . . . singing "We Shall Overcome"? You don't do that in a revolution. You don't do any singing, you're too busy swinging.

Malcolm's image of a bloody revolution galvanized a generation of black militants and set the stage for riots that would erupt in American ghettos for the rest of the decade. But he also sowed the seeds of his own demise. Open talk of black-on-white violence, of course, horrified whites and frightened many blacks. But it also elevated Malcolm to a position as black militancy's most infamous proponent, and this did not sit well with his mentor, Elijah Muhammad, who reserved such influence for himself. Even before the Detroit speech, Muhammad had tried to rein Malcolm in. When a Los

Angeles Muslim named Ronald Stokes was killed by police in 1962, Malcolm called for Black Muslims everywhere to retaliate, invoking the long-foreseen "War of Armageddon." Muhammad called it off, embarrassing Malcolm.

The turning point came three weeks after the Detroit speech, when reporters asked Malcolm what he thought of President Kennedy's assassination nine days earlier. He replied that "chickens coming home to roost never make me sad; they make me glad." This was too much for Muhammad, who had forbidden public criticism of Kennedy; amid widespread shock, he suspended Malcolm for three months. Malcolm spent the time touring the United States with his newest acolyte, the prizefighter Cassius Clay. Afterward, on March 8, 1964, Malcolm announced he was quitting the Nation to form a new group, the Organization of Afro-American Unity.

It was the beginning of the end. Malcolm spent much of the next year overseas, on a pilgrimage to Mecca and a tour of African and European capitals. In his absence, Harlem exploded in ten days of riots after an off-duty police officer killed a fifteen-year-old black boy. Helmeted police fired into crowds of angry blacks, who responded by throwing rocks and burning cars. Black nationalists who led the riots wasted no time placing the violence squarely in the context of Malcolm's new idea of a bloody "revolution." "There is only one thing that can correct the situation," one told a crowd, "and that's guerrilla warfare." All they needed to set New York ablaze, he went on, was "100 skilled revolutionaries who are ready to die." Such comments, however, went all but unnoticed in the white press.

What no one realized was that the first to die would be Malcolm himself. During his travels, tensions with the Nation escalated into death threats. Muhammad himself told Louis Farrakhan that "hypocrites like Malcolm should have their heads cut off"; an issue of the Nation's newspaper, *Muhammad Speaks*, actually carried a cartoon showing Malcolm's severed head bouncing free of his body. The end was all but preordained. On February 21, 1965, just days after Malcolm returned from Europe, he was about to address a nationalist meeting in Harlem when he was rushed by several Black Muslims. They opened fire with pistols and a sawed-off shotgun. He was dead within minutes, his body riven by twenty-one gunshot wounds. Malcolm's death, however, did little to stop his message; if anything, his popularity grew. Thirty thousand people attended a viewing of his body. His posthumous book, *The Autobiography of Malcolm X*, became mandatory reading for every budding black radical.

After Malcolm, the mantle of black militancy was passed to a newcomer on the national scene, a tall, slender twenty-four-year-old named Stokely Carmichael. A composed, natural leader and a gifted orator whose voice carried a hint of his Trinidadian birth, Carmichael emerged in the mid-1960s as a kind of Malcolm of the South. He was so charismatic that friends jokingly called him Stokely Starmichael; at the height of his influence, *Ebony* wrote that he "walks like Sidney Poitier, talks like Harry Belafonte and thinks like the post-Muslim Malcolm X." Carmichael was raised in the Bronx, and in 1964 he graduated from Howard University to become a full-time organizer for an emerging outfit called the Student Nonviolent Coordinating Committee, or SNCC, known as Snick. SNCC was formed in the wake of the 1960 Greensboro sit-ins and, until Carmichael's rise, quietly went about registering black voters in the South's most dangerous corners. From the beginning, SNCC attracted angry, erudite young blacks, including many Northern black nationalists, many of whom had little patience for King's plodding marches and lofty speeches. They wanted action. Now.

Heavily influenced by Malcolm's teachings, Carmichael was further radicalized as a SNCC coordinator during 1964's "Freedom Summer" voter-registration drive in Mississippi; watching blacks being beaten during a riot in Montgomery, Alabama, the following year, he suffered a breakdown followed by an epiphany. "I knew I could never be hit again," he recalled, "without hitting back." Afterward, Carmichael began charting an entirely new course for SNCC. Marches and riots might provide an emotional release, he reasoned, but the surest path to political power was the voting booth. He studied a single Alabama county, Lowndes—known as Bloody Lowndes for the violence directed against black organizers there—and saw that blacks outnumbered whites by a four-to-one margin. Yet only two black voters were registered in the entire county. What if, Carmichael reasoned, they registered enough blacks to elect black people to office?

Lowndes County became an unlikely testing ground for new concepts of black militancy. SNCC formed a political party, the Lowndes County Freedom Organization, and (fatefully) chose as its symbol a coiled panther; the party became known in the press as the Black Panther Party, a name that would, in time, inspire thousands of young blacks across the country. Taking a page from black nationalism, SNCC held classes for first-time voters in African history and literacy, played tapes of Malcolm's speeches, and produced pamphlets explaining the political system and how to cast a vote. "It's very simple," Carmichael told a reporter. "We intend to take over Lowndes County."

They didn't. All seven black candidates for office were defeated, thanks largely to ballot-stuffing tactics widely decried as illegal. It didn't matter. Carmichael and SNCC had set an example of how blacks could earn political power within the system that would inspire a generation of young black leaders. CANDIDATES LOSE, read the headline in SNCC's newsletter, BUT BLACK PANTHER STRONG.

By the summer of 1966, Carmichael and his SNCC followers were growing increasingly militant. Their emulation of Malcolm drove a wedge between Carmichael and moderate black leaders like King and the NAACP's Roy Wilkins. The brewing clash of ideologies came to a head during that summer's major civil rights event, a march from Memphis to Jackson, Mississippi. It had begun on June 5 as a one-man effort by activist James Meredith, the first black man to attend the University of Mississippi; when he was shot and wounded by a white supremacist, Carmichael, King, and other leaders amassed hordes of marchers in Mississippi to finish what he had started.

Tensions between the King and Carmichael camps were evident from the outset. While King wanted another Selma, a moment when whites could join blacks in calling for black voters to register, Carmichael argued successfully that whites should be excluded altogether. For security he brought in the Deacons for Defense, a group of armed Louisiana blacks who followed Robert Williams's philosophy of self-defense. Marching beneath a withering sun,

King overheard a SNCC volunteer say, "I'm not for that nonviolence stuff anymore. If one of those damn white Mississippi crackers touches me, I'm gonna knock the hell out of him." Each night King and Carmichael delivered speeches around their campfires. "I'm not going to beg the white man for anything I deserve," Carmichael said at one. "I'm gonna take it." When King's people attempted to sing "We Shall Overcome," Carmichael's troops sang a new version, "We Shall Overrun."

The moment that changed everything, when the civil rights movement began to morph into something new and frightening to many Americans, occurred on June 16, 1966, in the town of Greenwood. After he was arrested for pitching a tent at the local high school, Carmichael stormed out of the jail and marched to Broad Street Park, where a crowd waited. He leaped atop a tractor-trailer and shot a fist into the air. "This is the twenty-seventh time that I've been arrested," he announced. "And I ain't going to jail no more. The only way we gonna stop them white men from whuppin' us is to take over. We been saying freedom for six years and we ain't got nothin'. What we gonna start sayin' now is Black Power!"

"Black Power!" the crowd roared.

Another activist, Willie Ricks, jumped atop the trailer and joined Carmichael. "What do you want?" Ricks hollered.

"Black Power!"

"What do we want?"

"Black Power!"

Black Power. For the first time the rising tide of black anger had not only a new face, in Stokely Carmichael, but a name: Black Power. Carmichael's speech electrified the nation. The NAACP's Roy Wilkins called the term "the father of hatred and the mother of violence." In a speech the very next night in Greenwood, King himself told his audience, "Some people are telling us to be like our oppressor, who has a history of using Molotov cocktails, who has a history of dropping the atomic bomb, who has a history of lynching Negroes. Now people are telling me to stoop down to that level. I'm sick and tired of violence." But it was too late. The movement of white Freedom Riders and speeches by Dr. King was ending.

In its place a new movement was taking shape, but exactly what it would look like, no one could say. Carmichael himself, in a television appearance on *Face the Nation* and in later speeches, struggled to define Black Power. To him, it appeared to mean a grasp for economic and political power by a movement run by blacks—and only blacks. Yet his use of incendiary language—"when you talk about Black Power, you talk about bringing this nation to its knees"— only emboldened those whose vision of "power" meant burning, rioting, and worse. White America certainly had no difficulty defining Black Power. In a jarring juxtaposition, a *Life* cover that summer featured a tearful Elizabeth Taylor—in an unrelated story—beneath the headline PLOT TO GET WHITEY: RED-HOT YOUNG NEGROES PLAN A GHETTO WAR. The story, focusing on a fringe militant group inspired by Robert Williams, the Revolutionary Action Movement, known as RAM, noted: "In secret recesses of any ghetto in the U.S. there are dozens and hundreds of black men working resolutely toward an Armageddon in which Whitey is to be either destroyed or forced to his knees."

This, at least, was a conservative white interpretation of the black riots that had begun convulsing U.S. cities in 1964. Los Angeles's Watts neighborhood had burned in 1965, followed in 1966 by riots in twenty cities, including San Francisco, Oakland, Cleveland, and Omaha. The idea that these riots represented something other than the spontaneous frustrations of impoverished urban blacks—that these could be the first shots of an armed black revolution—came into sharp focus in 1967. The catalyst was a pair of nasty summer riots in Newark and Detroit, in which crowds of enraged blacks ransacked entire city blocks and engaged in street battles with police and hundreds of National Guardsmen. In the flames of Newark, the activist Tom Hayden, like many others in the Movement, saw a black rebellion. "The actions of white America are showing black people, especially the young, that they must prepare to fight back," he wrote. "The conditions slowly are being created for an American form of guerrilla warfare based in the slums. The riot represents a sign of this fundamental change."

No one could prove that black riots were a product of Black Power sloganeering, but they certainly pushed violent rhetoric toward new extremes. When Carmichael, seeking release from his administrative responsibilities, resigned the chairmanship of SNCC in May 1967 to embark on a speaking tour of Europe and Africa, he was replaced as Black Power's national spokesman by his successor, a fiery twenty-three-year-old militant named H. Rap Brown. While white radicals like Hayden swapped position papers as Detroit and Newark burned, Brown not only foresaw the spread of violence; he demanded it. During a July riot in the town of Cambridge on Maryland's Eastern Shore, he mounted the hood of a car and, in a rambling forty-five-minute speech, used the most explicit language yet in calling for the overthrow of White America.

"This ain't no riot, brother!" Brown declared. "This is a rebellion, and we got 400 years of reasons to tear this town apart! You don't have to be a big group to do it, brothers. In a town this size, three men can burn it down. That's what they call guerrilla warfare!" Brown's remarks, scribbled down by a *New York Times* reporter, went beyond calls for burning "the white man's" stores. "Don't love him to death! Shoot him to death!" Brown told the wildly cheering crowd. "You better get yourself some guns! . . . I know who my enemy is, and I know how to kill him. . . . When I get mad, I'm going out and look for a honky and I'm going to take out 400 years' worth of dues on him."

The incident thrust Rap Brown into the national spotlight. All that summer, in speeches from New Jersey to Texas, he escalated his calls for blacks "to wage guerrilla war on the honky white man," as he put it to an audience in Jersey City. "Violence is necessary; it is as American as cherry pie," he told a boisterous crowd outside a Washington, D.C., church on July 27. "Black people have been looting. I say there should be more shooting than looting, so if you loot, loot a gun store." In a speech in Queens, New York, on August 6, Brown called the Detroit and Newark riots "a dress rehearsal for revolution" and warned President Lyndon Johnson—whom he termed "the greatest outlaw in history"—that "if you play Nazis with us, we ain't gonna play Jews."

This kind of talk, by the leader of a nationally recognized group like SNCC, was unprecedented, a step beyond anything Carmichael or even Malcolm had dared put into words. It provoked widespread denunciations, congressional investigations, and something approaching horror among black leaders as well as white. For the moment, however, White America could do little to halt the spread of Black Power. As Rap Brown whipped black crowds into a frenzy, Stokely Carmichael took the angry word farther afield, introducing Black Power to adoring audiences in Copenhagen, London, Paris, several African capitals, and, significantly, Havana. As he had with Robert Williams, and would do to scores of white and black radicals in the years to come, Fidel Castro greeted Carmichael with open arms. Carmichael, in turn, met with guerrilla leaders from across the Third World and, placing Black Power's struggle in an international context, pledged solidarity with revolutionary movements from Uruguay to South Africa. When he returned to New York's Kennedy Airport on December 11, he received a hero's welcome. A crowd raised clenched fists and chanted, "Ungawa! Black Power!"

By then, however, Carmichael's power, if not his visibility, was waning. Riven by internal disputes, SNCC was crumbling. The Movement was surging beyond civil rights toward something darker and more confrontational. Yet still no one had answered the basic question: What was Black Power? What did it mean on the streets? An answer was on the way, it turned out, and it came clad in sleek black leather jackets, black berets, and cocked shotguns. Within days of his return from abroad, Carmichael met in Washington with members of a new group who would translate the bold words of Black Power into organization and action, transforming the nascent revolutionary movement and setting the stage for the underground groups to come. They called themselves Black Panthers.

Stokely Carmichael's work in Lowndes County had actually spawned a dozen or more tiny Black Power groups who called themselves Black Panthers, in New York, St. Louis, San Francisco, and other Northern cities. But only one of these would become *the* Black Panthers. This was the one that formed around a pair of Oakland college students, Huey Newton and Bobby Seale, who founded their Black Panther Party for Self-Defense four months after Carmichael's Greenwood speech, in October 1966. Like many they would attract in 1967 and 1968, Newton and Seale were working-class Southern transplants: The seventh child of a minister and a housewife, Newton had come from Louisiana as a boy, and Seale had come from Dallas. Newton—silkily handsome, thin-skinned, intellectual, a tortured soul—was the thinker, the visionary. Seale, six years older, served as the governor on Newton's fiery engine.

They became friends at Oakland's Merritt College, where Newton paid his tuition in part by burglarizing homes. Seale, following a dishonorable discharge from the air force, had joined the Robert Williams–inspired Revolutionary Action Movement; he met Newton at Merritt's Afro-American Association. Both were smitten by the entire canon of revolutionary literature circa 1966, especially *Negroes with Guns*, Frantz Fanon's *The Wretched of the Earth*, and anything written by Che Guevara. They read everything Mao wrote. But their idol was Malcolm, whose every word they treated as scripture; Newton later called the Panthers "a living testament to [Malcolm's] life work." As the thrill of Black Power swept black colleges and ghettos in the fall of 1966, the two decided to form a local group to protest police brutality and mount armed patrols to monitor police in black neighborhoods, as a group in Watts was doing. They pitched the idea to Merritt's Soul Student Advisory Council, which rejected it as impractical. When Seale took it to his RAM friends, they were even more emphatic: They called him suicidal.

And so, that fall, Newton and Seale sat down in the offices of the North Oakland Service Center and, engulfed by books and pamphlets issued by RAM, the Nation of Islam, and a half-dozen other militant groups, devised a program of their own. Newton dictated; Seale transcribed. The result was the Panthers' famous "ten-point program." Some of these points were practical, some not. They demanded full employment, good housing and education, an end to police brutality, and "freedom," but also the exemption of blacks from military service and the release of all blacks in every jail and prison. Before they had a single recruit, Newton named himself the party's leader—its "minister of defense"—while Seale became the chairman, the No. 2.

Few protest groups in U.S. history have risen to national prominence as quickly as the Panthers: They went from an idea in Huey Newton's head to the front pages of major newspapers in a scant seven months. Part of this was luck, part the enormous appeal to beleaguered urban blacks of the Panthers' message to police: Kill a black man, they warned, and retribution will follow. But the crucial factor in the Panthers' meteoric rise was Newton's genius for media and street theatrics, as demonstrated from their first confrontations with authority to the costumes they donned, black leather jackets, powder-blue shirts and turtlenecks, and especially the black berets they wore in honor of Che Guevara. Unlike other black-militant groups springing up that year, the Panthers not only sounded badass; they looked it.

In its first hundred days, the party consisted only of Newton, Seale, and a dozen or so of their friends. With little fanfare, they secured their first guns, learned how to use and clean them, opened a storefront office at Fifty-sixth and Grove in Oakland, and began their patrols, cruising the streets until they found a black citizen being questioned by police, typically at a traffic stop. The Panthers would step from their car, guns drawn, and remind the citizen of his rights; when a shaken patrolman asked what the hell they were doing, Newton, who had taken law school classes, told him of their right to bear arms. The Panthers generated curiosity and then, after a tense confrontation outside their office in early February 1967, respect.

An Oakland policeman stopped Newton's car; Seale and others were with him. At first Newton politely showed his driver's license and answered the officer's questions; he had his M1 rifle in clear view, Seale his 9mm. In short order three more patrol cars arrived. A crowd began to form. Up and down the street, people poked their heads from apartment windows. When an officer asked to see the guns, Newton refused. "Get away from the car," Newton said. "We don't want you around the car, and that's all there is to it."

"Who in the hell do you think you are?" the officer demanded.

"Who in the hell do you think *you* are," Newton replied.

At that point, Newton emerged from the car and loudly chambered a round in his rifle. When police tried to shoo away the growing crowd, Newton shouted for everyone to stay put, that they were within their rights to observe what was happening on a public street.

"What are you going to do with that gun?" an officer asked.

"What are you going to do with *your* gun?" Newton replied. "Because if you shoot at me or if you try to take this gun, I'm going to shoot back at you, swine."

The byplay continued like this for several long minutes. Each time Newton challenged the police, onlookers would clap and yell, "You know where it's at" or "Dig it!" Newton, it was clear, was acting out the fantasy of every black youth on the street. And, amazingly, he got away with it. The police retired without making any arrests.

Within days, word of these brazen new Panthers spread from Oakland across the Bay Area. The turning point came on February 21, 1967. Another of the new Panther groups, this one based in San Francisco, had invited Malcolm's widow, Betty Shabazz, to announce the formation of a Bay Area chapter of Malcolm's OAAU on the anniversary of his death; because the San Francisco Panthers disdained weaponry, they invited the Oakland Panthers to provide security. Newton, Seale, and their new recruits, all armed, escorted Shabazz from the airport to offices of the radical magazine *Ramparts*, where she gave an interview. They emerged afterward into a phalanx of newspapermen, television cameras—and police.

Shabazz had asked that her picture not be taken. When one photographer refused to lower his camera, Newton punched him. Several policemen raised their guns. When a few Panthers turned their back to watch Shabazz emerge from the building, Newton snapped, "Don't turn your back on these backshooting motherfuckers!" He chambered a round into his shotgun. A crowd formed. Both *Ramparts* editors and policemen raised their hands and told everyone to "cool it," but when one officer refused, Newton barked, "Don't point that gun at me!" When the officer still refused, he shouted, "Okay, you big fat racist pig, draw your gun! Draw it, you cowardly dog! I'm waiting." The officer lowered his weapon, defusing the situation, but the incident was caught on television cameras and made a powerful impact when it aired.

This was something entirely new to California and soon to the rest of the country: strong, proud black men with guns facing down startled white policemen. This, it appeared, was what Black Power would mean in the streets. Word of Huey Newton and these fearless new Black Panthers spread like a windswept fog. In the next few weeks the party attracted hundreds of new recruits, some of them gang members and ex-convicts; Newton made clear that the Panthers wanted the toughest, most badass street fighters he could find, and he got them.

None were more important than a tall, languid ex-con who studied Newton's bit of theater on the sidewalk that day outside the *Ramparts* office, where he worked. His name was Eldridge Cleaver, and his destiny would be to become Huey Newton's single most valuable partner and, later, his worst nightmare. Cleaver's legacy would be the destruction of the Black Panther

Party, but he was even more pivotal to what came after, to the underground movement of the 1970s. He became Black Power's fourth great voice, the oratorical bridge between open defiance of American authority and urban guerrilla warfare. Not only would he emerge as the guiding force behind the Black Liberation Army, but, having forged alliances between black convicts and white Bay Area radicals, he created the intellectual framework for what became the Symbionese Liberation Army.

There was no black voice, before or since, quite like Cleaver's. Born in rural Arkansas in 1935, he moved with his family to Phoenix and then to Watts, where as a teenager he fell into a life of drugs and petty theft. He spent much of the 1950s shuttling between reform schools and California prisons, eventually, in 1957, graduating to rape. Years later, in a series of essays that paved the way for the white-radical deification of hardened black prison inmates, he described his rape of white women as his first revolutionary act.

He wrote:

> To refine my technique, I started out by practicing on black girls in the ghetto—in the black ghetto where dark and vicious deeds appear not as aberrations or deviations from the norm, but as part of the sufficiency of the Evil of the day—and when I considered myself smooth enough, I crossed the tracks and sought out white prey. I did this consciously, deliberately, willfully, methodically. . . . Rape was an insurrectionary act. It delighted me that I was defying and trampling upon the white man's law, upon his system of values, and that I was defiling his women—and this point, I believe, was the most satisfying to me because I was very resentful over the historical fact of how the white man has used the black woman. I felt I was getting revenge.

Sentenced to prison for rape, first at San Quentin and later at Folsom, Cleaver (like Malcolm) read voraciously, joined the Nation of Islam, and became a leader in the state's burgeoning prison movement, pushing for books and classes in African history. In 1965 he wrote a radical Bay Area attorney named Beverly Axelrod, who took up his case. She gave some of Cleaver's letters to editors at *Ramparts*, who enjoyed them so much that they promised to hire him, as they did, when Axelrod managed to secure Cleaver's release, in December 1966. Cleaver, who became Axelrod's lover, said years later that he had been romantically "gaming" her in a cynical bid to gain his freedom.

At *Ramparts*, Cleaver became an instant celebrity, by far the most prominent black radical in the Bay Area. Angry, sometimes funny, and frequently sexual, his letters and articles portrayed Cleaver as a kind of cross between Malcolm and Barry White, an angry, charismatic lover man with his own revolutionary spin on hoary black stereotypes. Cleaver viewed blacks as sexual supermen, envied by whites and too often rejected by uppity black women. And, like Huey Newton, he argued that the most genuine "revolutionaries" were those who were most oppressed: black prison inmates and gangbangers—an idea that appealed strongly to white radicals yearning for a taste of black authenticity. Unlike Stokely Carmichael, Cleaver embraced white radicals, who adored him. They flocked to Black House, a kind of Black Power salon Cleaver co-founded, where he held court with every Movement figure who visited San Francisco. Cleaver's rise would be capped in 1968, when his letters and *Ramparts* articles were packaged into a memoir, *Soul on Ice*, an international bestseller that sold more than two million copies in just two years. Critics hailed Cleaver as a powerful new literary talent, a symbol of black political and sexual repression. The *New York Times* named *Soul on Ice* one of the ten best books of 1968.

After the confrontation outside *Ramparts*, Cleaver signed on as the Panthers' "information minister," editor of the party's new weekly newspaper, the *Black Panther*, and—in the public's mind, at least—Newton's intellectual equal. But while the Newton-Cleaver marriage gave the Panthers instant legitimacy in radical circles, it introduced an ideological rift that would eventually split the party. Newton and Seale were using "armed self-defense" as a recruiting tool, a way to lure members to man the education, welfare, and free-breakfast programs the Panthers were putting into place; for all their tough talk, they had no intention of actually hunting policemen. Cleaver did. He wanted the bloody fight Malcolm and Rap Brown foresaw: a genuine revolution, Vietnam-style guerrilla warfare in America. Many found this hard to take seriously, but Cleaver was serious. Once, when asked what he meant when he talked of an army, Cleaver responded, "A black liberation army! An army of angry niggas!"[2]

With Cleaver on board, the Panthers' profile rose quickly. After a sheriff's deputy killed an unarmed car thief named Denzil Dowell that April, the Panthers announced their own investigation. This outraged a group of state legislators, one of whom swore to "get" the Panthers by introducing a bill to ban the public display of loaded weapons. Newton's dramatic response would make the Panthers a household name. On May 2, 1967, Bobby Seale led a team of two dozen armed Panthers, clad in black leather and berets, to the California State Capitol building in Sacramento. A news crew, on hand for a talk Governor Ronald Reagan was giving to a group of schoolchildren on a nearby lawn, began filming.

Seale, wearing a .45 on his hip, was stopped by security guards at the top of the capitol steps. To his left stood a Panther holding a .347 Magnum; to his right was the party's first recruit, a teenager named Bobby Hutton, massaging a 12-gauge shotgun. One of the guards asked another, "Who in the hell are all these niggers with guns?"

"Where in the hell is the assembly?" Seale shouted. "Anybody here know where you go in and observe the assembly making these laws?"

When someone yelled that it was upstairs, Seale's group pushed past the guards, ascended a broad staircase, and marched into the packed assembly chamber. Pandemonium ensued. As guards began pushing the Panthers back toward the door, a guard snatched Hutton's shotgun. "Am I under arrest?" Hutton yelled. "What the hell you got my gun for? If I'm not under arrest, you give me my gun back!"

The Panthers went peacefully. Outside, as reporters crowded around, Seale read a statement, denouncing the proposed gun law and launching into a tirade against "racist police agencies throughout the country intensifying the terror, brutality, murder and repression of black people." This was the Panthers at their most theatrical, and it caused a sensation. Overnight, footage of armed black men boldly roaming the capitol steps stunned the nation.

All that summer, as Newton led the Panthers in demonstrations across the Bay Area, the party was inundated by calls from new recruits. Then came the moment that altered the course of Panther history. Early on the morning of October 28, 1967, Newton—who by his own estimate had already been stopped by police fifty or more times—was flagged down by an Oakland patrol car. A gunfight ensued. Newton walked away with at least one bullet hole in his abdomen. Two officers were badly wounded; one died. When Newton limped into an emergency room, he was arrested. He would not go free for three years.

The prosecution of Huey Newton would be one of the decade's centerpiece events, providing a rallying cry—"Free Huey!"—for a generation of Black Power advocates, drawing hundreds of recruits to the party and mobilizing thousands more to protests. But the impact on the Panthers was ultimately devastating. The absence of both Newton and Bobby Seale—who was serving a six-month sentence for his role in the confrontation on the capitol steps—created a leadership vacuum that was filled by Eldridge Cleaver. It was under Cleaver that the Panthers would drastically escalate their language of violence and insurrection to levels never before heard in America.

The audacity of this rhetoric, even from a vantage point of forty-five years, is shocking. It was the Panther newspaper, the *Black Panther*, that coined the phrase "Off the Pig"; under Cleaver, the *Panther* openly called for the murder of policemen, supplying tips on ambush tactics and ways to build bombs. "The only good pig," quipped Michael "Cetawayo" Tabor, a New York Panther, "is a dead pig." The Panther chief of staff, David Hilliard, was arrested after telling a crowd in San Francisco, "We will kill Richard Nixon." When Cleaver ran for president in 1968, he said of the White House, "We will burn the motherfucker down." Another Panther was quoted as saying, "We need black FBI agents to assassinate J. Edgar Hoover . . . and nigger CIA agents should kidnap the Rockefellers and the Kennedys."[3]

Panther rhetoric, in turn, inspired a host of black voices toward new extremes. A young poet, Nikki Giovanni, was among the mainstream black writers attracted to revolutionary themes. She wrote in a 1968 poem:

Nigger
Can you kill
Can you kill

Can a nigger kill
Can a nigger kill a honkie . . .
Can you splatter their brains in the street
Can you kill them . . .
Learn to kill niggers
Learn to be Black men.[4]

Much of this, the author Curtis J. Austin has observed, could be dismissed as "ghetto rhetoric." But the FBI, and especially urban police commissioners, could not ignore it, and with good reason. The escalation in Black Power rhetoric paralleled a rise in attacks on police. Between 1964 and 1969, assaults on Los Angeles patrolmen quintupled. Between 1967 and 1969, attacks on officers in New Jersey leaped by 41 percent. In Detroit they rose 70 percent in 1969 alone. In congressional testimony and press interviews, police officials in cities across the country blamed the rise in violence squarely on the Panthers and their ultraviolent rhetoric.

The Panthers drew the FBI's attention early on. In late 1967 agents began bugging party headquarters in Oakland, the first step in an anti-Panther drive that, as shown elsewhere in this book, would grow into an elaborate and illegal campaign of dirty tricks against Black Power groups, all of it designed to prevent the rise of what J. Edgar Hoover called "a black messiah": a single black leader who could unite the disparate voices of Black Power. Until that messiah rose, Hoover told a Senate committee in 1969, he considered the Panthers "the greatest threat to the internal security of the country."

In early 1968, the rise in Panther rhetoric led to heightened tensions with Bay Area police, especially in Oakland. The police launched scores of raids on Panther homes, briefly arresting Cleaver and Seale, and rumors flew that police were plotting to "wipe out" the Panthers. Then, on April 4, Martin Luther King was assassinated in Memphis. In Washington, D.C., Stokely Carmichael, now aligned with the Panthers, announced that White America had declared war on blacks. Riots broke out in more than 120 cities. In Oakland, two days later, Cleaver and a group of Panthers jumped into three cars and went looking for police to kill. They stopped at an intersection in West Oakland, Cleaver recalled years later, because he "needed to take a piss real badly." An Oakland patrolman pulled up behind. "Everybody all day was talking about taking some action," Cleaver recalled. "So we put together a little series of events to take place the next night, where we basically went out to ambush the cops. But it was an aborted ambush because the cops showed up too soon." When the patrol car pulled up, Cleaver said, the Panthers "got out and started shooting. That's what happened. People scattered and ran every which a-way."

Cleaver and young Bobby Hutton took refuge in the basement of a nearby home, where they engaged police in a ninety-minute gunfight. When the police used tear gas, Cleaver emerged shirtless—to show he was unarmed—alongside Hutton. Officers began shoving and kicking Hutton; when he stumbled, shots rang out. Hutton, hit at least six times, was killed. He became a martyr. Cleaver, granted bail, became a hero.

It was King's death and the image of brave Panthers seeking to avenge it that cemented the party's national reputation. For the first time many blacks who had resisted the martial calls of Black Power began to believe that white violence must be met with black violence. Emissaries arrived in Oakland from New York and dozens of other cities, all clamoring to start their own Panther chapters. In a matter of months, party membership went from hundreds to thousands; by late 1968 there would be Panther chapters in almost every major urban area. From a managerial point of view, it was chaos. A Central Committee was supposed to impose some kind of structure, but for the moment, Panther headquarters exercised little sway over these new affiliates.

It was, in some respects, the apex of the party's influence; looking back, there is no denying that the Panthers' "heroic" age was already passing. In September, after a two-month trial marked by rancorous demonstrations, Huey Newton was convicted of manslaughter and sentenced to two to fifteen years. Bobby Seale was indicted for taking part in demonstrations at the Democratic National Convention that August, becoming one of the "Chicago Eight." Eldridge Cleaver, released on bond after the April shootout, spent the rest of 1968 "campaigning" for president and promoting *Soul on Ice*. After refusing to appear for a court date on November 27, he vanished; some said he had fled to Canada, others to Cuba. The next month a weary Stokely

Carmichael boarded a freighter for a self-imposed exile in Guinea. "The revolution is not about dying," he observed. "It's about living."

In the absence of its best-known leaders, the party was ostensibly run by Newton's childhood friend and chief of staff, David Hilliard. But Hilliard was a weak leader, crass and profane, and by early 1969 the chapters were growing increasingly autonomous, straining ties between Oakland and the larger East Coast outposts, especially the ultramilitant New York chapter. Beset by police informers, Hilliard initiated a nationwide purge of suspect members, forbidding new initiates and further alienating not only his subordinates but the Panthers' radical white allies. The new Nixon administration's all-out war on the party led to mass arrests of Panthers in New York in April and May 1969 and in New Haven that May. By the summer of 1969 the party was spiraling toward anarchy.

Which is exactly when a crucial group of the Panthers' white allies mounted a kind of rescue operation. These were not just any allies. They were the crème de la crème, the national leadership of the dominant white Movement organization, Students for a Democratic Society, known as SDS. They called themselves Weatherman.

Part One

WEATHERMAN

"YOU SAY YOU WANT A REVOLUTION"

The Movement and the Emergence of Weatherman

> He's a real Weatherman
> Ripping up the mother land
> Making all his Weatherplans
> For everyone
> Knows just what he's fighting for
> Victory for people's war
> Trashes, bombs, kills pigs and more.
> The Weatherman
>
> *—Weatherman song, to the tune of*
> *the Beatles' "Nowhere Man"*

> Pig Amerika beware: There's an army growing right in
> your guts, and it's going to bring you down.
> *—Weatherman editorial, December 1969*

Weatherman, or the Weather Underground Organization, as it was eventually known, was the first and by far the largest group of people to launch a nationwide campaign of underground violence on American soil. A faction of the leading '60s-era protest group, Students for a Democratic Society (SDS), it boasted a membership that stood in sharp contrast to those of later underground groups, whose members tended to be fringe militants. Weatherman was composed of the cream of the protest movement, including some of its most visible activists; they may have been the country's first Ivy League revolutionaries. Much has been written about Weatherman, especially its "aboveground" origins and its early months in 1969, which were marked by all manner of bizarre behavior, not least its members' penchant for engaging in sexual orgies. Much less has been written about Weatherman's actual underground operations, which have remained cloaked in secrecy for more than four decades.

Partly as a result, Weatherman's multiyear bombing campaign has been misunderstood in fundamental ways. To cite just one canard, for much of its life, Weatherman's attacks were the work not of a hundred or more underground radicals, as was widely assumed, but of a core group of barely a dozen people; almost all its bombs, in fact, were built by the same capable young man: its bomb "guru." Nor, contrary to myth, did Weatherman's leaders, especially its best-known alumni, Bernardine Dohrn and Bill Ayers, operate from grinding poverty or ghetto anonymity: For much of their time underground, Dohrn and Ayers lived in a cozy California beach bungalow, while the group's East Coast leaders lived in a comfortable vacation rental in New York's Catskill Mountains. Of far greater significance is widespread confusion over what Weatherman set out to do. Its alumni have crafted an image of the group as benign urban guerrillas who never intended to hurt a soul, their only goal to damage symbols of American power: empty courthouses and university buildings, a Pentagon bathroom, the U.S. Capitol. This is what Weatherman eventually became. But it began as something else, something murderous, and was obliged to soften its tactics only after they proved unsustainable.

To begin to understand all this, one needs to understand the protest movements of the '60s, and to understand that turmoil, one must at least glance at the decade that produced all those angry young activists: the 1950s. For much of white America, the '50s was a time of suffocating conformity, when parents born during the Depression and empowered by winning a "good war" taught their children that America represented everything that was right and true in the world. These were the "happy days," when a booming economy sent wealth soaring and children, born by the millions, grew up in homes where every family seemed to have two cars in the driveway, a stereo cabinet, and, in fifty million homes by 1960, a television. How happy *were*

Americans? When a 1957 Gallup poll asked people whether they were "very happy, fairly happy, or not too happy," an astounding 96 percent answered very or fairly happy. "The employers will love this generation," University of California president Clark Kerr said in 1959. "They are not going to press many grievances . . . they are going to be easy to handle. There aren't going to be riots."

And then, as if overnight, things changed. More than anything else, it was the pictures young Americans began seeing on those new televisions in 1960—of stoic Southern blacks dragged away from all-white lunch counters, of black protesters being beaten bloody by red-faced Southern deputies—that laid the groundwork for the white protest movement. The violence and injustice itself was shameful enough, but it was what those pictures said about America, about what an entire generation of young people had been taught, that felt like a betrayal. America wasn't a land of equality. It wasn't a land of the good and the just and the righteous. It was all a lie.

Those were feelings, at least, that consumed many of the idealistic white students who joined the civil rights movement after those first sit-ins in Greensboro, North Carolina. There were only a trickle at first, but when pictures of Southern thugs beating the first Freedom Riders in 1961 were broadcast, the numbers grew. A host of white groups sprang up to work with SNCC in those first years, but by far the most influential was SDS, at the time an obscure youth branch of an even more obscure socialist education organization called the League for Industrial Democracy, which traced its origins to 1905.

SDS's emergence was spearheaded by a Freedom Rider named Tom Hayden, a onetime University of Michigan student who served as SDS's president in 1962 and 1963. It was Hayden who, at a conference of barely sixty SDSers and allies on the coast of Lake Huron, drafted the protest manifesto that became known as "The Port Huron Statement." Grandly billed as "an agenda for the generation," the fifty-page document by itself did not electrify or even mobilize campus activists across the country. But it did establish an agenda for SDS—broadly antiwar, antipoverty, and pro–civil rights—that over time would attract hundreds and then thousands of mostly white students across the nation. That the massive baby boom generation would produce a politically liberal or even radical voice had long been anticipated; the sociologist C. Wright Mills had actually written an open "Letter to the New Left" in 1960, asking what was taking so long. SDS and its intellectual allies, wanting to distance themselves from the communist "Old Left" that J. Edgar Hoover's FBI had destroyed, took the "New Left" mantle as their own. SDS thus became the core of the '60s New Left, much as the New Left became the core of the broader protest movement, "the Movement."

The Movement grew all through 1963 and 1964, propelled both by social shocks, such as the assassinations of President Kennedy and of three civil rights workers in Mississippi, and by the first whiffs of true campus unrest, especially the emergence of the Free Speech Movement at the University of California in Berkeley. Much of white activism was still drawn to the struggle for Southern civil rights, at least until 1966, when Stokely Carmichael's call for Black Power served as a warning that white protesters were no longer wanted, much less needed. It was then, when the white protest movement badly needed something new to protest, that the new war in Vietnam, accelerating in 1965, caught its attention.

SDS crouched unsteadily at the center of the gathering storm. Somewhat like a social fraternity, it existed as a string of campus chapters linked by a national office that attempted—through conventions, newsletters, and traveling emissaries—to direct the individual chapters, with mixed degrees of success. In practice, the chapters largely went their own way. But the highest echelon of SDS, its national leadership, did tend to draw the liveliest minds in the Movement, and their utterances were widely followed. All through 1965 and 1966 SDS members peopled myriad civil rights and antiwar demonstrations, hundreds of them, but a kind of malaise soon set in. Every month brought more and larger protests. Yet there seemed to be little improvement in black civil rights, and more American soldiers poured into Southeast Asia every day. Clearly, if SDS and the broader Movement were to bring about the fundamental changes they so badly wanted, a new set of tactics would be needed.

The first stirrings of something greater than mere protest, something momentous, could be heard in SDS leadership circles by the end of 1966. The first to voice them was the organization's national secretary that season, Greg Calvert, a twenty-nine-year-old history teacher from Iowa State who would be gone from SDS by the time others began going underground. It was Calvert who, in the face of widespread frustration at the speed of change, first began using Malcolm's word, "revolution," to characterize the level of struggle the Movement needed to bring to America. In a report to membership in November 1966 he wrote, "Let's quit playing games and stop the self-indulgent pretense of confusion. . . . I am finally convinced that a truly revolutionary movement must be built out of the deepest revolutionary demands and out of the strongest revolutionary hopes—the demand for and the hope of freedom."

This was still a long way from planning actual violence, but an intellectual foundation was being laid. Calvert's call struck a chord, as did the slogan he coined that swept the Movement that winter of 1966–67: "From protest to resistance." At least initially, no one was entirely sure what "resistance" meant. But out on college campuses, students quickly provided the answers. All through the first half of 1967, protesters who once silently carried signs began confronting authority. When a district attorney tried to confiscate copies of a student literary magazine at Cornell, a crowd of angry students sold it in brazen defiance; when six were arrested, others surrounded the police car and freed them. At Penn State student protesters occupied the president's office until he provided information about the university's practice of releasing student-organization lists to Congress.

But it was SDS itself that propelled by far the largest resistance movement: to the military draft. The first draft-resistance groups began springing up in early 1967 and were soon widespread, many students openly burning their draft cards or wearing a popular SDS button: NOT WITH MY LIFE YOU DON'T. This kind of open defiance to government authority, along with disclosures of U.S. bombing of North Vietnamese civilians, drew tens of thousands of young people into the Movement even as its intellectual leaders, especially in SDS, began musing about ever more militant ways to confront the government. Protests alone, they could see, were no longer enough.

As an SDSer named Dotson Rader put it:

> The meaninglessness of non-violent, "democratic" methods was becoming clear to us in the spring of 1967. The Civil Rights Movement was

dead. Pacifism was dead. Some Leftists—the Trotskyites, Maoists, radical socialists . . . some of the radicals in SDS, Stokely Carmichael, Rap Brown, Tom Hayden—knew it early. But it took the rest of us awhile to give up the sweet life of the democratic Left for revolt.[1]

One of the most striking characteristics of radical thought during the late 1960s was the flash-fire speed with which it evolved: An idea could be introduced, accepted, popularized, and taken to the "next level" in a matter of months, sometimes weeks. And so it was with the path of "resistance." No sooner had the broader Movement plunged into the realities of draft and other resistance than the keenest thinkers began pondering what came next. Defying the government was giving way to confronting the government. And there was only one place to go, intellectually, once the government was confronted.

It was Greg Calvert once more who first put it into words, at least publicly, in a front-page article in the *New York Times* in May 1967. The article, which attempted to take stock of student-resistance activities, suggested that violence was the Movement's logical next step, a contention it supported with a quote that Calvert quickly recanted: "We are working to build a guerrilla force in an urban environment." No other student leader seconded it, and because it suggested a tactic few in SDS had even considered, much less approved, it was broadly renounced. But not by everyone. The intellectual cat was now out of the bag, and as the Movement exploded into public consciousness during 1967's Summer of Love, the first voices could be heard saying that Greg Calvert was onto something.

After years of talk and restlessness 1968 changed everything. It was as if the earth itself was exploding in protest. Suddenly, as if in concert, students and working people around the world—in France, Germany, Great Britain, Mexico, Northern Ireland, Finland, Brazil, even in China, Czechoslovakia, Yugoslavia—rose up and demanded that their governments change. Every night on the evening news it was as if the same roll of film were being broadcast over and over from country after country, thousands of young people holding protest signs, students leaping over barricades, steel-helmeted police and soldiers staring impassively or, increasingly, beating them down. For those in power, it felt as if the world was crumbling around them. For those in the streets, it was as if the entire world was aflame. Suddenly there was a single word on everyone's lips: "revolution."

The revolution—a single global uprising of the "oppressed"—was happening, right now, all over the world and would soon come to America. It was an idea that seemed to wash over the Movement in a matter of minutes, easy to discuss, harder to grasp, harder still to actually believe. Yet it spread with stunning swiftness. In the summer of 1968, barely a year after Greg Calvert had been pilloried for suggesting that protesters become urban guerrillas, a study found that more than 350,000 young Americans considered themselves "revolutionaries." The term, of course, meant many things to many people. For most, unwilling or unable to accept the far-fetched notion that a violent uprising might topple the government, the word "revolution" became a kind of shorthand for fundamental change. When they used it, they meant a revolution in American norms, in the power structure, in civil rights, in attitudes toward the poor and dispossessed. No sane person, it was widely assumed, believed the U.S. government could actually be overthrown.

But others did believe it. For the hard core, for those who saw governments teetering everywhere, who felt that the Movement was doomed to failure, who despaired at the murders of change agents such as Martin Luther King and Robert Kennedy, 1968 bore signs of the apocalypse. For these activists, who might be called apocalyptic revolutionaries, there was a vivid and growing sense that the world was on the brink of historic, irreversible change and that the morally corrupt American government, murdering the Vietnamese, unleashing dogs on Southern blacks, and beating its protesters, was poised for imminent collapse. SDS's leadership happened to be populated by an outsized number of Jewish students, and for many of these the notion of challenging a U.S. government they imagined as the second coming of Nazi Germany had enormous appeal. All that was needed was a push. Castro had done it in Cuba, Lenin in Russia, Mao in China. Why not in America?

This was a powerful idea, at once outlandish and intoxicating, providing a rush of intellectual adrenaline as strong as any drug. It was also, as Kirkpatrick

Sale notes in his definitive history, *SDS: The Rise and Development of the Students for a Democratic Society*, the inevitable result of everything that had happened to that point in the 1960s:

> Revolution: how had it come to that? It was a blend of many things: bitterness, hatred, and alienation, hope, confidence, and conviction, energy, passion, and need. It was the pattern woven by all the threads of the sixties, the inevitable product of the awakened generation as it probed deeper and deeper into the character of its nation. . . .
>
> There was a primary sense, begun by no more than a reading of the morning papers and developed through the new perspectives and new analyses available to the Movement now, that the evils *in* America were the evils *of* America, inextricably a part of the total system. . . . Clearly something drastic would be necessary to eradicate those evils and alter that system: various reforms had been tried, confrontation had been tried, there had been civil-rights agitation, university pressures, antiwar marches, doorbell ringing, electoral action, student power, draft resistance demonstrations, campus uprisings, even tentative political violence—all to little avail. . . .
>
> Worse, those who wanted peaceable change, who tried to work through approved channels, seemed to be systematically ignored, ostracized, or—as with the Kennedys and King—eliminated. More was necessary, and in the words of [one SDS leader], "What it came to that year was that people came to the conclusion that the only way to stop the war was make a revolution, and the only way to stop racism was make a revolution." "The monster"— that was the recurrent phrase now—could not be altered, deviated, halted: it had to be destroyed.

Apocalyptic revolutionaries represented a strident new voice in the Movement, but they were able to draw from a wellspring of ideas that weren't entirely new: philosophies, arguments, books, and films that had sprung up around armed-resistance movements worldwide. They studied Lenin and Mao and Ho Chi Minh—it went without saying that revolutionaries were almost always communists—but their favorite blueprint was the Cuban

Revolution, their icon Ernesto "Che" Guevara, Castro's swashbuckling right-hand man. A handsome doctor, Che represented the thoughtful, "caring" revolutionary who resorted to violence only to fight an unjust government; by 1968 his poster could be found hanging in dormitories across America. The apocalyptic revolutionary's favorite movie was *The Battle of Algiers*, a 1966 film that portrayed heroic Algerian guerrillas doing battle against their French occupiers. In time, once people actually began going underground, their bible would become *Mini-Manual of the Urban Guerrilla*, written in 1969 by a Brazilian Marxist named Carlos Marighella; it outlined dozens of strategies and tactics, analyzing weapons, outlining ways to organize a guerrilla cell, even describing the best ways to rob a bank. A number of underground newspapers would excerpt Marighella's manual.

"We actually believed there was going to be a revolution," remembers a Weatherman named Paul Bradley.* "We believed the world was undergoing a massive transformation. We believed Third World countries would rise up and cause crises that would bring down the industrialized West, and we believed it was going to happen tomorrow, or maybe the day after tomorrow, like 1976. We really thought that would happen. I know I did."

For the moment, it was all just talk, and crazy talk at that. But by early 1968 apocalyptic revolutionaries—"kamikazes," one SDS report called them—were rising to the fore in every SDS chapter, prophesying the coming conflict. They always seemed to be the loudest, the angriest, the most voluble, and they refused to be shouted down. Chapter after chapter was split between armchair protesters and "action factions" who wanted action, often violent action, *right this second*. The spark could have happened anywhere. In the event, it happened at Columbia University in New York, where in April 1968 the SDS chapter's action faction grew outraged at the segregation of a proposed gymnasium and the university's ties to a Pentagon-sponsored think tank. After a peaceful protest, a group of SDSers occupied Hamilton Hall, Columbia's administration building, and refused to leave until the gym was scrapped and ties to the think tank were severed. When an administrator named Henry S. Coleman went to meet them, he was taken hostage and

---

*"Paul Bradley" is a pseudonym for a long-serving member of the Weather Underground.

barricaded into his office. Police surrounded the building but declined to storm it, worried about inflaming adjoining black neighborhoods. A kind of siege ensued, with the occupying students using bullhorns to harangue crowds of the curious.

Had all this happened in San Diego, it might have been dismissed as a random instance of especially aggressive protesters. But because it happened in New York, the world's media center, Columbia became an overnight phenomenon as images of angry, shouting students were beamed to television sets around the world. As far as the press was concerned, the star of the show was the student spokesman, a soft, husky New Jersey sophomore named Mark Rudd, whose dramatic poses—typically one fist raised, the other wrapped around a bullhorn—appeared seemingly everywhere, climaxing with the cover of *Newsweek*. For mainstream America Rudd became a dismaying symbol not only of SDS but of the Movement itself, the prototypical nice Jewish boy from the suburbs transformed into something new and angry by these strange times.

Behind the scenes, however, the driving force behind the occupation, and the man who would eventually craft the philosophical framework for Weatherman, was Rudd's best friend, a hyperintense, motormouthed Connecticut leftist named John Jacobs, universally known as JJ. Brilliant and handsome, with a streetwise style marked by beat-up leather jackets and slicked-back hair, JJ was already a legend at Columbia when the protests began. Some thought him a prophet, some a poseur, but either way he was surely the purest voice of the apocalyptic revolutionary. Where mainstream commentators viewed Columbia as a student protest, JJ told anyone who would listen that it was far, far more: the first step toward a genuine American revolution, concrete evidence that young people working together could bring the country's white elites to their knees. More than anyone else in the SDS universe, it was JJ who popularized the parallels between Columbia and the Cuban Revolution, who preached that a select group of hard-core rebels could, as Castro and Guevara had with Cuba, lead America into revolution. "At first everyone thought JJ was crazy," remembers his friend Howie Machtinger. "But then events kind of caught up with him, and suddenly what he was saying seemed almost sensible."

As outlandish as this idea might sound today, it emerged as a popular argument among apocalyptic radicals in 1968 and would endure as the rationalization behind almost every underground group of the 1970s. Known as the *foco* theory, it had been advanced in a 1967 book, *Revolution in the Revolution?*, by a French philosophy professor named Régis Debray. A friend of Guevara's who taught in Havana, Debray argued that small, fast-moving guerrilla groups, such as those Che commanded, could inspire a grassroots rebellion, even in the United States. Debray's theory, in turn, drew on what leftists call vanguardism, the notion that the most politically advanced members of any "proletariat" could draw the working class into revolution. Perhaps unsurprisingly, these ideas were catnip to budding revolutionaries like JJ, many of whom had no problem imagining themselves as American Ches. Their ardor was undiminished by their hero's inability to make the *foco* theory work in Bolivia, where soldiers had captured and executed Guevara in 1967.

Veterans of the Columbia occupation, which ended with police storming the occupied buildings and arresting many of the protesters, would eventually constitute the largest single group of Weathermen. In Columbia's aftermath, both JJ and Mark Rudd emerged as stars in the SDS firmament. While Rudd embarked on months of fund-raising trips, JJ fatefully fell in with another up-and-comer, a strikingly attractive twenty-six-year-old law student named Bernardine Dohrn. Dohrn was destined to become the glamorous leading lady of the American underground, unquestionably brilliant, cool, focused, militant, and highly sexual; J. Edgar Hoover would dub her "La Pasionaria of the Lunatic Left." A high school cheerleader in her Wisconsin hometown, she graduated from the University of Chicago in 1963 and, while working toward her law degree, began assisting a host of protest groups, including SDS.

Clad in a tight miniskirt and knee-high Italian boots, Dohrn burst onto the scene at Columbia, where she helped arrange bail bonds. Everyone who met her—every man, at least—seemed mesmerized. "Every guy I knew at Columbia, every single one, wanted to fuck her," remembers one SDSer, and Dohrn knew it. She liked to wear a button with the slogan CUNNILINGUS IS COOL, FELLATIO IS FUN. She and JJ were immediately smitten with each other. "Bernardine would be arguing political points at the table with blouse open to the navel, sort of leering at JJ," an SDSer named Steve Tappis recalled. "I couldn't concentrate on the arguments. Finally, I said, 'Bernardine! Would you please button your blouse?' She just pulled out one of her breasts and, in that cold way of hers, said, 'You like this tit? Take it.'" Another SDSer, Jim Mellen, recalled, "She used sex to explore and cement political alliances. Sex for her was a form of ideological activity."[2] Yet even many SDS women soon idolized Dohrn. Everyone "wanted to be in her favor, to be like her," a Weatherman named Susan Stern said years later. "She possessed a splendor all her own, like a queen . . . a high priestess, a mythological silhouette."

In the summer of 1968, buoyed by her sudden popularity, Dohrn mounted an out-of-left-field bid to become SDS's "inter-organizational secretary"— one of three coequal leadership positions—and, to widespread surprise, won election at the national convention that June. More than a few found her too beautiful to take seriously. When one questioner asked whether she was in fact a socialist, Dohrn took a moment, looked the man square in the eyes, and memorably replied, "I consider myself a revolutionary communist."

Together Dohrn and JJ became a force of nature in the SDS universe; years later, friends would term their loud bouts of sex "animal mating." From the beginning, they had their eyes on seizing overall control of SDS. They were stars, and that summer they took their newfound fame and ambitions to Chicago, which was the site not only of SDS's national headquarters but of that August's Democratic National Convention, which drew thousands of protesters into pitched battles with Chicago police. Their apartment, near downtown, became the epicenter of SDS politics, especially for those who shared JJ's apocalyptic views. Many of the brightest SDSers, including several who would achieve prominence in Weatherman, swung by that autumn to crash, drop acid, and ogle Dohrn as they listened to JJ's rambling, amphetamine-fueled soliloquies on Che and Debray and every other revolutionary topic imaginable. One was Jeff Jones, a handsome Southern California kid who looked—and some thought acted—like a dim-witted blond surfer. Another was Howie Machtinger, a scrappy University of Chicago PhD candidate. An SDS contingent from Ann Arbor, Michigan, was especially significant. It was led by Jim Mellen, a thirty-five-year-old activist; his protégé Bill Ayers, a lippy, hedonistic rich kid whose father was chairman of Chicago's Commonwealth Edison; Ayers's girlfriend, Diana Oughton; and their close friend Terry Robbins, a wiry, intense SDS ambassador at Kent State.

As this group coalesced around JJ and Dohrn in the winter of 1968–69, political violence was spreading on campuses across the country, much of it fueled by the Vietnam War's escalation and the new Nixon administration's vow to crack down on student protesters. By one count, incidents of bombings and arson, mostly Molotov cocktails thrown in the night, had increased to forty-one that fall, a 300 percent rise from the spring. ROTC facilities burned in Delaware, Texas, Berkeley, and Oregon and at Washington University in St. Louis, where an SDSer was convicted of arson. Campus buildings were bombed at Georgetown, the University of Michigan, New York University, and four California colleges. When the ROTC building at the University of Washington burned, students danced by the light of the flames, chanting, "This is number one / And the fun has just begun / Burn it down, burn it down, burn it down." For the first time underground newspapers began publishing instructions on the making of Molotov cocktails. Homemade bombing manuals began circulating at SDS meetings and rock concerts. A rash of bombings occurred in Detroit that winter; small devices exploded five times outside the city halls in Oakland and San Francisco.

To apocalyptic revolutionaries, it was a sign of the coming conflict. In Chicago, JJ and Dohrn were emboldened. By the spring, when they relocated to a spartan apartment on North Winthrop Avenue—JJ, it was said, had demolished their furniture in an LSD rampage—their circle had begun to think of themselves as the future of SDS and of the Movement. They planned to run for all the top leadership positions at the SDS convention that June, but to win they would need to defeat a set of rivals who were, if anything, even more strident and doctrinaire than they: a hard-core Maoist group called Progressive Labor, known as PL. As a statement of principles and a way of contrasting themselves with PL, they began writing what would become a defining, sixteen-thousand-word manifesto: the infamous "Weatherman paper." Chewing amphetamines like gum, JJ banged out most of it on a typewriter in the kitchen, passing around pages for the others to review. When they were done, he and ten others, including Dohrn, Mark Rudd, Jeff Jones, Howie Machtinger, Jim Mellen, Terry Robbins, and Bill Ayers, signed their names.

One Weatherman history terms the paper, a nearly impenetrable blizzard of Marxist jargon, "an almost mystical vision of a coming political Armageddon." ("Any close reading of the Weatherman paper," one SDSer quipped, "will drive you blind.") A crystallization of all JJ's pet ideas, the paper didn't just draw parallels between American student protests and the Third World guerrilla campaigns sprouting up around the world: It judged them all part and parcel of a single titanic global struggle between oppressed minorities and the agencies of U.S. imperialism. In other words, Mark Rudd hadn't just acted like Che at Columbia; he was, in fact, Che's comrade in arms. But the genius of JJ's argument was that it allowed white radicals to portray themselves as allies of these oppressed minorities by rallying behind the one group whose leaders—from Martin Luther King to Huey Newton—the JJs of the world adored even more than Che Guevara: American blacks. "I think in our hearts what all of us wanted to be," former SDS leader Cathy Wilkerson recalls, "was a Black Panther."

Wars like Vietnam came and went, but it was only the brewing revolution of American blacks, JJ prophesied, that had the potential to destroy the country. Every white revolutionary, he argued, was duty-bound to become 1969's version of John Brown, the Civil War–era antislavery zealot. "John Brown! Live like him!" became JJ's rallying cry. What this meant in reality was, like most protest-era rhetoric, open to interpretation. In the minds of apocalyptic radicals like JJ, white American protesters were destined to become Che-style guerrillas in the streets of America, rallying blacks and the white working class to a bloody revolution. For JJ and his allies talk of violence was no longer abstract. They wanted to bomb buildings and kill the policemen who were murdering blacks in the ghettos. Not many, it should be emphasized, shared this view: More than a few, even within the Movement, thought talk of anti-government violence was lunacy. JJ's group decided to name its manifesto after a Bob Dylan line: "You don't a need a weatherman to know which way the wind blows." Saner SDSers twisted this into a memorable quip: "You don't need a rectal thermometer to know who the assholes are."

The SDS convention took place at the Chicago Coliseum on Wednesday, June 18, 1969; nearly two thousand people attended. The Weathermen arrived as part of the larger RYM—Revolutionary Youth Movement—caucus, but both were consumed with the battle against their archrivals, PL. (The basic difference between the two groups was that PL adopted a Maoist philosophy of focusing on "workers," while Weatherman put its emphasis on the "oppressed," especially blacks.) The convention's first two days were consumed with the trappings of student-leftist gatherings, angry speeches, PL chants against RYM, RYM chants against PL, even fistfights. The turning point came on Friday night, when a delegate from the Black Panthers took the microphone and read a statement that condemned PL as "counterrevolutionary traitors" who, if their ideological positions did not change, "would be dealt with as such." It amounted to an ultimatum from the Panthers, whose approval every SDS leader sought like lost gold: Dump PL or else. PLers tried to drown out the Panthers, chanting "Read Mao" and "Bullshit!" When RYM supporters chanted the Panther slogan, "Power to the People!" PLers shouted back, "Power to the Workers!" Fistfights broke out. On stage, Mark Rudd called for a recess. As he finished, Dohrn rushed to the rostrum, eyes ablaze, and shouted that it was time to decide whether they could remain in the same organization as those who denied human rights to the oppressed. Anyone who agreed, she announced, should follow her. And with that, Dohrn and the leadership marched into an adjacent arena to decide what to do next.

The RYM caucus and its allies, maybe six hundred people, talked there for three hours, then resumed discussions Saturday morning. The debates lasted all that day. Finally Dohrn, pacing between a set of bleachers, delivered a slow, deliberate speech that detailed the case for expelling PL from SDS. "We are *not* a caucus," she concluded. "*We* are SDS." And with that, a vote was taken: By a five-to-one margin, PL was expelled. The leadership, led by Dohrn and Bill Ayers, then drafted a statement listing the reasons why. Around eleven everyone filed back into the main hall, and Dohrn strode to the rostrum. For twenty minutes she laid out every PL sin, real and imagined, terming the group reactionary, anticommunist, and "objectively" racist. When she announced PL's expulsion, chaos ensued. PLers chanted "Shame! Shame!" Dohrn led the RYM caucus out of the auditorium, leading their own chants: "Power to the People!" and "Ho, Ho, Ho Chi Minh!"

By Sunday confusion reigned. The PLers, refusing to acknowledge their expulsion, elected their own SDS leadership. At a church across town, the

RYM caucus elected theirs, all prominent Weathermen: Mark Rudd as national secretary, Bill Ayers as education secretary, Jeff Jones as the interorganizational secretary. By Monday morning there were, in effect, two functioning SDSes, but everyone understood that Weatherman had carried the day, in large part because its members had taken control of the national office in the days before the convention. Possession is nine-tenths of the law; Weatherman possessed the national office, and so it possessed SDS.

But in name only. The Weathermen who took control of SDS that summer envisioned an SDS unlike any other protest group before or since. Gone was the idea of a national office as a shaggy bureaucracy to guide SDS's far-flung chapters. In its place the Weathermen became, in effect, an überchapter of their own, one dedicated to the leadership's twin goals. The first was fanning out across the country to recruit members of the working class. The second was melding recruits with existing Weathermen for a massive protest march planned for October in which the new, far larger group would make its political debut, storming the streets of Chicago in an all-out attack on the police and symbols of government authority. They billed it as "the National Action," but in time it would become known as the Days of Rage.

Weatherman was born into Richard Nixon's divided America, in the final years of J. Edgar Hoover's FBI. It was a country, and a time, in which dissenters were watched and wiretapped by stern federal agents with spit-shined shoes and little patience for long-haired kids who mused about bombing government buildings. Two million people marched in antiwar demonstrations in the autumn of 1969 alone, images of angry demonstrators jamming the nightly news broadcasts where a fatherly Walter Cronkite warned Middle America that the country was coming apart at the seams. President Nixon, who gained office that January in large part on his promise to crack down on protesters, had no doubt that it was, and from his first days in office he pushed the FBI to do everything possible to undermine the antiwar movement. Even before Nixon, the Bureau had been doing exactly that, engaging in a broad harassment campaign against radicals, white and black alike, called

COINTELPRO, which consisted of everything from break-ins to fake letters intended to sow discord among protest groups. Weatherman had been on the FBI's radar from its inception. Months before its leaders began planning a campaign of underground violence, the FBI sensed the threat it posed. In September 1969 Hoover's right-hand man, William Sullivan, warned that Weatherman had "the potential to be far more damaging to the security of this nation than the Communist Party ever was, even at the height of its strength in the 1930s."[3]

For the moment, though, there wasn't much the FBI was able to do to counter Weatherman. Agents tried to recruit informants who might signal the group's plans, but they were all but impossible to come by; few in the Movement wanted anything to do with the FBI. Again and again, FBI memoranda moaned about the Bureau's inability to develop a single decent informant. As one agent complained, Weatherman's "degenerate living habits, their immoral conduct, and their use of drugs" made it "extremely difficult to find informants who fit this mold and are willing to live as they do." That fall the Bureau's Cincinnati office was able to insert a single informant into Weatherman's local branch, a man named Larry Grathwohl, who would in time provide a glimpse into the group's inner workings.

Without informants, the Bureau, led by its Chicago office, relied on wiretaps to keep track of Dohrn and the others. The twenty-eight-year-old agent who eventually headed the FBI's Weatherman investigations, William Dyson, began his wiretapping duties that summer, manning a set of taps every day from four to midnight in a windowless room deep in the Chicago bureau's building. "I *watched* them become the Weathermen!" Dyson remembered years later. "I was *with* them when they became the Weathermen! It was exciting. I was watching history. . . . I knew more about these people than they knew about themselves."

While the FBI lingered in the shadows, the day-to-day responsibility for monitoring Weatherman fell to Mayor Richard Daley's Chicago police. In the days when U.S. police departments viewed harassing student protesters as part of their daily jobs, the Chicago force employed an especially nasty "Red Squad" that relentlessly targeted the Weathermen, staking out the national office, following the leadership at all hours, and sometimes arresting them.

Dohrn and JJ, for example, spent a night in jail after police found drugs in their car at a traffic stop. In one memorable episode, a Columbia Weatherman named Robbie Roth—who would later become one of the Weather Underground's five leaders—was sitting in a third-floor apartment with two young women when a trio of detectives appeared at the door and began questioning them. Roth sensed that the men had been drinking; he could smell it on their breath. The climax of his interrogation, Roth says, came when the three pushed him out a window and dangled him by his ankles. One of Dohrn's friends, an earnest activist named Russell Neufeld, experienced an even more harrowing brush with the Chicago police. Arrested with two other Weathermen at a demonstration outside the federal building on September 26, Neufeld was dragged inside nearby police headquarters. "I was standing there with a guy named Joe Kelly, and these cops put .38-caliber guns in our mouths and said if we moved, they would blow our brains out," Neufeld recalls. "Then they took Danny Cohen and pistol-whipped him. I swear, they broke every bone in Danny's face, blood everywhere. Joe and I stood there with guns in our mouths, forced to watch. It was horrible."

While the FBI and Chicago police looked on, the new Weatherman leaders of SDS embarked on an uproarious six-month period, the second half of 1969, that would come to define them. It was then that the group's most bizarre behaviors took place: the street brawls, the women running topless through high schools, the forced breakups of Weatherman couples, the orgies. All of it was designed to transform Weatherman's five hundred or so core followers into the makings of JJ's dream: an "urban fighting force" to rally the working class toward revolution. Almost everything that happened that summer and fall, in fact, was designed in some way to "toughen up" a band of coffeehouse intellectuals whose only experience with actual violence, other than watching *The Battle of Algiers*, was throwing the occasional rock during a street demonstration. "We have one task," Bill Ayers announced at meeting after meeting, "and that is to make ourselves into tools of the revolution." The idea wasn't to go underground—not yet, anyway. For the moment, the focus was to be on recruiting, violent street demonstrations, and, come the fall, the Days of Rage in Chicago.

Few outside Weatherman itself thought that any of this, especially the Days of Rage, made much sense. When Mark Rudd met with leaders of the group that organized the largest mass protests of the era, the National Mobilization Committee—the "Mobe"—they adamantly refused to join forces, arguing that street fighting and battling police were counterproductive. The Panthers too thought the Days of Rage a bad idea. The Chicago Panthers' charismatic young leader, Fred Hampton, held shouting matches with Dohrn and other leaders; the Panthers refused to help, and Hampton actually went public with his opposition, calling the Days of Rage "Custeristic."

Inside Weatherman, especially in its male-dominated upper reaches, the surest way to lose face was to share these doubts. JJ set a macho tone, and a number of those who trailed in his wake, including Bill Ayers, Terry Robbins, and Howie Machtinger, were short young men who seemed to compensate by adopting façades of arrogant swagger, scoffing at anyone who dared question Weather dogma; several of them had begun carrying guns. When Rudd made the mistake of questioning the Days of Rage, Ayers and Robbins snorted. "How could you succumb to that liberal bullshit?" Robbins demanded. "We've got to do it. It's the only strategy to build the revolution." As Rudd wrote later, "The scene plays in my memory like a grade-B gangster flick. Billy looks on in smirking contempt as Terry dismisses me with a flick of his ever-present cigarette. 'How could you be so weak?' That settled it."

Yet even those whom Weatherman most wanted to emulate, the leaders of revolutionary Cuba, had their doubts. The extent of Weatherman's ties to the Cuban government has been a source of speculation for more than forty years, the subject of multiple FBI investigations that ended up proving little. It is clear that several Weathermen, including Ayers, enjoyed contacts with Cuban diplomats in New York and Canada that would endure for years to come. The genesis of the relationship can be traced at least to the days immediately after Weatherman took control of SDS, when Dohrn led a group, part of a larger delegation of protesters, in an extended visit to Havana. The Cubans treated Dohrn like visiting royalty, featuring her in government magazines and introducing her to dignitaries from throughout the revolutionary world. The highlight of the visit was a meeting with a delegation from North Vietnam, which seemed far more eager to discuss formation of a Viet Cong–style underground in America than half measures like street fighting. Their message was mixed: Even as they lectured Dohrn on ways this underground could be formed, they cautioned her "about not getting too far ahead of the masses," in Mark Rudd's words, which was exactly what Weatherman was doing. In the end, after giving the Weathermen rings forged from the metal of downed U.S. fighter planes, a North Vietnamese delegate simply urged the Weathermen to do their best. "The war is entering its final phase," he told Dohrn. "You must begin to wage armed struggle as soon as possible to become the vanguard and take leadership of the revolution."

Back in the United States, JJ and the other new SDS leaders were already preparing the ground. Within days of their convention victory, detachments of Weathermen, more than two hundred in all, began arriving in cities across the country: thirty in both Seattle and New York; twenty-five in Columbus, Ohio; fifteen in Denver; plus smaller groups scattered throughout the Midwest, in Detroit, Pittsburgh, Milwaukee, Cleveland, and Cincinnati. In each, members lived together in "collectives." The leadership, based in Chicago and now known as the Weather Bureau—JJ, Rudd, Ayers, Jeff Jones, and others— traveled among them, leading the collectives in increasingly outlandish protests aimed at rallying the working class, to whom they referred as "greasers" or, more commonly, "the grease." Their most common tactic was a series of "invasions" they mounted of blue-collar high schools and community colleges, in which Weathermen ran through the halls screaming and urging students to join them at the Days of Rage. In August, in the Detroit suburb of Warren, a group of Weatherwomen took over a classroom at Macomb Community College during exams and lectured the thirty or so confused students on the evils of racism and imperialism; when the teacher called the police, the Weatherwomen were arrested. A month later, in Pittsburgh, twenty-six Weatherwomen stormed the halls of South Hills High School, tossing leaflets, waving a North Vietnamese flag, and, when this didn't sufficiently engage male students, lifting their skirts and exposing their breasts. Once again, most of the Weatherwomen ended up in jail.

All through July, August, and into September, Weathermen led similar protests around the country, brawling with PLers in Boston and New York and fighting with police in Seattle and in Detroit, where on September 27 JJ led a march of sixty Weathermen that turned violent, the protesters pelting police with rocks and bottles. These actions were successful insofar as they boosted morale in the ranks and created a sense that Weatherman was actually "doing something." The problem, it soon became apparent, was that, for all the effort, Weatherman wasn't finding much of anyone in the "working class" who wanted to join its revolution. In several cases its representatives ended up in shoving matches with the very people they were trying to befriend. When Mark Rudd tried to recruit a band of tough-looking teens at a Milwaukee hamburger joint, they beat him so badly he had to be hospitalized.

Rudd, in fact, though he was still the symbol of SDS to many, was proving a less-than-inspiring leader. A telling snapshot, offered in Kirkpatrick Sale's *SDS*, came during his appearance at Columbia on September 25, in a speech in which he implored the audience to prepare for the revolution. "I've got myself a gun—has everyone here got a gun?" Rudd all but sneered. "*Anyone?* No? We-e-ll, you'd better fuckin' get your shit together!" When a non-Weatherman SDSer named Paul Rockwell approached the stage, insisting he had heard enough, Rudd took two menacing steps toward him. Rockwell barreled into Rudd and slammed him into the podium, at which point Rudd simply shrugged and slunk to one side of the stage. "Rudd's face was a picture of stunned fear," Sale wrote, "all his rhetoric having done nothing to overcome his ingrained middle-class unfamiliarity with, and anxiety about, violence."

Rudd could see his stock falling. With every passing day, power and influence were passing to the more aggressive leaders, Jeff Jones, Terry Robbins, and especially Bernardine Dohrn, who, as the leadership's sole female, seemed to hold every other Weatherman leader in thrall. "Power doesn't flow out of the barrel of a gun," Rudd snarled at Dohrn during one Weather Bureau meeting. "Power flows out of Bernardine's cunt."[4]

The heart of Weatherman's work remained in Chicago, where the leadership and their friends lived together in groups of five and six. The brutality they experienced there—especially from the Chicago police but also from others—would have a powerful impact on their eventual decision to go underground. One of Jeff Jones's friends, Jonathan Lerner, was given control of the national office, a set of second-story rooms at 1608 West Madison, on the edge of a ghetto. Lerner's tiny staff paid the bills, answered mail, and put out the SDS newspaper, *New Left Notes*. "The office was a terrifying place," Lerner recalls. "The presence of the cops was constant, sitting outside, following us to the bank. We were under siege by this group of black boys, ten, eleven years old. They would come up the fire escapes, race through, and steal people's purses. It was absurd. Eventually we boarded up all the windows to keep the kids out, put deadbolts on all the doors, and built a metal cage like an airlock to get in. None of it helped."

Another danger, though the leadership never publicized it, was the Panthers, whose offices were several blocks away. If SDS was a focus of police harassment, the Chicago Panthers were approaching open war with the police. Their derelict offices were regularly raided, their members stopped and frisked on an hourly basis. The Weathermen idolized the Panthers, but the relationship fast deteriorated. "The Panthers were in a stage of total madness," recalls Lerner. "As those months went on, as they became more paranoid and more crazy, they kind of took it out on us. To them our offices were much bigger, much nicer than theirs, we had lots of equipment, and cars, and the printing press. It rapidly developed into this rip-off relationship. That was emotionally horrible. You couldn't dare question it politically. It was completely insane." Tensions climaxed when a group of Panthers stormed the SDS office, jammed a gun into a girl's face, beat up the SDS printer, Ron Fliegelman, and ransacked the office, making off with typewriters and other equipment. Afterward, Bernardine Dohrn and others went to the Panther offices to complain, Lerner recalls, "and were basically kicked down the stairs."

For all the threats of political violence, however, the emotional violence Weathermen unleashed among themselves proved even more destructive. Throughout this period, the Weather Bureau issued a series of directives designed to mold every individual Weatherman—or "cadre"—into a revolutionary combatant. The most grueling of these practices, borrowed from the Maoist Chinese, was known as criticism/self-criticism, essentially a marathon all-night interrogation in which members were accused of every conceivable human weakness, from cowardice to insubordination. For many, these sessions were too much; dozens of Weathermen left the group as a result. This was the point: to weed out the weak and the unready, to break down all traces of individualism and transform the deponent into a tough, obedient, unquestioning soldier. Another initiative, which actually originated with a group of Detroit Weatherwomen, was the Smash Monogamy program, which ordained that every member of Weatherman break up with his or her romantic partner. The idea, again, was to sever individual Weathermen from every meaningful relationship except that with the group itself. Scores of Weather couples were forced to break up, though it was noted that Dohrn always seemed exempt; while she and JJ did break up during this period, Dohrn began an extended monogamous relationship with Jeff Jones.

The Smash Monogamy program led to Weatherman's most notorious initiative: orgies. The idea was to break down the last remaining personal barriers. As Terry Robbins put it, "People who fuck together fight together." One of the first, called the "national orgy," occurred in Columbus, Ohio, during a visit by the leadership. "We were doing booze, dope, and dancing," a Weatherman named Gerry Long recalled:

> And suddenly you could see the wheels turning in people's minds. Will it happen? When? How to get started? We knew it wouldn't happen of its own accord; somebody had to do something about it. We were constantly talking about asserting leadership in ambiguous situations, and here was a case in point. After a while, Jeff Jones went upstairs to the attic, where the mattresses were, with an old girlfriend. JJ sees them go up and follows, taking off his clothes, too, and lying down beside them. Finally, Billy [Ayers] yells, "It's time to do it!" and takes the hand of the woman he's been dancing with and goes up, too. Within minutes, there was a whole group of naked people looking down from the head of the stairs, saying, "Come on up!" I took the hand of this girl and exchanged a few pleasantries to give it a slightly personal quality, and then we fucked. And there were people fucking and thrashing around all over. They'd sort of roll over on you, and sometimes you found yourself spread over more than one person. The room was like some modern sculpture. There'd be all these humps in a row. You'd

see a knee and then buttocks and then three knees and four buttocks. They were all moving up and down, rolling around.

The next day there was a lingering awkwardness, Long recalls, until one woman piped up, "I'm sure they have to do it this way in Vietnam."[5]

"I was one of the people who instigated [the orgies], one in Chicago, one I remember, after a demonstration in Washington in November," recalls Jon Lerner, who was in the process of coming out. "Billy Ayers and I were the leaders in D.C. After the demonstration, about thirty of us came back to this house. Somebody had a bunch of acid. We sort of said, 'Let's all drop acid and have an orgy,' so we did. For me, it was sort of liberating, because I got a chance to have sex with some of the men I was after. The creepy thing was, I have a memory of several women who came out as lesbians having their first sex with women, and it was weird because everyone was sitting around watching. There were people who clearly didn't want to be there, standing on the sidelines, legs crossed. It was basically creepy."

Weatherman's taste for orgies proved short-lived, petering out within months. Mark Rudd thought all the sexual experimentation—from Smash Monogamy to orgies to homosexuality—was "disastrous," fostering petty jealousies, driving people out of the collectives, and introducing a level of sexual confusion that did little to focus cadres on the revolution. Worst of all, he recalls, was a resulting epidemic of sexually transmitted diseases, from gonorrhea and pelvic inflammatory disease to crab lice and genital infections they called Weather crud. For Rudd, the final straw came when he was having sex with a woman and noticed a crab in her eyebrow.

All of it—the organizing and recruiting, the orgies, the escalating violence—climaxed at the Days of Rage in October. Weatherman leaders crisscrossed the country, giving interviews in which they predicted it would be the largest, most violent mass protest the Movement had seen, something on par with an urban Armageddon. As Mark Rudd told an Ohio television station, "thousands and thousands" of protesters were coming to Chicago "to fight back, to fight the government, to fight their agents, the police." Exactly what that meant, no one was entirely sure. "We're not urging anybody to bring guns to Chicago," Bill Ayers said at the time. "We're not urging anybody to shoot from a crowd. But we're also going to make it clear that when a pig gets iced, that's a good thing, and that everyone who considers himself a revolutionary should be armed, should own a gun."[6] Two nights before the protest, leadership sent a team to detonate Weatherman's first bomb, a small one that destroyed the ten-foot bronze statue of a policeman in Haymarket Square, site of the violent 1886 labor rally in which eleven people (seven of them policemen) were killed. After the Weather bomb went off, a union official vowed that police were ready to meet violence head on. "We now feel," he said, "that it's kill or be killed."

After months of speechmaking and posturing, the long-awaited Days of Rage began on a cool Wednesday night, October 8, 1969, on a rise at the southern end of Lincoln Park. At dusk the Weathermen began gathering around a bonfire—most of the leadership, Dohrn, Bill Ayers, Jeff Jones, all ready for battle. Then they waited, and waited, and waited. By nightfall it was clear something was wrong. Thousands had been expected. At best two hundred people had shown up, almost all of them veteran Weathermen. Everyone stood around blinking, vaguely embarrassed, until one young man, glancing about nervously, muttered, "This is an awful small group to start a revolution."[7]

Small, but ready for havoc. Most were wearing some kind of helmet, goggles, or gas mask; beneath their clothes they hid lead pipes, chains, blackjacks, and their emergency contact information. At 10:25 p.m., after several desultory speeches, Jeff Jones stepped into the firelight and shouted the code words, "I am Marion Delgado!"—evoking the name of a five-year-old California boy who in 1947 had placed a concrete block on railroad tracks to derail an oncoming locomotive. With that, amid a volley of war whoops and echoing ululations—a bit of street theater taken directly from *The Battle of Algiers*—the attack began, some two hundred Weathermen running from the park into the wealthy neighborhood known as the Gold Coast. Chanting "Ho! Ho! Ho Chi Minh!" they tossed bricks through the bay windows of chandeliered apartment houses and bashed the windshields of dozens of cars. Racing toward downtown, they smashed more windows, at the Astor Tower Hotel, the Park Dearborn Hotel, and the Lake Shore Apartments. High above, a few irked residents threw ashtrays and flowerpots.

The police, dozens of whom had been lining Lincoln Park, were caught off guard; they had assumed that the demonstration would take place inside the park. Scrambling to stop the surging protesters, police managed to erect a roadblock in front of the Drake Hotel. Seeing it, the charging Weathermen veered a block east, then ran south into another roadblock, this one manned by thirty helmeted police officers. A melee ensued. Thirty protesters were beaten to the pavement. Others broke through and split into groups, which the police ran down, truncheons swinging, gunshots fired. Six Weathermen were shot, none seriously; dozens were hauled off to jail. By midnight it was over.

It took three days to bail many out of jail. The Weatherman contingent, once again two hundred strong, reassembled on Saturday, at first marching peacefully through downtown streets past double lines of Mayor Daley's finest. At a signal the war whoops again rose, and they broke into a run, swinging pipes at car windshields and chucking rocks. They never had a chance. This time uniformed officers, augmented by plainclothes detectives, appeared at every corner, mercilessly beating everyone with long hair until they fell, bloodied, into the gutters. More than 120 people were arrested. This time someone was seriously hurt: a city attorney named Richard Elrod, who charged at a Weatherman named Brian Flanagan, lost his balance, and hit his head, leaving him paralyzed from the neck down. Flanagan was indicted and later turned himself in; a jury eventually found him not guilty.

It was, all in all, a humiliating debut for Weatherman. Bail bonds alone cost SDS $2.3 million. All the group's top leaders were arrested and now faced criminal charges, typically assault and incitement to riot. But the Days of Rage event did achieve something important: It marked Weatherman as the leading player on the "heavy edge" of the New Left, the furthest left, the wildest, the craziest, the most committed. The leadership chose to declare victory. The next issue of *New Left Notes* argued:

> We came to Chicago to join the other side . . . to do material damage to pig Amerika and all that it's about . . . to do it in the road—in the open—so that white Amerika could dig on the opening of a new front . . . to attack . . . to vamp on those privileges and destroy the motherfucker from the inside. We did what we set out to do, and in the process turned a corner.

FROM HERE ON IT'S ONE BATTLE AFTER ANOTHER—WITH WHITE YOUTH JOINING IN THE FIGHT AND TAKING THE NECESSARY RISKS. PIG AMERIKA BEWARE. THERE'S AN ARMY GROWING IN YOUR GUTS AND IT'S GOING TO BRING YOU DOWN.

"The Days of Rage was really a shock to us, that nobody came but us," recalls Jon Lerner. "You know, we didn't step back and take a sober view of it. We took a reactive view, which was 'Well, if we're the only people who will do this, it's us against the world.' And after that, it was."

"The decision to go underground," says Russell Neufeld, "was largely a function of what happened to us in Chicago, the violence, the brutality. Things like getting a gun put in your mouth, it convinced a lot of us we really were living in a police state. [Going underground] seemed the logical next step."

It appears that the Weather Bureau decided to abolish SDS and go underground in the days immediately after the Days of Rage. The decision had certainly been made by the time the leadership gathered ten days later for a postmortem in a pair of cabins they rented in White Pines Forest State Park, in northern Illinois. Of those present, only Mark Rudd and Jim Mellen have given partial accounts, and both recall that the decision to go underground— to, in effect, attempt a Cuban-style revolution in the United States—was presented to them as a fait accompli. Both voiced doubts, suggesting that the Days of Rage had been a failure and that it might be time to reconnect with a Movement they were turning their backs on. Both were dismissed out of hand.

As Mellen remembered it: "The argument, as usual, was in personal terms. I didn't have the character to be a revolutionary. I lacked audacity. I couldn't do it. When I tried to point out that military action required exactly the kind of discipline that we'd rejected and a technical capacity [i.e., bomb making] we'd never bothered to master, JJ looked at me and said, 'Jim here is from the Six-Months-in-the-Library School of Sabotage.' Everybody laughed, and that was that."[8]

In a 2011 interview for this book, Rudd remembered being stunned by the sudden shift in strategy. They had mused about going underground for months—every self-styled revolutionary had—but Rudd had never truly believed they would go through with it. Just as startling, he says, was how the message was delivered: by Bernardine Dohrn, with preternatural cool, "as if she were suggesting we go for supper." As Rudd recalled it, Dohrn said, "We've learned from Che that the only way to make revolution is to actually begin armed struggle. . . . This is what we've been waiting for. The next step after the National Action is to move to a higher level of struggle, to build the underground. Street violence is an unsustainable tactic—it makes us too vulnerable and costs too much. We've got to be able to work clandestinely."[9]

Rudd couldn't believe it: They were planning to initiate actual violence, actual bombings, actual sabotage. It was surreal. Almost as shocking was Dohrn's final message: Weatherman's underground would be organized not by the Weather Bureau but by a new subset of leadership they were calling the Front Four: Dohrn herself, JJ, Jeff Jones, and the pugnacious Terry Robbins. All the others—Rudd, Mellen, Howie Machtinger, even Bill Ayers—would be relegated to secondary status. Only later would many of them realize that the crucial component in this equation was the little-known Robbins, that in the words of the writers Peter Collier and David Horowitz, who published a history of Weatherman in *Rolling Stone* in 1982, there was a "subtle passing of the torch from JJ, Weatherman's thinker, to Terry, who had proposed himself as Weatherman's doer." One Weatherman told them, "JJ had these fantasies, but it was Terry who was prepared to act them out."[10]

It was a fateful choice. To that point, Robbins had been a marginal member of leadership, an SDS stalwart best known as Ayers's best friend. A chain smoker, small, dark, and intense, Robbins came across to friends as warm and funny, as the sensitive poet he was; others, noting his caustic humor and macho posturing, found him, in the words of a Weatherman ally, Jonah Raskin, "menacing." Robbins was younger than the rest, having just turned twenty-two, but he talked tougher than almost anyone. He was the perfect fist at the end of JJ's arm, endlessly preoccupied—obsessed, some would say—with underground warfare. He would scribble bomb designs and ideas for sabotage in a notebook, remembered by Bill Ayers in his 2001 memoir, *Fugitive Days*:

Terry studied The Blaster's Handbook, a publication of the Explosives Department of E.I. du Pont Corporation, his cranky notebook lying open on the ratty sofa, each inflamed sketch coiled tight, busy with detail, poised to detonate on the page—pressure-trigger device, nipple time bomb, magnifying glass bomb, cigarette fuse, alarm clock time bomb, homemade grenade, walking booby trap, Bangalore torpedo, book trap, pressure-release gate trap, loose floorboard traps, whistle and pipe traps. . . .

There were detailed drawings of bridges—slab bridge, T-beam bridge, concrete cantilever bridge, truss bridge, suspension bridge—with wild X's indicating the pattern of placements that would drop every goddamned thing into the water or the ravine below, and architectural sketches of the skeletons of numerous buildings, with the requisite accompanying fury of X's designed to doom the thing, reduce it to chaos. There were maps of highways with notes on sabotage and destruction.

Page after page was piled with calculated steps for making high explosives with all-but-indecipherable formulae; the formula for nitroglycerin, the formula for mercury fulminate, for dynamite, for chloride of azode, for ammonium nitrate, for black powder. . . . The pigs need a strong dose of their own medicine, Terry said grimly, shoved down their throats. . . . And up their asses, too. A napalm enema for Nixon.

In retrospect, others would remember an inescapable air of violence that hung over Robbins. He came from a broken family and hinted that there had been violence; one of his many girlfriends later came forward to say he beat her. But what troubled some, including his principal lover that winter, Cathy Wilkerson, wasn't so much his comfort with violence as his preoccupation with death. He was constantly talking about the need for Weathermen to give their lives for the revolution, how he was willing to die for the struggle. His favorite movie that season was *Butch Cassidy and the Sundance Kid*, and his favorite scene was the last, when the two outlaws meet their fates charging headlong into a volley of bullets. More than one Weatherman alumnus, discussing Robbins, uses the term "death wish."

After the postmortem, the leadership scattered, some, like Bill Ayers, heading to a massive antiwar demonstration in Washington, and others, like

Mark Rudd, touring the collectives, making sure everyone understood leadership's latest pronouncements while assessing each cadre's capability for supervised violence. Weatherman's cultlike trappings, especially the withering crit/self-crit sessions, seemed to grow even more intense during this period as leadership attempted to break down the last vestiges of individuality in its followers, who strived in turn to parade their combat readiness. One story, probably apocryphal, tells of a young Weatherman who strangled a cat in front of his peers to demonstrate his willingness to kill.

Rudd wrote in his excellent 2009 memoir, *Underground*:

> [This] was the most notorious Weatherman period—more group sex, LSD acid tests, orgiastic rock music, violent street actions, and constant criticism, self-criticism sessions . . . [more] orgies to prove our revolutionary love for each other. . . . We were by now a classic cult, true believers surrounded by a hostile world that we rejected and that rejected us in return. We had a holy faith, revolution, which could not be shaken, as well as a strategy to get there, the foco theory. . . . We were the latest in a long line of revolutionaries from Mao to Fidel to Che to Ho Chi Minh, and the only white people prepared to engage in guerrilla warfare within the homeland.

Then, just before dawn on the morning of December 4, came the moment that for many Weathermen erased any doubt about the rumors of going underground. The telephone calls ricocheted from apartment to apartment with the stunning news: The Chicago police had murdered Panthers leader Fred Hampton in his bed. They had stormed the rooms where he and eight other Panthers were staying; an FBI informant had slipped him a powerful barbiturate, and Hampton was still asleep beside his girlfriend when police shot him twice in the head. For once radical propaganda was accurate: It amounted to an official assassination. Almost every Weatherman had the same thought: Am I next? "Was this our Kristallnacht?" Wilkerson wondered.[11] When the Panthers opened Hampton's apartment to show his bloody mattress to the public, hundreds filed by in astonishment, including Dohrn, Bill Ayers, and many other Weathermen. For most it was the final straw, the moment when their intellectual grasp of armed struggle gave way to rage. "It was the murder of Fred Hampton more than any other factor that compelled us to take up armed struggle," a Weatherman named David Gilbert wrote later. At a viewing of the body, Ayers pulled off the ring a Vietnamese activist had given him and placed it in Hampton's hands. As Ayers wrote later, "We were ready now, our dress rehearsal behind us, to plunge headlong into the whirlpool of violence."[12]

It was December 1969. Fred Hampton's murder was just one of a series of ominous events that heralded the nightmarish end of a tortured decade. Two days later in Altamont, California, Hells Angels knifed and killed a teenager in the unruly crowd watching Mick Jagger and the Rolling Stones perform at the infamous concert. The papers were still jammed with lurid stories of the massacre of five people at the hands of Charles Manson's hippie cult four months earlier. In later years each of these events would be cited as the unofficial end of the Age of Aquarius, or the death of the '60s, or the passing of the Woodstock Generation's dreams of love and hope.

But few gatherings illustrated the dark borderlands between the end of the '60s and the onset of the '70s more clearly than the one Weatherman held in the days between Christmas 1969 and New Year's 1970. Billed as the National War Council, or "Wargasm," it was the pep rally from Hell, a five-day orgy of violent rhetoric intended to set the stage for the underground revolution the leadership was now ready to begin. It was held in a tumbledown dance hall in the heart of a Flint, Michigan, ghetto; on his arrival, Mark Rudd, who continued to have doubts about their plans, fingered a hole in the plywood front door, the result of a shotgun slug that had killed a patron just the night before, and thought, "How appropriate." The Detroit collective had handled the decorations, hanging large psychedelic portraits of Castro, Che, Ho Chi Minh, Mao, Malcolm X, and Eldridge Cleaver. One wall was lined with posters of the fallen Fred Hampton. Above the stage they had hung their centerpiece, a six-foot cardboard machine gun.

Four hundred Weathermen and friends attended, all watched closely by local police, who patrolled the parking lots. The days were filled with calisthenics, karate classes, workshops; evenings, with Weatherman songs written by a popular Columbia SDSer named Ted Gold and others ("I'm dreaming of a white riot, just like the one October Eighth"), increasingly violent speeches, frenetic dancing, and copious amounts of illegal drugs. Every speaker tried to top the one before. "It's a wonderful thing to hit a pig," Rudd found himself telling the crowd. "It must be a really wonderful feeling to kill a pig or blow up a building." JJ hit the high notes. "We're against everything that's good and decent in honky America," he declared. "We will burn and loot and destroy. We are the incubation of your mother's nightmare."

But it was Dohrn's speech that people would talk about for years to come. For once she shed her cool façade and practically screamed for the crowd to avenge the murder of Fred Hampton by bringing violence and chaos, writ large or small, to white America. She told a story of an airline flight where, she claimed, she and JJ had run down the aisles stealing food from the other passengers' trays. "*That's* what we're about," she shouted, "being crazy motherfuckers and scaring the shit out of Honky America." She climaxed by heaping praise on the wild-eyed Charles Manson for his cult's murders, including that of Sharon Tate and Tate's unborn baby. "Dig it!" she famously cried. "First they killed those pigs, then they ate dinner in the same room with them. They even shoved a fork into the victim's stomach! Wild!" Soon everyone in the hall was raising their hands in four-finger salutes, signifying the fork shoved into the pregnant Sharon Tate's belly.

Most nights many of the delegates repaired to the nave of a nearby Catholic church for marathon bouts of group sex. Between all the orgies and the speeches and the karate classes, there was endless speculation about what the leadership was planning. No one was entirely sure what they would be asked to do, although it was assumed that bombings would be part of it. But what else? In one gathering they debated whether killing a white baby was a properly revolutionary act. Behind closed doors, meanwhile, the leadership was in fact finalizing a battle plan, discussing the whats and hows and whens of a struggle that until that point had been purely hypothetical. On New Year's Day 1970, as the last of the attendees rubbed their eyes at the dawn of a new decade, only one thing seemed certain: The Weathermen were going to war.

"AS TO KILLING PEOPLE, WE WERE PREPARED TO DO THAT"

Weatherman, January to March 1970

In the first days after Flint the Weatherman leadership began transitioning the group from a band of brainy protesters into something the country had never seen before: a true combat force determined to launch guerrilla warfare in the streets of America. They were the intellectual vanguard, they believed, and the Movement would follow them into bloody revolution, just as Castro had done in Cuba. Things, needless to say, would not go as planned. Those first two and a half months of 1970 proved the crucial period in determining Weatherman's fate. It entered with a defined public identity, laid detailed plans to adopt a new one, and by mid-March was on its way to becoming something else entirely. It is a period whose details few Weathermen have wanted to discuss publicly. It is the period, bluntly put, when Weatherman set out to kill people.

January began with the generals—Dohrn, Jeff Jones, & Co.—choosing their soldiers. Not everyone who'd been at Flint would go underground—far from it. The days afterward, in fact, are remembered as some of the most emotionally brutal in Weatherman's history, a time when the leadership spread across the country and purged the collectives of everyone they felt wasn't ready to be remade into an armed revolutionary. Anyone who wasn't willing to shed the trappings of bourgeois life—a wife, a boyfriend, a child, a job, anything—was unceremoniously thrown out of Weatherman. Anyone who questioned the leadership, who deviated from the political line, who hadn't demonstrated adequate bravery at the Days of Rage, who was considered weak or undependable or the least bit tentative: out. JJ christened this period "the consolidation."

"Everyone was waiting for what we called a 'tap on the shoulder'; we would say, I hope I get the tap on the shoulder," recalls Jonathan Lerner. "If you were tapped, you didn't talk about it. All that January people were sitting around waiting for the tap on the shoulder, which everyone wanted, because that was the thing to be: Go underground, be a fighter."

The purges began on January 2, when Bill Ayers arrived in Cincinnati to examine its collective. Mark Rudd took Cleveland, while Russ Neufeld and Cathy Wilkerson began slashing the deadwood out of Seattle on January 25. The purges led to the exile of probably a hundred or more Weathermen. Entire collectives disappeared in a matter of days, including Los Angeles, Denver, and Chicago. Seattle simply imploded, many of its members joining rival groups that soon melted into nothingness. No one was spared, though some of those who didn't make the cut were given consolation assignments; Jon Lerner, crushed by his rejection, was sent with three others on a mission to Cuba. Not everyone had to be purged. Many decided they simply didn't have the stomach for underground combat; some, like Neufeld and Brian Flanagan, decided they were better suited to help Weatherman in other ways. Still others, such as Jim Mellen, one of the Weatherman paper's eleven signers, thought the whole idea of guerrilla war was crazy. Mellen was watching the Super Bowl with JJ, Dohrn, and Ayers in Chicago when JJ remarked that anyone who quit now would have to be killed. For Mellen it was the final straw; he walked out of the house at halftime, never to return.[1] Within weeks there were probably no more than 150 active Weathermen left. Those who survived, however, were exactly the kind of people the leadership wanted: obedient soldiers, stripped of individualism, ready to attack "Amerika." A

symbolic end to their old lives came when the leadership closed SDS headquarters and donated its files to the University of Wisconsin. SDS was now
officially dead.

In January 1970 the first of the Weathermen began going "underground."
The term itself had many meanings to many people, but in general being
underground in America during the 1970s simply meant living under an
assumed identity. The underground wasn't a place; it was a lifestyle, a fugitive
lifestyle. There were many shades of it, though, especially with Weatherman.
Some, as in Sam Melville's circle, never got around to adopting new identities
and performed clandestine duties while carrying their actual identification.
Then there were the "aboveground" supporters, of whom Weatherman had
many, perhaps hundreds, far more than any subsequent underground group.
These would include onetime SDSers, purged Weathermen, friends, family,
and others in the Movement; by far the most useful were an array of determined radical attorneys. These people helped with a range of tasks, raising
money, arranging secret meetings, and acting as couriers. From time to time
some even pitched in to help with the group's bombings.

There is a mistaken notion that Weatherman somehow created the underground; it didn't. In fact, by the time its first members began to disappear, a
new kind of underground had been thriving in the United States for several
years. By far its largest concentration of members were military deserters and
draft dodgers fleeing service in Vietnam. The Pentagon listed 73,121 deserters in 1969, 89,088 more in 1970. Many turned themselves in, were arrested,
or fled to Canada. But draft-resistance groups estimated that between 35,000
and 50,000 deserters were living underground in the United States in 1970.
The FBI's central computer listed 75,000 additional criminal fugitives. Even
assuming some overlap between these groups, the hundred or so Weathermen amounted to a handful of new fish in a teeming underground sea.

This new American underground was enabled by a loose network of service providers, from sellers of false ID and cross-border smugglers to people
who would provide safe haven, sometimes in the new communes springing up around the country. One of the most surprising things about living
underground, in fact, was how often members helped out fellow travelers;

Weatherman cells would later shelter several outside fugitives. There were even specialized undergrounds, such as an archipelago of black supporters who sheltered fugitive Black Panthers, and a disciplined Catholic underground that helped hide draft resisters and other Movement figures. While the underground was not a place, certain places did draw the underground, especially cities with vibrant Movement politics. New York and the San Francisco Bay Area were the most popular, along with Boston and Seattle, where many Weathermen would eventually find sanctuary.

Living underground required self-discipline. By late 1969 lists of dos and don'ts were appearing regularly in the radical press. Among them: Avoid automobiles whenever possible; drivers are stopped and asked for identification far more than individuals using public transportation. Never drive at night; that's when most traffic stops are made. Avoid drugs and alcohol unless in a secure environment; both impair judgment. Assume that every telephone is tapped. If a phone must be used, make it a pay phone. One fugitive gave this advice in the *Liberated Guardian* newspaper:

> Cities are generally safer than rural areas or small towns. Avoid communes. Don't wear clothes that are likely to draw suspicion (i.e., military boots or jackets if you were in the Army). Don't turn up at well-known pads. . . . Your involvement in movement activities is up to you. But be aware that your jeopardy increases with the amount of involvement. . . . Once you have a name stick to it, unless you blow it and have to start again. . . . Use only a few trustworthy contacts in different locations to channel your mail. Place your letter in an envelope, omit the return address, send it in another envelope. . . . Avoid leaving fingerprints anywhere, wear gloves in handling letters. . . . Libraries are cool [but] don't check out books with suspicious titles [and] stay away from the out-of-town newspaper rack.

By 1970, thanks to the influx of deserters and draft dodgers, the underground had taken on a decidedly left-wing flavor. An armed robber who escaped from a Midwestern prison that year was startled to find how Movement sympathizers had transformed life on the run. Sitting in New York's Washington Square, he sang their praises to a *New York Times* reporter:

The Movement people are fabulous. They have a real underground that takes care of you. No matter where I went they made sure I had something to eat, they introduced me to others, they made me feel safe. . . . I've only been here three weeks now, but I feel completely different from all the other times I've been on the run. It's not a hassle like it was alone. I'm part of a community. The underground is much bigger than you'd think. It's all around. I could go from place to place for weeks and there'd always be a place I could stay and people to take care of me. . . . Whether you call us criminals or radicals, we've all been [screwed] by society, we're all on the lam together.

Among the first Weathermen to enter this strange new world was Jeff Jones, who related his introduction to it in his son Thai Jones's 2004 book, *A Radical Line.* His journey began in San Francisco that January, at a meal in a Chinatown restaurant, with "a man in a trench coat whom he had never seen before and would never see again." The man helped draft dodgers. After dim sum and tea, the stranger dipped into his pocket and, in exchange for cash, handed Jones an envelope filled with blank government documents: birth and baptismal certificates and draft cards. All Jones had to do was fill in the blanks and overnight he could be someone else.

As scores of Weathermen would do in the coming months, Jones began constructing not one but several false identities; if one was discovered, he had a second ready. Classifying himself 4F, he typed in names on the draft cards, sticking to "J" names: John, Jake, Jason. With a draft card and a false birth certificate, he was able to enroll in a three-hour driving course to obtain a California driver's license. By his own reckoning, Jones would take versions of this course more than twenty times. He researched which states required the least information for a license and spent weeks haunting small-town and out-of-the-way Department of Motor Vehicles offices.

"Building" false identities became a never-ending job for most people in the underground. In those early days, when a man in a trench coat couldn't be found, many Weathermen resorted to stealing purses and wallets and using driver's licenses they found inside. Eventually, petty theft came to be frowned upon as an unacceptable risk; worse, once a license was reported stolen, its use could get the thief arrested. Bill Ayers recalled once using a stolen license and credit card to rent a fancy car and buy new clothes, until Jeff Jones showed him how foolish he was being. (Shoplifting, however, was a common pastime; when Cathy Wilkerson needed a winter coat on her arrival in New York, she walked out of a boutique with one.) In time even dealing with ID brokers was deemed too risky. By the spring, most Weathermen had begun building false identities employing an old Communist Party trick: using the birth certificates of long-dead infants to file for Social Security cards and other government identification papers. Dead babies could be identified by searching old newspapers or, as Ayers did more than once, walking the grounds of remote cemeteries in search of infant graves dated between 1940 and 1950. Collecting their birth certificates became a "small industry," Ayers recalled; soon the group would amass hundreds of them.

"I used a blank birth certificate; somebody stole it for me," recalls Paul Bradley. "In time I had a pretty darn good set of ID. The only thing we couldn't figure out was credit cards, so we used cash for everything. For airplane flights, for rent, for everything."

As the last of the old collectives were purged that February, the survivors were herded into three sets of new underground collectives, sometimes called tribes, to be based in New York City, San Francisco, and the Midwest. Two tribes were based in Manhattan. One, tasked with gathering money and false identification, was headquartered in a Chinatown apartment under JJ's supervision; Mark Rudd took a bed there, along with Paul Bradley, Ron Fliegelman, the SDS printer, and others. The second tribe, led by Terry Robbins, was to plan and carry out East Coast bombings; its dozen or so members were initially spread across several Manhattan and Brooklyn apartments. In the Midwest, the collectives in Pittsburgh, Columbus, Milwaukee, and Cincinnati were shut down; the survivors gathered in Chicago, Detroit, Cleveland, and Buffalo under the loose supervision of Bill Ayers.

The rest of the leadership, including Bernardine Dohrn, Jeff Jones, and Howie Machtinger, along with fifteen or so others, made their way to San Francisco, where two apartments were rented, on Geary Street and in

Haight-Ashbury. Later Dohrn and Jones decided to distance themselves from the others, establishing a West Coast headquarters of sorts on a pink house-boat they rented at the Sausalito piers for $200 a month. The decision to relocate to the Bay Area, where SDS had little presence, was later a cause for some head-scratching. Some would cite San Francisco's importance as a center of the burgeoning youth culture, which was part of it. Another reason for the decision was Jeff Jones's familiarity with the area's New Left community. Yet another was the crucial presence of one of Dohrn's closest friends, the radical attorney Michael Kennedy, who would soon emerge as perhaps Weather's most useful aboveground supporter.

In those first days Dohrn and Jones found California liberating. All the hassle of Chicago—the police raids, the street fighting, the constant surveillance—seemed swept away in the cool seaside breezes. The houseboat had a fireplace and a metal ladder to the roof, where Dohrn sunbathed, sometimes topless. Overhead, seagulls swooped to and fro. As in New York, they established two collectives in San Francisco, one to gather money and false documentation, and a second, supervised by Machtinger, which prepared to stage bombings on the West Coast.

Outside the leadership, there was widespread confusion as to what kinds of actions were authorized (as there was for decades afterward). There would be bombings, everyone assumed, but what kind? "There was so much macho talk, you know, like the Panthers, 'Off the pigs,' 'Bomb the military back into the Stone Age,'" recalls Cathy Wilkerson. "But did that mean we were actually going to kill people? I never really knew." Bill Ayers and others would later insist there were never any plans to harm people, only symbols of power: courthouses, police stations, government buildings. The handful of Weathermen who crossed that line, Ayers claims, were rogues and outliers. This is a myth, pure and simple, designed to obscure what Weatherman actually planned. In the middle ranks, in fact, it was widely expected that Weathermen would become revolutionary murderers. "My image of what we were gonna be was undiluted terrorist action," recalls Jon Lerner. "I remember talking with Teddy Gold about putting a bomb on the [Chicago railroad] tracks at rush hour, to blow up people coming home from work. That's what I was looking forward to."

In fact, what constituted a legitimate target for a Weatherman bombing was the topic of sensitive discussions among the leadership at Flint. It was during these talks, according to Howard Machtinger and one other person who were present, that the leadership agreed that they would, in fact, kill people. But not just any people. The people Weatherman intended to kill were policemen. "If your definition of terrorism is, you don't care who gets hurt, we agreed we wouldn't do that," recalls Machtinger. "But as to causing damage, or literally killing people, we were prepared to do that." According to one side of the argument, says Machtinger, "if all Americans were compliant in the war, then everyone is a target. There are no innocents. That was always Terry and JJ's argument. But we did have a series of discussions about what you could do, and it was agreed that cops were legitimate targets. We didn't want to do things just around the war. We wanted to be seen targeting racism as well, so police were important." Military personnel were ruled to be legitimate targets as well.

The decision to attack policemen was an unspoken act of solidarity with the group whose approval mattered most to Weatherman leadership: Movement blacks, especially the Black Panthers, who reserved a special hatred for urban police. The death of Fred Hampton and the brutality of the Chicago police in general made almost everyone in the leadership eager to seek revenge against policemen. "In our hearts, I think what all of us wanted to be were Black Panthers," Cathy Wilkerson recalls. "And it was no secret what the Panthers wanted to do, which is what the Black Liberation Army did later, and that's kill policemen. It's all they wanted to do."

By the first week of February 1970, all three Weatherman groups—San Francisco, the Midwest, and New York—were more or less in place. Everyone, at least in the leadership, understood what would come next: bombings. Perhaps surprisingly, there appears to have been no coordination among the three groups, no overarching plan of attack. Instead, the field marshals in each group—Howie Machtinger in San Francisco, Bill Ayers in the Midwest, and Terry Robbins in New York—mapped out their initial actions independently. Given Weatherman's leadership culture, it is hardly surprising that a keen competition arose among the three men and their acolytes to see who could launch the first, and splashiest, attacks.

"The problem with Weather wasn't that people disagreed with our ideology," Machtinger says. "It was that they thought we were wimpy. The sense was, if we could do something dramatic, people would follow us. But we had to act fast. We had no idea what Terry and Billy were doing, they had no idea what we were doing, but everyone wanted to be first." Adds Wilkerson, "That was the real problem: all these macho guys with their macho posturing, seeing who could be the big man and strike first."

Working from the Geary Street apartment, Machtinger and the leadership were determined to strike quickly. They decided to mount an attack on the police, sending male-and-female teams—posing as lovebirds—to scout police stations throughout the Bay Area. They selected the sprawling Hall of Justice complex in Berkeley as their first target. No one involved would remember where they obtained the dynamite—"I don't remember that being a problem," Machtinger recalls—but they managed to assemble two pipe bombs at Geary Street. Each device carried two sticks of dynamite linked to an alarm clock. The devices were wiped with alcohol to remove any fingerprints.

The new Weatherman underground made its unannounced debut six weeks after Flint, late on the evening of Thursday, February 12, when five or six Weathermen edged into position around the Berkeley police complex. There had been no warning call; this was intended to be an ambush, pure and simple. Just before midnight, when shifts would change, sending dozens of off-duty policemen out to their cars, two Weathermen crept into the parking lot. One bomb was placed beside a detective's car; a second was tossed on the ground between cars. A few minutes after midnight, as officers began wandering outside, the first bomb detonated, its deep boom echoing through the downtown streets. Nearly thirty plate-glass windows in the adjoining municipal building shattered. More than two dozen officers were in the parking lot, and one, a reserve patrolman named Paul Morgan, was struck by shrapnel that mangled his left arm; he would later undergo six hours of surgery to save it. Thirty seconds later, as groups of stunned policemen slowly rose from the pavement, the second bomb went off, shattering more windows. Afterward, a half-dozen cops would be treated for bruises and broken eardrums.

"We wanted to do it at a shift change, frankly, to maximize deaths," says a Weatherman cadre who took part in the action that night. "They were cops, so anyone was fair game. Basically it was seen as a successful action. But others, yeah, were angry that a policeman didn't die. There was no one that was anti that. That was what we were trying to do."

Because Weatherman took no credit for the Berkeley bombing, it received none. Until now, no history or memoir of the group has mentioned it, much less its intent, which has allowed apologists like Bill Ayers to claim that Weatherman never intended to hurt people. Even at the time, the attack received little notice, in large part because there were so many bombings that winter. In just the two-week period before and afterward, from February 6 to February 21, 1970, there were seventeen incidents of significant radical violence in the United States, including two bombings by a Puerto Rican independence group in New York on February 9; a firebombing in Ypsilanti, Michigan, on February 11; the bombing of a police station in Danbury, Connecticut, that injured twenty-three people on February 13; another set of bombings in Berkeley, believed to be the work of black militants, on February 16; and sundry other bombings in Hartford, Boston, and Maryland.

One of the enduring mysteries of the Weatherman story centers on one of these seemingly unrelated incidents. It happened just four nights after the Berkeley bombing, on the evening of Monday, February 16. A steady rain was falling as a forty-four-year-old San Francisco police sergeant named Brian McDonnell sorted through bulletins at a Teletype machine inside the Park Police Station in the upper Haight neighborhood. At 10:45 p.m., with no warning, a bomb exploded on an outside window ledge, just feet from where McDonnell was standing. The device was packed with inch-long industrial fence staples, many of which erupted through the window and shredded McDonnell's face, severing his jugular vein and lodging in his brain; he was dead within two days. Detectives later surmised that the bomb had been timed to go off at the 11 p.m. shift change, much as the first Weatherman bomb had gone off at the Berkeley station.

The case has never been solved, but from the beginning San Francisco police suspected Weatherman. In 1972 detectives debriefed a Bay Area radical named Matthew Landy Steen, who claimed to have joined planning sessions for the action with Dohrn and Machtinger, among others. Two years later, in sworn testimony before a Senate committee, the FBI informant Larry Grathwohl claimed that Bill Ayers told a Weatherman meeting in Buffalo, New York, that Dohrn had supervised the attack; investigators, however, discounted this. They put more weight on stories told by a Weather associate named Karen Latimer, who emerged in the mid-1970s to tell of another meeting at which Dohrn presided and Machtinger oversaw the bomb building. According to a 2009 article in *San Francisco Weekly*, prosecutors came close to indicting Dohrn, Machtinger, and Jeff Jones in the late 1970s on Latimer's word alone.

The case lay fallow until 1999, when a task force of retired prosecutors and FBI agents reopened it as part of a drive to prosecute several unsolved '60s-era killings. Latimer's death, however, as well as a lack of any physical evidence, has to date precluded any indictment. Still, as late as 2010, authorities asked several Weathermen, including Machtinger, to give voice and handwriting samples. Few believe the case will ever be solved. Needless to say, the Weathermen who were in San Francisco at the time all deny any involvement. "That Berkeley action took weeks of planning," says one. "Given that, it's not like we could turn around and do another one four days later."

As Weatherman initiated its first attacks on police in February 1970, the most complex management task fell to twenty-five-year-old Bill Ayers, who found himself shuttling between collectives in Chicago, Detroit, Cleveland, and Buffalo. By the time of the Berkeley bombing on February 13, he had plans for similar actions under way in the Midwest. A vivid glimpse of Ayers in action during this period was later provided by Larry Grathwohl, the Cincinnati student who had joined Weatherman the previous fall.*

According to Grathwohl's account, Ayers chaired his first strategy meet-

---

*In the mid-1970s Grathwohl testified about Weatherman before a Senate subcommittee and subsequently wrote a book, *Bringing Down America*. Later he emerged as a kind of conservative gadfly who regularly appeared on Fox News and other cable channels to talk about Ayers and others he knew in the group. Grathwohl died in 2013.

ing in a vacant classroom at Wayne State University in Detroit. He led six Weathermen in a discussion of possible targets for a kidnapping or a bombing, including Vice President Spiro Agnew and Detroit's mayor. Grathwohl sensed that Ayers already had a target in mind, and watched as he guided the group toward it. At the time, three Detroit police officers were on trial in the deaths of three black youths during a 1967 riot. "Where did [those] pigs get the money to hire decent lawyers?" Ayers asked. "The Police Officers Association put up the money." When someone mentioned that the association had a headquarters downtown, Ayers pounced. "We blast that fucking building to hell," he said. "And we do it when the place is crowded. We wait for them to have a meeting, or a social event. Then we strike."[2]

The attack, Ayers indicated, would come at the same time that a second Weatherman group bombed the Detroit police's 13th Precinct house. Ayers unfolded a piece of paper on which he had drawn the neighborhood around the association headquarters. As the group studied it, he assigned each member a task, constructing disguises, securing a getaway car, and, for Grathwohl, scouting the target. Grathwohl, who was in regular contact with his FBI handlers, later told Ayers that he objected to his plan to place the bomb on a window ledge, which faced a restaurant called the Red Barn. "We'll blow out the Red Barn restaurant," he argued. "Maybe even kill a few innocent customers—and most of them are black."

According to Grathwohl's account, Ayers was unconcerned with killing innocent passersby, as was his best friend, Terry Robbins, in New York; both were regularly overheard to make comments to the effect that "collateral damage" was to be expected in any war. "We can't protect all the innocent people in the world," Ayers said, according to Grathwohl. "Some will get killed. Some of us will get killed. We have to accept that fact."

In the end, the two bombs, composed of forty-four sticks of dynamite, were placed exactly as Ayers planned, on the night of March 6, by which time Grathwohl had been transferred to another city. Detroit police found them before they exploded, however, either because they were built improperly or because Grathwohl alerted the FBI in time to remove them.

Another of Ayers's collectives, Cleveland, led by a Columbia SDS veteran named John Fuerst, was almost as ambitious. It was a group of six or seven that included two high school girls, one a sixteen-year-old dropout named Joanna Zilsel, who had made a life attending Weatherman and other demonstrations. Zilsel's parents were prominent progressives in the Cleveland area, but when her mother prevented her from attending the Days of Rage and Flint, she left home to join Weatherman. "We didn't have money, we didn't have anything, we were figuring things out on the fly; the only stuff we had we shoplifted," Zilsel recalls. "I think people were quite confused about what we were supposed to be doing. I know I was."

At one point, John Fuerst met with Bill Ayers. According to an informant— apparently one of the high schoolers—who spoke to the FBI in 1972, Ayers told Fuerst to focus on targets linked to the case of a militant convicted of murdering three Cleveland policemen, Ahmed Evans. How and what they did, however, was left to the Cleveland collective. "When [Fuerst] came back, he said, 'You know, we're on our own. That's just the way it is. All over the country there are cells, and everyone is doing their own thing,'" Zilsel says. "I don't remember hearing even a flavor of marching orders. It was more: Here we are, a group of individuals with a very strong commitment to making urgently needed change. The war had to be ended, racism had to be stopped, the system had to be changed. So we did the best we could."

The Cleveland collective launched its first action early on the morning of Monday, March 2. Their target was the home of a detective named Frank Schaeffer, president of the Fraternal Order of Police. At about 1:15 a.m., members of the collective crept into Schaeffer's front yard, Molotov cocktails ready to be lit. "We had a very clear plan, with designated responsibilities, signals and a driver," recalls Zilsel. "We went over this many, many times. And we were there and this young man, he was standing right beside me, he just lights the thing and throws it. With no coordination, just forgetting the plan. He just lost it. And we're like, 'Oh, my God, this is happening.' So I instantly said, 'There is no choice here, you have to follow through.' And so I [threw mine]. And we got away. It was just sheer panic and confusion." The firebombs ignited on the front porch. Wakened, Schaeffer and his son rushed out and extinguished the flames.

Oddly, it was the most aggressive of the Weatherman leaders, Terry Robbins, whose New York collective was the last to mobilize. Obliged to serve a six-week jail sentence following a demonstration, Robbins didn't arrive in Manhattan until late January, when actions proposed by the California and Midwestern groupings were well into the planning stages. Robbins, however, was determined that if his debut came last, it would be the splashiest.

A glimpse of Robbins's preparations comes from his girlfriend at the time, Cathy Wilkerson. Unlike Ayers, who granted subordinates wide latitude, Robbins took full control from the outset. At an initial meeting, the mood was grim—no jokes, no laughter. After months of airy talk, they were finally going to war. Robbins announced that he intended to launch three simultaneous firebombings. They discussed an array of targets, including buildings at Columbia and various police precincts. They made their move on the frigid night of Saturday, February 21, 1970. Robbins had gathered the makings of at least nine Molotov cocktails—each a glass bottle filled with gasoline, with a cloth inserted into its mouth, ignited by, of all things, a firecracker. That night everyone gathered around a gasoline can behind a supermarket, filled their bottles, and scattered to their targets. The first bomb was tossed at a patrol car outside the NYPD's Charles Street precinct at 1:30 a.m.; a second blew up in the street nearby. Neither caused any damage. Two hours later two more were thrown at navy and army recruitment booths near Brooklyn College; the booths were scorched. A fifth ignited on the steps of the Columbia University law library.

Robbins himself led a group into the Inwood neighborhood, at Manhattan's northern tip, to the redbrick home of John Murtagh, the judge overseeing the Panther 21 conspiracy trial. Murtagh was asleep inside with his wife and three children. Before placing the bombs, the group scrawled FREE THE PANTHER 21 and THE VIETCONG HAVE WON on the sidewalk. A neighbor called the police, who sent a patrol car. Before it arrived, the Weathermen placed three shopping bags containing Molotov cocktails beside the front door, on a window ledge, and beneath a car in the garage. All three went off at 4:30 a.m., blowing out two of the home's windows and scorching the car.*3

As a "political action," it was amateurish. On Sunday morning the bomb-ings drew headlines in the New York papers, but Weatherman's role went unreported; as in Berkeley, it had not sent a communiqué. Without it, "no one knew what they were about," Wilkerson recalled. "It didn't feel like we had accomplished anything. Firebombing had become routine. We could do them until we were blue in the face, and the government wouldn't really care."4

Robbins was disgusted with himself and the group for launching such an inconsequential attack. He began laying plans for something far more ambi-tious. First, though, they needed to get organized. The collective's members were scattered across the city, and when Wilkerson mentioned that her father was taking a Caribbean vacation, Robbins startled her by asking whether she could get a key to the family townhouse, on Eleventh Street in Greenwich Village. The suggestion hit Wilkerson "like a ton of bricks," she recalled, because it meant involving her family in her new underground life. She and her father, James, a radio executive, were estranged. Still, she went along, telephoning her father and telling him she had come down with the flu and needed a place to recuperate. He questioned her closely, then relented.

On Tuesday, February 24, Wilkerson visited the townhouse, on a quiet, tree-lined block just off Fifth Avenue, to see her father and stepmother off. She said nothing about anyone joining her there. Two hours later Teddy Gold and Terry Robbins arrived. Wilkerson, worried that a cousin might visit, pinned a note on the door saying she had the measles and would be watering the plants in her father's absence; she was confident the cousin wouldn't enter without at least a phone call. Robbins, meanwhile, toured the townhouse. It had four floors, plenty of bedrooms, and a subbasement with a workbench

---

*The details of the Robbins group's first actions are supplied by Wilkerson, who actually remembered that the Murtagh bombing happened on a different night from the other firebombings. However, newspaper articles at the time date them all to a single evening, February 21. Over the course of the next ten days, no other firebombings received mention in the New York press, suggesting that Wil-kerson's memory may be faulty and that all the Weather firebombings did happen on the same evening.

where James Wilkerson sometimes worked refinishing antique furniture. It would be a good spot for the technical work Robbins envisioned.

The following day, after five of them had moved in, Robbins chaired a meeting around the kitchen table.* Everyone agreed that the weekend actions had been a failure. Firebombings would no longer cut it; every ROTC building in America, it seemed, had been the target of Molotov cocktails. The answer, Robbins announced, was dynamite. Dynamite was actually safer, he insisted. It exploded only with the help of a triggering device, typically a blasting cap. They could buy it almost anywhere in New England. He had learned how to safely make a dynamite bomb, Robbins said. It was the only way to create an action large enough to get the government's attention. By that point, Robbins's authority was unquestioned. No one raised any objections.

That night in bed Robbins and Wilkerson had a long talk. In private, both admitted their fears. Robbins was secretly intimidated by the technical difficulties of building a bomb. As Wilkerson recalled it:

> [Terry] had been an English major during his brief stint in college, and a poet. Science was a foreign language, and he hated it for being undecipherable. Because this left him powerless, he felt terrified. He understood no more about what electricity or dynamite were made of than I did, and he was considerably less interested. . . . Terry's fear and dislike of anything technical could be overcome, I insisted. I tried to get him to see that it would be interesting to learn how all this worked. . . . [But] his fear, his courage, and his rage against injustice were feeding each other into a white heat. He was in a hurry, and didn't want to mull it over too much. . . .

> [His fear] could be overcome, he believed, by will. No one else seemed to be stepping up to the plate. Most people, even those in the movement, seemed willing to stand by while the United States rode roughshod over its victims. This infuriated Terry. We owed it to the Vietnamese to take some of the heat away from them. We owed the black movement to do the same.[5]

---

*Five people were living in the townhouse that week: Terry Robbins, Diana Oughton, Cathy Wilkerson, Teddy Gold, and Kathy Boudin. At least a half-dozen more members of the collective, including Brian Flanagan, lived elsewhere.

What worried Wilkerson most about their talk was Robbins's continuing fixation on *Butch Cassidy and the Sundance Kid* and its vision of young heroes going out "in a blaze of glory." If they failed, he swore, if they couldn't ignite a revolution, at least they would be symbols. Robbins was prepared to die for the cause. Wilkerson wasn't. Neither, she realized, were many of the others she knew in Weatherman. Not for the first time, she felt herself being carried along in a rushing river, powerless to stop.

On Saturday, February 28, the collective gathered to discuss targets: universities, police stations, ROTC buildings. Someone had seen a newspaper item about a dance at Fort Dix, an army base east of Philadelphia in New Jersey. Robbins seized on the idea of "taking the war" to the military but allowed other targets to be considered as well. Over the next few days they scouted half a dozen targets and got preparations under way. The dynamite proved easy to secure. On Monday, March 2—the day the Cleveland collective staged its attack—a member of JJ's tribe, Ron Fliegelman, did what Sam Melville hadn't realized he could do: He walked into the offices of New England Explosives in Keene, New Hampshire, presented the stolen driver's license of a New York rabbi, and laid out less than $60; he walked out with two fifty-pound cases of American Cyanamid dynamite, each case containing one hundred sticks.* The next day, neighbors on Eleventh Street watched as Teddy Gold supervised the unloading of crates from a van.

By Tuesday Robbins had decided on their target: the dance at Fort Dix. Dozens of army officers would be there with their sweethearts. They would strike, he announced, that Friday, March 6; this would be the same evening Bill Ayers carried out the failed bombings in Detroit, suggesting that Robbins and Ayers, who visited the townhouse that week, were trying to coordinate their strikes. Later, there would be speculation as to what the rest of the leadership had known of Robbins's plan. Ayers almost certainly knew. In the Chinatown collective, JJ and Mark Rudd knew. Blood, Robbins assured

---

*At the time, the sale of firecrackers was illegal in New Hampshire. The sale of dynamite wasn't. "You can buy dynamite easier than bananas," the state's attorney general complained in an interview with the *New York Times*.

Rudd that week, would run in the streets. When Rudd asked where, Robbins said, "We're gonna kill the pigs at a dance at Fort Dix."[6] In the years since, Bernardine Dohrn and Jeff Jones have downplayed their knowledge of the attack. A Weatherman confidant of both, however, asserts that privately the two have admitted they knew but were reluctant to confront Robbins.

On Thursday, March 5, Robbins chaired a final meeting in the townhouse kitchen, going over details and assignments for the attack. A new face was present; Diana Oughton, Ayers's girlfriend, who had been transferred to join the group. If Oughton was uncomfortable with the plan—an attack that, if successful, amounted to mass murder—she showed no sign. Neither did anyone else at the table. In fact, according to Cathy Wilkerson, there was no talk whatsoever about the decision to actually kill people. Years later she admitted that she had viewed those they planned to kill only as an "abstraction."[7]

There was, however, at least one naysayer. He will be called James. He was one of the Columbia alumni; he had been JJ's roommate at one point. James was a member of the collective who did not live in the townhouse. According to a longtime friend, "the target had been bothering him for days. Finally, right at the end, he went nuts. This was the night before. He just went crazy, crying and screaming, 'What are we doing? What are we doing?' And you know what Teddy Gold told him? [He said,] 'James, you have been my best friend for ten years. But you gotta calm down. I wouldn't want to have to kill you.' And he was serious."

That Thursday in the kitchen, they focused on practical details. There was some talk of how much dynamite to use. No one, least of all Robbins, knew how much damage a single stick would do or whether it would take one or ten sticks to blow up a building. Someone said dynamite did more damage if inserted into a pipe. Not much dynamite could go inside a pipe, however, so Robbins said he planned to pack roofing nails into the bomb as well, in order to do as much damage as possible. Wrapping up, he described the electrical circuit to trigger the explosion, as he had been taught. Someone asked if it would contain a safety switch, a way to test the bomb short of detonation. Robbins hadn't a clue. "Terry had been told to do it a certain way, and he was too insecure in his knowledge to debate it," Wilkerson remembered. "He cut off the discussion. He was the leader and he would take responsibility for how it was to be done. . . . No one else spoke up."[8]

By that evening Robbins had begun preparing his bombs at the workbench deep in the subbasement. He had far more dynamite than they needed, along with wire and a bomb-making text. No one knew what would happen when the bombs exploded at Fort Dix. They might be regarded as mass murderers; they might be heroes; they might be revolutionaries. In their minds Robbins and his acolytes were certain of only one thing: They would be striking back. It was Russia in 1905, and this was the road to a true revolution.

Everything was happening so fast. To members of the collective, what mattered most was striking back, and striking back now. No one took much time to ponder repercussions. At one point that week, Diana Oughton spoke with an old friend, Alan Howard. She admitted that the Days of Rage and Flint had achieved little and that the revolution would be possible only with mass support.

"We have a lot to learn," she said. "We'll make mistakes."[9]

They would have time for only one.

05

THE TOWNHOUSE

Weatherman, March to June 1970

That Friday, March 6, the day they planned to bomb the Fort Dix dance, everyone rose early at the townhouse. Terry Robbins and Diana Oughton disappeared into the subbasement to finish building the bombs. Teddy Gold walked to the Strand bookstore, where he ran into Kathy Boudin's mother, Jean. "Ted, Ted," Jean said, kissing Gold on his bearded cheek. She knew Gold stayed in touch with her daughter.

"Do you think Kathy will pick herself up and go to NYU Law School in the fall?" she asked.

"No," Gold said, his voice cracking from a cold.

"Is she living in Manhattan?"

"Sort of," Gold said. Jean Boudin rolled her eyes and smiled. She had been around leftists enough to know not to ask more.[1]

Back at the townhouse, Cathy Wilkerson busied herself stripping the beds and straightening the rooms. Her father and stepmother were due back from St. Kitts that afternoon, and everyone had to be gone, the house thoroughly cleaned, for their arrival. After Gold returned from the Strand,

Wilkerson tossed the sheets in a washer and started vacuuming. While others finished up the disguises they would wear that night, she unfolded an ironing board in the kitchen. Barefoot, her toes wriggling on the carpet, she had just begun pressing the wrinkles from a sheet when Gold came up the basement stairs. Robbins needed cotton balls, and Gold said he was running to the drugstore to buy some. Wilkerson nodded. Overhead, water coursed through the pipes. Kathy Boudin had just stepped into a second-floor shower.

A moment later, a few minutes before noon, as Wilkerson ironed sheets by the dull gray light of a kitchen window, everything—the townhouse collective, the Weatherman organization, every thought of armed revolution every student militant across the nation dared harbor—changed forever. Suddenly Wilkerson felt a shock wave ripple through the house, along with a deep rumbling from below. The ironing board began to vibrate. Everything seemed to happen in slow motion. Still standing, the hot iron in her hand, Wilkerson felt herself begin to fall as fissures appeared in the carpet at her feet. Geysers of splintered wood and plaster filled the air. A second, louder explosion came then, the floor gave way, and Wilkerson felt herself sinking. She had the presence of mind to toss the iron to one side. She was dimly aware of a dull red glow somewhere beneath her. When she stopped falling, everything went black. She could barely see.

The two explosions eviscerated the townhouse, destroying the first floor and blowing a great hole in its brick façade; above, the top floors hung like a set of trembling balconies, ready to fall at any moment. Up and down Eleventh Street windows blew out. Shattered glass sparkled like diamonds on the side-walks. All across Greenwich Village, heads turned at the sudden booms. A block away, walking on Fifth Avenue, Jean Boudin felt the explosion, stepped toward it, and saw the townhouse in flames. She had no idea her daughter was inside.

The first officers on the scene, a patrolman named Ronald Waite, who had been guarding a school crossing around the corner, and a Housing Authority cop named Vincent Calderone, who had just left a doctor's office nearby, arrived within moments of the explosions. Running up to the house, Waite tried to enter but was driven back by billowing white smoke; he dashed away, looking for help. Seeing no entry through the front of the townhouse,

Calderone sprinted through an adjoining house and circled to the rear of the Wilkerson home, where he encountered a padlocked door and barred windows.

Inside, Cathy Wilkerson was regaining her senses. Miraculously, she was unhurt. Her face was coated in soot and dust; she could barely see. She was seized by the need to find Robbins and Oughton. "Adam?" she called, using Robbins's code name. "Adam, are you there?"

Standing at the back door, Officer Calderone heard her words. As yet he had no sense that a crime had been committed; his only thoughts were of rescuing survivors. Fearing that the building would collapse at any moment, he drew his service revolver and fired several shots into the heavy padlock. It did nothing. Just then the house began to quiver, as if about to fall. Calderone backed away from the door.

"Adam?" Wilkerson asked once more. A voice answered, asking for help. It was Kathy Boudin, somewhere close by in the rubble.

"Are you okay?" Wilkerson asked.

"I can't see," Boudin said. It was the dust.

Wilkerson was dimly aware of flames. She sensed that they had barely ten or fifteen seconds before the fire reached them. Groping blindly, she inched left along the edge of what appeared to be a crater, reaching for Boudin. They touched hands, then grasped them. Wilkerson, still barefoot, took a step or two across the rubble, trying to reach what appeared to be a shaft of daylight in front of her. She could hear the flames building behind them. A few steps more, and she managed to pull herself and Boudin up a rise and out of the crater.

Just then a third explosion erupted from beneath the rubble at the back of the house. The force of it blew a massive hole in the wall of an adjoining building, which happened to house an apartment occupied by the actor Dustin Hoffman and his wife; Hoffman's desk fell into the hole. Behind the house, the blast knocked Officer Calderone from the door. As flames erupted from the rear windows, he stumbled and ran.

As he did, Wilkerson and Boudin clawed over the last of the rubble and emerged onto the sidewalk, dazed. Wilkerson wore nothing but blue jeans;

her blouse had been blown off. Boudin was nude. Other than cuts and bruises, the two women had not been seriously hurt.

A man in a white coat, a doctor passing the scene, helped them to their feet. A neighbor, Susan Wager, the ex-wife of the actor Henry Fonda, appeared and threw her coat around Boudin's shoulders.

"Is there anyone else in there?" she asked.

"Yes," Wilkerson mumbled as chunks of the townhouse's façade fell onto the sidewalk. "Maybe two."[2]

"Come on to my house and I'll give you something to wear," Wager said, leading the two shaken women down the sidewalk. Inside, she guided the pair to an upstairs bathroom, tossed towels on the floor outside, then jogged to a closet, where she pulled out two pairs of jeans, a pink sweater and a blue turtleneck, a pair of pink patent leather go-go boots, and a set of olive-green slippers. She left them outside the bathroom. A hand reached out and took them.

Regaining her senses, Wilkerson knew they had only minutes before the police arrived. She and Boudin showered quickly. When Wager left, Wilkerson crept from the bathroom and rifled through a set of closets in search of money or a subway token, anything they could use to flee. She found a token, then grabbed Boudin and trundled downstairs to the front door, where Wager's housekeeper said they shouldn't leave. The sound of sirens was already filling the air as Wilkerson insisted they needed to go to the drugstore and buy burn ointment. Before the woman could answer, they were out the door. They fast-walked down the sidewalk, hoping to avoid notice, and as the first fire trucks arrived behind them, made their way to the subway. And vanished.[3]

By twelve thirty, a half hour after the explosions, the hollowed-out skeleton of the townhouse was engulfed in angry flames, spewing thick clouds of smoke into the gray sky. A phalanx of fire trucks lined Eleventh Street, directing jets of water into the fire. In that first hour most of the firefighters assumed it was an accidental gas explosion, but the senior detective on the scene, Captain Bob McDermott of the First District, sensed that something was amiss. He put in a call to his boss, the chief of detectives whose men had arrested Sam Melville five months earlier: the crusty Albert Seedman.

"Captain McDermott just says it's like no gas explosion he ever saw," an aide told Seedman. "Like—it's unnatural."[4]

Seedman set up a command post in a basement across the street, which soon filled with the city's fire chiefs and a milling squadron of clean-cut FBI men. All that afternoon they watched as the fire consumed what remained of the townhouse. By dusk flames still raged at the rear, while the front had crumbled into a massive heap of smoking, red-hot rubble two stories high. Seedman, suspicious at the disappearance of the only known survivors, contacted James Wilkerson's office and learned that his daughter had been staying at the house. He got his first lead when a detective hustled up around 6 p.m. A records check, the detective said, indicated that Cathy Wilkerson belonged to Weatherman—"the wildest of the wildest," as he put it.

Seedman pondered the news all that evening as the rubble cooled and firefighters began to take shovels to the top layers. This was no gas leak, he felt sure. But why would Cathy Wilkerson bomb her father's home? Did she hate her father that much? Or was it something else? He was still chewing over matters around seven when there were shouts from the debris. They had found a body, a young man with red hair, lying crushed in the rubble with his mouth wide open. He was loaded into an ambulance and taken to the coroner's office for identification.

Cranes were wheeled in; all weekend they lifted the rubble and dumped it into waiting trucks to be taken to the Gansevoort Street pier, where police raked through it for clues. Sunday evening Seedman was at his command post when he got the news: The dead man was another Weatherman, Teddy Gold.* For Seedman, this changed everything. One Weatherman could be dismissed. Two meant this was no accident. This was a bomb factory.

The news broke in the Monday morning papers. At Columbia students

---

*In later years Gold's Weather comrades would speculate that he had returned to the townhouse from the drugstore in time to be killed. In all likelihood, he hadn't left yet. He was crushed beneath the basement's concrete staircase.

tried in vain to lower the flag in memory of the popular Ted Gold; when security stopped them, they scrawled on the flagpole's base, IN MEMORY OF TEDDY GOLD. FIGHT LIKE HIM. In the window of a store on West Eighth Street, a sign appeared: TED GOLD DIED FOR YOUR SINS.

Chaos broke out in the Weatherman ranks. In those first crazed hours, no one understood what had happened, much less what to do. Ron Fliegelman had been in Vermont buying more dynamite. After hiding it, he returned to New York to find JJ's collective in an uproar. "The collective was in a tizzy," Fliegelman recalls. "No one knew what to do. I gave a thought to giving up, and I had a gun pulled on me and was told I was not leaving." Mark Rudd didn't learn the news till that evening, when he returned to the Chinatown apartment to find everyone hunched over an early edition of the *Times*. TOWNHOUSE RAZED BY BLAST AND FIRE; MAN'S BODY FOUND, read the headline. They had no idea who was alive and who was dead. Rudd ran outside to a pay phone and with a single call managed to find Cathy Wilkerson and Kathy Boudin, who had most likely taken shelter at the Boudin family's house. He hurried over and heard everything from the two shaken women. Robbins and Diana Oughton were almost certainly dead. Ted Gold was missing.

All night Rudd worked the phones, rounding up the other members of the townhouse collective. Everyone gathered the next morning at a coffee shop on Fourteenth Street. They were in shock. For the moment Rudd concentrated on logistics, making sure people had safe places to stay. A few days later he managed to herd them to upstate New York for a day of shooting practice, just to get them out of the city. Outside New York, most Weathermen heard the news on their car radios. Most knew only that there had been an explosion; out in Denver, David Gilbert heard it had been a police attack. "We were just like, 'Oh, my God, Diana Oughton, Teddy Gold,'" remembers Joanna Zilsel, then a teenager in the Cleveland collective. "I had met them. It was like, Holy shit. This is the real thing. We're in a war. This is what the Vietnamese people are being subjected to every day. This is the ugliness of violence."

A crane was still gouging out loads of debris Tuesday morning when one of Seedman's detectives, Pete Perotta, thought he saw something. He held up his hand for the crane operator to stop. The man jumped to the ground alongside him. "Is that . . . ?" he asked.

"Holy Mary, Mother of God," Perotta breathed.[5]

He summoned Seedman and a group of FBI men from their command post. There, hanging from the teeth of the bucket, were bits and pieces of a human body: an arm with no hand, a shredded torso, a set of buttocks, a leg without a foot, all of it studded with roofing nails. They looked for a head but never found one. The coroner would later identify the remains as Diana Oughton's.*

The crane operator was just finishing his shift at five o'clock when Detective Perotta urged him to lift out one final load. The big bucket splashed into a hole in the middle of the rubble, now filled with seven feet of black rainwater. When the bucket rose, Perotta lifted his hand again. Between the bucket's teeth was a gray, basketball-sized globe. Perotta stepped closer and peered at the muddy orb. It was studded with roofing nails and encrusted with dripping protuberances. It took a moment for Perotta to realize what they were: blasting caps. Slowly it dawned on him: The entire blob was made of dynamite—enough explosive to blow up the entire block. Albert Seedman would say it was the single largest explosive device ever seen in Manhattan.

The block was evacuated, the bomb squad called in. Working through the night, they whisked the dynamite away, then found fifty-seven more bright-red sticks deep in the rubble, along with all the wristwatches, coils of orange fuse, and blasting caps Robbins had secreted in the subbasement. Seedman was terrified that one of his men might be killed if they stumbled on more dynamite. At his request, both James Wilkerson and his wife stepped in front of television cameras and beseeched their daughter to tell them how much more dynamite might be inside and how many bodies. They received no answer.

---

*Detectives sifting through the rubble that day also discovered an appointment card indicating that Kathy Boudin was scheduled to see her dentist Monday, March 9, three days after the explosion. Checking with the dentist later that week, they were amazed to find that she had kept it.

By the following Saturday the rubble had almost been cleared, the deep pool of rainwater drained, and detectives were able to begin inspecting what remained of the walls and foundation. That morning a detective glimpsed what appeared to be a piece of pinkish-brown rug wrapped around a sewer pipe in the subbasement. Only when he unrolled it did he realize he was holding human flesh. It was all that remained of a man's torso—and it was all they would ever find of Terry Robbins. It would be two months before he was tentatively identified.

Seedman and the NYPD had done all they could. This new mode of terrorism—massive bombs being placed by educated and highly mobile young radicals—was not their job to prevent. If the Weathermen were to be stopped before others died, it would be up to the FBI.

On Sunday, March 8, two days after the explosion, President Richard Nixon met with the FBI's aging director, J. Edgar Hoover, and White House staffers in the Oval Office. Nixon was alarmed at the spread of radical bombings, and not simply those attributed to Weatherman. Every day that winter seemed to bring a new incident of radical violence, random bombings from Rockefeller Center to San Francisco, shoot-outs with Black Panthers in Chicago and elsewhere. The Townhouse appeared to confirm the FBI's worst fears. Further, Nixon lectured Hoover, it was only a matter of time until Weatherman or some other radical group tried to assassinate him. Nixon said he wanted "everything possible" done to end the Weatherman threat.

Hoover promised he would see to it. The problem was, he had few arrows in his quiver. When Weathermen had begun disappearing underground that January, the FBI had been caught off guard. Agents had relied so completely on tapped telephones in Chicago that when the taps went silent, they had no sense where anyone had gone. The day of the townhouse explosion—an event so momentous in leftist circles that it came to be referred to simply as the Townhouse—the Bureau had precisely one significant informant inside Weatherman: the Cincinnati student Larry Grathwohl. Not long after, he was in Buffalo, studying a plan to bomb a power station in Niagara Falls, when Bill Ayers arrived and ordered him to New York. There Grathwohl managed to slip away and meet with FBI agents at a hotel. Overnight Weatherman had become the FBI's highest priority, and Hoover ordered the immediate arrest of any Weatherman Grathwohl could provide. Grathwohl groused that the leadership had fled. The only fugitive he knew in the city, he said, was a girl named Linda Evans, who had been indicted in Chicago. Worse, Grathwohl argued, an arrest would blow his cover, leaving the FBI with no informants inside the group whatsoever.

It didn't matter. Hoover wanted an arrest, pronto, and he got it. Grathwohl arranged to have breakfast with Evans on April 15, at a diner on East Twenty-third Street. FBI men were waiting. As it happened, so was Mark Rudd, who arrived early, sensed something was wrong, and calmly left, unnoticed, before Grathwohl arrived. When Grathwohl got there, he and Evans were arrested, along with another Weatherman, Dianne Donghi, whom they found at Grathwohl's hotel. Both women served brief jail terms. Grathwohl testified before a grand jury, then was whisked to San Francisco, where the FBI put him to work on surveillance duties, hoping he could spot Bill Ayers or anyone else in the leadership. He never did.

Hoover pressed ahead anyway. Two dozen Weathermen were named the targets of "intensive investigations," which meant that field offices had to report on their efforts to apprehend them on a weekly basis. The White House's paranoia grew after the discovery of an old Weatherman bomb cache in Chicago in late March, followed by a specious tip that the group planned to begin bombing commercial airline flights. On April 2, Attorney General John Mitchell announced a second set of major indictments against the group, charging a dozen top Weathermen with conspiracy and inciting riots in connection with the Days of Rage.

The combination of so enormous a perceived threat with so little intelligence persuaded Hoover's right-hand man, William Sullivan, that extraordinary measures were called for. For decades one of the FBI's most effective investigative methods had been the illegal break-in, "the black bag job." But an aging and increasingly cautious Hoover, concerned about potential lawsuits, had forbidden further black bag jobs in 1966. That winter, as

Weathermen began disappearing, Sullivan—without Hoover's knowledge—quietly sent word down the chain of command that break-ins were again acceptable. This directive was left intentionally vague, leading some FBI offices to initiate an entire range of illegal activities, from break-ins to opening mail.

Nowhere were these tactics embraced more enthusiastically than in the FBI's New York office, where agents worked out of an office building on East Sixty-ninth Street. After the Townhouse, thirty were quickly formed into a new Weatherman squad, dubbed Squad 47. Their exploits would, in time, bring the FBI to the brink of ruin.

Bernardine Dohrn learned of the Townhouse explosion just as she and Jeff Jones were about to sit down to a lasagna dinner at Michael and Eleanore Kennedy's Victorian mansion in San Francisco. Putting down the phone, Dohrn motioned to Michael to join her and Jones in another room. After a moment they emerged, Dohrn kissed Eleanore good-bye, and she and Jones disappeared into the night.

It took days to grasp it all. Terry, Diana, Teddy: all dead. Dozens of members had scattered and were nowhere to be found. The damage was incalculable. More than a few inside the organization felt that Weatherman would never recover. Others believed it would simply cease to exist. "After the Townhouse, it was just complete chaos," Cathy Wilkerson recalls. "There was no plan, no reality, zero. When reality hit, you know, the leadership was completely unresponsive for three or four weeks. Hundreds of people just disappeared. They were gone. Weather evaporated. It basically ceased to exist. Only later were some people contacted and brought back. Others, they were never found." In California Jeff Jones took a break, driving alone to his father's home outside Los Angeles, where he spent long days lounging on the couch, hiking the San Gabriel Hills, grieving, thinking. In the end, he decided he knew two things: He remained dedicated to the struggle, and he didn't want to die in some dank basement as the others had. When he returned to

Sausalito, he sat atop the houseboat with Dohrn and talked. If Weather was to live on, Jones and Dohrn agreed, changes were needed. They made three decisions. One was on a strategy going forward; this they kept to themselves for the moment. The second was to gather what remained of the original eleven Weatherman signers and present their new vision. If things went as planned, they wouldn't need to announce their third decision; it would be clear. Because there, atop a houseboat in Sausalito, Dohrn and Jones had decided to take control of Weatherman.

The call went out. In ones and twos, many of the remaining cadres began to trickle into the Bay Area over the next few weeks. Most were now officially fugitives, having failed to show up for court appearances on the Chicago indictments. Bill Ayers used a stolen credit card to rent a car and drove it cross-country with JJ, who spent the trip arguing the need for more and larger actions. After a month lying low in Philadelphia, Mark Rudd borrowed money from his parents and flew west, as did Cathy Wilkerson and Kathy Boudin. "There was Weather debris—that's what we called ourselves— coming into Berkeley at the rate of three a day," recalls Brian Flanagan, among the first arrivals. "Others we never found. They were just gone."

Many of the newcomers crowded into a first-floor apartment they had rented in April on Pine Street, on the Tenderloin side of Nob Hill. When that filled up, a second flat was rented nearby. Dohrn and Jones greeted each new arrival in person; hugs and tears were the order of the day. Gradually the post-Townhouse gloom began to lift. In its place a wave of relief swept the group. They had survived. They were among friends. They were free. "There was a certain amount of exhilaration that we'd gotten away with what we'd gotten away with," recalls Paul Bradley. "We weren't in jail like we were supposed to be. We were living in this beautiful city and going to the beach. So, yeah, it was good."

This "new" incarnation of Weatherman began to develop a style sharply different from its Midwest and East Coast origins. As wonky student leftists, SDS members had dressed conservatively, by '60s standards; the men had short hair. In San Francisco many Weathermen finally came face-to-face with what they insisted on calling "youth culture," that is, hippies, adorned with long hair, beards, beads, and bell-bottoms. In barely a year, while the Weather leadership had been consumed with purges, riots, and bombs, these shaggy kids seemed to have taken over a series of ever-larger antiwar demonstrations.

Sensing the change, and needing to blend into the Bay Area's laid-back Left, the Weathermen embraced the new look. Jeff Jones took the lead, growing a bushy beard and donning a leather cowboy hat; he acquired a pickup truck adorned with a large red rose and named it Suzie Q. Bill Ayers sported a leather vest and beads with no shirt, while Dohrn wore Grace Slick–style fishnet tops with no bra, a look that—if nothing else—kept men from staring at her face. The new hippie vibe tended to unsettle their militant friends back east. "It did seem like the California people had a different style," recalls Jonah Raskin, who visited Dohrn and Jones later that year. "I mean, no one in New York was driving around in a pickup truck with a red rose."

Others, however, sensed that the change was needed. "People had been overheated, you know, in Chicago," remembers Rick Ayers, Bill Ayers's brother, who had left the army to join Weatherman, "and before long, they realized we had to calm down, be cool, think, plan for the long term. The weird thing was, being underground, suddenly everyone was a lot calmer, a lot more zen. It was like, 'Eh, let's have another cup of tea.' Chill out. Relax. You know, we took our time."

While the leadership regrouped in San Francisco, what remained of Weather's underground structure collapsed as quickly as the townhouse itself. "It was crazy how many people we lost," recalls Brian Flanagan. "I remember asking Jeff Jones at one point, you know, what happened to Denver? And he kind of sighed and said, 'Those people are so far underground they don't even know they're still members.'" The Midwestern tribes—Cleveland, Pittsburgh, Buffalo—simply disappeared. Scores of Weathermen found themselves cast adrift, still committed to armed struggle but unable to regain contact. The teenaged Joanna Zilsel and a girlfriend left Cleveland headed for California, with vague plans of finding other Weathermen. They never did. Zilsel ended up in British Columbia, where she lives to this day.

Many settled back into "normal" lives within the Movement, where they would form a bulwark of Weather's aboveground support. But others refused to give up. One or two, such as Seattle's "Quarter Moon Tribe," later forged ties with Weather, functioning as minor-league affiliates. Still others struck out on their own.

A group of veterans of the Weather collective in Milwaukee formed around a young activist named Judith Cohen and two others; they had all been purged but kept the collective alive in hopes of regaining leadership's favor. "We decided to form a 'purgee' group," Cohen recalls. "This was my chance to get back in. We did some great little actions, on campuses, against ROTC, almost riots, busting into classrooms, a lot of civil disobedience. We weren't Weathermen. We were trying to be Weathermen, hoping they would invite us back in."

After the Townhouse, Cohen's group managed to recruit a half-dozen other local radicals, including a nineteen-year-old named Kirk Augustin, who had been at Flint and whose factory job paid the rent at the group's two apartments, near Marquette University. "The problem was, we didn't have a clue what to do," Augustin recalls. "The [national] leadership might issue these communiqués, but below that, it was just people trying to survive. These people, they were students, they didn't know how to make money, or fix a car, much less make a bomb. They had lived off their parents before that. To think of it as cadres and safe houses, that's too romantic. At our level, it was all about survival. The people in Milwaukee, they had been abandoned. We were supposed to try and do [actions]. That's a difficult thing to do. And essentially nothing got done. So everyone was constantly blaming each other, with all these constant power struggles and factions."

That summer the Milwaukee collective did its best to scout targets, mainly military installations. Several in the group went so far as to steal dynamite from a site in Lexington, Kentucky, that August. Augustin, now a software engineer in Oregon, demurs when asked whether this is true. "Uh . . . , let's just say it wouldn't be that hard to do," he says. "Getting explosives was easy."

"We stole it from a quarry," says Judith Cohen, who met the "raiding party" in St. Louis and ferried the dynamite back to Milwaukee. "But once we got back, we didn't know what to do with it. We had to go to the library to read how to, you know, make something out of it. I was torn. I remember this one guy, who knew what we were doing, he asked me, 'Does it matter to you if you blow up innocent people? I mean, you're keeping dynamite in a house, this could go off and people could die, what the fuck is the matter with you? Don't you have any morals?' You know, my jaw just kind of went up and down. I really hadn't thought of it that way. The whole thing was just unreal. It was like we were kids playacting. It was real and not real."

In the event, the collective couldn't bring themselves to actually bomb anything. The only explosions they triggered, Augustin recalls, came during "training sessions" in the Chequamegon-Nicolet National Forest. "There were always discussions of [actions,] but it was theoretical," Augustin says. "We did stuff for fun, blowing things up in the forest. The theory was, we were training. In reality, we were just playing around. We didn't have anything we wanted to do, so nothing ever happened." Their careers as would-be saboteurs ended when a problem developed with the dynamite. "The stuff that came back was leaking, and we realized it wasn't stable, that it could go at any time," Cohen recalls. "So we ended up throwing it in Lake Michigan."

Pressure from the FBI and the Milwaukee police, meanwhile, took its toll. A detective named Harry Makoutz succeeded in befriending one of the group's youngest members, a troubled teenager, who quickly told all. That October a trio of Weather sympathizers responded by attempting to detonate a grouping of gasoline cans on Makoutz's front porch; they failed to explode.[*] In the wake of the aborted attack, the pseudo-Weathermen and many of their allies were hauled before a grand jury. "Pretty much everyone spilled their guts," Augustin remembers.

While no additional indictments were forthcoming, what remained of the Milwaukee collective crumbled. "I don't even remember now how it all ended," Augustin says. "But you know, you start with this daydream. And bit by bit, that daydream becomes reality, and that's intimidating and difficult. Eventually it all just petered away."

"Yeah, I washed my hands of Weatherman," Cohen recalls. "We were like this zombie Weather group. We were trying to be like real Weathermen, when we were dead Weathermen. For so long, you know, you're in this delusional state, and then you emerge back into sanity."

---

[*]Two of the accused were later acquitted in a jury trial.

The summit meeting Bernardine Dohrn and Jeff Jones arranged took place in mid-May at a remote beach house they rented outside the northern California town of Mendocino, a haven for hippies and marijuana growers 150 miles up the coast from San Francisco. The setting was ideal, a large sunken living room lined with low couches, with bay windows overlooking the ocean, just the spot for the healing and quiet reason the two were counting on. Driving "Suzie Q" with a load of hay in back, Jones ferried everyone to the house in ones and twos, Howie Machtinger, then Kathy Boudin and Mark Rudd, looking a bit shell-shocked. Jones picked up JJ and Bill Ayers in a field near a distant bus station. Ayers later wrote that he had been struck by Jones's placid demeanor:

> He seemed shockingly serene, and though he was sad, sad, sad about the [townhouse] deaths, and particularly attentive to me because of Diana, I think, he was in no hurry to explore any political issues with us yet. . . . He said only that we would have plenty of time to sort things out. We should try to catch our breath for now, he said. We'll have plenty of time, he repeated, and that unremarkable phrase, a commonplace in most company, was jarring here because no comrade could have spoken it in the past several months without a barrage of derisive criticism. It was heresy, too, but it was calming, and I felt, oddly, that I wanted to cry.[6]

Instead of the heated debate most of the attendees expected, they were met by the unlikely sight of Dohrn in the kitchen, leaning over a pot of boiling pasta. Jones announced that meetings wouldn't even begin for a day or two. Until then, he said, they should all try to relax and enjoy one another's company. Everyone appeared relieved but JJ, who wouldn't shut up, going on and on about the battle plans they needed to draw up to avenge Terry and Diana and Teddy. They ate together, then watched the sun set over the Pacific and took long walks in the surrounding hills; after dinner they drank wine and smoked joints and talked about nothing. Both Dohrn and Jones paid special attention to Ayers, who was key to their plans. Dohrn took him for a walk and cried. Jones took him for a stroll alongside an adjoining cliff and said, "Bill, your best friend just killed your girlfriend, and it's okay for you to be angry about that and mourn."[7]

While personal issues were important, everyone understood there were larger issues on the table. It wasn't just studying their mistakes. In the four months since they had closed the SDS office, change within the Movement had accelerated. Everyone felt it. On April 30, 1970, President Nixon had announced that the United States was invading Cambodia. The campuses exploded. On May 4 National Guardsmen at Kent State University in Ohio fired into a crowd of protesters, killing four. Protests grew so widespread, and so virulent, that more than five hundred campuses were closed. But what struck many observers, especially those in Weatherman, was not what protesters were doing; it was who they were. Hundreds of thousands of hippies and "freaks" were pouring into the Movement, transforming it into something new and unfamiliar. What remained of the New Left was being lost in a sea of tie-dye and LSD; if Weatherman was to survive, it would need to swim with the new tide.

It was just one of so many things they had to deal with that week. Finally, after two or three days, with everyone but JJ able to relax, they began the meetings. Forty years later, everyone involved has a different memory of what was said and in what order. But much of the talk revolved around what went wrong at the Townhouse. "There were actually three arguments about the Townhouse," Howie Machtinger recalls. "JJ's view was, yeah, we screwed up, but we'll do better next time. Cathy Wilkerson argued that things went wrong because the collective was sexist, that everything had gone crazy because men monopolized the weapons. I thought that was beside the point. It was Bernardine who played the essential role in putting things back together. She is the one who saw clearly the contradiction between white privilege and crazy actions like Terry planned. So her argument was, you have to remove any legitimacy for that kind of action."

This was a jarring moment for everyone: What Dohrn was saying refuted almost everything most had been expecting for months: *We won't kill people.* Not even policemen. Dohrn stated clearly that JJ and Terry's proposed action at Fort Dix represented the very worst kind of politics. It would have turned millions of Americans against them. There could be no more actions like it. What Dohrn proposed adopting instead, and what Weatherman became, was what might be called the Sam Melville model of underground operations. They would bomb buildings of symbolic importance—courthouses, military bases, police stations—but only after warnings, and only at times when the buildings were likely to be empty. Weatherman had to be more "life affirming," Dohrn said, more in line with the mass protests breaking out everywhere. Their bombings, she said again and again, must push the mass movement toward renewed militancy. She called the new strategy "armed propaganda." A writer for the *Berkeley Tribe* called it "responsible terrorism."

"Weatherman never understood violence, we didn't," remembers Cathy Wilkerson. "It was purely an abstraction, until it wasn't. Then we were like Lady Macbeth. What do you do when you have blood on your hands? For us, we decided to take violence out of the equation."

No one but JJ had the will to oppose Dohrn. Dealing with her onetime lover, the young man who had spearheaded the writing of the original Weatherman paper, who had done more than anyone to push them into forming an American guerrilla force, was Dohrn's final task. On the last day she made the announcement. She had taken JJ aside first, alone, to break the news. As Bill Ayers remembered it, she told JJ, "'Where we're going . . . you're not welcome.' She said it slowly, formally, representing a consensus, and with that [JJ] was expelled." Mark Rudd, JJ's closest friend, was dismissed from the leadership. He would be allowed to stay on as a cadre in the San Francisco tribe.

That night Rudd and JJ retired to a bar in nearby Fort Bragg, where they drank and played pool. JJ was surprisingly sanguine. Rudd wrote that JJ told him:

> "Someone has to take the blame. Bernardine, Billy, and Jeff are right about the military error."
>
> "But everyone knew what was being planned," I said. . . .
>
> "It doesn't matter. We have to create the fiction that they were always right so that they can lead the organization."

Inevitably, the subject turned to one of JJ's favorite novels, *Darkness at Noon*, about the Stalin-era purges. "I always respected the fact that the old Bolshevik confessed for the sake of the revolution," JJ said. "There had to be a single unified revolutionary party, even under Stalin's leadership. The individual doesn't count; it's only the party and its place in history that's important."

He laughed. "At least they're not going to liquidate me," he said. "I'll be back."[8]

But JJ never came back. In fact, he never really recovered. Wanted by the FBI, he would wander the United States and Mexico for years, eventually settling in Vancouver. There, calling himself Wayne Curry, he worked odd jobs, ultimately making a living as a low-level marijuana dealer. He died of cancer in 1997, forgotten.

As sad as it was to his friends, Rudd wrote years later, "JJ's expulsion was a brilliant maneuver that successfully rewrote history. Suddenly no one remembered how universally accepted the old 'Fight the people, all white people are guilty' line was." No one would remember that they had tried to kill policemen. "Weather's history," Rudd wrote, "had been conveniently cleaned." A myth was born. "The myth, and this is always Bill Ayers's line, is that Weather never set out to kill people, and it's not true—we did," says Howie Machtinger. "You know, policemen were fair game. What Terry was gonna do, while it was over our line, it wasn't that far over our line, not like everyone said later. I mean, he wasn't on a different planet from where we were."

When the meetings ended, Dohrn sat down with a tape recorder and, in a single take, dictated Weatherman's first communiqué. Her voice was calm, her tone the thoughtful grad student. "Hello, this is Bernardine Dohrn," she began. "I'm going to read a declaration of war."

This initial declaration, soon to be quoted in newspapers around the country, gave no hint of the group's proposed retreat from murderous violence; if anything, it celebrated violence. The statement is notable in that it makes only a single reference to the war; as Dohrn makes clear, Weatherman's true motivation was fighting alongside the blacks they imagined were in revolt against the U.S. government:

> Black people have been fighting almost alone for years. We've known that our job is to lead white kids to armed revolution. . . . Kids know that the lines are drawn; revolution is touching all of our lives. Tens of thousands have learned that protest and marches don't do it. Revolutionary violence is the only way. Now we are adapting the classic guerrilla strategy of [Uruguay's] Tupamaros to our own situation here in the most technically advanced country in the world. . . .
>
> Within the next fourteen days we will attack a symbol or institution of Amerikan injustice. This is the way we celebrate the example of Eldridge Cleaver and H. Rap Brown and all black revolutionaries who first inspired us by their fight behind enemy lines for the liberation of their people.
>
> Never again will they fight alone.

It was a bold and, especially given the humiliation of the Townhouse, astonishingly arrogant statement. Weatherman was a shell of its former self; it had lost hundreds of supporters and dozens of members. Many believed it could never survive the emotional wreckage of the Townhouse. Yet Weatherman's challenge now was as much technical as logistical. If it was to actually carry out a "war" against the U.S. government, it needed to find a way to do so without getting any more of its members killed. The bomb Terry Robbins had been building had no "safety switch," that is, no way to test it short of detonation. Their first task, Dohrn and Jones were uncomfortably aware, was finding a way to build a safe bomb. "There was a flaw in our design," Cathy Wilkerson recalls. "Howie and the San Francisco people, they had been lucky, because the design wasn't safe, it was primitive. I was eager to fix it, for any number of reasons. I was eager to learn. There was a sense I was responsible for the Townhouse. And yes, a part of me wanted to finish what Terry had started."

In San Francisco, Wilkerson, Paul Bradley, and several others obtained chemistry and explosives manuals and began studying bomb design. "We just went to the store and bought books," Wilkerson recalls. "*Popular Mechanics* magazines. I needed all that stuff. I needed to figure out how electricity works. Protons, neutrons, I didn't know any of that stuff." The most serious work, however, was done back east. Even before Mendocino, Jeff Jones had returned to New York and sat down on a Central Park bench with Ron Fliegelman. "We were talking about the Townhouse, and I said, 'I don't want this to happen again,'" Fliegelman recalls. "He was talking politics, you know, 'This wouldn't have happened without bad politics,' and I said, basically, that's crap. You either know how to build something or you don't. He said, 'Well, what do we do?' And I said, 'This can never happen again. I'll take care of it.' And I did."

In all the thousands of words written about Weatherman in the past forty years, including six memoirs, three other books, two films, and countless news articles, not one devotes a single sentence to Ron Fliegelman. Yet it was Fliegelman who emerged as the group's unsung hero. Beginning that day in Central Park, he devoted hundreds of hours to the study of explosives and, in the process, became what Weatherman desperately needed: its bomb guru. "Without him," says Brian Flanagan, "there would be no Weather Underground."

In a group that at that point had shrunk to barely thirty or so members, many of whom were effete intellectuals, Fliegelman was the one person who knew how to strip down and reassemble guns, motorcycles, and radios, who knew how to weld, who could fix almost anything. He had always been this way. The son of a suburban Philadelphia doctor, Fliegelman had from an early age been fascinated by how things work. His grandfather, a steelworker, never objected when he returned home to find that little Ron had taken apart the alarm clock. By his teens he could disassemble and rebuild any kind of engine. He was never much in the classroom, dropping out of two colleges before washing up at Goddard College in Vermont, where Russell Neufeld, who became his lifelong friend, invited him to join Weatherman in Chicago. When SDS ran out of money to pay its printer, Fliegelman took over himself, cranking out hundreds of leaflets before crushing his hand in the machinery. Aimless up to that point in life, he discovered in Weatherman a new purpose, a new meaning. "I knew none of these people, and they didn't know me," he recalls. "But I was opposed to the war and racism, and I thought, 'This is pretty cool.'"

Squat and stout, with a bushy black beard, Fliegelman plunged headlong into the study of dynamite. "Everyone was afraid of the stuff, for good reason," he says. "What we were dealing with was a group of intellectuals who didn't know how to do anything with their hands. I did. I wasn't afraid of it, I knew it could be handled. When you're young and you're confident, you can do anything. So, yeah, you play with it, and try to build something. The timer is the whole thing, right? It's just electricity going into the blasting cap. Eventually I came up with a thing where I inserted a lightbulb, and when the bulb lit, the circuit was complete, and we were able to test things that way. If the light came on, it worked. The rest of it is simple."

It is perhaps appropriate that Weatherman's two principal bomb makers, Ron Fliegelman and Cathy Wilkerson, would in time come together and have a child. Forty years later Wilkerson, while acknowledging Fliegelman's primacy in explosives, isn't so certain her onetime boyfriend should take sole credit for Weatherman's bomb design. Fliegelman, however, has no doubt. "New York fixed the problem," he says with emphasis. "And we taught it to San Francisco. Cathy was the only technical one out there. She knew how to build the thing, but she was the only one out there who could do it." In the years to come, Fliegelman reckons he personally built the vast majority of the group's bombs, flying to the Bay Area on a number of occasions. "Maybe they did two or three things without me," he says, "but I doubt it."

In Weatherman's May 21 declaration of war, Dohrn had promised to attack a major symbol of American power within fourteen days. In Weather lore, and in previous histories, that is what they did. But the reality, according to several alumni, was not only far more complicated but far more embarrassing, not to mention harmful to the myth that Weather had now dedicated itself to solely nonviolent actions.

The actual "battle plan," such as it was, consisted of at least three actions. The first suggests that, its own propaganda aside, Weatherman was still actively considering high crimes. It went beyond anything ever attempted in radical circles to that point, and had it been successful, it might have altered the history of the underground. The action involved a small coterie of

Weathermen led by Howie Machtinger, who related his version of events to the author in 2011.

According to him, he was asked by the leadership to take the group on a super-secret mission to the state of Maine. Their task, Machtinger says, was the kidnapping of a member of the Rockefeller family, said to be at a summer home whose exact location has been lost to time. "I don't even remember which Rockefeller it was," he says. "I just remember we went up there, got a hotel, and drove around a lot, not even sure what we were supposed to do. We were there like a week, and eventually, you know, we didn't have any plan, we just kind of gave up." What Machtinger does remember, however, is the leadership's wrath when he returned in defeat to San Francisco. Though he had been one of the group's eleven founders and had been among those considered the early leadership, he was now abruptly dismissed from Weatherman and exiled to Seattle. "You know, there's this myth that Bernardine ruled out any violent actions after Mendocino, but it's just not true," Machtinger says. "The line is much blurrier than that. The fact is, we were prepared to do a political kidnapping, and in fact we tried to, but we weren't able to carry it out."

The second stage of the war plans involved something almost as dramatic: the bombings of major centers of power on both coasts. The targets were the San Francisco Hall of Justice, the massive concrete monolith that housed the courts and the police department, and the headquarters of the New York Police Department. The San Francisco bomb was placed in a men's room drain; a warning was phoned in, but the device failed to detonate, presumably because the Bay Area Weathermen had yet to master a working bomb design. Though rumors of the incident floated among FBI agents for years, details were only confirmed in David Gilbert's 2012 book, *Love and Struggle: My Life in SDS, the Weather Underground, and Beyond*. Afterward, Gilbert writes, "we had the awkward but necessary responsibility of telling the authorities [by telephone] exactly where the device was hidden so that the bomb squad could find and defuse it, thus giving police forensics an intact example of our circuit and components."[*9] By the June 4 deadline, in fact, neither the San

---

*Gilbert claims that the bomb was discovered after Weatherman phoned in its whereabouts. Retired FBI agents recall that it was found by a shaken janitor later that year.

Francisco nor New York actions had taken place. This was a significant set-back for the organization; war had been declared, actions had been promised, and nothing had happened. "Raising people's hopes that high isn't a good way to build trust in the underground," griped a letter writer to the *Berkeley Tribe*.

Weather's reputation was salvaged in the near term by its fledgling New York cell, which would come to play an outsized role in future actions. The cell's importance has never been publicly explored, largely because until now its members have declined to discuss its operations. But it was surprisingly small: Before the Townhouse, Weather could count as many as thirty-five active members in New York; afterward, while outsiders and aboveground supporters drifted in and out, the core of the "new" New York cell was rarely more than six people, including Ron Fliegelman. Its leader was Robbie Roth, the twenty-year-old student who had replaced Mark Rudd as head of Colum-bia's SDS chapter. Roth was a popular Weatherman, smart, generous, and easygoing, traits Dohrn and the others recognized. Weather's post-Mendocino leadership has usually been understood as comprising three people—Dohrn, Jeff Jones, and Bill Ayers—but in fact, Roth was named leadership's fourth member after the Townhouse.

Months later the New York cell's third prominent member, Eleanor Stein, would be named the fifth member of Weather's Central Committee. Stein was a classic "red diaper" baby, intense and committed. That June she, Roth, and Fliegelman were living with several others in an apartment they rented in a house on Amity Street in Cobble Hill, Brooklyn. ("That place took all the romance out of the underground for me," recalls Stein's ex-husband, Jonah Raskin, a Weatherman supporter who visited often. "A single apart-ment, upper floor, remaindered furniture, with a half-dozen people crammed inside.") Fliegelman had purchased dynamite in Vermont under an assumed name; he kept it in a garage they rented nearby. Forty years later, he shudders at the memory of that first bombing, at NYPD headquarters. "That first one was the scariest," he recalls. "Going into a public building, there was security, and you had to get past it. We had people who did the casings. We needed people who wouldn't be noticed, so they went in dressed like lawyers. Still, I was scared. Very scared. We knew if we did this, they would come after us."

The "casers" identified a second-floor men's room as an ideal spot to hide a bomb: It was just 125 feet from Police Commissioner Howard Leary's office. In the years to come, public bathrooms would become Weatherman's favorite target. Stall doors allowed a measure of privacy, and many bathrooms could be locked from within. At the Amity Street apartment, Fliegelman built the bomb, a large one, using his new design: about fifteen sticks of dynamite and a Westclox alarm clock purchased at a Radio Shack. The challenge was smuggling it into the building; they couldn't risk having a backpack or briefcase searched. In the end, Fliegelman says, they hollowed out a thick law book and placed the bomb inside. Exactly who walked it through security and placed it above a ceiling tile in the bathroom has never been disclosed, but by the afternoon of Tuesday, June 9, the bomb was in place. "It wasn't like they had metal detectors back then," Fliegelman says. "There was just a guy at a desk, and we walked right past him."

At 6:40 p.m. they phoned in the warning. "There is a bomb set to go off at police headquarters," said the male caller, who hung up without offering details. At that moment about 150 people were in the building. Police operators got this kind of call routinely in 1970; it was ignored. Seventeen minutes later, at 6:57, the bomb exploded, its deep boom ringing through the narrow streets and alleys of Little Italy. The blast demolished two walls of the bathroom and blew a hole in the floor twenty feet wide and forty feet long, destroyed a deputy commissioner's office on one side, shattered dozens of windows, and catapulted a cloud of soot and smoke into Centre Street; chunks of granite the size of cinder blocks crushed two cars below. Eight people were treated for injuries, none of them serious. Afterward, furious police inspectors stalked the wreckage. "We'll investigate this until our dying day," one told the *Daily News.*

Forty years later Weatherman bombings can blur together, a string of dates and buildings and communiqués. The NYPD headquarters attack, however, was unique, because it was unprecedented; it left the department and all city government deeply shaken. Commissioner Leary flew back from a conference in West Berlin; as he spoke to reporters at Kennedy airport in New York, headquarters was being evacuated after a copycat bomb threat.

Mayor John Lindsay vowed a "relentless" investigation; his residence, Gracie Mansion, was itself evacuated after a bomb threat. "Our problem," one police commander said, "is not the damage to the building or to our own morale. Our problem is the feeling that if the police cannot protect themselves, how can they protect anyone else?"

In the days immediately afterward, significant security precautions began appearing for the first time at police headquarters, major government buildings, and New York skyscrapers, a trend that would accelerate during the early 1970s. Civilians entering police facilities were forced to show identification, have their appointments confirmed, and be escorted when in the building. At J.C. Penney headquarters the company installed electronically coded door openers and television cameras. In other buildings the bathrooms began to be locked. The *Times*, for one, remained skeptical that anything could be done. "Nothing and no one can be made safe from a man determined to explode an infernal machine in a public building," it editorialized. "When the full implications of that truth sink in . . . New Yorkers are going to realize that they are living with a new urban anxiety."[10]

The NYPD bombing marked an abrupt change, too, in the tone of Weatherman's message. The communiqué issued afterward was a sharp turn away from the traditional New Left fight-alongside-the-blacks message. In place of the dense Marxist verbiage of the original Weatherman statement was something that sounded as though it were written in Haight-Ashbury rather than in some Ivy League apartment. It was a clear effort, the first of several, to connect with the burgeoning youth culture that had taken over much of the Movement in the wake of SDS's immolation:

> The pigs in this country are our enemies. . . . The pigs try to look invulnerable, but we keep finding their weaknesses. Thousands of kids, from Berkeley to the UN Plaza, keep tearing up and ROTC buildings keep coming down. Nixon invades Cambodia and hundreds of schools are shut down by strikes. Every time the pigs think they've stopped us, we come back a little stronger and a lot smarter. They guard their buildings and we walk right past their guards. They look for us—we get them first. They

built the Bank of America—kids burn it down. They outlaw grass, we build a culture of life and music.

At their apartment in Cobble Hill, the New York cell and its supporters were jubilant. "That first one, I remember, we had one heck of a celebration afterward," recalls Ron Fliegelman.

"RESPONSIBLE TERRORISM"

Weatherman, June 1970 to October 1970

On Friday, June 5, 1970, four days before the attack on NYPD headquarters, President Nixon summoned J. Edgar Hoover and CIA director Richard Helms to the Oval Office, along with the chiefs of the National Security Agency and the Defense Intelligence Agency. Nixon was furious. Everywhere he looked, the antiwar movement seemed to be turning increasingly violent. The deaths at Kent State were still fresh in the air. Weatherman had now declared war; its first attacks were promised any day. This had gone far beyond the Townhouse and random bombings. The president lectured Hoover and the others that "revolutionary terrorism" now represented the single greatest threat against American society. He demanded that the four agencies assemble a concerted, overarching intelligence plan to defeat its spread.

At the FBI, Hoover's No. 2 man, Bill Sullivan, already had such a plan well in hand. The following Monday, June 8, he convened the first of five meetings intended to tear down the walls between the FBI, the CIA, and their brethren, lift all restrictions on domestic intelligence gathering, and clear the way for all four agencies to institute every dirty trick in the FBI's old playbook: illegal break-ins, unilateral wiretapping, the opening of mail, even inserting informants into undergraduate classrooms. They called it the Huston Plan, after Tom Charles Huston, the twenty-nine-year-old Nixon aide who championed it alongside Sullivan. When Huston relayed the plan to Nixon on July 14, the president said he approved. There was just one problem: J. Edgar Hoover was dead set against the Huston Plan.

The old man had grown exceedingly cautious in his last years, fearful his legacy would be tarnished if the rampant illegalities he had ordered over the years burst into view. He had never liked working with the CIA and had rarely done so; he didn't want anyone, especially the FBI's institutional rivals, knowing the Bureau's secrets. But his main objection was the question of blame if this ever became public. Nixon had given only verbal approval. Hoover, who had no idea that Sullivan had already cleared FBI offices to engage in almost all these illegal tactics, had no doubt he and the FBI would take the fall.

Hoover had something else to hide: the Bureau's near-total inability to learn much of anything about Weatherman and other violence-prone radicals. With the loss of Larry Grathwohl, the FBI didn't have a single informant anywhere near Weatherman—not one. Nor did it any longer have any useful wiretaps. As a result, the Nixon administration was badly misreading Weatherman's status. No one at the FBI had any idea that the Townhouse had left the group in shambles. In fact, the startling explosion in the heart of New York City left senior officials believing exactly the opposite: that Weatherman constituted as dire a threat to national security as any the United States now faced. In the FBI's nightmare scenario, Weatherman would lead thousands of long-haired demonstrators into a campaign of sabotage and assassination.

Without informants, FBI agents across the country had first tried traditional investigative methods, interviewing Weatherman family and friends. This got them nowhere. A few agents were allowed to grow their hair long and linger at demonstrations, but it would take months if not years before they could be expected to infiltrate Weatherman or its allies. The fact was, the FBI had never attempted to root out an underground group like Weatherman. The legality of the tactics under consideration—or already under way—was unclear; no court, for instance, had yet ruled whether wiretaps could be installed without a court order. "Can I put an informant in a college classroom?" William Dyson, the agent put in charge of Weatherman cases, recalls wondering. "Can I penetrate any college organization? What can I do? And nobody had any rules or regulations. There was nothing."

Unsure and unconnected, Dyson and his peers had no clear sense of how to safely operate in this strange new world of long hair, drugs, and secrecy. The one thing everyone believed was that Weatherman would never be brought down by traditional methods. That brought extraordinary pressure to bend the rules. "There were certain people in the FBI who made the decision: We've got to take a step—anything to get rid of these people," Dyson recalls. "Anything! Not kill them, per se, but anything went. If we suspect somebody's involved in this, put a wiretap on them. Put a microphone in. Steal his mail. Do anything!"

Chief among those "certain people" was Bill Sullivan, who was assuming control over all the FBI's domestic investigations. A number of offices had already begun illegally opening the mail of Weatherman supporters; New York's Squad 47 purchased a small machine that steamed open envelopes. "We knew they were doing it," recalls Elizabeth Fink, who lived with several Weatherman supporters in Brooklyn. "Our mailman told us. They came and took our mail every two weeks. Like clockwork." Wiretaps were ramped up; the Bureau would eventually record more than thirteen thousand individual conversations. Sullivan had already sent word down the chain of command that "black bag jobs" were to be resumed—without Hoover's knowledge. These illegal burglaries (typically designed to place listening devices in the homes of Weather sympathizers) would eventually center on known supporters such as Bernardine Dohrn's sister, Jennifer.

The most zealous of the FBI's burglars belonged to Squad 47. All its break-ins fit the same pattern. One of its alumni, Donald Strickland, today an attorney in Hartford, Connecticut, says that when an agent sought approval for a break-in, he wrote a memo to Squad 47's supervisor, an avuncular Irishman named John Kearney, asking for an "intensive investigation." Kearney, in turn, would clear the job with a senior administrator at FBI headquarters, often the Bureau's No. 3 man, Mark Felt, best known to history as the reporter Bob Woodward's infamous "Deep Throat" source. Once a burglary was approved, up to twenty agents would stake out the site. In New York most of the bag jobs took place in apartment buildings. There was generally no need for an actual break-in; a building superintendent would almost always hand over a key. Half the agents would wait for the target to leave and follow him or her, reporting back to supervisors if the subject was returning; the other agents would then enter the apartment. Once inside, they would silently fan out, guns drawn, to make sure no one was there.

"We'd give 'em ten to fifteen minutes to get out of the neighborhood, then we'd go," Strickland recalls. "You never knew who might have stayed inside. It could have been Bill Ayers and Bernardine Dohrn themselves. So that was pretty hairy."

Once the coast was clear, each agent had a specific duty. One or two would bag and remove the trash. Others would insert tiny microphones into the overhead lights, taking special care to bug the bedroom—"where we knew all the skullduggery talk took place," Strickland says. Another agent would be assigned to make copies of any address books and personal correspondence. The squad had a special camera built into a briefcase, and two agents were assigned to photograph the apartment. In most cases the FBI burglars were able to finish their tasks in thirty minutes or less.

Still, such tactics made many agents uncomfortable, few more so than William Dyson. "We were going to end up with FBI agents arrested," he remembers thinking at the time. "Not because what they did was wrong, but because nobody knew what was right and wrong."

J. Edgar Hoover sensed this as well. After Nixon approved the Huston Plan, Hoover demanded an audience with the president. "In view of the crisis of terrorism," Nixon told him, he found the plan "justified and reasonable." But Hoover would have none of it. Nixon, fearing a scandal if Hoover resigned in protest, relented. The Huston Plan was dead. But as his own men continued pursuing these tactics behind Hoover's back, the FBI remained the leading edge of the illegal campaign against antiwar radicals. The Bureau was, in effect, going it alone, and in the end it would pay the price.

———————

By midsummer Ron Fliegelman's new bomb design had migrated to the Bay Area, allowing Weatherman to finally begin launching actions on both coasts. Cathy Wilkerson acknowledges that she helped build the first two bombs, small ones they decided to detonate at the sprawling Presidio military base, near the tip of the San Francisco peninsula. The twin bombings may have been viewed as experimental, in that there was no communiqué or claim of responsibility released afterward. The first device, described in newspapers the next day as a pipe bomb two inches in diameter, was left in a trash can in a parking garage outside the Armed Service Police Headquarters. The second was placed at the base of a twenty-five-foot outdoor model of a Nike-Ajax missile. The bomb in the trash can was spotted. A police bomb squad was en route, in fact, when it went off just before 1 a.m. on Sunday, July 26, blowing a hole in an adjacent cinder block wall and scattering debris across a military policeman's desk. The second bomb went off without a hitch, destroying the missile model. No one was hurt.

A brief communiqué, Weatherman's third, was issued later that day, but in Detroit, where two days earlier Dohrn, Ayers, and eleven other Weathermen had been indicted for "conspiracy to commit terrorism." Rich in the groovy jargon the group had begun using in an effort to reach the counterculture, the communiqué was timed to coincide with the eleventh anniversary of the Cuban Revolution. "Today we attack with rocks, riots and bombs the greatest killer pig ever known to man—Amerikan imperialism," it read. "A year ago people thought it can't happen here. Look at where we've come. . . . [Attorney General John] Mitchell indicts 8 or 10 or 13; thousands of freaks plot to build a new world on the ruins of honk America. And to General Mitchell we say: 'Don't look for us, Dog; we'll find you first.'"

Weatherman's bombing tactics were still in their infancy, but in coming months the group would establish routines that varied little over time. Planning was typically done at a safe house, while the bombs themselves were built in a hotel room booked for the occasion, the better to safeguard the rest of the organization should something go wrong. Components were bought off the shelf, the wiring and Westclox clocks purchased at a Radio Shack. Fingerprints were wiped clean.

A unique glimpse of a Weatherman bombing is offered in an unpublished manuscript written by a young radical named Marvin Doyle, who worked closely with the leadership beginning in 1971.* In it, he gives a detailed portrait of the intense days leading to a bombing, including interaction between the national leadership and local cadres and coordination between West and East Coast bomb makers. The action Doyle describes was actually a double bombing, in August 1971, at two offices of the California Department of Corrections. Dohrn, he writes, placed great emphasis on the need for local cadres to physically build the bomb and write the communiqué. For technical guidance, though, Ron Fliegelman was flown in from New York. Doyle describes Fliegelman as "roly-poly, with a big black beard, wire-rimmed glasses, and a Santa Claus twinkle in his eye that inspired confidence."

They did their initial work at an apartment they rented in San Francisco's Sunset district:

> We sat down together in the [apartment], with [Paul Bradley] in attendance, going over [Fliegelman's] sketches of the model circuit, with its safety light and a second safety circuit, or shunt, that connected the odd poles of the switch. The next day, we brought out the hardware and constructed a trial timing device together, soldering together a circuit connecting batteries, safety light, shunt, switch, blasting cap, and a pocket watch with the minute hand removed. One wire was soldered to a screw driven into the face of the watch and at the other end of the circuit was a wire soldered to the hour hand. When the hand reached the screw, the circuit was closed.
>
> At twilight, we drove down to the south end of Ocean Beach, planted a cap in the sand and armed the device. Once the circuit was activated and the safety light stayed off, we flipped the switch that opened the circuit

---

*"Marvin Doyle" is a pseudonym. The author now works for a Washington-area think tank, where no one knows his history as a 1970s-era radical.

connecting the battery, clock and cap and stood back a few feet. The surf was pounding at our backs and the sky was getting darker as we waited out the short interval we had set on the pocket watch. At the expected moment, more or less, there was a dull thud and a burst of sand exploded into the air. The test was right.

Afterward, Jeff Jones took Doyle to inspect the dynamite they would use, kept in a rented garage in an industrial area. They closely inspected the paper wrapping, looking for beads of "sweat" that might indicate that the explosives had begun deteriorating. There were none. Two days before the action, the bombing team began moving into a hotel room, this one on Lombard Street, to finish its preparations. They assembled their disguises, mostly wigs and fake mustaches, along with the wiring, two alarm clocks, and ten sticks of dynamite.

Arrivals and departures from the motel were tightly rationed—we didn't want it to look like a dope dealer had set up shop. The electrical equipment was brought in first. [Fliegelman] and I started working on the wiring that first night. Remove the minute hand from the pocket watch and drive a small screw into the face of the dial, soldering it fast. That way you can set the detonation eleven hours or so ahead, with a timing circuit that closes when the hour hand touches the screw. One wire is attached to the screw, another connected to the hour hand, and these wires lead back around to each other in a loop that also includes a nine-volt battery, the blasting cap, the safety switch, and the safety light—the all-important warning that goes on if by accident the timing circuit . . . shorts out. . . .

As much as possible, [Fliegelman] had me solder the connections, after several extensive practice sessions, and under his close supervision. We had the thing pretty well built and were testing the connections by midmorning Friday, when one of the boys from LA delivered the shoebox full of TNT. [Dohrn] was in and out, keeping the East Coast informed and nailing down arrangements for afterwards, when quite a few people would want to be out of town.

On the day of the action, parts of the bomb itself were slid into a shoe box. Fliegelman cut a small hole in one end, through which the safety switch and the light would be visible. Doyle had been chosen to carry the bomb to the target in a Pan Am flight bag. The final task was packing the detonating circuit into the sticks of dynamite:

> [Fliegelman] and I did this together, four hands carefully moulding and fitting the package together, looking up into each other's eyes every so often to share the immediate experience of our consciousness and resolve. Everyone else in the room—three or four others—seemed to finish what they were doing in time to watch the lid go on the box and be taped down. [Bradley] slid the box into the airline bag, switch and light facing up, then zippered the bag shut and hung it on my shoulder. Hugs and kisses all around and out the door into the bright California sunshine.

Bradley drove Doyle to the Corrections building on the downtown waterfront. There was no security. They simply walked into the lobby and stepped to the elevator. Doyle had scouted the location, moving a ceiling panel on an upper floor where they would plant the bomb.

> [Bradley] was unusually quiet, unusually sparing with his customary bonhomie. "This is it, eh? Not much you can say," was all he offered as we slid into one of the old cars. . . . [At the Corrections building] we would be looking for vending machines if anyone asked, but were confused about which floor they were on. [Arriving at the floor, Bradley] went ahead to the alcove. The hallway was empty as I followed him. Step around the corner, crisply now. The drop-ceiling panel is still out of place. I step into the corner and squat under the hole, bracing myself against the wall. [Bradley] steps up on my shoulders, as we practiced, and I stand. He sticks his head in the hole and takes a quick look around, spots the place he wants to put the package, then beckons me to hand it up. Unzip the bag, flip the switch that arms the bomb. Oh my God! I didn't even look at the light! A subliminal flash—we could all be dead!—buried instantaneously by some bluff feral nerve. Alive! Let's do this and stay alive. Up the parcel goes, my hands to

his, into the hole. Squat again, step down, turn. One last moment of serious vulnerability, stepping back out into the main hall—all clear, nobody there, nobody looking. Split up. Leave in opposite directions. Don't walk too fast. It's two-thirty. Nine and a half hours to go.

We did it!

In keeping with the leadership's insistence that local cadres do as much work as possible, Doyle himself called in the warning to police from a pay phone that night. He didn't see or hear the explosion, which demolished a pair of empty offices. Afterward, when police began investigating, everyone left the city for several days.

"[Actions] were terrifying, just terrifying," Paul Bradley recalls forty years later. "You just do it."

They were doing it. After all that had happened—Chicago, Flint, the Townhouse—they were finally launching a true armed struggle in America. It all sounded so dramatic. Yet the day-to-day reality of the Weathermen's lives was anything but. Many, especially those in San Francisco, lived on the edge of poverty. "I lived on Bisquick," Cathy Wilkerson recalls. "Lots and lots of biscuits."

For those outside the leadership, the emotional tumult that followed in the wake of the Townhouse gave way that summer to stretches of grinding boredom. Much of their time was spent waiting for orders, reading, taking long walks, smoking pot, building IDs, and perfecting disguises. Bill Ayers joked that you could always tell a Weatherman by their bad hair-dye jobs. Until the leadership issued a new set of marching orders, many cadres wondered what to do.

Between actions, for instance, the New Yorkers struggled to define their roles as "revolutionaries." Should their work be limited to bombings? When money ran low—and it was always low—would true revolutionaries meekly wait for another donation from a radical lawyer or a family member? Or simply take what they needed? In the apartment in Cobble Hill, they debated whether to rob a bank, as other radical groups would do in the years to come. "The thinking was, we were revolutionaries, this is what revolutionaries do," Fliegelman says. "In Uruguay the Tupamaros robbed banks. I mean, we were declaring war on the country. So whatever you have to do, you do."

In the end, after considerable debate, Fliegelman says, they decided to stage a robbery. But not a bank. The logistics seemed far too daunting. Instead, once they finally mustered the courage to rob something, Fliegelman says with a sigh, "it was a steakhouse. In Westchester County. Two of us walked into the restaurant. And there was a driver outside. There was a cashier. They were scared to death. They pulled guns on the cashier and asked for all the money and they were given all the money. It wasn't very much, a thousand or two."

Afterward everyone felt awful. What if someone—a proletariat worker— had been shot? Would revolutionary ends have justified it? The entire exercise was humiliating, at once far too ambitious and yet, as Ivy League students just months before, somehow beneath them. Weatherman's goal was the overthrow of the legitimate government of the United States of America. Yet they could barely summon the nerve to rob a steakhouse. Would the vaunted Tupamaros have robbed a steakhouse?

"I think we felt, this is just too hard for us," says Fliegelman. "This is not what we are. You're walking into a restaurant with a loaded gun. Are we willing to actually shoot someone? I guess we weren't. We're not thugs. We don't rob people. [Our feelings] had to do with the middle-class white people we really were."

One of the great mysteries of the Weatherman story involves the sources of its funding. Of the half-dozen largest underground groups active during the 1970s, it was one of only two that did not resort to armed robbery to raise money. Many have assumed that because a number of prominent Weathermen were the children of wealthy families—Bill Ayers and Cathy Wilkerson are often cited—they lived off donations from family and friends. While some families did help, money remained a chronic problem for many

Weathermen. In San Francisco, Jeff Jones and the cadres he was responsible for lived on $1,200 a month and kept to strict budgets. At various times the FBI launched probes into traveler's-check and credit-card scams it suspected the organization was using for money, but nothing ever came of them.

In fact, the single largest source of funding appears to have been donations from Movement sympathizers. Most gave willingly; others, it appeared, had to be persuaded. "I remember this one guy they targeted in Brooklyn, a rich guy, Fred something, his father founded [a toy company]," recalls Elizabeth Fink. "They find out he has like twenty-five grand. So they have this party, eight or nine people, all of them Weatherman or connected to the underground. Fred is the only one not in the underground. He just thinks they're fun. I don't know what happened, but the next morning I heard they got every cent of that money, all twenty-five grand."

Among Weatherman's financiers, by far the most important single source of money was a group of radical attorneys in Chicago, New York, San Francisco, and Los Angeles. Almost all belonged to the National Lawyers Guild, a network of left-wing lawyers founded in 1937 as an alternative to the American Bar Association. "Money? It was the lawyers, all of it," says Ron Fliegelman, a sentiment echoed by several other Weather alumni. Of the dozen or so attorneys mentioned as key supporters, only a handful will admit helping out. One is Dennis Cunningham, then a Chicago attorney who represented Black Panthers. "I gave them money, sure, and I raised even more," he says. "Without the lawyers, I'm telling you, they couldn't have survived."

"You gotta understand, honey, we were lawyers, but we were revolutionaries in our hearts," says Elizabeth Fink. "We didn't have the balls to go underground, you see, but those who did, they were our heroes. You can't believe the excitement of helping the underground, the romance of it, the intrigue. It was enthralling, and addictive. Any of us—Dennis, me, a bunch of us—we would've done anything for these people. Money, strategy, passports, whatever it was we could do, you just did it. This was the revolution, baby, and they were the fighters. But a lot of what they did, you know, was because they had attorneys like Dennis and me and a lot of others aboveground helping out."

By far the most important attorney in Weatherman's support network was

Michael Kennedy, who in 1970 was emerging as one of the Bay Area's most prominent radical lawyers. Born in 1937 and raised in California's San Joaquin Valley, Kennedy had gone to Berkeley, then Hastings law school, before heading to New York in 1968 to work with a leftist lawyers' group, the Emergency Civil Liberties Committee. There he forged a close friendship with several high-profile liberal attorneys, including Kathy Boudin's father, Leonard, and William Kunstler. In 1969 Kennedy relocated to San Francisco, where he caused a splash representing infamous pornographers, the Mitchell brothers.

Michael and his wife, Eleanore, were among Bernardine Dohrn's closest friends in the Bay Area; the two women even went to the gynecologist together. Michael served as a useful conduit to the Movement and beyond. "Michael Kennedy was the key," recalls Dennis Cunningham, a close friend of Dohrn's, who visited her in San Francisco. "I went out there and got in touch with him, and he got me in touch with them. Bernardine had a lot of confidence in Michael. He was the most important friend they had."*

Although he denies any significant role, Michael Kennedy was nevertheless drawn into what would become the strangest political action in Weatherman's history: the prison escape of LSD guru Timothy Leary. A onetime Harvard lecturer who had transformed himself into the nation's preeminent exponent of psychedelic drugs, Leary had drawn a ten-year sentence after an arrest for possession of two marijuana cigarettes in Laguna Beach, California; sent to the California Men's Colony in San Luis Obispo, he hired Kennedy to handle his appeal. Leary's wife, Rosemary, meanwhile, reached out to the country's largest illegal distributor of LSD—a ragtag bunch of Orange County– and Maui-based hippies who called themselves the Brotherhood of Eternal Love— in hopes they might bankroll an effort to rescue him. The amount involved is in dispute; most sources say $25,000, others $50,000. In fact, one of the Brotherhood's leaders, Travis Ashbrook, told Leary's biographer years later that he and another dealer gave an intermediary $17,000 to cover the costs.

---

*Michael Kennedy declined to comment for the record.

According to Jeff Jones's son Thai's book *A Radical Line*, Jones made the pickup on the Santa Monica Pier. A woman sat on a bench, placing a brown paper bag at her feet. A moment later Jones wandered up and sat beside her, placing an identical bag filled with clothes next to hers. After a minute Jones took the woman's bag, rose, and walked off. Inside he found bundles of hundred-dollar bills and several doses of acid, to be used as a celebration once Leary had been freed.

Michael Kennedy has always denied any role in Leary's escape; an FBI investigation of his involvement ended in 1977 with no indictments returned. But Leary, in multiple interviews before his death in 1996, repeatedly characterized Kennedy as the driving force behind everything that happened. "Kennedy masterminded my escape from prison in such a way that there was no way he could possibly be imprisoned," Leary told an interviewer in 1991. "He did nothing illegal, but he was my spiritual counselor. He directed and announced it."[1]

Weatherman's involvement was controversial within the group. Leary was not a political but a cultural figure; some cadres felt helping him escape was a risky sideshow. "We were opportunistically glomming on to the counterculture," Mark Rudd has written. "The Leary jailbreak appeared to me to be a transparent attempt to insinuate ourselves with our potential base, the flower children."[2] Others suggested that if anyone was to be broken out of prison, it should be a heavyweight black revolutionary, such as Huey Newton. "Huey Newton was in a maximum-security prison and it would have required guns and bloodshed and we were not capable of doing that," Jeff Jones recalled. "This was doable and had a lot going for it. It was a real poke in the eye to California and the drug laws. It was a big 'fuck you.'"[3]

Weatherman's entire Bay Area apparatus was employed in the brewing escape, which was planned in minute detail. A date was set: the night of Saturday, September 12, three days before Leary was scheduled to return to New York for trial on yet another set of drug charges. That Friday, Leary later told the FBI, Michael Kennedy's law partner, Joe Rhine, visited him and laid out the details. Leary would always insist he never knew that his rescuers were to be Weathermen; Kennedy, he said, had mentioned only that they would be "political people." The escape itself turned out to be child's play. San Luis

Obispo was a minimum-security prison—which made it easy the next night for Leary to simply walk out of his cell and climb atop a building near the wall. From there he began shimmying along a hundred-foot horizontal cable, fighting exhaustion and at one point freezing when a prison patrol car passed beneath him. Crossing the outer wall, he reached a telephone pole, then climbed down and leaped into a ravine along Highway 1. By and by a car coasted to a stop alongside him.

In later years Leary maintained that two young women using code names were in the car. In a 1974 interview with the FBI, however, he indicated that the driver was in fact "the brother of a well-known political radical," a description that best fits one of Weatherman's ablest cadres, John Willard Davis, Rennie Davis's brother. As Leary stripped off his prison denims, the car headed through the town of Morro Bay and soon stopped on a beachfront road. Led across the dunes, Leary spotted a gray-haired man and an unidentified woman alongside a battered camper. The man was Clayton Van Lydegraf, a fifty-five-year-old Communist Party veteran from Seattle who had emerged as one of Weatherman's most reliable aboveground supporters. The handy Van Lydegraf, who would leave a lasting mark on the organization, had fixed up the camper with Mark Rudd's help. He and the woman guided Leary inside, dyed his hair, and for the first time told him he was in the hands of Weatherman. Outside, another reliable cadre, Paul Bradley, collected Leary's prison clothes and drove south, eventually dumping them in a gas station restroom near Los Angeles in hopes of misleading police.

Van Lydegraf, meanwhile, drove Leary north in the camper as a second car trailed behind, monitoring a police scanner. Like Rudd, the old communist wasn't thrilled by his duties. "I was against this whole thing from the start," he told Leary, "and if it was up to me you'd still be rotting in jail."[4] Leary sat in the back, sipping chilled wine, all the way to their destination, a duplex in a North Oakland slum. There was no sign of pursuit. The next day Van Lydegraf drove Leary north again, heading up Interstate 5 into far northern California, where they pulled into a remote campsite deep in the woods between the towns of Lakehead and Weed. The next night Bernardine Dohrn, Bill Ayers, and Jeff Jones arrived to welcome him.

Leary was transfixed by Dohrn. His description of her would eventually appear in countless articles. She dressed, he said, "like no one else in the out crowd," with "cashmere sweaters and black Capezio flats," possessed of "unforgettable sex appeal" and "the most amazing legs," like "the rah-rah leader of the crazy motherfuckers from the Girls Athletic Association running down the aisles of American Airlines borrowing food from people's plates." Leary volunteered to join Weatherman underground. Dohrn demurred, saying he was far too hot. She thought he should leave the country, perhaps join the Black Panther leader Eldridge Cleaver, who had fled to Algeria. They wrote a pair of communiqués around the campfire. Dohrn's was a transparent attempt to curry favor with the counterculture:

> Dr. Leary was being held against his will and against the will of millions of kids in this country. He was a political prisoner, captured for the work he did in helping all of us begin the task of creating a new culture on the barren wasteland that has been imposed on this country by Democrats, Republicans, capitalists and creeps. LSD, and grass, like the herbs and cactus and mushrooms of the American Indians and countless civilizations that have existed on this planet, will help us make a future world where it will be possible to live in peace. Now we are at war. . . . We are outlaws, we are free!

Leary's was predictably florid. He wrote, in part:

> There is the day of laughing Krishna and the day of Grim Shiva. Brothers and sisters, this is a war for survival. Ask Huey and Angela. They dig it. Ask the wild free animals. . . . To shoot a genocidal robot policeman in the defense of life is a sacred act. . . . Listen, the hour is late. Total war is upon us. Fight to live or you'll die. Freedom is life. Freedom will live.

The escape was news around the world and probably did more to elevate Weatherman's visibility than any single bombing. At a press conference in San Francisco, Michael Kennedy characterized it as "a merger of dope and dynamite. . . . There is now a merger of Timothy and the Weathermen. This portends more destruction to the American government than anything in history." In Washington a simmering J. Edgar Hoover, asked about Leary, sniped, "We'll have him in ten days."

The next morning the group split up, Dohrn and the others promising to see Leary again in three days. Once again Van Lydegraf drove Leary north in the camper, eventually coming to a stop on a country lane outside the town of Monroe, northeast of Seattle. A mile down the lane stood a farmhouse occupied until a few days earlier by Bill Ayers's brother, Rick, and his pregnant girlfriend. Rick had deserted from the army to join Weatherman and would soon emerge as its West Coast logistics expert. "I didn't even know about Leary until afterward," he recalls forty years later. "I just knew someone was coming. So we all cleared out."

Leary's wife, Rosemary, was waiting at the house. When Dohrn and the others finally arrived, Leary insisted they all go see the Woodstock concert movie; at the theater, a totally stoned Leary, his head now shaved, ate popcorn and hollered comments at the screen while Dohrn and Jones sat behind him, wishing he would shut up.

Both Learys had been given fake driver's licenses. The next morning Dohrn told Leary it would be necessary to fly to Chicago to get the passports needed to travel to Algeria. "Tim was quite shocked when he found out we weren't handing him a preprinted, ready-to-go passport," Jones recalled. "That was a capability we did not have."[5] Rick Ayers recalls: "Leary was, like, 'Fuck, I'm out, let's hijack a plane and get outta here,' and the leadership was, like, 'Man, cool out.'"

On September 23, having used the fake licenses to secure passports at a Chicago passport office, the Learys boarded a flight to Paris, eventually making their way to Algiers. There they held court with a host of Movement figures, including Eldridge Cleaver and Dohrn's sister, Jennifer. It was the beginning of a multiyear international odyssey that would end in embarrassment for everyone involved.

The Leary escape created a surge of momentum for Weatherman, one the leadership could not afford to waste. Everyone sensed they were nearing some kind of turning point. After Kent State and the campus riots in May, there were worrisome signs that the mass movement was flagging. The Nixon White House, it was clear, could not be influenced by demonstrations, no matter how large; that era was passing. By that fall, one author notes, "activists faced three options: go underground and fight the establishment by any means necessary, drop out and do their own thing, or turn their energies toward other causes."[6]

Events beyond Weatherman's control, meanwhile, had dealt the underground's allure a severe blow. Early on the morning of August 24, three weeks before the Leary escape, four militants in Madison, Wisconsin, packed nearly a ton of explosives into a stolen Ford Econoline van and parked it beside the University of Wisconsin's Sterling Hall, which housed the Army Mathematics Research Center; it was the same building Jeff Jones, during a campus appearance, had urged "trashing" a year before. The resulting explosion, exponentially larger than anything Weatherman ever attempted, could be heard thirty miles away. It gutted the six-story building. Damage was put at $6 million; at the time, it was the single most destructive act of sabotage in U.S. history. Worse, a postdoctoral researcher named Robert Fassnacht, working inside the building, was killed. He left a wife and three children.

Literally overnight, the Madison bombing transformed the national conversation from a focus on Nixon's misdeeds—Cambodia, Kent State—to those of self-styled revolutionaries. Midnight bombings that until that point seemed brave or romantic or even heroic suddenly appeared callous and uncaring at least, murderous at worst. For the first time a generation of militants comfortable with revolutionary rhetoric were forced to confront its consequences. "It isn't just the radicals who set the bomb in a lighted, occupied building who are guilty," editorialized the *Wisconsin State Journal*. "The blood is on the hands of anyone who has encouraged them, anyone who has talked recklessly of 'revolution,' anyone who has chided with mild disparagement the violence of extremists while hinting that the cause is right all the same." Reporters who sought reactions from young radicals found many not only chagrined but prepared to denounce the use of violence altogether. "Blowing up the CIA building will not bring home the troops," a Detroit radical observed. "Bombings are suicidal and are not bringing any change except more repression." In a widely quoted speech at Kansas State University three weeks later, President Nixon cited the Madison bombing in a virulent denunciation of student revolutionaries, "the violent and radical few, the rock throwers and the obscenity shouters" who would "tear America down."

Weatherman's leadership was determined to keep the underground option alive. Even before the Leary escape, plans had been laid for an ambitious "fall offensive" to demonstrate the group's resurgence and reach. In late September Ron Fliegelman and others traveled from New York to Chicago for the first bombing. "That was us, New York, and some aboveground friends," he recalls. Their action was to be a symbol of Weatherman's Phoenix-like rise from the ashes of the Townhouse: the very same Haymarket police statue they had destroyed a year earlier. The statue had been rebuilt, but on the morning of October 5, Fliegelman detonated a dynamite bomb that destroyed it once again.*

At a New York press conference the next day, Jennifer Dohrn, taking a step toward becoming Weatherman's aboveground spokesperson, along with the Yippie activist Abbie Hoffman, played a recording of her sister Bernardine reading Weatherman's communiqué aloud. It promised a series of bombings "from Santa Barbara to Boston" in the days ahead and, using the group's groovy new "youth culture" patois, struck an almost plaintive tone, all but begging Movement activists to stay the course:

> Today many student leaders have cut their hair and called for peace. They say young people shouldn't provoke the government. And they receive in return promises of peaceful change. . . . Don't be tricked by talk. Arm yourselves and shoot to live! We are building a culture and a society that can resist genocide. It is a culture of total resistance to mind-controlling maniacs; a culture of high-energy sisters getting it on, of hippie acid-smiles and communes and freedom to be the farthest-out people we can be.

This time all the bombs went off.

At 1:27 a.m. on October 8, two days after the press conference, the first

---

*The statue would eventually be rebuilt yet again, this time inside a protected courtyard.

demolished an empty courtroom in the Marin County Courthouse, north of San Francisco. Two months earlier police there had killed a seventeen-year-old black teenager named Jonathan Jackson who was attempting to free three San Quentin prisoners at a hearing. The bombing was carried out by Weathermen working from the Pine Street apartment in San Francisco; Mark Rudd had scouted the site. Ninety minutes later the Seattle underground group Quarter Moon Tribe, which the exiled Howard Machtinger had joined, detonated a bomb in a set of lockers in an ROTC building at the University of Washington. The explosion destroyed a vacant office. Ninety minutes later a group calling itself the Perfect Park Home Garden Society detonated a bomb against a wall of a National Guard Armory in Santa Barbara, California. Damage was minimal. (The Seattle group was directly affiliated with Weatherman; the Santa Barbara group was believed to be.)

Twenty-four hours later, having returned from Chicago, members of the New York cell detonated a large bomb behind a telephone booth on the third floor of a traffic court in Queens. Warnings were called in; no one was injured. A communiqué said the explosion was in support of an inmate riot that week at the Queens House of Detention. Four days later a fifth and final bomb went off in Cambridge, Massachusetts, at Harvard University's empty Center for International Affairs, Henry Kissinger's alma mater. A communiqué took credit on behalf of Weatherman's "women's brigade," initially called the Proud Eagle Tribe. This was believed to be a group of several Weatherwomen, including Kathy Boudin, and friends.

The bombings prompted a blizzard of bomb threats around the country, including dozens phoned in to major airports—so many that the Federal Aviation Administration was obliged to issue a nationwide alert calling for tightened security measures. At the Pentagon senior officials issued an order for increased National Guard security at military installations. In Washington, D.C., Attorney General John Mitchell termed the attacks the work of "psychopaths." In Key Biscayne, Florida, the White House press secretary, Ron Ziegler, told reporters that the president had ordered the FBI to investigate. A new crime bill had been introduced, to which Republicans had added a clause doubling fines and jail time for bombings and making it a federal crime to bomb any building whose occupants received federal funding. Nixon,

Ziegler said, had told White House staff that the new bombings "are further evidence of the need for speedy Congressional action." Reaction in the mainstream press followed suit. As a *Times* editorial put it:

> Presumably the Weatherman and their ilk believe their outrages are furthering the cause of revolution in this "oppressive society." The reverse is much more the case. Every building bombed, every person killed or wounded by bombs horrifies and makes more angry the great majority of the American people who abhor all political violence. . . . The bombings and other acts of terrorism are helping move this nation to the right; they foster repression and reaction.[7]

It was a valid point. It wasn't just the White House that was cracking down. In state legislatures, public dismay at radical bombings had triggered a rush to pass new restrictions on the sale and storage of dynamite. A Senate investigation revealed that thefts of dynamite from quarries and construction sites had risen from 12,381 pounds in 1969 to 18,989 pounds in just the first five months of 1970. Yet, as Ron Fliegelman had shown, dynamite could be purchased far more easily than stolen. In Michigan a pair of UPI reporters walked into a hardware store and, without showing identification or signing any paperwork, were able to buy twelve sticks of dynamite for just $3. When the two reporters walked into a pharmacy next door, they were forced to prove they were twenty-one and sign a logbook before being allowed to buy a two-ounce bottle of cough syrup containing codeine. At the beginning of 1970, some twenty-three states had little or no dynamite regulation; by that fall, perhaps unsurprisingly, almost all had passed or were considering new restrictions on dynamite sales.[8]

Not that it mattered to Weatherman. By one alumnus's estimate the group already had enough dynamite under lock and key to allow it to bomb a new building every month for the next thirty years.

THE WRONG SIDE OF HISTORY

Weatherman and the FBI,
October 1970 to April 1971

Hundreds of anonymous tips flowed into FBI offices after the October bomb-ings, most of them spurious, as with the caller who claimed that Weatherman was planning to steal biological weapons from the army's Fort Detrick, in Maryland, and poison a major city's water supply. The attacks put enormous pressure on the FBI to make arrests, but while any number of radicals were detained that autumn, none were Weathermen. It was, in fact, a wildly uneven manhunt. The group was a top priority for the New York, Chicago, and San Francisco offices, but despite all the demands and directives from headquar-ters, a number of FBI stations had simply refused to form Weatherman squads, seeing no pressing local need. When Wesley Swearingen, a veteran agent involved in both the Sam Melville and Townhouse investigations, was trans-ferred from New York to Los Angeles that spring, he asked to be assigned to the Weatherman squad. He was told there wasn't one. "Wes, you don't under-stand," a supervisor told him. "There arc no Weathermen in Los Angeles."[1]

Almost immediately, however, Swearingen found one. The owner of a construction-supply store in Tucson had called police, suspicious of a young man to whom he had sold fifty pounds of dynamite. The man had showed a California driver's license in the name of William Allen Friedman. When another agent showed it to Swearingen, he recognized the photo as John Fuerst, the Columbia SDSer who had headed the Cleveland collective until fleeing after the Townhouse. Swearingen traced "William Friedman" to an address in the beachside town of Venice, California, swiftly identifying five other radicals at the same address.

"Hell," Swearingen said, "these are Weathermen."

Reluctantly the Los Angeles FBI office formed a Weatherman squad. Fuerst had vanished, but Swearingen alone eventually opened more than two hundred wiretaps. When these found little to prove that the remaining five radicals in Venice were Weathermen—they apparently weren't—Swearingen and other agents followed in Squad 47's footsteps and began breaking into the homes and offices of their friends.

The Fuerst investigation opened a new front in the government's pursuit of Weatherman. It was led by a sharply dressed Washington lawyer named Guy L. Goodwin. As the newly named chief of the Justice Department's special litigation service of the internal security and criminal division, Goodwin would become Weatherman's own Inspector Javert, a relentless prosecutor who used grand juries to interrogate—terrorize, his critics charged—just about anyone ever linked to the group. The syndicated columnist Jack Anderson termed him President Nixon's "Witch-Finder General." In fact, Goodwin was a liberal Democrat who was deeply opposed to the Vietnam War and secretly disdainful of the Nixon administration. But he put his job first. In time, acting as a kind of traveling prosecutor, he would convene more than a dozen grand juries across the country, remaining calm and professional even in the face of the angriest Weather supporters. Once, when demonstrators pelted him with urine and oil outside a Seattle courthouse, Goodwin shrugged and told an associate, "Calm down. Kids will be kids."[2]

In one of his first grand juries, Goodwin subpoenaed the five Venice suspects to testify in Tucson. The only concrete evidence he could muster was the fact that Fuerst had used one of their cars. When all refused to testify, Goodwin had them jailed for contempt. In the meantime, Wes Swearingen and other Los Angeles agents burglarized all their new residences and then the homes of four of their attorneys; no usable evidence was ever found. When the grand jury expired six months later, the "Tucson Five," as they were known by then, were freed. Goodwin subpoenaed them once more. Facing eighteen more months in jail, three testified. Cited for contempt, another appealed all the way to the Supreme Court, which reversed the citation. Fuerst was eventually indicted but never captured. Many years later he turned himself in to authorities in Tucson. The case was dismissed.

Guy Goodwin, however, was just getting started.

After the October bombings Weatherman's leadership gathered for a postmortem in New York. It was probably the first time all four of its members—along with its soon-to-be-named fifth, Eleanor Stein—had been in one place since Flint. It had been an incredible six months since Mendocino, a period in which they had managed to rebuild the organization, perfect a safer bomb design, and launch a sharply different kind of nationwide bombing campaign from the one JJ and Terry Robbins and many other Weathermen had envisioned. Everyone was exhausted. They needed time to rest, regroup, and plan.

Along with members of the New York cell, the leaders rented a house near the beach in Hampton Bays, toward the eastern end of Long Island. Jeff Jones passed out the last of the California acid and led everyone in gathering seashells. On Thanksgiving Stein cooked a turkey while the men played touch football. In the evenings they smoked pot, listened to Bob Dylan's new album, *New Morning*, and tried to take stock of everything that had happened in the eight frenetic months since the Townhouse. They had achieved so much. They had struck at the government in six cities. No one had been hurt. No one had been arrested. Yet, for all they had achieved, it was hard to argue that Weatherman had done much to further the underground cause. They had imagined they would be an intellectual vanguard whose actions would draw others into the underground and trigger the revolution they wanted so badly. But it wasn't happening.

Major protest bombings were on the rise, it was true; by one count, there were 330 in 1970, almost one a day, more than three times the number reported in 1969. Almost all, however, like the one in Madison, appeared the work of "one-off" student rage. No significant new underground groups had formed. And while Weatherman retained real prestige as the "heavy edge" of the New Left, the Madison bombing had done incalculable damage to the group's cause, at once repelling would-be allies and demonstrating that public tolerance of radical violence was on the wane. In a Gallup poll that winter, only 8 percent of college students surveyed expressed a "highly favorable" view of Weatherman, while 47 percent had a "highly unfavorable" view, one point less than for the ultraconservative John Birch Society.[3] Weatherman itself, while operational, was far smaller than it had been before the Townhouse; by Thanksgiving, it probably had less than fifty active members, perhaps as few as thirty.

Change was in the air. You could see it on the streets. The media, from *Time* to the *Saturday Evening Post*, was calling it a revolution, but it was not at all the revolution Weatherman expected. Everyone called it something different: the Age of Aquarius, Woodstock Nation, Alternative Society, the counterculture. After five years of scoffing and hand-wringing at the riotous change in its children, much of mainstream America had begun to embrace it: the drugs, the music, the long hair, the bell-bottom pants, the distaste for authority. A best-selling book that winter, *The Greening of America*, by a Yale professor named Charles Reich, announced it loud and clear:

> There is a revolution coming. It will not be like revolutions of the past. It will originate with the individual and with culture, and it will change the political structure only as its final act. It will not require violence to succeed, and it cannot be successfully resisted by violence. . . . This is the revolution of the new generation. . . . Their protest and rebellion, their culture, clothes, music, drugs, and liberated life-style.[4]

It was true. America, it turned out, had fallen in love with everything about this groovy new counterculture—except its politics. Those like Weatherman who had predicted a revolution in America ended up being half-right. A revolution was arriving, but it was a cultural rather than a political phenomenon. It was the height of irony: Much of America wanted to dress like

Bernardine Dohrn, smoke pot like Bernardine Dohrn, and listen to Bernardine Dohrn's music, but it honestly didn't want to hear a word she had to say. The Movement had preached endlessly about freedom, to dress as you like, eat what you like, smoke what you like: "You can do what you want" was the famous line from the 1971 movie *Harold and Maude*. As these new values seeped into the American mind-set during 1970, 1971, and 1972, it turned out that what most Americans wanted to do was focus not on politics—and certainly not on overthrowing the government—but on themselves. It was the dawning of what Tom Wolfe called the "Me" Decade. Terry H. Anderson gives this vivid portrait of its beginnings circa 1971:

> Liberal cities turned exotic as freaks and ethnics created a hip cultural renaissance. Street art flourished; color flooded the nation. Chicanos painted murals at high schools and "walls of fire" on buildings. Black men wore jumbo Afros and the women sported vivid African dress. Young men with shaved heads and robes beat tambourines and chanted on corners, "Krishna, Krishna, Hare Krishna." Hip capitalists invaded the streets, setting up shops: Artisans wearing bandanas and bellbottoms sold jewelry, bells, and leather, as sunlight streamed through cut glass. Communards in ragged bib overalls sold loaves of whole-wheat bread at co-ops and organically grown vegetables at farmers' markets. Freak flags flew, curling, waving across America. Carpenters wearing ponytails moved into decaying neighborhoods, paint and lumber in hand, and began urban homesteading. Longhairs blew bubbles or lofted Frisbees in the park. Tribes of young men and women skinny-dipped at beaches and hippie hollows.[5]

The irony was that even as Middle America adopted the Movement's look and feel, the Movement itself was slowly coming apart. In part, it was due to the dawning realization that demonstrations alone would never end the war or influence the White House. Nixon had started his "Vietnamization" of the war; American soldiers had begun streaming home. Suddenly protesting the war didn't seem so urgent. Thousands of young people were giving up politics, many of them flocking to the hippie communes springing up all over the United States. By 1971, the Associated Press estimated, three thousand communes had opened, taking in three million people. But the real problem was that the Movement had become a victim of its own success. By empowering women, it created the women's liberation movement. By calling out corporate polluters, it helped spawn the modern environmental movement. In the countercultural mainstreaming of 1970, 1971, and 1972, these two causes and many others exploded into the national consciousness, diverting the attentions of many who had built their lives around protesting the war and racism. This shift was symbolized by the decision at *Rat*, the underground paper where Sam Melville's girlfriend, Jane Alpert, once worked, to give up coverage of the "revolution" altogether and focus exclusively on women's issues.

"[The past two years] haven't been good for anyone, and on balance they haven't been good for the left at all," the writer David Horowitz observed that winter. "The main motion is in other directions, towards new lifestyles rather than new constituencies, toward political communes and collectives rather than parties and coalitions, toward underground violence rather than aboveground organizing."

Sipping coffee in the mornings at Hampton Bays, Dohrn and the others sensed they might be sliding toward the wrong side of history. They had achieved much, they agreed, but they had made mistakes, and not just at the Townhouse. They had led a banzai charge, and no one had followed. They had been stunningly arrogant, and dismissive of their critics. Worst of all, they had walked away from their only source of real power: the vast network of SDS, now in ruins. Without SDS, they had no power. Without SDS, they were isolated. They were alone.

"By then the question was becoming 'Why are we doing this?'" recalls Brian Flanagan. "People started saying it was a mistake jettisoning SDS, and it clearly was. Then, once you took real violence off the table, once you said we weren't going to kill policemen, what were we gonna do, blow up bathrooms the rest of our lives?"

They had burned too many bridges, and they knew it. That winter, for the first time, some of their aboveground allies began openly appealing for support from the rest of the Movement, something the leadership had never thought would be necessary. Returning from a trip to Algiers, Jennifer Dohrn made clear that Weatherman couldn't bring about a revolution on its own. "Revolution," she told the *Liberated Guardian*, "means moving on all different kinds of levels. . . . If they're doing a bombing, well, then we should be planning how we're going to be out on the street [in support], not how we should be doing a bombing too. To coordinate stuff moves so many more people, and it's really a way of increasing our strength, building solidarity among us."

A more plaintive note was struck by two imprisoned Weatherwomen, Linda Evans and Judy Clark, who released a letter from a Chicago jail in which they appealed to their fellow radicals not to forget Weatherman. "I wonder how many old friends of people who are underground think to talk about them with people," Clark wrote. "Think how effective it would be in making those underground figures into real life and blood people, massifying that understanding so that more and more people can develop a consciousness about aiding and abetting fugitives, developing their own sense of security, breaking down that feeling of separateness between under[ground] and over[ground]." Evans added: "[This] makes them real people, not superstar myths. People don't seem to understand how important the creation of the underground is to the future of the struggle—how important it is for all of us to help them survive—support them totally, openly when they have the misfortune to get caught. . . . Talk with friends about ways they survive, ways we can help them—just to make the whole thing more real than visions of people hiding in basements, putting on wigs occasionally to carry a bomb into a building."

"Superstar myths" hiding in basements: Eight months after the Townhouse, that's what they had become. Somehow, Dohrn knew, they had to begin to rebuild all those bridges, make themselves real again to the Movement. They started writing in the mornings after coffee, all of them contributing to the essay they decided to call, in another nod to Dylan, "New Morning, Changing Weather." It was the longest and most mature document they had produced to date. Gone was much of the hippie-dippy "youth culture" jargon that came to be associated with Jeff Jones and Bill Ayers. In its place was something they had never tried before, genuine humility, infused into a sober accounting of Weatherman's first year. The tone came to be identified with Dohrn; when "New Morning" was released, on December 6, 1970, only her signature was appended.

"New Morning" was a stark admission not only of Weatherman's failure to draw others into revolutionary violence but of how thoroughly the world had moved away from its tactics in just a year. "It has been nine months since the townhouse explosion," it read "In that time, the future of our revolution has changed decisively." Weatherman, too, needed to change, the statement went on. In language that represented a sharp reversal from communiqués issued as recently as that September, it rejected almost everything Weatherman had represented up to the Townhouse, admitting that "the townhouse forever destroyed our belief that armed struggle is the only real revolutionary struggle." It acknowledged its "military error" and apologized not only for its "technical inexperience" but for a tendency "to consider only bombings or picking up the gun as revolutionary, with the glorification of the heavier the better." Gone were the calls for supporting black revolutionaries. In their place were more attempts to reach out to hippies and freaks, announcing that "grass and organic consciousness expanding drugs" were now "weapons of the revolution." Dohrn even changed the name of the group, rejecting "Weatherman" as sexist. They would now be called the Weather Underground.

"New Morning" drew criticism from a number of leading radicals, none more important than the Panther 21, the group of New York Black Panthers still engaged in a mass conspiracy trial. The "21" issued an open letter criticizing Weather's retreat from revolutionary violence, as well as its unwillingness to raise money or help the jailed Panthers in any significant way. The letter put Weather's leadership in a delicate position. Everyone knew what many Panthers wanted to do: kill policemen, the exact strategy Weather had now disavowed. The 21's letter, in effect, forced Weather to publicly choose between its old principles and those it would now embrace, supporting black revolutionaries or renouncing deadly violence. In the end, in a decision that came back to haunt everyone involved, Dohrn decided to take what many saw as the coward's way out. The leadership responded to the 21 with complete silence. They said nothing.

"That right there is the moment when they abandoned the blacks, abandoned everything they ever said about helping the blacks, and we all knew it," says one radical attorney of the period. "Bernardine, Billy, that pretty boy Jeff Jones, all of them, they decided they didn't want to die, they didn't want to go to jail. So they walked out on everything they believed so they could stay free and stay alive."

After "New Morning" the New York leadership returned to their apartment on Amity Street in Brooklyn, the others to San Francisco. It was around this time, it appears, that Dohrn, Jones, and Ayers abandoned their Sausalito houseboat for a modern gated home in the waterside suburb of Tiburon. At least two friends remember visiting them there. "They were living in a big, glamorous house in Tiburon, with a beautiful deck, four bedrooms, totally empty," recalls Jon Lerner. "I remember I walked into the kitchen, and someone looked outside and noticed an unmarked panel van across the street. The three of them panicked and said, 'Let's get outta here,' and so we packed them up and left. I assume they went back at some point. It was a false alarm."

The Tiburon house symbolized a dichotomy that was beginning to trouble many in Weather's lower ranks. While leadership lived in a waterfront home, their followers, many still huddled in a single apartment on Pine Street in San Francisco, were living on the edge of poverty. The resentment would grow in the coming months. "They wouldn't let us have jobs, you know, they would give us twenty bucks now and then," says Cathy Wilkerson, who remains resentful forty years later. "In time the difference between the top and the bottom became really gross. Offensive. Their position was that if you wanted money, you should raise money. Well, most of us couldn't do that. They would go to good restaurants that we could not afford. If we went with them, we had to pay for ourselves, unless business was discussed, and they would pay."

One Weather alumnus remembers visiting Bill Ayers and opening the refrigerator to find a stick of butter. "Butter!" he exclaims today. "I couldn't afford a piece of bread, and they had butter!" Ayers's brother Rick was especially incensed. At one point, while underground in Los Angeles, he was so poor he lived for months in a tent in a city park. "They never seemed to have jobs," he recalled. "They lived off radical lawyers and moneyed friends who told them what they wanted to hear—what courageous revolutionaries they were—while all the rest of us did the shit work and went around blowing things up to maintain their reputations. While some of us were dangerously poor, they always ate good food and they always slept between clean sheets."[6]

For the leadership, at least, life was good—so good that worries of complacency set in. "There were a lot of people who were getting sloppy, their IDs were bad, their wigs were bad, their hair dye was bad," remembers Rick Ayers, who warned his brother they were taking too many chances. "I was a stickler. I recall I really thought they were getting sloppy in San Francisco, and I told them so."

Rick's concerns rose that winter when, during a single two-month period, a number of Weathermen survived encounters with their FBI pursuers. The first was Rick Ayers himself, who was then living in a remote farmhouse north of Seattle. His girlfriend had given birth that summer, and at one point the couple crossed into Canada to register their daughter under their real names in Vancouver. Not long after, their landlord's teenaged son warned them that federal agents had arrived to arrest them. "We were gone within an hour," Ayers recalls. "We lost the car and everything else. Apparently we had been photographed at the Vancouver train station, and it had taken them months to find us." (It was after this episode that Ayers relocated to Los Angeles.)

The second incident involved one of Weather's young attorneys, a Harvard graduate named Donald Stang. On January 22, 1971, security guards at the Standard Oil building on Bush Street in San Francisco discovered Stang in an eleventh-floor restroom. Over his head they saw he had unscrewed a ceiling vent. When police were called, they found he was carrying a diagram of what appeared to be the building's heating system. With no evidence of any crime, Stang was not arrested, but the FBI clearly believed he was scouting a location to be bombed.*

By far the most dangerous encounter occurred a month earlier, on December 16, on Manhattan's East Side. Bill Ayers and several others, including Ron

---

*Reached at his Oakland-area home in 2013, Stang declined to discuss the incident, saying it was all "a misunderstanding."

Fliegelman, decided to take in a movie at a theater on East Sixty-eighth Street, which happened to be around the corner from the FBI's New York offices. Fliegelman was with his new girlfriend, Judy Clark. As luck would have it, an FBI agent passing the theater recognized Clark as she walked inside. "There were four or five of us in the theater," recalls Fliegelman. "We knew something was wrong. Someone in front of us was looking back at us. I remember some-body came back and asked Judy who she was, then asked her to come back with them. At the back, she ran. And they had to run after her. There was an emergency exit by the screen, and we all went to that and got away. It was close."

Even as Clark broke into a run, her FBI pursuers watched in amazement as she pulled out a notebook and actually began eating its pages. "When we caught her, oh, God, she was kicking and screaming and spitting at us," recalls Don Shackleford, a Squad 47 agent who helped make the arrest. "She called us every name in the book."

Clark, who was wanted on charges connected with the Days of Rage, would eventually be sentenced to nine months in the Cook County Jail, serve four, and resume a long and colorful career helping underground groups. While she told the FBI nothing of value, her arrest had immediate repercussions. When agents examined her driver's license, they found it was in the name of a long-dead infant named Yvette Kirby, the first inkling the Bureau received that this was how Weather was building its false identities. On December 21, five days after her capture, the FBI's San Francisco office dispatched a team of agents to the San Francisco Department of Health to begin examining all dead-infant birth certificates from the 1940s that had been issued during the previous year, paying close attention to those issued between January and April, when Weather cadres were first arriving in the Bay Area.

It took a dozen agents six weeks to complete the search, but when they did, they suspected they had hit pay dirt: Twenty-seven birth certificates had been issued. Cross-indexing these names with driver's licenses issued by the Department of Motor Vehicles, they found that eighteen of these long-dead infants had been issued new driver's licenses in the previous year. All, they suspected, were Weathermen. Studying the license photos and signatures, the agents tentatively identified at least a dozen Weathermen, including Mark Rudd and Kathy Boudin.

The real find, though, came when they examined a license issued on March 13, 1970—a week after the Townhouse—to a woman named Lorraine Anne Jellins. The baby by that name had been born in 1944 and died days later. Jellins was a dead ringer for Bernardine Dohrn. The signature matched. Checking motor-vehicle registrations, they found that Lorraine Jellins had registered a 1954 Chevrolet pickup truck: It was Jeff Jones's beloved Suzie Q. The truck had been issued parking tickets in Sausalito in May and in San Francisco in September. An arrest warrant for the unpaid tickets was immediately issued. Best of all, the FBI found an address in San Francisco. The owner was listed as a young doctor.

The doctor and his home were put under surveillance, but the Bureau wasn't willing to wait. According to FBI memoranda, "a highly confidential source" was identified at the doctor's on February 27, meaning the FBI broke into the apartment. Inside, they found a driver's license that had been issued to Norman Kenneth Bailey. The photo was of Jeff Jones. They also found a bill indicating that Lorraine Jellins had been examined at St. Francis Memorial Hospital on January 28, a month earlier. Checking hospital records, agents discovered a Dr. Robert E. Shapiro had seen Jellins at eleven fifteen that morning. The previous appointment, at eleven, had been for Eleanore Kennedy, Michael Kennedy's wife. Jellins was Dohrn. There was no doubt. An areawide alert was issued for Jones's truck. Neither Jones nor Dohrn, however, was found.

As luck would have it, they were at that very moment in Washington, D.C. The next day they bombed the U.S. Capitol.

The Capitol bombing on March 1, 1971, was the rare Weatherman action in which all, or almost all, the leadership gathered to take part. Ron Fliegelman believes he built the bomb, though his memory is hazy. Security in the building at the time was all but nonexistent; a visitor's bags weren't searched, and there were no metal detectors. According to several sources, Bernardine Dohrn and Kathy Boudin simply left the bomb behind a toilet in a first-floor men's room on the Senate side of the building. According to an account Jeff

Jones gave years later, it failed to explode, forcing a second team of Weathermen to sneak back inside and rearm it. After a warning call, the bomb finally detonated at 1:30 a.m., demolishing the restroom, heavily damaging an adjacent barbershop, and blowing out windows in a Senate dining room down a corridor. Damage was estimated at $300,000. On ABC News, anchorman Howard K. Smith noted that it was the first attack on the Capitol since the British burned it in 1814.

Much like the bombing of New York police headquarters nine months earlier, the Capitol bombing had a lasting and dramatic impact on security measures in Washington. For the first time, Capitol police began inspecting all purses and parcels brought into the building. All employees were issued photo identification cards. Gallery attendants received training in identifying suspicious persons. Seldom-used nooks and corridors were closed off. In the following year, the Capitol police force was increased in size to 1,000 officers from 622. Patronage appointments, until then routine, were stopped. Training was formalized. The department purchased its first bomb-sniffing dogs.

The roving prosecutor, Guy Goodwin, was brought in to lead a grand-jury investigation of the bombing. It turned into a fiasco. In a flurry of headlines, a nineteen-year-old demonstrator named Leslie Bacon was arrested—and later released—while several of her friends, including the Yippie activists Stew Alpert and Judy Gumbo, were subpoenaed to testify. Gumbo appeared with the Weather Underground logo—a neon rainbow—painted on her forehead. Alpert wore a sequined dress with appliqué spelling out BERNARDINE. Yet another Yippie, noting that Goodwin was looking for urban guerrillas, showed up in a gorilla suit. In the end no indictments were returned. "We didn't do it," Gumbo said when asked about the bombing. "But we dug it."

Days after the Capitol bombing, Jones and Dohrn returned to San Francisco with no sense that the FBI knew their identities or that agents were searching for Jones's truck. But as luck would have it, it wasn't the truck that got them into trouble. It was a single, innocuous money order, for all of $650.

It came from Dohrn's friend Dennis Cunningham. On the morning of

Thursday, March 4, the Chicago attorney walked into a Western Union office on West North Avenue and slid a wad of cash—$650, as he recalls—to the clerk. He used a fake name, Herman Schaefer, as he had done before, to send a money order to a "Duane Lee Compton" in San Francisco. Afterward he returned to his office, unaware he was being watched by FBI agents. Within minutes word was relayed to the Bureau in San Francisco, where dozens of agents were pursuing Weatherman leads. None had any evidence the money order was connected to the underground, much less knew who Duane Lee Compton was; most agents assumed he must be some aboveground supporter. "We were gonna set up a surveillance," recalls one agent, Max Noel, now retired. "The theory was, they would send an aboveground person, and we would follow them. This was the only plan. When we questioned this, the fact that there was no secondary plan if a fugitive arrived, the supervisors pooh-poohed the idea and told us not to worry."

By early afternoon a team of agents was in place at a Western Union office on Market Street in downtown San Francisco. One worked the counter. Another stood ready in a backroom with a camera. Two or three "beards"— long-haired street agents—lingered in the lobby, while two more teams sat in cars outside. For hours they waited. No one appeared. Finally, at seven thirty that evening, a customer asked for the money order from Chicago. He was a young man, tall and blond, with a bushy beard. At first glance, several agents thought it might be Jeff Jones himself. As the man left, two of the beards bumped into him. Afterward both whispered into their radios that it was Jones.

Chaos erupted among the FBI contingent. Jones was a Top Ten fugitive (on the FBI's Ten Most Wanted Fugitives List), and there were strict rules for arresting a Top Ten. "FBI regs say an SAC must be present to arrest a Top Ten," Max Noel recalls. "If he isn't, we would have to explain it to headquarters. So it was total turmoil deciding what to do." As the agents argued, the man who might be Jeff Jones stepped into a waiting Volvo sedan.*

---

*The lone disparity between versions of this incident involves what car was being driven. Jones remembers he was driving Suzie Q. Three FBI agents present that day recall he was driving a Volvo sedan.

Behind the wheel the agents could see a young woman. Some thought it was Cathy Wilkerson. It wasn't. It was Bernardine Dohrn.

As Jones remembered that day years later, he and Dohrn had just finished a meeting in the Tenderloin district and were on their way to meet Bill Ayers for dinner at a Chinese restaurant. Stepping into the Western Union office, Jones immediately sensed that something was amiss. Three men were lounging inside, wearing what he sized up as hippie attire straight out of a dinner-theater production of *Hair*. As he took his place in line, his mind raced. Were they FBI? If they knew who he was, he would already be under arrest. If they didn't and he ran, they would be suspicious.

He waited as the line inched forward. In a back office an FBI agent began snapping photographs. When his turn came, Jones slipped his driver's license under the glass and received his money. He stepped outside onto the sidewalk, keeping his head. Sliding into the car, he turned to Dohrn. "There were three guys in there, and I didn't like the looks of them," he said. She told him a man had just walked by and glanced at their license plate. As they pulled from the curb, Jones stared in the rearview mirror. He saw a black sedan ease from its parking space, take a slow U-turn, and begin to follow them.

"Then the parade began," Max Noel continues. Neither the pursued nor the pursuers, however, were entirely sure this was real; the agents weren't certain who they were following, and Jones and Dohrn weren't certain they were being followed. Unsure, Dohrn drove north from Market, then turned left onto California Street. One FBI car trailed behind, while two others drove parallel streets. The procession continued for several blocks until Dohrn, taking no chances, suddenly took a sharp left turn onto Mason Street. The FBI car behind her, caught unawares, stopped at the light, then radioed to the other two cars to take up the pursuit. In the resulting confusion, neither was able to spot the speeding Volvo. "They lost 'em," Noel recalls.

It was the first time anyone in the FBI had so much as laid eyes on Weatherman's leadership in more than a year. "It was shattering," Noel continues. "So afterward everyone came back to the office. The supervisors said it couldn't have possibly been Jeff Jones. Then they developed the film, looked at the photos, [and said,] 'It sure looks like Jeff Jones.' We had his prints from Western Union, and finally the fingerprint guy came and ID'd it as Jones. Well, you can imagine the uproar. The concern was how we explain this to headquarters."

As agents debated what to do, Jones and Dohrn met Bill Ayers and other friends at the restaurant. Safely inside, Jones began to doubt himself. It was not at all clear that they had been pursued. The men at Western Union couldn't really have been FBI agents, could they? He told himself he was being paranoid. Still, once dinner concluded, Jones suggested to John Willard Davis that they switch cars. Handing him the keys, Jones and Dohrn took Davis's car home.

"By this time it was evening," Max Noel continues. "So we start this huge canvass around the 1000 block of California at Mason, where the car was lost. Then one of the agents leaving to go home, driving down Market, he sees the Volvo, parked right outside a laundry. They set up a surveillance on the vehicle." The stakeout began at eleven. A few minutes after midnight agents saw a young man walk up and unlock the car. It was Davis. Agents leaped from their cars and rushed him, guns drawn. Davis raised his hands and went peacefully. They took him to the Hall of Justice, where, during hours of questioning, he denied knowing anyone named Jeff Jones. The Volvo, he insisted, belonged to his parents, which the FBI confirmed.

"So they had to release him the following morning," Noel says. "We watched him walk up to a pay phone on Van Ness and start making calls, obviously warning everyone. Everyone in the office was assigned to saturate that neighborhood up on California and Mason. We knocked on every door, but it was fruitless. Nothing ever came of it."

When Jeff Jones heard what happened, he realized the danger they were in. He had registered a car using the same name he used to pay the electric bill for the Pine Street apartment. It was only a matter of time, he suspected, before the FBI made the connection and raided the apartment. He realized that Weather's entire Bay Area infrastructure—the fake IDs, their cars, the apartments—was tainted. He telephoned Pine Street and told everyone to leave immediately. They did so, leaving their belongings behind. Years later, remembering an episode that came to be known in Weather lore as "the Encirclement," some of those involved would recall running out just as FBI agents stormed the flat.

That wasn't the way it happened. In fact, despite knocking on every door in the neighborhood, the FBI didn't find the connection. A week later, however, a Chinese American landlord telephoned the San Francisco office saying a group of young white people had disappeared from an apartment he owned at 1038 Pine Street; when he pushed his way inside, he found what appeared to be bomb-making equipment. Max Noel and three other agents were at the apartment within the hour.

"We found what was essentially their West Coast bomb factory," Noel recalls. "There were stacks of communist, Cuban and antigovernment literature, Maoist tracts. Disguise kits. And lots of bomb-making equipment, pliers and wires and pipes and tools, one big block of C-4 plastic explosive. We called in the bomb squad." Agents later identified fingerprints taken from the apartment as those of every significant Weatherman believed to be on the West Coast.

Not that it mattered. They were all gone.

The day after the FBI almost captured Dohrn and Jones, Friday, March 5, 1971, people began gathering in New York for the one-year anniversary of the Townhouse. Down on Eleventh Street the rubble of the Wilkerson residence had been cleared; all that remained was a vacant lot fronted by a high plywood barrier. Someone had painted the words WEATHERMAN PARK across the top; beneath it hung a few posters and hastily scrawled slogans: POWER TO THE UNDERGROUND, read one.

The next afternoon Abbie Hoffman led a procession up Fifth Avenue from Washington Square. Everyone gathered in front of the townhouse. "Terry, Teddy, and Diana were fighting to make this a free country, which it's not," Hoffman told the crowd. "They saw the nature of the beast imperialism and were ready to give their lives to destroy it. They paid the ultimate sacrifice. They made a mistake. They weren't careful with explosives. From now on we've got to be careful."

It was the last anyone would hear of the Weather Underground for months. What none of the protesters gathered at "Weatherman Park" that day realized, however, was that an entirely new front of the underground struggle was poised to open, one that was far more desperate, and far more deadly. It happened barely sixty days later, on the far side of Manhattan.

Part Two

———————————

THE BLACK LIBERATION ARMY

08

"AN ARMY OF ANGRY NIGGAS"

The Birth of the Black Liberation Army,
Spring 1971

The idea of a Black Liberation Army emerged from conditions in Black communities; conditions of poverty, indecent housing, massive unemployment, poor medical care, and inferior education. The idea came about because Black people are not free or equal in this country. Because ninety percent of the men and women in this country's prisons are Black and Third World. Because ten-year-old children are shot down in our streets. Because dope has saturated our communities, preying on the disillusionment and frustration of our children. The concept of the BLA arose because of the political, social, and economic oppression of Black people in this country. And where there is oppression, there will be resistance. The BLA is part of that resistance movement. The Black Liberation Army stands for freedom and justice for all people.

—*Joanne Chesimard, aka Assata Shakur*

MAY 1971 | NEW YORK CITY

Along the Hudson River, high on Manhattan's left shoulder, Riverside Park was a green finger of calm, an oasis of playgrounds and gardens a world away from the angry traffic on the parkway over by the river. That warm May evening, the 19th, the park was in bloom, a dazzle of pink and crimson on the Japanese dwarf cherry and crab apple trees.

One man who lived on the park, at 404 Riverside Drive, was Frank Hogan, known as Mr. Integrity, who had been the New York district attorney since taking over from Thomas Dewey all the way back in 1941. The week before, Hogan had wrapped up the longest case in state history, the trial of the Panther 21, and while the proceedings were finally over, policemen still sat outside his building around the clock. Weatherman had firebombed the home of the presiding judge, John Murtagh, the year before. It was May 1971. No one was taking any chances.

At 9 p.m. a green-and-white cruiser relieved the officers. Inside sat a pair of thirty-nine-year-old patrolmen, Thomas Curry and Nicholas Binetti. Darkness had fallen barely fifteen minutes later when, to their dismay, a dark Maverick suddenly sped past, going the wrong way down 112th Street, a one-way street. Officer Binetti wheeled the squad car into a sharp U-turn and gave chase as the Maverick swerved left onto Riverside Drive.

Six blocks south, at 106th Street, Binetti managed to pull alongside the speeding Maverick. At that moment the driver, one of two or three black men inside, crouched in his seat. From the passenger side the ugly nose of a .45-caliber submachine gun appeared. In a split second a geyser of bullets blasted the patrol car. The windshield exploded. Officer Binetti was struck eight times, in the neck, stomach, and arms. Officer Curry was hit in the face, neck, and chest; one bullet severed his optic nerve. The patrol car veered to its left and smashed into a stone staircase beneath a statue of the Civil War general Franz Sigel. The Maverick roared away, vanishing into the gloom.

A few moments later, after briefly losing consciousness, Officer Binetti came to. Glancing to his right, he saw his partner lying outside the car, his uniform stained with blood. Before passing out once more, Binetti managed to palm the car radio. "Twenty-six Boy Charlie, 26 Boy Charlie," he murmured. "We've been shot. We've been shot."[1]

Three miles north of the shooting, the eight grimy towers of the Colonial Park Houses stood on the west side of the Harlem River, beside the site of the old Polo Grounds, the hallowed baseball stadium where Bobby Thomson hit the "shot heard 'round the world" for the New York Giants that defeated the Brooklyn Dodgers in a 1951 pennant playoff game. The Colonial Park buildings, fourteen stories tall, were home to hundreds of poor black families, who on sultry summer nights could gaze out their kitchen windows south across the tenements of Harlem toward the glittering office towers of Midtown. Colonial Park was a rough place, the kind of project cops from the nearby 32nd Precinct—the "Three Two"—entered with care.

Two nights after the shootings on Riverside Drive, two officers from the Three Two, Waverly Jones, thirty-three, and Joseph Piagentini, twenty-eight, stepped from their squad car and walked into Colonial Park to answer a call about a woman hurt in a knife fight. When the woman refused their help, the two ambled back to their car. As they did they passed two young black men lounging against the fender of a parked car. The men fell in behind them. A moment later the men drew pistols and opened fire.

Officer Jones, who was black, was struck three times, first in the back of the head, then twice in the spine. He died instantly. The second gunman fired repeatedly into Officer Piagentini, who fell to the sidewalk but, as the gunman cursed him, refused to die. The first gunman then reached down and removed Officer Jones's .38, hefting it in his hand, feeling its weight, as if he were taking a souvenir. The second gunman wrenched Piagentini's weapon from its holster even as the dying officer flailed at him. Once he had it, he fired every bullet in its chamber into the fallen cop.

Still Piagentini wouldn't die. The first gunman stepped to his prone body, pointed his own .45 downward, and fired a single shot. Then both shooters turned and walked away. Behind them, Officer Piagentini, in his last moments of life, began crawling toward the safety of a green hedge, a trail of blood in his wake. The next morning the coroner would count twenty-two bullet holes in his body.

A few hundred feet away, a passerby named Richard Hill heard the shots. Running to the scene, he glimpsed what he thought to be a clump of bloody clothes on the sidewalk. Then the clump moved. Hill sprinted toward the two fallen men, snatched up a walkie-talkie from the pavement, and yelled, "Mayday! Mayday! Two cops shot!"

That same evening, two packages were delivered, one to the *New York Times*, a second to WLIB, a Harlem radio station. Each carried a license plate, the same plates seen on the Maverick whose occupants shot Officers Curry and Binetti. The *Times* package also contained a .45-caliber cartridge and a typewritten message. It read:

May 19th 1971

All power to the people.

Here are the license plates sort [*sic*] after by the fascist state pig police. We send them in order to exhibit the potential power of oppressed peoples to acquire revolutionary justice.

The armed goons of this racist government will again meet the guns of oppressed Third World People as long as they occupy our community and murder our brothers and sisters in the name of American law and order; just as the fascist Marines and Army occupy Vietnam in the name of democracy and murder Vietnamese people in the name of American imperialism are confronted with the guns of the Vietnamese Liberation Army, the domestic armed forces of raciscm [*sic*] and oppression will be confronted with the guns of the Black Liberation Army, who will mete out in the tradition of Malcolm and all true revolutionaries real justice. We are revolutionary justice. All power to the people.

Three nights later, a second pair of packages arrived at WLIB. This time the typewritten letter read:

Revolutionary justice has been meted out again by righteous brothers of the Black Liberation Army with the death of two Gestapo pigs gunned down as so many of our brothers have been gunned down in the past. But this time no racist class jury will acquite [*sic*] them. Revolutionary justice is ours!

Every policeman, lackey or running dog of the ruling class must make his or her choice now. Either side with the people: poor and oppressed, or die for the oppressor. Trying to stop what is going down is like trying to stop history, for as long as there are those who will dare live for freedom there are men and women who dare to unhorse the emperor.

All power to the people.

Up at the Three Two, where detectives confirmed that both letters came from the same typewriter, and at the FBI offices on Sixty-ninth Street, white men read the two notes, turned to one another, and asked:

What the hell was the Black Liberation Army?

More than forty years later, a handful of historians are still asking the same question—"handful" being a generous characterization of the few obscure academic papers and police procedurals that constitute all known publications on the Black Liberation Army, known as the BLA. The paucity of literature is a reflection of the deep confusion and ambivalence the BLA engendered in its heyday. Many policemen, along with BLA members themselves, considered the group a murderous black counterpart to the Weathermen. Mainstream politicians, afraid of alienating black voters, played down this talk entirely. Following suit, most of the white-dominated press dismissed the BLA as a ragtag collection of street thugs. To the press, at least, poorly educated, self-proclaimed black guerrillas who murdered policemen were not credible revolutionaries. But self-proclaimed white guerrillas from good schools who bombed vacant buildings were.

At the height of its infamy, many questioned whether the BLA even existed, the theory being that every time a black militant shot a policeman, he announced himself as a member of the BLA. The group itself was maddeningly difficult to pin down. It had no leadership or structure the press could point to, no Bernardine Dohrn, no Bill Ayers, not even a Mark Rudd to rely on for public statements. Other than the odd bare-bones communiqué, BLA members were utterly mute, a policy its adherents have clung to for decades;

before now, onetime BLA fighters had yet to issue a meaningful word about the group's internal dynamics, much less its crimes. Now as then, the BLA is viewed as semimythic, but to rank-and-file policemen who hunted its members across the country, there was nothing imaginary about the BLA. The machine guns its "soldiers" fired, the grenades they threw, the policemen they killed, the banks they robbed—it was all very real. Between tokes and giggles the Weathermen may have mused about "offing the pigs," but after the Townhouse they just talked the talk. To men in uniform, it was only the BLA who walked the walk.

In fact, the Black Liberation Army was a credible group of violent urban guerrillas, the first and only black underground of its kind in U.S. history. In one sense the BLA was a cluster of deadly acorns that rolled free when the mighty oak of the Black Panther Party fell and shattered; it was a splinter group of the Panthers, much as Weatherman split off from SDS. In another sense, it was the logical culmination of the Black Power movement: After years of black "revolutionaries" calling for armed attacks against the police and federal government, one group, the BLA, finally followed through.

How it happened is a complex story. As FBI records make clear, the Black Liberation Army was an idea long before it was a reality. Any number of '60s-era militant groups had taken some form of the name. A group of three who plotted to blow up the Statue of Liberty in 1965 called itself the Black Liberation Front. A group of eight who engaged in sniper attacks on Detroit police in 1970 called itself the Black Liberation Army Strike Force. The actual BLA was a concept of the Black Panthers; the idea of a Panther underground had existed as long as the party itself. Talk of a black underground was a staple of Huey Newton's early speeches, and by 1968 the party's rules anticipated its establishment, stating that "no party member can join any other army force other than the Black Liberation Army." Many Panther chapters offered weapons training, and several claimed to be training paramilitary units. But even at the height of the party's influence, the BLA existed only in the minds of the most militant Panthers, as an urban guerrilla force that might form in some dimly imagined future.

The actual BLA emerged during the Black Panther Party's implosion in the spring of 1971, a traumatic process that prompted several chapters, most notably New York, to secede from the party. In fact, the story of the BLA is in large part the story of the New York Panthers. Hundreds of black men and women, from Harlem to Bedford-Stuyvesant, joined the New York chapter, but for the sake of this narrative, two boyhood friends mattered most. Their names at birth were Nathaniel Burns and Anthony Coston. Born in 1944, Burns was a lean, charismatic thug nicknamed Beany in the neighborhood gangs where he fought as a teen; years later, after changing his name to Sekou Odinga, he would emerge as the most admired revolutionary of his age, a savvy urban guerrilla who traveled the globe, robbed banks, and engineered prison breakouts during an underground career spanning twelve years. Coston, a squat, muscled gangbanger known in his youth as Shotgun, would become Lumumba Shakur. His career would prove far shorter.

Like a surprising number of people who ascended to leadership positions in the BLA, the two were the children of Southern migrants who grew up in the South Jamaica section of Queens, a historically white neighborhood that during the 1950s became a favored destination for hundreds of middle-income black families streaming into New York from the Deep South. Odinga and Shakur, as they will be called, met at Edgar D. Shimer Junior High, where Odinga recalls meeting Shakur in the assistant principal's office. Both boys were troublemakers. Odinga's father, Albert Burns, a laborer with a fourth-grade education, had come north from Mississippi in the 1930s and saved enough money to buy a two-story home, where Sekou was the fourth of seven children. Like his friends, the teenaged Odinga joined a gang, the Sinners, whose members busied themselves with muggings and fistfights with rival gangs like the Bishops and the Chaplains. In 1961, when he was sixteen, he was arrested for a mugging and sent to the state prison in Comstock, New York.

At Comstock Odinga renewed his friendship with Shakur, who had spent his childhood ricocheting among the homes of relatives in Virginia, Philadelphia, Atlantic City, and eventually Queens. Both were in the process of discovering the teachings of Malcolm X. Both, however, were startled to find Shakur's father way ahead of them. As Shakur wrote:

In the summer of 1962, my father came to see me. He was telling me about the family, but he seemed reluctant about something. Then my father dropped it on me and it blew my mind, because I was thinking about how I was going to say the same thing to him. He asked me my opinion of Brother Malcolm X. I told my father that, "Malcolm X is a very beautiful brother and all the brothers in prison love Brother Malcolm X." I also told my father that I was a black nationalist and a Muslim but I could not relate to praying. I never before saw anything that affected my father like what I just said. His facial expression became one of complete satisfaction. . . . We must have talked for about four hours.[2]

From that day on, the elder Coston, now known as Aba Shakur, acted as a spiritual guide for his son and his friends, a role he continued for many in the Black Panthers and the BLA. Shortly after, his son adopted the name Lumumba Shakur. His older brother James, an elfin intellectual who would also take leadership positions in the Panthers and BLA, took the name Zayd Shakur. The Shakurs, in turn, introduced Odinga to Malcolm X's teachings. "Aba was very, very influential; you could almost say he was the father of our little movement," Odinga recalls. "People like me, Lumumba, Zayd, lots of others later on, everybody was exposed to Aba. He sent Malcolm's writings to us at Comstock. When Lumumba finished reading, he gave it to me. Those were the first books I had ever read. It was Aba and those years in Comstock that made me the man I became later."

Odinga was the first to be released, in December 1963. "I went in angry and foolish, and I came out the same way, but looking for direction," he remembers. "I went in search of Malcolm and saw him preaching on a street corner. He was mesmerizing." Odinga was drifting from job to job, smoking weed and gambling, when he finally glimpsed a way to follow the vague new path he sensed lay before him. While he was visiting the 1964 World's Fair in Queens, New York, a group of "beautiful black sisters" at the African Pavilion asked him to model a series of dashikis and other colorful African garb. Odinga was entranced. He befriended the girls, began wearing dashikis, and soon learned to make his own, which he sold to friends. A year later he shed his identity as Nathaniel Burns and, inspired by the Guinean nationalist

Sékou Touré, legally changed his name to Sekou Odinga. When Shakur emerged from prison, he joined Odinga's circle. The two took an apartment in Harlem, where they turned heads as some of the first to wear dashikis in the street.

Their hopes of joining Malcolm X's entourage evaporated with Malcolm's assassination in February 1965. In the wake of his death, scores of black nationalist groups sprang up. Odinga and Shakur joined the Panthers, proudly donning the black berets and standing guard outside the group's New York headquarters on Seventh Avenue in Harlem. From the beginning, the Panther leadership in California was ill at ease with its New York recruits. Many of the New Yorkers, steeped in Malcolm's teachings, had risen from gangs and served in prison; they were far more streetwise, confrontational, and Afrocentric than the Californians. "We had studied black history and African history," Odinga recalls. "They were more into the politics of communities in California. We were more African. They were more American." One of the first open disagreements between the two groups, in fact, came when headquarters attempted to ban the wearing of dashikis and the taking of African names. When the New Yorkers objected, a Panther delegation headed by Eldridge Cleaver was sent east to enforce the order.

"Lumumba and I met with them," Odinga recalls. "It got ugly for a minute or two. They said, 'We are the party. If you are part of the party, you will follow orders.' We said, 'We will follow your leadership, but not blindly.' Arguments stretched on for weeks. Most of the rank and file was on our side. Finally we compromised. We agreed to wear black leather to BPP functions. The rest of the time, dashikis."

Oakland's wariness was reflected in the leadership it chose in New York, a group of SNCC veterans based in Brooklyn. Shakur was made section leader in Harlem, Odinga in the Bronx. Odinga was also named minister of education and took responsibility for the political-education classes all new Panthers were obliged to attend. Both took part in the full array of Panther activities, the free breakfasts, the lectures, appearances at myriad demonstrations. But from the beginning, Odinga and Shakur had a second, secret agenda, the same one later pursued by the Black Liberation Army: They wanted to kill cops.

And they tried. Along with twenty other Panthers, they concocted an ambitious plan to attack a series of policemen and precincts. Bombs were built, sniper positions set. But two of the Panthers turned out to be police detectives, and before the plan could be set into motion, the NYPD swooped in and arrested almost everyone, including Shakur. Of those involved in the Panther plot, only one avoided arrest: Sekou Odinga. He was hiding in an upper-floor apartment near Brooklyn's Prospect Park when a squad of officers crept up the stairs to arrest him. Asleep at the time, Odinga woke when he heard a noise. Pressing his ear to the door, he sensed what was happening. He heard footsteps on the roof. He was surrounded. He stepped into the bathroom, glanced around, and saw what he would have to do. Struggling into his clothes, he grabbed a carbine by his bedside and yelled, "Who's there?"

"The police! Open the door!"

"Gimme a minute. I'm putting my clothes on."

Once he had the speaker's attention, Odinga stepped to the front door and loudly clicked a round into the gun's chamber.

"He's got a gun!" came the shout. "He's got a gun!"

As the police scattered for cover, Odinga raced into the bathroom, where a tiny window, no more than twelve inches wide, opened. Outside was a four-story drop to an alley below. Leaving his rifle behind, he squeezed through the window and slid one hand onto a concrete drainpipe that ran down the building. Leaving the safety of the window, he clasped the drainpipe with both hands and both feet and began shimmying down. He managed to descend about ten feet when a voice cried out from below: "There he is! There he is!"

Odinga sprang from the wall and jumped, landing nearly thirty feet below on the roof of a one-story garage. As he landed, his knee struck his chin and nearly knocked him unconscious. He stood, woozy, and heard the cries of policemen all around. Stepping to the edge of the roof, he leaped into a tree, only to have the branches break, dropping him to the pavement below. He limped to a nearby brownstone, tried its door, found it locked, then tried another, and another and another, until he found an unlocked basement door. Inside, he curled himself into a ball and hid behind an oil tank.

Police cordoned off the block and began a house-to-house search. For hours Odinga listened as they tromped about. His luck held. No one came into the basement. When darkness fell, he uncoiled his aching body, stepped from the basement, hailed a gypsy cab, and vanished.

The legal odyssey of Lumumba Shakur and the rest of Panther 21 falls outside the narrative of this book. All told, their mass trial lasted more than eight months, from September 1970 to May 1971; at the time, it was the longest and most expensive trial in New York history. "The 21" became a cause célèbre for the city's white radicals, as well as many wealthy liberals. The legendary Park Avenue party thrown by the composer Leonard Bernstein—which inspired writer Tom Wolfe to coin the term "radical chic"—was a fund-raiser for the 21; the most prominent Panther in attendance (and the centerpiece of Wolfe's article) was Field Marshal Don Cox, who, while little remembered today, would go on to become a guiding force behind the BLA. Celebrities adored the New York Panthers; when Shakur's slender, intellectual brother, Zayd, was arrested, his bail was posted by none other than Jane Fonda. Zayd Shakur, so slight his peers jokingly called him the "field mouse" rather than field marshal, would go on to become an influential member of the BLA.

The BLA was ultimately a by-product of tensions between the smooth, cliquish Panthers of the West Coast and the angry, Afrocentric, dashiki-wearing Panthers of New York—tensions that rose during the Panther 21 trial. Throughout the proceedings, the New York Panthers clamored for money—for lawyers, bail, and expenses—that Oakland was unable to supply. Relations worsened when headquarters insisted on dispatching a stream of California Panthers to New York to fill the leadership vacuum left by the 21's incarceration. The California Panthers, especially a field marshal named Thomas Jolly, smirked at the dashikis, openly courted female Panthers, and seemed to freely spend what remained of the chapter's cash. "Panthers on the street, we felt put upon, abused, distrusted," recalls Thomas "Blood" McCreary, then a Brooklyn Panther. "You don't trust our new leaders? They treated us like a bunch of idiots, fucking our women and stealing our money. These motherfuckers, they were running amok."

Tensions rose further still when Huey Newton, his murder conviction reversed on appeal, emerged from prison and reassumed leadership of the Panthers in August 1970. The party Newton now oversaw, however, was nothing like the one he had known. It had grown from a handful of chapters to more than fifty, with thousands of new members Newton had never met. He had few skills to lead such an organization, much less one hounded on every front by the FBI and riven with dissent. Even as Newton began making his first tentative speeches as a free man, rumors flew that he was in fact a shell of his former self, holed up in an Oakland penthouse snorting mounds of cocaine.

Maybe the most contentious issue Newton faced was the question of armed struggle, the question of whether the Panthers really should, as their rhetoric promised, go to war against American police. A few Panthers, notably Eldridge Cleaver, had always called for armed revolution, and right away. Some rank-and-file Panthers, especially in New York, agreed. Once Cleaver disappeared, however, few in the national leadership were prepared actually to build and arm the guerrilla force he envisioned, even on a standby basis. The one leader who argued for doing so was a twenty-three-year-old Panther named Elmer "Geronimo" Pratt. A Green Beret in Vietnam, Pratt had been the Southern California chapter's "minister of defense." When Newton went to prison, Pratt took it upon himself to organize underground cadres within several Panther chapters. The leadership grudgingly consented.

Once a chastened Newton emerged from prison, however, he wanted little to do with talk of revolution, which he dismissed as fantasy. This kind of talk prompted grumbling from, of all places, the North African country of Algeria, where Cleaver, after months trying to find a safe haven, had remade himself as head of the Panthers' new "international section." The story of Cleaver's time in Algiers is a key untold chapter of the Black Liberation Army story. After fleeing a court date in November 1968, Cleaver had gone to Cuba, where he'd hoped to set up camps to train revolutionaries he believed would start a guerrilla war in the United States. In fact, Fidel Castro refused to allow him to even give interviews, much less set up camps. Incensed, Cleaver demanded to leave. Castro resisted—that is, until a reporter spotted Cleaver and broke the news that he was in Cuba. In June 1969, after Cleaver had cooled his heels in Havana for six months, a Cuban diplomat walked him onto an Aeroflot flight and escorted him to Algiers, where he was reunited with his wife, Kathleen.

Algiers in the summer of 1969 was perhaps the perfect place, and the perfect moment, for Eldridge Cleaver. Since winning its bloody war for independence from France in 1962, the government had forged close relations with the Soviet Union and allowed scores of revolutionary groups, from Angola to Palestine, to maintain offices in its diplomatic community. A London paper termed Algiers in 1969 the "headquarters of world revolution." Cleaver, figuring he could demand an embassy too, invited any number of other Panther fugitives to join him. A half dozen followed suit, including a trio of California skyjackers; Donald Cox of "radical chic" fame, a Panther field marshal fleeing a murder indictment in Baltimore, who arrived in May 1970; and Sekou Odinga, who with two other Panthers reached Algiers via Havana three months later. Cox became Cleaver's aide-de-camp, Odinga his unofficial No. 3 man.

It took a full year of on-and-off negotiations, however, for the Algerian government to approve official recognition of the "international section" of the Black Panther Party. While waiting, Cleaver embarked on a series of trips, leading Panther delegations to the Soviet Union, China, North Vietnam, and his personal favorite, North Korea, where he spent two months. In Algiers, Cleaver rented a spacious apartment in the Pointe Pescade section, where he gave frequent interviews. Finally, in June 1970, Cleaver received the Algerian government's formal recognition, which came with a monthly stipend, identification cards, the right to obtain visas, and, best of all, the Panthers' own embassy, a white two-story villa in the suburb of El Biar previously used by the North Vietnamese. Cleaver held a press conference to announce it all, telling reporters the "Nixon clique had begun to group the black people in concentration camps, escalating repression to the level of overt fascist terror against those who dare resist the oppression of the diabolical system under which the blacks of the United States are suffering. We reject the temple of slavery, which is the United States of America, and we intend to transform it into a social system of liberty and peace."[3]

Huey Newton emerged from prison just as Cleaver established himself in his new Panther embassy. Their rivalry was intense and very personal. It was stoked by the FBI's notorious COINTELPRO program: Agents forged dozens of letters between various Panthers passing on spurious allegations that Newton was plotting to kill Cleaver and vice versa. The two clashed almost immediately over Cleaver's call to raise a guerrilla army to fight the U.S. government. All this, as it happened, coincided with a trip Geronimo Pratt was making through Southern chapters in his ongoing attempts to organize just such a clandestine force. After Pratt was arrested in Dallas that December, Newton expelled him from the party. When several militant New York Panthers protested, Newton announced he was expelling them, too.

From Algiers, Cleaver called loudly for Geronimo Pratt and the New York Panthers to be reinstated. Newton refused. By late January 1971 rumors of an impending split in the party were approaching a fever pitch, especially in New York, where stories sprouted daily that Newtonite assassins were arriving at any moment to wipe out the East Coast leadership. Newton realized it was time for a public display of unity. But with Cleaver marooned in Algeria, the best he could do was a transatlantic phone call between the two, which was to air, live, on Jim Dunbar's *A.M. San Francisco* television talk show on February 26. Cleaver reluctantly agreed, but he suspected he was walking into a trap. All manner of wild rumors were flying from Algiers to Oakland: that Cleaver had ordered several Panthers murdered; that he was preparing a violent overthrow of the party; that he was secretly dealing drugs and guns; that he was insane. Even their doctrinal differences could be embarrassing if aired on live television.

Both men went ahead. It was a disaster. As Newton sat in a Bay Area television studio, Cleaver opened the conversation by insisting that the New York Panthers be reinstated. Newton again refused, saying those purged had plunged "into counterproductive avenues of violence and adventurism." Cleaver was just getting started. Terming the Central Committee "inept," he demanded their resignation. When Newton again refused, the two men simply talked past each other. The high point came when Cleaver denounced Newton personally, called for immediate guerrilla warfare against the U.S. government, and said that he would now direct the "real" Black Panther party from Algiers. Afterward Newton expelled Cleaver. Cleaver then expelled Newton.

For days, confusion reigned. Chapter leaders across the country telephoned Oakland for guidance and held meetings among themselves. Nothing as formal as a nationwide vote ensued, but had there been, the results would have been clear within a week: The vast majority of Panther chapters remained loyal to Oakland, to Newton. Party histories inevitably call this period the Split; in fact, it was less a split than a single-city secession. Only New York—many of its members, anyway—wanted to side with Cleaver. One account tells of a tense meeting in Harlem between several East Coast leaders, including some from as far afield as Rhode Island and Baltimore. Only the Harlem, Brooklyn, Queens, and Bronx branches pledged allegiance to Cleaver. Afterward, New York's intellectual leader, Zayd Shakur, who remained in regular contact with Cleaver in Algeria, told other members they would establish the new East Coast Black Panther Party by taking over the old Panther headquarters, the Harlem storefront on Seventh Avenue. A new newspaper, *Right On!*, would be published to spread the word.

Amid the chaos of those early March days, the only constant was the rumor of imminent warfare between the East and West Coast Panthers. Zayd Shakur repeatedly told reporters that Newton had dispatched as many as seventy-five "robots" to wipe out the New York leadership. Overnight, the Panther offices in Harlem and the Bronx were transformed into fortresses. Guns were stockpiled. Windows were boarded. At any minute, Shakur warned, Newton's assassins would strike.

Then, on the afternoon of Monday, March 8, came the spark. Robert Webb was a charismatic twenty-two-year-old Panther field marshal from the Bay Area who had come to Harlem the previous spring with two other Panthers in an effort to reassert Oakland's control. Webb, however, warmed to the New Yorkers; when his companions were unceremoniously sent back to California, he stayed behind, emerging as a popular leader known as Coffee Man. "Coffee Man saw how we worked, and he hooked up with us," a one-time Panther named Cyril Innis recalls. "He became one of us, and that made the powers that be very, very nervous."

That Monday afternoon, in front of a Chock Full o' Nuts restaurant at the corner of 125th Street and Seventh Avenue, Webb confronted a rival Panther selling newspapers. Exactly what happened has never been explained, but Webb, who was carrying his customary .357 Magnum, ended up dead on the sidewalk, a single bullet hole in the back of his head. The Harlem Panthers would later claim he had been killed by a Newtonite assassin, but no arrest was ever made. In an FBI memo written to J. Edgar Hoover a month later, an agent in New York credited COINTELPRO "activities" with causing Webb's murder. Webb's death electrified the New York Panthers, who were convinced that the long-awaited war had begun.

"Right then, that's when the BLA started," Cyril Innis recalls. "Certain people were told to go underground. Who made the decisions? I wish I knew. To this day, I don't really know."

The full story of the Black Liberation Army's origins will probably never be told. Too many people have died, then and since; too many who lived still worry about being prosecuted for the killings that began that chaotic spring. One man who will talk, however, was perhaps the BLA's most important organizer. His name in 1971 was Richard "Dhoruba" Moore. Forty years later, after a legal odyssey as strange as any in U.S. history, he is known as Dhoruba bin-Wahad.

Dhoruba Moore, as he will be called, was twenty-six that spring. He was an unlikely underground commander, a rangy, motormouthed peacock and curbside intellectual whose rambling soliloquies on every conceivable topic tended to draw snickers from Panthers and reporters alike. Like Sekou Odinga and other Panthers, he was a onetime gang member who had been radicalized in prison. A talented recruiter, Dhoruba had been arrested and become one of the more notorious of the Panther 21, thanks to his penchant for outrageous courtroom outbursts.

That March, as tensions escalated between West and East Coast Panthers, Dhoruba and another 21 defendant, Michael "Cetawayo" Tabor, made bail and were released from custody. When the party split and open warfare appeared imminent, both men decided to join Cleaver in Algiers. With two others, they jumped bail and made their way to Montreal, where flights had been arranged. At the last moment, however, Dhoruba was informed that his papers weren't ready; he couldn't go. When Tabor boarded a plane to Algiers, Dhoruba was left behind. At that point, he had to make a choice. If he returned to New York, where he imagined Newton's assassins were combing the streets in search of him, he was going back to fight—fight the West Coast Panthers and the New York police and anyone else who threatened them. "What else would we do? Join the Salvation Army?" Dhoruba recalls. "This was war."

War meant one thing: mobilizing the underground, the nascent Black Liberation Army. "It was our plan when we came back to build an underground, to use the infrastructure we had in place, that would attack the police who had killed our people," Dhoruba recalls. "We would strike back, and that's what we did, or what we tried to do."

Returning to New York, Dhoruba began gathering his people, many of whom had been put on alert that winter. By and large, those first BLA recruits were men, and a few women, with arms or medical training, whom Dhoruba felt he could trust. They came mostly from three neighborhoods, including the Brownsville section of Brooklyn, where Dhoruba had worked as a Panther recruiter, and South Jamaica, the home of many of the "heaviest" Panthers, including the Shakur brothers and Sekou Odinga. A third source of recruits was the Washington Heights chapter of the National Committee to Combat Fascism, a Panther-affiliated group many would-be Panthers had joined when the party's ranks were closed to new members in 1969. "Jamaica, Brownsville, and Washington Heights—that's where almost all the initial BLA cadres came from," Dhoruba recalls. "Andrew Jackson, Frank Fields, Assata Shakur—they all came from the Washington Heights chapter. I'd had Washington Heights on the down low for months. They were half expecting this."

The cell that coalesced around Dhoruba Moore was only one of several that formed that spring in the chaos after Robert Webb's death—an estimated fifty to eighty Panthers were in some stage of going underground—but it was the first to act. Several safe-house apartments were already in place, an archipelago of dingy flats scattered through Harlem and the Bronx. What amounted to the group's headquarters was a shambling three-story townhouse at 757 Beck Street in the Bronx, where Dhoruba stored the group's weapons, including several hand grenades and a machine gun. Bunking off and on there were a dozen or so Panthers, all in their twenties, several of whom were destined for prominence within the BLA; these included Frank "Heavy" Fields, a chunky New York University dropout; Andrew Jackson, a suave, smooth-skinned Queens Panther; and sixteen-year-old Mark Holder, who had been at Robert Webb's side when he was murdered. The townhouse doubled as their hospital. Friends at a radical-run clinic in the Bronx had stolen a closetful of medical supplies for them. The group's medical expert— she knew first aid, at least—was Joanne Chesimard, later known as Assata Shakur, a smart, attractive City College student who would eventually become the BLA's most infamous member.

The Beck Street cell's first priority was money for food and rent. To get it, Dhoruba says, they began robbing heroin dealers, which brought the additional benefit of fighting the drug trade, a longtime Panther priority. "I knew all these major drug dudes, Nicky Barnes, Tito Johnson, Albie Simmons, from the Bronx and from prison," Dhoruba recalls. "It was the natural place to get money. So when we first went underground, we started taking down heroin dealers. We were really rolling these motherfuckers. And they gave us information. When we rolled Tito, he says, 'There's a lot of pressure, we can't work, the cops are all over us wanting information on you.' That's how we found the police were trying to use the dealers against us. We bashed down a lot of doors, man. We were like black cops."

After several weeks, when neither the police nor a Panther assassination squad had found them, the talk at 757 Beck turned to revenge for Robert Webb's murder. Their target was obvious: the East Coast office of the Newton-controlled Black Panther newspaper, on Northern Boulevard in Queens. The office was run by a popular thirty-two-year-old Panther named Sam Napier. They watched it for days. As police later pieced together events, seven members of the Beck Street underground, led more or less by Dhoruba, piled into a U-Haul truck and drove to Queens on the afternoon of April 17. Shooing away a number of women and children in the office, the group bound Napier with a venetian blind cord, tortured him, shot him four times, then set his body on fire.

To those white radicals who had rallied to the Panther 21's defense, the sudden outbreak of violence was deeply unsettling. One of those caught in the political cross-currents was a twenty-three-year-old volunteer on the 21's defense committee named Silvia Baraldini. She was an expatriate Italian businessman's daughter who had grown up in Washington, D.C., and radicalized at the University of Wisconsin; in the next dozen years Baraldini would go on to one of the more colorful careers of any underground figure. "Suddenly, you know, all these Panthers we knew were killing each other," she remembers. "None of us, the whites I mean, had any clue what was really going on."

One might expect Napier's gruesome murder to have intensified West Coast–East Coast violence. Instead, it ended it. The BLA never again targeted a Panther for death. Instead, barely a month later, its members would ambush four police officers, killing two. Contemporary accounts portrayed the May shootings of Officers Curry and Binetti and the murders of Officers Jones and Piagentini as attacks that erupted out of nowhere, with no warning. In fact, the BLA's abrupt change in focus arose from a little-noticed incident in Harlem a full month earlier, on April 19, just two days after Sam Napier's death.

That afternoon two patrolmen, Arthur Plate and Howard Steward, were cruising on West 121st Street when a pedestrian flagged them down and, motioning toward a trio of black men, said he had overheard them discussing plans for a robbery. The officers emerged from the car, approached the three men and ordered them into the foyer at 215 West 121st to be searched. Two complied. The third drew a pistol and opened fire. A wild gunfight ensued inside the vestibule. Officer Plate was struck in the face and fell to the floor, critically wounded. Officer Steward, struck in the thigh, ducked, drew his gun, and fired all six shots in his service revolver. His bullets killed one of the men, twenty-year-old Harold Russell, and injured a twenty-three-year-old named Anthony "Kimu" White. A third man, wounded in the shoulder, charged out the door and made his escape. Police identified him as Robert Vickers.[4]

All three men, it turned out, were Cleaverite Panthers; the two survivors, in fact, would become active members of the BLA. For the police, it was just another nasty shooting; the NYPD had no idea the men were Panthers and no clue that anything called the Black Liberation Army yet existed. For Dhoruba Moore's new BLA, however, the gunfight was a call to arms. The wounded Robert Vickers made his way to 757 Beck Street, where Joanne Chesimard nursed him back to health.

"He comes back to Beck Street," Dhoruba recalls, "and we decide that of course retaliation is appropriate. And it could be on Malcolm X's birthday. So we decided to announce the debut of the BLA, the first black underground, on Malcolm's birthday. May 19."

The full story of those first two BLA attacks, on May 19 and 21, 1971, probably will never be told. After three trials and years of litigation, Dhoruba, whose fingerprints were found on one of the communiqués, would be convicted of his involvement. Forty years later, he will not discuss what happened. But all available evidence indicates that the two shootings were actually carried out by two unrelated groups of Panthers who knew nothing of each other's plans. The May 19 shootings of Officers Binetti and Curry were the work of Panthers from 757 Beck Street, including Frank Fields, who was killed later that year. The May 21 murders of Officers Jones and Piagentini, as will be seen, were carried out by a group of out-of-state Panthers who happened to be visiting New York and, it appears, were inspired by the May 19 attacks. Dhoruba Moore, one surmises, wrote the communiqués for both incidents, even though he had no idea who was behind the second incident; presumably this was done to make the attacks appear related and the BLA more dangerous.

All Dhoruba will say today is that he regrets targeting patrolmen.

"The tactical mistake we made was killing the cops in uniform," he says, "when we should've killed the higher-ups. That would've been more effective."

In spearheading the BLA's formation, Dhoruba expected it would take guidance, if not direct orders, from Eldridge Cleaver and his military adviser, Donald Cox, in far-off Algiers. In the wake of the split, Cleaver certainly appeared ready to launch his long-predicted guerrilla war in the United

States. He seemingly had command of every gun and gadget a modern guerrilla leader might need, all of it tucked away in his beloved Panther embassy. He seldom left the grounds, spending much of his time smoking hashish and talking on the telephone. But even as his personal world shrank, Cleaver's introduction to the other Third World revolutionaries broadened his worldview: In his mind, he was now not only the leader of black revolutionary America but a leader of the global revolutionary movement. What money he raised, much of it from a Panther support group in Paris, went into a Marxist library—he kept an account at a London bookseller—and newfangled electronic equipment, including cameras and machines to make how-to and revolutionary videotapes he intended to distribute around the world. His pride and joy was a giant map of the world that filled one entire wall of his communications room. When a British reporter visited, Cleaver demonstrated how the map worked:

> Cleaver begins flicking switches on a consul, and slowly, all over the world, lights come up. There is one color for the Panther headquarters in America, another color for liberation groups engaged in armed struggle in Africa, Brazil, Vietnam. There is another color for "solidarity" groups. "We have a solidarity group in China," Cleaver says with a laugh. "Its chairman is Chairman Mao." Finally one last light goes on, much bigger than all the rest, and bright red. It is in Algiers. "That is the Witchdoctor," Cleaver says with a grin. He gesticulates in the direction of the map. "We will make videotapes of the struggles going on all over the world. . . . [But] we don't call it videotape. We call it voodoo. Because it has, like, magical properties. You know how electricity moves? It's kind of mysterious. . . . It's invisible."

With the Panther split in February 1971, Cleaver's dreams seemed to be coming true. After years of calling for guerrilla warfare in the United States, militant Panthers began flocking to New York to take arms. Policemen were murdered. Communiqués were issued. Given his role as a beacon of revolutionary violence, one might have expected Cleaver to anoint himself chairman of the BLA. He didn't. In fact, Cleaver ordained that the BLA would have no leader. Not him. Not anyone. Under guidelines set by Cleaver and

Don Cox, the BLA's structure would be the exact opposite of the Weather Underground's. Where Weather cadres did nothing without direction from leadership, Cleaver and Cox wanted BLA units to operate independently, with no central coordination whatsoever. A system of autonomous cells, Cox reasoned, would be much harder for the government to subdue; a single leader could be defeated with a single arrest. This sounded fine in theory; in practice it led to anarchy. "I never understood the concept of an organization without leadership," recalls Brooklyn BLA member Blood McCreary. "I always thought that was going to be difficult, and it was. When we got into the field, we were supposed to be autonomous, and you'd be two or three cells trying to do their own thing. I remember once two cells showed up to rob the same bank. It happened outside the Bronx Zoo, at a Manufacturers Hanover. So not having leadership, that was a problem."

A decentralized structure, however, had the added virtue of distancing Cleaver from BLA violence. The Algerian government, while happy to host revolutionary groups, made clear to all of them it would not condone acts of violence initiated on its own soil; worse, from Cleaver's point of view, were hints that the government might be warming to a U.S. government more than a little interested in Algerian energy reserves. In practice this meant that while Cleaver spent day and night proselytizing bloody revolution, he seldom if ever mentioned the Black Liberation Army by name, much less publicly condoned its acts. His position in Algiers was too insecure. Rather than speak over an international phone line he suspected—correctly—that the FBI had tapped, Cleaver laid out his initial plans for the BLA in a set of "voodoo" tapes, which his favorite courier—a striking young Puerto Rican radical named Denise Oliver—brought to New York.

Cleaver's subsequent relationship with the BLA was as complex as the man himself. He was a writer at heart and sensed he was best suited to be an inspirational rather than operational leader. "He was not a military man; he only thought he was," Sekou Odinga recalls. "It was D.C. [Donald Cox] who had the military mind; he was a brilliant strategist. It may have looked like Cleaver was leading the BLA, but he wasn't. He just talked the talk. But the decisions— the *decisions*—were made by D.C. and me and Cetawayo [Michael Tabor]. Cleaver didn't even know most of these guys. But they were our comrades."

Communication between BLA leaders in New York and the Algerian Panthers was problematic at best. Zayd Shakur and, after his release from jail, his brother Lumumba spoke to Algiers on a regular basis, but the calls were expensive, and when money ran low, volunteers at the Seventh Avenue headquarters resorted to using stolen credit cards. When they managed to get through, surviving transcripts of FBI wiretaps indicate, Cleaver rarely came to the telephone. The calls were usually taken instead by Donald Cox or Odinga, who, keenly aware of FBI wiretaps, were obliged to speak in circumscribed terms. "Not only was Cleaver not leading the BLA, remember, he didn't know most of them, he wasn't even from New York," Odinga remembers. "Zayd, Denise, they called and talked to me. Lumumba made sure I got all the info. I talked to them every day. I was in contact with dozens of people underground. Believe me, everything that was going on, I knew about."

The problem, Odinga says, was that knowledge of events did not translate into influence. Cleaver, for instance, wanted to call their new underground the Afro-American Liberation Army. Dhoruba Moore says the New York Panthers simply ignored this. "Outside of an advisory role, we had no role," Odinga goes on. "I made suggestions, sure, but they were not listening to what I said. They made their own decisions. I was not leading anything. As far as I know, no one person was leading anything. I kept telling them, 'Go slow, organize, get yourselves together.' But once [Robert] Webb got killed, things got outta control. Lumumba and Zayd, they're trying to control things, but they can't. I said, 'Slow down, I'm gonna come help,' and they said, 'Nah, it's too late for that.' Things just got too crazy."

"To follow Algeria, that was the initial plan," Dhoruba recalls. "When the split went down, we were following the instructions from Eldridge and D.C. in Algiers. Denise Oliver brought back these audiotapes from them, with guidelines, so we could read them out to people, our people, but also people Geronimo [Pratt] had organized in California and the South. But then everything changed. The reality on the ground was, people were scrambling and running for their lives. After [the police shootings on] May 19, it became a real war between the police and us. It got harder to talk to Algeria."

What most interested Cleaver, and the subject he returned to again and again in his transatlantic phone calls, was the need to establish an aboveground network to support the BLA. Guerrilla units could not survive long, he knew, without donations, without volunteers to serve as couriers and press agents, without community support. A Panther named Bernice Jones was keeping the old Seventh Avenue headquarters open in Harlem, but as police pressure skyrocketed after the May attacks, many volunteers simply melted away. Those who remained came under relentless surveillance and harassment from the FBI and NYPD. By the summer there would be fewer than a dozen people working with Jones. "Everyone is just too scared," Lumumba Shakur complained in one call to Algeria. "They all running and hiding in fear."

While subordinates fielded harried calls from Harlem, Cleaver resorted to doing what he did best: writing. He started a newspaper to compete with the official Panther organ, *The Black Panther*. Cleaver's paper, *Right On!*, was aimed squarely at the recruitment and education of black urban guerrillas; its language was even more violent than that found in *The Black Panther*. Its first issue, which hit the streets two weeks after Webb's death, explained the split, called for New York Panthers to rally behind Cleaver, and featured a back-page cartoon showing a black man with a pistol aimed at a policeman. IN THE SPIRIT OF ROBERT WEBB, the caption read, WE HAVE NO HANG UPS ABOUT REVOLUTIONARY VIOLENCE.

A second issue, "The New Urban Guerrilla," published May 17, just hours before the first police shootings, went even further. In an article detailing the death of one Panther, the author wrote, "His spirit will live in all revolutionaries who pick up the gun to off their oppressors." There was a photo of Richard Nixon with a noose around his neck, and a cartoon drawing of a child holding a pistol to a policeman's head. THE 9MM & HOW TO USE IT, the caption read.

The assassination of two New York police officers and the critical wounding of two more was so jarring that its reverberations were felt all the way to the White House, where on May 26, five days after the shootings, President Nixon summoned J. Edgar Hoover and Attorney General John Mitchell to the Oval Office. Was this the beginning, Nixon wondered, of the violent black uprising they had always feared? Or just street thugs run amok? Hoover hadn't a clue, but Nixon told him to use every means necessary to stamp out this Black Liberation Army, or whatever it was. Hoover ordered every available New York agent into the case, which he code-named NEWKILL. At the FBI's Sixty-ninth Street offices, a new squad, numbered 43A, was formed.

From the beginning, however, this was the NYPD's case, which presented Mayor John Lindsay with a set of delicate problems. Presidential primaries began in a scant ten months, and many believed Lindsay wanted to run again, as he eventually did. Lindsay's image as a candidate, however, was built on a reputation for having kept New York's bubbling racial stew from boiling over. Talk of a black conspiracy to kill policemen struck directly at his prospects, not that it mattered to police-union officials. "We're in a war," Edward J. Kiernan, the head of the union, growled to a group of reporters. "It's open season on cops in this city. I refuse to stand by and permit my men to be gunned down while the Lindsay administration does nothing to protect them. Accordingly, I am instructing them to secure their own shotguns and carry them on patrol at all times."

"You think that'll make a difference?" a reporter asked.

"I dunno," Kiernan said. "But we'll do whatever is necessary. If we have to patrol this city in tanks, that's what we'll do. This is war."

Black leaders, fearing police reprisals, denounced these and similar "emotional calls for shotgun justice," in the words of Manhattan borough president Percy Sutton. City Hall did everything possible to tamp down racial tensions. Asked if there really was a Black Liberation Army targeting cops, Police Commissioner Patrick Murphy told reporters there was "no proof." When Murphy subsequently announced that police cruisers in high-crime areas would be followed by unmarked backup cars, he denied that it was to protect the police. Rather, he said, it would "counteract possible overreacting by policemen."

As the police dragnet spread, Dhoruba Moore and his comrades began efforts to raise money, robbing a series of heroin dealers and social clubs. In the predawn hours of June 5, he and three men barged into an after-hours club in the Bronx called the Triple O. Waving a .45-caliber submachine gun,

Dhoruba ordered the two dozen patrons to strip; when one man was a bit slow, Dhoruba fired a burst of bullets into a wall over the man's head. Once everyone's clothes were piled on the floor, Dhoruba's companions began searching them for cash and jewelry.

The gunfire was loud enough that officers in a passing police cruiser heard it. Sensing a robbery in progress, they radioed for backup. Within minutes police from five patrol cars were outside, guns drawn. They called for everyone to come out. No one came. After several minutes ticked by, one officer opened the door and crept up the staircase to the second-floor club. He found thirty or so people still putting on their clothes. "What's going on here?" he demanded.

"Beats me," one man replied. "We just minding our own business."

"We heard shooting."

"Some dudes tried to rip us off," another said. "But they gone now."

Then the man who had drawn Dhoruba's fire piped up. "No way, that's him!" he said, pointing out Dhoruba, who was attempting to blend in with the patrons. "And him. And him. And him."

Dhoruba and his men were led away in handcuffs, a matter of hours, as it happened, after the FBI had identified his fingerprints on the BLA communiqués. The newspapers all trumpeted the arrests, suggesting that the men behind the May attacks had all been caught, or soon would be. Fears of police reprisals and race riots began to ebb. Investigations of the Beck Street Panthers, who quickly scattered, would drag on for months, but as far as police were concerned, the mystery of the May attacks was more or less solved. All that remained was to track down the remaining suspects. This Black Liberation Army, the thinking went, was just another silly name dreamed up by the radical element to lend credence to its crimes. Few in law enforcement, or anywhere else for that matter, appear to have given serious thought to the idea that the BLA was very real, and just getting started.

09

THE RISE OF THE BLA

The Black Liberation Army,
June 1971 to February 1972

> *faceless brothers of the night*
> *who swim through the city*
> *like fish in the sea*
> *never resting in your search*
> *and destroy mission*
> *against the system*
> *i know how lonely you are*
> *and my heart reaches out to you . . .*
>
> *as repression grows*
> *it becomes more difficult for us*
> *to continue our struggle here*
> *but we persist*
> *until the final day*
> *when we shall join you*
> *in the sea of blood*
> *that will flow in the streets*
> *of babylon.*
>
> *—A poem appearing in Eldridge Cleaver's*
> Right On! Black Community News Service,
> *Fall 1971*

There were three versions of the story of the Black Liberation Army playing out in New York as that hot summer of 1971 wore on: what the public knew, what the police suspected, and what was actually happening. To the public, the attacks in May had swiftly become old news after the arrests of Dhoruba Moore and his three comrades; the NYPD, it was assumed, would make more arrests, as they usually did; as for the BLA itself, few believed it was anything more than a name typed on a letter. The police, however, were starting to suspect that something was afoot. All through June and July detectives chased reports of onetime Panthers robbing drug dealers and social clubs across Queens, the Bronx, and Brooklyn. Something was going on.

What was happening, it is now clear, was that after the chaos that spring, the BLA was beginning to consolidate. By July the Panthers who had gone underground—perhaps fifty or sixty total—had coalesced into two main cells: one based in the Bronx, one in Brooklyn, each divided into "subcells," and each, as Eldridge Cleaver had ordained, operating independently. All were beginning to realize that it was far easier to talk about guerrilla warfare than to engage in it.

"We had no idea—no idea—what we were up against," remembers Blood McCreary, who was busy robbing drug dealers in Brooklyn. "We had really hoped that established revolutionary organizations, that they could point to us and say that unless certain things are dealt with in society, this is what you're going to be dealing with. But we were so young, we didn't know what we were doing. The cops, the government, man, they were killing us. Everywhere we looked, there were cops."

The BLA's most pressing problem, however, was a lack of aboveground support, something Cleaver and Sekou Odinga in far-off Algiers constantly harped on. Other than *Right On!*, whose next issue wouldn't appear until August, there was none. Barely a dozen people now manned the Panthers' Seventh Avenue storefront as their every move was tracked by the NYPD and the FBI. Both searched for links to the underground, but other than the intermittent calls to Algeria, all monitored by the FBI, there were none to be found. The calls, in fact, only revealed the tensions among those few volunteers still supporting Cleaver. At one point, Lumumba Shakur and the *Right*

On! editor, Denise Oliver, got into a bitter argument. "I hit her in the titty!" Shakur crowed to Odinga in Algiers. Cleaver was forced to intervene.

With no donations, the BLA cadres turned to armed robbery. Their targets, as Dhoruba Moore's experience demonstrated, were black social clubs and drug dealers; almost all these robberies are lost to history. "There were actions all over the five boroughs," recalls Blood McCreary. "There were people in the drug business who were setting up others for us to move on. We raised a lot of money that way, and we were letting them know that drugs would not be tolerated anymore."

One of the few surviving accounts of these robberies involves a murderous twenty-year-old BLA recruit whose zeal for gunplay and wide-ranging travels would make him perhaps the single deadliest revolutionary of the decade. His name was Twymon Ford Meyers. A onetime gang member with a long juvenile record of muggings and robberies, Meyers had spent much of his time in the Panthers selling newspapers. His real talent, though, was violence: He used a gun more freely than almost anyone else in the BLA. "Twymon is the baby of three or four kids, and they were all thugs," recalls McCreary. "Twymon was political, you know, but he was really a gangster. He had done a lot of time [in jail], and there was only one clear thing in his mind. He always told me, 'I will die before I go back in jail.'"

On the night of August 4, 1971, Meyers and a trio of BLA members burst into Thelma's Lounge on the corner of Seventh Avenue and 148th Street in Harlem. After robbing the thirty patrons of $6,000, they commandeered a gypsy cab to make their escape. When the cab sagged in heavy traffic three blocks south, police cars arrived. Meyers leaped from the cab, whipped out a .30-caliber automatic rifle, and began firing wildly up and down the street. Police hunched behind their cruisers and fired back; during the exchange the cabdriver was hit and killed. Meyers threw down his gun and ran. The others surrendered and were charged with murder. For the moment, the authorities had no sense that the shooting might be tied to the fledgling BLA.

"Of all the deaths Twymon was involved in, the one with that cabdriver bothered him the most," recalls McCreary. "Shot right in the head. Twymon always said that really fucked with him. He always said, 'That motherfucker had nothing to do with anything.' I remember when he got back to the safe house that night, that cab had just exploded. The women, they picked car glass out of his hair for two or three hours."

The larger of the two BLA cells, which included the remnants of the Panthers living at 757 Beck Street, was commanded by a burly thirty-eight-year-old army veteran named John Thomas. Another onetime resident of South Jamaica, Thomas was a heavy drinker who surrounded himself with a dozen of the most violent new BLA members, including Twymon Meyers. Realizing that drug rip-offs alone wouldn't raise enough money to feed and shelter his people, he resolved to begin robbing banks. They hit the first one, in Queens, on July 29, but it was a slapdash job. A more rigorous second robbery, at a Bankers Trust branch on August 23, involved half a dozen BLA members. As four of them trained their guns on the customers, two others leaped over the teller cages, rifled several drawers, and ran with the others to a waiting getaway car with about $7,700.* None of the robbers wore masks. Security cameras easily recorded their every move. Within days both the FBI and the NYPD were searching for them.

It was then that Thomas decided New York was getting too hot for his people. Dhoruba's arrest also worried him, as did the arrest of several BLA soldiers attempting to set up new operations in Detroit. Thomas announced they were leaving the city. If they were to form a legitimate guerrilla army, he explained, they needed intensive training, and for that Thomas decided to set up a kind of training camp in an area where no one was looking for them, in the South.

At that point the story of the BLA, for the police at least, took a surprising turn—in San Francisco. On the evening of Saturday, August 28, a police sergeant named George Kowalski was cruising the rough streets of the Mission District alone when two black men in a dark Oldsmobile stopped in front of him. One opened fire with a submachine gun. Kowalski ducked,

---

*Three weeks later Thomas, Mark Holder, Frank Fields, and Joanne Chesimard were indicted for the robbery. According to a BLA member captured and interviewed by the NYPD in 1973, the participants were Thomas, his girlfriend Ignae Gittens, Holder, Fields, Chesimard, and Andrew Jackson. Jackson was later tried and acquitted of involvement. Forty years later New York detectives who have extensively researched the BLA say they doubt Chesimard was present; they believe the second woman was another female BLA member.

found himself unharmed, then gave chase, leading to a wild pursuit through city streets that ended when the driver of the Oldsmobile lost control of the car, sliding into a curb, and was surrounded by police. Both men emerged with hands held high.

The two, Anthony Bottom and Albert Washington, turned out to be Black Panthers, and after detectives began questioning nineteen-year-old Bottom, he gave them quite a story. According to Bottom, he was part of a group of Panthers who had staged a series of minor Bay Area bombings stretching back at least a year; they would later be charged with the murder of a San Francisco policeman as well. But what stunned his questioners was when Bottom volunteered that he and Washington had been among five San Francisco Panthers who had journeyed east that May and murdered two New York policemen, Waverly Jones and Joseph Piagentini. Bottom's information eventually led to the arrests of the others, including a lithe Panther named Herman Bell, who had fled with several others for New Orleans, where, police learned, they had begun robbing banks. The Bell-Bottom Panthers weren't officially members of the BLA, but they might as well have been. Dhoruba Moore had been more than willing to take responsibility for their killings in New York.

In Washington, FBI officials watched all these events with mounting alarm. The BLA was fulfilling every warning about black militancy J. Edgar Hoover had made. "During the past several months, the Cleaver Faction of the Black Panther Party has moved on a course of increased violence, lawlessness and terror," Hoover wrote every FBI office on September 24. "I consider their potential for violence and disruption greater today than ever before. . . . [T]his Bureau must approach its investigation of extremist activity with renewed vigor and imagination."

For once Hoover was right. Not that it made a bit of difference.

At just about the moment Anthony Bottom and Albert Washington were arrested in San Francisco, members of John Thomas's BLA cell began arriving in Atlanta. There were seventeen of them in all, by far the largest single BLA group ever assembled. The No. 2 man, Andrew Jackson, a veteran of 757 Beck

Street, was there, as was Joanne Chesimard and Twymon Meyers. Some came in a rented Ryder van piled high with guns and books, others by car, the last few by Greyhound bus.* Several checked into the Bellview Hotel on Auburn Avenue. Within days they found their new headquarters, a large frame home they rented on Fayetteville Road in a semirural area of DeKalb County, on the city's eastern reaches. This would be the BLA's first training camp.

"Atlanta was supposed to be a school, a training ground; we were sending everyone there," recalls Blood McCreary. "Once you got through Atlanta, you were supposed to be ready for anything."

Once they moved in, Thomas began showing everyone how to clean, strip, and fire pistols and rifles. Classes were held in mapmaking, use of a compass, and robbery techniques. Chesimard led sessions in first aid. Every few days they drove the van into a wooded area, where Thomas had everyone shoot on jerry-rigged firing ranges. Other times they tried to learn wilderness skills, something none of them, city dwellers as they were, knew much about.

After three weeks the money began to run low. Thomas sent everyone into Atlanta to fan out and identify a bank to rob. When the group reassembled that evening, he gave a long talk to the group on how to stage an efficient robbery. Everyone was told to take notes, and afterward Thomas reviewed all the members' notebooks to make sure his message had sunk in. He then scouted the location himself and announced they had found their target: a branch of the Fulton National Bank on Peters Street. To rehearse, they built a sandbox in which they constructed a model of the bank and its surroundings. Thomas moved around the sandbox, drawing arrows with a stick and discussing each member's role.

In preparation, Meyers and a young recruit named Fred Hilton were sent into downtown Atlanta to steal a car, only to return, crestfallen, without one. Unable to hotwire a car themselves, they ended up robbing a garage attendant who refused to hand over a vehicle. Irked, Thomas sent Meyers and another teenager, Samuel Cooper, to try again. This time they walked into a downtown garage, pointed a pistol at the attendant, and were just about to steal a

---

*The story of the BLA's sojourn in Atlanta is based on interviews two captured BLA members gave to the NYPD months later, along with newspaper accounts of their crimes and interviews with policemen who investigated them.

car when a woman drove up. Meyers shoved the attendant out of sight while Cooper politely accepted the unknowing woman's keys and handed her a ticket. They then drove off in her car.

They robbed the bank on October 7, covering the customers and quickly leaping the cages. Afterward, flush with cash, Thomas decided to establish a second safe house outside Atlanta. Joanne Chesimard led a scouting team of five members to Greenville, South Carolina, but after a week of searching for a suitable retreat they received word from Thomas to begin looking in Chattanooga, Tennessee. Chesimard's group arrived there on October 14, checking into three rooms at the Rosetta Motel on Thirty-seventh Street. They later moved into a set of apartments. In the following days Thomas sent several members shuttling back and forth between the two cities, redistributing the group's guns, ammunition, and belongings.

He then announced that it was time to begin their long-planned war. To all of them that meant one thing: killing policemen. Thomas selected the two youngest members, Twymon Meyers and Freddie Hilton, for the honor of the first kill. The two teens had borne the brunt of his anger more than once, for mishandling stolen cars and for crashing the Ryder van into a tree and having to abandon it. Now, Thomas announced, they must prove they were worthy of the BLA. They would go into the streets of Atlanta, alone, and kill.

A few minutes after midnight on the morning of November 3, 1971, a twenty-seven-year-old Atlanta police officer named James Greene walked out of Grandma's Biscuits with a late-night snack: a cup of coffee and a ham biscuit. He climbed into his patrol wagon and drove to a darkened service station on Memorial Drive across from a cemetery. He had just finished the sandwich when Twymon Meyers and Freddie Hilton materialized from the shadows on both sides of the wagon, raised their .38-caliber pistols, and opened fire with no warning. Greene never had a chance. Struck by three bullets, he would be dead by morning.

Meyers and Hilton opened the car door, tore off Greene's badge with such force that they ripped his shirt, and took his pistol. When they returned to the house on Fayetteville Road, one BLA member would recall months later, they were triumphant, brandishing the police revolver and the badge, announcing, "We did it! We did it!"

John Thomas was pleased; he dispatched the two to the Chattanooga apartments to hide out. At the same time he summoned two other members, Cooper and Ronald Anderson, to return from Tennessee. When they arrived, Thomas led them into a bedroom where Jackson was waiting. "You know what happened?" Thomas asked.

They knew. "Your two brothers did it," he continued. Motioning toward Jackson, he said, "You all have the next one." The next morning Cooper woke to find Jackson caressing Officer Greene's stolen revolver. "The pigs got nice guns," he remarked.

On November 7, four days after the murder of Officer Greene, Andrew Jackson led his two young charges into Atlanta to kill a second policeman. Instead, after a passing patrolman noticed their guns, they ended up getting arrested outside a convenience store. When the news reached John Thomas, he ordered an immediate evacuation. The group piled everything into two cars and drove to the apartments in Chattanooga, where they pored over the newspapers for any sign of what was happening back in Atlanta. After four days, once it became clear that Jackson and the others would not be released anytime soon, Thomas announced that everyone was returning to New York. On the morning of November 11, the remaining nine members of the cell drove east out of Chattanooga in two cars, crossing the Smoky Mountains into North Carolina.

Everything went smoothly until one of the cars was stopped by a sheriff's deputy named Ted Elmore in Catawba County, North Carolina. A gunfight broke out. Elmore was shot and left paralyzed; four of the group's members were arrested. The others rendezvoused in Norfolk, Virginia, and decided they couldn't afford to return to New York, where too many people knew them. Instead, Thomas led four of them to Florida, where they were later accused of robbing a bank in Miami and robbing a gun store in Tampa. On December 30 they checked into a hotel in the small town of Odessa, north of Tampa; when a hotel employee became suspicious, police were called. FBI agents arrived on the scene the next day. Thomas and his girlfriend went quietly. Another BLA member, Frank Fields—probably one of the three men who attacked Officers Curry and Binetti—ran, and an FBI agent opened fire; a bullet struck Fields in the eye, killing him.

The implosion of John Thomas's cell scattered nearly twenty BLA militants all across the Southeast. As a new year, 1972, dawned, Thomas sat in a Tampa jail awaiting bank-robbery charges; four others were behind bars in North Carolina. Andrew Jackson and two others, arrested in Atlanta, had managed to escape from a county jail and made their way into Florida as well, where they spent two months picking tomatoes alongside migrant workers in an effort to raise money for the bus fare back north. The others trickled back to New York in ones and twos. Marooned outside Tampa, Twymon Meyers and the teenaged Mark Holder stuffed dozens of guns into three suitcases, stole a car, and drove back. Holder was arrested with most of the guns in Philadelphia three weeks later.

The sudden loss of a dozen men did little to dissuade the BLA members still in New York; if anything, it motivated them to strike back, to show authorities that they remained viable and strong. At the time there were still at least two active New York subcells, both devoted to armed robbery, mostly of drug dealers and social clubs. Even before the loss of Thomas and so many of his men, one of these cells had also talked about heading south. In December this group, led by a twenty-eight-year-old ex-marine named Ronald Carter, embarked on a multistate odyssey whose bloody climax would shake the city of New York to its core and trigger a national debate about the BLA that would, in a small way, reverberate in the 1972 presidential primaries.

The full story of the Carter cell has never been told; only three members remain alive, and one, Blood McCreary, tells his version of events here for the first time. Because of the crimes involved, however, his account is incomplete and, in at least one regard, open to doubt. McCreary, for example, states that the Carter group chose to leave New York after the Shakur brothers, Lumumba and Zayd, decided "to make a cell for Assata," that is, for Joanne Chesimard, the Thomas cell's most prominent survivor.

As McCreary tells the story, the group had hoped to receive guidance of some sort from Algeria. A meeting was arranged with Cleaver's emissary, the fiery poet Denise Oliver. "That cell came about from Algeria, or it was supposed to," McCreary recalls. "Denise had been over there, and she came back with instructions from Eldridge. You know, Algeria, they had some good [ideas], but they didn't really run us. Anyway, Denise was to meet with us and give us the information from Algeria. [Several of us], we all showed up to meet Denise. That meeting didn't go down, because Assata wanted to get back to Atlanta, 'cause shit was going down there. But she didn't go; things were too fucked up. So when she stayed, it was decided to create a new cell for Assata."

This new cell, led by Carter and Chesimard, soon fled New York for Miami, which McCreary says was the plan all along. A more likely explanation for their sudden departure involves a bizarre episode in Queens on December 20, 1971. At nine thirty that morning, two patrolmen in a squad car spied four people in a green Pontiac—one woman and three men—parked in front of a Bankers Trust branch on Grand Avenue at Forty-ninth Street, acting suspiciously. When the cruiser approached, the Pontiac pulled away from the curb. Following at a safe distance, the officers checked its license plate and discovered that the car had been stolen.

When the cruiser lit its rolling lights, the Pontiac took off, racing to the corner of Flushing Avenue and Fifty-seventh Street, where it turned southwest, toward Brooklyn. As the chase continued, someone in the Pontiac rolled down a window and lobbed something toward the cruiser. It was, of all things, a hand grenade—an M-26 fragmentation grenade, to be exact, the kind used by the U.S. Army in Vietnam. To the officers' amazement, it exploded beside the cruiser, wrecking it. As the officers leaped, unhurt, from the burning car, the Pontiac roared off toward Brooklyn, where a few minutes later its occupants jumped out, rushed toward a man at a Sunoco gas station, and stole his car. Later the man identified Joanne Chesimard as one of his assailants.* The NYPD immediately issued a thirteen-state alarm calling for her arrest.

---

*Chesimard's identification, while likely, is not ironclad. The witness, Paul Costa, also identified another BLA member, Andrew Jackson, who was in Florida at the time.

As police suspected, the attack was almost certainly the work of Chesimard and the Carter cell. In the BLA's first-ever phone call to the press, a caller to United Press International (UPI) took credit in the name of the Attica Brigade of the Afro-American Liberation Army—Cleaver's name for the BLA—saying, "We have more grenades, and we will be back." The police dragnet would explain why Chesimard, Carter, McCreary, and three other comrades swiftly relocated to the Miami area. There they rented an apartment in the beachfront city of Hollywood and began scouting banks. They probably didn't know that at that very moment they had become the third BLA group at large in the state of Florida.

They pulled off a quick bank robbery in Miami, running out in less than five minutes. Much as John Thomas had done after his robberies in New York, the cell took its cash and began making plans. Carter and Chesimard, in fact, envisioned sharply expanding the BLA's reach, creating a string of safe houses across the Midwest. Within days they had left Miami, scattering to rent apartments in Cleveland, Milwaukee, St. Louis, and Kansas City. Carter and McCreary then returned to New York, where they met with Zayd Shakur, who was still in touch with Algeria. They agreed that their immediate focus should be freeing those who had been captured, especially Dhoruba Moore and, at Chesimard's urging, her boyfriend, who had been arrested in Detroit. "We were going to break them out," McCreary recalls. "I went with Assata to Detroit and looked things over, but it was clear it would never work. It was obvious we could never get near them."

Afterward, members of the cell rendezvoused at their new Cleveland safe house, a set of three apartments on East Eighty-fourth Street. Once it became clear that there was no easy way to free the prisoners, two new plans were sketched out. Both involved actions in New York. "Cleveland was our new home," McCreary remembers, "but New York City was to be our battleground." All through the first days of 1972, BLA members shuttled back and forth between Cleveland and New York; after the Thomas group's shootout in North Carolina, they eschewed cars and began traveling by Greyhound bus. The drawback was the Pennsylvania State Police's penchant for boarding buses to search for drugs. "Every time they came on board, you know, we were strapped [with guns]," McCreary recalls with a shiver. "Those were some pretty hot moments."

In short order the Cleveland cell grew in size to nine, as McCreary tracked down three soldiers who had lost their way, including Twymon Meyers, whom he stumbled across one night in the East Village, and a new recruit, Henry "Sha Sha" Brown. In Cleveland they quickly went to work on an audacious plan that had originated with Cleaver and Don Cox in Algeria. Black guerrillas had launched a civil war in the South African country of Zimbabwe, and the white-led government had responded with a string of indiscriminate killings. Cleaver suggested that the Cleveland cell attempt to storm the Zimbabwean Consulate in New York.

"We wanted to make a signature statement in New York, something that would get us noticed internationally," says McCreary. "So we scouted out [the consulate]; it was off Park Avenue in the Fifties. We went in. We could see it was gonna be too much trouble. Too much traffic, it just didn't work out. So we found out [the diplomats] all lived in homes on Long Island, like in a compound. The place was guarded by these huge dogs, Rhodesian ridgebacks. So we go out there to poison these dogs, and needless to say, it didn't work. And so we went to the alternate plan. And I don't want to talk about that."

And with good reason. The Carter cell's "alternate plan" almost certainly led to one of the most gruesome murders in the history of New York.

The night of January 27, 1972, was freezing; frigid winter winds whistled down the garbage-strewn streets of New York's East Village. Snow was on the way. Down on Avenue B two young patrolmen were walking their beat. Greg Foster, who was twenty-two, was black. Rocco Laurie, a year older, was white. The two had served together as marines in Vietnam and, as close friends, had received permission to be partners, patrolling one of New York's most dangerous and drug-ridden neighborhoods.

The two were walking south along Avenue B around ten thirty when they noticed a car parked in front of a hydrant. They ducked into a luncheonette across the street, the Shrimp Boat, and asked the owner if he knew the car. He stepped outside and shook his head no. Satisfied, Foster and Laurie turned and began to walk back north. As they did, three black men passed, parting to allow the officers to walk between them. One of the men wore a long black coat, another a green fatigue jacket and a black Australian-style bush hat.

A moment after the officers passed, the three men suddenly turned and drew pistols, a .38 automatic and two 9mm automatics. Foster and Laurie were a few strides away when the men began firing directly into their backs. Foster was hit eight times and fell in a heap onto the icy pavement. Six bullets hit Laurie. All but one struck his arms and legs, but the last pierced his neck, and he staggered forward, clutching at his throat before dropping to his knees and falling, slowly, onto his side. As the two men lay dying, their assassins marched calmly toward them. A witness later claimed one of the shooters hollered, "Shoot 'em in the balls," and all three again opened fire.

Three bullets were fired directly into Foster's eyes; two were shot into Laurie's groin. When both men lay still, two of the assassins reached down and wrenched loose their pistols. They ran toward a waiting Chrysler, while the third man, apparently intoxicated by the moment, reportedly danced a jig over the dead men's bodies, firing his pistol into the air Wild West–style. Startled to be left behind, he ran off alone, disappearing into the night.

The whine of police sirens echoed within minutes, and the first several officers to respond, all answering a disturbance call two blocks away, were quickly on the scene. What they found was stomach turning. Greg Foster's head had been destroyed; a sludge of blood and brain matter formed a three-foot puddle around his corpse. Rocco Laurie had been shot to pieces, bullet wounds up and down his body. An ambulance took Laurie to Bellevue Hospital, where he died. Almost everyone who responded had the same thought: These were planned assassinations, no doubt by the same people who had murdered Officers Piagentini and Jones eight months before, this so-called Black Liberation Army. It took only a few hours to confirm it. Fingerprints found in the getaway car suggested that the assassins were Ronald Carter, Twymon Meyers, and at least one other member of the Cleveland cell.

The Foster-Laurie murders presented Mayor John Lindsay's administration with much the same dilemma it had confronted after the first attacks the previous May. Within hours, in fact, a series of debates erupted within the police department and the mayor's office: Were these planned assassinations or something else? If they were the work of the same group behind the attacks in May, as was widely assumed, did this mean there actually was a genuine Black Liberation Army? Was there really a nationwide black conspiracy to murder policemen? And if so, should the public be told?

What police knew was this: Ten officers had now been attacked and seven killed in a nine-month span in New York, San Francisco, North Carolina, and Atlanta, seemingly all by onetime Panthers claiming to be a Black Liberation Army. Some of these attacks were linked; some were not. Many in the NYPD believed that this constituted a legitimate national conspiracy. But others, including several aides in Mayor Lindsay's office, felt that the killings were unrelated. There was no black army, they argued; this was the work of a few disgruntled Panthers borrowing a discarded Panther term to make it appear as if there was.

The pivotal figure in these debates was a newcomer to the NYPD, a deputy police commissioner named Robert Daley. Daley had been a *New York Times* reporter who had attracted the attention of Police Commissioner Patrick Murphy while writing a profile of him; when Murphy offered him the department's top public-relations job, Daley accepted. He was a divisive figure, a publicity hound who, as the *Times* itself noted later, "was always mugging for the cameras." What Daley loved most was a good detective yarn, and the story of the BLA was one of the best he had seen. Gunsmoke had barely cleared over Foster and Laurie's bodies when he began arguing that the NYPD had an obligation to go public with its suspicions that the murders constituted a planned assassination by a national conspiracy of black militants.

This kind of talk startled aides to Mayor Lindsay, who had announced his campaign for the presidency a month earlier. Talk of black terrorists loose in the streets would undercut his candidacy, inflame race relations, and have every cop in the city looking askance at young black men. Lindsay's combative press secretary, Tom Morgan, made clear to everyone that he didn't want to see a single word about black conspiracies in the press.

Swarmed by reporters the morning after the murders, the chief of detectives, Albert Seedman, went along, pooh-poohing the conspiracy angle. But the next day, a Saturday, the UPI office received a handwritten communiqué, signed by the "George Jackson Squad of the Black Liberation Army."* Mailed the previous day, it referenced "the pigs wiped out in lower Manhattan last night" and promised: "This is the start of our spring offensive. There is more to come."

This was too much for Daley. That same afternoon—even as citizens in far-off Arizona were voting in the caucuses, in which Lindsay placed second to Edmund Muskie—Daley strode into an East Village precinct house and, standing before a bank of microphones, raised Rocco Laurie's blood-drenched shirt for all to see. He called the murders assassinations, carried out by a conspiracy of urban guerrillas—black urban guerrillas. "Always in the past the police have been quiet about this conspiracy because of fear of accusations of racism," he said. "But it isn't the black community that is doing this, it is a few dozen black criminal thugs. . . . It's terribly serious, much more serious than people seem to think. The police are the last barrier before chaos."

Suddenly the rhetorical cat was out of the bag. The mayor's people were apoplectic. But the New York newspapers, sensing a story too hot to handle, downplayed Daley's dramatic press conference; the *Times* buried the story on page 35. Talk of a black conspiracy ebbed for several days as reporters focused on the officers' funerals, which were massive affairs, with hundreds of uniformed officers lining Fifth Avenue in front of St. Patrick's Cathedral. But Daley would not let up. In off-the-record chats all that week, he told reporters that there was a true national conspiracy, that the NYPD's intelligence, gathered over the previous seven months, confirmed the existence of a Black Liberation Army, with hundreds of would-be assassins divided into revolutionary cells. For the most part, no one believed him; no

---

*Jackson was a California prison inmate and best-selling author who had been killed the previous August. See chapter 12 for details.

one, at least, printed more of his theories. It was all too inflammatory, too far-fetched.

Finally, a week after the murders, a *Times* reporter cornered a reluctant Commissioner Murphy. All available evidence, Murphy admitted, suggested that the Foster-Laurie murders were in fact the work not of a national conspiracy to kill police but of roving bands of militants—"crazies," Murphy termed them—who moved from city to city, murdering policemen. Daley, however, went much further. He told the *Times* there was a BLA that was "nationwide in scope," adding, "We have here a very, very dangerous and criminal conspiracy. The public really doesn't seem to be aware of it. The time is over when the Police Department should keep its mouth shut on this kind of thing."

Working with incomplete information, neither man was entirely correct. The BLA was far too disorganized and far too decentralized to be called a true national conspiracy. But it was more than "roving" bands of "crazies." Daley would not be deterred. Over the vocal opposition of the Manhattan district attorney, Frank Hogan, he persuaded Commissioner Murphy to hold an unusual press conference on Tuesday, February 8, in which Murphy detailed the BLA's involvement not only in the Foster-Laurie murders but also in the May attacks and the attacks on policemen in San Francisco and Atlanta. He named nine BLA figures sought by police, including Ronald Carter, Joanne Chesimard, and Twymon Meyers. Prosecutors had adamantly opposed going public, arguing that it would complicate any case they brought. The mayor's office objected as well, finally persuading Murphy not to use the word "conspiracy."

But the debate—and the killings—were far from over.

The murders of Greg Foster and Rocco Laurie have never officially been solved. But there is little doubt that the killers came from the Ronald Carter–Joanne Chesimard cell based in Cleveland. While political debates raged in Manhattan, Carter and his eight comrades pored over New York newspapers, following the investigation. After two weeks they began to fear they had stayed too long in one place. "So we took a vote," Blood McCreary remembers. "We decided to go to St. Louis."

A safe house there was already in place. On Monday, February 14, they rented a U-Haul truck, which the group crammed with furniture, books, mattresses, and personal belongings. The next morning they left the city in a three-vehicle caravan heading toward St. Louis. "On long trips I drove," says McCreary, whose family was originally from South Carolina. "I had the Southern manners—you know, 'Yes, sir,' 'Whatever you say, sir'—which we needed at toll booths or if we got stopped. Our younger guys, Twymon and them, they didn't have the manners. If a cop car stopped us, they always wanted to shoot."

They reached the St. Louis safe house without incident. "It was late afternoon," says McCreary. "Later we decided to go looking for out-of-state newspapers. Four of us went: me, Twymon, Ronald Carter, and Sha-Sha Brown. We drove downtown looking for a newsstand. That was a mistake. Seemed like everything was closed. Then I saw the cop's car."

It was 9:30 p.m. when the two St. Louis patrolmen, cruising North Grand Avenue in a black neighborhood, spotted a green 1967 Oldsmobile sporting, of all things, a set of cardboard Michigan license plates. The cruiser lit its rolling lights. McCreary was behind the wheel. "I said, 'We got lights,'" he remembers, "and Ronnie leaned forward—he was in the backseat—and said, 'Be cool, just pull over.'"

One officer hung back while the second walked to the driver's-side window. "We had all been taught that, if you get stopped, the first thing you do is roll down all the car windows," McCreary says. "That way, if you have to shoot, you don't want glass exploding all over you. So we rolled down our windows. I took out my wallet. When he came to the car, I had everything in my hand. Everything he needed was in my hand. But you know, it wasn't right. The car had Michigan temporary plates. It was registered in Florida. My driver's license was my alias, Frank Reece of Windsor, North Carolina. Poor cop, he was as confused as anything. [He says,] 'I'm going to have to ask you guys to step outta the car.' And you know, I was doing everything I could to get outta this. I kept saying, 'Why is that necessary? Why?'"

"We all had on shoulder holsters," McCreary says. "Twymon was beside me in the front. I saw he had the 9mm between his legs. In the trunk we had like seventeen different guns, an M16, a bunch of Browning 9mms. I had a .357. Sha Sha had a nine-mill. I had been through several situations with Twymon, and I knew that when he was about to shoot, he always started rocking. Rocking back and forth. And I realized he had started rocking in his seat. I'm talking to the cop, and I feel Twymon pulling at my sleeve. He wants me to lean back so he can shoot the cop. I know he's about to shoot, and I'm trying everything I can do to make this cop go away. . . .

"The cop keeps saying, 'Get out of the car.'

"I keep saying, 'Officer, why is that necessary? All our papers are in order. Why is that necessary?'

"And finally, you know, he had enough. He said, 'Nigger, get out of the fucking car!' And when he said that, I just leaned back and all I saw then was red and blue streaks of fire going past my face. Twymon was shooting, and then, well, the whole car kind of exploded."

The officer beside the car fell, struck in the stomach and legs. As the Olds roared off, he fired all six shots in his revolver. As luck would have it, two narcotics officers were on a stakeout a block away and heard the shooting. They gave chase. Spying their pursuit, McCreary mashed the accelerator, hitting speeds close to 100 miles per hour as the Olds zigzagged through narrow streets toward the Mississippi River waterfront. By the time he got there, there were four police cars behind him, their sirens echoing through the downtown streets. When one approached his fender, he swung the steering wheel violently to the left. The Olds veered into a vicious left turn, turning completely around, until it hopped a curb, all four tires blown, and came to rest against a high chain-link fence bordering a vacant lot.

When the car stopped, McCreary turned to face Ronnie Carter, only to find him slumped forward, a sick gurgling noise coming from his throat. He had been shot in the chest; an autopsy would reveal that he had accidentally been killed by a BLA bullet fired by Sha Sha Brown. McCreary leaped outside. A hail of bullets drove him toward the chain-link fence. "We were trying to get to the trunk," he recalls. "If we could've gotten the M16 or the .30-06, we would've gotten away."

Up and down the wide boulevard, policemen were crouching behind their cruisers, firing. The three BLA men ran to the fence. McCreary turned and provided covering fire as Meyers and Sha Sha Brown climbed it and vaulted into the vacant lot. When he ran out of ammunition, McCreary threw down his pistol and surrendered. The police captured Brown a few blocks away, bleeding from a wound in his wrist. Only Twymon Meyers managed to get away, disappearing into the night.

In the first confused hours after the incident, there was nothing to link it to the BLA; both McCreary and Brown gave false names. What triggered a barrage of early-morning phone calls to New York was the discovery that a pistol Brown had thrown down had until two weeks before belonged to Officer Rocco Laurie. This changed everything: For the first time the NYPD felt obliged to reveal everything they knew.

At a press conference two days later, Commissioner Murphy called on the White House, the attorney general, and the FBI "to give the highest priority to the hunt" for the Foster-Laurie assassins and the BLA. After Murphy spoke, the NYPD's assistant chief inspector, Arthur Grubert, detailed the attacks on police in New York, San Francisco, and Atlanta and gave reporters the most reasoned, lucid overview of the BLA to date. He noted:

> Intelligence fails to identify a formal structure of a firm organization known as the Black Liberation Army. It is more likely that various extremist individuals, 75 to 100 in number, are making use of the name Black Liberation Army in order to give some semblance of legitimacy to these homicidal acts. These individuals form and dissolve and reform in small groups, or cells.

The NYPD might not want to call the BLA a true "army," but what it described sounded martial enough. The *Times*'s skepticism, for instance, began to fall away. The headline of its front-page story on February 17 was EVIDENCE OF "LIBERATION ARMY" SAID TO RISE. It was then, with its notoriety near a zenith, that the BLA went utterly silent. Not a single word would be heard again for months.

10

"WE GOT PRETTY SMALL"

*The Weather Underground and
the FBI, 1971–72*

The Weather leadership's narrow escape from the FBI in March 1971, and
the unprecedented raid on one of its San Francisco apartments—what came
to be known in Weather lore as "the Encirclement"—marked a turning point
for the organization. Though it would continue to mount actions and issue
communiqués, Weather would never again be as active or as relevant as it was
during its first year underground.

Its numbers were dwindling. There is ample evidence, in fact, that after
mid-1971 Weather was a far smaller organization than has been previously
understood. Four hundred radicals had attended the Flint War Council.
Maybe a hundred went underground. Maybe fifty remained active after the
Townhouse. The precise number of later cadres may never be known, in part
because many people called themselves Weathermen despite doing little clandestine work. In 1972, for example, the Los Angeles collective consisted of
six or seven people who never participated in a single bombing. One estimate
puts thirty-five people underground during the 1972–73 time frame, a count

endorsed by several alumni. But the number who actually performed clandestine work, who carried out bombings after the middle of 1971, was smaller still.

"We lost most of the people after the Townhouse," says Ron Fliegelman. "After the Encirclement, we lost even more. I'm telling you, we were down to ten or fifteen. The leadership, me, the Cathys [Cathy Wilkerson and Kathy Boudin], Paul Bradley. The core group, the ones who did things, was ten or twelve people, no more than fifteen."

"That wasn't necessarily a bad thing," says Brian Flanagan. "People like me, who were aboveground, could do a lot more things. I mean, how many people did you really need underground at that point?"

"It's true, we got pretty small," says Rick Ayers. "A lot of people went up [aboveground]. We sent a lot of people up. That was actually a conscious decision. We wanted a new sort of organization, with members aboveground, where they could do more for us. So you had an underground structure where the members weren't all fugitives."

In the wake of the Encirclement, the leadership and the San Francisco cadres scattered. "After the Encirclement, we had to do what was essential, which was fall back on support," recalls Ayers, who had moved to Los Angeles. "We ran to a lot of friends and asked for help, but it slowed things down, for sure. We had to devise other ways and other kinds of ID. It was like starting over. Again." Many cadres fled to new cities and new identities to await orders that, in some cases, didn't come for months. David Gilbert went to ground in Denver, while others fled to Seattle. Mark Rudd, now thoroughly alienated from the leadership, fled active work altogether, resettling with his girlfriend in Santa Fe. Others simply melted away. Still others fell victim to the paranoia that gripped the underground after the San Francisco raid.

One such situation involved a former Kent State student who had rented the apartment on Pine Street. As several Weather alumni tell it, the student was experimenting with gay life, and the habits he developed in San Francisco worried many. "He would pick up guys at bathhouses and bring them back to the safe houses, and you can't do that, not without being compromised," recalls Paul Bradley. After the Encirclement, the student was transferred to New

York, where his problems continued. "None of us had dealt with gay issues at that point," recalls Fliegelman. "He would go off and do stuff, and he could be compromised, so he ended up having to leave."

The Encirclement obliged Robbie Roth's busy New York collective to scatter as well. Eleanor Stein sat on the floor of its apartment in Cobble Hill, Brooklyn, spread out a piece of butcher paper, and charted all the connections between the West Coast and East Coast IDs; there were enough, it was decided, that the New Yorkers needed to relocate.

"I remember it took a solid week to scrub every surface of that place, erasing every fingerprint," recalls Jonah Raskin, a frequent visitor. "It was an unbelievable headache."

The whereabouts of the West Coast leadership—Bernardine Dohrn, Bill Ayers, and Jeff Jones—after they left San Francisco in spring 1971 have remained a secret for forty years. In his memoir *Fugitive Days*, Bill Ayers portrays their lives as nomadic, moving between working-class hideouts, including "a perch above a goat shed on a commune, and later in the grounds-keepers' quarters of a mansion near Laurel Canyon [in Los Angeles]" as well as "a basement room in a monastery in Mundelein [Illinois] . . . and a stone house on the Olympic Peninsula [in Washington state]." However complete this list may be, the one place Ayers doesn't mention is the actual home the leadership found shortly after the Encirclement, which would serve as the group's informal West Coast headquarters for several years. It was not, as Ayers wanted his readers to believe, some decrepit flat in an out-of-the-way slum. In fact, it was a sunny bungalow just steps from the ocean in Hermosa Beach, an Orange County beach community thronged with surfers and hippies.

"It was really cozy, you could hear the surf," recalls Marvin Doyle. "It was on this little street on an alley, jammed in against other similar places, with a postage-stamp-sized patio. The rooms were decorated in 'tasteful hippie.' Bernardine had rococo tastes, a lot of pillows and nice patterned cloths on the furniture, in rich colors and textures. I remember she used madras bedspreads for curtains."

The Bay Area, however, was far too important for Weather to abandon. From the moment they left, in fact, Dohrn was determined to reestablish a presence there. "It was a power center, of the Left, and you didn't want the

FBI to beat you, you wanted to show them you couldn't be defeated, that you could come back hard and fast," recalls Doyle, who, in the absence of other San Francisco cadres, emerged as a key intermediary in Dohrn's orbit. The first Weatherman to return to the city was Paul Bradley, who was developing a lifelong love for the area. He managed to rent a secluded carriage house on Vallejo Street in the Russian Hill section; it was perfect, nestled in a garden behind an apartment building, with a single entrance to the street. Bradley lived there for several years; out-of-town visitors, including the leadership, were always welcome. Later a second flat was rented, in the Sunset area. Once he was established, Dohrn asked him to approach Doyle.

Thin, with long, scraggly hair, Doyle had lingered on the edges of Weather for the previous year. Bradley had approached him months earlier and asked to use his telephone for calls and his home address as a mail drop. Wary but secretly thrilled, Doyle had agreed. At one point, aware that he was being considered for active membership, he had ridden with Bradley to the Point Reyes National Seashore, north of San Francisco, for a rendezvous with Dohrn, who dazzled him. "She was spellbinding," Doyle recalls. "Sexy, brilliant, and immensely articulate. And she had this boldness, on a higher level than I'd ever been exposed to. The power and the intellect, she just blew you away."

Then, in the weeks after the Encirclement, Bradley came to him once more. "Man, we're really desperate for cash," Bradley said, and Doyle handed over his last $1,500 from a fellowship. After that, Doyle's responsibilities grew. One day that spring a Weatherman drove him to a remote garage in the Sunset district, which to Doyle's surprise held not only Jeff Jones's beloved pickup truck, Suzie Q, but all of Jones's and Dohrn's belongings, abandoned after the Encirclement. After wiping the truck for fingerprints—it was later sold—the men loaded everything into a camper, after which Bradley arrived and told Doyle to drive. Without a clue about their destination, Doyle drove south, arriving later that day south of Los Angeles, where he drove into a warren of alleys alongside the ocean in Hermosa Beach. It was there that Doyle saw the leadership's new home and forged a relationship with Dohrn.

For weeks after the Encirclement, Dohrn remained leery of San Francisco. But Weather had many allies in the Bay Area, so she began slipping into the city on a regular basis, often meeting Doyle in parks and at restaurants. "We would sit and talk for like two hours, in Ghirardelli Square a lot and elsewhere," he remembers. "She would say, 'Go do this, go talk to this guy and say this.' We hit it off real well. I basically became her gopher." And, in time, her lover. "Yeah, I remember she returned from the East at one point, to L.A., and with this other couple we went to a Grateful Dead concert," Doyle recalls. "We ended up in bed. We had a kind of summer fling."

Dohrn's sudden availability, it would appear, coincided with the breakup of her relationship with Jones. Neither has ever spoken publicly about what happened. Some within the organization blamed Jones for the Encirclement, leading to speculation that Dohrn had soured on him as a result. The fact that she subsequently entered into a long-term relationship with Bill Ayers led still others to believe there had been a love triangle at work. Whatever happened, the dissolution of the Dohrn-Jones union had a few obvious repercussions. "It was a big deal," recalls Paul Bradley, who was close to Dohrn. "My memory is the three of them kept it pretty close to the vest until the last minute, when an announcement was made. It actually went surprisingly smoothly."

After the breakup, Jones decided to relocate to the East Coast. Eleanor Stein happened to be visiting from New York, and the two drove across the country. They eventually arrived at what would become Weather's ad hoc New York headquarters, a remote four-bedroom rental house with a pond on an acre of land deep in the Catskill Mountains, a few hours' drive north of Manhattan. The New York cell had moved in after the Encirclement; Ron Fliegelman and one or two others lived there with Stein and Jones for more than a year. Taking long walks, watching the morning mist rise over the Pepacton Reservoir, Jones began to relax, even after he saw his wanted poster at the post office in the nearest town, Delhi. He started a garden, planting cucumbers and tomatoes. He and Stein were opposites—a communist-raised New York intellectual and a California surfer type—but in those early days in the Catskills, they fell in love. Like Dohrn and Ayers, they would eventually marry. Forty years later both couples remain together.

Jeff Jones's tranquil new life in the mountains was in many ways a symbol of the changes the Weather Underground was undergoing. The *New York*

Times began printing the Pentagon Papers that June; the antiwar movement was slowing noticeably. They had gone underground with dreams of triggering a Castro-style revolution in America. It hadn't happened. Only the deluded still believed it would. By any measure, their grand vision of rallying young Americans to a bloody revolution had failed; they had succeeded only in surviving. At a bungalow in Hermosa Beach, at a secluded carriage house on San Francisco's Russian Hill, at a dewy rental house in the Catskills, what remained of the Weathermen needed time to take stock.

"After the Encirclement, things really slowed down," says Rick Ayers. "It began a time when things were much slower, more time between actions, more time to think. Everybody needed to chill out."

Nowhere was the change in tone more evident than in the group's new approach to bombings. Until the Encirclement, Weather had always taken the initiative; afterward, almost all its bombings were staged in reaction to specific events. A case in point was the first action it carried out after the San Francisco raids: the twin California bombings described by Marvin Doyle in chapter 6. They came in retaliation for the August 21 killing at San Quentin State Prison of a charismatic inmate named George Jackson, whose best-selling memoir, *Soledad Brother*, had fueled a newfound interest in prison conditions in Bay Area radical circles. The planning was done at the new Sunset apartment. "It was a typical San Francisco apartment, elongated windows, scruffy furniture," Doyle recalls. "A lot of hanging out there, a lot of intense meetings, people coming and going. That's where Ron and people from New York would stay when they came out. That was kind of the center of gravity the whole summer."

The bomb Doyle and Paul Bradley placed above a second-floor ceiling tile in the Department of Corrections office in San Francisco's historic Ferry Building demolished a small psychiatric clinic. A second bomb wrecked a sixth-floor restroom at the department's headquarters in Sacramento. No one was injured in either explosion. The communiqué, mailed to the *San Francisco Examiner*, was a departure from previous Weather missives, a lengthy diatribe denouncing the treatment of American blacks and especially black prisoners: "Black and Brown people inside the jails are doing all they can— must they fight alone even now? White people on the outside have a deep responsibility to enter the battle at every level. Each of us can turn our grief into the righteous anger and our anger into action. Two small bombs do not cool our rage. . . . We view our actions as simply a first expression of our love and respect for George Jackson and the warriors of San Quentin."

Weather's interest in prison conditions deepened two weeks later, on September 13, when the killing of twenty-nine inmates and ten state personnel during a rebellion at New York's Attica prison sparked widespread calls for reform. The New York cell, comfortably ensconced in their Catskill Mountains hideaway, staged their first post-Encirclement action four days later. Ron Fliegelman, as usual, built the bomb, which was smuggled into a ninth-floor washroom outside the offices of Russell G. Oswald, commissioner of the New York Department of Correctional Services in Albany. Early that evening a warning was called in to the *Albany Times-Union*. The building was quickly cleared, and at seven thirty the bomb detonated, destroying the washroom. No one was injured. "Tonight we attacked the head offices of the New York State Department of Corrections," the forthcoming communiqué read. "We must continue to make the Rockefellers, Oswalds, Reagans and Nixons pay for their crimes. We only wish we could do more to show the courageous prisoners at Attica, San Quentin and the other 20th century slave ships that they are not alone in their fight for the right to live."

The final Weather Underground bombing of 1971 came on October 15, when the group's "Proud Eagle" affiliate detonated a small bomb above a ceiling panel in a fourth-floor women's restroom at the Grover M. Hermann Building at the Massachusetts Institute of Technology. The early-morning explosion slightly damaged an adjacent office used by the onetime White House aide William Bundy. A two-page communiqué sent to the *Boston Globe* blamed Bundy's role in crafting the war in Vietnam.

When Weathermen did get around to bombing things, the preparation and execution remained fraught with risk. Long-haired young people lingering outside courthouses and police stations late at night tended to draw attention in the early 1970s. It occurred to Dohrn, and to others in the leadership, that disguises alone wouldn't ensure their safety. Thus the question arose: What could they take along to reliably deflect a policeman's curiosity? One answer was children.

No beat cop, they reasoned, would suspect a family with kids out for an evening stroll. It was a brilliant idea; the only problem was, no one in Weather had children. A handful of supporters did, however, and this was how one of Dohrn's friends, the Chicago attorney Dennis Cunningham, saw his family drawn into clandestineness. Cunningham, as we have seen, had emerged as a key conduit for the money that paid the leadership's living expenses. He adored Dohrn and considered her one of the most talented minds he had ever encountered.

If anything, Cunningham's wife, Mona, a tall, thin actress in Chicago's Second City theater troupe, was even more dazzled. A budding revolutionary herself, Mona had actually attended the Flint Wargasm, taking along Marvin Doyle, who happened to be a relative of her husband's. Mona was so smitten by Dohrn, in fact, that when she gave birth to her fourth child, in June 1970, she named her Bernadine. The Cunninghams, however, had been having marital troubles, and their work with the underground added a new strain to their disagreements. Then, in the fall of 1970, Dohrn invited the couple to California. It was a relaxing trip; the Cunninghams accompanied Dohrn and Jeff Jones on a tour of California campgrounds in an old camper. It was during this trip, Cunningham recalls, that Dohrn floated the idea of the couple joining them underground.

"She said, you know, 'Maybe you should just fade out, disappear and come out here, maybe [live] down around Santa Rosa,'" Cunningham recalls. "It made no sense to me. What would I do? I couldn't figure out what the fuck she was talking about." In Chicago Cunningham had a bustling practice defending all manner of radicals, including the late Fred Hampton and many other black activists. He couldn't just leave. But Mona Cunningham seemed intrigued. Dohrn was surprisingly candid, encouraging Mona to come alone, Dennis recalls: "She was like all of them, Mark Rudd, all of them, she just came out and said it, 'You're really going to stay in this fucking monogamy?'"

After a tense discussion, Dennis announced he was returning to Chicago.

Mona stayed behind, Dennis says, "to learn about things. I think she stayed a week or ten days before she came back to Chicago." As that winter wore on, Mona talked often of going underground. Eventually, the following June, the Cunninghams separated.

Which is how, in the summer of 1971, Mona Cunningham, now going by her maiden name, Mona Mellis, left Chicago and moved west, initially into an Oregon commune, then into a flat in San Francisco's Haight-Ashbury. She brought all four of her children: Delia, who turned eight that year; her younger brother, Joey; another daughter, Miranda; and the baby, Bernadine. Dohrn welcomed Mona with open arms, continuing what would become a long friendship; the two often referred to themselves as sisters. At the same time, Mona began an extended affair with Bill Ayers. But of all the relationships renewed by the Mellis family's move to San Francisco, it was the one between Dohrn and eight-year-old Delia Mellis that would endure. Dohrn "was like a favorite aunt, or an older sister, just very cool and very fun to be with," remembers Delia, today a faculty member affiliated with Bard College in New York.

The move into Dohrn's orbit introduced young Delia to a strange new world of intrigue she found thrilling. "There were secret things, and I kept them secret," she recalls. "We would go see Bernardine and Billy, and Mom would say, 'Don't say anything about this at school, don't tell your dad, don't tell your grandparents.' I knew what was happening, what they were doing, and why. I knew the FBI was all around, and it was dangerous. I never told a soul."

When Dohrn was visiting from Hermosa Beach, Delia would join her in the Sunset-area apartment. But before long she began accompanying her on outings, first around San Francisco, then to Hermosa Beach and other destinations she can only vaguely remember. In those early months Mona would drop Delia off at Golden Gate Park's Conservatory of Flowers, a Victorian-era greenhouse, where her mother showed her how to watch for police. Once they were sure they weren't followed, Mona would leave, and Delia would wander among the greenery until Dohrn or Bill Ayers or Paul Bradley would mysteriously appear to take her away. In Hermosa Beach, Dohrn and Ayers— now "Molly and Mike"—would take her shopping and to the movies. They insisted on calling Delia by her code name, "Sunflower," which Delia secretly loathed.

"I went to L.A. a bunch of times," Delia recalls. "I would play while they had meetings. There was a lot of time in cars. Bernardine and Billy always had cool cars, fifties cars. We would go to movies, old films, Chaplin films. Later I started going on trips, into the countryside, to other cities, trips on airplanes, on trains, cross-country, once or twice to upstate New York, where I think we stayed when Jeff Jones moved there. I knew they loved spending time with us, my siblings included, but I also knew we were good cover. The two things went together well. I know Mom was really into that, that we were helping. Did we scout out bombing targets? Yeah, I think so. I never actually saw anything explode, but it was always discussed. 'We had a great action. We're going to be discussing an action.'"

In time, Delia came to know almost all the remaining Weathermen, though their ever-changing code names perplexed her. "I totally loved Cathy Wilkerson. Cathy was 'Susie.' Paul Bradley introduced me to comic books. He was 'Jack.' Robbie Roth was 'Jimmy.' Rick Ayers was 'Skip.' I didn't like it when Bernardine changed from 'Molly' to 'Rose' and Billy went from 'Mike' to 'Joe.' It was confusing."

The second Mellis daughter, Miranda, who was three when the family moved to San Francisco, fell into Wilkerson's orbit. "I was not allowed to go near Delia, because she was Bernardine's," Wilkerson recalls. "So Miranda and I, we would hitchhike to Santa Cruz and walk on the beach all day. She remembers none of it. It had nothing to do with actions." Even the baby, Bernadine—everyone called her by her nickname, "Redbird"—was used. "I used to take the baby, little Bernadine, down to Hermosa Beach and leave her with 'Big' Bernardine all the time," recalls Marvin Doyle. "It was cover, sure, but it was also a respite for Mona." Paul Bradley recalls a trip in which he was obliged to ferry the baby back north on a commercial flight.

It took time for Dennis Cunningham, who remained in Chicago, to realize what had happened. "[Dohrn] had been interested in me [going underground]," he says, "but they definitely wanted Mona out there, because I think what they wanted most was my kids, to use as 'beards.' I know what Mona did. I know how many of these 'trips' Delia went on with Bernardine. She and the other kids went on actions. Did it upset me? Well, I was indifferent at first, then a little fearful, sure."

As the months stretched into years, all four of Mona Mellis's children grew accustomed to traveling with the Weathermen. Wilkerson drove cross-country with Delia and Miranda at least once. The children were useful ornaments, but other factors were at work. Several of the Weatherwomen were approaching thirty, and a few, like Dohrn and Wilkerson, were struggling with the issue of motherhood. Says Wilkerson of her time with Miranda, "It was all about my biological clock. I had always been a 'kid person,' and then I had given up kids for the revolution." Delia believes she and her siblings served not only as cover but as surrogate children until these women could become mothers themselves. "Bernardine once told me we were the reason she decided to become a mother," Delia remembers. "Until then, she had been wrapped up in this idea that she couldn't and still remain a feminist."

Dennis Cunningham, it turned out, wasn't the only person keeping tabs on what Mona Mellis was up to in San Francisco. At least one of his friends was an FBI informer, and it didn't take long before Mona drew the Bureau's scrutiny. "We got word that Mona was coming out to do her thing with Bernardine," a retired Bay Area FBI agent named William Reagan recalls. "She had been on our radar, but it wasn't till she came out here that things got serious."

"Willie" Reagan wasn't just any FBI man: He was one of the first agents in the Bureau's history to work exclusively undercover. After transferring from Florida, Reagan had been among the first San Francisco agents to begin wearing long hair and hippie attire in 1969; most used this disguise only to infiltrate public meetings and demonstrations. Heavily bearded, a dead ringer for the rock singer David Crosby, Reagan had tracked Weather fugitives in vain since the group's earliest days, hanging out with Abbie Hoffman and other Yippie leaders in hopes of sniffing them out. He had been one of the "beards" on Market Street the day of the Encirclement.

Reagan thought Mona Mellis was the best lead the FBI had gleaned in eighteen frustrating months hunting the Weather leadership. When she and her children rented the apartment in Haight-Ashbury, Reagan moved into the same building. Riffing on his Florida background, he posed as "Bill

Raymond," a fugitive Gulf Coast gambler now working as an accountant for a group of marijuana farmers. "Mona was sharp," Reagan recalls. "I remember the first time I met her, walking up the apartment stairs, probably December '71, she said, 'Who are you?' I said, 'I'm your new neighbor.' She goes, 'How did you get this apartment? I've had friends who wanted to move into this building, and they couldn't get in.' I gave her this long explanation about how I knew some people in the Haight [Haight Ashbury], and that seemed to satisfy her."

Both the FBI and the San Francisco police kept Mona's building under around-the-clock surveillance. They followed most of her visitors, not that it mattered. "We didn't have anything close to modern surveillance procedures," Reagan says with a sigh. "Half the time we had no idea who we were following. They were really good at losing our guys." SFPD detectives, meanwhile, zealously searched the Mellis family's trash. "Oh, God, worst trash you've ever smelled," recalls one retired detective. "Her kids were vegetarians, and those diapers, oh, Jesus. . . ." As the weeks ticked by, Reagan made a habit of encountering Mona in the hallways. They became friendly. Mona was in the process of coming out as a lesbian, and Reagan began accompanying her to a lesbian bar, Maud's, where they played pool.

That winter, in fact, Reagan grew close enough to Mona that she asked him to babysit her children—the very same children who were hanging out with the Weather leadership. But neither the children nor Mona ever said a meaningful word about Bernardine Dohrn or the Weather Underground. The FBI didn't have a clue about Delia's visits with Dohrn; in fact, Reagan didn't learn of Dohrn's relationship with the Mellis children until he was interviewed for this book. At only one point during the six or seven months he lived in their building, he says, did he sense Weather's presence. It came in the spring of 1972, when he agreed to drive Mona to a music festival in Colorado. At the last moment she canceled, then asked Reagan if he would take one of her girlfriends instead. The trip never happened, but Reagan did catch one tantalizing glimpse of the girlfriend when Mona briefly opened her apartment door. The young woman, whoever she was, was wearing a bright red wig, and for a fleeting moment Reagan thought it was Dohrn. He never met her, or saw her again, and shortly afterward transferred to British

Columbia, where he spent the next two years tracking sightings of Weather fugitives. "I don't know whether that was Bernardine or not," he says. "It haunts me to this day."

North of the city, in Marin County, another FBI agent, Bud Watkins, had his own chances to pursue the Weather leadership. Michael Kennedy's law partner, Joe Rhine, had a home on a remote hillside near Point Reyes, and one of his neighbors told a story of encountering Rhine with a woman while out walking. The woman repeatedly turned her face away from the neighbor's gaze, making him suspicious, and during a subsequent visit to the post office the neighbor spied Dohrn's wanted poster. He was certain the woman he had seen was Dohrn, but the FBI, despite another long surveillance, was never able to confirm it.

Watkins felt he got much closer to capturing Kathy Boudin. The Bureau had flagged her fake driver's license, and when the license was entered into a state database following a speeding violation in Marin, Watkins and another agent had an all-points bulletin issued on the car. It was found a few days later in San Anselmo, parked near the home of an attorney with well-known radical sympathies. Surveillance on the car, however, indicated that it had been abandoned. Boudin was never found.

By the beginning of 1972, Weather's energies were ebbing. They were down to fifteen or so active members, and almost all were questioning their reason for being. "There were long periods when not much got done," remembers Ron Fliegelman. "We met with people to raise money, we talked about politics. You read, you talked. It was never boring. It was pleasant."

Weather's leadership, especially Dohrn, spent much of 1972 traveling the country in an effort to rebuild the political and intellectual alliances it had so cavalierly burned after destroying SDS. "By mid-'71 we realized we had pissed too many people off," says Marvin Doyle. "It was time to rebuild those bridges, and Bernardine was really good at that. She was completely sincere."

For most of America, however, Weather simply disappeared. During all of 1972, in fact, it mounted only one action, though its target was significant:

the Pentagon. This lone bombing can be understood in the context of input the leadership was receiving from other radical groups, who felt that protest bombings no longer had much purpose. For Weather to give up bombings altogether, however, would be to disavow everything it had achieved to that point. Dohrn and Ayers, at least, agreed on a new tack: fewer bombings, bigger targets.

A description of the Pentagon bombing is included in Bill Ayers's *Fugitive Days*, and while he uses pseudonyms, it seems clear that members of the New York cell were responsible. The key participant, "Aaron," appears to be a thinly disguised Ron Fliegelman. Fliegelman says he does not remember the incident. "Aaron," Ayers writes, "was the backbone of the group—entirely committed and trustworthy, hardworking and dependable. . . . A guy we all believed could easily survive in the Australian Outback or the Siberian wilderness for weeks with nothing but a pocket knife. . . . The model middle cadre."

The Pentagon was the second of Weather's three "dream" targets, the others being the Capitol, bombed a year earlier, and the White House, which they had "cased" by mingling with tours. "Aaron" was one of three Weathermen who studied the Pentagon off and on for months; the others, a woman Ayers calls "Anna" and a man he calls "Zeke," may well have been Robbie Roth and any one of several female Weathermen. They deposited their dynamite in a rented storage locker and, in keeping with tradition, took a cheap apartment they paid for by the week. "Anna" was their scout, walking into the Pentagon most mornings amid the crowds of incoming office workers. She wore a dark wig and thick glasses, dressed in a suit and carrying a briefcase, and covered her fingertips in clear nail polish, the better to obscure any fingerprints she left behind. In the days before the military tightened its security procedures, she was able to prowl the long miles of hallways unchallenged, usually leaving by 11 a.m. Back at the apartment, she drew elaborate maps from memory. Ayers writes:

> I can do it, she said finally, pulling out her sketches and maps. Here—she
> pointed to an isolated hallway in the basement of the Air Force section—
> I've been here four times, never seen another person, and there's a woman's

room halfway down, right here. She made an X on the map. There's a drain on the floor, narrow but big enough, I think, she said. One more visit was planned in order to unscrew the cover and take the dimensions of the space.

Anna was in the next day at 9:00 AM, and was in the women's room and the stall by 9:10 AM. She locked the door, hung up her jacket, and pulled plastic gloves, a screwdriver, and [a] tape measure from her briefcase. The grated cover was gunky but easy to pop off once the screws were out, and there was a comfortable 4-inch diameter that ran down for over a foot. Anna replaced the drain cover, wiped the area down and was back at the apartment by 10:00 AM.

"Aaron" had the bomb ready when she returned, a foot-long packet of dynamite with fishing line and a hook tied to one end so that it could be lowered into the drain; the final decision to move forward was made only after calls with Dohrn and Ayers. Afterward "Aaron" slid the bomb beneath the papers in Anna's briefcase, and she returned to the Pentagon to place it in the drain. While "Anna and Zeke" left town, "Aaron" spent the rest of the afternoon wiping down the apartment, cleaning the storage locker, and paying their remaining bills. He called in the first warning to the *Washington Post*, making just one slipup: He said a bomb would detonate on the eighth floor, but the Pentagon has only five. At eleven thirty "Aaron" phoned a second warning to the Pentagon's emergency line. The bomb went off just before 1 a.m., right on schedule, demolishing the fourth-floor restroom and sending thousands of gallons of water cascading onto a shopping concourse below.

Among the Weathermen, this was a major strategic victory, a strike inside the heart of America's war machine, by far the most audacious bombing in the group's short history. However, 1972 was not 1970, and in the ensuing days the tenor of mainstream press coverage was far more scathing than after bombings just two years before. In an especially stinging comment, the *New York Times* editorialized:

The bomb explosion at the Pentagon represents a return to the mindless display of violence as a means of registering dissent from the violence of war. The ultraradicals who boast of responsibility for this pointless act

stand totally discredited by the overwhelming mass of the student generation whom they once hoped to enlist in their anarchist ranks. . . . It is
important to recognize the culprits for what they are—not idealistic activists but vandals posing as revolutionaries.

By 1972 the lassitude that pervaded the Weather Underground had spread to
its government pursuers. The roving prosecutor, Guy Goodwin, was still
convening grand juries, but not one had led to a significant arrest, much less
a conviction. The FBI's feckless work, meanwhile, reached a turning point
that spring. For two solid years agents across the country had engaged in a
variety of illegal activities designed to track down Weather's leadership: illegal wiretapping, mail opening, and dozens of break-ins, much of it targeting
the group's families, friends, and supporters—anyone, in short, who might
have the first idea where they were hiding. But by May 1972, when J. Edgar
Hoover died at the age of seventy-seven, the Bureau had precisely one arrest
to show for the risks it had taken: that of Judy Clark outside a Manhattan theater, a matter of sheer luck. Conventional methods had gotten them nowhere.

Privately many officers in the busiest Weatherman squad, New York's
Squad 47, thought Weather no longer warranted the resources the Bureau
was devoting to it; among the nicknames agents pinned on the group was
"the terrible toilet bombers." They even penned a bit of doggerel: "Weatherman, Weatherman, what do you do? Blow up a toilet every year or two."
When the squad's supervisor, John Kearney, retired that June, his men gathered to present him with a gift. "We haven't managed to actually capture any
of the Weather leadership," an agent announced, "but we have come awfully
close." And with a flourish, he produced a clear plastic evidence envelope and
presented it to Kearney, who grinned when he saw its contents: a pair of Bernardine Dohrn's sister Jennifer's panties.

Kearney's replacement was a veteran agent named Horace Beckwith, who
had been working radical cases, including the Sam Melville bombings, since
1966. Beckwith was deeply frustrated by the Bureau's inability to make
arrests. In an attempt to reinvigorate the investigations, senior agents from

around the country gathered in Quantico, Virginia, that June. At such gatherings agents typically referred to ongoing practices of questionable legality—the wiretaps, the break-ins—by euphemisms. That day, however, a Detroit agent rose during the afternoon session and exasperatedly blurted out: "We're doing bag jobs, wires, and [opening] mail. What else can we do?"

The outburst rattled at least one headquarters official, Edward Miller, who headed the internal intelligence division; afterward, he approached a group of senior agents and asked, "Do you think I should be hearing all this?" Indeed, there seemed to be widespread confusion at the top levels of the Bureau as to what methods had been approved and who had approved them. Hoover was dead. His right-hand man, Bill Sullivan, had resigned. No one left in their wake seemed entirely sure what was legal and what wasn't.

Indeed, the legality of many of the FBI's tactics was already being debated in two major court cases, both of which climaxed that June. The first occurred in Detroit, where two years earlier most of the Weatherman leadership had been indicted in a federal court. One of their attorneys, a young New York firebrand named Gerald Lefcourt, repeatedly told the presiding judge, Damon J. Keith, that his clients' families had been the subject of months of illegal burglaries, wiretaps, and "espionage techniques." The press, for the most part, ignored his claims. But Keith, in a startling decision issued June 5, 1972, ordered the government to disclose whether it had actually used burglaries, sabotage, or electronic surveillance techniques in its investigations. Two weeks later, on June 19, the Supreme Court ruled in an unrelated case that warrantless wiretapping was in fact illegal. That same day the U.S. attorney general, Richard Kleindienst, issued a written directive ordering the FBI to immediately stop any and all wiretaps and burglaries that hadn't been authorized by a court. Forty years later Don Strickland insists that no such order was relayed to the agents in Squad 47. "Nobody told us about it, I can tell you that—no one," he says. "We just kept doing what we'd been doing."

Questions about wiretaps and black bag jobs lingered all that summer in the chaos that pervaded FBI headquarters after Hoover's death. A new director, L. Patrick Gray, was named, but for months no one seemed to have a clear sense of how aggressively he wanted to pursue the Weather Underground, which had detonated exactly one bomb in the previous nine months.

Finally, at a meeting of supervisors on August 29, Ed Miller pointedly asked Gray whether black bag jobs would still be allowed. According to Miller, Gray said they would. At the subsequent meeting, Miller recalled, "Gray stood up and he did tell them. He said he had decided to approve surreptitious entries, 'but I want you to make damn sure that none of these are done without prior bureau authorization.'" Afterward Miller telephoned one of his aides, Robert Shackleford, to say break-ins would be resumed. "That's good," Shackleford said, "because they're going on anyway."[1]

Later that fall, reacting to the terrorist attacks at the Olympic Games in Munich, President Nixon issued a secret presidential directive calling for an all-out counterterrorism campaign. In Gray's mind, at least, this included actions against the Weather Underground. He told his No. 2 man, Mark Felt, that he wanted the Weathermen "hunted to exhaustion." Newly emboldened, Squad 47 renewed its illegal activities with a vengeance, initiating black bag jobs against the friends and families of twenty-six Weather fugitives. It was all very secret and all, very clearly now, illegal. That October, in fact, the Justice Department unceremoniously dropped its case against the leadership in Detroit rather than disclose what the FBI was doing. To the Bureau's lasting regret, their activities would not remain secret for long.

11

BLOOD IN THE STREETS OF BABYLON

The Black Liberation Army, 1973

> *I understand I am*
> *Slightly out of fashion.*
> *The in-crowd wants no part of me.*
> *Someone said that I am too sixties*
> *Black.*
> *Someone else told me I had failed to mellow.*
>
> —*Poem by Joanne Chesimard,*
> *aka Assata Shakur*

The year 1973 was pivotal in postwar U.S. history, the year the Vietnam War was effectively lost, the Watergate scandal unraveled, the '60s era finally ended, and "the wave of student uprisings and radicalism," one author notes, "ran its course." The Movement was dead. Abbie Hoffman, arrested on drug charges, went underground, writing a "travel" column for *Crawdaddy* magazine about his clandestine life. H. Rap Brown was in prison. Huey Newton fled to Cuba. Timothy Leary was arrested in Afghanistan and returned to give grand jury testimony against the Weather Underground. The previous autumn the government of Algeria had finally thrown the Panthers out of their beloved embassy. Washing up in Paris, Eldridge Cleaver glumly told reporters the revolution was over; he had lost.

A new conservative mood was afoot, a reaction to '60s excesses, especially the wave of drugs whose abuses and attendant violence had turned swaths of cities from San Francisco to New York into what the press liked to call war zones. Crime soared. The harsh Rockefeller drug laws passed in New York. The White House called for the death penalty. Nothing worked. It was, the author Andreas Killen notes, "a genuine low point in American history."

Nowhere was the clash between revolutionary diehards and a public newly incensed at drugs and violence more vividly on display than in the bloody final months of the Black Liberation Army. The BLA's last chapter began in the darkness before dawn on October 23, 1972. Lower Manhattan was quiet that morning, but deep inside the Manhattan House of Detention, the granite fortress known as the Tombs, seven men were busy at work—with hacksaw blades. One was Anthony "Kimu" White, a twenty-four-year-old BLA recruit. White had been in jail since taking part in the Harlem shootout that helped give birth to the BLA, the Plate Steward incident in April 1971.

After a headcount at 6:15 a.m., the seven men began sawing through four steel bars in their fourth-floor cell area. Once finished, they crawled across a thirty-foot gangplank spanning an unused area of the jail that had been damaged in a 1970 rebellion. At the end of the gangplank, the men crawled up a sixteen-foot wall to a tiny window, where they sawed through another set of steel bars. Squeezing through, they dropped a bedsheet ladder to a parking lot forty feet below. A guard spotted them at 6:25 a.m., just as the last inmate leaped to the pavement and dashed into the gathering dawn. It was the first escape from the Tombs since it opened in 1941.* And though no one knew it, it would reinvigorate what remained of the Black Liberation Army in New York.

Kimu White wasted little time reuniting with his comrades in the New York BLA cell, one of only two cells still at large; the other was a group of West Coast exiles robbing banks in the New Orleans area. The New York cell was down to fifteen or so desperate members, hunted, scattered, constantly on the move among squalid apartments in Harlem, Brooklyn, and the Bronx. The wild-eyed Twymon Meyers was one, along with his pals Avon White and Fred Hilton, who had rejoined the BLA after serving brief terms

---

*Authorities later arrested two of the men's girlfriends and accused them of smuggling in hacksaw blades.

in North Carolina jails after the November 1971 shooting of a sheriff's deputy. To the extent that these last survivors had any true leadership, it had fallen to the unlikeliest field marshal in the annals of black revolutionaries: twenty-five-year-old Joanne Chesimard, who was poised to become the most wanted female in New York history.

Chesimard went by many names. Her family knew her as Joey. In underground circles, where she would become an icon, she would be known as Assata Shakur. She had grown up in Queens with a troubled mother, but she was smart and pretty. Small and quiet, she had been a student at City College before she began running with the Panthers. She attended her share of protests, but otherwise little is known of her Panther career until an incident in March 1971—during the violence of the Panther split—when she was shot in the stomach during some kind of robbery at a Midtown Manhattan hotel, probably an early BLA drug rip-off. She had been with Dhoruba Moore at 757 Beck Street, where she distinguished herself as a medic, and later with the BLA contingent in Atlanta. She was little known to the public during her years underground, but her notoriety skyrocketed once her career came to an end. It was then that the *New York Daily News* dubbed her "Sister Love." It was then that the NYPD began referring to her as the "heart and soul" of the BLA.

Whatever you called her, no one could deny she became a defining symbol of the underground era. Where Bernardine Dohrn's name sometimes drew snickers from the most hard-core radicals, Chesimard would be viewed in the underground as perhaps the purest expression of revolutionary ardor, a ferocious, machine-gun-toting, grenade-tossing, spitting-mad Bonnie Parker for the 1970s, an archetype for a series of badass heroines heralded in *Foxy Brown*, *Get Christie Love!*, and other blaxploitation films of the day. It was a powerful image: In time, Chesimard's visage would hang alongside those of Che Guevara and Malcolm X on the walls of scores of revolutionary venues. But while she was an angry young woman who almost certainly robbed banks and conspired in attacks on policemen, Chesimard left many more questions than answers in her wake. Forty years ago the NYPD cast her as the BLA's last and greatest leader, blaming her for scores of crimes. There proved precious little evidence to back up these assertions, however, and today the handful of detectives still investigating the old BLA cases question almost all of these claims.

"Chesimard," rasps one New York investigator, "is no fucking saint, but was she the heart and soul of the BLA? Hell, no. The guys back then demonized her because, unlike the others, she was educated. She was young and pretty. I can point to at least two other women in the BLA who were more important than Joanne Chesimard ever was. We created that myth. The cops did." Adds a longtime BLA attorney, Robert Boyle, "Assata was never this massively important figure the police portrayed her as. She was important, but the police made up this mythic image of a super black woman, with the afro and the machine gun. She was never that."

Divining the truth about Chesimard is not easy. During the 1970s few journalists took the trouble to learn her story; what little they wrote came from police, whose theories proved unsupportable. Since then she has been the subject of two books, an autobiography and a memoir written by her aunt, who was also her attorney; both are notable for dwelling solely on her early and later life, leaving a gaping hole where one expects to find details of her career with the BLA. What is known is that in 1972, in the months after the Foster-Laurie murders, Chesimard and the other BLA survivors limped back from St. Louis and Cleveland and Miami to the only city they knew, New York, and attempted to regroup. No coherent story of their lives that year has ever emerged, only allegations of various outer-borough armed robberies that eventually led to trials and, typically, not-guilty verdicts. When it was finally over, the FBI and the NYPD would take some bare-bones statements from captured BLA members, but the few documents that survive give little sense of the desperate lives they must have led.

Typical was the statement given by BLA member Ronald Anderson, a veteran of the Atlanta training camp. Anderson was one of the three BLA men who escaped from an Atlanta jail in November 1971 and spent the following weeks picking tomatoes in Florida. According to his statement, the trio finally raised enough cash for the long bus trip back to New York in January 1972. They hid in a relative's home in the Bronx for a month, living on money from one of their mothers. After that they split up. Lumumba Shakur found an apartment for Anderson and John Thomas's onetime No. 2, Andrew

Jackson, on Dean Street in Brooklyn, where they lived with two Panther women who supported them by working as prostitutes in a Manhattan massage parlor. That spring, Anderson said, they finally met with Joanne Chesimard in the Brownsville section of Brooklyn. She said she was leading a bank-robbery gang with Twymon Meyers and two other BLA soldiers and offered them a place in it; Anderson insists that he declined.

By the beginning of 1973, both the FBI and NYPD investigations of the BLA were languishing. In the ten months since the shoot-out in St. Louis, precisely two BLA members had been captured. When an NYPD lieutenant named James Motherway arrived at his new assignment in the Major Case Squad's Thirteenth Division, he found morale among the detectives low. No fewer than eight groups were hunting the BLA at that point—including detective squads in Queens, Brooklyn, and the Bronx, plus district attorneys in Brooklyn and Queens—apparently without talking with one another, much less the FBI. The NYPD was further hamstrung by two bugaboos of mid-1970s policing: the department's newfound sensitivities about race, and a lengthy corruption inquiry.

A snapshot of the situation is offered in Motherway's unpublished memoir. "So what's the problem?" he recalls asking the assembled BLA investigators one morning in early 1973. No one responded. At first no one wanted to be seen criticizing the department—"the kiss of death," in Motherway's words. "Maybe these pussies are afraid to talk, but I'm not," a bellicose detective named Joe Tidmarsh finally piped up. "You wanna know what's wrong? I'll tell ya. The bosses won't turn us loose. We have a dozen leads they won't let us follow. Did you know we aren't allowed to go into Harlem after dark?"

"No," Motherway said, skeptical. "I didn't."

"Yeah," Tidmarsh went on, "the Deputy Chief [of detectives] is afraid we'll cause a riot or shoot someone. It might ruin his chance for promotion." Another detective chimed in, "Did you know we have a tap on Twymon Meyers's mother's phone? Last week we hear her telling her niece that she was going to meet 'baby.' That's Twymon. Here she's going to meet the guy we know has killed a half-dozen cops and we couldn't tail her because it was nighttime in Harlem."

Motherway left the meeting shaken. By coincidence, a few days later the new chief of detectives, Louis Cottell, sent an inspector to find out why the BLA cases were stalled. Motherway was the last of the squad's lieutenants to be interviewed. Certain he was risking his career, he decided to relay the detectives' complaints. Three days later the deputy chief was replaced. The squad now reported directly to Cottell. Morale rose. Detectives were allowed into Harlem at night. Suddenly they began aggressively pursuing a host of new leads.

One involved two BLA members, Woody Green and Kimu White, the Tombs escapee. One detective learned that Green's wedding anniversary was January 23. Certain Green would see his wife, he asked for surveillance. Motherway approved it. That evening detectives followed Green's wife to the Big T Lounge in Bushwick, Brooklyn. Sipping coffee in unmarked cars outside, they spotted Green walking into the bar at midnight. Two detectives, Cleave Bethea and Philip Hogan, were sent in to confirm the identification. As they entered, they made eye contact with Green, who was standing at the bar alongside White and a dozen patrons. Suddenly both Green and White drew pistols and opened fire.

Hit by bullets in the left arm and leg, Bethea fell to the floor and passed out. Hogan, struck in the shoulder, rolled through the lounge's door onto the sidewalk. Nine detectives leaped from their cars, unsheathed pistols, and laid shotguns across the hoods of parked cars. Inside, the bar went quiet. The patrons flattened themselves on the floor. Within minutes more than a dozen patrol cars began squealing to stops all around. When two detectives attempted to peer through the lounge's window, gunfire erupted from within, sending them scurrying for cover. Up and down the street, cops returned fire. Their bullets blasted the Big T Lounge to shreds, smashing windows and riddling the walls behind the bar. When everything finally went quiet, a detective crawled through the front door. He found White and Green dead on the floor. Miraculously, none of the other patrons were injured.

To the press, it was just another BLA shoot-out; the *Daily News* carried the story on page 8, while the *Times* chose page 48. To Joanne Chesimard and the remaining members of the BLA, however, it was as if the NYPD had violated a months-long ceasefire. Months later, a rare glimpse of the group's inner workings at the time would be provided by a captured BLA soldier, Avon White. According to White, Chesimard convened a strategy meeting the night after the shootout in a ratty safe-house apartment in the Bronx. She argued for immediate retaliation. The others—a soldier named Melvin Kearney, Zayd Shakur, Freddie Hilton—agreed. That same night they stole a car in Brooklyn. Guns, they had.

The next evening, Thursday, January 25, a frigid north wind was blowing as two brothers, Officers Carlo and Vincent Imperato, climbed into their radio car at the East New York Avenue station in Brooklyn. It was a routine patrol, at least until seven forty-five, when Carlo, who was driving, stopped at a red light on Newport Street.

Glancing to his left, Carlo was startled to see a black man in a raincoat step out of a parked car and aim an automatic rifle directly at him. It was a BLA man, Melvin Kearney.

"Duck!" Carlo yelled.

Bullets shattered the driver's-side window; one struck Carlo in the left shoulder, and flying glass gashed his brother's arm. Vincent drew his revolver and squeezed off two shots as Carlo mashed the accelerator and the patrol car surged forward, barreling through the intersection. Behind them Kearney kept firing; police would find twenty-three bullet casings scattered on the pavement. The brothers drove themselves to Brookdale Hospital, where they were treated and released.*

COP BROTHERS SHOT IN B'KLYN AMBUSH, screamed the *Daily News* headline the next day. The police commissioner, Patrick Murphy, chose his words carefully: "We are very disturbed at this time because this was a deliberate attack without provocation. I'm very troubled, upset and angry about this

---

*According to Avon White, gunmen that night were Kearney, Zayd Shakur, and Fred Hilton. Only Kearney, armed with a Browning automatic, appears to have fired. Shakur and Hilton remained in the parked car. The shooting of the Imperato brothers led to a change in NYPD policy that remains in place to this day: Relatives can no longer ride in the same squad car.

trend of violence shown against the police. This violence must cease. We ask the public to condemn this behavior."

Everyone assumed it was the BLA. After a year in the shadows, the shooting thrust the group back onto the front pages. As it happened, the Imperato shootings came just days after a series of attacks in New Orleans in which a black radical named Mark Essex shot nineteen people, killing nine, including five police officers; some believed that Essex was a member of the BLA. Suddenly the dormant debate about the BLA's existence reignited. In a lengthy article, the *New York Times* asked the central question: "Are there really organized cells of blacks dedicated to the ambush of urban patrolmen? Or if nothing that extensive, are there a handful of 'guerrilla' assassins moving from city to city and getting help from friends along the way? . . . Talk of conspiracy has become virtually a reflex response to such incidents in the last few years, and yet in no single case has it ever been substantiated."[1] The *Times* polled police officials across the country. Some believed that the BLA was a nationwide conspiracy. Most scoffed at the idea.

Whatever was happening, the NYPD was taking no chances. The morning after the Imperato shootings, Mayor Lindsay approved the police commissioner's plan to flood the northern sections of Brooklyn with officers allotted a thousand hours of overtime. Meanwhile, safely back in the Bronx, Chesimard, Zayd Shakur, and the others were incensed that the Imperato brothers had survived. They plotted a follow-up attack, this time determined to take a life—"the reasoning being," Avon White told the NYPD months later, "that the pigs did not die in Brooklyn."

On the evening of Saturday, January 27, two nights after the Imperato attack, the group split into two squads and walked out into the chilly night to hunt and kill a cop. Chesimard and Meyers spent several hours canvassing the streets of the Bronx but were unable to find a suitable ambush target. The second group, the same trio who had attacked the Imperatos, took a stolen red GTO and patrolled Queens. Eventually they parked on Baisley Boulevard in the St. Albans section and took their positions around an intersection, waiting for a patrol car to stop. Kearney sagged inside a phone booth. Across the way, Hilton hid a machine pistol beneath his coat. Shakur watched the oncoming traffic, nursing a hidden shotgun.

Finally, a little past midnight, a patrol car containing two officers stopped in their sights. All three men whipped out their guns and began firing. The driver, Officer Roy Pollina, ducked down and hit the gas, smashing into the fender of a car in front of him. A bullet grazed his forehead. As the firing continued, Pollina regained his senses and raced from the scene. His partner suffered a shoulder wound. Police would find twenty-eight shell casings at the intersection.

The next day, confronted by two attacks in fifty-three hours, the mayor threw out any pretense of diplomacy. At a press conference Lindsay announced that an extra six thousand police officers were being hired at a cost of $13 million. Asked if he considered the BLA attacks a "crisis situation," he replied, "When you have a pattern like these vicious attacks of police officers, I would call it a crisis. No one is going to rest until this group is arrested and brought to justice."

The newspapers began to change their tone. On January 26, in a story pegged to the police shootings in New Orleans, the *Times* headline had read, OFFICIALS DOUBT A PLOT BY BLACKS TO KILL WHITE POLICEMEN. Three mornings later, after two new BLA ambushes, the headline read, LIBERATION UNIT RATED AS MURDEROUS.

The furor over the BLA's sudden legitimization climaxed two weeks later, when *New York* magazine published an excerpt from a forthcoming book called *Target Blue*. It was written by none other than Robert Daley, the NYPD's onetime spokesman—he had resigned—and while it covered many topics, the most explosive parts dealt with the BLA. Using information gleaned while in office, Daley laid bare the story of the 1971 New York and San Francisco attacks and argued they were the work of a single, nationwide militant group. For the first time the debate over the BLA washed into the national press, though many writers and book reviewers remained skeptical. As Gerald M. Astor, who termed Daley "a pistol-packin' flack with literary ambitions," noted in a review of *Target Blue* in *Washington Monthly*:

> Conspiracy claims by the cops have a bad habit of collapsing. . . . A top
> police investigator of the recent assaults . . . has said of the conspiracy the-
> ory: "A few dozen guys in different places happen to know each other and

share a certain affinity, so one of them sits down at a typewriter and taps out B.L.A. But in numbers and in administrative structure they don't make it an army."

The irony was that Daley was largely correct. While hardly an army, the BLA was real, and it was a multistate conspiracy, if a desperate and sloppy one. But the fact that the man promoting this idea was also promoting a book did little to convince the skeptics. Still, the growing acceptance of the BLA's existence, at least in New York, had an impact in the streets, where shootings by jittery policemen were becoming almost routine. Every day or two brought a new incident, most having nothing to do with the BLA. When gunfire struck a squad car on Long Island, the papers were filled with stories about the BLA invading the suburbs; it turned out to be a stray bullet from a firing range. A single day, March 6, brought a pair of Bronx shootings. In the first, police tried to stop a gypsy cab they believed had been carjacked. When the car pulled over, three men jumped out and sprayed the cruiser with gunfire; this may well have been Twymon Meyers and two confederates. (POLICE CAR BLASTED BY BRONX GUNMAN, read the *Daily News* headline.) Twenty minutes earlier, a pair of patrolmen cruising 168th Street thought they recognized Meyers. When they called him by name, he ran. At Franklin Avenue, he tried to flag a cab. When the cab wouldn't stop, Meyers turned and fired a pistol at the pursuing officers. One, William Hoy, got out and chased Meyers on foot through crowds to Fulton Avenue until, after running for blocks, Meyers vanished. "It was him," Hoy said later. "I know his picture better than my own kids'."

In those tense late-winter weeks, BLA soldiers emerged as New York's new boogeymen, spotted at every robbery, blamed for every unexplained shooting. Meyers was one of three BLA soldiers named in the April 10 robbery of a bank on Northern Boulevard in Queens. Another, named Victor Cumberbatch, was so spooked that he pulled a gun on two telephone repairmen, thinking they were police; the Brooklyn district attorney tried to indict him for kidnapping. Other soldiers were blamed for a string of supermarket and bodega robberies. When a new police commissioner, Donald F. Cawley, took office that April, one of his first actions was to summon the chief of detectives, Louis Cottell, into his Centre Street office and make clear his top priority.

"The Black Liberation Army," Cawley growled. "Get the bastards." He added: "Louie, think big."[2]

Cottell, in turn, brought in a plumpish, sandy-haired deputy chief named Harold Schryver, a twenty-seven-year NYPD veteran. Given wide latitude to apprehend the BLA's leadership, Schryver consolidated the three detective squads working BLA cases. To analyze the myriad threads of information the squads had gathered, he hit upon the novel idea of entering it all into a Hazeltine 2000 computer he arranged for the department to rent. Two detectives were sent to training courses to figure out how to use it. Detectives were still mastering the computer's intricacies when, on May 2, the word came from New Jersey. It was Joanne Chesimard.

Later there would be considerable speculation about where they were headed, the BLA's last two intellectual leaders, Joanne Chesimard and little Zayd Shakur, the "field mouse," who was a long way from the moment when Jane Fonda bailed him out of jail three years before. Some said they were heading to hide with family members in Philadelphia or Atlantic City. Others thought they were en route to Washington. Their destination, however, was beside the point. What mattered was their desperate need to escape the police dragnet in New York, and the poor choices they made that night of May 2 in order to do so. In fact, they were breaking every rule of underground survival. They were driving in a car, they were driving at night, and worst of all, they were driving on the New Jersey Turnpike, a highway, then as now, where state troopers had a reputation for stopping and searching cars driven by black men.

A little before midnight they drove out of the city and stopped their battered white Pontiac LeMans for snacks at the Alexander Hamilton rest stop north of Newark. Forty-five minutes later, at twelve forty-five, they were speeding south, passing through the central New Jersey city of New Brunswick, when they saw the trooper behind them, lights rolling. Their driver, a onetime Panther named Clark Squire, pulled to the side of the highway. The trooper, twenty-nine-year-old James M. Harper, called for backup even before approaching the car, which was standard procedure; he later said he stopped the car because it had a faulty taillight. A second trooper, thirty-five-year-old Werner Foerster, pulled up moments later. As it happened, the three cars were now lined up barely two hundred yards south of state police headquarters.

Trooper Harper took Squire's driver's license, then asked him to stand behind the car with Trooper Foerster. Harper next leaned into the car to examine the serial number on the driver's-side door. As he did, he noticed that the woman sitting in the front seat seemed fidgety. The small, light-skinned man in the backseat sat frozen, his eyes glassy.

Suddenly, from behind the car, Foerster said, "Jim, look what I found." Harper looked back and saw Foerster holding up a clip from an automatic pistol. He quickly turned his attention back to the man and the woman inside the car and told them not to move. He saw Joanne Chesimard reach beneath her right leg. A moment later the gun was in her hand. She fired from barely three feet away. "Her eyes went wide open, her teeth were showing," Harper testified months later. "She fired a shot. I felt the pain in my shoulder."

Staggering, Harper managed to draw his revolver and fire several shots into the car, striking both Chesimard and Zayd Shakur. One bullet struck Shakur flush in the chest, mortally wounding him. Behind the car, Clark Squire and Trooper Foerster began grappling. At some point Squire grabbed Foerster's gun and shot him in the head.

Harper, now outnumbered three to one, ran for the headquarters building. As he did, Squire jumped back in the Le Mans and drove off. When Harper reached the building, he managed to say, "I've been shot," before collapsing. A description of the Le Mans was immediately broadcast. Minutes later a trooper saw it parked on the side of the turnpike, five miles south. As he screeched to a stop he saw a man running away, toward a wooded area. He yelled for him to halt, then fired a wild shot when he didn't; Squire was found hiding in nearby woods the next day. The trooper found Chesimard lying beside the car, bleeding lightly from a wound in the chest, and Shakur, who was dead. Chesimard was taken to a hospital, where she recovered.

The next day Joanne Chesimard's face—puffy, with full lips and a medium

Afro—stared out from the front of every New York newspaper; the *Daily News* coverage spread across six pages, two just of photos. It was a singular moment in underground history, the first time the press was obliged to introduce and attempt to explain a black revolutionary—and an attractive woman at that—to a mainstream audience. The *Daily News* termed Chesimard not only "the high priestess of the cop-hating Black Liberation Army" but a "black Joan of Arc." The *Times* called her the "soul" of the BLA. Yet even then the news failed to catch the national imagination. As it had from the start, the BLA remained largely a New York story. It would take time for Chesimard's legend to spread.

Two contrasting funerals ensued. In East Brunswick, New Jersey, the governor led a crowd of 3,500 mourners at Trooper Werner Foerster's simple twenty-minute service. His body was taken to a cemetery in a procession of five hundred police cars. Meanwhile, in Harlem, Zayd Shakur, his body wrapped in a white shroud, lay in state at the Marcus Jackson Funeral Home. Hundreds of people, almost all of them black, filed past; fliers outside urged readers to "Support the Black Liberation Army."

"The blood was no super nigger, or super star," a BLA communiqué announced. "He was just a nigger that was tired of the Racist Pig cops shooting down unarmed brothers and sisters in the streets. . . . The nigger felt the correct method for obtaining liberation here in Babylon was through Revolutionary violence. . . . We will bury our dead, clean our guns and prepare for the next battle."

Joanne Chesimard's capture was a crushing blow for the dozen or so BLA members still hiding in New York. Eldridge Cleaver's onetime courier, Denise Oliver, now living underground with the BLA's Andrew Jackson, wrote of their mounting desperation in a diary the NYPD later discovered. "Each day only brings more bad news, more deaths, more captures," she wrote. "Old friends hit the dust . . . and we are helpless . . . in touch with nothing but the TV. . . . Sexless, but comrades." The day after Chesimard's capture, she wrote: "I don't know if [Jackson] turning himself in is the answer.

But to keep running seems futile. In the end, jail or death is the resolution. So why postpone it?"

Both the FBI and the NYPD, now working together, sensed the momentum shifting. "In my view, the BLA (and related groups) are hard pressed to find the type of 'home base' support they need to conduct their terrorist tactics at this time," New York's police commissioner, Don Cawley, wrote in a memo to his top men on May 30. "In short, they are on the run and appear to be leaderless. . . . The best defense is a good offense. We should quickly move forward and place as much pressure on these revolutionaries as possible."

Suddenly doors began opening. That spring, either just before or after Chesimard's capture, three FBI agents who had been working BLA cases since the beginning—Jim Murphy, Bob McCartin, and a youngster named Danny Coulson—secured an informant. "We really believed in pursuing informants; that had been our highest priority for two years," McCartin recalls. "And finally, you know, we got one." The informant was a jailed BLA member's girlfriend; she too faced charges and began cooperating with the FBI to avoid them. Her identity, which has never been revealed, is being withheld here as well; the woman is alive today and in her sixties.

The informant, who remained in contact with several other group members' companions, furnished tips that allowed the FBI to identify a series of BLA hideouts and rendezvous points. The first involved a meeting between two of the BLA's most wanted members: Freddie Hilton and Twymon Meyers, the teenagers who had assassinated Officer James Greene in Atlanta in 1971. The pair was planning to meet on the morning of June 7 on New Lots Avenue in Brooklyn; both the FBI and the NYPD were waiting. A vivid glimpse of what happened next was given in Danny Coulson's 1999 memoir, *No Heroes.*

The FBI contingent was holed up in an elderly gentleman's apartment across the street. ("I don't take to no cop killers," the man explained, "so you can use the place.") A group of NYPD detectives dressed as a construction crew sprawled across a stoop down the street; as the FBI men watched, the cops cracked open two six packs of beer and lazily passed them around. Up and down the street, FBI agents and NYPD officers crawled into sniper positions along the rooftops.

A few minutes before eleven Freddie Hilton appeared, as promised. He walked halfway up the block and peered down toward the construction crew, which made a little show of guzzling their beers. In the apartment above, Danny Coulson took out a .308-caliber Remington sniper rifle and trained it on Hilton's chest. Through the scope, he could make out the slight bulge on Hilton's hip.

"Murph," he radioed Jim Murphy, "put it out that he has a pistol in his waistband, left side, butt forward."

Suddenly the distant cry of a police siren could be heard. As the FBI men exchanged glances, it drew nearer. On the sidewalk, Hilton glanced up and down the street, then studied the surrounding buildings. Coulson eased back into the darkened apartment. As each moment passed, the siren grew nearer until, to Coulson's dismay, a patrol car appeared at the head of the street. "Shit, there it is, down to our left," an FBI man whispered. Once again Coulson trained his rifle on Hilton's chest, ready to fire if he made a move toward the approaching car.

As the others watched, the patrol car slid down the street. As it approached Hilton, he edged into the shadow of a doorway. The car passed him and came to a stop sixty feet beyond, in front of the building at 440 New Lots. Hilton stepped out of the doorway and watched as two uniformed officers got out, trotted up the steps, and disappeared inside. With Coulson's rifle still trained on his chest, Hilton, evidently curious, sauntered down toward the patrol car. As he did, shots rang out from the rooftop. Hilton jumped in surprise, then craned his neck skyward. He never saw the two NYPD detectives who barreled into him from behind, tackling him to the pavement.

It took several minutes for everyone to understand what had happened. As it turned out, a woman living at 440 New Lots had seen plainclothes officers on her roof and, mistaking them for burglars, called the Liberty Avenue station, which dispatched the patrol car. The responding officers crept up a stairwell to the roof entry, where, through the crack of a door, they glimpsed what appeared to be a man pointing a shotgun at them. One officer fired three shots through the door, hitting forty-four-year-old Williams Jakes of the Major Case Squad in the stomach. "We're police officers!" the men on the roof shouted. The officer in the stairwell tossed his police hat through the door. A badge came whistling down the stairs in response. It was friendly fire.

Fred Hilton was handcuffed, bundled into a police car, and taken for fingerprinting, after which he was shoved into a car full of FBI men for the short drive to a federal magistrate. "So who are you guys?" Hilton asked at one point. Coulson, Murphy, and the others introduced themselves. "Oh, I heard of you guys," Hilton said, daring a smile. "We know who's chasing us, you know."

"Fred," Coulson said, "if you know our names, why didn't you just call us and surrender? Our number's in the book, you know."

"You guys just don't get it, do you?" Hilton snapped. "We're at war. The people are at war with this fascist government. I'm a soldier on my side, and you guys are soldiers on your side, and we won't ever surrender." Coulson twisted to face him. "No, Freddie, we're not at war," he said. "If we were at war, you'd have a great big hole in your chest from my rifle." Fred Hilton said no more.[3]

Once again Twymon Meyers had gotten away, but later that day Jim Murphy got a follow-up tip from their informant, this one on the BLA's dashing Andrew Jackson. According to the informant, Jackson was holed up with Denise Oliver in a flat at 158th and Amsterdam Avenue in Harlem. FBI agents surrounded the building the next morning. Jim Murphy and another agent swung a battering ram, knocking the apartment's door off its hinges. An agent named Errol Meyers barged inside, then into the bedroom, where Jackson was in bed with Oliver. Slowly he put up his hands. "Don't shoot, man," he said. "Don't shoot."

After three high-profile arrests orchestrated by the FBI, it was time for the NYPD's retooled, computerized BLA squad to make its mark. The good news, as far as Chief Harold Schryver was concerned, was that there were only a handful of hardened BLA soldiers still at large; the bad news was that they were the most desperate and dangerous of all. In mid-September, days after the onetime Panther Herman Bell and several others were arrested for a string of bank robberies in New Orleans, the New York Transit Police received a tip that a BLA soldier named Robert "Seth" Hayes, wanted for shooting a transit cop that June, was holed up in a tenement apartment at 1801 Bryant Avenue in the Bronx. Surveillance suggested that a number of people appeared to be living with him, including three women and at least one infant.

Early in the evening of September 17, police quietly surrounded the building. The apartment, a double-sized unit with doors labeled "B" and "C," was on the first floor. Just before eight o'clock a group of nine NYPD detectives carrying battering rams hustled inside the building and rushed the two doors. Door B, a metal door, refused to budge; after two strikes from a battering ram, neither would Door C. At that point someone inside the apartment opened fire with a shotgun. One final heave of the battering ram and Door C flew open. Six detectives rushed into the dim apartment, whose sole adornment appeared to be a poster of George Jackson on one wall. Hayes emerged from a bedroom, holding a shotgun at his waist. He fired, striking a detective named Melvin Betty in the hand. Betty staggered back into the corridor.

The apartment erupted in gunfire as Hayes disappeared back into the bedroom, the detectives firing wildly in his direction. Inside, a woman began screaming, "My baby! My baby is in here!" It was bedlam. Two detectives tried to duck into the living room, only to be driven back by fire from an unseen gunman. Hayes poked his shotgun out from the bedroom door and fired another blast. A pair of detectives grabbed the smoking barrel, pushed Hayes back inside the room, and tackled him on a bed as a woman and her seventeen-day-old daughter screamed in a corner.

For a moment the apartment went silent. Detectives furiously reloaded their weapons, at one point sliding pistols across the floor to beef up their arsenal. Suddenly a detective named Maximo Jimenez, struck by a glancing bullet in the buttocks, saw something rolling out of the living room toward him. It was a smoke bomb. Thinking fast, Jimenez reached out his foot and kicked it back into the living room, which began to fill with smoke. "We were shouting things like, 'You're surrounded, throw out your guns and come out with your hands up,'" one detective later told the *Daily News*. "What they were shouting back wasn't printable." After several more staccato exchanges of gunfire, someone from within the living room shouted, "We give up!"

Coughing and hacking, two BLA soldiers, Melvin Kearney—wanted in connection with the police shootings early that year—and Avon White, walked out, hands in the air. The trio's three girlfriends eventually scurried out through the smoke as well. Three detectives were wounded. In a press conference afterward Police Commissioner Cawley—overjoyed—called the raid "a monumental event."

It was almost over. With most of the BLA now off the streets, the head of the Major Case Squad, Harold Schryver, decided to make an all-out effort to bring in the last and deadliest of its gunmen, Twymon Meyers. The morning after the Bronx gunfight, the FBI named him to its Ten Most Wanted Fugitives list. Leads came in slowly, most on buildings in the South Bronx where Meyers had been seen. They found apartments on 117th and 118th Streets that he had used months before. Finally, in October, they unearthed a hideout on 116th Street that hadn't been reoccupied in the weeks since Meyers had left. The apartment was filthy, strewn with trash, and infested with rats. In the garbage detectives found a receipt for a money order issued by a store in the Bronx. At the store a clerk handed over the original order, made out to a real estate company. A visit to the real estate company revealed that the money had been used to rent an apartment at 263 West 118th Street, which also had not been reoccupied since Meyers had last used it. Inside detectives found a copy of the *Amsterdam News* with the page carrying apartment listings torn out. They concluded that Meyers was using it to rent his hideouts.

Unfortunately there were more than a hundred such listings in every issue, far too many to canvass. Then, on November 7, came the break. One of Meyers's bank-robbing partners, Joe Lee Jones, surrendered to the FBI on an old charge of deserting from the army. NYPD detectives interrogated him the next day. Jones, who was deathly afraid of Meyers, said Meyers moved apartments every few weeks. He had no idea where he was. But he mentioned a remark by Meyers's girlfriend in which she spoke of moving into a freshly painted flat. Detectives checked the *Amsterdam News*: Only eleven places were advertised as newly painted. It took six days to rule out ten of them. On November 14 they discreetly interviewed neighbors around the eleventh, a third-floor set of rooms in a tenement at 625 Tinton Avenue in the Bronx. From their descriptions the occupants had to be Meyers and his girlfriend.

Both the NYPD and the FBI sent every man they had. By early afternoon, when the girlfriend left the building and was positively identified, there were nearly 150 policemen and federal agents in the area, about a dozen undercover men on Tinton Avenue itself. Armed with flak jackets, shotguns, and automatic weapons, they were ready for war.

The day stretched by with no sign of Meyers. Finally, around 7:15 p.m., a man wearing a ski cap emerged from the building. He looked like Meyers.

It was, in fact, Meyers. Unaware of the small army around him, he strolled around the corner onto 152nd Street, then disappeared into a bodega. When he came out, a detective named Kernal Holland was closest to him. Holland knew that Meyers usually carried an automatic pistol beneath his coat. When Meyers turned down the street, Holland stepped forward, grabbed his arm, and barked, "Freeze! Police!"

Meyers wheeled. His eyes met Holland's and widened. He took two steps back, pulled a 9mm submachine gun, and opened fire. Holland rolled to the pavement and shot back. The quiet Bronx neighborhood exploded as FBI men and plainclothesmen up and down the street drew their guns and fired. Wounded, Meyers wildly fired his 9mm, then frantically drew a second submachine gun from beneath his coat. It was no use. No one could have survived the blizzard of bullets directed his way. Twymon Meyers, out for a stroll on a cold New York night, was cut to pieces.

His funeral in Harlem made a deep impression on any number of white radicals who attended. The young Italian émigré Silvia Baraldini, who would later rob banks alongside black militants, gave a friend a religious icon to place inside the coffin. "You had to run this gauntlet of police sharpshooters to go into the funeral," she remembers. "Seeing all these sharpshooters, on practically every rooftop in Harlem, you realized there really was a war going on. I think that was the day I decided to join them."

It was over—the shooting, at least. A few stragglers would pull a bank job or two in coming months, but the BLA's days as a legitimate urban guerrilla force were at an end. The trials of its members would stretch on for years, with one or two serving as rallying points for what remained of the radical underground. The memory of the BLA itself blurred and then dimmed and then, in the minds of an American public that took little notice of it anyway, winked out altogether.

Even in custody BLA fighters refused to surrender. Henry "Sha Sha" Brown, captured in St. Louis, managed to escape but was recaptured a week later. Melvin Kearney, held on the eighth floor of the Brooklyn House of Detention, tied together bedsheets and shimmied out a window, only to fall to his death when they unraveled.

Forty-two years later six onetime BLA fighters remain alive in U.S. prisons. The murders of Greg Foster and Rocco Laurie of the NYPD remain officially unsolved. Of the dozens of onetime Panthers who served in the BLA, only a handful would soldier on, and only one would make his mark doing so. In 1973, still a fugitive, still the only veteran of Eldridge Cleaver's Algerian adventure vowing to continue the struggle, the man known as Sekou Odinga melted into the shadows of New York City and, with a handful of recruits, began robbing banks.

Part Three

THE SECOND
WAVE

12

THE DRAGON UNLEASHED

*The Rise of the Symbionese Liberation Army,
November 1973 to February 1974*

> Believe me, my friend, with the time and the incentive
> that these brothers have to read, study and think, you will
> find no class or category more aware, more embittered,
> desperate or dedicated to the ultimate remedy—revolution.
> The most dedicated, the best of our kind—you will find
> them in the Folsoms, San Quentins, and Soledads. They
> live like there was no tomorrow.
>
> —*George Jackson*, **Soledad Brother**

> When the prison gates fly open, the real dragons will
> emerge.
>
> —*Ho Chi Minh*

The death of Twymon Meyers in 1973 should have signaled an end to what
remained of the underground movement. The BLA had now been defeated.
Only the Weather Underground soldiered on, a shadow of its former self, its
isolated leadership groping for some kind of return to relevance. The '60s
were over. America was moving on. With the war all but complete, underground violence seemed a relic of a fast-receding era, vanishing as quickly as
peace signs.

In fact, the American underground was poised for an explosive rebirth, one that would spawn headlines unlike any seen before, along with a series of "second generation" protest bombers. This new eruption of armed cells would be peopled by a motley collection of wannabes and never-weres, those who had missed the Weather and BLA trains or who saw in those organizations' exploits a path toward the greater meaning so many radicals sought once the seismic energies of the 1960s faded. They emerged in far-flung corners of the country: in the Bay Area, in the Pacific Northwest, in New England, in New York. Most modeled themselves on Weather or the BLA, reading, rereading, and underlining their Mao and Debray and Marighella, even rediscovering the rigors of criticism/self-criticism. But what made the new cells distinct from their forerunners was that they no longer drew their inspiration from the war or the civil rights movement. Their intellectual fuel emanated instead from a new source of shimmering radical energy: U.S. prisons, especially those in California.

That jailed criminals would link up with the underground movement had long been foreseen. The rhetoric of violent revolution had found hundreds, perhaps thousands, of eager adherents inside U.S. prisons from its first utterances in the mid-1960s. Nowhere did prisoners pore over Debray and Che and Marighella more avidly than in California, where their interest attracted the notice of those who wanted a revolution just as badly: white radicals in San Francisco, Oakland, and especially the college city of Berkeley. This unlikely alliance, between charismatic black inmates and adoring white radicals, provided the underground with the long-sought messiah it ardently sought, thereby prolonging the life of a movement that had been on its last legs.

Ironically, the figure who paved the way for all this was a white man, Caryl Chessman, a convicted rapist who, during the 1950s, launched a tireless legal and literary assault on the California prison system from his cell at San Quentin. What began as a stream of writs and lawsuits evolved into a series of best-selling memoirs in which Chessman put the prison system's brutality on trial. By the time he was finally executed, in 1960, he had drawn clemency appeals from such liberal icons as Eleanor Roosevelt and Norman Mailer. During the 1960s hundreds of California inmates mimicked Chessman's tactics, churning out thousands of clemency petitions and memoirs of their own—so many that as late as 1967 inmates on San Quentin's Death Row were punished if discovered attempting to write their life stories.

Few snatched up Chessman's gauntlet more skillfully than the first important group of postwar prison radicals, the Black Muslims, whose leader, Elijah Muhammad, himself a onetime convict, had begun recruiting convicts during the 1950s. Malcolm X preached that prisoners held a special place in the Black Muslim world, symbolizing "white society's crime of keeping black men oppressed and deprived and ignorant, and unable to get decent jobs, turning them into criminals."

By the early 1960s there were mosques at several California prisons, including San Quentin, Folsom, and Soledad. The wardens tried to outlaw their meetings, leading to an escalating series of confrontations that climaxed with shootings that killed Muslim inmates in 1961 and again in 1963. By 1967, after a bloody riot at San Quentin, California prison facilities had embarked on a cycle of violence and retaliatory crackdowns that would endure for years. It brought racial polarization, along with an avalanche of legal challenges and, among black inmates at least, racial unity and a taste for open confrontation with guards and wardens. The first inmate to emerge as a public figure from this turmoil, Eldridge Cleaver, as we have seen, almost single-handedly rallied white radicals to the prison-reform movement and, in so doing, built the foundation of the black inmate/white radical alliance that ensued. By 1970 the protests of Bay Area radicals were all but permanent fixtures outside the walls at San Quentin.

For apocalyptic revolutionaries, who had long sought a constituency to rise up and fight alongside them, black inmates seemed to represent the Holy Grail. Weatherman, after all, had invested thousands of hours attempting to rally working-class youth, high school students, and black liberals and had earned little in return but snickers and shrugs. Finally, in California's toughest prisons, radicals found what appeared to be a loyal following. By 1968 black inmates were reported to be forming clandestine chapters of the Black Panthers and a hard-core Marxist group called the Black Guerrilla Family, both of which operated extensive, secret Marxist political-education groups, including courses on revolutionary theory and bomb making. In 1971 a House subcommittee identified the most popular books requested by black inmates as *The Autobiography of Malcolm X*, H. Rap Brown's *Die Nigger Die*, and Cleaver's *Soul on Ice*.

It was Cleaver, starting in 1968, who loudly and repeatedly began predicting that black inmates would soon rise up and form the leading edge of the revolution. This kind of talk produced something approaching rapture in a certain brand of white revolutionary, to the point that, in a phenomenon the author Eric Cummins terms "convict cultism," by the early 1970s "convicts who were released from California prisons frequently enjoyed instant hero status in radical organizations." As a Movement radical named Betsy Carr put it, "I was completely fascinated with [black inmates]—the glamour, the bizarreness. It was my Hollywood. I'd never discussed anything with any of them, just watched in total awe."

By 1971 scores of Bay Area radicals were volunteering and protesting at California prisons. More than a few of the black inmates they befriended, however, turned out to be opportunists who parroted Marxist philosophy in hopes of luring their new white friends into helping them make parole or, in extreme cases, escape. The classic case came in October 1972, when several members of Venceremos, a leading Bay Area activist group, ambushed a car transporting a black prisoner named Ronald Beaty outside Chino's California Institute for Men. A guard was killed in the ensuing gunfight. Their plan, authorities learned later, was to form guerrilla training camps in the California mountains, from which they would launch the long-awaited revolution in American cities. These hopes were dashed, however, when Beaty was recaptured. He not only implicated much of the Venceremos leadership; he also said he had only pretended to be a revolutionary to gain his freedom.

For a brief window of time, between 1968 and 1972 or so, many in the Movement's most radical corners ardently believed that black inmates held the key not only to the underground's future but to the specter of revolution itself. All that remained was the emergence of someone to lead them. Ever since Cleaver fled to Algeria, white revolutionaries, especially in the Bay Area, had been seeking that new messiah, a strong man who could unite white radicals and black inmates in the revolution. In 1970 they found him, the fifth great voice of the era's black militants. His name was George Jackson.

On paper George Jackson resembled Eldridge Cleaver. Like Cleaver's, Jackson's family immigrated to Southern California during the 1950s; there, like Cleaver, he became a teenaged thug who stole cars, robbed liquor stores, and wanted, deep in his soul, to someday become a writer. But whereas Cleaver could grin and charm and talk for hours, Jackson was a thug with a fountain pen, far angrier and prone to violent language than Cleaver had ever been.

Jackson was born in Chicago in 1941. His family moved to Watts in Los Angeles when he was fourteen. A gangbanger with a long criminal record, by his own admission he staged his first mugging at the age of twelve. After a burglary at fifteen he was sentenced to a California Youth Authority Camp. He escaped and fled to Chicago, then got himself arrested after knifing a man and was dragged back to Los Angeles in shackles. He escaped again. He was recaptured again. Paroled, he was arrested in 1961 for a $70 gas-station stickup in Bakersfield. When he pled guilty, the judge gave him a sentence of one year to life. On his prison admission form, Jackson stated that his ambition was "to become a successful writer." He was nineteen.

George Jackson would spend his entire adult life behind the walls of California prisons, initially in a juvenile facility, then San Quentin, and later Soledad, a hulking fortress outside the farm town of Salinas, an hour south of San Francisco. He was an extraordinarily violent prisoner, earning forty-seven disciplinary actions in just under ten years, an average of one every ten weeks. At his first stop he and his friend James Carr—best known for burning down his elementary school at the age of nine—worked as muscle for Mexican gangs, then branched out into loan-sharking and homosexual pimping. Jackson was investigated for a murder, as he would be several times, but nothing came of it. Transferred to San Quentin, Jackson, by then a chiseled six-footer—it was said that he performed a thousand fingertip push-ups every morning—joined the black Capone Gang, where he established himself as a feared debt collector, so adept at threatening other inmates that he took to buying debts from other prisoners to collect himself. He was angry, sullen, irascible, and legendarily mean-spirited.

"He was the meanest mother I ever saw, inside or out," a white prisoner once recalled. "And you want to know why he was what dumbass people call a prison leader? 'Cause everyone was shit-scared of him. . . . I mean, he was into everything when I was inside. Dope, booze, peddling ass—you name it. Strong-arm. Hit man." John Irwin, a board member of the United Prisoners Union, recalled, "We hated his guts. . . . He was a mean, rotten son of a bitch. He was a bully . . . an unscrupulous bully."[1]

The stories of Jackson's prowess as a prison fighter, especially after he began studying martial arts, are legion. The time he was seen swinging a length of pipe during a riot in 1967. The times he took pals into the showers and, just for the fun of it, screamed, "ATTACK!" and began beating other inmates bloody. "He was pound for pound the toughest guy I ever knew," an inmate named Johnny Spain recalled.

No doubt part of Jackson's anger arose from his 1965 parole review, where his own father testified that his son was better off in prison. It was in the wake of this setback, during long months in solitary confinement, that Jackson began reading radical literature an older inmate gave him. Like a generation of black inmates from Malcolm X to Dhoruba Moore to Sekou Odinga, he discovered not only the power of the written word but the revolutionary views espoused by Frantz Fanon, Malcolm, and Che. He began to see himself as a victim of white society, a viewpoint he developed at length in letters to his family.

On January 13, 1970, as Jeff Jones and Bernardine Dohrn were settling into a San Francisco apartment two hours north, came the events that would transform George Jackson from anonymous convict to the Bay Area Left's messiah. Racial tensions were running high that day when Soledad officials released fifteen black and white prisoners into a new exercise yard alongside the notorious O Wing, the prison's maximum-security ward. A fistfight broke out. Standing above the yard, a white guard named O. G. Miller raised his carbine and—with no whistle being blown, no warning rounds being fired—shot four bullets. All, an investigation showed later, were aimed at the black prisoners; a supervisor would freely admit that Miller had been trying to protect the whites. Three black inmates fell dead.

Immediately talk of reprisal flashed through the black population not just of Soledad but of San Quentin, Folsom, and every other significant

California prison. At Soledad George Jackson's voice was among the loudest. Revenge among inmate gangs had always been the law: If a white prisoner killed a black, the blacks would retaliate, and vice versa. Jackson argued that this policy should now be extended to the guards. "There had been talk goin' around for some time that the officers were subject to the same treatment that the inmates were getting," one inmate recalled. "And I think there was a kind of concerted kind of thing goin' on to where one would be taken from all the institutions. It was a thing like when one [prisoner] gets knocked in Folsom, then one [guard] will go in Quentin, one will go in Soledad, one will go in Tehachapi, all down the line."[2]

Meanwhile, a grand jury began reviewing the killings. On January 16, after a television report that the grand jury had ruled the deaths "justifiable homicide," the Soledad inmates took their revenge. A young, inexperienced guard named John Mills was alone on the floor of Soledad's Y Wing, where Jackson was housed. A group of inmates grabbed him by the throat, beat him up, and threw him over a third-floor railing. Mills struck the concrete floor below with a thud, tried to rise, then fell dead. The cell block exploded in cheers.

Jackson and two other inmates were detained, placed in solitary, and charged with Mills's murder; as a serial offender, Jackson faced the gas chamber. The case of the "Soledad Brothers," as the three were soon dubbed, would have a profound impact on the California prison system, the Left, and ultimately the underground. The key figure was a radical attorney named Fay Stender, who agreed to represent Jackson after she made a name for herself as Huey Newton's co-counsel in his murder trial. A plain woman with a smoldering sexuality, Stender was utterly entranced by the black inmates she represented. Although married with two children, she would enter into a sexual relationship with Jackson, as she had with Newton.

She was a genius at public relations. As she'd done with Newton, she intended to put the entire white "system" on trial by portraying Jackson as an innocent victim being persecuted for his revolutionary beliefs. Enlisting white activists from across California, Stender formed the Soledad Brothers Defense Committee, which soon blossomed into a full-blown bureaucracy with seven subcommittees and a Who's Who of radical-chic supporters, including Jane

Fonda, Pete Seeger, Allen Ginsberg, Tom Hayden, and a striking UCLA professor named Angela Davis. The committee turned Jackson into a cause célèbre for the radical Left, pumping out a stream of posters, pamphlets, buttons, bumper stickers, and fund-raising letters while staging bake sales, poetry readings, and art auctions. The Grateful Dead even played a benefit concert.

Under Stender's guidance, George Jackson emerged as the living symbol of everything the Bay Area Left yearned for: strong, black, prideful, masculine, and undeniably sexual. John Irwin, who was called to testify for Jackson's defense, noticed how naïve and starstruck Stender and her supporters were. "It was mostly women who were doing the organizing," he told the writer David Horowitz years later. "They had each picked their favorite Soledad Brother and were kind of ooh-ing and ah-ing over them, like teenagers with movie stars. I couldn't believe it." A New York radical named Gregory Armstrong met Jackson and summarized his appeal this way:

> Everything about him is flashing and shining and glistening and his body seems to ripple like a cat's. As he moves forward to take my hand, I literally feel myself being pulled into the vortex of his energy. There is no way I can look away. He gives me a sudden radiant smile of sheer sensual delight, the kind of smile you save for someone you really love. As we take each other's hands, I have a sense of becoming almost a part of his very physical being.

But Jackson's most valuable asset, as Fay Stender saw, was his writing. It was she who discovered the letters he had penned to family and friends and contacted Bantam Books about publishing them; Gregory Armstrong, in fact, was Jackson's editor there. He and Stender combed through Jackson's writings, editing them heavily—they chose, for instance, not to publish the letter in which Jackson fantasized about poisoning Chicago's water supply— in an effort to portray him as an American Dreyfus. Stender draped him in the trappings of an intellectual, giving him a set of horn-rimmed glasses and luring the French philosopher Jean Genet to write a preface for his book. It worked spectacularly. Published in October 1970, *Soledad Brother: The Prison Letters of George Jackson* was an immediate best seller, a critical and commercial sensation. The *New York Times* called it "one of the most significant and important documents since the first black was pushed off the ship at Jamestown colony."

Soledad Brother made Jackson an international literary sensation, much as *Soul on Ice* did for Cleaver. But in the end it brought little but heartache to Jackson himself. The first blow fell on his brother, Jonathan Jackson, a bright, sensitive student at Pasadena's Blair High School. Jonathan became obsessed with the Soledad Brothers case; he regularly visited George and attended his hearings. George, in turn, assigned Jonathan to be Angela Davis's bodyguard. It was Angela who gave Jonathan his first gun, a .380-caliber Browning with a thirteen-round clip. On August 5, 1970, after a long visit with George, she bought him another, a shotgun, at a San Francisco pawnshop.

Whether a conspiracy was afoot to help George escape from prison would never be proven. What is known for certain is that two mornings later, at ten forty-five on August 7, Jonathan walked into the Marin County Courthouse and took a seat at the rear of Judge Harold Haley's courtroom. In the dock were three of George's revolutionary friends, all San Quentin inmates. One, James McClain, was in the process of being retried for the stabbing of a guard. The other two, Ruchell Magee and William Christmas, had been called as witnesses.

Suddenly Jonathan stood up, pulled a sawed-off shotgun from beneath his overcoat, and shouted, "All right, gentlemen. I'm taking over now." He produced several more guns and tossed them to Magee and McClain, then called Judge Haley forward and taped the shotgun to his chin. After several minutes of confusion, the four men took the judge, a prosecutor, and three woman jurors as hostages and walked outside to a yellow van Jonathan had rented. A witness later said McClain shouted, "Free or release the Soledad Brothers by twelve thirty or they all die!"

Several minutes ticked by when McClain couldn't figure out how to operate the van, and he and Jonathan were obliged to switch places. By that point police and sheriff's deputies had surrounded the area. As Jonathan drove toward the frontage road, a shot rang out. In a flash dozens of officers opened fire on the van. Jonathan, wounded, pulled the trigger on the shotgun, blowing off Judge Haley's face. By the time the shooting stopped, Jonathan,

McClain, and Christmas were dead. Ruchell Magee and the prosecutor were badly wounded. Angela Davis was arrested in New York two months later and brought back to trial; she was eventually exonerated of all counts linked to the shoot-out, emerged as a radical icon herself, and remained famous for years after the world had forgotten Jonathan Jackson. Jonathan, who was given a Black Panther funeral, became the radical Left's newest martyr; more than one underground group would ultimately take his name as theirs.

George Jackson spent the year after his brother's death writing the book that he believed would be his legacy. He never lived to see it published. On August 21, 1971, with his trial already under way, someone, almost certainly one of Jackson's attorneys, managed to slip him a gun. He used it to take over San Quentin's internal detention block. As he did, witnesses later reported, he repeatedly shouted, "The Dragon has come!" Six guards and two white prisoners were taken hostage; five were later found dead in Jackson's cell, their throats slit. Jackson later bolted into the prison yard, where snipers immediately killed him with a single shot to the middle of his back. Six men were dead. It was the bloodiest day in the history of the California prison system.

In a split second George Jackson went from messiah to martyr. Two thousand attended his funeral at a church in Oakland; during the services the Weather Underground detonated bombs in protest, one in San Francisco—the incident Marvin Doyle wrote about—and a second in Sacramento. At San Quentin officials so feared a violent reaction that they prepared for an armed invasion of the prison. In the end not much happened. But although he was quickly forgotten by mainstream America, the memory of George Jackson—and his brother—would inspire several underground groups in the next few years, the last of which would not be broken up until thirteen years later, in 1984. There are Bay Area radicals who hang George Jackson's picture in honor to this day.

Jackson's final literary offering, *Blood in My Eye*, was published six months after his death, in February 1972. It is an amazing document, a straightforward call for a bloody black-led revolution in the streets of America and a vivid testimony to how thoroughly he had internalized everything he had read in Debray and other revolutionary sources. Jackson had written much of it while in solitary, grieving for his brother, and later friends would come forward to say how totally he had lost touch with reality there.

Jackson wrote:

> We must accept the eventuality of bringing the U.S.A. to its knees; accept the closing off of critical sections of the city with barbed wire, armored pig carriers crisscrossing the streets, soldiers everywhere, tommy guns pointed at stomach level, smoke curling black against the daylight sky, the smell of cordite, house-to-house searches, doors being kicked in, the commonness of death.

Blood in My Eye was largely dismissed by critics; the *Times* reviewer said it suffered from "slapdash urgency" and "lacks the visceral brilliance, the epistolary panache" of Jackson's first book. It was avidly read, however, by prison revolutionaries, especially in California, where it was viewed as a messiah's final call to arms. Among its most passionate readers was a slender, soft-spoken inmate at the California Medical Facility at Vacaville, the state prison system's psychiatric treatment center, an hour north of San Francisco.

His name was Donald DeFreeze.

Of the hundreds of self-styled revolutionaries in the California prison system, Donald DeFreeze was among the least likely to lead an underground army. He was neither a charismatic leader like George Jackson nor a gifted writer like Eldridge Cleaver nor physically intimidating; he hadn't even done time in a brutal "prestige" facility like San Quentin. Behind prison walls he was never a leader. In the real world he was scarcely remembered at all. But he was a well-read black prisoner, and for the impressionable white radicals he would eventually take underground, that was enough.

DeFreeze's story was a sad one. Born in Cleveland in 1943, the eldest of eight children, he was a bright, sensitive child whose alcoholic father, it was later claimed, regularly beat him, sometimes with a baseball bat or a hammer. After a series of arrests for stealing cars and a gun—he said he wanted to kill his father—DeFreeze at fourteen ran away to Buffalo, New York, where he lived with a cousin and then a Baptist minister who pulled the teenager into his raucous fundamentalist church, an experience that would eventually inform DeFreeze's life underground. Once again, though, he got into trouble, and he was shipped to a juvenile facility in Elmira for stealing a car. He was released at eighteen, and washed up alone and aimless in Newark, New Jersey.

DeFreeze was a quiet man, five foot nine, slender; he often spoke with the hint of an affected Jamaican lilt. Against all odds, he found stability and structure in Newark. He became a housepainter, a diligent one, and married an older woman, twenty-three-year-old Gloria Thomas, who had three children of her own. They were a mismatched pair, Thomas energetic and immaculate, DeFreeze a sullen loner with wounded eyes. Thomas was every inch a striver, friends recall, and hectored DeFreeze to make more money. He tried for a time, starting his own interior decoration outfit, the House of DeFreeze, but it went nowhere. They began to fight. Thomas did most of the hollering, yelling at DeFreeze as if he were one of her children. He began to withdraw, disappearing at night and sometimes for days at a time. Later there were stories he had turned to house burglary and armed robbery.

He began buying guns, tinkering with them in a basement workshop at their apartment house in East Orange. It was there, on the morning of March 9, 1965, two years into his new life, that the trouble began. Neighbors heard a loud bang, and the building began to fill with smoke. When police arrived, DeFreeze told them it was just a firecracker. A search revealed an unexploded bomb housed in a bamboo stem, presumably a twin to the one that exploded. DeFreeze was arrested, then indicted for illegally discharging a firearm. His wife was apoplectic. His landlord evicted them. Just as he had done as a boy, DeFreeze reacted by running away, this time to Southern California. Three weeks later he was arrested while hitchhiking on the San Bernardino Freeway; in his briefcase officers found a sawed-off shotgun, a sharpened butter knife, and a homemade tear-gas bomb. After his release he returned to Newark, only to be arrested again, carrying a homemade bomb. To this day, no one has a clue what he was up to. He was years away from being a revolutionary—he wasn't remotely political, in fact—and there was never an accusation that he used a bomb in anger. People in Newark, however, suspected the worst. After rumors spread that he was a violent Black Muslim, DeFreeze was unable to secure any more housepainting jobs. He convinced his wife they would have a better chance starting over in Los Angeles. And so the family moved to California.

There, it would appear, while working intermittently as a short-order cook and a painter, DeFreeze indulged his interest in guns by moonlighting as a black-market gunrunner, selling pistols and rifles to street gangs and, it was said, to members of the new Black Panther Party. His home life remained unstable. He drank, he disappeared for days, they fought; the family made do on a $370 monthly welfare check. And DeFreeze's penchant for bizarre arrests continued. In 1967 he was arrested for running a red light—on a bicycle. In its basket officers found a pistol and two homemade bombs. DeFreeze drew probation. That December he was arrested yet again, for carrying an unlicensed pistol; a check revealed that it was one of two hundred weapons stolen from a military-supply warehouse. DeFreeze cooperated, offering to lead police to the entire cache, but once arriving at an apartment house he leaped from a second-story window and escaped. Four days later he was recaptured. This time he dutifully escorted the police to his partner's flat, where they found the guns.

Once more, thanks to his cooperation, he drew probation. A court psychologist found DeFreeze "emotionally confused and conflicted with deep-rooted feelings of inadequacy." Afterward DeFreeze tried to go straight, taking a course in aircraft assembly, but Lockheed turned him away when they discovered his criminal record. In the summer of 1969 his wife demanded they leave Los Angeles. This time DeFreeze chose his hometown, Cleveland, but the family's stay came to an end after only a few months, when DeFreeze was arrested on the roof of a bank with burglary tools. His wife left him. DeFreeze returned, alone, to Los Angeles, where his wanderings finally came to an abrupt end a few weeks later, in November 1969. It was then, police said later, that he robbed a woman of a $1,000 cashier's check, tried in vain to cash it, then led officers on a foot chase, firing at them until he ran out of bullets. His probation revoked, he was sent to prison, at Vacaville, for a minimum of five years. It is not clear that a soul in the world cared.

Like Malcolm X and Sekou Odinga and Eldridge Cleaver before him, Donald DeFreeze got something from prison that he had never known: time to read, time to develop his mind. He started with pornography and men's magazines but, soaking up the revolutionary tenor of California prisons, soon found the book, and the man, that explained it all: *Soledad Brother* by George Jackson. Reading Jackson, DeFreeze was suddenly able to understand his strange jumble of a life. None of it, he discovered, was really his fault. The black man never had a chance. *He* never had a chance. Moreover, he wasn't really a criminal. He had been fighting for his economic freedom, for his dignity, and a repressive white government had jailed him for it. He was a political prisoner. In time DeFreeze branched out, reading the books Jackson recommended—Mao, Lenin, Che, then Fanon and Debray and the rest—and while he never became entirely conversant in left-wing ideology, he found adventure and excitement and purpose. Marxism even explained his wife: She wasn't a striving harpy; she was just bourgeois.

In 1970, not long after DeFreeze arrived, Vacaville formally approved the charter for a two-year-old Black Culture Association. The BCA, as it was known, met two nights a week in the prison library, one for informal classes in black history, literature, and similar topics, the second a social evening, typically with a presentation by a guest speaker, poetry, music, or a film. BCA meetings came wrapped in the full regalia of black liberation; each began with clenched-fist salutes, a Swahili chant, and the hoisting of a Black Liberation Army flag. Almost to a man, BCA members adopted African-sounding names that some could never quite learn how to spell. After DeFreeze joined, he began calling himself "Cinque M'tume," usually shortened to "Cin."

With the BCA's help, DeFreeze, like scores of other inmates, soon lost himself in a world of revolutionary fantasy, imagining that he would escape from prison and lead the urban revolt his idol, George Jackson, called for. As one of the BCA's white tutors put it:

> There were inmates at Vacaville who had mapped out the revolution from
> beginning to end, leaving nothing out in between. They knew what time

the revolution would start in the morning and what day. They knew how to form a vanguard and how it would split up into cadres from the east and the west and the north and the south. To hear them talk you would think that they knew exactly how to do away with the system. The guards would hear this shit twenty-four hours a day, seven days a week. There were people who could quote long passages from Che and Mao and Marx and revolutionaries that I had never heard of. '

DeFreeze was Exhibit A of this kind of prisoner, and it was in the BCA that he met many of the white volunteers he would eventually lead underground. He briefly lost touch with these friends, if not his revolutionary dreams, after being transferred to Soledad in December 1972. Then, on the night of March 5, 1973, as the police in far-off New York swept the streets in search of Joanne Chesimard and the remnants of the BLA, a Soledad guard in a prison truck dropped DeFreeze off at a collection of boilers at the fence line. It was 12:15 a.m., the first—and last—shift of DeFreeze's new job as a boiler attendant. The guard was to check on him through the night. But the moment he drove off, DeFreeze jogged to the twelve-foot-high wire fence, climbed it, tearing his jeans in the process, and dropped to the far side. By the time the guard returned, at 12:40, he had vanished into the night.

At that moment DeFreeze became a free man, an escaped prisoner, and, his fevered mind was convinced, the leader of the bloody revolution that would soon sweep America. A hundred miles north, in Berkeley, in San Francisco, in the ghettos of Oakland, vanguard troops were waiting for his command; he knew it. He just had to reach them. In the cold, damp hours before dawn, DeFreeze walked east to Highway 101, where he flagged down a man driving a Ford pickup who took him ten miles north to the farming town of Gonzales. A Chicano laborer, accepting his explanation that he had been robbed, took DeFreeze into his home, gave him a bowl of soup, and, after he took a nap, allowed him to telephone friends in the Bay Area Left.

It was early; most weren't home. Finally one, whose identity was never divulged, drove down with a change of clothes and picked up DeFreeze after lunch. On the drive north, DeFreeze spoke of the joys of reading Fanon,

Debray, Marighella, Lenin, and others, especially George Jackson. With Jackson gone, DeFreeze remarked, the revolution had no leader. It was clear who DeFreeze thought Jackson's replacement should be. Arriving in Oakland, DeFreeze took out a list of names, people who had visited him in prison and spoken fervently of the need for a revolutionary alliance of black prisoners and white radicals. Here, however, he got his first sense of the yawning gap between cell-block sloganeering and 1973 America. Of the four or five people he managed to find that first day, not one would take him in.

"Hide you out?" one Berkeley student asked in exasperation. "I can't be harboring no convicts. That's cops-and-robbers shit."[4]

Finally, late that night, DeFreeze's friend dropped him off outside Peking House, a revolutionary commune in Berkeley whose members had volunteered at Vacaville. According to lore, when the door was opened, DeFreeze's first words were "Looka here, you know, I'm here. Let's start the revolution." A friend of a friend allowed DeFreeze to sleep in her apartment that first night. It was on the second night that Donald DeFreeze, soon to anoint himself "General Field Marshal Cinque" of the Symbionese Liberation Army, found his way into the bed of his first recruit, an attractive twenty-two-year-old pharmacist's daughter named Patricia Soltysik. Her family called her Pat. She preferred "Mizmoon." She was a sometime Berkeley student, a sometime lesbian, and a self-avowed revolutionary feminist. She was also a janitor. When she wasn't mopping floors, Soltysik would become DeFreeze's partner in their revolutionary assault on America.

In those early days, with no one looking that hard for DeFreeze, the two were free to drift through the bizarre bazaar that was 1973 Berkeley, a college town deep in a post-1960s intellectual hangover, a haven for aging radicals who could still talk eagerly about the coming revolution but no longer had the energy to do much about it. Berkeley's Free Speech movement had helped launch the Movement in 1964, but its best and brightest had long since moved on to other causes; in their absence, the calls for revolution had fallen to the wayward souls who still flocked to Berkeley from across the country: the street preachers, the deluded, the lost. The Bay Area Left remained as vital as ever, still teeming with radicals devoted to every conceivable cause, but those who clung to the idea of "armed struggle" and the viability of an underground now ran less to the brainy Ivy Leaguers of the Weather Underground than to the escaped convicts, janitors, runaways, and angry lesbians who would eventually, under DeFreeze's leadership, become the Symbionese Liberation Army. America had changed that much in three short years. In 1970 those who called for violent revolution were viewed by many as an intellectual vanguard; in 1973 they were widely dismissed as lunatics.

Berkeley was probably the only place the SLA could have been born. It was among the few enclaves left in the United States where the notion of armed struggle was taken even the slightest bit seriously. A dozen or so flyspeck underground groups were scattered through the hills around town; about the only people who heard their calls for revolution were those sitting next to them on the couch. A few, however, tried to mount isolated actions. During DeFreeze's time in Berkeley members of a radical commune called the Tribal Thumb Collective were arrested for a bank robbery. Police tied another group, the August Seventh Guerrilla Movement, to a series of murders and a bizarre incident in which a cabdriver was briefly kidnapped; the ransom note demanded that Bay Area cabbies go on strike to force the release of radical convicts. This kind of violence was woven deeply into the fabric of the Bay Area in 1973. San Francisco's mysterious Zodiac Killer was still at large. The SLA's exploits would parallel a series of fourteen Bay Area murders by a small group of black militants dubbed the Zebra Killers.

In this environment DeFreeze and Mizmoon had little trouble gathering a guerrilla cell of their own, including a former lover of hers and DeFreeze's friends from the Vacaville BCA. Most of their recruits were in their twenties and active in the prison movement. A few had worked with Venceremos. All believed that, with the help of black prisoners, they could use U.S. ghettos to launch the kind of urban warfare that their hero George Jackson had prophesied. Eventually they would number eight:

Nancy Ling Perry, "Fahizah": Tiny, barely four foot eleven, the daughter of conservative parents, Perry grew up in Santa Rosa, California, and earned an English degree at Berkeley in 1970. A heavy drug user, reeling from a broken marriage, she was selling juice from a gypsy cart on campus when she was drawn into the SLA.

Willie Wolfe, "Cujo": Raised in Connecticut, the son of a wealthy doctor, Wolfe graduated from a Massachusetts boarding school before drifting west to enroll at Berkeley in 1971. Quiet but committed, he lived for a time at Peking House and spent every free hour working with inmates at Vacaville.

Camilla Hall, "Gabi": Originally from Minnesota, Hall, a heavyset lesbian with short blond hair and thick glasses, arrived in Berkeley in 1971, taking an apartment on Channing Way. Mizmoon was her upstairs neighbor; they had been lovers.

Russell Little, "Osceola": A University of Florida dropout, Little washed up in Berkeley in 1972, rooming with his best friend, Willie Wolfe, at Peking House. Drawn into the Vacaville BCA "to search out the revolutionaries, political prisoners and prisoners of war," he became convinced that underground warfare was still tenable, that groups like Weather had failed in large part because they were afraid to take lives.

Joseph Remiro, "Bo": Remiro was the ultimate angry Vietnam veteran, a hyperactive, hotheaded former infantryman who returned to the United States determined to strike back at the government that sent him overseas. He spent much of his time holding weapons classes for Bay Area radicals. When Little and Wolfe left Peking House, they moved in with Remiro.

Bill Harris, "General Teko": The oldest of the recruits at twenty-eight, Harris was another Vietnam veteran. After returning and earning a master's degree in urban education at the University of Indiana, he moved to Oakland in 1972 in search of a teaching job. A heavy LSD user, Harris ended up sorting mail at the Berkeley post office and spent his spare time volunteering with black prisoners at the Vacaville BCA.

Emily Harris, "Yolanda": Married to Bill, Emily was a peppy Chi Omega at Indiana University until falling for Harris and internalizing his radical politics. She worked as a typist at Berkeley.

Angela Atwood, "General Gelina": A flamboyant young actress from the New Jersey suburbs, Atwood met the Harrises while studying theater at Indiana. She joined the couple in Oakland and, between roles in local plays, worked as a waitress at the Great Electric Underground restaurant. When her marriage broke up, in 1973, she moved into the Harrises' spare bedroom.

Pieced together from the most committed of those at Peking House and their friends, this group came together in fits and starts during mid-1973, gathering momentum once DeFreeze and Mizmoon moved into an apartment on East Seventeenth Street, in a ghetto section of Oakland, that June. Nancy Perry was the first to join, bringing along Willie Wolfe and his pals Russ Little and the angry Joe Remiro; before DeFreeze appeared, the four, all BCA volunteers, had formed a nascent underground cell of their own with prisoners at Vacaville; the "Partisans' Vanguard Party," however, existed only in their minds.

These recruits found DeFreeze brimming with ideas for a revolutionary army. He and Mizmoon had been scribbling organizational charts and rules for weeks. From the beginning there was a surreal quality to the aborning SLA, an exaggerated sense of deluded grandiosity, of playacting. DeFreeze envisioned not only a Symbionese Liberation Army—"symbionese" was derived from the word "symbiosis"—but a Symbionese Federated Republic, a Court of the People, and units labeled mobility, medical, provision, and communication. The SLA's ideology, however, was even hazier than its imagined structure. It sought to abolish prisons, marriage, and rent while attacking "racism, sexism, ageism, capitalism, fascism, individualism, possessiveness, competitiveness and all other institutions that have made and sustained capitalism."

In practice, DeFreeze and his acolytes did their best to mimic routines pioneered by Weather: the calisthenics, the weapons training, the study of Marxist texts, even the grueling "crit/self-crit." But all of it was in service to a worldview that veered between comical and truly insane. Where Weather's leadership now called itself the Central Committee, DeFreeze styled himself General Field Marshal Cinque—pronounced "sin-kay." Where Weather took banal code names—Jack, Molly, Mike—the SLA chose monikers out of some imagined African revolution: Fahiza, Cujo, Teko. Where Weather's communiqués alternated between hippie jargon and sober Marxism, the SLA's would arrive unmoored from all reality, a notion enshrined by its favored salutation, a line that sounded as if uttered by the villain in a 1930s-era Buck Rogers serial: "DEATH TO THE FASCIST INSECT THAT PREYS UPON THE LIFE OF THE PEOPLE!"

It's entirely possible that the SLA would have remained just a fixture of Donald DeFreeze's fevered imagination if not for the sudden arrival of yet another escaped prisoner, this one from Vacaville, in August. His name was Thero Wheeler. Wheeler was a friend of DeFreeze's and an inmate leader, every bit as revolutionary-minded but a tad more level-headed.

When Wheeler was brought to a rendezvous in Palo Alto, he was surprised to see DeFreeze waiting; he had no idea that his old pal had helped arrange the escape. Wheeler and his girlfriend, a young heiress and Venceremos associate named Mary Alice Siem, began hanging out with Mizmoon and Nancy Perry. There, Wheeler told reporters months later, DeFreeze eagerly brought out a notebook adorned with the SLA's symbol, a seven-headed cobra, in which he had scribbled detailed organizational and battle plans for his new underground army. "He handed me this book, you know, with all these cobras on the cover," Wheeler remembered. "He asked me to read it. I did and I thought, man, this is really shit. I told him it was a bunch of garbage, it wasn't realistic as far as revolution was concerned. Actually, it was bullshit, it was suicide."

DeFreeze was crestfallen but undeterred. He needed Wheeler badly, because Wheeler had the contacts—to Venceremos, to the Black Panthers, to people who could sell them guns—that he didn't. DeFreeze was uncomfortably aware that, other than the nine recruits he had fielded so far—some still of uncertain loyalty—not a single other radical group they had approached had shown the slightest interest in joining forces with them. He pressed ahead nonetheless. They stole weapons, burglarizing the homes of leftists they knew. Up in the Berkeley hills, Joe Remiro showed them how to fire the guns; he taught them karate, too.

All through the fall they debated their first action. An attack on an Avis rental car office—for supporting the "fascist governments" of Portugal, Israel, and others, a draft communiqué explained—was planned but then postponed, as was an assassination of the director of the California prison system, Raymond Procunier. Finally, one evening in October, Thero Wheeler launched into a rant about Marcus Foster, the superintendent of the Oakland school system. Foster, the city's first black school administrator, was a nationally respected figure, but he had angered the Black Panthers and other radical groups by suggesting that police be brought in to curb school violence and by proposing that students carry identification cards. In Wheeler's mind this amounted to a fascist plot against black youth.

DeFreeze listened, then leaned forward, and in a tone that halted any further discussion, breathed, "That nigger is gonna die."

The unofficial birth of the Symbionese Liberation Army came on November 6, 1973, just eight days before the killing of Twymon Meyers and the unofficial death of the Black Liberation Army. No one would ever be entirely sure who the participants were; according to most accounts, it was DeFreeze, Mizmoon, and little Nancy Perry. Whoever it was, they were in place a few minutes after seven that dark, chilly evening, two of them in the parking lot of the Oakland Board of Education, leaning against a wall. A third was crouched in nearby foliage. Just then two men emerged from the building. The first, a deputy superintendent named Robert Blackburn, glanced at the pair in the shadows as he passed, his car keys already in his hand. His best friend, Marcus Foster, the superintendent Oakland had hired away from

Philadelphia, was walking just a few steps behind him when the first shots rang out.

Blackburn whirled around just in time to see the muzzle flashes as the two figures behind him began firing into Foster. There was an explosion, and Blackburn felt a searing pain in his back, a load of buckshot fired from the bushes. He lurched forward just as a second blast struck him a glancing blow. Blackburn staggered, nearly falling, before stumbling almost sixty feet to an outside door. Inside, he slumped to the floor and shouted, "Help! Get help!"

Police were on the scene within minutes. They found a group of school officials standing over Foster's dead body. Blackburn, taken to the hospital, survived. The shooters had vanished, but detectives found footprints in the bushes and bullet casings. When they examined a spent slug, they noticed something odd: The tip had been drilled out. Chemists would later discover that each of the bullets fired at Foster that night had been filled with potassium cyanide. The superintendent had been shot to pieces, five bullets fired into his back, two more in the front, the last hitting him in the leg.

The Symbionese Liberation Army's "war" against the United States had begun, but the reaction to its first attack was not at all what DeFreeze had expected. Far from drawing cheers from Bay Area radical groups, Foster's assassination provoked near-universal condemnation. Black leaders denounced the murder of one of their own; thousands would turn out to attend one of three memorial services. The Panthers decried the "brutal and senseless murder" and initially suggested that "powerful fascist elements" were behind it. Not until the next day did the strange communiqué with the seven-headed cobra arrive at a Berkeley radio station, KPFA. It was from the "Symbionese Liberation Army Western Regional Youth Unit," and it explained Foster's murder as the result of his "fascist" student-identification program. "To those who would bear the hopes and future of our people," it read in part, "let the voice of their guns express the words of freedom."

Public reaction to the strange communiqué was muted; in the Bay Area, the SLA missive was viewed as yet another bizarre message from yet another bizarre group no one had heard of. The most notable reaction was a yawning silence from the radical left, especially from the prisons, the one place from which DeFreeze might have expected to hear voices of support. Instead:

nothing. The fact was, even for those who still espoused revolution, the assassination of a black leader seemed incomprehensible. Months later, when the SLA became a focus of national interest, the prevailing view of Foster's murder was voiced by none other than Bernardine Dohrn, who issued a statement from the safety of her bungalow in Hermosa Beach. "We do not comprehend the execution of Marcus Foster," she wrote, "and respond very soberly to the death of a black person who is not a recognized enemy of the people."

The following week, after the Oakland school system suspended the ID program to "reassess community and student feelings," the SLA issued a second communiqué defending itself, mentioning Foster's onetime membership on the Philadelphia Crime Commission:

> The forces of the Symbionese Liberation Army . . . remind the enemy rich ruling class that the people will always understand the effectiveness and tactics of revolutionary justice, and will never be deceived by the distortions and lies of the fascist news media. Marcus Foster has been likened to one of our slain leaders. We ask, who ever heard of a Martin Luther King on the Philadelphia Crime Commission? . . . We are well aware the fascist news media seeks to condition us by repressing the truth.

The manhunt for Foster's killers prompted immediate changes in the SLA. Thero Wheeler, wanting no part of a murder rap, fled. DeFreeze, however, only redoubled his preparations for war. Along with Mizmoon, he and most of the others moved into a house in suburban Clayton, just north of Berkeley, where they introduced themselves to neighbors as the DeVoto family. Behind nailed-down shutters and window shades, they spent their days in a furious routine of calisthenics, weapons training, bomb building, and writing. They wrote at least ten separate communiqués, each intended to be a public explanation of a bombing of some multinational corporation, or the assassination of one of its executives; the targets included companies such as ITT, Bank of America, and General Tire. The other members, including the Harrises and Angela Atwood, were frequent visitors.

For the moment, at least, they were able to operate safely and secretly at the Clayton house; as yet the police had no clue who the SLA was, much less where it was hiding. Then, suddenly, came the moment that changed everything. On the night of January 10, 1974, a policeman in the adjoining suburb of Concord, David Duge, spied a van moving slowly down a residential street. Thinking it might be burglars casing the neighborhood, he pulled it over. Inside were Joe Remiro and Russ Little. They said they were lost, which was true. A check of their driver's licenses came back clean. But something about the pair struck Duge as suspicious. When he asked Remiro to step out of the car, he saw the bulge beneath his untucked shirt.

Their eyes met. Remiro went for his gun. Officer Duge ducked behind his cruiser. When he stuck his head out, Remiro fired two shots. Duge fired two back. After a second exchange of fire, Remiro sprinted into the darkness. With a squeal of tires, Russ Little drove off in the van. After Duge radioed for help, a second cruiser arrived. They had just driven forward a single block when, to their amazement, they saw the van driving back toward them. Little, guessing that police would follow his trail, had circled back. The officers leaped from their cars and pointed their guns at the van. Little emerged, hands held high.

Police swarmed into the area in search of Joe Remiro. Finally, just before dawn, an officer saw someone dart between two houses just a few blocks from the shooting site. When a second officer arrived, they walked up a darkened driveway, one officer loudly pumping a shell into the chamber of a shotgun. From the darkness someone called out, "I've had it. I give up." Remiro was led away in handcuffs.

By sunrise, no one in the police ranks yet had any sense that Remiro and Little were part of the SLA, much less that DeFreeze and three others were living barely two blocks away. As luck would have it, the SLA learned of the arrests before the police learned of their whereabouts. At six fifteen that evening neighbors saw a Buick Riviera wheel out of the "DeVoto family's" sloping driveway, moving so fast that its undercarriage struck the pavement with a *whomp*. Before leaving, DeFreeze and the others had drenched the home with gasoline and gunpowder, lit a fuse, and run. The conflagration they planned, however, didn't come off. There wasn't enough oxygen in the enclosed house, and when the first fire truck appeared, the blaze was quickly put out.

The firemen saw everything: two gunpowder bombs, an aerosol-can bomb, not to mention the thousands of pages of loose paper and notebooks—the plans, the charts, the communiqués, their research—that laid out the who, what, when, where, and how of everything the SLA had been doing. The SLA was gone; the Harrises and Angela Atwood disappeared that same day. But police now had a clear idea what and who they were up against. They might have learned much more had anyone bothered to study a green spiral notebook found at the house. It was adorned with Nancy Perry's tiny handwriting. One page was a numbered list of subjects she planned to research at the library. They included the Touche Ross accounting firm, the University of California Board of Regents, and Bank of America. Only later would police realize the significance of item No. 1. It read: "That daughter of Hearst."

13

"PATTY HAS BEEN KIDNAPPED"

The Symbionese Liberation Army,
February to May 1974

On the fateful evening of Monday, February 4, 1974, Patricia Campbell Hearst was a very wealthy nobody, at once an anonymous daughter of one of America's richest families and just another headstrong nineteen-year-old trying to chart a life for herself with her fiancé in a five-room duplex on Benvenue Avenue, at the edge of the Berkeley campus. To acquaintances, Patty was, like many nineteen-year-olds, a bit of a cipher, possessed of a personality as yet ill-defined, which would, in time, allow millions of Americans to make their own easy judgments of her. But to close friends Patty was a teen rebel and not an especially sympathetic one at that. She had been the only student at her private school who refused to wear a uniform, who drove a car, and who referred to farmworkers as "miserable fucking migrant people." She squabbled with her mother and sometimes her father, Randolph, who helped lead the family media empire, a vast constellation of magazines including *Cosmopolitan*, television stations, and newspapers, most notably the *San Francisco Examiner*.

As a seventeen-year-old at the Crystal Springs School for Girls in Hillsborough, California, Patty had begun an affair with her math instructor, a twenty-three-year-old named Steven Weed. After she graduated, she joined him at Berkeley, where Weed was a graduate student in philosophy; Patty studied art history. In the fall of 1972 they moved into their apartment, where they spent much of their time alone doing the things young lovers do: cooking quiet meals, shopping, and strolling Berkeley's galleries and coffeehouses. They lived on money from her parents and Weed's teaching job.

That Monday night, a little after nine, Patty was cleaning the kitchen when Weed answered a knock at the door. Three people, believed to be DeFreeze, Bill Harris, and Angela Atwood, barged into the apartment. A wine bottle was pushed in Weed's face. "Keep your head down or you're dead," someone said as he was shoved to the floor. Atwood ran into the living room and tackled Patty. "Oh, no, no, not me!" Patty cried.

After DeFreeze hit Weed several times with a rifle butt, the trio forced Patty down the outside stairs, firing a volley of bullets over the heads of a pair of curious neighbors. They stuffed Patty, now blindfolded and gagged, into the trunk of a stolen Chevy, its hapless owner still trussed up on the rear floorboards. They drove up into the Berkeley hills, stopped, and transferred Patty to a second car, leaving the Chevy's owner tied up in his car. In a half hour they were back at the new apartment they had rented in Daly City, a gritty suburb on San Francisco's southern border. Inside they forced Patty into a fetid closet and slammed the door, warning her not to touch her blindfold or gag. When she briefly panicked, she heard a voice outside the door say, "It's only a closet, for Christ sake."

Back in Berkeley, Weed staggered out of the apartment and made it to Cowell Hospital; Berkeley police were soon on the scene, followed by the FBI. Soon afterward, one of Patty's sisters broke the news to Randolph Hearst and his wife, Catherine. "Patty has been kidnapped," she said. Hearst calmly asked that police embargo the news, which they managed to do till the next day, when the Oakland newspaper indicated that it was prepared to publish, at which point the embargo was lifted. From the beginning the FBI suspected the SLA, having found a box of cyanide-tipped bullets left behind at Patty's apartment, presumably a kind of calling card. Weed couldn't identify any of the suspects, although he thought he recognized a photo of Thero Wheeler, who had left the group weeks earlier.

For three days Patty's kidnapping remained a mystery. Then, on Thursday, February 7, a receptionist at Berkeley's KPFA radio station slit open an envelope and found a communiqué issued by the "Symbionese Liberation Army Western Regional Adult Unit." Written as an order of "The Court of the People," it identified Patty as a "prisoner of war" and Randolph Hearst as a "corporate enemy of the people." There was no ransom demand, just an order that the communiqué be reprinted "in full, in all newspapers, and all other forms of media."

The SLA's appearance on the stage transformed the kidnapping of Patty Hearst into what would become, after Watergate, probably the greatest media event of the 1970s. Before it was over, her face would appear seven times on the cover of *Newsweek* alone. Almost all the coverage, especially once the story grew more complicated, would be devoted to Patty: who she was and what she represented, why she did what she did, what it meant, what it symbolized for an America struggling to come to grips with the political and emotional fallout from the 1960s even as the Nixon White House was being revealed to be every bit as corrupt as all those long-haired radicals said it was.

What is notable is how little analysis was devoted to the SLA. From the beginning, the media simply mocked it: the silly cobra heads, the purple prose. The *Kansas City Times*, for one, noting the "paranoia, the messianic posturing," the "childish fascination with queer names and elaborate symbols," compared the SLA to the Ku Klux Klan, concluding that it was "sick." The *Richmond News Leader* went a step further, belittling the SLA's pronouncements as "childish imaginings of a make-believe world—little girls and boys playing dress-up in mommy's and daddy's clothes." Others threw off reasoned analysis altogether, terming the SLA a bunch of "crazies" and "psychos."

It was true that the SLA's ideas, devised by a black ex-convict with little formal education, paled before those advanced by the Ivy League denizens of the Weather Underground; from the beginning, it was always more akin to a cult. But the media's mockery was more than just a commentary on the SLA's hazy theorizing. It was a mark of how far—and how far to the right—much of America had come in its rejection not only of '60s-era violence and protest but of an entire canon of liberal thought, especially parental permissiveness, the overindulgence of academic freedoms, and the coddling of criminals. Just four years earlier the Weather Underground's bombings had been viewed, however briefly, as a semilegitimate response to Nixon-era policies. The SLA was granted no such credibility. They were just psychos.

Many days that February Randolph Hearst would step outside his suburban mansion and answer questions from the growing media contingent. For the moment, all he could do was appeal for Patty's safe return. Then, on Tuesday, February 12, after five days of agonized waiting, the SLA's next communication arrived at KPFA: eight pages of communiqués and two audiotapes, one from DeFreeze, one from Patty. "These people aren't just a bunch of nuts," Patty said. "They've been really honest with me but they're perfectly willing to die for what they're doing. I'm here because I'm a member of a ruling-class family." It was DeFreeze's tape that set the stage for one of the decade's strangest episodes. In the comically stilted language he employed in all the SLA's communications, he announced that the SLA "court" had ordained that, before it could consider releasing Patty, the Hearsts would need to carry out a "good faith" gesture by giving out food to the "oppressed" people of the Bay Area. The demand was oddly specific: $70 worth of food, to anyone who needed it, on Tuesdays, Thursdays, and Saturdays for the next four weeks. "If you can get the food thing organized before the nineteenth," Patty said, "then that's okay and it will just speed up my release."

Randolph Hearst told reporters the "food demand" was "impossible to meet"; one estimate put the cost at $133 million, another at $400 million. Hearst promised to study the offer and suggest an alternative. Before he could, another pair of tapes arrived three days later, one each from DeFreeze and Patty. In his, DeFreeze appeared to back away from the food demand, saying the SLA might accept an alternative. Patty seconded this, saying, "They weren't trying to present an unreasonable request. It was never intended to feed the whole state. So whatever you come up with basically is okay."

The SLA had demanded that the food handouts begin on Tuesday, February 19, and it named a series of charity groups that could help organize them. That day Hearst again stepped before the microphones in front of his mansion and announced he was forming a $2 million foundation to distribute food to the needy, a program called People in Need. Telephone lines were established to draw volunteers. Several of the groups the SLA named said they would help; others, including the Black Panthers, refused, saying they could not approve of kidnappings. Hearst promised the first distribution would take place on Friday, February 22. As final preparations were under way that Thursday, another SLA communiqué was delivered, left at a black church in San Francisco. In it, DeFreeze dismissed Hearst's $2 million offer as "throwing a few crumbs to the people" and demanded $4 million more in handouts.

It was a colossal—and chaotic—undertaking, tons of donated and purchased groceries loaded onto rented trucks at a San Francisco warehouse, then ferried to supermarkets in black neighborhoods across the Bay Area. Hundreds of people waited in lines. When trucks arrived late, crowds surrounded them. Fights broke out. In some cases workers simply tossed bags of food out of the trucks; at a distribution center in East Oakland, several people were injured after being struck by frozen turkeys. By day's end, at which point Hearst had hoped to deliver food to twenty thousand people, maybe nine thousand got some. Later distributions, eventually five in all, went more smoothly. They continued through March over the protests of California conservatives, whose sentiments were symbolized by Governor Ronald Reagan's memorable quip: "It's just too bad we can't have an epidemic of botulism."

The SLA's emergence once again put the remnants of the Weather Underground in a quandary, much as the Panther 21's request for aid had done three years earlier. "The Patty Hearst thing was great, giving out the food, all of that was great," recalls Weather's Paul Bradley, who was working as an auto mechanic in San Francisco. "Of course, we all thought their rhetoric was ridiculous, and none of us paid much attention to the Marcus Foster killing, a horrible thing. Frankly, everybody was confused by the SLA. It was led by this black guy, so it was hard for us to be critical. It was hard to condemn it, too."

Weather's ambivalence was reflected in the lone communiqué it issued on the SLA, on February 20. While wishing for Patty's safety, it noted: "We must acknowledge that this audacious intervention has carried forward the basic public questions and starkly dramatized what many have come to understand through their own experience: It will be necessary to organize and to destroy this racist and cruel system."

It was not Weather's finest moment: In 2006, when Bernardine Dohrn, Bill Ayers, and Jeff Jones published a collection of Weather communiqués, their commentary on the SLA was notably absent.

Through much of the chaos Patty Hearst remained where she had been since the first hours after her kidnapping: in a bedroom closet in a rented tract house in Daly City. She described her ordeal in excruciating detail in her 1982 memoir, *Every Secret Thing*. From the beginning DeFreeze was a regular presence in that closet, describing the SLA to Patty as a vast army with training camps and ties to guerrilla groups around the world. When Patty said she had never heard of the SLA, which was a lie, the others began calling her "Marie Antoinette," joking that she lived inside a cocoon of wealth.

DeFreeze promised she would not be mistreated unless she tried to escape, at which point she would be executed. He would talk for hours, bombarding her with lectures on the SLA's worldview, from the inhumanity of the prison system to the plight of the oppressed to the evils of ruling-class families like the Hearsts. Between lectures they fed her and led her to the bathroom, still blindfolded, and in time Patty learned all their names: Bo, Fahizah, Cujo, Teko, and more. On her third day in the closet DeFreeze announced that her formal interrogation was beginning, and he handled it himself, firing questions at her about her upbringing, her education, and her family's media holdings. It lasted for days. She told them everything they wanted to know.

From the closet she could hear them talk. They were practically giddy at the publicity they were receiving. When it was time to issue a communiqué, DeFreeze sat with her in the closet, a tape recorder in his lap. Patty was happy to make the tapes. It was the only way she had to communicate with the world. As the days wore on, the others began taking turns sitting outside her door, talking to her for hours, usually a litany of SLA propaganda, quoting Mao, talking about the prisons, the oppressed. They just went on and on. Patty marveled at how sincere they seemed, how they genuinely seemed to believe they were leading a revolution that would in time change America forever. Alone in the closet she veered wildly between hope and despair.

Slowly the group began to accept her as something other than a prisoner. When she grew weak from inactivity, sometimes unable to walk to the bathroom without help, they had her do calisthenics. The women watched as she bathed. DeFreeze remained obsessed with the idea of an FBI raid, and in an effort to bolster their defenses he taught Patty to break down and use a shotgun. But it was her seeming acceptance of their political views that truly changed her status. Patty considered herself "apolitical" and didn't care a whit about Mao or prison conditions; she thought these people were suicidal. But in an effort to improve her plight, she began agreeing with every point they made, until finally they gave her books to read, Cleaver's *Soul on Ice*, George Jackson, Marx, Mao. They began letting her out of the closet, still blindfolded, to sit in on their political discussions, where she did her best to appear an eager student. She memorized the SLA's rules and asked an endless stream of questions, every one of which the others were thrilled to answer. In time they stopped calling her "Marie Antoinette." They called her "Tiny" instead.

Patty had no idea what they had planned for her. At one point DeFreeze spoke of trading her for Joe Remiro and Russ Little. Another time he suggested she might face a choice: Join the SLA or be executed. "You know, we've kind of gotten to like you," he said. "So we don't really want to kill you, if we don't have to. Think about it."

For the moment, though, DeFreeze let the subject lapse. Then, in late March, seven weeks after the kidnapping, the group suddenly abandoned its Daly City safe house for a cramped, one-bedroom apartment on Golden Gate Drive in San Francisco; DeFreeze was convinced an FBI raid was imminent. To make the trip, Patty was taken from her closet and maneuvered into a plastic garbage can, which was placed in the trunk of a car. At the new flat she was again led into a closet. One evening, as her political education continued, she was brought into the living room and told about "revolutionary sex." Anyone in the SLA was free to have sex with anyone else, they told her; no one was forced to, but it was considered "comradely" to accept any sexual offer. That night Willie Wolfe came to the closet and wordlessly had sex with Patty. Several days later DeFreeze began visiting her as well. Patty remembers lying there "like a rag doll," just waiting for the sex to be over.

They had been in the new apartment only a few days when DeFreeze came to the closet and finally made the proposal that changed Patty's life forever. "The War Council has decided you can join us if you want to," he told her. "Or you can be released, and go home again."

Patty wrote later that she never believed they would release her; the choice, she felt, was between joining them or death. Without a moment's hesitation, she blurted, "I want to join you."

"You'll be an urban guerrilla, fighting for the people."

"Yes," she said. "I want to fight for the people."

Over the next week Patty endured blindfolded talks with all eight SLA members, assuring each that she was genuinely committed to their cause. Finally she was led into a meeting where DeFreeze told her to remove her blindfold. When she did, she saw the others, for the first time, grinning at her. "As General Field Marshal," DeFreeze announced, "I welcome you to the Symbionese Liberation Army!"

Patty's first thought was what ugly, depressingly ordinary people they all were: Their voices had been so much more impressive. "Now that you've seen us," Angela Atwood asked, "what do you think?"

"Oh, you're all so attractive!" Patty lied.

"Well," DeFreeze said, "all freedom fighters are beautiful."

Overnight Patty was accepted into the group. She was issued combat boots, a carbine, and a new name, "Tania," after a noted Cuban revolutionary. She began using the SLA's communal toothbrush, which she found disgusting. She lined up in the morning for DeFreeze's inspections and stifled laughter as she watched the others engage in "combat exercises," darting around the apartment pretending to shoot each other, "like cowboys and Indians," she wrote later. Once her own training began, they started preparing the communiqué that would announce her enlistment to the outside world—a publicity coup, DeFreeze promised, pronouncing the word "coop." Everyone contributed to the script Patty read into the tape recorder. In it, she announced she was joining the SLA voluntarily and launched into a tirade against her father that was so "over the top," she wrote later, she was certain he would realize she was doing this simply to remain alive.

The communiqué, issued April 3, ignited a media firestorm and triggered a national debate about Patty and her motivations. America's embrace of this discussion, coming as it did smack in the middle of the Watergate investigations, might be understood as a welcome diversion from weightier matters. As for Patty herself, she always insisted her decision to join the SLA was purely a question of survival. In time, though, the lengths she would go to in order to "belong" would cause many who knew her, and millions who didn't, to question her actions. Her quandary, in fact, confronted her almost immediately. They were running low on money, and she was startled to hear DeFreeze and the others debating the merits of various banks they wanted to rob.

Once they identified their target, a branch of the Hibernia Bank on Noriega Street, they rehearsed the robbery in exhaustive detail. Patty couldn't believe they would actually go through with it; the whole idea seemed so surreal. If they did, she was certain she would be killed. Yet there she was, her carbine clasped to her side, as the group filed out of the Golden Gate apartment on the bright, sunny morning of Monday, April 15. It was the first time Patty had been outdoors in weeks. As they drove in two rented cars toward the bank, she marveled at the blue of the sky, the green of the trees. They pulled up around the corner from the bank just before ten. DeFreeze, with Patty and Gabi Hall, was first through the door; there were eighteen employees and six customers inside. Guns hidden, the trio strolled to a desk.

As they did, Mizmoon and Nancy Perry burst inside, guns drawn. Just then the clip fell out of Perry's rifle, clattering to the floor, bullets spilling everywhere. Patty produced her carbine, DeFreeze a submachine gun. "This is a holdup!" DeFreeze shouted. "The first motherfucker who don't lay down on the floor gets shot in the head!"

It went like clockwork, everyone rushing around shouting, "SLA! SLA!" as they herded the tellers and customers to one side and scooped cash from the drawers. Patty stood moored in the lobby, until she remembered what she was supposed to say. Several customers heard her say, in a small voice but clearly, "This is Tania Hearst."

They were finished in minutes. DeFreeze began calling out numbers, the signal for each to leave. Just as they turned toward the front door, a fifty-nine-year-old liquor store owner named Pete Markoff entered the bank. Just behind was his pal Gene Brennan, a seventy-year-old pensioner. Seeing the robbery in progress, Markoff turned to run. For some reason Nancy Perry opened fire. Markoff fell, a .30-caliber bullet striking his right buttock. Brennan was hit in the hand. "I've been shot!" he yelled. "I've been shot!" As customers from a nearby bar spilled out to see what was happening, the SLA sprinted from the bank, DeFreeze turning to fire a burst at the onlookers, scattering them. The group hustled into the getaway cars and were gone in an instant. The take came to $10,600. Back at their apartment, the mood was euphoric. DeFreeze presented Patty with a pistol as reward for her performance.

The Hibernia robbery was a turning point. The bank-camera photo of Patty calmly holding a gun on customers, soon to become one of the decade's iconic images, provided the first evidence that she had in fact joined the group. Initially the San Francisco papers withheld judgment. A *Chronicle* headline suggested SHE MAY HAVE BEEN COERCED; the Hearsts' *Examiner* asked, WAS PATTY A PUPPET? But the U.S. attorney general, William Saxbe, had no such doubt. In Washington he told reporters that Patty "was not a reluctant participant." His comments set the tone for a transformation in the pursuit of the SLA, which had been lackluster; California's attorney general suggested that police had been "timid" out of concern for Patty's safety. In fact, police hadn't even identified all the SLA's members. After the robbery they did, and wanted posters sprouted in post offices across the state. Arrest warrants were finally issued. San Francisco's mayor, Joseph Alioto, denounced the SLA as "killers, extortionists and third-rate intellectuals," claiming, "We have indulged them long enough."

At the flat on Golden Gate, DeFreeze began to worry. He promised it was only a matter of time before the FBI found them. He genuinely believed that agents were checking every house in San Francisco in an effort to quash the revolution. He said no one could leave the apartment, which was a problem; after two days they ran out of food. At that point DeFreeze announced that the answer was to recruit new soldiers the FBI didn't know. Taking Bill Harris with him, he marched out of the apartment and, to the others' dismay, began knocking on other doors in the building, introducing himself as "General Cinque of the SLA" and asking the occupants to join up. After one woman slammed the door in their faces, DeFreeze was convinced that recruitment in their own building might be a tad unwise.

Not that this stopped him. He and Harris strode out into the surrounding neighborhood and began knocking on other doors. Amazingly, this strategy worked. After several more doors were slammed in their faces, a black woman who happened to be a Black Muslim said she would help. The next day she brought them food. A few days after that she found a new apartment where they could hide, on Oakdale Avenue in a black neighborhood. To ensure that they made it there safely, DeFreeze had Angela Atwood, the amateur actress, experiment with disguises, daubing black theatrical makeup on all the white faces. The women donned Afro wigs; Patty, it's said, made a thoroughly convincing black girl. DeFreeze chose to dress in drag; apparently he made quite a fetching woman. On the way out they trashed the flat, scrawling antigovernment slogans on the walls and throwing papers into a makeshift acid bath they brewed in the bathtub. No sooner had they left, however, than word came that the new apartment was not quite ready.

The woman found them a shabby hotel, where they waited for two days, pacing and reading. Once they moved into the new apartment, they again relied on the woman, now augmented by three Black Muslim men, to buy their groceries. Now that they had money, DeFreeze began saying it was time to initiate combat operations. They would drive the streets of San Francisco hunting for policemen to kill, as the BLA had done. But before they could begin, Randolph Hearst announced a $50,000 reward for Patty's return. Suddenly DeFreeze began eyeing their Muslim helpers with suspicion. After several days he decided that remaining in the Bay Area was too risky. They would don their disguises once more and move their theater of operations to a city he knew well, or thought he did: Los Angeles.

They drove south in three vans the Muslim men rented for them, arriving in Los Angeles on May 10. The first day they cruised the black neighborhoods in South Central until they spotted a house on West Eighty-fourth Street with a FOR RENT sign. After they moved in, the first order of business was shedding their disguises. "Willie and I looked like shit in black makeup," Bill Harris said much later. "It was just too phony."[1] For several days everything went smoothly, each of them running out to pick up the groceries and clothes they needed.

By this point, Patty wrote later, she was losing her grip on her old identity. After three months of intermittent death threats, then untold hours of political indoctrination, she had grown "numb" and was increasingly willing to do whatever DeFreeze and the others told her to do. A cynic might deride her intellectual weakness, and many later did; a supporter might say this was a nineteen-year-old's way of coping. Whatever it was, by the time the SLA moved to Los Angeles, Patty came to believe that her safety depended solely on her obedience; if she ever mulled an actual escape attempt, much less insubordination, she didn't mention it later. She simply did what she was told.

It took all of six days in Los Angeles for trouble to start. On May 16 Patty and the Harrises went shopping at Mel's Sporting Goods in neighboring Inglewood. When the Harrises went inside—Patty remained outside in a Volkswagen van—a security guard noticed Harris stuffing a pair of socks into his jacket. The couple paid for other items, but after they walked outside, the guard confronted Harris about the socks. When Harris refused to go back inside, a struggle ensued. Emily jumped on the guard's back. Other employees rushed out and joined the fight.

Suddenly Patty began firing a carbine from the van—the first time she had fired a gun in anger, it appears—bullets shattering the store's front windows. The Harrises sprinted to the van. Patty drove off in a squeal of tires, the guard leaping into his own car to give chase. At a stoplight the Harrises jumped out and ordered a young black man out of his car. "We're from the SLA and we need your car," Harris shouted, and the man hastily obliged;

when Harris noticed the guard a few cars back, he pointed his rifle, and the guard slammed into reverse, leaving the scene. After commandeering and switching to a second car, a station wagon, Patty and the Harrises drove off, but the dimwitted decision to identify themselves as "the SLA" quickly brought the FBI into the matter. By nightfall news of the SLA's surprising arrival in Los Angeles headlined the evening newscasts.

For the next several hours the desperate trio ricocheted through the city, commandeering a series of vehicles from frightened Angelenos, briefly taking two drivers hostage. Every hour they stopped at a pay phone and called the emergency numbers they had arranged, but neither DeFreeze nor anyone else ever answered. They continued like this all through the night, giving up only late the next morning. It was then, unable to make contact, that they decided to take shelter in a strangely appropriate place, the fantasy capital of California: Disneyland.

Identifying himself as a member of the SLA wasn't Bill Harris's worst blunder that frantic day in Los Angeles. When the FBI searched the Volkswagen van they had abandoned, they found a parking ticket issued three days earlier outside a house on 833 West Eighty-fourth Street, where at that very moment DeFreeze and the rest of the SLA were watching news broadcasts with mounting alarm. And with good reason. By ten o'clock that night FBI agents and LAPD officers were creeping into the neighborhood. Staying well back, they watched the house in silence for several hours, seeing no signs of activity. Finally, just before dawn on May 17, they approached a neighbor, who identified photos of the Harrises as people he had seen at the house at 833. By 8:50 a.m. police had the house surrounded, at which point an LAPD sergeant took out a bullhorn and ordered everyone inside to come out with their hands up. When no one answered, tear gas canisters were fired inside. Minutes later, SWAT teams crashed through the front and back doors. The house was empty.

DeFreeze and the others had fled. They drove around for several hours, it appears, before stopping at about 4 a.m. It was then, at a small stucco house at 1466 East Fifty-fourth Street, four miles away, that a hard-partying thirty-five-year-old named Christine Johnson answered a soft knock on her front door. She and a group of friends had been drinking wine and listening to music all night; theirs was the only house on the block with lights still on. Opening the door, Johnson and her friend Minnie Lewis found a stranger: DeFreeze. "I saw your lights, sisters," he said. "My name is Cinque. I need your help."

The name meant nothing to the two women. DeFreeze said he and his friends needed a place to stay for a few hours. He admitted, sheepishly, that police were looking for them, not an unusual circumstance in this neighborhood. He pulled out $100 and promised there would be no trouble. Johnson whispered for a moment with her friend, then took the money and said they could stay for a little while.

At that moment there were six people in the house, Johnson and Lewis, a parking lot attendant named Freddie Freeman, seventeen-year-old Brenda Daniels, and two sleeping children. Freeman helped DeFreeze unload the vans, which took twenty minutes. There were boxes packed with documents, a footlocker, sleeping bags, and, to Freeman's dismay, nineteen guns, including four .30-caliber carbines, a Browning .30-06, and seven sawed-off shotguns. There were also four thousand bullets, some of them in bandoliers. DeFreeze and Freeman lugged it all inside and stacked it in the kitchen.

They hid the vans in an alley around the corner, then went to look at an apartment house where Freeman suggested they could find a permanent home. By the time DeFreeze returned, Johnson was having second thoughts about sharing their home with these odd strangers. Not only were "Cinque's" friends all white; they were white people with pistols jammed in their belts. They had watched in dismay as one of the girls, apparently Nancy Perry, filled several bottles with gasoline. An hour later, after sending Lewis's two children to school, Johnson and Lewis popped several pills, swigged a few last beers, and went to sleep.

People, including a stream of preschool children, filed in and out of the house all morning. DeFreeze sent Brenda Daniels for groceries. One of Daniels's girlfriends came by for what she called "a wake-up beer." Freeman's supervisor arrived to pick him up for work, but Freeman waved him off, figuring to make some money off Cinque and his strange white friends. At midmorning DeFreeze gave Freeman $450 and told him to go buy them a car. Through it all, he and his acolytes stood at the windows in shifts, taking turns grabbing naps. At the top of every hour DeFreeze picked up the telephone and dialed one of the designated pay phones, hoping to find Bill Harris. No one answered.

It was growing hot. By noon, the sky a brilliant blue, the temperature had risen into the eighties. As before, DeFreeze made no effort to hide who they were. He seemed to genuinely believe that, because they were fighting in the name of black people, black people would support them, or at least would not alert the police. When asked, he said he had come to Los Angeles to start a revolution, to kill police. Told that the neighborhood was dominated by a local gang, the Crips, DeFreeze said he hoped to meet some, pledging to make them "right-on revolutionaries." Each of the visitors scurried back outside to spread the word that the SLA was at Christine Johnson's house. Up and down the street, people shook their heads in disbelief. Others whispered in their yards. Phones rang. The news spread. A sixty-three-year-old grandfather named James Reed stopped by the house to drop off some collard greens. Two white girls wearing pistols smiled at him and said hi.

The day stretched on. When Johnson finally stirred, beers and joints were passed. Around three, Minnie Lewis's children returned from school. One, an eleven-year-old named Timmy, marveled at all the guns.

"Who are you?" he asked DeFreeze.

"We're your mama's friends."

"No, you're not. I know all my mama's friends."

DeFreeze told the boy to sit down. Suddenly Timmy, apparently a more avid consumer of mass media than his mother, recognized him.

"Are you Donald DeFreeze?" he asked.

"No."

Timmy darted out the back door and ran toward his grandmother's house. DeFreeze kept watching the street. Something wasn't right. There were too many people around, too many police cruisers driving idly by. Johnson, now awake, still drunk, assured him that police in the neighborhood were nothing new. But DeFreeze didn't like it. There was still no word from Hearst and the

Harrises. He kept glancing at the street, wondering where Freddie Freeman had gone with his $450.

"He ought to be back by now," he kept saying.

Another police car cruised past.

"We gotta get outta here," DeFreeze told Mizmoon. "It's getting too hot."

"Why?" she replied. "It's hot everywhere."

A few minutes later, trouble arrived—but not at all the kind DeFreeze had feared. An angry grandmother, Mary Carr, came storming through the front door and, ignoring DeFreeze and the armed white people for a moment, found her daughter, Minnie Lewis, passed out on a bed. "Is everybody here drunk?" she demanded.

The teenager, Brenda Daniels, took her elbow and whispered that there were two white women in the other bedroom. Making bombs.

This was too much for Mary Carr. She marched into the kitchen, where DeFreeze had wandered, studiously avoiding her.

"You get out of this place right now!" she hollered.

DeFreeze mumbled something about black people sticking together. Mary Carr took two of her grandchildren by the collar, stalked out the front door, and went in search of a policeman. She didn't have to look far. Hundreds of men in blue were already streaming into the area.

The LAPD knew they were close. A search of the house on West Eighty-fourth Street produced a trove of evidence: gas masks, a radio, three suitcases packed with clothing, a bag of medical supplies, one of Angela Atwood's poems. "Now is the time—we're all alive," one couplet read. "Eat it Pig!" Neighbors described the two vans. Dozens of police cruisers began criss-crossing the area, and at 12:20 p.m. a pair of Metro Squad cops spotted the vans in an alley on East Fifty-third. Black plainclothes detectives began filtering into the surrounding streets.

Neighbors did the rest. At two o'clock one called the FBI to say the SLA was hiding at 1462 East Fifty-fourth Street—next door. A caller to the LAPD phoned in an address on South Compton—around the corner. By three, when a meeting of senior LAPD and FBI officials convened at the Newton Street Station, the noose was tightening. By four o'clock, when police set up a command post in a tow-truck office a few blocks down East Fifty-fourth, four houses had been pinpointed. At four twenty a perimeter was established. By five, 127 FBI agents and more than two hundred police officers, including two SWAT teams, had surrounded the area. When Mary Carr found her way to the command post, the last piece fell into place.

Inside the house at 1466 East Fifty-fourth, DeFreeze sensed it. The block was slowly draining of people. Minnie Lewis disappeared. Freddie Freeman never returned. The Harrises were nowhere to be found. Christine Johnson, an epileptic, collapsed in the kitchen, and DeFreeze dragged her to a couch. When Brenda Daniels went for more groceries, police took her into custody. By five thirty, besides Johnson, the only occupants of the house other than the SLA were a neighbor named Clarence Ross, taking pulls from a pint bottle of whiskey, and Minnie Lewis's eight-year-old son, Tony, who was watching cartoons.

At one point, a neighbor girl—curious to "see the SLA"—wandered into the house and told DeFreeze police were in the area. She followed him into the kitchen, where he drank from a jug of Boone's Farm wine. The end was near, DeFreeze said. He was ready. "But we're gonna take a lot of mother-fucking pigs with us," he promised.

Everyone knew what was coming. Even news reporters had arrived on the scene; one tried to interview a next-door neighbor, Mattie Morrison, who told him to get lost. Detectives crept up to houses up and down the block, warning residents to leave or remain inside; most ignored them, peering from their porches, waiting. By 5:40 p.m. the SWAT teams, eighteen men in all, had hustled into place, one team splayed behind cars and bungalows in front of the house, another on the block behind. At 5:44 their leader raised his bullhorn:

"Occupants of fourteen-sixty-six East Fifty-fourth Street, this is the Los Angeles Police Department speaking. Come out with your hands up. Comply immediately and you will not be harmed."

The house was still. After a pause the announcement was repeated. Down

Sam Melville, below left, and Jane Alpert, below right, led the first significant radical bombing group, which detonated nearly a dozen bombs around Manhattan in the second half of 1969. Above, detectives nose through the wreckage of a Commerce Department office the group bombed in Foley Square that September.

Bernardine Dohrn, left, brainy and charismatic, emerged as the queen of the 1970s-era underground: "La Pasionaria of the Lunatic Left," as J. Edgar Hoover termed her. She spent much of her time underground in a beachside bungalow in Southern California, sometimes using a supporter's small children as cover when scouting the Weather Underground's bombing targets.

Above, Weatherman leadership at the notorious Days of Rage protest, Chicago, October 1969; left to right, Jim Mellen, Peter Clapp, John "JJ" Jacobs, and best friends Bill Ayers and Terry Robbins. At right, Jeff Jones, the dashing Weatherman who orchestrated the disastrous "inversion" strategy that led to the group's demise.

Above, March 6, 1970: New York firefighters work to extinguish fires after the deadly Townhouse explosion in Greenwich Village that left three Weathermen dead and forever altered the trajectory of the underground movement. Below left, Cathy Wilkerson, one of the Townhouse's two survivors, became a West Coast bomb maker for the group. Below right, Ron Fliegelman, the Weather Underground's unsung hero, perfected a bomb design and became the group's explosives guru. He later fathered a daughter with Wilkerson.

Above, May 19, 1972: Pentagon officers guard the women's restroom where a Weather Underground bomb exploded, destroying it. Below left, Clayton Van Lydegraf, the aging Communist who led the internal purge that destroyed the group. Below right, Mark Rudd, the hero of the 1968 Columbia riots who was marginalized after going underground and eventually surrendered in September 1977.

Joanne Chesimard, a.k.a. Assata Shakur, at left, being led into a New Jersey jail, January 29, 1976. Hailed as the "heart and soul" of the Black Liberation Army—an overstatement, some say—Chesimard was an archetype for a string of machine-gun-toting blaxploitation-film heroines during the 1970s. Below left, Richard "Dhoruba" Moore, the BLA's most important early organizer, escorted by New York detectives after his arrest, June 5, 1971. Below, Twymon Ford Meyers, the young BLA gunman who may have been the underground era's deadliest soldier.

At right, Deputy Police Commissioner Robert Daley and two New York police officials examine the East Village scene of the BLA's gruesome murders of Officers Gregory Foster and Rocco Laurie, January 27, 1972. Chalk outlines on the sidewalk indicate the position of the officers' fallen bodies.

New York police and fire engines responding to the FALN's bombing of the Fraunces Tavern restaurant, which killed four diners, January 24, 1975. Oscar López, top left, was the FALN's mastermind, a onetime community organizer in Chicago who orchestrated dozens of bombings and armed raids in New York and Chicago between 1974 and 1980. Marie Haydee Torres, bottom left, was convicted of planting the deadly FALN bomb at Mobil Oil headquarters in New York in 1977. Willie Morales, top right, survived an accidental explosion that blew off nine of his fingers and much of his face in July 1978. His subsequent escape from Bellevue Hospital's prison ward was one of the underground's crowning achievements.

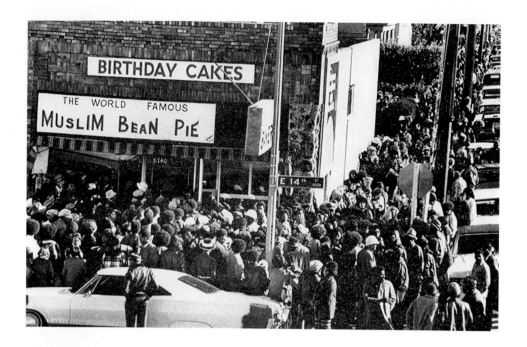

Above, February 22, 1974: Hundreds of Oakland residents line up for the Randolph Hearst family's initial food giveaway, part of the ransom the Symbionese Liberation Army demanded for the release of Hearst's daughter, Patty. At left, Patty during a 1972 vacation in Greece.

Opposite, clockwise from top left: A surveillance-camera photo of Patty Hearst in her first appearance as an SLA soldier during the robbery of a Hibernia Bank branch in San Francisco, April 15, 1974. The eight members of the SLA's first incarnation; Donald DeFreeze, the escaped prisoner who styled himself "General Field Marshal Cinque," stands in the middle of the back row. A woman and her children flee the SLA shoot-out in South Central Los Angeles, May 17, 1974.

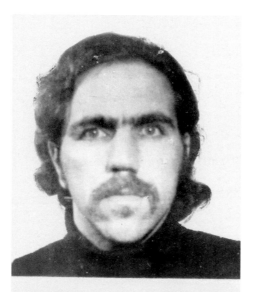

RAYMOND LUC LEVASSEUR

Ray Levasseur, at left, a French Canadian radical, led the most unusual of the 1970s-era underground groups: two blue-collar couples (later three) and their children who detonated bombs and robbed banks up and down the East Coast between 1976 and 1984. Above, police and fire officials examine the damages from the group's first bombing, of Boston's Suffolk County Courthouse, 1976.

Opposite top, several members of the group as portrayed in an FBI circular around 1982. Bottom, Levasseur in 1989.

RAYMOND LUC LEVASSEUR

RICHARD C. WILLIAMS

RICHARD C. WILLIAMS

RICHARD C. WILLIAMS

JEREMY

THOMAS WILLIAM MANNING

THOMAS WILLIAM MANNING

THOMAS WILLIAM MANNING

CAROL ANN MANNING

Sekou Odinga, above, perhaps the most respected militant of his age, masterminded more than a dozen bank robberies and took part in a pair of daring jailbreaks during an underground career that spanned thirteen years. His partner Mutulu Shakur, left, was the cocaine-addled head of "the Family," the ragtag alliance of black and white radicals that staged the era's bloodiest raid, the $1.6 million robbery of a Brink's armored car in suburban Nanuet, New York, October 20, 1981.

Opposite: Marilyn Buck, top left and center, the only white member of the Black Liberation Army, walked away from a federal prison to become Odinga and Shakur's aide-de-camp. Buck, together with Silvia Baraldini, top right, formed the nucleus of the band of radical women the Family nicknamed "the white edge." Bottom: the U-Haul trailer and a police cruiser pockmarked by bullets fired in the shoot-out following the Brink's robbery.

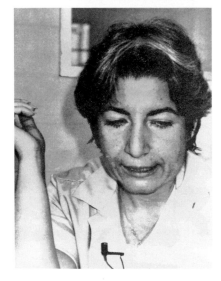

Those who joined the underground struggle met a variety of fates. Assata Shakur, top left, lives in Cuba. She remains a wanted fugitive today. Dhoruba bin-Wahad, above, is an activist living in the Atlanta area. Top right, Bill Ayers, Bernardine Dohrn, and their son, Zayd Dohrn, outside a New York federal courthouse in 1982. Ayers, also pictured at center right, is an author, activist, and retired professor of education at the University of Illinois, Chicago. Silvia Baraldini, right, lives in Rome.

the block television crews raised their cameras, correspondents their microphones. The evening news was just minutes away. All three networks went to the scene live.

The house remained silent. Behind it, a SWAT marksman could see a refrigerator being moved to blockade the back door. "People in the yellow frame house with the stone porch, address fourteen-sixty-six East Fifty-fourth Street, this is the Los Angeles Police Department   "

Suddenly there was movement on the front porch.

"The front door," one of the police walkie-talkies squawked. "Somebody's coming out."

It was the eight-year-old, Tony, curious what all the noise was about. He hopped down the front steps, drifted toward the sidewalk, and froze, wide-eyed. Everywhere he looked were men with guns.

"Come this way, over here," a SWAT team member called.

Tony was a statue.

A policeman scurried up, grabbed the boy, and carried him away in his arms. Tony began screaming, "Mama! Mama!"

A minute later Clarence Ross stepped onto the front porch, hands clasped behind his head. He and Tony were led around the corner, where SWAT leaders fired questions at them. Ross said little. But Tony gave a good description of DeFreeze, his people, and their weapons. As he did, the SWAT team at the front of the house endlessly repeated its bullhorn announcements, eventually eighteen times in all.

With nightfall barely two hours away, the LAPD wanted to avoid an all-night siege in a tough neighborhood. They decided to bring matters to a head. At 5:53, nine minutes after the first warning, a pair of Flite-Rite rockets streaked from the street, shattering a front window and exploding in Christine Johnson's living room. Wisps of tear gas could be seen wafting through the windows. From inside came the SLA's reply: a burst of machine-gun fire from an M1. Bullets chattered against the side of an apartment house across the street. Up and down the block, officers rose and fired their weapons into the house.

The entire neighborhood seemed to explode in gunfire. For five full minutes bullets whizzed and ricocheted everywhere, all of it broadcast live on television. Policemen ran to and fro. Everywhere residents ducked, climbed out windows, and sprinted for cover. Dozens more tear gas canisters were fired into the house, one hundred in all. Clouds of gas enveloped the house and front yard.

Then, at 6:40, after almost an hour of confusing gunfire, black smoke could be seen pouring from a rear window. Police would later theorize that one of their tear gas canisters had ignited the gasoline Nancy Perry had been seen pouring into bottles. Then Christine Johnson wobbled into the front yard, where police whisked her away. By then the first flames could be seen.

"Cease fire!" a SWAT leader barked. "Cease fire!"

Another officer lifted his bullhorn. "Come on out, the house is on fire," he announced. "You will not be harmed."

The only reply was a sustained burst of automatic-weapon fire. The police again opened fire. Then, at 6:47, came a lull in the shooting. Police would later discover that DeFreeze and his soldiers had chopped a hole in the kitchen floor and wriggled into the eighteen-inch crawlspace beneath the house. It was then, as the firing continued, that officers behind the house saw a tiny woman in combat fatigues emerge from a hole in the crawlspace. It was Nancy Ling Perry, "Fahizah." She took a step forward and, spying SWAT officers in the alley, raised a pistol and fired. Police fired back. Two bullets struck her in the back, severing her spinal cord, and she fell dead. Camilla Hall—"Gabi"—emerged from the crawlspace firing a pistol. A bullet struck her flush in the forehead, killing her. Officers watched as a pair of hands grabbed her ankles and dragged her back inside.

By then the house was engulfed in flames. Even then the SLA kept firing from the crawlspace. Finally, at 6:58, the roof began to collapse. The walls caved in. All that was left was an inferno, black smoke billowing into the early-evening sky, visible for miles. Three neighboring houses caught fire as well. All around, the police, the reporters, all of Los Angeles, were spellbound. For several minutes bullets and a pipe bomb or two could be heard exploding inside. A few minutes later the first fire engines began to move in.

The deadliest single day in the short history of America's radical underground was over. Six people were dead; not a single lawman had been hurt.

Later that night, when police began sifting through the rubble, they found DeFreeze, Mizmoon Soltysik, and Willie Wolfe in a rear corner of the crawl-space, burned to cinders, crushed, gas masks melted to their faces. Angela Atwood lay nearby. Nancy Perry had been buried beneath a falling wall. Camilla Hall's body wasn't found for two days. But that was it. The one person the LAPD, and all of America, most wanted to find, Patty Hearst, was nowhere to be found.

For days police cars cruised the neighborhood, hoping to catch a glimpse of her. What the police never learned was that others were searching as well: a team from the Weather Underground led by Bill Ayers's brother Rick. "We really thought groups like the SLA were nuts and horrible, and yet we felt some responsibility," Ayers recalls. "We could recognize that level of craziness, and that someone needed to get a hold of them and say, 'Just chill.' We just tried to find them, just drove around looking for them. We felt it was bad for everyone, and we thought, I don't know, that we could save them."

But Patty Hearst was gone.

14

WHAT PATTY HEARST WROUGHT

The Rise of the Post-SLA Underground

As Patty Hearst and the Harrises drove south from Los Angeles toward the city of Anaheim that day, May 17, 1974, their car radio was alive with reports of the LAPD's failure to capture their comrades in the house on Eighty-fourth Street. Harris roared with laughter and pounded the wheel every time an announcer repeated the news that the SLA had gotten away. The laughter stopped, however, once they checked into a hotel room down the road from Disneyland late that afternoon. Flipping on the television, Harris watched for a moment, confused, thinking at first that the scenes of policemen creeping toward a house on every channel were recordings of the morning raid on Eighty-fourth Street. With mounting horror, he finally realized this was a second raid, being shown live.

"That's our people in there!" Emily Harris screamed.

They watched it all, live, for hours, the firefight, the flames, the burning house, the bodies. Harris shouted at the television throughout, demanding that the three stage a rescue attempt, then realizing its futility, finally collapsing in Emily's arms in tears, blaming himself as Patty, curled up on the floor, trembled.

"It's all my fault," Harris kept saying. "I killed them. . . . Oh, I wish I was there. . . . I wish I was dead, too."

Shell-shocked, they spent that weekend at the hotel, then drove to Costa Mesa, where they stayed for a week at another hotel, watching the news, going over what had happened, going over their mistakes, before each of them swore their renewed allegiance to continue the SLA's struggle. On Memorial Day, ten days after the conflagration on Fifty-fourth Street, they drove north on Interstate 5, returning to the Bay Area, the only place they had friends they felt they could trust, who might hide them.

Their car broke down as soon as they reached San Francisco. After two days lugging a heavy duffel bag packed with guns between hotels, they managed to rent an apartment in Oakland. For the next few days they lay about inside, swilling jug wine as the Harrises squabbled, over money, over their plans, over sex; when Emily denied him, Harris simply mounted Patty, who felt powerless to object. Most of all they discussed who might be safe to approach. It was Emily who finally came up with a promising name: Kathy Soliah, one of Angela Atwood's waitressing friends. It turned out to be a fateful choice.

By all rights, the fiery destruction of the SLA should have brought an end to what little remained of the underground movement. Instead, it reinvigorated it. Where the vast majority of Americans viewed the SLA as a tiny, bizarre cult, those still inclined to believe in armed struggle envied the SLA's "achievements": the food program; the humbling of the Hearsts, millionaire capitalists; and most of all the publicity, the endless magazine covers and television coverage. For the first time in years the underground was part of the national conversation again. To those few who still yearned to hear it, the message was clear: Armed underground struggle was still a viable alternative, even in mid-1970s America, and its new crucible was Berkeley.

Within two years, in fact, four significant new bombing groups would emerge, three of whose founders either came from the Bay Area Left or had visited Berkeley in attempts to join the underground. Two new radical journals began publishing, the first since the death of Eldridge Cleaver's *Right On!*, both devoted to chronicling underground bombings and the printing of communiqués. Within weeks of the SLA's immolation, a series of public events—the trial of Joanne Chesimard, massive rallies in support of Attica plaintiffs, and the unlikely reemergence of the Weather Underground— would provide opportunities for scores of new underground members to meet, mingle, plot, and plan. The bombings, robberies, and deaths that resulted would, against all odds, extend the life of the radical underground into the 1980s.

It all began, in a way, with Kathy Soliah, who was twenty-seven that spring. Tall, with straight brown hair and a strong jawline—in some photos she bore a passing resemblance to Bernardine Dohrn—Soliah had waitressed with Angela Atwood before both women quit in anger after their manager ordered them to wear low-cut blouses. Like Atwood, Soliah was an amateur actress, and like Atwood she had wanted to join the SLA; according to Patty Hearst, Bill Harris had rejected Soliah, saying she was "too flaky to be trusted with the SLA's underground activities."

She was, in some ways, the SLA's biggest fan. News of their deaths incensed her. In the following days she cobbled together a protest rally. Held on June 2, 1974, in a corner of Berkeley's Ho Chi Minh Park, it drew four hundred or so onlookers, many of whom seemed to drift into the park out of curiosity; the FBI filmed the proceedings from a nearby building. Along the front of the stage, someone had lined up bottles of DeFreeze's favorite beverage, Akadama Plum Wine. Soliah took the microphone wearing pink bellbottoms, a turtleneck sweater, and enormous sunglasses. "I am a soldier of the SLA," she began.

> Cinque, Willie, Camilla, Mizmoon and Fahizah were viciously attacked and murdered by five hundred pigs in LA while the whole nation watched. I believe that Gelina and her comrades fought until the last minute. And though I would like to have her be here with me right now, I know that she

lived happy and she died happy. And in that sense, I am so very proud of her. SLA soldiers, although I know it's not necessary to say, keep fighting. I'm with you.

The Harrises read about Soliah's appearance in the newspapers and decided to contact her. Emily made the approach, slipping Soliah's aunt a note asking to meet at a Berkeley bookstore. Soliah appeared overjoyed. They gathered the next night at an Oakland drive-in; *The Sting* was playing. The Harrises spent hours telling Soliah every last detail of what happened in Los Angeles. Soliah swore that many in Berkeley still supported the SLA; she and her boyfriend, Jim Kilgore, in fact, were ready to sign up then and there. For the moment, though, Harris was less concerned with new recruits than with finding a safe place to hide. When he mentioned the possibility of heading to New York, Soliah said she knew someone who might be able to take them. His name was Jack Scott. He was, of all things, a radical sports writer, a onetime college athletic director who went on to write for *Ramparts*.

Scott had already spread word around Berkeley that he wanted to meet the SLA, but not to chauffeur them. He wanted to write their story. A meeting was arranged at the Oakland apartment. Scott said he was happy to drive them to New York, provided that they went unarmed; Harris objected, and their argument stretched toward dawn. Finally they agreed the guns would remain in the trunk. On June 7 Patty and the Harrises recorded a new communiqué for release; in it, Harris announced that the SLA lived on, now operating as a unit of something called the New World Liberation Front. The name meant nothing to police. Afterward everyone piled into three cars and drove east, toward the mountains. It was the beginning of what the press would later call Patty's "lost year."

Kathy Soliah did more than save the SLA. For weeks she had been fretting about the bad publicity the SLA was getting. So, with a group of radicals, she helped form a study group called the Bay Area Research Collective, known as BARC, which began publishing *Dragon*, a mimeographed journal that would become the landmark paper for underground groups. *Dragon* quickly grew beyond an initial focus on the SLA. Between 1975 and 1977 it would publish bombing news and communiqués from almost all the second-generation underground groups, especially those on the West Coast. But *Dragon* was more than just a clearinghouse for the underground. In an early announcement BARC indicated that it was affiliated with this New World Liberation Front, or NWLF.*

This being Berkeley in 1974, no one took this kind of talk seriously, not even the FBI. The NWLF might be a genuine new underground group, or it might, like so many others, exist only on paper. But something was afoot. During a jailhouse interview in late May, the SLA's Joe Remiro told a local author, John Bryan, of a May 25 "emergency meeting" in which a number of Bay Area radical groups had formed a new umbrella organization to coordinate the activities of the SLA, the NWLF, and others. In a subsequent issue, *Dragon* carried a letter, supposedly from the NWLF, in which it invited anyone and everyone to detonate their bombs in the name of the NWLF, a tactic it acknowledged made the group seem larger than it was. At least initially, the group's invitation was met with a yawning silence.

Then, on August 5, came the first NWLF bomb, a dud, left outside an office of the General Motors Acceptance Corp. in suburban Burlingame, California. A communiqué announced "greetings and love to the Symbionese Liberation Army." Three nights later came another—another dud—left outside a San Francisco GM dealership. In September two NWLF bombs shattered windows late at night outside two Bay Area offices of Dean Witter, a stock brokerage firm. After that the bombs began going off, on average, every sixteen days. On October 2 one damaged a women's bathroom at a San Francisco Sheraton; on October 5, a Sheraton in Los Angeles; on October 30, the home of a retired ITT executive in Silicon Valley; on November 6, seven meter-maid motorcycles in a Berkeley parking lot. By the end of 1974 eleven NWLF bombs had gone off, at which point the Bay Area press, long accustomed to random radical bombings, was obliged to take notice.

---

*Some sources claim that the name New World Liberation Front originated in a statement by Eldridge Cleaver in 1969. Cleaver envisioned it as an alliance of radical whites and Third World blacks.

The NWLF would become one of the great mysteries of the underground era. At first the FBI assumed that Bill Harris and the SLA were responsible. But NWLF bombs would still be exploding long after Harris and his acolytes were off the streets. They would go on year after year, in fact, mostly in California, until, in time, the NWLF would be credited with planting more bombs than any other underground group, more than twice as many as the Weather Underground. The truth about the group, or at least part of it, would not emerge for years.

Of the bombing groups that rose to public view beginning in 1974, perhaps the most surprising was the resurgent Weather Underground. It had been a long time coming. For Weather, 1972 and 1973 amounted to lost years, during which time they all but disappeared from public consciousness. Looking back today, few Weather alumni can remember much that happened then, in large part because very little did. Between May 1972, when it struck the Pentagon, and March 1974, when it attacked a federal building in San Francisco, Weather staged only two small bombings. By October 1973, when a three-year-old set of indictments against the leadership was dropped in Detroit, the *New York Times* called the group "dormant."

These were the years when the Movement slowed and then died, fracturing into dozens of radical shards. The final blow was the long, slow end of the Vietnam War, symbolized by the signing of the Paris Peace Accords, in January 1973. A few weeks later Weather issued a statement hailing the North Vietnamese "victory," but it was a short, desultory thing, noticed by few. The fact was, for many in the underground, the end of the war brought a kind of emotional vertigo, a rare moment of celebration followed by the morning-after realization that a dominant focus of their lives had suddenly disappeared. Without the war to protest, and without any sense that their bombings had changed the American condition, Weather had all but stopped doing them.

"We, like most of the Left, began to evaporate after the Vietnam War began ending," recalls Paul Bradley. "By '72 things were settling down. We read a lot, met with people, tried to raise money. There was a lot of talk about the role of armed actions, because we had done a lot of them and nothing had changed. There was a sense we should do something else, but there was no sense what that something else was."

For the moment, they did very little. It was during this period, in fact, that a number of Weathermen began taking actual jobs. In Los Angeles Rick Ayers worked as a housepainter and gardener. In San Francisco Bradley found work as a mechanic at a foreign-car dealership. He rode a cable car to work. His bosses adored him, handing him the garage keys, and Bradley returned their loyalty, at one point declining to attend a Weather retreat because he feared losing his job.

At the highest levels, however, only a handful of cosmetic changes were made. The leadership was rebranded the Central Committee; at one point the group's name was changed to the strangely corporate-sounding Weather Underground Organization. In May 1973 the New York cell roused itself to bomb a trio of police cars in Queens after a cop killed a ten-year-old black boy named Clifford Glover. Three years earlier Weatherman had been in the headlines on a regular basis. The morning after the Glover bombing the *Times* couldn't even get its name straight; its article suggested the group at some point had renamed itself "Weather People." No one knew; no one particularly cared. Coverage of the year's second bombing that September was just as dismissive. In protest of the CIA-backed coup in Chile, Weather detonated a bomb on the ninth floor of ITT headquarters in Manhattan, demolishing several empty rooms. Responsibility calls went to the *Post* and the *Times*, which seemed skeptical that Weather even still existed.

"If yesterday's bombing was indeed done by people connected with the Weatherman [sic]," the *Times* reported, "it would be one of the few times since the fall of 1970 that the violent splinter of Students for a Democratic Society has been heard from."

It was, all in all, a grim period for a group of intellectual firebrands who four years earlier had been public figures, giving interviews to *Time* and *Newsweek*. Bernardine Dohrn and Bill Ayers, it appears, spent much of it in their Hermosa Beach bungalow, squiring Mona Mellis's children to old movies and ice cream shops. Jeff Jones and the New York cell remained in their

Catskills hideaway. After the dropping of federal indictments, many Weathermen were no longer fugitives; while Dohrn and others were still wanted on state charges linked to the Days of Rage, Bill Ayers and Ron Fliegelman were now free to walk into FBI headquarters without fear of arrest. Dozens of agents were still looking for dozens of Weathermen—still breaking into their families' homes, in fact—but the only new arrest they made was dumb luck, when Howie Machtinger stumbled into a stakeout outside his brother's Manhattan apartment in September 1973. He made bail and promptly returned underground, releasing a statement thumbing his nose at the FBI as he did.

For a group as aimless as Weather, dissension was probably inevitable. As the months wore on with little sense of new direction, complaints bubbled up from the ranks, especially from those few dozen members who hadn't taken active roles in the bombings or leadership. Some were simply tired of living near the poverty line. A handful of gays and lesbians griped that leadership wasn't attentive to their needs. The loudest complaints, though, emanated from several young women who began to self-identify as radical feminists. The Central Committee discouraged them from joining outside feminist groups, prompting gripes that the leadership had been corrupted by "white male superiority." Efforts were made to placate these women. They were allowed to form a "women's brigade" within the organization that bombed a Department of Health, Education and Welfare building in San Francisco in March 1974. At one point it issued an entire white paper on the importance of feminism, not that it helped; one male Weatherman recalls a "Weatherwomen's" conclave in Marin County whose members emerged to insist that no male Weatherman could even talk with a female Weatherman without asking permission. This grousing culminated in a 1973 article in *Ms.* magazine by none other than Jane Alpert, Sam Melville's onetime girlfriend, who had been underground for three years, mostly working as a rabbi's secretary in Denver. Alpert, who had visited Bernardine Dohrn, Mark Rudd, and other Weathermen, announced that she was rejecting the underground because of "sexist" leadership that "exploited" women. Not long after, she surrendered to authorities.

A rare glimpse of this turmoil is afforded by a little-noticed internal history of Weather released by a band of dissidents in 1976. According to this document, matters came to a head in October 1973, when the Central Committee, fearing open revolt, developed a plan for "reorganization." The leadership realized that the complaints were symptoms of a far larger problem facing the group, a crisis at the core of its identity: If the Weather Underground wasn't going to bomb things, what would it do instead? The answer turned out to be surprisingly simple. For four years they had detonated bombs to get people to read the written statements they released. What if they simply went on releasing their writings without the bombs? What if they put all their writing into one package? The idea of a book was born.

From the outset, it was Bill Ayers's baby. By one account, he had been noodling with a political manifesto for months. According to the internal history, the Central Committee sold the idea as a program embodied in three slogans: "Educate Ourselves, Organize Ourselves, Activate Ourselves Around a Written Program." The project was less about politics than what businessmen call team building: They needed to get everyone on the same page—literally. The job of writing the book, which took all of 1973, has been described in Ayers's and other memoirs as a rare collaborative endeavor, with the manuscript being passed among writers throughout the organization. Borrowing a line from Mao—"a single spark can start a prairie fire"—they decided to call it *Prairie Fire: The Politics of Anti-Imperialism*.

The dissidents' history, however, suggests a far more contentious process. According to this version, Ayers's draft was "no good" and "strongly -criticized." A second draft was authorized, this one overseen by the old Communist Party hand who had driven the Timothy Leary getaway car, Clayton Van Lydegraf. It was a poor choice. Thirty years older than his peers, Van Lydegraf was a unique figure in Weather, a doctrinaire Maoist who had been deeply involved in Seattle's vibrant leftist politics since his days as a Boeing machinist after World War II. Bouncing among myriad communist groups, he emerged during the 1960s as a mentor to Seattle radicals and an author of several influential pamphlets, one of which caught the attention of John "JJ" Jacobs, who drew him into Weatherman. Van Lydegraf was an ardent proponent of armed struggle and disdained any retreat from it.

As it turned out, Van Lydegraf was one of two aging communists who got involved. The second was Eleanor Stein's mother, sixty-year-old Annie Stein, a chain-smoking activist who had long been active in New York left-wing politics. A former schoolteacher, she focused on fighting racism in the New York schools. During Weather's "lost years" she became a political mentor to her daughter and Jeff Jones. Sometimes the couple would slip into New York to sip coffee with Annie at one of her favorite delis. Other times they would take walks in the Catskills. Annie Stein was a traditional communist who believed that a social revolution would arise only from organizing "the masses," not from bombing buildings. By 1973 she and Van Lydegraf had become something like intellectual rivals, each determined to imprint their ideas on the leadership and in the pages of *Prairie Fire*.

After Bill Ayers's first draft was rejected, the internal history says, responsibility for a second draft was given to an "experienced and trusted comrade"—clearly Van Lydegraf—who enrolled several of the radical feminists. Distinctions between this group's "revolutionary" line, emphasizing Weather's support for women and people of color, are easily lost on any mainstream reader. But they clearly led to a series of internal debates that turned ugly. The history says the Central Committee "fought tooth and nail" for their version—which included Annie Stein's emphasis on the "international working class"—"and discouraged struggle against them by saying it was sectarian and factional." There were arguments over almost everything, from how to "position" the book to how to publish it.

"It was really a struggle between Annie and Van," recalls Howie Machtinger, who wrote sections of the manuscript. "They both considered themselves to the left of the Communist Party and the Chinese. But they were different. The emphasis on armed struggle, that was Van. The emphasis on organizational work with the masses, that was Annie. I read the thing as a compromise of their positions."

A power struggle ensued, its details now all but lost to history. What is clear is that Ayers and the Central Committee won; Van Lydegraf was expelled from Weather at some point in 1974. The resulting bitterness would eventually come back to haunt everyone involved.

The completed manuscript of *Prairie Fire*, which ran to 156 pages, ended up as a wide-ranging survey of 1970s-era radical views, featuring histories of the American Left, the rise of 1960s-era radicals, SDS, and the Vietnam

War. It laid out Weather's take on every conceivable political topic, from slavery and feminism to Native Americans and independence struggles in the African nation of Guinea-Bissau. Always, though, it circled back to the absolute necessity of violent revolutionary struggle against the U.S. government:

> We are a guerrilla organization. We are Communist men and women, underground in the United States for more than four years. . . .
>
> Our intention is to disrupt the empire, to incapacitate it, to put pressure on the cracks, to make it hard to carry out its bloody functioning against the people of the world, to join the world struggle, to attack from the inside.
>
> Our intention is to engage the enemy, to wear away at him, to harass him, to isolate him, to expose every weakness, to pounce, to reveal his vulnerability.
>
> Our intention is to encourage the people to provoke the leaps in confidence and consciousness, to stir the imagination, to popularize power, to agitate, to organize, to join in every way possible the people's day-to-day struggle.
>
> Our intention is to form an underground, a clandestine political organization engaged in every form of struggle, protected from the eyes and ears and weapons of the state, a base against repression, to accumulate lessons, experience and constant practice, a base from which to attack. . . .
>
> The only path to the final defeat of imperialism and the building of socialism is revolutionary war. Revolution is the most powerful resource of the people. . . . Many people have given their lives in this struggle and many more will have to.

As the manuscript neared completion, the question became how to publish it. They decided they couldn't risk engaging a traditional publishing house, even a radical one, so they chose to print and distribute the book themselves—no small task for a band of fugitives. But against the odds, the production of *Prairie Fire* was a triumph of Weather's logistical prowess. Almost everything was done in Boston, where the Central Committee's Robbie Roth and several New Yorkers had relocated. They rented the basement of a brownstone, purchased a multilith offset printer, and put it in a back room. In the front the handy Ron Fliegelman, with help from Mark Rudd, built a Potemkin-village outer office, complete with a reception desk and filing cabinets, in case they had uninvited visitors. Fliegelman supervised the printing press. They cranked out five thousand copies of the book, each assembled by hand, with gloves. According to one participant, a second printing was done in Eugene, Oregon.

It was an ambitious project, especially given the plans to distribute the book nationally. For that, more people were needed. At that point the leadership began reaching out to more than a dozen Weathermen who had been exiled or marginalized, hoping to lure them into becoming the foot soldiers they needed. Many accepted, including Howie Machtinger, still lurking around New York, and Jeff Jones's old pal Jon Lerner; both were assigned to a new collective in Boston. Mark Rudd, having long since abandoned New Mexico for a Pennsylvania farmhouse, came as well, moving with his girlfriend to Yonkers, New York.

By the spring of 1974 the book was ready to be released. As if needing to remind the public it still existed, Weather then launched a trio of new attacks, its first since the ITT bombing six months earlier. In protest of the SLA killings, the San Francisco cell bombed an office of the California attorney general. In New York, as a protest against the state's draconian drug laws, Fliegelman made a stink bomb his group rolled into a banquet feting Governor Nelson Rockefeller. "Yeah, a stink bomb, why not?" Fliegelman says today. "I guess we were trying to change things up a little." The final action came on June 13, barely a month before *Prairie Fire*'s release, when Weather detonated a large bomb that wrecked most of the twenty-ninth floor of Gulf Oil headquarters in Pittsburgh. Exactly as a traditional publisher might arrange a book excerpt in the pages of *Time* or *Newsweek*, Weather included an excerpt from *Prairie Fire* in its communiqué.

"Some of those late actions, I think we got a little sloppy, maybe a little dangerous," Fliegelman recalls. "I remember one time one of us took a bomb on an airplane, which we shouldn't have done." Asked if this was the Gulf action in Pittsburgh, a rare Weather bombing off the coasts, he shrugs and says, "Maybe."

Finally, everything was set. On the night of July 23, 1974, teams of volunteers dropped off copies of *Prairie Fire* at alternative bookstores and radical organizations in a dozen cities, from San Francisco to Madison, Wisconsin, to Philadelphia and New York. Silvia Baraldini never forgot walking into the Brooklyn Women's School to find them. "They just arrived, out of nowhere, a big pile of books," she says. "We were all told we had to study this book. And we did. Our desire to read the book was due to the mystique of Weatherman. We thought they were doing important things. They were *underground*."

Prairie Fire was widely read in radical circles and noticed in the mainstream, garnering a brief article in the *New York Times*. For the leadership, the taste of relevancy proved intoxicating and would lead to a series of plans that transformed what remained of the organization. The book's impact was felt outside the group as well. Like *Dragon*, *Prairie Fire* served as an invitation to new groups to take up the cause of "armed struggle" even as Weather's leaders, increasingly preoccupied with the printed word, showed little interest in new bombings themselves. Others heard the call, however, and within months of *Prairie Fire*'s appearance, they began to strike.

On its face, it was just another political rally, nearly twenty thousand people streaming into Madison Square Garden carrying angry placards and posters that night, October 27, 1974, three months after *Prairie Fire*'s publication. They had come to hear radical icons, such as Angela Davis and Jane Fonda, raise their fists and deliver speeches calling for change. What almost no one understood, save perhaps for the handful of people building the bombs, was that this rally heralded not only the debut of a new political movement but a new barrage of political terror, all the work of a group of militants who would emerge as the most determined bombers in U.S. history. All but forgotten today, they would go on to bomb dozens of U.S. skyscrapers and landmarks, raid presidential campaign offices, and kill more innocents than any other underground group.

They weren't black nationalists. They weren't aging hippies. Or the Palestinians, or the Croatians, or any of the other groups that resorted to terror tactics around the world during the 1970s. They were Puerto Ricans.

Their first bomb, though no one realized it at the time, had exploded at 12:55 a.m. on a hot summer night two months before the Garden rally, on August 31, 1974, in Damrosch Park outside Lincoln Center on Manhattan's West Side. The explosion did little but tear up a row of hedges. Sifting through the debris, the NYPD bomb squad found the remains of several propane tanks. No one claimed responsibility, and the incident was quickly forgotten.

A month later, on the night of September 28, two small bombs exploded across the river in Newark, New Jersey, in an alley between City Hall and police headquarters. No one was injured; there was no communiqué. The blasts came in the wake of rioting in which two Puerto Ricans had been killed. At the time Newark police had no clue the incidents were linked.

All of this, it appeared, served as a rehearsal for the onslaught that began on October 26, 1974, the morning before the Garden rally. At 2:55 a.m. a large bomb exploded beside a Mercury Comet parked outside the Marine Midland Bank in New York's Financial District.* The car was lifted into the air and smashed down on its roof, wobbling like an overturned turtle as the first patrol cars arrived; the bomb, which police later estimated to contain forty sticks of dynamite, shattered windows as high as eight floors up in surrounding buildings.

A few minutes later a second bomb detonated, outside the Exxon Building at Rockefeller Center in Midtown, again shattering windows but injuring no one. Ten minutes later a third exploded, outside the Banco de Ponce a block west, destroying the front door and blowing out windows as high as thirty-one stories up in adjoining buildings. As police began sifting through

---

*It was the same bank Sam Melville had bombed in the days after the Woodstock festival five years earlier, in September 1969.

the debris they were startled by the distant booms of a fourth and fifth bomb, one exploding outside the Union Carbide Building on Forty-eighth Street, the other at Lever House, on Park Avenue at Fifty-third Street. Both blew out windows, but no one was hurt.

Minutes later a caller to the Associated Press directed reporters to a communiqué inside a phone booth at Broadway and Seventy-third Street. The eight-paragraph note claimed the bombings on behalf of a group neither the NYPD nor the FBI had ever heard of: Fuerzas Armadas de Liberación Nacional Puertorriqueña, Spanish for "Armed Forces of Puerto Rican National Liberation." The communiqué was emblazoned with a logo: a five-point star with the initials FALN inside. The text called for independence for Puerto Rico and the release of five "political prisoners," all Puerto Rican militants who had carried out two attacks in Washington more than twenty years before: an attempted assassination of President Harry Truman in 1950 and a machine-gun attack on the floor of Congress in 1954. The five bombings, it said, were "a significant step in the formation of an anti-imperialist front in the United States, which will support and fight for the national liberation of Puerto Rico, and educate the American people about the murderous and genocidal policies of the Yanki capitalists through the world."

Both the NYPD and the FBI mobilized, but behind the scenes there was little real urgency, at least at first. Bombs had been going off in New York for five years, and more than a few had been placed by the odd Puerto Rican radical, most of whom had been arrested. At first blush this seemed more of the same. The NYPD catalogued the evidence, but as they suspected, there were no fingerprints, nor anything else to identify the bombers. In time the probe's momentum waned. At some point someone would make a mistake, and then arrests would be made.

Then six weeks later, just before 11 p.m. on December 11, a call came in to an NYPD precinct house in East Harlem. A woman with a Latin accent said there was a dead body inside an abandoned building. An officer named Ray Flynn responded, along with a rookie named Angel Poggi, a Puerto Rican officer who was enjoying his first full day of police work. When the two reached the building, they found it boarded up. There was no sign of activity. They left, figuring it had been a hoax.

A few minutes later the woman called again. The body was inside the building, she said. With a sigh, Flynn and Poggi returned. Flynn headed down a flight of steps to check basement windows. Poggi stepped up to the front entrance, a set of double doors. He pushed on the left door, which budged an inch or so. Poggi thought the body might be blocking the door. He took out a flashlight and peered inside. He could just make out a pile of debris blocking the doors and, above, what appeared to be remnants of a spider web hanging from the ceiling. Poggi gave the right door a shove. The explosion blew him into the air and vaulted his body out into the street, where it landed on the pavement, crumpled and shredded with slivers of wood and glass. Flynn raced to the cruiser and called for an ambulance, which spirited Poggi, still alive, to Metropolitan Hospital. Permanently disfigured, Angel Poggi would lose his right eye and much of the vision in his left and suffer a ringing in his ears for years afterward.

A woman telephoned the Associated Press several minutes later, claimed the attack on behalf of the FALN, and directed police to a communiqué in a phone booth at Fifty-second Street and Tenth Avenue. The single piece of paper, emblazoned with the same star logo as the October bombings, cited Comando Tomás López de Victoria, a Puerto Rican revolutionary, and said the attack was revenge for the death of a Puerto Rican musician named Martin Perez, who had hanged himself while in custody at the NYPD's 25th Precinct ten days earlier.

Suddenly the NYPD's investigation of this FALN gained momentum. If these people were targeting cops, it was time to get serious.

When Lou Vizi, a caustic thirty-one-year-old Philadelphian, transferred to the FBI's New York offices that summer after spending his first year in the Bureau chasing moonshiners across eastern Kentucky, he was thrilled to be back in a big Eastern city—at first. Then he sized up his twenty or so fellow agents in the Puerto Rican Security Squad. Most had gray hair and paunches. "Half these guys had been in that squad since World War Two," Vizi recalls. "They never went out in the streets. You couldn't dynamite 'em away from their desks. They had cases that, I swear, had been open for twenty years. We had zero resources, not a single radio, and one car the supervisor took home at night. When you went out on a lead, you had to take the subway."

There wasn't much to do. The Puerto Rican independence movement that turned violent on the island during the 1950s had spawned two series of bombings in New York but little of note in three years. Vizi, the youngest member of the squad, spent weeks probing an old case involving a group of supposed dissidents before realizing that the group no longer existed. It was a lonely job until Don Wofford—a genial thirty-three-year-old North Carolinian who had joined the Bureau two years earlier, after serving in Vietnam as an army hospital administrator—arrived at the squad on October 25, two days before the Garden rally.* Wofford and Vizi, both army veterans eager for action, found themselves running down leads together. When the older agents lost interest in the case—let the NYPD handle it, they muttered—the two young bucks kept at it. "None of the old guys wanted any part of that case," Vizi recalls. "Are you kidding? All that work? Riding the subway? They gave it to us instead."

Not that the young men, who had never actually investigated a bomb case, much less met an actual Puerto Rican, had much to offer. At one point Vizi was sent to NYPD headquarters, where someone pulled him into a meeting of deputy chiefs, one of whom asked what the FBI knew about the FALN. "Nothing," Vizi was obliged to stammer. "We've never heard of these guys either."

That, for the most part, was the extent of FBI-NYPD cooperation. The police kept the evidence to themselves, leaving Wofford and Vizi to begin combing through the Puerto Rican squad's files. They had chased a few leads, accomplishing nothing, when the booby-trapped bomb maimed Angel Poggi. They stood around the crime scene, powerless to help, while the NYPD gathered evidence. One thing, however, was clear.

"Don and I started realizing this was going to get a lot worse," Vizi recalls.

---

*Wofford joined the FBI in 1972 to avoid a second stint in Vietnam. The oldest student in his class at the FBI Academy, he served two years in Norfolk, Virginia, before his transfer to New York.

"These guys were serious. We tried to warn people, warn our supervisor, but no one was listening. It was no use." And then it happened.

Friday, January 24, 1975. It was a frigid noontime on Wall Street; a brisk winter wind whistled through the steel-and-concrete canyons. On the sidewalks bankers and traders and their assistants pressed down their hats and gathered their overcoats as they trudged out to grab sandwiches and hot cups of coffee. On Broad Street there was a steady flow of men—almost all men, in fact—moving into the colonnaded front doors of Fraunces Tavern, a red-brick restaurant that was one of the oldest buildings in New York. It opened in 1762 and had been a favorite of George Washington's. Washington, in fact, gave an emotional farewell address to his officers there in 1785.

Two centuries later Fraunces was a clubby Wall Street lunch spot, defined by white table linens, attentive waiters, and Revolutionary-era portraits. It had three dining areas: the bustling room inside the front doors, the private 250-member Anglers Club upstairs, and, set behind a pair of fire doors down a hallway, an annex building that housed the Bissell dining room. It was there, at an oval table set just inside the doors, that a group of six young executives were having what should have been a routine business lunch. Three of the men were bankers at J. P. Morgan & Co.; the others were clients. Lunch had been a last-minute decision, a chance to break from a long meeting and get to know one another.

Three of the men sat with their backs to the doors. Frank Connor, a thirty-three-year-old father of two, was a Morgan man, a finance executive who rode a commuter train into Manhattan from his home in Fair Lawn, New Jersey. Jim Gezork worked for Scott Paper in Philadelphia. Beside him sat Alex Berger, the thirty-two-year-old son of German Jewish refugees who worked for the chemical company Rohm & Haas in Philadelphia. Berger and his wife were expecting their first child, a son, in three months.

Around one o'clock, their meals almost finished, they called for the check. Five minutes later, with all three dining rooms packed with patrons, a waiter across the room saw an unkempt man in a trench coat step through the double doors and look around. Standing beside the oval table where the six executives were readying to leave, the man appeared out of place; the waiter thought he might be one of the homeless people who sometimes wandered into the restaurant. The waiter glanced away, and when he looked up, the man was gone. A few minutes after that another diner approached the stairs that led up to the Anglers Club. The waiter noticed a large gray duffel bag someone had inexplicably plopped down at the base of the stairs. Not wanting anyone to trip, he nudged it to one side of the staircase with his foot.

The duffel, which carried a bomb consisting of roughly ten sticks of dynamite and a propane tank, detonated at 1:22 p.m. The immense explosion collapsed the staircase and blew a hole in the floor seven feet wide. Windows and plate-glass doors shattered in buildings up and down Broad Street; a truck parked outside was wrecked, tossed on its side. The thin wall to the Bissell dining room evaporated. Sitting behind it, Frank Connor and Alex Berger were killed instantly; Jim Gezork would die on the operating table. All around, bodies were thrown into the air, people somersaulting through a blizzard of deadly flying glass. Knives and forks zinged through the restaurant like angry bees, impaling a number of diners; doctors would later remove cutlery from a dozen or more patrons. More than forty people were badly injured in the Bissell dining room alone. The force of the explosion erupted upward as well, sending a single floor nail firing through the ceiling like a bullet, where it tore through the bottom of a chair and ripped into the body of a sixty-six-year-old banker named Harold Sherburne, killing him.

Chaos ensued. In a flash waiters and patrons from the main dining room, which remained unharmed behind a thick brick wall, scrambled through the wreckage and dragged dazed and bleeding men out onto the sidewalk. The blast echoed through the Wall Street area, sending scores of office workers, plus firemen at a nearby station house, into the streets to see what was wrong. A priest from Our Lady of the Rosary Church on State Street was among the first to arrive; he knelt in the wreckage, administering last rites. Within minutes the whine of sirens filled the air. Wounded men writhed in pools of blood beside the gutters as the first police cars arrived. Quickly the streets filled with cops, fire engines, ambulances, and crowds of the curious. By nightfall four men would be declared dead. It was the worst terrorist attack on U.S. soil since an anarchist bomb hidden in a horse-drawn cart killed thirty-five people on Wall Street in 1920.

Don Wofford and Lou Vizi were in a car on FDR Drive when they heard the news on the radio. They stopped, telephoned their supervisor, Harry Hogue, and asked whether the FALN might be involved.

"A tavern? The FALN isn't gonna blow up a tavern," Hogue replied "Believe me, it's probably just a gas explosion."

"We're going down there anyway," Wofford said.

"Well, okay, but I'm telling you, it's just a gas explosion."

Wofford and Vizi were among the first FBI men on the scene. By the time they arrived, a caller had taken responsibility for the attack on behalf of the FALN, directing police to a communiqué inside a phone booth. By that evening Don Wofford, barely two years out of the FBI Academy, found himself leading the Bureau's investigation, which he named FRANBOMB. In those early hours, backed by nearly fifty agents, he and Vizi began scribbling assignments on note cards and handing them to other agents, who flooded the streets looking for eyewitnesses. No one had much of anything useful to say. The NYPD came up with sketches of two Hispanic men seen in the area, but they never came to anything. The NYPD managed to identify the duffel bag's maker, and detectives fanned out in hopes of finding who sold it. The components of the bombs detonated to date—the Timex wristwatches, the batteries, the propane tanks—were studied in detail. They were all the same, in all likelihood the work of a single bomb maker. There was little else to be learned.

But that wasn't Wofford's central problem. From the beginning, the Fraunces Tavern investigation—and the broader probe of the FALN—was hamstrung by the strange new rules of policing in the mid-1970s. Until 1972 the NYPD, like the FBI, had maintained extensive files on all manner of Puerto Rican radical groups. But after complaints from left-wing civil rights groups, many files, along with scores of files on similar radicals, had been destroyed. "We haven't done any surveillance of Puerto Rican political groups in several years," one detective griped to the *New York Times*. "We've been forbidden from even attending meetings as observers. The truth is we have no good contacts inside the radical Puerto Rican community and we were completely unprepared for the FALN when it sprung up."[1]

The FBI, however, unlike much of the American public, knew a lot about Puerto Rican terrorism. Then as now, it's hard to identify an issue of such national significance about which so many Americans knew—and cared—so little. Yet there had been people in Puerto Rico, a U.S.-owned territory roughly three times the size of Rhode Island, who had been fighting for its independence almost since Christopher Columbus stepped onto a beach there in 1493. The indigenous Taino revolted against the Spanish in 1511. They lost. Native-born islanders (*criollos*) took to arms for reform in 1809. They lost. Anti-Spanish conspiracies—one history counts more than thirty—popped up throughout the nineteenth century. Full-blown revolts against Spain erupted in 1868 and again in 1897. Each left its leaders in prison, with sundry followers skulking off to jungle lairs or U.S. cities to begin plotting anew.

When the United States gained control of the island in 1898, after the Spanish-American War, it appeared the nationalists had given up their guns for political debate. The Puerto Rico Independence Party was formed in 1912, though its cause was soon subsumed by the more powerful Nationalist Party, formed in 1922. The new party's leaders loudly called for independence, but unfortunately—and this has always been the irony for Puerto Rican nationalists—the vast majority of Puerto Ricans were happy being part of the United States. The Nationalist Party was defeated again and again at the polls, and before long its frustrated leaders decided it was time to return to violence.

The 1930s saw a series of Nationalist marches that devolved into melees, along with various assassination attempts against U.S. judges and governors. Things simmered until 1948, when a U.S.-appointed governor forced through the infamous Law 53, forbidding public calls for independence. Two years later, when the United States moved to declare Puerto Rico a semiautonomous commonwealth, nationalists launched a series of coordinated attacks on police and government buildings across the island, in Mayagüez, Jayuya, Arecibo, and, most notably, in the capital of San Juan, where gunmen sprayed the governor's mansion with bullets. The army moved in, and every major nationalist leader was arrested.

Then, on November 1, 1950, as the White House was being renovated and President Truman was living at Blair House, two Puerto Rican revolutionaries tried to rush the building and assassinate him. They succeeded only in forcing a shoot-out with guards, one of whom was killed. One attacker was killed, too; the other was sentenced to death, until Truman commuted his sentence.*

Four years later, in 1954, four more Puerto Rican revolutionaries filed into the balcony of the U.S. House of Representatives, quietly recited the Lord's Prayer, then rose, whipped out guns, and opened fire on a crowd of congressmen below. Five legislators were hit, one of them, Alvin M. Bentley of Michigan, struck in the chest. All recovered. The shooters were arrested and given life sentences; gaining their freedom had been a priority for every Puerto Rican radical since.

For the next decade the independence movement lay dormant. By the mid-1960s, however, with revolutionary movements springing up in postcolonial Asia, Africa, and, most notably, Cuba, a new breed of armed militant appeared in Puerto Rico: Marxist by outlook, impatient by nature, and eager to resort to violence to free the island from the hated *yanquis*. Among the most energetic of these firebrands was a salsa musician named Filiberto Ojeda Ríos. Born in the town of Naguabo in 1933, Ojeda Ríos was intelligent enough to enter the University of Puerto Rico at fifteen. In 1950, after a family argument over his future, he dropped out and moved to New York City, where he married, fathered the first of his four children, and played guitar and trumpet in salsa bands. Another musician recruited him into a Marxist study circle, where he was radicalized and joined the July 26 Movement, which supported Fidel Castro in his struggle against the Cuban government. Ojeda Ríos dreamed of launching a similar struggle in Puerto Rico, to which he returned in 1955. Six years later he moved to Cuba, where he

---

*This man, Oscar Collazo, served twenty-nine years in prison until ordered released by President Carter in 1979. Collazo was among several Puerto Rican nationalists decorated by Fidel Castro that same year.

attended the University of Havana and was recruited into Cuba's intelligence service, the General Intelligence Directorate, known as the DGI. At the time, the DGI's goal was spreading Castro's revolution into the countries of the Caribbean and Latin America.

Puerto Rico was in Castro's sights from the beginning. Accounts of DGI history indicate that Ojeda Ríos was given extensive training in sabotage and spycraft and dispatched to Puerto Rico in 1963, about the same time, perhaps coincidentally, that the first modern Puerto Rican revolutionary group, known as MAPA, emerged. Police quickly arrested MAPA's leaders, however, and Ojeda Ríos returned to Cuba, where with other Puerto Rican exiles he continued to plan for revolution. According to Puerto Rican newspaper accounts, a turning point came when, during a 1966 meeting with Castro himself, Ojeda Ríos received approval to form an armed resistance group that would carry out sabotage in both Puerto Rico and the U.S. mainland, backed by Cuban arms and money.

The group Ojeda Ríos formed, the Armed Revolutionary Independence Movement, known by its Spanish initials, MIRA, became one of an alphabet soup of ragtag revolutionary groups that sprang up on the island in the late 1960s. MIRA launched its first attacks in 1969, detonating bombs outside police stations and government installations. Unlike other island groups, it also established a New York cell, which staged a series of thirty-five or so minor bombings in the city beginning in November 1969, including a pipe bomb that exploded outside the main branch of the public library and one that didn't outside the General Electric building. MIRA's little-noticed campaign, relegated to the back pages of city newspapers, climaxed with explosions inside two Bronx movie theaters on May 1, 1970, two months after destruction of the Weatherman townhouse. Ten people suffered minor injuries.

Two weeks later police arrested a Puerto Rican radical named Carlos Feliciano as he placed a hollowed-out loaf of bread outside an army recruiting station in the Bronx. The bread was fresh, as was the bomb nestled inside. Feliciano was a MIRA operative who had served five years for a murder committed after the 1950 uprisings. A father of six, he was alleged to have committed all thirty-five bombings, charged with two, and convicted of one. In Puerto Rico police swooped in and arrested Ojeda Ríos, who promptly skipped bail and disappeared. This marked the end of MIRA, although its attacks continued for a short time in New York, with more than a hundred oddly tiny bombings stretching into 1971. The devices consisted of chemicals secreted inside cigarette packs and Ping-Pong balls. The detonations caused minimal damage—for example, a grand total of $50 from the cigarette pack that exploded in the carpet department of B. Altman & Co. in March 1971. Afterward police arrested two Puerto Rican students who claimed to be MIRA members, perhaps its last; they received jail terms of five and seven years.

By 1975 MIRA was a dimming memory, but its mastermind, Ojeda Ríos, remained at large. Many in the FBI, especially those with experience in Puerto Rico, suspected that he had now graduated from exploding Ping-Pong balls to indiscriminate murder. But where he was, or where this FALN would strike next, no one had a clue.

Don Wofford and Lou Vizi studied the three FALN communiqués carefully. Dense with Marxist verbiage, they seemed to hold echoes of Weather texts. A number of agents suspected the FALN was a cover for Weather, that the older group was taking on a new cause under a new name; just that summer, *Prairie Fire* had called for Puerto Rican independence. Others suggested the group was a tool of Cuban intelligence. Wofford's supervisor, Harry Hogue, suggested that they study the acres of files the squad had built over the years: "The answers are in the files. Believe me, the files will solve this case." Privately, Wofford scoffed. "The answers are in the files, my ass," he muttered to Vizi. "These people are new. They're cutting edge. They're not the same old guys we've been chasing for years." Still, Wofford did begin thumbing through the files, which clerks wheeled to his desk by the cartload. As he read, one *independista* in particular drew his attention. His name was Julio Rosado.

A former newspaper reporter in San Juan, Rosado embodied the independence cause in New York. His name seemed to be on every protest permit. He and his brothers, Andres and Luis, had been thoroughly investigated during the MIRA bombings; by Wofford's count, there were ten volumes of reports on Julio alone. "As far as suspects, the Rosados were head and shoulders above everyone," Wofford recalls. "They knew everybody in the movement. They were everywhere. They *were* the movement. The older agents still had an informant or two, and when we asked who could pull off something like Fraunces, who had the vision and leadership, Julio's name came zinging back every time. Julio, Julio, Julio, Julio. It was all we heard. He became my main focus."

On the day after the bombing, Wofford dispatched a pair of agents to interview Rosado at his apartment, on Brooklyn's Eastern Parkway. They returned to Sixty-ninth Street excited, reporting that Rosado, confronted at his apartment door, had gone white and begun shaking the moment they fired questions at him. Before he slammed the door in their faces, the two agents got the strong sense he had something to hide.

Wofford had the Rosado brothers placed under twenty-four-hour surveillance. Julio's apartment was in Brooklyn, while agents rented an apartment across from Andres and Luis's building, on Manhattan's Second Avenue, training binoculars on every entrance. Trailing the trio through the streets of New York proved challenging, however. All three seemed to be expert at countersurveillance techniques, jumping in and out of subway cars at the last minute, even sliding through the back doors of stores, to elude their pursuers. "These people were good; they were amazing," Lou Vizi recalls. "Let me tell you, they taught *us* about surveillance. We were so young, we had to learn all this stuff."

The second focus of the FBI's investigation, meanwhile, took shape in Spanish Harlem, where Wofford was intrigued by a Puerto Rican activist who had organized protests over the death of the young artist in the Angel Poggi case. Her name was Dylcia Pagan, and like Julio Rosado, she had worked as a journalist, first as a gossip columnist for a Spanish-language newspaper, then as a producer developing children's programming at the local CBS affiliate and other stations. "She was a real dynamo," Wofford recalls. "She seemed to know everyone in Spanish Harlem." Wofford put Pagan under round-the-clock surveillance, usually posting teams on rooftops near her apartment.

For the moment, however, neither Pagan nor the Rosado brothers were leading them anywhere. Wofford pressed the U.S. attorney's office for warrants to search or bug their apartments, but prosecutors turned him down every time, saying he didn't have probable cause. In one meeting Lou Vizi lost his temper. "I was just screaming at the guy, 'What do you want? What do we have to give you to get this warrant?'" he recalls. "My supervisor had to drag me out of there."

Other FBI offices were scarcely more helpful. Wofford expected the San Juan office, which had been chasing Ojeda Ríos and other revolutionaries for years, to be a trove of leads. To his dismay, San Juan refused even to respond to many of his inquiries. He and Vizi appealed to headquarters but ran smack into the realities of FBI bureaucracy. Individual SACs (special agents in charge) ran their offices as personal fiefdoms, and with J. Edgar Hoover dead and gone, there was no one in Washington willing to make San Juan play ball. "We sent hundreds of leads to San Juan," Vizi recalls. "You could wait till retirement and never get anything. Eventually I remember the San Juan SAC sent us something that basically said, 'Stop busting our balls. The bombs are going off in New York, not here. It's your problem.'"

Wofford, Vizi, and dozens of other agents were still working around the clock when, on the night of April 2, the FALN struck again. The first bomb exploded at 11:42 p.m., on the southwest corner of Madison Avenue and Twenty-seventh Street, shattering four large plate-glass windows in the New York Life Insurance Building. Five minutes later the second bomb detonated, outside the Metropolitan Life Insurance building at Park Avenue and Twenty-fifth Street, shattering sixty windows. A pedestrian was struck by flying glass and treated at Bellevue Hospital. At midnight the third bomb exploded, outside the Bankers Trust Company on Park Avenue at Forty-eighth Street. Ten minutes later a fourth and final bomb exploded, amid a pile of green trash bags outside a Blimpie fast-food restaurant, next door to the American Bank and Trust Co. on Forty-sixth Street at Fifth Avenue.

At 1 a.m. someone with a Spanish accent called the Associated Press and directed police to a communiqué inside an Eighty-eighth Street pay phone. The communiqué was dramatically different from previous missives; while again demanding the release of Puerto Rican prisoners and condemning CIA "repression," it was almost apologetic about the Fraunces Tavern bombing:

"Our attack on January 24, 1975, was not in any way directed against working-class people or innocent North Americans. The targets of our attack were bankers, stock brokers and important corporate executives of monopolies and multi-national corporations."

Wofford and Vizi spent days orchestrating agents who canvassed all four bomb sites looking for witnesses. The bomb components, analyzed by the NYPD's bomb squad, produced no new leads. "No one saw shit," Vizi told Wofford one afternoon as he slumped at his desk. "Same logo, same typewriter, same everything. We got nothing."

The only good news was that the FALN, presumably in reaction to criticism it had received for the deaths at Fraunces Tavern, had returned to nighttime bombings that put fewer people at risk. Wofford was now convinced that the FALN was a genuine new radical group and that the only way to stop it was to become the FBI's one-man clearinghouse for everything FALN. He was still studying the old reports that June when the FALN suddenly opened a new theater of operations.

Just after midnight on June 14, 1975, two young couples, Bill and Sara Evans and Jim and Cynthia Teitelbaum, strolled through the warm night air in The Loop section of downtown Chicago, a world away from the FALN bombings in New York.* They were walking past the First National Bank at the corner of Monroe and Dearborn when they noticed a curly-haired man with a bushy mustache crouching by the front entrance. Thinking he was homeless, they turned away and headed down the street to a bar, where they enjoyed a nightcap. Afterward, heading back to their car, the two couples again passed in front of the bank and spied a camera bag on the sidewalk.

Curious, Jim Teitelbaum picked it up and carried it to the car, where he slid into the backseat. As Bill Evans, at the wheel, drove away from the curb, Teitelbaum struggled with the bag's zipper, which seemed to be covered in a sticky substance. After a few moments he managed to open the bag. Peering

---

*The names are pseudonyms. The couples were never publicly identified.

inside, he saw a tangle of wires, a small propane tank, and several sticks of what could only be dynamite.

"It's a bomb!" he shouted.

Evans screeched to a halt at the curb. Teitelbaum opened the car door and threw the bag onto the sidewalk as the others scrambled out the other side into the street. As the bag landed, all its components, including the dynamite, tumbled out onto the pavement.

It didn't explode. Teitelbaum and Evans exchanged glances. Should they run? Or abandon it on the sidewalk? Deciding he couldn't risk harming an innocent pedestrian, Teitelbaum leaped from the car and gave the bomb a hard kick toward the Mid-Continental Plaza Building. He had just turned and taken several running steps toward the car when the dynamite exploded. The boom reverberated through the streets. Its force threw Teitelbaum to the pavement. Patting himself down, he found he was miraculously uninjured, save for a few pieces of shrapnel that had seared into his back. Windows shattered up and down the streets.

Chicago police were on the scene in minutes. The bomb left a foot-wide crater in the sidewalk. Twenty minutes later, as uniformed officers began roping off the area, the distant boom of another explosion echoed through the night. The second bomb detonated in front of the United Bank of America, shattering windows but injuring no one. Ten minutes later a woman called the Associated Press, claimed the bombings in the name of the FALN, and directed police to a communiqué in a phone booth at Chicago's Union Station. When police retrieved it, they discovered that it spoke of three bombs, the third at the Federal Building. A search there lasted into the next day but uncovered nothing.

The Chicago bombings triggered a vigorous debate between the FBI's New York and Chicago offices. Older agents, accustomed to MIRA and similarly lackluster Puerto Rican groups, argued that this was more of the same, most likely one or two angry New Yorkers who had set off bombs in Chicago to make themselves appear more significant than they were. Wofford and Vizi didn't believe it. They suspected something larger afoot, especially after the Weather Underground took credit for a June 16 bombing at a New York branch of the Banco de Ponce that the FALN had already bombed. (Thirty years later Weatherman David Gilbert acknowledged that he had set this bomb himself.) Wofford and Vizi, working fourteen hours a day six days a week, scoured their yellowing reports for anything that might link the FALN to the Weather Underground or to their mutual friends in Cuban intelligence, an effort that gained steam after Fidel Castro announced publicly that August that the Cuban government would give the FALN whatever support it could. For the moment, though, the FALN itself remained a phantom.

Then, on October 27, the anniversary of the first bombings in New York, came the most ambitious set of attacks to date. Just after midnight, in the span of a single hour, ten pipe bombs detonated in three cities: two in Washington, outside the State Department and the Bureau of Indian Affairs; five in New York, outside four banks and the United Nations; and three in Chicago, outside the Continental National Bank, IBM Plaza, and the Sears Tower. The explosion at Continental, two blocks from the FBI office, was so loud it shook the night supervisor's desk. A guard at the Chicago Standard Oil Building, meanwhile, reacting to the echoing booms, searched the surrounding plaza and stumbled upon something strange: an abandoned bouquet of roses in green florist's paper. Inside, to his horror, he glimpsed five sticks of dynamite. A member of the Chicago bomb squad, Frank Kasky, arrived in time to disarm the device. Kasky's work gave authorities their first unexploded FALN device.

Damage from the ten bombs came to a quarter of a million dollars. A caller to the Associated Press directed authorities to a communiqué in New York, which thanked Castro for his "moral support." In twelve months the FALN had now detonated twenty-five bombs. In Washington FBI supervisors were growing impatient. Shouting matches erupted between Washington and Chicago, where agents for the first time were sent burrowing into the Puerto Rican community, much of it centered on Humboldt Park. They managed to identify a handful of neighborhood leaders who had spoken favorably of Puerto Rican independence, including a high school principal named José López and a reverend named José Torres. Neither said much. At one point agents interviewed Torres's twenty-three-year-old son, Carlos. They found him polite and respectful, wrote up a report, and forgot about it, with no clue whatsoever that they had just spoken to one of the FALN's masterminds.

"THE BELFAST OF NORTH AMERICA"

*Patty Hearst, the SLA, and the Mad Bombers
of San Francisco*

In the final days of June 1974, a month before the publication of *Prairie Fire* and six weeks before Richard Nixon's resignation, Patty Hearst found herself sitting beside the sports writer Jack Scott in the back of a blue Ford LTD being driven by his parents, an elderly Las Vegas couple who had happily agreed to drive the country's most wanted fugitive across the country. All Patty wanted was a way out of a police dragnet. All Scott wanted was a book. Bill and Emily Harris followed in separate cars. After five days the group reached New York, heading to Scott's Upper West Side apartment.

Thus began what the press would call Patty's "lost year," a period when she and what remained of the Symbionese Liberation Army vanished from view. By this point, Patty wrote years later, she had abandoned any hope of leaving the group or escaping; she thought of herself as an SLA soldier and was resigned to whatever fate that brought. Those first few months they spent on the East Coast. Scott and his wife rented a farm in the Pennsylvania countryside, outside Scranton, where Patty was joined by the Harrises and a new recruit named Wendy Yoshimura, a Berkeley radical who had helped detonate several bombs in the Bay Area in 1971 and 1972. Back in California, Kathy Soliah was promising to gather new SLA members; once she did, Harris said, they would return west and renew combat operations. In the meantime they busied themselves doing calisthenics, reading, and arguing; Harris was a volatile martinet, forever screaming at Emily and the others over slights real and imagined. The Scotts visited every week and several times actually brought along friends, including a Canadian writer who began interviewing them all for the book Scott hoped to write but never would.

At the end of July the Scotts suddenly announced that the farm was no longer safe. Everyone moved to a second farmhouse, this one outside the remote New York village of Jeffersonville, which, as it happened, was barely fifty miles south of the vacation home where Jeff Jones and Weather's New York cell were hiding. They remained there for two months, out of sight, until word finally arrived from Soliah. She had the recruits ready; better yet, the trial of their onetime SLA comrades Joe Remiro and Russ Little had been moved to Sacramento. Harris approved a plan for everyone to rendezvous in the California capital. There they would try to break their friends out of jail.

In the last week of September the Scotts took Patty and drove west. The trip was uneventful, save for a traffic stop one night in Indiana. In Utah they turned south for Las Vegas, where Scott deposited Patty at a motel until someone could fetch her. Two days later Kathy Soliah's boyfriend, Jim Kilgore, arrived, a .38 pistol jammed in his belt. They took an overnight bus to Sacramento, where Soliah had rented a house—"basically a wooden shack," Hearst called it—in a rundown neighborhood near downtown.

There Patty met the new recruits Soliah had rounded up. In addition to Kilgore, they were Soliah's laid-back brother Steve, her sister Jo, and a pugnacious Berkeley housepainter named Mike Bortin. Everyone was warm and kind, which Patty needed after four months stuck with the bickering Harrises, and for two weeks she was able to relax. Everyone sat around talking, hashing over the SLA's errors; the Soliahs felt strongly that the group needed to read up on conventional Marxist texts to craft a message to win the hearts and minds of the Bay Area Left. They fed everyone by shoplifting.

Everything changed the moment the Harrises arrived. Bill, the little general, antagonized everyone by spouting orders and excoriating anyone who questioned him; he was Donald DeFreeze's anointed successor, and he expected his "troops" to give him the respect they had given their fallen leader. When Wendy Yoshimura returned from the East Coast, a screaming match with Harris ensued, and she left for a time. The Harrises fought constantly, and more than once Bill punched Emily, blackening her eye. Between arguments the group did its best to plot the escape of Remiro and Little. But for weeks not much happened. The new recruits shuttled between San Francisco and Sacramento; when visiting the capital, they debated targets, strategies, and politics. As for Patty Hearst, she was just happy to still be alive.

The FBI's inability to find Patty and the Harrises, in the wake of Watergate and accompanying leaks and investigations into the Hoover-era black bag jobs and abuses, was yet another blow to its faltering reputation. At every press conference, at every dinner, Director Clarence Kelley was pelted with questions: Why couldn't they find Patty Hearst? Where was she? The Bureau tried everything, prevailing on the *Journal of the California Dental Association* to publish the fugitives' dental records, even printing wanted posters in Spanish—a first—which it distributed to police in Mexico and Central America. By the end of 1974, however, they hadn't uncovered a single significant lead.

The break finally came on January 31, 1975, when Jack Scott's tipsy brother, Walter, wobbled into a Scranton, Pennsylvania, police station at 2 a.m. Walter Scott, who was forty-one, was a renowned fantasist in Scranton's bars, an ex-marine who often claimed to be doing secret work for the government. Even so, police had to listen when he claimed that his chatty brother had been hiding Patty Hearst on a nearby farm. By dawn Walter was being debriefed by the FBI. He knew the farm was somewhere in neighboring Wayne County, and from his description agents were able to find it. When they finally searched it, they found not only Bill Harris's fingerprints, on a piece of glass, but Wendy Yoshimura's, on a newspaper stuffed under a mattress. A grand jury began hearing testimony about the Scotts, who swiftly disappeared, but it was the discovery of Yoshimura's prints that would prove more significant.

Even as news broke of the FBI's find—the Scott family would be in the headlines for months—the SLA finally turned from talk to action. On February 25, with the group almost out of money, two of the new recruits, Jim Kilgore and Mike Bortin, robbed a branch of the Guild Savings & Loan in a Sacramento strip mall, racing out with $3,729; the police never had a clue it was the SLA. Around the same time the newcomers finally convinced Bill Harris that his plans to free Remiro and Little were suicidal and abandoned them. On March 1, the pair tried to escape anyway, rushing a pair of guards as Little jabbed a sharpened pencil four inches into one guard's throat; the two were finally tackled and subdued as Remiro was unlocking a gun cabinet.

Afterward Bill Harris ordered that the robbery proceeds be used to buy cars and guns and rent two additional apartments for the group. But the cash, which ran out shortly, did nothing to reduce the growing tensions within the aspiring guerrilla band. Harris seemed to live in a state of constant rage. His primary target was Hearst, whom he endlessly denounced as worthless and unable to shed her bourgeois hang-ups; more than once, she claimed later, he punched her in the face, too. Harris was almost as incensed at Bortin, who refused to give up his LSD habit despite the SLA's rules against drugs. Sometimes, when Harris was off on a tirade, his target would respond by raising the single criticism he had no answer for: Harris, the others felt, was not a credible field general because he was white. "Only a black or a Third World person can understand the plight of the oppressed masses," Patty quoted Emily Harris as saying. They would love a black general, everyone agreed, if only they could find one.

But nothing produced more schisms within the group than sex. As they remained marooned inside three grungy Sacramento apartments, the gamesmanship devolved into a kind of sexual *Lord of the Flies*. When Bill Harris began sleeping with Kathy Soliah, Emily retaliated by sleeping with Steve Soliah. When Harris, in a jealous rage, confronted Steve with a gun, Steve left Emily and started sleeping with Hearst. Emily, in turn, began sleeping with Jim Kilgore. When that didn't work out, Kilgore began sleeping with Wendy Yoshimura, who flitted in and out of the group. Everyone was having sex with everyone, it seemed, and everyone was angry about it. When they weren't arguing about sex, they were arguing about what to do next. After they robbed Guild Savings, Harris wanted to hit a larger bank. By Patty's count they cased at least fifteen Sacramento-area banks before deciding on a branch of the Crocker National Bank in suburban Carmichael. Harris wanted this to be an "SLA action," meaning they would announce their responsibility, letting the world know that the SLA was again operational. The newcomers angrily resisted, arguing that, with only eight members, they were too weak to confront police. Kilgore and Bortin, their confidence growing, challenged Harris's ability to lead the Crocker National action. Harris won out by shouting everyone else down.

As they readied for the bank job, everyone buying new guns and firing at targets in a wooded area, news broke of the FBI's discoveries in Pennsylvania. Suddenly, after almost a year of silence, the SLA was again front-page news. Harris saw no reason to leave Sacramento; not even the Scotts knew they were in the city. Finally, on April 21, after a month of preparations, all eight of them piled into cars and drove toward the Crocker branch. As five of the group burst into the lobby, screaming for everyone to "get your noses in the carpet," one woman paused. Her name was Myrna Opsahl. She was forty-two that morning, and she had come to the bank with three other women to deposit money from their church. According to witnesses, Opsahl was cradling a heavy adding machine, and rather than fall to the floor, she hesitated. Emily Harris turned and blasted Opsahl with a shotgun. Years later she would claim that the gun went off accidentally. Barely five minutes later the robbers raced from the bank, leaving Myrna Opsahl to bleed to death. Hearst, sitting in a getaway car, joined the others inside a waiting van. When one of them wondered aloud whether the bleeding woman would live, Hearst wrote later, Emily Harris snapped, "Oh she's dead. But it really doesn't matter. She was a bourgeois pig anyway."

The murder of Myrna Opsahl, and press accounts that labeled the Crocker National job an "SLA-style" robbery, convinced the group that it was time to leave Sacramento. The new recruits took news of Opsahl's death the hardest; for the first time, Patty said later, the romance of revolutionary violence began to fade. The decision was made to return to where it all began, the only place most of the SLA members felt at all safe: San Francisco.

Kathy Soliah and Jim Kilgore took Patty and rented an apartment on Geneva Avenue, above a dry cleaner's on the city's southern outskirts. Everyone else followed a few days later, bringing their weapons and belongings in a pair of U-Haul trucks. A game of musical apartments ensued. Emily Harris announced that she couldn't stand living with Bill anymore, so Bill moved to a second flat, in Daly City; the others took turns living with him. In the end Emily and Jim Kilgore moved in with Hearst. The new recruits, meanwhile, all took jobs, Kathy Soliah waitressing under an assumed name at the Sir Francis Drake Hotel while the others returned to housepainting, eventually securing a sizable contract to repaint a set of apartments in Pacifica, south of the city. Two of Wendy Yoshimura's radical girlfriends began attending the SLA's internal meetings, hoping to join.

Once they were settled, Harris announced that they were renewing their war against the fascist U.S. government. In DeFreeze's honor, he said, they should carry out his dream and begin killing policemen. If they killed enough, he reasoned, the police would crack down on the oppressed minorities of the Bay Area, who would then rise up and begin the revolution. "That's a terrible, disgusting idea," one of the prospective members said. "One of the women I work with is married to a policeman, and he is a very nice person."

"We're revolutionaries and we should be killing pigs and pigs' families," Emily Harris responded.

"You people are sick," the woman said, and stormed out.[1]

Mike Bortin just rolled his eyes. "All you people do is talk," he said. "I think you're all a bunch of sissies. If you want to go out and kill some pigs, you ought to just go out and do it."

Harris insisted they needed a plan and challenged Bortin to devise one. A few nights later Bortin took Hearst and cruised past a coffee shop called Miz Brown's in the Mission District. It was filled with police, on and off duty. At the group's next meeting Bortin proposed that they walk in with guns blazing; they could kill a dozen cops before anyone knew what was happening. Harris scoffed. They could never win a shoot-out with trained professionals. "You people analyze everything to death," Bortin said before storming out.

In Bortin's absence the other newcomers argued that the safest attacks would be nocturnal, Weather-style bombings. The debate raged for days, until Bortin finally returned and plunked down a package of plastic explosives, the kind used on construction sites. "Here's your explosives," he told Harris. "All you need is some blasting caps and you're good to go."

Later there would be considerable confusion about the rump SLA's bombings, in large part because they were carried out in the name of the New World Liberation Front, the umbrella group Harris had endorsed a full year before. In the interim a group calling itself the NWLF had already detonated thirty bombs in the Bay Area. Patty Hearst, and much of the press, would later come to believe that the SLA was the only branch of the NWLF, that Harris and his acolytes had carried out *all* the bombings, but as later events would show, that was clearly not true. It's all but certain that, as Bortin's introduction of explosives indicated, the SLA hadn't yet bombed a thing.

But it would now. Rejoining the group, Wendy Yoshimura served as its explosives expert. Everyone gathered in the Geneva Avenue flat to watch her build a pipe bomb—gunpowder jammed into a two-inch pipe. She and Harris burned the powder in different recipes on a mattress in the rear courtyard until one afternoon when Hearst noticed smoke billowing from behind the building. Apparently they had left something burning. Just then there was a pounding at the door. "Fire department!" a voice shouted. Firemen rushed into the apartment, dragging hoses behind them, and quickly extinguished the fire. When Yoshimura explained she had seen teenagers playing with matches earlier in the day, they left. Afterward everyone was able to laugh about it.

Harris chose the first two targets: police stations in the Mission District and on Taraval Street. Overruling Yoshimura, he insisted on building the bombs himself, packing toilet paper in with the gunpowder, despite Yoshimura's insistence that there was no need. On the night of August 7, Patty and Jo Soliah took one of the bombs in a plastic bag and strolled by the Mission station; once they were certain no one was watching, Soliah slid it under a parked police car. Yoshimura and the others returned to the apartment with their bomb still intact, insisting there were too many people around the Taraval Street station to plant it. The next morning, when they checked the newspapers, they found a small item about a dud bomb found under a Mission

District police car. Harris was apoplectic, his face red and trembling as he excoriated everyone for incompetence and insubordination.

Mike Bortin, always ready to challenge Harris, teased him mercilessly. "Great job," he smirked. For once Harris had little to say.

The next day they built three new bombs, minus the toilet paper, and drove to a remote area of Sonoma County to test them. They were tiny, only three inches long, but they detonated. Harris announced that they would strike next at the police department in Emeryville, beside Berkeley on San Francisco Bay. Emily Harris and Steve Soliah planted the bomb on August 13, Soliah scrambling up a slope to slide it under a patrol car. Minutes later it went off, destroying the car. Writing the communiqué proved harder than the bombing. Harris wanted to rename themselves the Jonathan Jackson unit of the New World Liberation Front. Kilgore objected, saying that suggested they were black revolutionaries. Eventually they compromised, calling themselves the Jonathan Jackson/Sam Melville unit of the NWLF. "Remember, pigs," the communiqué read in part. "Every time you strap on your gun, the next bullet may be speeding toward your head, the next bomb may be under the seat of your car." In the only nod to the SLA, they used DeFreeze's old signoff line: "Death to the Fascist Insect That Preys on the Life of the People."

Bursting with confidence now, Harris announced that their next action would be simultaneous attacks in Los Angeles and at the site of Jonathan Jackson's death, the Marin County Courthouse. Harris built the bombs, bigger ones this time, gunpowder packed with concrete nails inside a foot-long pipe. He called it an "anti-personnel" bomb and rigged up a contraption that would affix it to the bottom of a car and, in theory, detonate when the car moved. Steve Soliah, riding a bicycle, placed the first bomb at the courthouse, outside the sheriff's office. Another they slid under a police car. Both went off with no problem. They dropped off the communiqué outside a radio station.

Later Harris returned, incensed, from Los Angeles with Jim Kilgore and Kathy Soliah, who was sporting a new black eye. Their "mission" had degenerated into farce. They had gotten into an argument over what to bomb. Sitting in traffic, Kilgore got so mad he punched Soliah in the face, at which point Harris began punching him, even as drivers behind them began honking their horns. Later that night, having calmed down, they managed to slide two bombs under a pair of police cars, one in Hollywood, the other in East Los Angeles; afterward they checked into a motel, switched on the television, and waited for news of their triumphant attacks. Unfortunately, Harris's new triggering device didn't work. When the first cruiser was driven off, the bomb just lay there in a trash bag in the street, at which point two young boys found it and began kicking it around like a soccer ball. When the bomb fell out of the garbage bag, an adult saw it and called the police. Rushing to check nearby cars, they found the second bomb before it could explode. "Everything," Hearst wrote later, "pretty much spiraled out of control after that."

Back in San Francisco violent arguments broke out, all exacerbated by ongoing sexual tensions within the group. Everything came to a head one long night at the Geneva Avenue apartment when, amid clouds of cigarette smoke, half-eaten pizza crusts, and beer and wine bottles, Harris announced that the only cure for the SLA's dysfunction was black leadership. He proposed approaching a paroled San Quentin inmate they knew and asking him to take over. The newcomers hated the idea, afraid to bring in outsiders. As Harris and Kilgore screamed at each other, Emily Harris lamented the loss of the clarity DeFreeze had brought to the "old" SLA. Kilgore's response provided an unwitting epitaph for the group: "That's all a bunch of crap! What did the old SLA ever accomplish? You killed a black man, kidnapped a little teenaged girl and robbed a bank. What the hell did that amount to?"[2]

Finally, with half the group screaming and red-faced and the other half in tears, Harris shouted, "That's it! It's all over!" He and Emily were going in search of black leadership. The others could do as they pleased. The next day the Harrises rented an apartment on Precita Avenue in Bernal Heights, not far from San Francisco General Hospital. And just like that, with no good-byes, they were gone. Patty and the others moved into the remaining safe house, in Daly City. It was then, on August 29, that the Soliahs' father, Martin, appeared in San Francisco and informed his three children that the FBI was looking for them. Harris ordered everyone to leave the Daly City flat; to make sure they did, he gave the landlord notice. Thrown out, Hearst and the others were cruising the Outer Mission District one evening when they saw a FOR RENT sign at a small apartment building. The address was 625 Morse Street.

For the next two weeks there was little communication between the Harrises and the others. Patty heard that the couple had found their would-be black messiah, lying stoned in a bush at a rally. For the first time she began thinking of turning herself in. She was exhausted. The SLA was falling apart. But the others persuaded her to stay. "You're a symbol of the revolution," one told her. "You give the people hope."

By midsummer the FBI had finally picked up the SLA's trail. One of Jack Scott's friends, who had visited the group in Pennsylvania, gave agents Wendy Yoshimura's alias, "Joan Shimada." Someone by that name had registered a car in New Jersey, then sold it to a girl named Cathy Turcich. When agents visited the Turcich family on July 19, her parents volunteered that Cathy's sister was one of Yoshimura's oldest friends; she was waitressing in San Francisco, in fact, and was in touch with her. When agents visited the restaurant, the Plate of Brasse, they found that Turcich had disappeared. But when they showed employees photos of Yoshimura's known associates, someone picked out a photo of a waitress named Kathleen Anger. It was Kathy Soliah. Soliah was also gone; a call from New Jersey had tipped everyone off. Both the FBI and the police, however, were well aware that Soliah and her friends were behind BARC, the pro-SLA group that published *Dragon*. A week later, playing a hunch, a Sacramento police detective ran all the BARC group's fingerprints against one found on the Crocker Bank getaway car. It was Jim Kilgore's.

The FBI poured men into Sacramento. But the break came after agents struck up a relationship with Martin Soliah, who lived in Palmdale, in the high desert east of Los Angeles. He was horrified to learn that his children might be mixed up with the SLA. He tried to reach them but couldn't, then managed to arrange a dinner on August 29 in San Francisco. The FBI agreed to let him go alone. When Martin came clean, telling his children he was working with the Bureau, Kathy exploded. "How could you do such a thing?" she demanded. "Don't you know you can't trust the FBI?" They spent seven hours walking and talking, the father beseeching the children to come home, the children denying everything.

Martin Soliah returned, crestfallen, to the FBI agents waiting at his hotel. The family meeting seemed a total loss—until he mentioned one thing. At some point his son Steve had volunteered that he and Michael Bortin and Jim Kilgore were still painting houses. Within days agents fanned out across the Bay Area, showing photos of the SLA to supervisors at every painting job they could find. It took two weeks, but on the morning of Monday, September 15, a pair of agents approached Bill Osgood, manager of the Pacifica Apartments, and showed him the SLA photos. "That one," Osgood said, pointing to a picture of Bortin. That was "John Henderson," he said, the boss of the "hippie painters" repainting the apartments.

At 10:30 a.m. the two agents, sitting in a parked car, saw Kathy and Jo Soliah drive up. Surveillance teams took up positions all around the complex. At 5:30, when the Soliahs were finished for the day, agents followed their 1967 Ford as it drove into San Francisco, eventually stopping at 625 Morse, where the women disappeared inside. The next morning agents spied Steve Soliah leaving the apartment, followed him to Pacifica, and at day's end trailed him to a second address, 288 Precita in Bernal Heights.

By the next morning, Wednesday, September 17, teams of FBI agents and SFPD inspectors were in place. At 10:50 they spotted a man who might be Bill Harris, wearing cut-off jeans, as he emerged from the Precita building, stretched, then disappeared back inside. At 11:30 they watched as the man and a woman who might be Emily Harris came out and went for a jog. All day agents watched the pair come and go, at one point trailing them inside a Laundromat, but they couldn't be sure it was the Harrises. The man had jet-black hair; Harris's was brown. The woman looked nothing like Emily Harris.

All that night and into the morning agents at the San Francisco office debated what to do. None could be sure it was the Harrises. And there was no sign of Patty Hearst. Finally, at a 9:00 a.m. meeting, the agent in charge, Charles Bates, told his men to arrest the couple if they went jogging again. At least they could be sure they weren't carrying guns. As luck would have it, the couple emerged from the Precita building at 12:50, the man in purple running shorts, and proceeded to go for a jog. An FBI car cruised behind.

At 1:12 the couple were walking slowly back toward 288 Precita. As they approached the front door four agents sprang from a parked sedan.

"We're the FBI!" one shouted.

Without a word Bill Harris raised his hands. Emily, however, turned and ran—only to confront two agents directly behind her, one with a shotgun pointed at her chest. "You motherfuckin' sons of bitches!" she shouted. "You sons of bitches!" Emily was taken away in handcuffs. Agents took Bill Harris's fingerprints in the car. "It's him," someone said.

Agents stormed the house. It was empty. There was no sign of Hearst. An hour later a handful of FBI men moved in on 625 Morse. The building had two apartments, one on the second floor, the other on the third; they couldn't be sure which one was Steve Soliah's. Taking a risk, they approached a man in the garage, who turned out to be the owner. No one was living on the second floor, he said. But three new tenants, a man and two young women, were living on the third. The "girls," he said, were up there right now.

"What's the best way up there?" the ranking agent, Tom Padden, asked.

"Up the back stairs," the landlord said.

Leaving the other agents to cover the front, Padden and an SFPD inspector named Tim Casey unsheathed their pistols and crept up the wooden stairway at the rear of the building. Padden went first, taking each step slowly, quietly. Just before reaching the landing outside the apartment, he glanced back at Casey, who was holding a .357 Magnum. Casey nodded.

Padden stepped onto the landing, a .38 in his outstretched right hand. There was a Dutch door to the apartment; the upper half was open to the air. Peering inside, Padden was startled to come face-to-face with Wendy Yoshimura, standing in the kitchen. "FBI!" he barked. "Freeze!"

Yoshimura froze. Then Padden saw the second girl, sitting at the kitchen table. She stood and turned to run.

"Freeze or I'll blow her head off!" Padden yelled.

The other girl stopped. Inspector Casey burst into the kitchen, his Magnum pointed at her back.

"Patty!" he said.

She turned around slowly. He could see her face now. At which point Patty Hearst did about the only thing she could. She peed.

It was over. The capture of Patty Hearst was front-page news around the world and would remain so for months. At the federal courthouse newsmen and photographers mobbed the car as she was hustled inside. She was arraigned on charges of robbing the Hibernia Bank, then taken to the San Mateo County jail. Asked her occupation, she famously replied: "Urban guerrilla." The FBI arrested Steve Soliah later that day, but amazingly there were no agents at the Pacifica apartment house where the others spent the day painting. When news of the arrests hit the radio, all of them—Kathy and Jo Soliah, Mike Bortin, Jim Kilgore—disappeared and went underground.

A side benefit of the arrests, Bay Area officials announced with relief, would be the end to the manic series of bombings carried out in the name of the New World Liberation Front; police assumed that the NWLF was a cover for Bill Harris and the SLA, with perhaps a few stray radicals contributing to the campaign. The bombings had become a fixture of daily life in the Bay Area, like the fog. After its debut in August 1974 the NWLF had accelerated the pace of its actions in 1975, detonating thirty-seven explosive devices by the time Hearst was captured, an average of one every week for nine months. Its targets, almost all struck by bombs left outside buildings late at night, included Pacific Gas and Electric transformers and substations, U.S. Air Force radar sites, KRON-TV, the California Department of Corrections, the firing range at San Quentin prison, the Marin County Courthouse, and the home of a Safeway Stores board member. Almost all of NWLF's communiqués complained about some aspect of Bay Area life, typically railing against conditions at area jails, slumlords, and labor disputes. There were so many bombings that an FBI man termed San Francisco "the Belfast of North America." To date, no one had been seriously injured.

Neither the Bureau nor the Bay Area police, despite ample reward offers, had been able to make a single arrest. The NWLF communiqués were mailed fast and furiously, some with unidentifiable fingerprints, each in the name of another NWLF "combat unit": People's Force No. 1, which preferred bombing General Motors facilities; People's Force No. 2, which hit the air force sites; People's Force No. 4, which struck PG&E transformers; the Lucio

Cabanas unit, named after a Mexican guerrilla leader, which bombed everything; the Nat Turner/John Brown unit, which bombed the corrections department. At the FBI's San Francisco office, the working assumption was that all these "units" were essentially just the SLA, the profusion of names an effort to make the NWLF appear larger than it actually was.

Within days of Hearst's capture, however, that assumption was already being challenged. When a bomb damaged a PG&E substation in San Carlos on October 13, a communiqué arrived in the NWLF's name. Two more NWLF bombs exploded by Halloween, one outside the army's Fort Ord. Things took an unexpected turn in November. After San Francisco voters approved a series of ballot initiatives designed to curb police power, the police responded with a ticket-writing blitz, issuing three times as many parking tickets as normal. On November 16 the NWLF unveiled a dramatic response of its own, pouring liquid steel into the locks of hundreds of city parking meters. "They got 400 to 500 meters," a police spokesman told the Associated Press, "including a bunch in front of police headquarters." The NWLF communiqué, signed by the "People's Forces Training Unit," threatened to sabotage every parking meter in San Francisco if the police didn't stop writing so many tickets.

That the NWLF's underground campaign had taken a seriocomic turn did little to stem the FBI's frustration that the group apparently remained alive and well. It was then, just as San Franciscans were beginning to accept the idea that the bombings might continue, that things got strange. To that point the NWLF had delivered its communiqués the old-fashioned way, leaving them outside radio stations and newspaper offices late at night or taping them inside telephone booths. Now, the police heard, someone was delivering them by hand. In January 1976, after two more bombings during the holidays, the *San Francisco Chronicle* publicly identified the NWLF's shadowy courier as a gentleman calling himself Jacques Rogiers. Tall and thin, with bushy brown hair and a broomlike mustache, Rogiers turned out to be a thirty-seven-year-old convicted marijuana dealer whose real name, it appeared, was Jack Rogers.* At Soledad and San Quentin he had written for

---

*Or, according to government prosecutors, John Hazinski.

radical inmate newspapers. Prison administrators thought he was basically harmless, if a tad unhinged; one internal assessment noted that Rogiers supported the SLA and "appears not to have good contact with reality and is living a fantasy life."[3]

Maybe so, but after his release from San Quentin in 1974, Rogiers found quite a few new friends living much the same fantasy life on the streets of San Francisco. He made a deep impression on several. "Of all the hundreds of clients I've ever represented, the two largest influences on me were Huey Newton and Jacques Rogiers," recalls Tony Serra, the ponytailed radical attorney who eventually represented Rogiers. "Jacques was like a holy man, a guru, a wise man. I've never known anyone before or since like him."

Rogiers's entry into underground causes was a tangled affair. In June 1975 the high-profile president of the United Prisoners Union, an ex-con named Wilbur "Popeye" Jackson—he had played a key role in organizing the SLA food drives—was shot dead on a San Francisco street, along with his girlfriend. Jackson had been publicly critical of the NWLF, saying it should be bombing buildings filled with people instead of empty ones. A letter to the *Chronicle* claimed credit for Jackson's murder on behalf of the NWLF. But the NWLF hadn't done it. Bill Harris had fired off a letter saying so, which at the time had contributed to the notion that the NWLF and the SLA were actually the same group.

Out of nowhere, and with little or no track record in Bay Area radical politics, Rogiers had announced he was forming a group called the People's Court in an effort to determine the truth behind Jackson's murder. He eventually published a forty-four-page pamphlet exonerating the NWLF. The NWLF apparently liked what it read; within weeks Rogiers had taken up his courier duties and, after his unmasking in the *Chronicle*, effectively emerged as the public face of the NWLF. With the help of several young assistants, Rogiers worked out of a cluttered flat on Valencia Street; he called his little operation People's Information Relay 1. Under police questioning, Rogiers insisted he wasn't a member of the NWLF and didn't know anyone who was. He claimed he simply took delivery of communiqués and relayed them to the press. It was far from clear whether any of this actually broke any laws. For the moment the police were powerless to do anything but keep Rogiers under watch.

On the eve of Patty Hearst's trial, in mid-January, things took an abrupt and ominous turn. Until then, despite having detonated forty-five bombs in the previous sixteen months, the NWLF had largely been dismissed as another harmless Bay Area oddity; its bombs hadn't hurt anyone, and most went off in the dead of night at remote locations. Then, on Saturday, January 10, 1976, the day after an NWLF communiqué reiterated demands for improved health care in city jails, a package arrived at the home of a San Francisco supervisor—the equivalent of a city councilman—named John Barbagelata. His daughters, Marina, fourteen, and Elena, twelve, picked up the mail and, while walking back inside, began pitching the package back and forth. "Hey," one joked, "this could be a bomb!" Their mother, noting the strange typed address identifying her husband as "the people's choice," decided to take no chances. She placed the package on a rear patio.

A half hour later the president of the board of supervisors, Quentin Kopp, brought his mail from home and dropped it in his City Hall office. The largest piece was a package wrapped in plain brown paper. When his assistant began opening it, she noticed an inner wrapping of aluminum foil. Suspicious, she suggested they call the police. Detectives were soon on the scene. Inside the package they found a box of See's hard candy. Inside the candy box they found a bomb. After Kopp phoned the Barbagelata home, police raced there and found an identical bomb in the strange package left on the patio.

Mayor George Moscone angrily denounced the bombing attempts, which were widely assumed to be the work of the New World Liberation Front. On Monday an anonymous caller to media outlets confirmed as much, insisting the NWLF wasn't actually trying to hurt anyone. "Listen carefully," a young woman's voice told a *Chronicle* reporter. "A half stick of dynamite and a six-second-delay fuse constructed with great care demonstrates that this was not an attempt to kill." Pressed by reporters, Rogiers said City Hall had only itself to blame for ignoring the NWLF's communiqués. "They keep stepping up their actions," he said. "When are the supervisors going to take them seriously? They've gone right up to the edge. Next time they're liable to say, 'They won't take us seriously. Now let's kill one of them.'"

Patty Hearst's trial began four days after delivery of what came to be known as "the candy box bombs." For the next two weeks the NWLF busied itself elsewhere, launching a series of new bombings—none, however, linked in any way to the proceedings. On Saturday, January 31, it attempted to bomb five PG&E transformers in San Geronimo. The next night it blew up another landlord's car and bombed the home of a landlord who owned an apartment building that had burned, killing several poor residents. The next night a bomb went off outside the home of the Bank of California's chairman. Rogiers merrily delivered the communiqués, as he had before. Across Valencia detectives watched him come and go, unable to stop him. Rogiers shot them a middle finger from time to time and showed no signs of distancing himself from the underground. Within weeks, in fact, he began publishing a new journal, called *TUG: The Urban Guerrilla*, which was essentially a counterpart to the *Dragon*, a repository for bombing communiqués.

Finally, during the third week of Hearst's trial, the NWLF turned its attention to the proceedings, if mildly. One afternoon a bomb threat was telephoned to the courthouse, forcing an early adjournment. Then, on February 12, a bomb went off beside a guesthouse at the Hearst family's fabled San Simeon estate, near San Luis Obispo, 150 miles south of San Francisco. It caused about $1 million in damage. An anonymous caller took credit on behalf of the NWLF, demanding that the Hearsts put up bail money for the Harrises. Afterward Randolph Hearst was beside himself. "These people, they're just a bunch of maniacs," he told a wire-service reporter. "Just a bunch of maniacs."

The following week Patty Hearst broke down in tears on the witness stand, insisting her life was in danger. Asked who would want to harm her, she sniffed, "The New World Liberation Front."

The break the FBI so badly wanted, it appeared, came that same week, after police in Lagunitas, an unincorporated area of Marin County, were called to the scene of a shoot-out at a local home. Two Berkeley radicals were arrested. They turned out to be members of the New Dawn Collective, a tiny group of activists that operated a bookstore and published communiqués from a new underground group that called itself the Emiliano Zapata unit of the NWLF.

The Zapata unit had claimed credit for eight bombings in recent months, most against Safeway Stores.

The shoot-out, police learned, arose after members of New Dawn had attempted to raid the home of a local drug dealer, apparently in search of money, à la the Black Liberation Army. A search of the suspects' van found reams of Zapata and NWLF literature. That, in turn, led to the address of a Spanish-style bungalow in the town of Richmond, mere blocks from the home where the SLA had hidden out two years earlier. Just before dawn on February 21, thirty FBI agents and local SWAT teams surrounded the house, broke down the door, and dragged out six New Dawn members in handcuffs. Inside, agents found 150 pounds of explosives, most of it stolen from a Santa Cruz–area quarry a year earlier, as well as still more Zapata and NWLF communiqués.

FBI officials were jubilant; one crowed to the *Chronicle* that they had "broken the back" of the NWLF. But they hadn't. The San Simeon bombing came the very next day, and after exhaustive questioning of the New Dawn suspects, the FBI was forced to admit that those arrested were members of the Zapata unit but not of the NWLF. They had merely been using the NWLF name.

The Hearst trial went on, undisturbed, for the next month. Then, on March 11, after three more unrelated bombings, the NWLF struck at another Hearst estate, Wyntoon, on 67,000 heavily wooded acres near Mount Shasta in far northern California. A woman caller to KRON-TV in San Francisco took credit for a bombing, again demanding that the Hearsts contribute $250,000 to the Harris defense fund, but the Hearsts said there hadn't been any explosion. It took almost five hours to find the bomb, partially exploded, in the basement of the remote mansion, which was roughly six miles from the nearest road. A few floorboards were splintered, but the FBI was left to marvel at the persistence of a group that had climbed a perimeter fence, trudged through miles of forest, and found a way to break into the mansion and plant the bomb, all without being detected by caretakers.

Nine days later Patty Hearst's trial came to an end, with a guilty verdict. The judge gave her thirty-five years, later reduced to seven. She would serve only twenty-two months; President Jimmy Carter commuted her sentence in early 1979. President Bill Clinton granted her a full pardon in 2001. Bill and

Emily Harris pled guilty to charges of kidnapping and ended up serving eight years. The rest of the SLA had vanished.

If the Patty Hearst saga was finally at an end, the mystery of the New World Liberation Front still had several colorful chapters remaining. A grand jury had begun hearing testimony against Jacques Rogiers. The investigation dragged on for months. Through it all the NWLF kept up its bombing campaign, albeit at a slower pace; between March and December 1976 it managed only seven attacks. The most significant was a bomb planted in a window box attached to Supervisor Dianne Feinstein's home in Pacific Heights on December 14. A maid noticed a fruit punch can among the flowers the next morning. Feinstein's daughter, a Berkeley sophomore, glanced through a window and saw "some liquid, and the letters E-X-P-L." Police arrived and found a pocket watch timing device lying on the sidewalk. The bomb had misfired at 2:14 a.m.

Feinstein was apoplectic. "The time has come," she told reporters, "when the fear and intimidation that everyone feels has got to stop. I don't think that going around putting bombs on people's houses accomplishes a thing." Later that day an NWLF communiqué delivered to media outlets demanded improvements in health conditions at the city jails.

A month later, on January 23, 1977, Jacques Rogiers was finally arrested on charges of threatening public officials and conspiracy. After a press conference he took a vow of silence, refusing to say a word to anyone. The next day the NWLF issued a communiqué threatening three supervisors with death if Rogiers should die in jail. It then commenced its most intense spate of bombings in months. After three bombings in the four days leading up to Rogiers's arrest—the targets, once again, were PG&E transformers—it detonated four more bombs in the following week, a campaign that climaxed on the night of February 4, the day Rogiers was formally indicted. One bomb exploded inside a women's room at the Federal Building. An hour later a second went off, directly beneath a green Volvo station wagon in the driveway of District Attorney Joseph Freitas's San Francisco home. The car, an officer noted, "was blown to smithereens." The NWLF communiqué warned prosecutors not to make Rogiers a "scapegoat" and once again threatened the supervisors, saying, "If necessary, the poor and oppressed will take freedom over your dead bodies." Mayor Moscone, irate, denounced the bombings as an "effort to terrorize and even paralyze city government."

Afterward the NWLF fell silent for six long weeks. Then, on the night of March 22, it again targeted Supervisor John Barbagelata. An unusual bomb—actually a single blasting cap tied to a broom handle—was tossed toward his home on Portola Drive. It landed in a neighbor's yard, obliterating a swing set. The Barbagelata family, gathered in their kitchen fifteen feet away, fell to the floor in panic. No one was hurt.

In the following weeks, as preparations for Rogiers's trial began, the NWLF returned to bombing unrelated targets, mostly PG&E transformers, as well as a bomb tossed toward a home once owned by a PG&E board member. The trial began in mid-May. It featured testimony from Supervisors Kopp, Barbagelata, and Feinstein, along with vigorous attempts to link Rogiers to these and other bombings. Rogiers and his attorney, Tony Serra, spent much of the proceedings smoking marijuana—in the courthouse. "Jacques had the finest marijuana I ever had," Serra recalls. "He insisted—*insisted*—we get stoned whenever we went to court. We'd go into the stairwell and smoke grass before court, at lunch, and after court. *Tons* of it. I can remember walking into court—I remember it so clearly—literally floating into court. I can still feel it, every step, just kind of floating up to the bench."

It was an unorthodox but ultimately successful strategy. Once the judge ruled that Rogiers had been acting as a journalist, the defense grew confident. On June 7 the jury announced its verdict: not guilty. Serra and Rogiers exchanged hugs. Afterward "there was a big party scheduled to celebrate the victory," Serra recalls. "Jacques was a hero, in his world, for his righteous character and demeanor. I remember all of us waiting at this party, waiting and waiting. He never showed up. And no one ever saw him again. No one. I never saw or spoke to him again, and I don't know anyone who did. He disappeared. I was told he went to the mountains and became a monk and never again ventured into society. He was just gone. It was almost Christlike."

Jacques Rogiers's days as the public face of the NWLF were over. Almost forty years later his fate remains a mystery.

And still the NWLF bombings went on. There were ten more that summer, all directed against Coors beer distributors in sympathy with a workers' strike. None did significant damage. Then, after twin bombings at another PG&E facility and the Marin County Courthouse on August 29, 1977, the NWLF suddenly unveiled a new target: the rich. On September 1 a bomb was planted outside the Pacific Union Club—it didn't explode—and the next night at the Olympic Country Club; it did explode. A week later a powerful bomb exploded at the San Francisco Opera House, destroying the limousine entrance. "As long as poor people are forced to live in unsafe, unhealthy housing," the communiqué read, "ruling class functions will be threatened."

The three bombings triggered a civic uproar exponentially louder than any other NWLF actions to date. Blowing up a PG&E transformer was something the San Francisco elites could safely ignore; blowing up the opera was another thing altogether. The police could only sigh. "Hell," one detective griped to the *Chronicle*, "they've been bombing on a regular basis for months—even years—and now all of a sudden, people are excited because some guy goes to Nob Hill to have lunch with the board chairman and all he hears about is the bomb. Then he goes out to the Olympic Club for a round and it's the same thing. He's gonna get mad."[4]

The *Chronicle* published a "box score" of Bay Area bombings dating to 1971. No one had an exact count, the paper noted, but the number was easily more than one hundred, credited to seven radical groups. By far the most active, by the *Chronicle*'s count, was the NWLF, with sixty-four, followed by the Chicano Liberation Front, with nine; the Zapata unit, with eight; and a group calling itself Americans for Justice, with six. The most popular targets were PG&E, bombed twenty-three times, followed by the U.S. government and Safeway stores, with nine each. The FBI had posted rewards for information on the NWLF but had nothing to show for it. "We believe they're not an extremely large group," one agent told the paper. "But who knows?"

The one new element to the new bombings was Tony Serra's debut as the NWLF's spokesman. "They called my office," Serra recalls. "I didn't know who it was. He asked if I would take over communications. I said sure. I got a call every few weeks. It was like, 'Go to Fifth and Mission, there's a phone booth.' So I go. The phone rings. 'All right, Tony, look across the street, do you see the pillars holding up the billboard? Go over there, on the right side, there is a parcel.' This happened like six times, and always, along with the communiqué, there would be at least two bags of [marijuana]. I held a press conference, always well attended, and put out the communiqué."

Then that fall, without explanation, the calls stopped. There were two more NWLF bombings in October, followed by an explosion outside a Union 76 refinery in the town of Rodeo on November 10. Then nothing. The NWLF went utterly silent for five long months. At the FBI offices in San Francisco, agents debated what was happening. Had the NWLF simply given up? No one knew. Finally, on March 14, 1978, another bomb went off, outside a PG&E substation in suburban Concord; a communiqué expressed support for a coal miners' strike. After four years and a hundred or so bombings—the precise number remains in dispute—this would prove the final NWLF action, the final communiqué. At the FBI agents waited for the bombings to resume; they never would. "When the bombs stopped, we kept wanting them to start again, because with nothing new to work on, everything just went cold," recalls Stockton Buck, an agent on the NWLF case.

Not for a full five years would the truth about the New World Liberation Front, or much of it, finally emerge. It was as strange a tale as any in the annals of the radical resistance. The NWLF, it turned out, had been the only underground group to dissolve after an axe murder.

The full story of the New World Liberation Front will never be known. The fact is, other than a handful of county prosecutors and FBI agents, no one (aside from the author of a 1978 master's thesis, written long before the group was revealed) tried very hard to learn it, much less write it. Not a single pamphlet, magazine article, or book has ever been published analyzing the

NWLF, which detonated more explosive devices than any other radical underground group, nearly twice as many as the Weather Underground.

What's clear is that there were at least three separate combat "units" of the NWLF, none of which appeared to know the first thing about the others. All were responding to the Bay Area Research Collective's 1974 call for radical groups to unite under one banner. The first group was Bill Harris and the rump SLA, which was responsible for two bombings in August 1975. The second group was the Emiliano Zapata unit, which detonated eight bombs later that year.

The vast majority of NWLF actions, however, probably seventy or more, were carried out by a third group, which can be viewed as the "actual" NWLF. This one centered on a deeply troubled man named Ronald Huffman. Remarkably little is known about him. From the scant public record it appears he was born in Oregon in 1939. His parents worked at a mental hospital. He had a difficult upbringing, that much is clear; a stepfather, it was later claimed, beat him with a hose. He was arrested at sixteen for burglary; in 1963, when he was twenty-three, there was an arrest for smuggling balloons filled with heroin across the Mexican border, followed a few years later by a marijuana arrest.

By 1971, when he turned thirty-one, Huffman seems to have been a small-time marijuana dealer in the San Jose area, a balding radical typically adorned in biker regalia; his customers called him "Revolutionary Ron." According to Stockton Buck, who became the FBI's expert on Huffman, Huffman met his girlfriend—and future bombing confederate—Maureen Minton in 1971 or 1972. A bit more is known about Minton. She grew up in Mountain View, in today's Silicon Valley, the daughter of a family who owned one of the town's oldest stores, Minton Lumber. Described as a quiet hippie girl, she graduated with honors from Berkeley in 1970, then, in search of a peaceful life, moved to an island commune near Vancouver, British Columbia. She met Huffman on a return visit to the Bay Area. The two lived for a time in rural Canada, Buck says, before relocating to Santa Cruz, California, two hours south of San Francisco, in 1973. Not long after, they rented a bungalow in a remote mountainous area ten miles north called Bonny Doon. Among their neighbors was the noted science fiction writer Robert Heinlein.

Here the couple comes into clearer focus. Huffman—"Revolutionary Ron"—was a colorful if little-noticed character on the streets of Santa Cruz. Minton worked as a volunteer at Planned Parenthood and at some point began to study nursing at Cabrillo College. From all available evidence, however, their lives were overwhelmingly focused on two things, and two things only: marijuana and bombs. They constructed an elaborate marijuana farm in the dense foliage around their new home, four enormous plots of cannabis plants, some as high as ten feet tall. The surrounding brush, much of it manzanita bushes, was so thick that Huffman was forced to cut tunnels through the greenery just to reach his plants. An intricate system of water hoses snaked through tree limbs to irrigate the marijuana. Elsewhere water pools were dug. Huffman's weed, it was said, was of the highest quality. It was probably what Tony Serra was smoking at Jacques Rogiers's trial.

Watering and harvesting the marijuana was a full-time job, but Huffman and Minton had spare time, and they appear to have used much of it building the New World Liberation Front. To this day no one knows whether the NWLF had two members or dozens; Stockton Buck guesses it may have been six or seven, but no one other than Huffman and Minton would ever be publicly identified. Years later the FBI used fingerprint evidence almost exclusively to build an NWLF case. By doing so, it was able to establish that the couple had been engaged in underground activities as early as 1973, when they first moved to Santa Cruz. Their first known action, actually just a communiqué, was mailed to the *Chronicle* on October 1, 1973, commenting on the Weather Underground bombing of an IT&T office on Madison Avenue in New York. Oddly, it was sent in the name of Weather as well, though fingerprints later established that it was Huffman and Minton's work. It demanded that the state open free health clinics for the poor. There was no actual bombing.

If the IT&T communiqué represented the couple's initial attempt to dip their toes into the underground pool, they soon realized they wanted an identity of their own. Their first actual bombing, it appears, came on November 27, 1973, at a PG&E substation in Cupertino; this was three weeks after the SLA's assassination of Marcus Foster. A communiqué, sent in the name of "Americans for Justice," demanded a 10 percent reduction in utility rates. The explosion briefly cut off power to four surrounding communities. Months later, in February and March 1974, the same group claimed responsibility for three bombings outside Shell Oil facilities in Berkeley, Coalinga, and San Ramon; the communiqués demanded that Shell give away its products for free.

The Americans for Justice bombings garnered few headlines, but they happened to coincide with the SLA's rise and kidnapping of Patty Hearst. That spring, after DeFreeze and the others were killed in Los Angeles, BARC made its open invitation asking other groups to carry out bombings in the name of the New World Liberation Front. Huffman and Minton, it appears, were the first to accept. Their subsequent bombings were all in the name of the NWLF. The first known NWLF action, the dud bomb found outside a General Motors facility in suburban Burlingame in August 1974, was theirs, fingerprints on the communiqué confirmed. So was the Sheraton bombing that October and several—but not all—of the bombings that provided the backdrop to Hearst's trial. It was Huffman and Minton who carried out the campaign against the San Francisco supervisors. The notorious "candy box" bombs delivered to Supervisors Barbagelata and Kopp were the couple's work. So was the December 1976 bomb found in Dianne Feinstein's flower box.

In all, the FBI would be able to tie Huffman and Minton to only sixteen bombings and attempted bombings between 1973 and their final attack in 1978. In all likelihood, the vast majority of the other NWLF bombings were theirs as well. Little is known about life inside their remote marijuana compound, or of their relationship with Jacques Rogiers. It's possible that the couple simply mailed their communiqués to Rogiers anonymously; it's possible they never met. It's also possible, as some suggest, that Rogiers made his living selling Huffman's marijuana in San Francisco. Nor is there any clue as to why Huffman and Minton stopped their bombings in 1978. "We just could never learn much about them," recalls Madeleine Boriss, then a Santa Cruz prosecutor. "We could never find any real friends or associates. It was just them." They did have a dog. His name, perhaps unsurprisingly, was Che.

But Huffman, it is clear, was never the most stable soul. According to a relative interviewed by prosecutors, he was prone to violent mood swings. In the wake of the final NWLF bombing, in 1978, there is considerable evidence that Huffman began losing his grip on reality. Feral dogs and coyotes roamed the Bonny Doon area in those days, and Huffman became obsessed with them, calling them "demon dogs" whose incessant howling was the voice of Satan. Psychiatrists would later debate whether Huffman was schizophrenic, drug-addled, or just a weird guy, but what's unavoidable is the sense that, as 1979 wore on, the focus of his anger became Maureen Minton.

The couple had a worker named Dennis Morgan, who helped tend the marijuana farm. Morgan later told prosecutors he became increasingly frightened of Huffman. According to Morgan, Huffman developed a long list of complaints against Minton: She hadn't watered the weed enough, or she'd watered it too much. She'd neglected to give Che his heartworm medicine. She didn't respect Huffman's grandfather. Huffman's lawyer would later claim that his client believed that Minton herself was possessed by demons. That September Minton told an aunt that, all demons aside, Huffman was incensed that she had had an abortion against his wishes. Morgan later swore that Huffman told him he was "getting rid of Minton and [finding] himself a new lady. One who could bear him children."

Whatever the reason, there is little doubt as to what happened on the bright Sunday morning of September 23, 1979. Standing in their yard, Huffman ordered Minton to kneel before him. For some reason he slid a draftsman's knife into her mouth. Then, lifting a long-handled axe, he swung it viciously down onto her skull, all but splitting her head in two. Minton died instantly. Huffman then took a two-by-four and beat her body, hoping, his attorney would later claim, to knock the demons out of her corpse. Apparently unsatisfied, he then took a scalpel and cut out a section of her brain. His attorney would insist that Huffman believed Minton's brain matter had magical powers.

A few hours later Huffman packed a suitcase and threw it in his car, along with $32,000 in cash, ten bags of marijuana, a book (*The Greatest Story Ever Told*), and a paper sack containing a portion of Minton's brain. He drove down to the Pacific Coast Highway and turned north toward San Francisco. A few miles up the road, just past the beach at Greyhound Rock, he picked up a German hitchhiker, driving off so quickly he left the young man's girlfriend in the road. Huffman, who appeared highly agitated, was talking a mile a minute, and the poor German couldn't understand a word he was saying. He pleaded with Huffman to stop the car, at which point Huffman produced a knife and began slashing at him. A struggle ensued, during which the car skidded to a stop outside the Short Stop Market in Half Moon Bay.

The hitchhiker leaped from the car and raced toward a young man named Corey Baker, who was standing in the parking lot. Huffman emerged and began yelling something unintelligible. Baker approached him, noticing a strange whitish-gray substance on his hands. He thought it was fish guts. It wasn't. He told Huffman to calm down and go wash his hands. Huffman responded by punching him, grabbing a fountain pen, and attempting to poke out his eyes. Baker ran. Huffman drove off. An hour later a police car managed to force him off the road near the town of Pacifica. Huffman got out of the car, swearing and spitting, his eyes rolling back in his head. When an officer pulled his gun, Huffman held up his book and the bag of brains, as if to shield himself. Officers wrestled him to the ground. Later, when they visited the cottage, they found Minton's body. Huffman was tossed into jail.

Once he calmed down, Huffman telephoned Tony Serra, who agreed to represent him. At that point, Serra insists, this was a simple murder case. He had no clue that Huffman was behind the NWLF bombings; the authorities wouldn't learn of the connection for months. Not long after the arrest, Serra says, Huffman attempted to hang himself in his cell. Cut down at the last minute, he was rushed to a hospital, where doctors saved his life. But there was lingering brain damage of some sort. Afterward, Serra says, Huffman's speech became slurred, the name Tony came out "Dunny." At the hospital Huffman motioned for Serra to lean in close. "Dunny," he whispered.

"He told me where he had buried all his cash, hundreds of thousands of dollars, plus a huge freezer of marijuana," Serra remembers. "I go, 'Far fucking out!' So I go out there one night, with two shovels, two friends, and we dig where he told us, beneath a ladder in this old shed. And we found this massive freezer. I was so pumped! Wow, five hundred pounds of marijuana! And then we open it and the thing is empty!" Serra later returned to the cottage and dug dozens of holes in the yard. He never found a thing.

The first hint authorities received that Huffman might be involved in bombings came a few months after his arrest, when an informant suggested as much to the San Jose police, who passed the tip on to the FBI. "It was really vague, you know, that Huffman might be good for some bombings," recalls Stockton Buck. Huffman and Minton's fingerprints were forwarded to the Bureau, which began checking them against unidentified prints found on NWLF and other communiqués as far back as 1971. Among the first hits they got were those found on the candy box bombs. Eventually the FBI made sixteen matches in all. Many NWLF communiqués held no identifiable prints, however, so it's possible Huffman and Minton sent many of those as well. The only other evidence emerged after the new occupant of their Bonny Doon bungalow found a package buried in the yard. Inside was $30,000 in decomposed cash, along with hundreds of pages of NWLF literature: communiqués, codes, manifestos, surveillance rules, revolutionary tracts, and munitions manuals.

Amazingly, Huffman's ties to the NWLF remained a secret for four years. For much of this time he remained in jail as psychiatrists debated whether he was fit to stand trial for Minton's murder. Finally, in April 1983, he was ruled fit. The trial took place in Monterey. Huffman pled not guilty by reason of insanity; about the only sound he made during the proceedings was an occasional doglike growl. Tony Serra told the jury Huffman was "stark raving mad." Another defense attorney termed him "absolutely wacko." The jury disagreed, finding him guilty of second-degree murder.

The following week federal prosecutors finally unsealed a months-old indictment against Huffman for the NWLF bombings; because each carried a five-year statute of limitations, he was charged with conspiracy. The story made the front pages of the San Francisco papers but disappeared after a day or two. Outside the Bay Area it was all but ignored. The last NWLF bomb had detonated barely five years before, but it might as well have been fifty, so thoroughly had the world changed. The *Chronicle* story sounded as if the NWLF arose during the Dark Ages, terming Huffman, probably the decade's most prolific bomber, "part of a world that eventually disappeared."

In the end Ronald Huffman pled guilty and went to prison. No one connected with his case, including his attorneys, has a clue what happened to him after that. An administrator in the Santa Cruz County district attorney's office, however, confirms that Huffman died in a California state prison in 1999. Where he is buried, or whether anyone cared, remains a mystery.

HARD TIMES

The Death of the Weather Underground

The release of *Prairie Fire* on July 24, 1974, proved a transformative moment for the remaining members of what was now known as the Weather Underground Organization. The book itself, distributed to alternative bookstores, coffeehouses, and left-wing hangouts from coast to coast, successfully reintroduced the group to radical conversations everywhere. At some point, *Prairie Fire* morphed into something far more than simply a book. It became the first step in Weather's most crazily audacious plan ever: a grand scheme for the entire leadership not only to "resurface" publicly but to do so while simultaneously gathering the radical left into a single overarching coalition that they themselves—Jeff Jones, Bill Ayers, Bernardine Dohrn, Eleanor Stein, and Robbie Roth—would emerge to personally command.

What's more, it was all to be done in secret. In hindsight it was almost laughably brazen: The radical left, home to some of the most suspicious people in U.S. politics, was literally going to be *fooled* into returning Weather's leadership to the exalted positions they had abandoned on leaving SDS four years before.

The plan sprang from months of anguished discussion of Weather's irrelevancy. By 1974 it had become an open point of debate among the leadership: They were achieving precisely nothing. Remaining underground wasn't having the slightest influence on anyone in the radical left; it was only cutting them off from a movement seemingly reenergized by the Watergate scandal and the myriad FBI and CIA abuses already spilling into the press. Staying underground "was an increasingly high-cost fantasy," Bill Ayers recalled. "What was it accomplishing?" Dohrn herself agreed, noting in a 2004 interview that "to do what we were doing, in the sense of doing a couple actions a year and releasing communiqués, seemed inappropriate [in 1975]. And I think it was inappropriate. It didn't have the kind of shock value and interpretive value that it had during the war." Jeff Jones was even more blunt, also in a 2004 interview: "The underground had run its course by 1975."[1]

The initial idea, which came to be known as "inversion," emerged from talks Jones had with Eleanor Stein's mother, Annie. "There was a feeling," recalls Dohrn's friend Russell Neufeld, who emerged as a key player in Weather's new plans, "and Annie Stein was its most passionate advocate—Annie had super-strong opinions on almost everything—that Weather had squandered its ties to the Movement and needed to find a way to regain its leadership. Annie convinced Jeff and Eleanor of a lot of this, and Jeff and Eleanor convinced the rest of the leadership." There was skepticism at first, but Jones and Eleanor pushed. This, they argued, was their last, best chance to ever be political leaders again. "The idea was, Weatherman's leadership was going to take control of what remained of the Movement," recalls Cathy Wilkerson. "It was beyond ridiculous. We could never get away with it. Any person in their right mind should have known we were behind this, but you know, we were all enveloped in the vapor. Leadership, it was like a drug. We really thought we were the Chosen People."

As it unfolded, the conspiracy had two thrusts, one open and honest, the other secret and dishonest. The honest component would capitalize on *Prairie Fire*'s popularity by establishing a second publication, envisioned as a quarterly radical newsmagazine, called *Osawatomie*, named for the Kansas town where the abolitionist John Brown, long a Weather icon, first saw battle in 1856. The slender periodical, dense with left-wing position papers and occasional reportage on events such as a busing controversy in Boston, debuted in 1975.

The dishonest part of the plan involved the formation of a new aboveground group whose stated purpose was spreading *Prairie Fire*'s message via discussion groups across the country. This group, the vehicle that leadership secretly hoped to ride back to national prominence, was called the Prairie Fire Distribution Committee, or PFDC, and its first twenty or so members, many of whom had physically distributed the book that summer, portrayed themselves as entirely unrelated to Weather, as simply good-hearted radicals inspired by *Prairie Fire*'s message to try to knit the disparate threads of the Left into a single tapestry. The only ones briefed on the Central Committee's actual goals were the five close allies it had secretly selected to run the PFDC. These included Russell Neufeld; Dohrn's sister Jennifer; Jeff Jones's college pal Jon Lerner; and a fervent onetime Weatherman named Laura Whitehorn. At first Neufeld and Lerner resisted.

"The creation of the front organization, the secret organization, it's one of the things I deeply regret, being a shill," says Lerner. "I remember objecting very much to the idea, because I didn't like the manipulative part of it, and I didn't think it was going to work. The Laura Whitehorns of the world, they thought it was just a great idea. And I allowed myself to be bludgeoned into it, and it was about my needing to belong to the group emotionally. We were manipulating the PFDC the entire time. The entire time."

"I don't think I understood all of that until much later," remembers Neufeld. "Initially I thought it was just a way to build an aboveground support group. Only later did I learn everything, and it made me very uncomfortable. For me the contradiction was, we were building this mass organization, when in fact we were manipulating them all into being pawns of our leadership. It became very manipulative."

It all started simply enough, in the fall of 1974, when the new PFDC leaders began wooing friends during a series of picnics and parties in the Boston area. "A lot of people swallowed our entire line, that we had nothing to do with Weather," Lerner says. "But a lot of people, including people who came to these picnics, did not join us, because I think they understood right away that this was a front for Weather. Me, I thought it was obvious."

Neufeld and other volunteers, meanwhile, drove a battered Volkswagen bus to campuses around the country, convening discussion groups and handing out copies of *Prairie Fire*. "I was constantly being asked whether this was a front for Weather," he recalls. "I didn't want to lie outright, so I kept saying, 'I really can't talk about that.'"

To Neufeld's surprise, they were able to sign up dozens of new members, eventually more than a hundred. PFDC chapters were established in Boston, Philadelphia, San Francisco, and Chicago. In Brooklyn Silvia Baraldini prevailed on the two dozen or so members of the Assata Shakur Defense Committee to join en masse, despite her concerns that *Prairie Fire* seemed to be deemphasizing the black struggle in favor of a classic Marxist philosophy of working alongside the "international working class." "I read it, and I was skeptical, this glorification of white working-class stuff," Baraldini recalls. "I was stupid. I fell for it. It wasn't Weather, but it had that Weather mystique, and that was a powerful thing. We didn't realize their leadership had already abandoned any pretense at being true revolutionaries and wanted only to surface and take control of the Left and enjoy the middle-class lives they had left behind. None of us knew how we were being manipulated."

The second step in Weather's plan was transforming the PFDC into a permanent group, the Prairie Fire Organizing Committee, or PFOC. The change was announced at a July 1975 convention in Boston, where doubts about Weather's influence lingered. "I couldn't believe how many people were buying into this," recalls Elizabeth Fink. "To me it was blindingly obvious Weather was behind it." It was in Boston that the third and final step of Weather's plan was unveiled: a second PFOC conference, this one scheduled for January 1976, aimed at uniting dozens of radical groups—white, black, and Hispanic—beneath a single banner. Jeff Jones, in a bit of candor, came up with the name: the Hard Times Conference. There, the PFOC leadership, secretly controlled by the Central Committee, would be elected to lead the new coalition. Once Weather's leadership resurfaced and dealt with its legal troubles, they would be free to take over the group outright.

The Hard Times Conference, then, became a kind of Hail Mary pass for Weather's leadership, their last shot at regaining all they had thrown away. From the summer of 1975 on, all the PFOC's efforts—with Jones and the

Central Committee pulling strings behind the scenes—were focused on luring radical groups to the conference, which was to be held at the University of Illinois's Chicago campus. No group was too small to invite. Jonathan Lerner reached out to Native Americans. Silvia Baraldini recruited blacks in the South. Again and again Russell Neufeld, who moved to Chicago to supervise the preparations, was obliged to deny that Weather was involved. "Jeff was the one most involved in the day to day details," he recalls. "I was constantly being asked by Jeff to carry out Weatherman's wishes, and this troubled me. It became very manipulative. We just lied so much."

Among the preparatory steps was an unusual "cadre school" the Central Committee convened at a home in a gated community outside the town of Bend, Oregon. About twenty Weathermen attended, including several who had been invited back into the group; most took buses across the country from Boston. They masqueraded as graduate students on an anthropology field trip. Rick Ayers, who arranged everything, posed as their professor. The purpose of the five-day retreat was teaching Weather's new political "line," that is, the Marxist-Leninist philosophy set out in the pages of *Prairie Fire*. Annie Stein was on hand for guidance. "That really represented Annie's intellectual triumph," recalls Howard Machtinger, who attended.

"We read a lot of Lenin, read and discussed, and then we had physical education, exercises, and running," recalls Lerner. "I remember Bernardine Dohrn wearing big wedge sandals, running in these high sandals. The politics was strange, because it represented a real shift away from our early suspicion of Marxism and Lenin and was an adoption of classic commie rhetoric. It was like stepping backward into the old days. But it made people comfortable. It was known."

The months leading up to the Hard Times Conference were a blizzard of activity. Inside Weather the leadership debated endlessly whether to publicly "surface" two, three, or all five of its members. A team of lawyers led by Kathy Boudin's father, Leonard, was assembled to negotiate the surrenders. All were highly aware of the FBI break-ins, and at least one of the attorneys, it was later claimed, reached out to friends in the Democratic Party to see if they might strike some form of immunity deal in exchange for public testimony against the FBI.

The final weapon in Weather's public-relations arsenal was an attempt to burnish its image in the American mainstream. It was, of all things, a movie. After reading *Prairie Fire*, a documentarian named Emile de Antonio was startled to realize that Weather was still active. "What the hell," he mused, "is an essentially white, middle-class revolutionary group doing in America in 1975?" Through mutual friends he arranged a meeting with Jeff Jones and Eleanor Stein in the distant Brooklyn precinct of Sheepshead Bay at Lundy's, a restaurant where Stein's family often held celebrations. Jones immediately recognized the potential of a sympathetic film, both to clean up Weather's image and as a fund-raising vehicle. He agreed to be interviewed once de Antonio promised to hide their faces, give the leadership "final cut," and refuse to cooperate with any government subpoenas.

The filming, which took place over three days in Los Angeles in April 1975, was cloaked in secrecy. De Antonio and his cinematographer, Haskell Wexler, best known for *One Flew Over the Cukoo's Nest*, rendezvoused with Jones in an alley. Jones handed them each a pair of sunglasses, painted black, then guided them into a waiting station wagon, which he drove aimlessly for a half hour before arriving at a Weather safe house with the windows boarded. There, behind a cheesecloth drape to guard their identities, five of the best-known Weathermen—Jones, Dohrn, Ayers, and the two Townhouse survivors, Cathy Wilkerson and Kathy Boudin—were interviewed by the filmmakers.

The resulting eighty-eight-minute film, *Underground*, spliced footage of 1960s demonstrations with shots of the five Weathermen talking in shadow. Other than a moment when Jones described the bombing of the U.S. Capitol, they kept their answers general and a bit self-righteous. There was little they hadn't said before in one communiqué or another; some in the ranks thought the resulting procession of talking heads so boring, they referred to the film as *Jaws*. Yet Jones, after approving the final cut at Wexler's Malibu home, thought it all grand. "I remember talking about the film with Jeff," recalls Mark Rudd. "He was so excited about it, almost like a little kid."

The film was to be released in mid-1976, but it began generating news months before. De Antonio was served with a subpoena, and he responded by holding a press conference where he brandished a petition of support from thirty-two Hollywood grandees, including Jack Nicholson, Warren Beatty, and Mel Brooks. The ensuing publicity obliged the government to back off, and it eventually allowed de Antonio to market the movie as "the film the FBI didn't want you to see."

Underground's release was still months away on Friday, January 30, 1976, when the first delegates began arriving at the University of Illinois's Chicago campus for the Hard Times Conference. Russell Neufeld watched nervously as they wandered in and registered. He knew what was riding on the conference's success. "This was the moment, this was huge," he remembers. "This was the one way Weather's leadership could come back to relevance." The turnout was promising, more than two thousand delegates in all, representing dozens of radical groups, from the Puerto Rican Socialist Party and the American Indian Movement to the Black Workers Coalition and the Republic of New Afrika. Clearly, Neufeld saw, they had tapped into some kind of yearning for a national radical coalition. Meanwhile Jeff Jones and Eleanor Stein paced a nearby hotel room, unable to attend. In the auditorium Annie Stein stood behind the curtain, watching, darting off every now and then to relay reports of the proceedings to Jones and her daughter.

Everything began smoothly enough. Jennifer Dohrn delivered an opening address calling on the delegates to devise a new agenda for the Left that would empower and protect the working class. "We have to develop a program for the working class as a whole in this period to fight the [economic] depression," she said. It was soon clear, however, that the conference's organizers, who were all white, did not fully comprehend the needs of the delegates, who weren't.

"I was almost lynched by a group of vegetarians because I hadn't provided enough nonmeat meals in the cafeteria," Neufeld recalls with a shudder. "There were a lot of little things like that, stuff I just didn't understand. Every time something went wrong, I was constantly being accused of being a racist. That was just devastating to me. I felt I was fucking up, like my head was just going to explode."

Much of the conference work was done in breakout groups, and by Saturday it was clear that many of them had little interest in the conference's agenda. A Black Caucus formed, and word soon spread that it was none too pleased with the emphasis on "working class" issues over black issues. A feminist caucus arose as well and was just as incensed at the lack of attention being paid to women's issues. "Jeff Jones wanted these people ordered and controlled, and there was just no way," Neufeld says. "My pushback [to him] was to respect the process, that people had opinions, that they couldn't be ordered around."

The ominous rumblings finally broke into the open during the closing session, when black delegates spent nearly an hour excoriating the organizers as racists and demanding that any new radical coalition be run by blacks. By nightfall confusion reigned. "I don't think [Jeff] initially appreciated how bad it was," Neufeld says. "In fact, I know he didn't. And it was bad. Very bad."

By that evening it was clear there would be no radical coalition for Weather or anyone else to control. Recriminations began the next morning, when thirty PFOCers gathered in a member's Chicago apartment. "That's when I first heard some of the non-Weather people start saying things like 'Where did this whole conference idea come from?'" recalls Lerner. "They were finally starting to smell the rat."

An investigation of sorts was soon under way. It was spearheaded by a band of West Coast members led by none other than Clayton Van Lydegraf, the graying communist lifer who, having been thrown out of Weather, had joined the PFOC. Granted an opportunity to take his revenge, he proceeded to do so with grim determination, practically overnight emerging as the PFOC's avenging angel. One by one, he and his acolytes pulled in Neufeld and other PFOC leaders and grilled them, a process that soon devolved into a Stalin-like purge—"everything but the bullets," as one participant put it.

"I remember Clayton came to New York and that's when we first heard of Weather's plan and resurfacing and all that," remembers Silvia Baraldini. "We heard there was a huge confrontation between Clayton and Annie Stein. We were just amazed. How could they actually believe they could resurface and take control of the Movement when people like the BLA were struggling to survive and they've been living well? It was just incredibly arrogant. Everyone was outraged."

For weeks there was chaos. No one knew who to trust. People scattered. The last Weather collectives in Boston imploded, the printing press abandoned, everyone running for the safety of family and friends. In time, Van Lydegraf's crusade took shape. He took Russell Neufeld to Chicago and forced him to apologize to everyone he had lied to. It was a wrenching experience for everyone involved. "There was a week or two that spring, when the whole thing was collapsing, that I just remember walking the streets, crying," recalls Jon Lerner.

But as the months wore on, it became clear that purging the PFOC was only the first step in Van Lydegraf's plan. Slowly word spread that he intended to purge the Weather Underground itself. Once again, one by one, a number of the original Weathermen, including Bernardine Dohrn herself, were summoned to San Francisco, where they submitted to criticism/self-criticism sessions said to have been more grueling than any others in the group's history. None of those involved have ever spoken in detail of what took place. "It was rough, yeah," recalls Cathy Wilkerson, who submitted to a rigorous examination. "They felt we had betrayed the black cause, and I guess they were right. But the fact is, by then, like a lot of people, I was so burned out I didn't really care." What she recalled about her final meeting with Van Lydegraf was walking out afterward to the startling realization that she was being followed. It was the first hint that law enforcement, after years of trying, had finally managed to infiltrate what remained of the group.

The culmination of Van Lydegraf's crusade came over Thanksgiving weekend 1976, when he unveiled his findings at a PFOC summit in San Francisco, essentially a series of white papers that indicted the Central Committee for a host of "counterrevolutionary" crimes, from betraying the PFOC to abandoning the black cause to attempting to "destroy" feminists, gays, and lesbians in Weather's ranks. Dohrn, Bill Ayers, and all the others were summarily expelled; Van Lydegraf ordered that no one could have any contact with them. The centerpiece of his findings was an extraordinary tape recording of Dohrn in which she admitted, among a kaleidoscope of offenses, engaging in "naked white supremacy, white superiority, and chauvinist arrogance." The tone was set in the first line: "I am making this tape," Dohrn intoned, in the voice so many remembered from Weatherman's declaration of war in May 1970, "to acknowledge, repudiate, and denounce the counterrevolutionary politics and direction of the Weather Underground Organization." She spread the blame, naming Bill Ayers and Jeff Jones as her co-conspirators. "Why did we do this?" she asked. "I don't really know. We followed the classic path of white so-called revolutionaries who sold out the revolution."

It all had the air of sad anticlimax. Dohrn's statement reeked as much of fatigue and self-loathing as of surrender. But if her words arrived draped in melodrama and Marxist dogma, there was no denying their essential truth: The Weathermen had, in fact, sold out their dreams in return for their own personal safety. One could argue that those dreams had actually died six years earlier, in the accidental explosion on Eleventh Street, after which no one in the leadership had any stomach for the violence they had so casually embraced and urged on others. In every conceivable way, the young intellectuals who had come together in 1969 to form Weatherman had utterly failed: failed to lead the radical left over the barricades into armed underground struggle; failed to fight or support the black militants they championed; failed to force agencies of the American "ruling class" into a single change more significant than the spread of metal detectors and guard dogs.

The Weather Underground was dead. Its survivors scattered, many of them unsure what to do next. For those still wanted on old criminal charges, most arising from the Days of Rage, the first order of business was confronting what had once been the unthinkable: surrender. Feelers from various lawyers began going out in early 1977. It was a measure of how thoroughly America had turned its back on the tumultuous 1960s that, for the most part, law enforcement yawned. When the first Weathermen, Robbie Roth and Phoebe Hirsch, appeared unannounced at a Chicago courthouse that April, the officer on duty told them to come back the next day. They eventually received probation and were fined a grand total of $1,000 each.

Next went Paul Bradley, who abandoned his beloved cottage house in San Francisco's Russian Hill neighborhood and, with Michael Kennedy at his side, turned himself in to Chicago prosecutors. He too got probation. "I remember in 1977 Bernardine apologized to me," Bradley recalls. "She said, 'You know,

I'm really sorry, who'd have thought it'd end up like this.' I said, 'Forget it, it's been great. How else could I have lived in San Francisco for seven years?'"

Howie Machtinger soon followed. After fleeing Boston, he had moved to Vancouver, where he found refuge with, of all people, John "JJ" Jacobs. But the young student who had inspired Weather's creation had never adjusted to life outside the organization. He had become a heavy drug user. "I began to think JJ was totally crazy," Machtinger recalls. "He was stoned all the time. Very erratic." In time Machtinger moved to Seattle, where he took a job as a sports counselor at a recreation center. In his spare time he read Stalin. Finally, in May 1978, he returned to Chicago, where he faced assault charges from the Days of Rage. He too received probation.

One of the stranger partings involved the two bomb makers, Cathy Wilkerson and Ron Fliegelman. By 1977 the couple had been living together for several years—first in Yonkers, New York, later in San Francisco—in a tenuous relationship arranged by the leadership in an effort to keep both of them content. "When everything started falling apart, my first thought was 'I can get out of this now,'" Wilkerson recalls. "Then I thought, 'Wait, I should get pregnant first.' So I did." (As did Dohrn and Eleanor Stein; all three women gave birth during 1977 and 1978.) When their daughter was born, Wilkerson and Fliegelman went their separate ways. Wilkerson, who was wanted on charges related to the Townhouse, went back into hiding, taking her daughter to an apartment in a gritty neighborhood of Chicago's South Side. Fliegelman, who wasn't sought, simply returned to his parents' home in Philadelphia. Within weeks he began working at the same school for troubled children he had left on joining SDS in 1969. "For me it was really seamless," he recalls with a shrug. "No one—the FBI, no one—ever came looking for me."

Of those who surrendered in 1977, the only one to attract serious media attention was Mark Rudd, the star of the Columbia unrest nine years earlier. A crowd of more than a hundred reporters and photographers jostled him as he and his attorney walked through New York's Foley Square toward the Criminal Courts Building that September.

"Hey, Mark," someone shouted. "Say something like the old days at Columbia."

"I've got something to say," Rudd replied as he fended off the crowd. "I hope no one is picking my pocket."

The press seemed to be the only ones who cared. A reporter who visited Columbia couldn't find anyone who knew Rudd's name. When the campus newspaper asked a hundred freshmen who Mark Rudd was, eight knew. Rudd eventually pled guilty to misdemeanor assault charges in New York and in Chicago. Like the others, he received probation and a fine.

By year's end barely a half-dozen significant Weathermen remained at large. Dohrn and Ayers appear to have left their Hermosa Beach bungalow in the mid-1970s and taken a place in San Francisco. In the wake of Weather's collapse they moved to New York, where Dohrn waitressed and Ayers worked as a baker's assistant. Of all the "Weather debris," the one who suffered the toughest transition was Jeff Jones, who was roundly blamed for the disastrous "inversion" strategy. For a time he and Eleanor Stein threw a mattress into a van and lived out of it, shuttling between parking spaces in the farthest reaches of Brooklyn and the Bronx. They tried to set up meetings with old friends, but people either shunned them or failed to show. In time Stein bowed to pressure from her own friends; the couple separated. Broke, Jones washed up in an apartment in Jersey City, New Jersey, paying his rent with the only job he could find: as a bicycle messenger.

There was a bizarre coda—actually, two—to the Weather Underground's demise. Clayton Van Lydegraf, it turned out, didn't want to just purge Weather's leadership. He wanted to assume it. At the Thanksgiving 1976 gathering of PFOC leaders in San Francisco, he argued in favor of launching a new underground bombing campaign. The New York delegation, spearheaded by Silvia Baraldini, thought he had lost his mind. "We kept asking, 'Who the fuck is this Clayton Van Lydegraf?'" says Elizabeth Fink. "'Who is he to tell you what to do?'"

"I remember Russell Neufeld saying, 'We have to wake up and realize we are not going to be Ho Chi Minh,'" says Baraldini. "Really, though, things broke down over race. We went out there with black people. There was an enormous fight over the role of black people in the PFOC. What I remember is that a group of us decided to leave [the PFOC. Clayton] took us in a van and talked to us for hours, [saying,] 'You can't just leave, we need you, you need to fight for [the blacks].' They just begged us not to let everything go down the tubes."

When Baraldini and the New Yorkers resigned anyway, Van Lydegraf and two couples decided to go it alone. For months they had convened regularly to read and discuss communist texts. Then, in the spring of 1977, they began weapons training, sort of, firing BB guns at tin cans at an impromptu firing range in the desert outside Barstow. To train for high-speed car chases, sort of, they took spins around a go-cart track. In all this they were helped immeasurably by Van Lydegraf's roommate of two years, named Ralph, and Ralph's close friend Dick, who turned out to be a pair of undercover FBI agents, Richard Giannotti and William Reagan—the same William Reagan who had grown close to Mona Mellis way back in 1971. Cathy Wilkerson had been right about being followed: In its death throes the Weather Underground had finally been penetrated by the FBI.

In November 1977, believing that Van Lydegraf's little band was about to bomb a California state senator's office, the FBI swooped in and arrested all five of them. All were thrown in jail for short stints, at which point any reasonable observer might have believed the days of the Weather Underground's attacks on "Amerika" were over. But even then, in 1977, there remained a handful who would not give up.

It was one of the ironies of the underground era that, just as the Weather Underground began to disintegrate, so did its main pursuer, the FBI's last true black-bag specialists, Squad 47. Members of the squad had precious little to show for the previous six years. Other than Leonard Handelsman, a Weatherman in the Cleveland collective who apparently fled after the Townhouse, the only figure of note to be arrested since 1971 had been Howie Machtinger, who promptly disappeared back into the underground. Sixty members of Squad 47 soldiered on, though, staking out relatives' homes and, when so inclined, breaking into them in a vain effort to find Bernardine Dohrn or anyone else on their list of known Weathermen. By 1976 a sense of defeat and resignation permeated the squad's offices on East Sixty-ninth Street. At one point Lou Vizi, the FALN investigator, grew excited when a Squad 47 agent mentioned they had discovered a fingerprint on a Weather communiqué. It belonged to a member of the Prairie Fire Organizing Committee. "Man, that's great!" Vizi remembers blurting.

The Squad 47 man pulled a face. "Why?" he asked.

"Why?" Vizi repeated. "You can take it to a grand jury. You got a print! We'd kill to have a print."

The Squad 47 man just sighed. "We've been down that road," he said, shaking his head. "The guy'll just say someone showed it to him, or it was an old piece of paper. Believe me, nothing will happen."

And nothing ever did. In the end Squad 47's downfall was pure happenstance. By 1976 disclosure of the FBI's COINTELPRO program had prompted the Justice Department to open a number of investigations, including probes into work against Martin Luther King and a host of black-power groups. The Socialist Workers Party (SWP) had filed suit, charging that they had been subjected to COINTELPRO-like tactics as well. Reviewing those charges fell to Bill Gardner, a lawyer who ran the criminal section of the department's Civil Rights Division.

Every few days during the spring of 1976, Gardner walked over from his office in the Todd Building to FBI headquarters, where a pile of the Bureau's SWP files would be awaiting him in a conference room. He had received a top security clearance in order to perform the review, but the Bureau took no chances: As Gardner sorted through the files, a pleasant FBI agent—Gardner thought of him as his babysitter—always sat in one corner, watching. The Keith decision in June 1972 made any warrantless electronic surveillance or break-ins against domestic organizations strictly illegal; any violations Gardner found that occurred after that date he fully expected to prosecute.

But a funny thing happened as Gardner was thumbing through the files. There was no indication whatsoever that the FBI had performed illegal surveillance of the SWP. But for some reason, someone had inserted dozens of the Bureau's Weather Underground files into those he was reviewing. When he glanced at these, Gardner realized in an instant that Squad 47 had been carrying out buggings and break-ins well after June 1972. The files cited dozens of instances, maybe hundreds, all the way into 1975. It was all there in black and white, in the FBI's own files. There was no way anyone in the Bureau could deny it.

Gardner, sensing he was onto something big, went straight to Stan Pottinger's office. Pottinger, a suave government attorney who would go on to a successful career as a novelist, ran the Civil Rights division. Pottinger, in turn, took the matter to the U.S. attorney general, Edward Levi, a former president of the University of Chicago appointed by President Ford. Levi appeared personally offended. The FBI had repeatedly sworn that these kinds of black bag jobs were history. He immediately authorized a task force to investigate Squad 47.

Gardner led the group of six attorneys. To investigate the men of Squad 47, the FBI lent them a group of agents, whose unpopular assignment soon earned them the nickname "The Dirty Dozen." A grand jury was impaneled in Washington to hear testimony. Gardner was not expecting serious difficulties. It seemed an open-and-shut case; the only question was whether Squad 47 was a rogue unit or something authorized by top FBI officials. "We had a series of smoking guns right from the start," Gardner recalls. "There was absolutely no question as to the blatant illegality. The question was how high up the chain it went. We divided into teams. We ran our investigation in a traditional pyramid style: Start with the ground agents, then their supervisors, then see how far up the ladder it goes."

One by one the agents of Squad 47 were interviewed. To a man, they hired lawyers and said nothing. Gardner and his team begged and wheedled and negotiated but got nowhere. They called a string of agents before the grand jury, but all took the fifth, including Don Strickland, by then an attorney in Hartford, Connecticut. "I remember Pottinger just begging me in the grand jury, 'I want you to talk to us,'" recalls Strickland. "And I wouldn't. No one would."

In the meantime, members of the "Dirty Dozen" descended on the FBI's Sixty-ninth Street offices with search warrants. They gathered documents from desks and safes, including one in SAC Horace Beckwith's office.* The men of Squad 47 panicked, furiously disposing of thousands of pages of Weather-related internal documents. "Everyone was running scared, guys were just scared to death," remembers Richard Hahn, then an agent on the FALN case. "Guys were literally burning files, tossing them in bags and taking them home to throw in their fireplaces. I know. I watched 'em do it. Before long you couldn't find a single folder in the New York office with the name Weather Underground on it."

Finally a single agent, identified by retired agents as Michael Kirchenbauer, agreed to tell the truth in return for immunity. Then the dam burst. One by one the men of Squad 47 sat for prosecutors and spoke up. "Some of us felt that what the Bureau did constituted a far greater danger to society than what the Weathermen ever did," recalls one prosecutor on the case, Stephen Horn. "When you looked the beast in the eye, and we interviewed all of them, you got a sense of how this started out as a somewhat regulated activity that just mushroomed. It was so much easier than regular police work. It was all Squad 47 did, in effect. They were seduced by this, and this just got totally out of control. They were going in everyone's house, mail openings, you name it. They were literally running amok. And they just didn't get the illegality of it all. I remember one agent saying to me in an interview, in a defensive tone, 'You gotta remember we cleared a lot of people by bagging their houses.'"

The Justice Department, however, had little interest in arresting street agents, who were only following orders. They wanted their superiors. By the first weeks of 1977, Bill Gardner and his team were prepared to do something no prosecutor had ever done: secure a felony indictment against an FBI supervisor. Their target was John Kearney, the avuncular Irishman who had retired as Squad 47's supervisor five years earlier. Kearney now worked in security for Wells Fargo in Massachusetts, but "flipping him"—that is, forcing his testimony as part of a plea agreement—was their best hope of gathering evidence

---

*In 1976 *Time* magazine carried a story that detailed how a major break in the case came when agents in the "Dirty Dozen" uncovered piles of incriminating Weatherman files in an office safe maintained by the onetime New York assistant director John Malone. Today neither Bill Gardner nor other prosecutors interviewed for this book can remember any such discovery. The only important FBI documents investigators found, Gardner emphasizes, were those he himself found at FBI headquarters at the outset of the investigation.

against those higher in the Bureau, conceivably all the way to the FBI's No. 2 man in 1972, Mark Felt, who had since retired.

Negotiations with Kearney's attorney, Hubert Santos, were going nowhere. Kearney "felt like he was doing the right thing, that they were doing everything the Bureau wanted them to do," Gardner recalls. "But deep down they knew the Bureau was doing something wrong. I know John Kearney wrestled with that. We were pushing him for a plea to get our investigation going. Hubert kept telling us, 'John can do a plea for a misdemeanor, he can't plead to a felony, because he doesn't feel guilty.' We needed a felony. Someone had to turn. We had a couple of SACs in our sights, and we needed a plea to go after them."

The Squad 47 investigation paused that winter when the new Carter administration entered office. A wizened Atlanta jurist, Griffin Bell, took over as attorney general. Gardner's team drafted a fat memo on the case for Bell's review. His reaction was not what they had hoped. While President Ford's attorney general, Edward Levi, "had been very offended by everything he learned about this, Bell was a completely different guy," Gardner recalls. "He was far more bothered by how this would disrupt the Bureau. When he was briefed on this, we heard he was quoted as saying, 'What's this got to do with civil rights?'" Still, unwilling to quash an investigation his men were excited about pursuing, Bell reluctantly allowed them to move ahead.

They did. On April 7, 1977—smack in the middle of the FALN grand jury proceedings—another federal grand jury in New York handed up a five-count indictment against Kearney that included two counts of conspiracy, two counts of obstruction of correspondence, and a single count of unlawful wiretapping. The *New York Times* carried the news on page 1. Morale among the agents plummeted. "It killed us," remembers Lou Vizi of the FALN squad. "It just killed us."

This was more than routine bellyaching. One week later, when Kearney was scheduled to appear in court to make his plea—not guilty—three hundred stone-faced FBI agents gathered on the steps of the federal courthouse in Foley Square in protest. It was an assembly unprecedented in FBI history, not to mention saturated in irony. Here were the men (and precisely two women) of the FBI—the agency that for a decade had been the bane of student protesters, whose undercover agents had secretly circulated through thousands of antiwar rallies, who had bugged and burgled and wiretapped long-haired activists, whose crew cuts and shined shoes marked them as the antithesis of the entire protest generation—turning to the very tactics they had been trying to stop for years. Attired in dark suits, they stood silent until a car drove up carrying Kearney and his wife. When the couple stepped from the car, the agents broke out into applause. Their spokesman, an agent named Patrick Connor, burst forth in a stout defense of Kearney.

These agents are here, he announced in what the *Times* called "a ringing baritone," "to demonstrate their personal loyalty to you and to give testament to your just and moral leadership over a period of years in the fight against the enemies of our nation, namely anarchy and terrorism." When the full truth "is before the American people and their voice is heard, your vindication will be assured."

In Washington the FBI director, Clarence Kelley, issued a statement decrying the indictment. Behind the scenes he and others strongly protested the move. "Judge Bell was just overwhelmed by the public reaction, he was lobbied heavily by the law enforcement community that this was a horrible, horrible thing to be prosecuting the FBI," Gardner recalls. "I can't tell you how many Saturday mornings I had with that guy where he was just wringing his hands. 'Have you read *A Man Called Intrepid*?' he would say. 'The Bureau's been doing this stuff since World War Two. This is gonna destroy the Bureau.' He was deeply troubled. He kept telling us, 'How am I gonna reform the Bureau with you guys prosecuting them all the time?'"

Yet Gardner's team forged ahead. Confident that they could eventually wring a plea agreement from Kearney, they turned to a related case, the proposed indictment of six FBI officials—including Horace Beckwith, Kearney's successor at Squad 47, and Wallace LaPrade, the official in charge of the New York office—on charges of perjury and conspiracy for lying about Weatherman cases before a grand jury. An assistant attorney general, Benjamin Civiletti, approved seeking the indictments. But this time Attorney General Bell put his foot down. "Civiletti came back to us and basically said, 'He doesn't want to do this,'" recalls Steve Horn. "'He wants you to skip all these layers and go straight to the top.'"

Gardner's team was crestfallen. This meant rethinking all their work to focus solely on the indictment of the top three FBI officials from 1972, Acting Director L. Patrick Gray, Acting Associate Director Mark Felt, and Assistant Director Ed Miller. Before that could be done, however, Bell ordered Gardner's men to interview senior White House officials from that era—the Watergate era—to see whether any had sanctioned Squad 47's activities. To a man, the prosecutors rolled their eyes; this, they were sure, was a wild goose chase. It took months. One of Gardner's men interviewed the Nixon aide John Ehrlichman in an Arizona prison, where he was serving time on Watergate charges. Another interviewed H. R. Haldeman. Yet another, an attorney named Frank Martin, traveled to California and actually interviewed Richard Nixon himself, at his retirement home in San Clemente.

No one admitted knowing a thing about Squad 47. Judge Bell was not impressed. When Gardner's team once again put the matter of broader FBI indictments on his desk, Bell said no. They could indict Gray, Felt, and Miller if they must. But no one else. In December 1977, after weeks of tense discussions among themselves, Gardner and his team did something no one could remember any other Justice Department prosecutors doing in the past century: They resigned.

Judge Bell carried the day. Four months later, in April 1978, a Washington grand jury handed up indictments against Gray, Felt, and Miller.* Felt, for one, thought the charges were outrageous. Later, after appearing in court, the three defendants were taken to a marshal's office, where they were photographed and fingerprinted. As Felt held out his fingers, Gray stood beside him, washing his hands in a basin.

"Pat," Felt asked, "how many years of service have you given your country?"

"Twenty-six years," Gray replied.

"This is the reward which your country has for you."

It was another moment steeped in irony. After the Weather Underground's seven-year bombing campaign, three senior FBI men were heading toward a criminal trial—and not a single Weatherman.

---

*The indictment against the FBI's John Kearney was simultaneously dropped.

"WELCOME TO FEAR CITY"

The FALN, 1976 to 1978

By the spring of 1976, as both the Weather Underground and its Squad 47 pursuers began to implode, what appeared to be the most lethal of the remaining underground groups, the FALN, had all but vanished. It hadn't claimed responsibility for a single action since the ten "anniversary" bombings the previous October. No one had a clue why. Maybe it had run out of dynamite. Maybe its members were in jail on unrelated charges. Maybe, like the NWLF, the FALN had given up.

The FBI hadn't. In Chicago agents studied every facet of the unexploded bomb found in a bundle of roses outside Standard Oil the previous October. They had the FBI lab analyze the flowers and the wrapping paper but found nothing of use. The one lead they unearthed involved the dynamite, which the lab discerned had been custom-made for use in building the Heron Dam in New Mexico, completed in 1971. The Albuquerque office interviewed workers at the site and identified a Chicano activist named Pedro Archuleta as the possible thief. Archuleta, however, had vanished. Agents also found that several of the October bombs had been secreted inside a certain brand of leather shaving kit, scraps of which were recovered at the scenes. In New York detectives fanned out across the city and discovered a luggage store in the Bronx whose owner claimed he had sold dozens of the kits to a curly-haired Hispanic man. A police artist drew up a sketch, but no one recognized the face.

Then suddenly, after eight months of silence, the thunder of FALN bombs once again echoed through the canyons of downtown Chicago. At 10:45 on the night of June 7, 1976, bundles of dynamite exploded simultaneously in a pair of trash cans, one outside the Hancock Building, the second at Bank Leumi, an Israeli bank a block from City Hall, the probable target. No one was hurt. All across downtown police and security guards scrambled to check for more bombs and, to their dismay, found one in a trash can outside police headquarters. The area was cleared of pedestrians just as the bomb exploded at 11:00. But no one found the last device, which detonated outside the First National Bank of Chicago. Damage at all the sites was minimal.

By the next morning no communiqués had been found, but the FBI lab confirmed that the dynamite was the same as that stolen from the Heron Dam, meaning it was the FALN. Three weeks later they struck again, this time in New York: four small bombs exploding in the dead of night outside two bank branches, the Pan Am Building, and the NYPD's 40th Precinct house. By this point there was a sense that the FALN attacks were growing almost routine: Four bombs drew all of five paragraphs in the *Times*.

The FBI, however, couldn't be so sanguine. The New York bombs exploded just a week before the largest celebration in postwar history: the Bicentennial, on July 4, 1976. A massive fireworks display was planned above the Statue of Liberty, among many events across the country. It was an ideal time, and an ideal place, for radical groups such as the FALN to strike, as several officials told the Senate Internal Security Subcommittee that June. The FBI, working closely with the NYPD, organized hundreds of teams to stake out virtually every landmark and skyscraper in New York, hoping they could catch the FALN in the act. But the holiday came and went with no bombings.

The attacks, in fact, came a week later, but in dismayingly tiny packages. On July 12 ten incendiaries placed inside cigarette packs, identical to those used by MIRA four years earlier, burst into flames at a series of Manhattan department stores, including Gimbel's, Lord & Taylor, and the flagship Macy's at Herald Square. All the fires were quickly extinguished. A caller to the *New York Post* pointed police to an FALN communiqué, which said the action was in protest of the Puerto Rican delegation at the Democratic National Convention that began that week at Madison Square Garden. A month later it happened again, flash fires erupting in the lingerie section at a Korvette's, in the coat section at Gimbel's, and in a third-floor dress section at Macy's. Sprinklers doused confused shoppers, who ran from the building. All three stores evacuated several floors before returning to normal.

At that point a new FBI supervisor, Paul Brana, encouraged by the Bicentennial cooperation between the FBI and the NYPD, proposed a second citywide dragnet, this one to coincide with the second anniversary of the FALN's debut in late October. They called it "Operation Catch a Bomber"; it took months to arrange. As meetings stretched on that September, the FALN struck twice more, in Chicago on September 10 and New York on September 21. The Chicago bombs were left in a restroom at the Lake Shore Drive Holiday Inn and in a government office. Damage was minimal; a communiqué noted that a "free and socialist Puerto Rico, if necessary, will be written in red blood." The New York bomb was more harrowing, demolishing a twenty-fourth-story stairwell at the New York Hilton, where Puerto Rico's governor was to be honored at a banquet that night.

In late October Operation Catch a Bomber went forward, flooding the streets around New York landmarks with hundreds of FBI agents and detectives. It was a complete bust. At the FBI offices on Sixty-ninth Street, Don Wofford and Lou Vizi were at their wits' end. At one point, in desperation, they brought in a psychic. Nothing worked.

And then they got lucky.

Deep in the rough Puerto Rican neighborhoods around Chicago's Humboldt Park, there lived an emaciated young man named Raul Velez. He rented a small flat on the third floor of a run-down building at 2659 West Haddon Avenue, five miles northwest of the skyscrapers downtown, and for the past several days he had been watching his new neighbors, a pair of Hispanic men, as they moved things into an apartment across the hallway. They had just purchased the building, they told him, and would be refurbishing it over the next several weeks. Velez studied them closely as they hauled in a suitcase, a footlocker, a large zippered bag, and several packages that looked like Christmas gifts. The two men stayed inside the apartment during the day and disappeared at night.

Velez was short on cash, and so in the early hours of November 3, 1976—a week after Operation Catch a Bomber in New York—he jimmied the lock on his neighbors' door and made his way inside, hoping to steal whatever he could find for sale to a pawn shop or a pal. Given the remodeling plans, Velez expected to find power tools. Instead, as his eyes adjusted to the gloom inside the apartment, he saw piles of boxes and spools of what appeared to be clothesline. It was labeled PRIME-A-DET. Velez had no idea what it was, but he recognized the red sticks packed into the footlocker: dynamite. Hundreds of sticks of dynamite. He sorted through the rest and found a shotgun, two rifles, walkie-talkies, and what he later learned were blasting caps.

Velez struggled to drag it all across the hall into his own apartment, and once he did, he telephoned a friend, George Dunn, who he knew had contacts on the street. Dunn drove over, saw Velez's surprising score, and by midmorning had helped him move it all a second time, to Dunn's apartment, several blocks away on Washtenaw Avenue.

It was just a little before noon when Detective John Dugan of the Chicago Police Gangs Unit got a call from one of his snitches, who told him someone named Dunn was spreading the word that he had dynamite to sell. The snitch had agreed to meet Dunn at 1 p.m., at a garage on Rockwell Street. When Dugan and his partner drove up, they saw their informant hunched over a footlocker with Dunn. The two cops walked up, tossed both men against a wall, and found themselves staring at what appeared to be hundreds of red sticks of dynamite.

At first glance Dugan couldn't believe it was real. But it was, as men from the bomb squad soon confirmed. All told, there were 216 sticks of it, plus an eighty-pound box of raw explosives, plus blasting caps and hundreds of feet of detonating cord—enough to blow up just about any building in Chicago.

Dunn confessed everything, and afterward Detective Dugan swung by and handcuffed Raul Velez. Dugan, thinking he had stumbled on a brewing gang war or even a terrorist plot, wanted to search the apartment Velez had burglarized, but his commander, lost in the minutiae of a busy afternoon, ordered him to finish his paperwork before the end of his shift to avoid any overtime. Dugan appealed to his sergeant, who was curious as well, and while Dugan's partner completed the paperwork, the two men drove to the building on West Haddon. On the way they radioed for a Spanish-speaking officer to meet them there.

Reaching the third floor, Dugan was surprised to find the apartment's front and rear doors wide open. There was no furniture, just a single table. On the floor they found a typewriter, some wire, and a dusting of white powder. On the table they found a piece of white paper covered with writing in Spanish. The Spanish-speaking officer glanced at it and gasped. It was a communiqué from the FALN.

They called the bomb squad, which suspected they had found an FALN safe house and telephoned a senior FBI agent, Tom Deans. Within an hour a dozen FBI men were on site, studying every corner of the forlorn apartment. Warrants were obtained, and the super directed agents to a storage area where the two Hispanic men had appeared to be doing some kind of work. Busting the lock, the agents found a trove of bomb-making paraphernalia: batteries, propane tanks, wiring, chemicals, wristwatches, a book that had been hollowed out, and photos of several downtown buildings. There were also piles of documents.

Deans realized this was the first FALN safe house ever found, but they appeared even luckier than that. The two Hispanic men had claimed to own the building; it was only a matter of time, Dean surmised, before they could be identified. After bagging and tagging all the evidence, they took the building's handyman downtown. He told them his father had bought the building on behalf of his son-in-law, who was the real owner. He identified the son-in-law as none other than Carlos Torres, the same man whom agents had found so cooperative when interviewed months before.

Torres was identified as one of the two Hispanic men whose things Raul Velez had stolen. The other was identified after helpfully leaving his résumé among the papers agents seized. He was Oscar López, a Vietnam veteran whose brother was principal at Chicago's Puerto Rican High School. Both had vanished from their apartments near Humboldt Park. Stakeouts were arrayed around relatives' homes, but both couples appeared to be long gone.

The next day Tom Deans persuaded the U.S. attorney's office to issue a warrant for Carlos Torres on weapons charges. All that was known of Torres was that he attended the University of Illinois, Chicago Circle Campus. His wife, Haydee, was said to be three months pregnant. López, meanwhile, was well known in the city's Puerto Rican neighborhoods. He had been a community organizer who put together protests on behalf of a dozen Puerto Rican causes in the early 1970s. His common-law wife, Lucy Rodriguez, worked for the federal government, as an equal-employment specialist in the Chicago offices of the Environmental Protection Agency.

As one set of FBI agents spread out in search of Torres and López, another pored over everything found at the West Haddon building. Of all the evidence the FBI gathered, the most curious bit was a copy of a letter mailed to a Maria Cueto, who was identified as executive director of the National Commission on Hispanic Affairs (NCHA). The letter was a request for funding from a church in Texas. A phone call determined that the commission was affiliated with the Episcopal Church. What on earth, investigators wondered, was its correspondence doing in an FALN safe house?

It turned out that the NCHA operated out of basement offices at the Episcopal Church's national headquarters in Midtown Manhattan. FBI agents interviewed Cueto there on November 18, two weeks after the discoveries in Chicago. An Episcopal lay worker from Phoenix whose aunt sat on the church's Board of Guardians, she politely explained that the NCHA gave money to Hispanic groups involved in all manner of self-help, educational, and commercial efforts. Yes, she said, she knew Carlos Torres. He was a member of her board; he had been in the city as recently as October, in fact, on church business. López had been on the board for a time as well, as had Pedro Archuleta, the man now suspected of stealing the dynamite the FALN had been using. Another suspect, Julio Rosado, had also been a board member; his brother Luis was one of the NCHA's consultants.

The news flashed through all the FBI investigators and federal prosecutors in New York, Chicago, and Washington. Don Wofford's head was practically spinning, trying to grasp it all. They had to say it out loud to make themselves believe it: Virtually everyone the FBI now knew to be linked to the FALN, virtually everyone they had ever considered a serious suspect, seemed to be connected to a legitimate charity that was part of the Episcopal Church's minority-outreach efforts. It made no sense whatsoever, but what other conclusion was there to be drawn than that the church was being used as a front for terrorism?

To this day, forty years after its formation, no one outside the FALN is exactly sure how it came to be. As with the Black Liberation Army, none of the group's original members has ever spoken a meaningful word about its founding, its evolution, or its crimes. What seems clear, however, is that the FALN was born, of all places, in the hallways of a rough Chicago high school.

The story begins long before, though, in the impoverished mountain village of San Sebastián, in northwest Puerto Rico, where during the early 1950s two brothers surnamed López were growing up on their family's fourteen-acre farm. Oscar, born in 1943, was seven years older than José. They had no electricity, indoor plumbing, or running water; José would recall that he didn't see a television until he was nine years old. The family raised pigs and cattle and ate only what they could wrench from the soil with their own hands.

It was never enough. Around the time José was born, his father immigrated to Chicago, where a small number of Puerto Ricans had preceded him. He found work in a factory making steel pipe and in 1957 sent for Oscar and his sister. José and his mother followed two years later. The Lópezes lived with six other families in a filthy, roach-infested building at the corner of Wood and Haddon streets. It was a Polish neighborhood, and the Poles detested the Puerto Ricans. When Oscar and José walked to school, the Polish women made displays of sweeping the sidewalks in front of the homes, forcing the boys to walk in the street. Some spit at them. "Dirty Puerto Ricans," they muttered.

Both Oscar and José were highly intelligent, not that teachers noticed. At the neighborhood school the boys were herded from the classroom into a set of walk-in closets reserved for children who spoke little or no English; the school had no Spanish-speaking teachers. While the Anglo and Polish children received their lessons, the Puerto Rican kids simply sat in the closets, waiting for a friendly teacher to stick her head in every now and then and attempt to give a lesson.

Shortly after José's arrival a cluster of heavy pipes fell and crushed his father's right hand, rendering him unable to work. He left the family. The boys' mother, who couldn't read or write and spoke no English, was obliged to take a 90-cent-an-hour job at the Rainbow Cleaners on Division Street, walking the twenty blocks back and forth twice a day to save the quarter in bus fare. The family barely managed to scrape by, and perhaps unsurprisingly José and Oscar developed deep reserves of anger and resentment, as did many of their parents' friends. In the early 1960s, when the Cuban Revolution was still shiny and new, some of these friends joined pro-Castro groups. One, a local barber, would bring José and Oscar pamphlets, which they read with zeal. Both boys eagerly listened in when the older men griped about the anti-Latin bias they fought each day, how things were better under Castro, how Puerto Rico itself would be better off independent like Cuba.

When he was old enough, Oscar joined the army and was sent to Vietnam. José remained behind, working a paper route to help his mother. He read front to back the newspapers he tossed and soon became interested in politics. One of the old Polish precinct captains drew him into election work in 1964, hoping he could build bridges to the Puerto Ricans, and José immersed himself in the era's radical writings, reading up on Malcolm X and Puerto Rican history. A top student and a conservative dresser, he was elected student council president at Tuley High School, then president of a citywide student group. He threw himself into student politics, protesting against the war, calling for Puerto Rican independence, and making alliances with black student groups. He went on to Loyola University, and upon graduation in 1971, at the age of twenty-one, took a job teaching history at his old high school.

Tuley High, an otherwise unremarkable redbrick building on North Claremont Avenue, named for an influential nineteenth-century judge, would become the unlikely cradle of the FALN. Tuley's most notable alumni were Notre Dame football coach Knute Rockne and the writer Saul Bellow. While the surrounding neighborhoods changed during the 1950s and 1960s, the school didn't. When José López joined the faculty, Tuley was already a seething cauldron of Puerto Rican resentment. A majority of the students were now Latin, an astounding 70 percent of whom dropped out before graduation. Yet the administration seemed deaf to their needs. There remained few Spanish-speaking teachers. Puerto Rican families ate beans with almost every meal, yet the principal, Herbert Fink, refused to serve beans in the cafeteria. It is a point of pride among many Puerto Ricans to hear a man out, yet when parents brought the principal complaints, Fink routinely cut them off. Jokes about Puerto Rican laziness were routine. On one of his first days at work, José ambled into the teachers' lounge and saw an instructor dozing beneath a sign that read, DO NOT DISTURB. PUERTO RICANS AT WORK. Everywhere he looked José saw Puerto Ricans ridiculed and ignored.

He began to agitate for change. He found an ally in a school counselor, Carmen Valentín, who would later become an FALN member. One of his history students, Dickie Jimenez, got involved; he too would eventually join the FALN. But José's greatest ally proved to be his brother, Oscar, who returned from Vietnam to become a social worker in his old neighborhood. Where José was studious and conservative, Oscar was a sidewalk whirlwind, sturdily built, handsome, a mass of bushy curls over a full, dark mustache. As a staff member at the Northwest Community Organization, Oscar stalked the streets around Tuley High in an old army jacket, fighting to improve the full range of Puerto Rican ills in Chicago, agitating for bilingual education, immunization programs, and job opportunities—unemployment ran at 33 percent in the Puerto Rican neighborhoods—and against gangs and slumlords.

Of all the issues that confronted Chicago's Puerto Ricans, the most volatile was the situation at Tuley High. In late 1972, under Oscar López's leadership, a group of parents organized and demanded that the school board replace Principal Fink with a Spanish-speaking administrator; they further demanded that a new school under construction be named after the Puerto Rican baseball star Roberto Clemente. When the board ignored its pleas, López led fifty protesters in a peaceful occupation of Tuley's office and social room. They sent a delegation to meet with a member of the board; when a crowd of seventy-five policemen materialized outside, they agreed to leave the building.

They returned two days later to occupy the lunchroom. Again police arrived. This time López and the protesters refused to leave, and police resorted to dragging many of them outside. There the protesters, joined by dozens of angry students, proceeded to hurl bricks and rocks at the cops, who responded by arresting sixteen of them. The school had to be closed for the day. López led a delegation that met later that evening with the city's deputy mayor, and this time the city listened. Five days after the melee, the school board gave in, removing Principal Fink and announcing that the new neighborhood school would be named after Roberto Clemente, a name it carries to this day.

How Oscar López and his allies at Tuley High morphed from earnest community activists into the murderous bombers of the FALN has never been explained. It happened quickly, that much is clear; barely eighteen months separated the Tuley protests from the first FALN bombings in New York. To this day many in law enforcement assume that at some point López and his circle were recruited by Puerto Rico's leading revolutionary, Filiberto Ojeda Ríos, the MIRA mastermind. According to 1982 Senate testimony by Daniel James, a journalist who interviewed several Cuban defectors, Ojeda Ríos had returned to New York after jumping bail following his 1970 arrest in Puerto Rico. In 1974, working with Cuban agents assigned to the United Nations, he was said to have gathered a band of onetime MIRA sympathizers and melded them with new recruits, presumably including the López group, giving them training in bomb making, sabotage, and spycraft. This theory, while never proven, suggests that the FALN was at least initially a creature of Cuban intelligence. No one, however, has ever suggested that the Cuban government had an operational role in its bombings.

In fact, while Cuban intelligence may well have played a role in the FALN's formation, there is evidence that another group was at least as influential: the Weather Underground. The two groups' unlikely alliance, which has never been publicly explored, can best be understood in the context of Weather's burning need circa 1974 to reassert its relevancy in far-left politics. Their partnership, it would appear, began with a single handwritten letter, sent by a friend of Rafael Cancel Miranda, one of the nationalists imprisoned for their roles in the 1954 attack on Congress. After stays at Alcatraz and Leavenworth, Cancel Miranda in 1971 was being held at the federal prison in Marion, Illinois. A prison strike was under way, and in the letter he sought legal support from a group of radical attorneys representing Attica defendants. A volunteer named Mara Siegel read the letter. She and another attorney, Michael Deutsch, drove to Marion. "Mara and Michael went down to Marion and Rafael just blew them away," remembers Elizabeth Fink, one of the Attica attorneys and a friend of everyone involved. "Then they started going to visit the others. And their stories just blew them away."

Deutsch and Siegel, who later became an attorney at Deutsch's People's Law Office (PLO), agreed to take on Cancel Miranda's appeal; the PLO later represented other Puerto Rican prisoners as well.* Word of their cause spread quickly. Bill Ayers made the plight of Puerto Rico a major section of *Prairie Fire*. The FALN-Weather alliance, it appears, existed on both the underground and aboveground levels. Much of the public foundation was laid by Weather's supporters in New York, among them Annie Stein and Julie Nichamin, an organizer of the radical tours of Cuba known as Venceremos Brigades.

"I was there when the call was put out for the 1974 Madison Square Garden event; that was written in Annie Stein's apartment," recalls Elizabeth Fink. "Julie Nichamin was the main person, she was the driving force, and she was totally hooked up to Weatherman. Judy Clark"—the onetime Weather cadre arrested in a Manhattan theater in 1970—"was there; no one was tighter with Weather than Judy. And a bunch of others. Everybody was there. It was all interconnected. This was in May 1974. Did we know there was to be an underground component? Honey, that's all we were about. This was the revolution. It wasn't unspoken. It was the politics. It was everything we were about."

The key to the FALN's early success was help provided by the National Commission on Hispanic Affairs and its director, Maria Cueto. Described

---

*Among the PLO's other attorneys was Dennis Cunningham, who led the FBI to Bernardine Dohrn and Jeff Jones in the Weather "Encirclement."

as a quiet, determined single woman, Cueto refused to talk to investigators and to the end of her life refused to discuss the FALN. Years of investigation created suspicion, but found little concrete evidence, of her involvement. But her attorney was Elizabeth Fink, and after Cueto's death, in 2012, Fink confirmed her onetime client's key role in the FALN. According to Fink, it was Cueto who arranged to name a half-dozen FALN members, including Oscar López and Carlos Torres, to positions on the NCHA's board, which allowed her to quietly pay them thousands of dollars in Episcopal Church monies that, in essence, funded the FALN's birth.

"Maria was the quartermaster of the FALN, the person who arranged the money, the travel, the person who arranged everything, who made everything happen," Fink recalls. "The church had this special house in Greenwich, Connecticut, and I know the FALN had meetings there. Remember, Maria was doing all this with the FALN at the same time she was running this amazing social-action ministry, helping Hispanics."

Cueto and the NCHA, however, were only half the equation. Without dynamite and the expertise to use it, the FALN would never have sprung to life. For that it turned to its allies in the Weather Underground. Law enforcement for years speculated that Weather had played a role in the FALN's formation. According to Charles Wells, a longtime member of the NYPD bomb squad, bombs built by the Weather Underground and FALN were of identical design. All of them, he explains, featured a single screw set into a clock at the "9"; the bomb detonated when the minute hand struck the screw.

But the concrete evidence of Weather's involvement came from its own bomb guru, Ron Fliegelman. "We gave them the training," he acknowledged during a September 2012 interview. "We did that, sure. Was it me? I shouldn't say. I don't want to go there."

By Thanksgiving 1976, with the startling disclosure that nearly a dozen suspects had some kind of affiliation with its NCHA charity, the headquarters of the Episcopal Church became the unlikely epicenter of the FALN investigation. Church officials initially gave the FBI free rein. In a search of the

NCHA's basement office agents found a receipt taped to the bottom of Maria Cueto's desk. It was for a Smith Corona typewriter. Agents knew that the FALN's communiqués had been typed on a Smith Corona. They hustled to the Brooklyn store that sold the machine but found nothing of use; the name on the receipt was an alias. The FBI lab had determined that the communiqués had been photocopied on a Gestetner copy machine; a search of Gestetner's records indicated that such a machine had been sold to the NCHA in 1974, on the eve of the first bombings. It was now being used by another office, and it would take a round of subpoenas to get it.

Lou Vizi, meanwhile, met with the church's top bishops and found them happy to furnish the NCHA's financial records. He sensed they were intimidated by Cueto and her people, whose political leanings were far to the left of their own. "They were appalled," Vizi remembers. "These were very nice people who had been stampeded into this charity stuff by their own guilt. The church treasurer got all the records for me, but they were a mess. He said, 'We tried a thousand times to use proper accounting methods with these people, and every time higher-ups would say, "Don't come down too hard, we don't want any problems."' So no one was paying too much attention to where the church's money was going, there were no receipts for a lot of this."

The NCHA's patchwork records, however, provided a trove of tantalizing leads. Some $53,000 of church money, for instance, had gone to a Puerto Rican school in Chicago José López had founded, where Oscar López and several other FALN members had briefly worked. The NCHA had even purchased airline tickets for Carlos Torres, López, and other FALN suspects. Matching these itineraries against the FALN's attacks, agents felt they could establish a pattern of various suspects traveling to New York and Chicago within days of any number of FALN bombings. López, for one, had flown into New York the day before the first bombings in October and left shortly after.

For the briefest of moments Vizi and Don Wofford felt they were on the verge of breaking the case. If Maria Cueto or her assistant, twenty-seven-year-old Raisa Nemikin, could be persuaded to cooperate, the entire FALN might be dragged into the sunlight. But when agents went to the women's homes to question them further, both denied knowing anything about the FALN.

Shortly thereafter they hired attorneys, an act that immediately sapped momentum from the FBI's investigation. If the two women had to be pulled before a grand jury, it could start a process that might take weeks, if not months.

Cueto was called to testify first, on January 10, 1977. She refused even to take the oath. When the judge ordered her to do so, she still refused and was jailed. Her attorney, Liz Fink, filed a series of motions asking for more time, and Cueto was released. Two weeks later Fink fired her first broadside, filing motions to quash all subpoenas in the case on the ground that they violated Cueto and Nemikin's rights to freedom of religion. Citing the FBI's notorious COINTELPRO programs, Fink argued further that the subpoenas were part of a systematic pattern of FBI harassment against Puerto Rican independence and radical groups.

Buttressing these charges was a parallel set of filings by none other than Paul Moore, the progressive bishop of the Episcopal Diocese of New York. In an affidavit he echoed Fink's charges and alleged that the subpoenas were designed to "prevent the church from funding progressive Hispanic groups." To the FBI's surprise, this was the first sign of a sharp split in church ranks, Moore and a group of liberal bishops on one side, some of the national leadership on the other. Behind the scenes, the halls of Episcopal headquarters were rife with rumors—that Cueto was the FALN's secret kingpin, and that FBI agents had been allowed to rampage through file cabinets monitored only by, in the words of a *Times* reporter, "a half-blind custodian called Buggsy."[1]

On February 4 Judge Lawrence Pierce rejected the defense motions and ordered Raisa Nemikin to testify. Ten days later she took the oath but refused to say another word. Then, on February 18, just hours before Nemikin was scheduled to reappear, two powerful bombs exploded in Chicago, one outside the U.S. Gypsum Building, the other at the giant Merchandise Mart. No one was hurt, but water pipes burst at the mart, causing millions of dollars in damage. There was no communiqué, but the FBI felt certain it was the FALN attempting to send a message.

That morning, in the Manhattan grand jury room, the federal prosecutor on the case, a Harvard Law graduate named Thomas Engel, bestowed immunity on Raisa Nemikin, meaning she couldn't be prosecuted for anything she said. Engel asked Nemikin when she last saw Carlos Torres, what she knew about the FALN, and whether she knew anyone involved in the Fraunces bombing. After each question Nemikin stepped outside to consult with her attorney, then returned and refused to answer the question.

In a hearing that afternoon Engel asked Judge Pierce to cite Nemikin for contempt and jail her until she answered his questions. Her attorney, the ubiquitous Liz Fink, called the demand "outrageous" and argued that her client's rights were being violated. A ruling was postponed for eight days. Afterward Nemikin read a statement to reporters outside the courthouse in which she characterized the entire proceeding as a government vendetta against the NCHA and progressive Hispanics.

That night, just before midnight, large bombs exploded outside two New York skyscrapers, the Gulf and Western Building and the Chrysler Building, where two men were injured by flying glass. A caller to WCBS radio directed police to a communiqué, which, after demanding the release of Puerto Rican political prisoners, ended with a new demand: "Stop the Illegal Use of The Grand Jury." Up at the FBI's offices, Wofford and Vizi smiled. Clearly they had struck a nerve.

The following Monday, Fink unleashed a new legal broadside, alleging that her phones, as well as those of several of her radical colleagues, were being tapped by the government. The filing did just as Fink hoped, turning the attention of the judge and the newspapers toward allegations—apparently unfounded—of government wrongdoing. The proceedings began to slow down, with daily hearings and allegations and a series of press conferences on the courthouse steps. Friends and supporters began filling the courtroom, hissing and booing. The judge eventually ruled both Cueto and Nemikin in contempt and tossed both women in jail. Two weeks later, on March 20, the FALN responded, detonating bombs outside a New York bank and, for the first time, directly below the FBI offices on Sixty-ninth Street. One man struck by flying glass was taken to the hospital. A communiqué sent to the *New York Post* again protested the grand jury proceedings.

While lawyers jousted, Wofford and Vizi pressed on. Maria Cueto's jailing gave them an opportunity. When she vacated her Brooklyn apartment, the building's landlord allowed agents to search it. Inside, the super remarked that Cueto had altered the bedroom closet, affixing hasps and locks and constructing three wooden shelves. Wofford and Vizi had an idea of what Cueto had used those shelves for. On March 22 the NYPD brought in a bomb-sniffing dog, which, when shown the closet, became excited. A later analysis of the shelving, however, proved inconclusive. Despite this, Wofford felt sure Cueto had stored at least some of the FALN's dynamite.

Vizi, meanwhile, was supervising a review of every person associated in any way with Cueto and the NCHA. One man, a board member, was named Guillermo "Willie" Morales. He lived in Queens. An FBI surveillance team watched him on the street and managed to snap a photo. When Vizi saw it, he immediately recognized the face; it was the face in the sketch the FBI had gotten from the owner of the Bronx luggage store—the one who sold the bags holding FALN bombs. "Identical," Vizi remembers. "It was absolutely identical."

The shop owner had retired to Florida. Vizi mailed him a photo of Morales, then waited for a response from agents in Florida. "So he looks at it," Vizi recalls, "and says, 'It's not him.' I said to our guys, 'Ask him what the difference is, I can't see any difference.' He says, 'I can't tell you exactly, but it's not him.'" Irked, Vizi sent agents to interview Morales. They returned to report that Morales was nothing but polite, unworried, unruffled. He was just an activist helping a good cause, nothing like the uncooperative Maria Cueto. "We believed him, and I just kind of let it go," Vizi recalls. "That was the biggest mistake I made in the twenty-five years I was in the FBI."

Because the very polite Willie Morales, agents would later learn to their dismay, turned out to be the FALN's bomb maker.

With Maria Cueto and Raisa Nemikin sitting mute in a New York jail, prosecutors began pressing other FALN suspects. The Chicano activist suspected of stealing the group's dynamite, Pedro Archuleta, had been found and was called before grand juries in Chicago and New York. He too refused to cooperate. He too was jailed. Once again the FALN responded, setting off nine tiny incendiaries at Macy's, Gimbel's, and Bloomingdale's in New York on April 9. A communiqué cited the grand juries.

It was a mark of the times that much of the public—at least the small slice paying attention to the proceedings—seemed far more willing to believe that the FBI was wiretapping radical attorneys than the frankly bizarre notion that two demure church ladies might be working for a terrorist group. Cueto and Nemikin, in fact, drew support from a variety of quarters. That spring hundreds of four-inch stickers began appearing on New York street signs and lampposts, especially in Hispanic neighborhoods. Each featured, against the backdrop of a Puerto Rican flag, a rifle, the letters FALN, and three sayings in Spanish: FREEDOM FOR PUERTO RICO, FREEDOM FOR THE 5 NATIONALIST PRISONERS, and END THE GRAND JURY. The FBI tried analyzing the stickers but couldn't even discover who was posting them.

Far worse, the National Council of Churches got involved, announcing that the FALN grand juries amounted to an illegal harassment of all churches and all Hispanics. A new group, Joint Strategy for Social Action, began rallying progressive ministers across the country, who responded by writing letters and newsletter articles of their own, all attacking the FBI for its illegal campaign against the churches. Supervisors at FBI headquarters, already reeling from John Kearney's indictment, were in no mood for even a hint of further extracurricular shenanigans. Inspectors from Washington began appearing at Wofford's and Vizi's desks, demanding to know what laws they had broken. Suddenly every agent working the FALN case found himself on the defensive.

Things were even worse in Chicago. There prosecutors had subpoenaed a half-dozen of Carlos Torres's and Oscar López's relatives, all of whom refused to testify and, as in New York, responded with legal motions alleging illegal government wiretapping. It took six full months for a judge to sort through it all, during which time the grand jury investigation ground to a halt. When a judge finally ruled in favor of the government that June, three of those subpoenaed, including López's brother José López, were thrown in jail. The FALN responded with a rare daytime attack, on June 4, detonating a bomb on the fifth floor of Chicago's City Hall–County Building, not far from the mayor's office. Damages were estimated at $50,000. The following month a group of FALN supporters launched another counterattack, suing the FBI, the U.S. attorney general, and several individual agents for harassment.

All of it—the internal bickering, the inability to find Torres and López, most of all the controversy over the Episcopal Church—convinced FBI headquarters that the situation was spiraling out of control. The answer, it was decided, was to install a single supervisor who could coordinate the disparate strands of the investigation. Roger Young, a trim, diplomatic forty-four-year-old inspector with a background in intelligence cases, drew the task. The first thing Young did was ask for the FALN file. What he received instead was several cartloads of files. Thumbing through them, he saw that supervisors had opened a new case on every FALN bombing, an obvious effort to avoid any criticism that they were spying on a domestic group. There was no single repository for FALN intelligence, no overarching analysis whatsoever.

Much of his job, Young could see, would simply be building relationships between the far-flung field agents. No one knew anyone, which made it easier to ignore their requests. He called a conference of FALN agents in Virginia that June, only to have the most important office, New York, refuse to attend. Citing John Kearney's indictment, New York supervisors said they were unsure whether such a conference was even legal under terms of the Privacy Act. They weren't taking any chances that the ACLU would find out and start picketing the office.

By midsummer 1977, despite Roger Young's best efforts, energy was fast ebbing from the FALN investigations. The grand juries were getting nowhere; Maria Cueto, Raisa Nemikin, and a half-dozen others were stuck sitting in jail, utterly mute. In New York the FALN squad was reorganized and rolled into a new, enlarged bomb squad. Supervisors transferred; new ones arrived. Several new cases—bombings by the Jewish Defense League, anti-Castro Cubans, Croatian separatists—each drew a stream of agents away from pursuing leads on the FALN.

Out in the streets, no one cared. Inflation was rising, cocaine and other drugs were rampant, crime was out of control; on the radar of an American's daily worries in 1977, the FALN registered not at all. Among workaday Americans, few gave a whit about Puerto Rico, much less its independence. Bombs had been exploding in the United States for a decade now and would probably be exploding for decades more: Who cared whether they were planted by crazy Puerto Ricans, crazy blacks, crazy hippies, or crazy aliens from outer space? They were just bombs, a new fact of American life.

Nowhere was this sense of resignation more evident than in New York, a city that seemed to be entering its death throes. Gotham's financial crisis had devolved into a new ring of urban hell. When police went on strike, someone posted a sign near LaGuardia Airport that read, WELCOME TO FEAR CITY. Every night fires burned out of control in the Bronx. On July 13 the city suffered a massive blackout, leading to widespread looting. Yet even then all anyone wanted to talk about was the crazed murderer stalking young lovers in the outer boroughs—the ".44 Caliber Killer," some called him, others "Son of Sam." In the early hours of Sunday, July 31, he opened fire on a couple necking on a quiet Brooklyn street, killing the girl, his sixth murder victim.

Between bombings, riots, blackouts, and serial killers, the last shreds of civilization appeared to be disintegrating. The city, it seemed, was slowly being lowered into its grave. From Staten Island to Riverdale to Kew Gardens, most New Yorkers found it easy to ignore the distant thud of the FALN's bombs. Like muggings and garbage and heroin and the homeless, they were simply part of life in a dying city, a softly throbbing bass line deep in the rhythms of a funeral dirge.

A wilting summer heat was already rising from the sidewalks of Manhattan on the morning of Wednesday, August 3, 1977, when a slender young woman—a girl, really—walked into the Employment Services office at Mobil Oil headquarters on East Forty-second Street a little before nine. It was three days after Son of Sam's latest killing; FRIGHTENED SUBURBS ON GUARD, blared the *Post*'s front-page headline. The girl, who wore a straw hat and enormous sunglasses, asked the receptionist for a job application, took one, then sat at an empty desk to fill it out. She wrote her name as "Sandra Peters," then paused and glanced around the room, smiling at one or two other job seekers. After a moment the girl rose and returned to the receptionist, saying she needed more information before she could complete the form. Then she turned to leave—until the receptionist stopped her, saying she needed the form back, completed or not. The girl smiled, returned the form, then walked out. No one noticed the umbrella she left hanging from a coatrack.

Fifteen minutes later and a block away, a man walked out of the U.S. Defense Department's twenty-first-floor office in the Christian Science Building, at the corner of Madison Avenue and Forty-fourth Street. In the hallway he passed a co-worker just as she glanced at a windowsill and noticed a lady's handbag tucked awkwardly behind the Venetian blinds. Curious, the two took the bag inside their office and tried to open it, thinking they might find a driver's license and return it to the owner. But the zipper wouldn't work; it appeared to be glued shut. A supervisor, Thomas J. Sweeney, walked over to help. Someone produced a cigarette lighter, and Sweeney applied it to the zipper, attempting to melt the glue. It worked. Sweeney unzipped the bag and, to his astonishment, found himself staring at a tangle of wires and an alarm clock. He called for everyone in the office to move to the opposite end. All fifteen people were crouching behind desks at a far set of windows when, twenty seconds later, at 9:37, the bomb exploded, blowing a hole in a concrete wall, shattering windows, and sending the office door careening into the hallway. Miraculously, no one was hurt.

Three minutes later, at 9:40, a call came in to the WABC-TV *Eyewitness News* desk. The caller was out of breath, so nervous he garbled his identification, saying, "This is the F.L.A.N." He told a clerk that bombs had been set at 410 Park Avenue, the site of a Chase Manhattan branch; 1270 Avenue of the Americas, the site of several Latin American consulates; 245 Park Avenue, the American Brands Building; and Mobil Oil's headquarters. Five minutes later a second call came in to *Eyewitness News*. This time the caller repeated the same information but added that additional bombs had been placed in both towers of the World Trade Center. A few minutes after that, yet another call was made, to the *New York Post*, saying an FALN communiqué could be found at the base of the Cuban revolutionary José Martí's statue in Central Park.

Within minutes sirens began echoing across Manhattan as police scrambled to rope off and search the targeted buildings. A pair of uniformed officers were the first to arrive at Mobil headquarters, where they began scanning the lobby for a bomb. As they did, Charles Steinberg and Ivan Gerson, two managers from a small employment agency, sat inside the Employment Services office, waiting to see if any jobs were available for their applicants. They had been sitting for almost ten minutes when the bomb—hidden in the umbrella left on the coatrack—detonated beside them. The force of the blast could be felt for blocks. The room's windows exploded outward, propelling a storm of blue-green glass across Forty-second Street. Pedestrians dived for cover.

Steinberg, a twenty-six-year-old newlywed, collapsed like a doll, his suit covered in blood; he died instantly. The office was wrecked: bits of furniture jutting from the walls, glass everywhere, and seven other people scattered around, left bloodied and moaning. In minutes police arrived on the scene and began evacuating the building. Two men with critical injuries, mostly the result of flying glass, were carted to Bellevue Hospital, along with five others, including a man who suffered a heart attack during the evacuation. There's "a lot of blood and a big pile of human mess," a cop told a *Daily News* reporter. "That's all I can call it. Human mess."

A summer rainstorm blew in as bystanders milled about beneath their umbrellas, trying to understand what had happened.

"They say it's that Puerto Rican group," a woman remarked.

"The FALN," a black man replied.

"What do they want, anyway?" the woman asked.

"I think they want freedom for Puerto Rico."

"For who? Puerto Rico isn't free?"

"They don't think so."[2]

Across the city, police and security guards began evacuating the other targeted buildings. It quickly became a mammoth undertaking: Hundreds, soon thousands, of office workers hustled out into the morning rain, standing beneath umbrellas in clumps on Park Avenue, on the Avenue of the Americas, and especially at the World Trade Center downtown, where Port Authority officers with bullhorns herded all 35,000 people in the two towers out into the streets. It was the first evacuation in the Trade Center's four-year history; the resulting crowds soon snarled traffic across Lower Manhattan. People craned their necks, staring upward, waiting for something to explode.

Even as the evacuations got under way, city switchboards lit up with bomb threats and warnings, a trickle at first, then dozens, then hundreds. Some claimed to be from the FALN, others from Palestinian groups, while still others came from wary citizens who suddenly thought every stray trash bag or coffee cup might be hiding a bomb. Police operators alone took more than two hundred calls, most of which the NYPD was forced to ignore. Still, seven floors of the Empire State Building were cleared when someone called in a bomb threat on the eighty-second floor. All day, up and down Manhattan, chaos reigned. By nightfall more than 100,000 people had been evacuated from their offices. Many went home. Others lingered nearby, watching police murmur into walkie-talkies and shaking their heads at what life in New York had come to.

"First Son of Sam, now this," a woman moaned to the *Daily News*. "You don't get any peace around here anymore."

The *Times* went a step further, editorializing that Friday: "For those who have lived through this mad week in New York there is a shared sense of outrage and impotence. Is New York City, after all, a failed ultra-urban experiment in which people eventually crack, social order eventually collapses, and reason ultimately yields to despair?"

A weary Mayor Abraham Beame—hip-deep in a spirited primary challenge from the likes of Bella Abzug, Mario Cuomo, and Ed Koch—scuffed through piles of bloodstained glass at the Mobil building, telling reporters, "This is an outrageous act of terrorism."[3] At three o'clock he stood at a City Hall podium alongside the police chief, Michael J. Codd, and promised that new detectives would be added to the FALN probe, adding that, yes, this could be done without drawing manpower from the Son of Sam case.* "The FBI has an excellent idea who these people are," Beame said of the FALN, "but they haven't been able to catch them in the act." The latest communiqué, fished from a niche in the José Martí statue, gave the police little new to pursue. It railed against imperialist corporations, demanded the release of "political prisoners" and an "End to Grand Jury Abuse!" then closed, oddly, with the words "Victory to the Palestinian Struggle!"†

The next day the bomb threats and warnings erupted again, leading to the evacuation of several more office buildings. They would persist for days, climaxing the following week when LaGuardia Airport had to be shut down. NYPD detectives, under intense pressure to make an arrest, burst into an apartment in the Bronx and arrested a twenty-seven-year-old Puerto Rican militant. They found guns and copier machines and FALN stickers. The *Daily News* and the *Post* played it up as a break in the case, but it wasn't; the man was eventually freed.

The FBI, meanwhile, descended on Mobil headquarters. The wreckage made a deep impression on Roger Young. "I remember walking through there and literally having to step over a pool of blood," he recalls. But the emotion counted less than the evidence. From the receptionist's wrecked desk agents managed to fish out the form the girl carrying the umbrella had left behind. Within days word came from the FBI lab: They had identified a single print on it. It was a right middle finger, and it belonged to Carlos Torres's twenty-two-year-old wife, Marie Haydee Torres. One month later FBI officials were able to stand at a City Hall podium beside the police chief and announce her indictment. It came on the same day, September 7, that Carlos Torres and Oscar López were indicted on explosives charges in Chicago. It was progress, not that anyone had a clue where López and the Torreses might be hiding.

---

*Seven days after the bombings, the "Son of Sam" killer, a mentally unbalanced man named David Berkowitz, was finally arrested.

†Five days after the Mobil Oil bombing, an office worker at one of the targeted buildings, 1270 Avenue of the Americas, glimpsed an envelope lying on an eighth-floor windowsill. Inside it police discovered an unexploded FALN bomb, apparently a dud that had been intended to detonate along with the two other August 3 explosions. Despite repeated NYPD searches, no other FALN bombs were found.

The FBI was attempting to pressure their friends and family, but the FALN's aboveground supporters were proving to be a combative lot. In New York agents detained three longtime suspects, Julio Rosado and his two brothers, Andres and Luis. When a judge ordered them to provide handwriting and voice samples, they refused and were thrown in jail until they did; so vocal were the forty or so supporters who appeared in court that day—they repeatedly hissed at the judge—that federal marshals had to clear the courtroom. An identical scene played out in Chicago, where López's brother José, along with Roberto Caldero and Pedro Archuleta, were ordered to jail when they refused to answer a judge's questions. Their hearing, held under tight security, was marked by repeated shouts and hisses from a crowd of seventy supporters, obliging Judge James B. Parsons to laconically remind them that "this is not a ball game."

There matters lay until October. Then, late on the night of the tenth, a homeless man— apparently an addled one—was nosing through a trash basket in front of the General Motors Building, across from the southeast corner of Central Park. He discovered a shoe box, opened it, and found himself staring at a wristwatch, some wires, and two sticks of dynamite, one sawed in half. For some reason he disconnected the wiring, tossed the full stick of dynamite back in the trash, then deposited the half stick, the watch, and the wires in a concrete planter, where it was noticed early the next morning by two FBI agents walking by on unrelated business. The bomb squad removed all the explosives.* A caller to the *New York Post* claimed credit for the FALN, saying the attempted bombing was to protest First Lady Rosalynn Carter's visit to Puerto Rico that week. A communiqué, one of the oddest yet, was later found in a Midtown phone booth. It was a diatribe against Australia, whose diplomats had blocked a resolution to have the United Nations take up the question of Puerto Rican independence.

The homeless man's bomb wasn't the only one that failed to detonate. That same night, a worker in the Damaged Mail section at the Main Post Office in Chicago spied a large manila envelope lying on a windowsill. Opening it, he

---

*Just before 4:00 that afternoon a pipe bomb exploded in a fountain outside the New York Public Library, lightly damaging a statue. This explosion was probably not an FALN bomb, the FBI concluded.

found a wristwatch and four sticks of dynamite wrapped in polka-dot wrapping paper. The bomb had been set to go off the previous night but hadn't.

Four days later, on October 15, three Hispanic children were passing by a National Guard Armory on South Calumet Avenue in Chicago. Suddenly one of them, a girl maybe ten years old, spied something on a window ledge. It was a package of some sort, wrapped in newspaper. As her two friends watched, the girl unwrapped it and was surprised to see a clock, some wires, and several sticks of what she realized was dynamite. Carefully rewrapping the bomb in her hands, the girl and her friends scurried to the armory's front door, pressed the bell, and told the custodian who answered that they had found a bomb. He didn't believe them but took the package anyway. Not until he reached the basement did he unwrap the parcel and see that it was in fact a bomb. He called the Chicago police, who searched the building and found a second bomb, this one placed in wrapping paper, on another windowsill. The newspaper was dated October 10, indicating that the bombs had probably been timed to go off with the others on October 11. Analysis of the dynamite confirmed what the FBI suspected: These were FALN bombs, from the same batch of dynamite found on West Haddon a year earlier.

In Washington Roger Young pondered the four dud bombs in New York and Chicago for days. This made no sense. One dud might be a bad or misplaced wire. But four? Something, he realized, was wrong with the FALN. With its explosives. He could feel it. He called the FBI lab's assistant director, Tom Kelleher, who explained that the bombs probably hadn't gone off because the detonators malfunctioned. Or—and this caught Young's attention—the dynamite might be going bad. All the FALN dynamite had come from the single batch stolen nine years earlier.

Some dynamite, Kelleher explained, has a shelf life, especially if not properly maintained. It can become unstable. Vibrations from a passing bus, even the footsteps of an encroaching mouse, might set it off; the children in Chicago had been very lucky. Whether the rest of the FALN's dynamite had gone bad was impossible to know. But if it had, and if it was stored en masse, as at the West Haddon bomb factory, an accidental explosion could destroy an entire apartment block. For several long nights Young lay in bed, thinking about those children in Chicago. The more he pondered, the more he realized he couldn't take the risk of that happening again.

Over the next several days Young and Kelleher had a series of long, quiet conversations. Eventually, after Young had a late-night spark of inspiration, they came up with the outlines of a plan. It was audacious, to say the least. In fact, it was unlike anything ever attempted in the history of the FBI. If their superiors learned of its details, both men realized, they might be fired or worse. They swore each other to secrecy and promised never to put anything about it in writing. Kelleher said he needed time to work out the technical details. Young promised to wait but soon realized he couldn't take the chance. It was all so outlandish it might never work, but he had to take the chance, and he had to do it now.

And so, a few days later, Young flew to Chicago and drove to the Metropolitan Correctional Center. He had the warden gather the FALN supporters—Oscar López's brothers, José and Juan, and another man—in a room. When he stepped inside, he could feel hatred radiating from the prisoners like bad cologne. You don't have to say a thing, Young began. Just listen. Slowly he told them what he knew. The FALN's dynamite was getting old. There was a chance it had become unstable. It's one thing to bomb a National Guard armory or a Wall Street bank in protest of something you believe in. But if that dynamite went off by accident, children might die. Whole families might die. No one wanted that. That was not what the FALN was about.

Silence. No one said a word. Then Young unveiled his offer. If someone was able to get word to the FALN, he said, the FBI was prepared to make a deal. In return for handing over the last of the Heron Dam dynamite, he continued, he would personally see to it that the FBI gave the FALN replacement dynamite, stick for stick. He would make the exchange in person, one on one, at any location the FALN chose.

Silence. Young looked around the room. He could hear them breathing. He scanned the faces around him. Their hatred was only building. No one said a word, but he could tell they thought it was some kind of stupid trick. And it was. What Young didn't say was that, back in Washington, Tom Kelleher was working to build a case of fake dynamite—actual dynamite that had been chemically altered so as never to explode. Further, Kelleher was attempting to construct something altogether new, a newfangled global positioning chip that could be inserted into every stick of explosive the FALN accepted.

But it was not to be. After several minutes without another word spoken, Young left the room, the jail doors clanging loudly behind him. He never heard a peep about the offer from the FALN or anyone else, and he wouldn't speak of it again for thirty-five years.

18

"ARMED REVOLUTIONARY LOVE"

The Odyssey of Ray Levasseur

> Now is the time to show our love for our people and
> our hatred of injustice and oppression. Armed revolution-
> ary love means not standing around while the oppres-
> sor strangles the life out of our people with his jackboot.
> There will never be a better time to fight and die than
> now—cutting the throats of kamp kammanders and fas-
> cist agents.
>
> *—Ray Luc Levasseur, in a 1976 letter celebrating*
> *the birth of his first daughter*

It was the morning of April 22, 1976. The streets of downtown Boston
were thronged with people on their way to work. Across from the gray granite façade of the Suffolk County Courthouse, a slender hippie girl stepped
through the crowds into the subway station. At a pay phone, glancing about
nervously, she dialed the courthouse switchboard. "This is no joke," the girl,
whose name was Pat Gros, told the operator. "This is the Sam Melville Jonathan Jackson unit. A bomb will go off in the probation office in twenty
minutes."

It was 8:52. Replacing the receiver, Pat walked up to the street, fighting
her nerves. She had never done anything like this before. None of them had.
She was only doing it, she knew, out of fear that the group's fiery leader, the
father of her infant daughter, would reject her. "I was scared shitless," Pat

recalls thirty-five years later. "This was our initiation, you know. I was just so in love with him, I had to show I was willing to be part of that armed struggle."

The bomb was scheduled to go off at 9:12. By 9:00, with her eyes fixed on the courthouse entrance, Pat realized with a start that no one was being evacuated. Frightened, she scurried back into the subway and again called the switchboard, repeating her warning. About five minutes later she saw a stream of people beginning to leave the courthouse. They were mostly judges; security was apparently evacuating the most important people first. Still, she noticed, no effort was being made to block the doors. People were still streaming in.

One of them was a man named Edmund Narine, a student who bounded up the courthouse steps heading for the Probation Office upstairs, where he needed to get a piece of paper showing he had no criminal record in order to get his cabbie's license. In Room 206 he took a spot in line, amiably chatting with another waiting man; neither noticed a backpack tossed against one wall. Suddenly, at precisely 9:12, there was a deafening explosion, and Narine's vision went pink. Only later would he realize he was seeing the world through his own blood.

The blast wrecked the Probation Office, injuring twenty-two people, including Edmund Narine, who would lose his left leg below the knee. Sirens echoed across downtown Boston. Ambulances arrived to cart off bloody, moaning men and women. Crowds of the curious began milling outside, just as they had at Fraunces Tavern and the Townhouse. Across the street Pat Gros turned her back and ran.

They called themselves the Sam Melville Jonathan Jackson unit—the SMJJ for short—though they later changed the name to the United Freedom Front. Whatever you called them, they were hands down the most unusual of the 1970s underground groups: two blue-collar couples—later three—who robbed banks, engaged in deadly shoot-outs with police, and bombed courthouses, military installations, and multinational corporations, all while raising small children, eventually nine in all. They were an inspiration for the 1988 movie *Running on Empty*, starring the teenaged actor River Phoenix. But while the cinematic family had retired from underground work, their real-life counterparts remained active and violent year after year after year, eventually triggering one of the largest manhunts in modern U.S. history.

The SMJJ arose from the prison movement, as the SLA did, but in an unlikely corner of the country: the state of Maine. Its leader and guiding light was a brawny, tattooed Vietnam veteran named Raymond Luc Levasseur.* Long before he went underground, Levasseur was an arresting figure in Portland's bustling radical community, a Marx-spouting ex-convict stalking the snowy streets in a Ho Chi Minh goatee, black beret, and knee-length black leather jacket, a ponytail flopping down his neck. What most remember was not his chiseled prisoner's face but the dark intensity of his deep-set black eyes—"like a cross between Rasputin and Jesus Christ," as one friend puts it. Uncompromising, confrontational, and very, very angry at the world, Levasseur radiated charisma. "Ray had a big ego, a big heart, and a hard shell," recalls one of his many lovers. "When he walked into a room, he was very tough and puffed up, but the moment that scowl turned into a smile, it just melted you."

The story of Ray Levasseur's journey underground provides a rare window on the emotional and political development of the 1970s revolutionaries. It begins in the village of Springvale, just outside the southern Maine mill town of Sanford, where a series of textile and shoe factories lined the Mousam River. Levasseur was born there in 1946, the older of two sons in a second-generation French Canadian family. His struggles with authority began with a distant and dictatorial father, who spent long periods away working as an air force mechanic, leaving the boys to be raised by their mother, Jeanette, in a series of ratty apartments. Exacerbating these struggles were prejudices in 1950s-era Maine against French Canadians, who were seen, in Levasseur's words, as "docile and dumb." Fifty years later he can still recall the stinging jokes: "What's a French Canadian? A nigger turned inside out." The

*The name rhymes with "harasser."

Protestant kids smirked at poor children like him, calling them "frogs." From an early age he yearned for their acceptance.

Two things made Ray Levasseur different from other mill town boys: a vague sense that he was meant for something better than life in the mills and, especially as he grew into adulthood, a deep-seated belief that the world should be fair and just, that poor people—"the oppressed," he would come to call them—were being held back by a rich and powerful white elite. His first act of revolt came against the nuns who taught his sixth-grade classes; when one smacked him in the forehead with an eraser, Ray implored his mother to let him attend public school, and she did. In high school he grew to be a strapping six-footer, big enough to start on the football team and handsome enough to snag a Protestant cheerleader as his girlfriend.

He thrived for a time, until football season ended during his senior year and he began to confront his future. His father, who himself disdained all things French Canadian, told him that whatever he did, he should never take a job in the mills. Ray began skipping school, hanging out at a pool hall, smoking, drinking, and getting into fights. Mostly he fought kids from neighboring Biddeford, but there was a small college nearby, and he and his pals mugged the college kids and stole their beer; he beat one so badly he ended up in the hospital.

After graduating at the bottom of his class in 1964, Ray reluctantly took a summer job in one of the mills, cranking out shoe heels and sabotaging the big machine when he needed a break. Frustrated and aimless, he usually began drinking when his shift ended at dawn; weekends he spent at the Maine beaches, drinking and fighting, earning his first night in jail for beating up a sailor at Old Orchard Beach. This wasn't what he wanted in life, he realized, so that fall he took his last $50 and hitchhiked down Interstate 95 to Boston, where he bunked with a girl he'd met at the beach. He got a job loading fish at the docks, where the older men nicknamed him "Animal" for his continuing penchant for fistfights. In one episode, at the Newport Folk Festival during the summer of 1965—he saw Dylan go electric—he got into a fight with another drunk for urinating too close to his car. He had the fellow on the ground and was pounding him senseless when the man's friend came up behind Ray and swung a hammer full force into the right side of his head, nearly popping out his right eye.

Ray never understood why he fought. Maybe to impress girls. Maybe out of frustration. He was certain this wasn't how his life was meant to go. But he had no idea how to escape the cycle of boozing and brawling. In Boston he was arrested twice for assault, then sued by both victims, after which his court-appointed attorney told him the judge would dismiss the suits if he entered the army. So he did.

It was December 1965; Ray was nineteen. The war in Vietnam was fast escalating, but he was still busy with his own fights. He got into one the night before he left for Fort Dix, New Jersey, then got arrested for going AWOL when he sneaked off one weekend to see a girlfriend in Boston, then arrested again the day before leaving for Vietnam; a military policeman accosted him for drunkenness, and Ray spit on him. The irony, lost on Ray at the time, was that when they sent him to an actual war, he did no fighting at all. He spent his year in Southeast Asia supervising Vietnamese laborers, building quonset huts, guarding payroll shipments, and smoking copious amounts of marijuana.

He returned from Vietnam in December 1967, a burly twenty-one-year-old. After a thirty-day leave visiting his girlfriend in Boston, he was assigned to Fort Campbell, Kentucky, where he was given little to do. He remained angry and deeply confused by his experiences overseas, having little grasp of Vietnamese history or geopolitics. For the first time in his life he suddenly wanted to understand the world. What was the war even about? Why had several of his friends died? Having made it through high school without reading an entire book, he purchased his first, *The Diary of Che Guevara*, and downed it like a starving dog. He found Che's odyssey enthralling, especially the notion that a small group, with the right leaders, could topple an entire government and change the course of history. His curiosity grew when, walking the streets outside Fort Campbell, he saw the aging signs of the Jim Crow South: COLORED ONLY. FOR WHITES ONLY. The prejudices burdening Southern blacks, it dawned on him, were not unlike those directed against French Canadians in Maine. To whites, he saw, they were all "niggers." Thus began his lifelong identification with blacks.

At a party he met and befriended a woman named Jan Phillips, an organizer for a civil rights group called the Southern Conference Education

Fund. Sensing an eager student, Phillips plied him with works by Stokely Carmichael, Martin Luther King, and Fidel Castro and invited him to his first demonstrations. He read every book, some twice. It was 1968, the year Dr. King was killed, and by that summer Ray felt like a new man, with a new vision and a new course in life, devoted to fighting the war and white prejudice in all its twisted forms. His girlfriend, Kathie Flynn, came to Kentucky, they got married, and he began taking night courses at Austin Peay State University, across the state line in Clarksville, Tennessee. When he learned he could qualify for a discharge if he went to college, he applied and was accepted as a full-time student.

Almost overnight Ray transformed himself from a confused, aimless army private to a campus radical. Growing his brown hair long, pinning peace symbols to his army jacket, he became a fixture at the few antiwar rallies around Clarksville and helped start a radical campus newspaper. He traveled to antiwar conferences in Atlanta and Louisville and marched side by side with young black men and women, raising his fist with theirs and shouting angry slogans. For the first time in his life he had found a purpose, a calling, and he loved it.

Like many of his friends, he also loved marijuana. Excellent Vietnamese weed was streaming into Fort Campbell in hundreds of packages mailed by U.S. servicemen, and Levasseur had started selling some of it, first at a black club in Hopkinsville, Kentucky, later to his college pals in Clarksville. One morning in February 1969 he was awakened at his apartment by the crashing of fists on his front door, and though he managed to flush his stash down the toilet, it was too late. One of his customers turned out to be an undercover cop.

He and Kathie were both arrested; their photo appeared on the front page of the Clarksville newspaper. They made bail, then got evicted from their apartment, at which point prosecutors allowed them to return to Boston until their trial that fall. Just like that, it was over: the new life in college, the civil rights marches, the work against the war. Deeply depressed, Levasseur washed up on a couch at Kathie's family home, watching Neil Armstrong take man's first steps on the moon and thinking, "This means nothing. The ghettos are in flames, and the world is turning to shit." He took his old job on the docks.

Levasseur now faced twenty years in prison. He had no money to hire a lawyer. After a final blowout weekend at Woodstock, he and Kathie reluctantly hitchhiked back to Clarksville for their trial. In the courtroom the prosecutor lambasted them as a "scourge to society." It was over in two days. Kathie got two years. Levasseur got two-to-five. Her family bailed her out, pending an appeal, but refused to help him.* He ended up in the Montgomery County Jail while his case too was appealed.

To say Ray Levasseur was an angry young man is like saying Mozart could play the piano. His anger was volcanic, all-encompassing, an emotional virus that was sinking into his bones, reshaping him, twisting him. Nothing about any of this seemed remotely fair. The government had sent him to Vietnam. The government, he felt, was now punishing him for antiwar work. His family—and Kathie's—had abandoned him. He was utterly alone, in a grimy Southern jail, and when he finally couldn't take it anymore, he exploded: at the bologna.

The bologna they served in the Montgomery County Jail, Levasseur decided, was moldy. At night, in his cell, he hollered at the black prisoners that they should mount a hunger strike, that moldy bologna was a violation of their rights as men. The black prisoners agreed and elected him their spokesman. He presented the sheriff and a crowd of beefy deputies with a list of demands. The very next morning they hauled him out in handcuffs and dragged him back to the courthouse, where the prosecutor called him a troublemaker and said, "We believe Mr. Levasseur would be more comfortable at the state penitentiary."

He was bused to the maximum-security state prison at Nashville and tossed into a holding area with hardened murderers and rapists. On the first day he struck up a conversation with a trio of young black men who had been convicted of killing a Nashville patrolman. They were in the cafeteria line, discussing Coltrane and Marx, when he noticed that the line was splitting in two at the entrance, blacks to the left, whites to the right. Unsure what to do, and unwilling to offend his new black friends, he joined the black line. Inside,

---

*Kathie Flynn lost her appeal, jumped bail, and lived underground for a period of months. According to Levasseur, she eventually turned herself in to authorities.

the cafeteria—blacks sitting only with blacks, whites with whites—was loud with the sound of a hundred inmate conversations. When he took his food-laden tray and walked toward a table full of black men, the din began to subside. By the time he sat down, the cafeteria had gone silent. One of the blacks leaned over and said, "Now you know what it's like."

From that day on Ray hung with the black inmates, eating, boxing, and playing basketball with them. Their stories of white hatred and bigotry only fueled his burgeoning radical worldview. From his cell he sent for every radical newspaper the guards would let him receive. He read of the Panthers and George Jackson and the Weathermen and all the young people who were calling themselves revolutionaries, who were actually fighting for the oppressed. He yearned to join them. Then, as he read more of Che and Mao and Ho Chi Minh and Lenin, he began to daydream about leading his own underground army; Ho had started with barely ten followers. It only took one man, Levasseur saw, one visionary leader to start it all. He dreamed of becoming the American Che.

A born proselytizer, he eagerly spread this new radical message to his black friends, which didn't sit well with prison officials. He was labeled a "racial agitator" and in the summer of 1970 was transferred to the state's toughest prison, Brushy Mountain, where Martin Luther King's assassin, James Earl Ray, was doing time. There, in his new cell, Ray found a welcoming note that read, "You're dead, nigger lover." Spending much of his time in solitary, he wasted no time agitating for parole, and in the spring of 1971 he earned it, on the condition that he leave the state. That May, six months after arriving, he was finally released. He stepped outside Brushy Mountain's high walls, raised a clenched fist to his friends in the cell block, thrust a defiant middle finger to the administration building, then boarded a bus for the long trip back to Maine.

Back in Sanford on parole, he took a job at a friend's Sunoco station, then quit it for a job making concrete blocks, then quit that to work construction in the resort town of Kennebunkport. He hung a portrait of Che on the refrigerator in his apartment. He began taking drugs, a little at first, then more, marijuana and amphetamines mostly, washed down with cheap scotch. He lived in a state of simmering rage, at a government that had sent him to Vietnam, that had thrown him into a maximum-security prison for a two-bit marijuana bust, that beat down the blacks and the poor and anyone who wasn't white and rich. All that summer he rode his bicycle past Kennebunkport's seaside mansions and dreamed of burning them down. Then, that August, George Jackson was killed. "George murdered, I'm insane with hate," Ray wrote in the diary he had started in prison. Three weeks later came Attica: "Attica Attica Attica, the massacre burns in my mind for weeks."

He knew he couldn't go on like this, a druggy life in a dead-end job. Then he read an interview with the president of the University of Maine at Augusta, who was recruiting underprivileged students, including blacks and ex-cons. Levasseur wrote him a letter, challenging him to let him enroll. To his amazement, the college telephoned.

"Could you be ready to enroll in January?" the woman asked.

"Shit, yeah," he breathed.

At the university, where the GI Bill paid his tuition and janitorial work his rent, he returned to the role of campus radical, starting a chapter of Vietnam Veterans Against the War. As if making up for lost time, he threw himself into antiwar work with a vengeance, staging a series of marches and demonstrations where he clutched a microphone and exhorted the audiences—including one of a thousand or more, labeled the largest in state history—to take to the streets. Overnight he became a public figure in Maine, a highly visible antiwar activist and a regular presence on television news; his mother took to calling to tell him to change his shirt. For Levasseur the high point came when he led a crowd of protesters that rocked Vice President Spiro Agnew's limousine after he delivered a speech in Augusta; his proudest moment, he often said, came when he spit into Agnew's open window and barely missed hitting him in the face.

And then, after nine frenzied months, it ended. American troops were streaming back from Vietnam, and what remained of the antiwar movement began fading away. That September of 1972, seeking a new cause, Levasseur printed up a thousand fliers calling for a demonstration to mark the one-year anniversary of the Attica rebellion. Stapled on bulletin boards across Augusta, it compared the Attica killings to harsh punishments of prisoners in Maine, demanding that "the economic, racist, sexist exploitation and oppression of human beings must end!!!" A handful of ex-cons, eager to improve conditions at the Maine State Prison, responded, and with their support Levasseur formed a new group, the Greater Maine Committee to Secure Justice for Prisoners. He plunged into a months-long study of Maine prisons, compiling lists of inmate beatings and suspicious deaths. In early 1973, working with inmate leaders at the state prison, he issued a press release citing prisoner grievances and making fourteen demands, from better medical care to elimination of segregation cells and mailroom censorship. "We are the convicted class," it concluded. "We have been pushed over the line from which there can be no retreat. . . . We will never give up."

He became a regular presence at the Maine State Prison, caucusing with inmates as the guards glared. Outside the walls he attracted an entourage of tough-eyed ex-convicts, many of them members of Maine's Iron Horsemen motorcycle gang. Stalking the streets of Augusta, always on the way to some critical meeting or demonstration, wearing do-rags, black shirts, and a long black leather jacket, a pistol sometimes jammed in his belt, he began affecting the gang's look.

By the spring of 1973, however, after fifteen months of nonstop organizing, Ray was beginning to burn out. That May, desperate to wean himself from the scotch-and-amphetamines diet that fueled him, he drove his motorcycle across Canada, then down into California, where he sought in vain to meet the Bay Area radicals he had read about. His dreams of becoming an American Che, placed on hold since leaving prison, returned at gale force; alone at night, he read everything he could find on the tactics of guerrilla warfare. "The underground thing was always there, all the time," he remembers today. "That's what I really wanted to do. I needed to hook up with people who saw the need to take things to another level. I just couldn't find anyone."

His return to Maine marked the final phase in his revolutionary development. That winter he began meeting with another prison-rights group, the

Portland-based Statewide Correctional Alliance for Reform (SCAR), and by the spring the two groups had merged. He found an apartment in Portland, enrolled at the University of Maine branch there, and spent every extra hour in community work, teaching high school equivalency classes in the jails, meeting with prisoners across the state to air their grievances, even leading karate classes at SCAR's new headquarters, on the second floor of an old seamen's hall on the waterfront. Levasseur had it named George Jackson Hall.

From the outset, however, he and his motley collection of bikers and ex-convicts mixed uneasily with the other SCAR volunteers. "It was a bit of a culture clash," remembers Alan Caron, SCAR's executive director at the time. "SCAR was a bunch of minimum-security guys, with mostly drug-related offenses. We were kind of late-sixties political, Crosby, Stills & Nash political. Ray was pretty far out there politically. His hero was Joseph Stalin. Our view was 'Hey, you gotta have everybody involved.' Well, that turned out to be deplorable naïveté. Ray came in slowly, quietly, did the work, teaching the GED in jails, built a network of supporters, then before I knew it, they began to push to make the group a white version of the Black Panther Party."

For the next year Levasseur seemed to be everywhere, speaking at Portland-area schools, attending inmate-rights conferences in Boston, lecturing about George Jackson and Che and Mao and all his heroes to groups at the SCAR hall, starting a SCAR-backed bail fund for the indigent, even testifying in favor of inmate rights before the legislature. He remained an angry young man, it was true, but for the first time he found himself working side by side with social workers, local clergy, and other volunteers devoted to helping Portland's needy; it was the Episcopal Church, in fact, that gave him the $3,000 he needed to start SCAR's bail fund. To outsiders Levasseur remained a fearsome presence. But not to the priests, professors, and pupils reporters would interview about him in the years to come. They used words like "brilliant," "committed," and "compassionate."

It was in Portland that he made three friends who would be at his side in coming years. Two were his lovers. Pat Gros, a slender, cheerful hippie girl who had fled her Maryland home in 1967 for San Francisco's Summer of

Love, had ricocheted among dozens of demonstrations and secretarial jobs until washing up, aimless and adrift, in Portland, where she endured a green-card marriage to a German puppeteer until Ray caught her eye at a demonstration. The sight of rugged Ray Levasseur, with his black beret and radiant smile, simply melted her. Going to work as a SCAR volunteer, she was transfixed. To Ray she was just another girl whose bed was always available.

The second woman had a more distinctive background. Pretty, with long dark hair, Linda Coleman grew up in a Long Island mansion, the daughter of a prominent family that traced its ancestry to Manhattan's original settlers; her grandmother was Joan Whitney Payson, the owner of the New York Mets baseball team. Shuttled between relatives as a girl, then banished to boarding school, Coleman fled Hampshire College that fall for Portland with a new-found thirst for radical politics and a shameful secret: She was rich, thanks to a $150,000 trust fund she received on her twenty-first birthday. Eager to shed her white-skin privilege, she began working at the SCAR offices between classes at a local hospital. She too glimpsed Levasseur at a demonstration, was struck by his charisma, and was soon sharing his bed. Levasseur liked Coleman. He liked her money even more. Neither she nor Pat Gros pushed for a commitment. "You gotta understand, Ray makes no commitments," quips one old friend. "His only commitment is to the revolution."

The third friend was Tom Manning, a handsome South Boston ex-con with a volcanic temper and great artistic talent. Like Levasseur, Manning had returned from Vietnam angry and aimless; after robbing a liquor store, he was sent to Massachusetts's grim Walpole State Prison, where he nearly died after being knifed by another prisoner. After his release he had met and married a sixteen-year-old runaway from Kezar Falls, Maine; he and Carol had settled in Portland, where she gave birth to a boy they named Jeremy. When Manning saw SCAR's newspaper, he signed up as a volunteer and quickly emerged as Levasseur's loyal sidekick, a position he would maintain for years.

This was 1974, the high-water mark of the SLA and the second-generation underground groups, and Levasseur had begun peppering his conversations and lectures around Portland with references to the need to "take things to the next level," to consider that violent revolution might be the only way to bring permanent change to "Amerika." SCAR's director, Alan Caron, thought such talk was delusional and risked alienating their supporters. By that summer it was clear the two men were heading for a showdown. "It was a choice between Alan and Ray," recalls a onetime SCAR member. "On one side you had the armchair revolutionaries. On the other were the real revolutionaries. They had these huge arguments. With Ray there were always these vague discussions of violence and the absolute necessity of violence. 'Sometimes you gotta go there, and the time is getting close! We're being attacked! You know, we have to fight back.'"

Many found this kind of talk frightening. "I remember at my last meeting with Tommy and Ray," Caron recalls, "Tommy spent a lot of time describing to me, while Levasseur chortled, what revolutionaries in Africa were doing to moderate leaders. They were killing them. And he goes, 'A lot can be learned from Africa, you know.' I was convinced by then that they were certifiably insane, or coked up on speed. Whatever it was, these guys were way, way out there. The last time I saw them, they came to the SCAR office and physically attacked me, beat me up, and told me to keep my mouth shut. I literally lived in fear of being killed for years after that."

The showdown finally came in August 1974, and Levasseur and a dozen of his SCAR acolytes resigned. Rather than start a competing group, Levasseur decided to take an entirely new tack, opening a ramshackle two-room bookstore on downtown Portland's main street, Congress Street. The Red Star North Bookstore, adorned with a large red star in the window and posters of Che and Ho Chi Minh, sold only radical literature, including the Berkeley papers and *Dragon*. The workers were volunteers. At night Levasseur led a study group that pored over his favorite Marxist texts. "It was tough for a lot of us to keep up with Ray's intellectual capacity," remembers Linda Coleman.

From the outset the bookstore drew the close attention of Portland police. Detectives sat outside at all hours, photographing everyone who came and went. Levasseur would stand in the doorway, staring at them over his uplifted index finger. Tensions quickly escalated. By the fall someone had begun sliding notes under the bookstore's door, threatening to rape the women volunteers and kill the men. Each note was adorned with swastikas and Ku Klux Klan signs. Down at the harbor, meanwhile, the SCAR office began receiving taped phone calls of screaming women, machine-gun fire, and a bugle playing taps.

Then, near the height of tensions, a bizarre scandal struck the Portland Police Department. A policeman was arrested for soliciting three other officers to perform the vigilante-style execution of a trio of criminals; the city council initiated a series of hearings. Levasseur believed what everyone in Portland's radical circles believed: that there was a genuine, Central America-style death squad operating inside the Portland police, and that it was this group that was terrorizing SCAR and the bookstore. On the street there were rumors that the death squad had a list of twenty or more local trouble-makers to kill. Levasseur's name was said to be at the top. As everyone expected, it was Levasseur who led the demonstrations outside Portland's city hall.

That fall, just as the bookstore opened and the police scandal broke, Tom Manning confided to Levasseur a secret that changed their lives forever. His brother-in-law, Manning said, was a onetime SDS radical named Cameron Bishop, who was on the FBI's list of Ten Most Wanted Fugitives. He knew people in the Weather Underground. And he wanted to talk to Levasseur about his dream: starting an underground unit that would strike back at Amerika.

Cameron Bishop was a legend in radical circles. In February 1969, as a twenty-six-year-old SDS organizer at Colorado State University, he had committed perhaps the first major act of antiwar sabotage: the dynamiting of four electrical transmission towers that served a Colorado defense plant. He became only the second American charged in peacetime under a World War I–era sabotage law, and in April 1969 he became the first self-styled revolutionary placed on the FBI's Most Wanted List. Bishop vanished into the underground, eventually, as luck would have it, meeting Tom Manning's sister Mary while hitchhiking through a Maine blizzard in 1971. They had married and settled in Rhode Island, where Mary gave birth to two children and Bishop held a factory job.

Levasseur met Bishop in a Boston fast-food joint and was dazzled. After five years in hiding Bishop badly wanted back in the revolutionary game. He was everything Levasseur dreamed he would be: the son of poor sheep farmers, a onetime army paratrooper, and a tough talker who praised the SLA and dismissed the Weathermen as "bourgeois rich kids." Together, Bishop proposed, they could launch a bombing campaign that would bring the American ruling class to its knees. Afterward Levasseur returned to Portland, exhilarated. "This was my opportunity," he recalls. "This was everything I had been waiting for."

Almost immediately, however, a problem arose. "Things started moving too fast," Levasseur remembers. "I got a call from Tom: Cameron's picture had run on a Rhode Island TV station, and Mary and Cameron and their kids were coming up to Portland. I was like, 'What?' He's a Top Ten fugitive! I've got a death squad here. We're under round-the-clock surveillance! What the fuck?" Within days the Bishops moved in with the Mannings at their cramped apartment in the Munjoy Hill neighborhood. Mary Bishop went to work at the bookstore. Cameron Bishop began urging Levasseur to form an underground cell—immediately. When Levasseur protested that they had no money, no way of supporting themselves, Bishop said they would do what the BLA and the SLA had done: rob banks.

"Cameron was a big fan of expropriations," Levasseur remembers. "But he had never done one. He had an attitude, and a gun, but he'd never done it. Cameron was really pushing this. I thought it was totally premature. I was game for a lot, but robbing a bank? That was ludicrous. None of us had experience at anything like that. That was just too much. I really resisted. On the other hand, I felt a commitment to Tom and Cameron. I felt myself getting drawn into it."

In desperation Levasseur began casting about for an alternative. An ex-con friend suggested sticking up a Portland department store on payroll day. Levasseur had ethical concerns, refusing to rob any store that was locally owned. "Expropriation is only justified if it's a large company that's already ripping the people off," he says. "So no mom-and-pop stores. It had to be part of the ruling class." They studied the job for weeks, and after satisfying himself that the store was owned by the ruling class, they decided to move. Levasseur declines to divulge details—he was never linked to the robbery—but finally, in November, the store was robbed. "We didn't get much, a few thousand dollars," he says. "It was mostly checks."

The robbery, however, did little to quell Bishop's demands that they immediately go underground. Levasseur stalled. His politics may have been radical, but in matters of risk he was highly conservative; planning and precision were hallmarks of his underground career. Levasseur and Bishop were still debating whether and when to go underground when, just before Christmas, Portland police raided the bookstore and arrested Levasseur for carrying an open can of beer. By the time he made bail he could feel control of matters slipping away. Tom Manning had inexplicably beaten up his landlord and now had a court date looming; he could be sent to jail if they remained aboveground. Worse, Levasseur had borrowed a girlfriend's car for the store robbery; she had gotten angry and was threatening to turn them in.

"There was a craziness that was building," Levasseur recalls. "Things were just moving too fast. When I first met with Cameron, I envisioned something planned out, something careful. But things were pushing us. Cameron kept going, 'We gotta go. We gotta go.'"

Then came the final straw. Linda Coleman walked into the bookstore one morning and discovered that it had been ransacked. On the floor she found Mary Bishop whimpering in a fetal position. She had been raped, she said, by two men who held a broken bottle against her neck. Levasseur had no doubt as to who was responsible: the Portland police, the fascist pigs who wanted them all dead. Bishop again demanded they go underground. Facing a kaleidoscope of pressures, real and imagined—the police, Manning's court date, the vengeful girlfriend, his commitment to the Bishops, not to mention his long-held dream of forming his own underground cell—Levasseur capitulated. By the next day he and the Mannings and Bishops had vanished from Portland's streets.*

---

*Pat Gros and Linda Coleman, who did not join the others underground, attempted to keep the bookstore open for several weeks, then quit and shut its doors.

That first week they hid in a friend's farmhouse in York County, six adults—Levasseur had brought yet another girlfriend along—and three small children, sleeping where they could and stacking their guns over the fireplace. Levasseur soon rented a house in Somersworth, a mill town just across the New Hampshire border. They were armed and underground now but not yet at the point of no return.

Again Bishop urged that they should rob a bank. Levasseur continued to resist. He needed to study how this was done, he said again and again. Finally, after weeks of discussion, he agreed to accompany Bishop back to Rhode Island, where Bishop said he knew several banks they could hit. "Cameron said he knew the area. I said, 'What does that mean?' [He says,] 'I know the roads, I know banks with armored cars just rolling in. There's all kinds of money there!' We just had this nebulous idea that there was something ripe there, ready to pick. That's how fucked up it was. We had all these guns, we had Marighella's *Mini-Manual* [*of the Urban Guerrilla*] with all these passages I had underlined. Basically we were impatient, we were desperate, and we were stupid."

They began scouting Rhode Island banks, sitting outside branches all around Providence for hours at a time, not quite sure what they were looking for. Which is what they were doing on the morning of March 12, 1975, the two of them slumped in a white 1967 Chevy in a Dunkin' Donuts parking lot across from the Old Stone Bank in East Greenwich. Levasseur was in the backseat, a .38 jabbed in his belt. Bishop was behind the wheel, cradling two pistols in a paper sack. Tom Manning had just stepped into the doughnut shop when Bishop spied two men—clearly plainclothes detectives—approaching the car.

"What do we do?" Levasseur asked.

"I got solid ID," Bishop said. "Don't worry about it."

Which were the last words Bishop spoke to Levasseur before the detectives placed them under arrest. As it turned out, a woman had seen them two days before, long-haired men in a car full of guns, telephoned police, and described the car. A sawed-off shotgun was found in the trunk, along with a map showing the route of a Purolator armored car. When the police ran Bishop's fingerprints, they realized who they had detained. The arrest of a Top Ten fugitive made national headlines. Photos of both men graced the front pages in Maine.

It was over.

19

BOMBS AND DIAPERS

Ray Levasseur's Odyssey,
Part II

Cameron Bishop was taken to Denver to face the old sabotage charges. Levasseur was detained on a weapons charge. To his amazement, he was granted bail; the authorities had no idea of his plans for revolutionary action. Linda Coleman dipped into her trust fund to pay a Boston bondsman $3,000, the first of a series of outlays that would keep Levasseur afloat in the coming months. A friend drove down to Rhode Island with Pat Gros to pick him up, and they chugged a celebratory six-pack on the drive to his mother's home in Maine. That night he and Gros made love in a guest room, conceiving what would become their first child.

Then Mary Bishop telephoned from Denver. She pleaded with Levasseur to come west to form a legal defense committee for her husband. He didn't want to go—Tom Manning was sitting in a Boston apartment, penniless, waiting for direction—but he did; Bishop, after all, seemed to be his last hope of joining the revolution. Levasseur took Coleman and drove cross-country to Colorado, where they joined Mary Bishop in a ranch house Coleman rented for them. That started the problems. The house was too nice, Coleman felt, and thus not properly revolutionary. She was deeply confused, unsure whether her money was going to true revolutionary purposes or just beer. They began to argue, with Levasseur barking that she was giving him money with strings attached.

The problems mounted when Bishop's family raised his bail. The Bishops turned out to be well-to-do sheep farmers—not at all the blue-collar people Levasseur had imagined—and, worse, Bishop seemed in no hurry to restart their underground army. "Cameron had always been very big on how it was every revolutionary's duty to escape, but he didn't want to skip bail," Levasseur recalls. "I said, 'This is it. It's time to go. We got unfinished business.' And he kept stalling. Then Mary gets wind of this, and she wants no part of it. So she makes it very uncomfortable for me to be there. One night she got mad and threw a pot at me in the kitchen, so I left." Before doing so, he and Bishop arranged a "call schedule" whereby Levasseur would telephone him at a series of pay phones once he returned east. Weeks later, when Levasseur began making the appointed calls, Bishop failed to appear for a single one.

Levasseur returned to New England in July 1975 on a bus, confused and depressed. Manning was now a fugitive, having failed to appear for his court date, and Levasseur soon would be; he had no intention of returning to Rhode Island to face his charges. Once it grew clear that Bishop was not rejoining them, it was obvious that if they were ever to set up an underground cell, they would have to do it alone.

"Our thinking," Levasseur recalls, "was seriously idealistic or serious tunnel vision. We wanted to be part of what these other groups—the SLA, Weather—were doing out there. We felt, there's a fucking war going on out there, and we want to be part of it. We wanted to be somewhere between the Weather Underground and the BLA. Weather had done some good actions. I liked *Prairie Fire*. But we felt we would have to go beyond what they were doing. The BLA, they also had good actions, but I didn't want to be just a squad that targeted police. That was too narrow. Not that I objected on moral grounds. I had no problems offing cops. None. But it was just beyond our capability. It would be way too much heat for us, and I didn't think we could withstand that."

Two men didn't make much of an army, however. What they needed was recruits. Renting an apartment in Portsmouth, New Hampshire—later they rented a second in Springfield, Massachusetts—they began sending out feelers to their ex-convict friends. Their first recruit turned out to be an unfortunate one, Joey Aceto, a diminutive twenty-two-year-old burglar paroled in Maine that April; Aceto had been in and out of institutions since boyhood and, unbeknownst to Levasseur, had a record of drug use, suicide attempts, and snitching on fellow inmates. At the Springfield apartment Levasseur mounted an elaborate indoctrination for Aceto, plying him with revolutionary books Aceto did his best to understand.

The next task was raising money. Much of their time was spent driving back and forth to Portsmouth, where they began casing their first bank. This time they were determined to do things correctly. Levasseur studied the bank's layout and personnel in detail, tailing the manager to his home, then devised an elaborate getaway plan by sea, arranging for a shady lobster boat captain to spirit them away from Portsmouth by boat. On their first rehearsal run, however, the boat began taking on water and had to be beached on a sandbar.

That scrubbed the Portsmouth robbery. Angry and running low on money, they cast about for a new bank to target. Levasseur remembered a branch of the Northeast Bank of Westbrook he had thought of casing in the Lunt's Corner area of Portland. On impulse they decided to rob it. On October 4, 1975, just days after abandoning the New Hampshire bank, Manning drove a stolen car up to the Portland bank. Levasseur—wearing a black afro wig and heavy dark sunglasses—led Aceto and a last-minute addition, another ex-con pal, into the bank, guns drawn. As they did, Levasseur glanced toward the drive-through window and gasped.

"There's a cop at the window!" he shouted. "Come on!"

As luck would have it, an off-duty policeman named Paul Lewis was sitting in his wife's car at the drive-through window. Hearing a commotion behind him, he realized that the bank was being robbed. Shoving his wife out of the car, he took the wheel, made a screaming U-turn, and arrived in front of the bank just as the three robbers sprinted from the entrance, dropping bags of cash in their haste to get into the getaway car. Manning slammed the accelerator and shot down a side road into a wooded area; when they spied Lewis giving chase, Manning veered to a stop at the curb. Lewis did the same, reaching for the pistol beneath the seat—only to realize that the gun was in his car, not his wife's. At least one of the robbers pulled a .45-caliber pistol and squeezed off several rounds that hit the front of Lewis's car. As Lewis cowered behind the wheel, powerless to respond, the robbers drove off.

Though they made their getaway—the take was barely $2,000—the incident left Levasseur shaken. This was not a game. This was life and death. He swore to himself he would never be so careless again. He began studying everything he could find on bank robberies; when he read how a Canadian revolutionary group, the Front de libération du Québec, never stayed inside a bank more than five minutes, he pledged to rob banks even faster. And in the short term, he realized, they would have to strike again. Linda Coleman was paying for almost everything, but even her pocketbook wasn't bottomless.

They found the next bank in Augusta, a branch of the Bank of Maine. Again Levasseur tried to be creative. He built a fake bomb using road flares—"They look just like dynamite," he says—and left it at a supermarket across town. On the morning of December 12 he phoned in the bomb threat. Once half the Augusta police force responded, they hit the bank, Levasseur, Manning, and Aceto charging inside, guns drawn, while Manning's wife, Carol, stayed outside, driving the getaway car; it was the first and only time she would take part in one of the group's actions. Levasseur and Aceto vaulted the counters and in less than a minute made it out the door with $12,000. They got away clean.

Finally they had done something right. Fearing a police dragnet in Maine, they decided to relocate to New York City for a few weeks, taking an apartment on the Lower East Side and attending several parties packed with radicals. At one someone whispered that Bernardine Dohrn was in attendance. At a party at William Kunstler's apartment, people said the SLA's would-be memoirist, Jack Scott, was there. One evening Linda Coleman brought Levasseur to her family mansion on Long Island. He left shaking his head. He found the display of wealth obscene.

They couldn't decide what to do next. They needed more money, that much was clear. The three men—Levasseur, Manning, and Aceto—fell to arguing. Levasseur wanted time to plan, to look at banks and potential bombing targets. Manning wanted to rob a market they knew in Portland;

Levasseur insisted that the target wasn't properly revolutionary. Aceto argued for killing policemen. "Aceto just wanted to kill cops," Levasseur recalls. "I got sick of it. We had some pretty intense arguments. We didn't have enough money to mount a political action, and I was starting to sour on the idea of more expropriations. We had already done two, and where had that gotten us? I told them, 'Before I'll steal from some mom-and-pop store, I'll find a job.' That view was not always very popular."

They split up. Searching for a remote place to live, Levasseur drove his battered brown Chevy to the town of Calais, in far northern Maine on the Canadian border, where he rented a spartan apartment. He was soon joined by Pat Gros, who that January had given birth to their first child, a daughter they named Carmen. Ray missed the birth, but mother and child's arrival in Calais made a deep impression on him. For the first time he had a family to support; after months of treating Gros as just another girl, he fell in love with her in those winter months in northern Maine, building her a kitchen table from two-by-fours and slow-dancing to the radio at night. He wrote her an impassioned letter to mark the beginning of their new family, in which he tried to explain his philosophy of "armed love."

> *To me you are just as much my sister—a comrade—a revolutionary—another young warrior to add to the voice—our voice—the voice of the oppressed. . . . My love is for the oppressed. Blacks, Browns, Native Americans, poor whites, rising women. With me it's the mill workers, shoe shop workers, cleaning women, the millions of unemployed laborers. . . . Armed love [means] picking up the gun with one hand and reaching out to the oppressed people and fellow comrades with the other. . . . So—what I feel is what Comrade George Jackson called, "Perfect love, perfect hate, that's the insides of me." Love for the oppressed—death for the oppressor. . . . Armed love is deep and lasting and I will take it to the wall and beyond. I believe we can all be together and happy some day. Building the new life.*

Levasseur and Gros's idyll in Calais was marred only by the arrival of the sullen Joey Aceto. When Levasseur took a construction job, he returned home most days to find Aceto swilling cheap wine, demanding they do something. Levasseur suggested that Aceto get a job; he wouldn't. Finally, after papering over their differences with Tom Manning, everyone rendezvoused in Portland to organize the new cell. Linda Coleman showed up, as did a new recruit, a bushy-haired twenty-seven-year-old ex-con named Richard "Dickie" Picariello, who had been an inmate leader at Maine State Prison.

In a series of meetings at a Ramada Inn outside the city, they chugged beers and debated everything: what to call themselves, what actions to mount, who would actually go underground. Eventually they decided to call themselves the Sam Melville Jonathan Jackson unit. As for actions, Picariello argued for prison breakouts and assassinations. Asked whom he wanted to kill, he mentioned utility executives who were raising electric rates, a suggestion that startled Coleman. "Dickie wanted to off Maine Power & Light officials because of rate hikes: I'm like, 'What?'" she recalls. "I think that was the first time I began having second thoughts."

Levasseur's argument, as usual, won the day. Like Weather and the FALN, they would attack symbols of the fascist U.S. government. The only question was whether to bomb empty buildings or full ones. The women, especially Gros and Carol Manning, argued for empty. But Levasseur would not be deterred. Anyone who got hurt, he announced, was "collateral damage" in their war against the government. The final step was the dynamite. Levasseur had no idea how to get some: Could they just buy it? He dispatched Coleman to a law library. She came back with bad news: Ex-cons couldn't buy dynamite in Maine. They would have to steal it.

After the last meeting, in March 1976, everyone scattered. Levasseur and Gros returned to Calais. Picariello promised to look into stealing dynamite but ended up buying fifty sticks instead, from an underworld contact in Portland. He and Aceto met Coleman in a crowded parking lot, where they opened the back of their battered station wagon and, with a flourish, pulled free a blanket to reveal the explosives. Stunned, Coleman hurriedly closed the car, fearing that someone would see. Her concerns grew as Picariello and Aceto downed beers on the long drive north. At one point she suggested that maybe she should drive. It was then she realized she couldn't do this anymore. "Dickie and Joey were just too crazy," she recalls. "They just seemed intent on doing whatever it took to get themselves thrown back into prison."

Back in Calais things quickly unraveled. Coleman read a letter of resignation. The next morning Aceto stomped off to the bus depot and left for Portland. He cared little for bombings; he wanted to rob banks or kill cops. Levasseur didn't bother attempting to dissuade Coleman, but losing Aceto was a risk: He might talk. They agreed to send Picariello to Portland to deliver a threat: If Aceto said anything about their plans, they swore to harm his family. In the event, Picariello and Aceto got to talking and ended up striking a deal. Picariello, who thought himself every bit as worthy a revolutionary leader as Levasseur, promised Aceto that if he would help him bomb something, Picariello would help him rob a bank. Maine would now have two genuine revolutionary cells; theirs, they decided, would be named the Fred Hampton unit, after the Panther leader killed in 1969.

That left the Sam Melville Jonathan Jackson unit with precisely four members—Levasseur and Gros, Tom and Carol Manning—and fifty sticks of dynamite. The defections didn't matter to Levasseur. He had read a *Boston Globe* article mentioning long lists of parolees kept at the Suffolk County Courthouse in Boston. If they could destroy those lists, he reasoned, the authorities would be powerless to keep track of thousands of ex-convicts. That, he announced to the group, was exactly the kind of place they should try to bomb.

To this day, Levasseur won't discuss that first bombing, but he doesn't deny that he planted the device. Building bombs was never hard for him; he had helped his grandfather blow up tree stumps as a boy, and with diagrams in the *Dragon* and other radical manuals he found it easy to hook the blasting caps to a tiny Westclox wristwatch. In time he became so expert he authored his own hundred-page manual.

The bombing of the Suffolk County Courthouse on April 22, 1976, was a sensation throughout New England. News that twenty-two people had been injured, including the would-be cabdriver, Edmund Narine, stunned Boston. Coverage took up several full pages in the *Globe*. Afterward Governor Michael Dukakis made a televised address to deplore the attack, then, with the city's mayor, led a march of thousands of citizens through the downtown area, dubbed a "procession against violence." The injuries, and the reaction to them, left Levasseur and the others stunned.

"There was time for them to clear the building, but they didn't," Levasseur says. "I was sick, all of us were, that we had hurt someone. Pat was really upset." Recalls Pat, "I was just in shock. People were not supposed to get hurt. Everyone felt shitty." She made Levasseur swear he wouldn't hurt more people. He promised to try.

That first SMJJ communiqué, mailed to a Boston alternative newspaper, struck the same melodramatic notes Levasseur used in his diary and his letters to Gros. "This is but the sound before the fury of those who are oppressed," it began, going on to list a series of demands to reform prisons in Maine and Massachusetts. "We wish to make it clear at this time, that if these demands are not justly dealt with, there will be further attacks against the criminal ruling class."

Back in Portland, Dickie Picariello read reports of the bombing and knew it was Levasseur's work. He wanted to bomb something, too. The problem was, Levasseur had his dynamite. Picariello telephoned Calais and begged for a few sticks, but Levasseur refused, insisting he didn't have enough to share. Irked, Picariello took matters into his own hands. He and Aceto broke into an explosives warehouse in New Boston, New Hampshire, and stole fifteen cases of dynamite and blasting caps. On May 11 they walked into the headquarters of the Central Maine Power Company and wandered the halls until they found places to leave the two bombs they had managed to assemble. Afterward they called in a warning—the building was safely evacuated, and no one was hurt in the two explosions—and mailed a communiqué to the Augusta newspaper. Three days later they robbed a bank in the town of Orono.

A bizarre competition thus developed between the two rival revolutionary cells. Levasseur struck next. Early on Monday, June 21, he left a small bomb in a grocery sack beside the front door of the Middlesex County Courthouse in Lowell, Massachusetts. It exploded at 6:16 a.m., showering a janitor with broken glass. They had called in a warning ahead of time, then made a second call to claim responsibility and direct police to a communiqué taped inside a pay phone in nearby Lawrence. It called for reforms at Tom Manning's alma mater, the Walpole State Prison.

In Boston FBI agents didn't know what to think: In two short months New England had suffered three bombings from what appeared to be two separate groups. To confuse matters further, there was already a Sam Melville Jonathan Jackson unit in California, an offshoot of the New World Liberation Front. Reached by reporters, Jacques Rogiers claimed he was "ninety-nine percent certain" the Boston bombing had been done by an NWLF "combat unit." Determined to sort things out, the FBI assembled a task force. They quickly picked up a tip that Dickie Picariello was involved.

FBI agents began watching Picariello's Portland apartment just as the strange contest between the two underground cells reached its climax. The occasion was Sunday, July 4, 1976, the American Bicentennial. Still working out of his apartment in northern Maine, Levasseur had an action scheduled, but it was Picariello and Aceto who planned something spectacular: a series of bombings of eight separate targets, including courthouses, post offices, and an Eastern Airlines passenger jet. The drama began early on the morning of Friday, July 2, when the two, along with another Maine ex-con, planted bombs at a National Guard Armory in Dorchester, Massachusetts, at the Essex County Superior Courthouse, and under an Eastern Airlines Electra prop jet at Boston's Logan Airport. The plane was destroyed, the buildings were damaged, but no one was hurt. Agents watching Picariello's flat inexplicably failed to see him leave.

Nor did anyone see the trio of ex-cons later that Friday when, just before midnight, they detonated yet another bomb, outside the post office in Seabrook, New Hampshire, heavily damaging the building. But on the third night, the Saturday before Bicentennial Sunday, agents spotted Picariello, Aceto, and two partners as they left Portland, heading south. They followed the four to a state police barracks outside Topsfield, Massachusetts, where they watched as two men got out, apparently with bombs at the ready. When the agents moved in, Aceto led them on a high-speed chase, eventually losing control of his car and crashing into a stone wall. Inside agents found guns and forty-six sticks of dynamite, most of it rigged as bombs.* The others were arrested later.

That same night Levasseur left a bomb outside a branch of the First National Bank of Boston in the town of Revere.† It blew up the next morning without incident, but such was the media furor over the Picariello-Aceto bombings and arrests, almost no one in New England noticed: The *Globe* gave the bombing a tiny story on an inside page. Levasseur was incensed, since his communiqué, the group's third, marked a sharp change in their public face. For the first time he had put aside his calls for prison reform and, having studied and admired the FALN's work, authored a florid call for Puerto Rican independence and the release of all Puerto Rican "political prisoners." No one cared.

His irritation, however, was quickly overcome by fear. It was only a matter of time, he knew, before Aceto talked. And so, picking up Gros and their baby, he and the Mannings did the only thing they could: They ran.

Their new home, the first of many to come, was a squalid flat in the New Hampshire village of Suncook. Levasseur took a midnight-shift job in a tannery, scraping and cleaning rancid, bloody cowhides. The Mannings found a place in Vermont. As yet, neither Levasseur nor Tom Manning had been identified publicly, but they knew that Joey Aceto was talking. FBI agents were fanning out to talk to everyone. Family. Friends. The SCAR people. The ex-cons. It was only a matter of time, Levasseur knew, before their faces would be staring out from the bulletin boards of every post office in New England. They were now cut off from anyone they had ever known.

They were alone. From Debray's and Marighella's revolutionary texts Levasseur knew that his little group had fallen victim to every guerrilla cell's

---

*Agents later recovered the rest of Picariello's dynamite, almost six hundred pounds of it, buried near Portland.
†Levasseur had hoped to place a bomb at a bank in downtown Boston but discovered that police security linked to the Bicentennial celebration made it impossible.

main vulnerabilities: the danger of early days and the danger of extreme isolation. He pored over his books to find out what to do. He started with identification, the foundation of every underground life. He had secured his first fake driver's license in Calais, simply calling the motor vehicle bureau and asking for a duplicate in the name of a man he read had died in a motorcycle accident. It was easy: At the time Maine licenses didn't have photos. The only problem was, the dead man had the wrong color eyes and happened to be three inches too tall. What they needed, Levasseur saw, was solid photo IDs, something to stand up to a policeman's perusal. In Suncook he began doing as the Weathermen had: visiting courthouses to harvest the birth certificates of dead infants, then using them to secure Social Security cards and driver's licenses. Gathering IDs, in fact, would become the one constant in their lives for years to come. When anyone in the group had spare time, they used it to "build ID." Eventually Levasseur alone would build more than a dozen identities.

With no hope of outside support, they began stockpiling materials for a life underground that would be self-sufficient and sustainable: programmable Bearcat scanners, one for each household and car, the better to monitor the police; more reliable cars, one for each of them, to replace the junkers everyone was driving; plus bulletproof vests, guns, ammunition, dynamite, and a place to store it all. Neither Levasseur nor Manning had anywhere near the money that was needed, nor was manual labor likely to raise it anytime soon, so after much agonizing, they decided to mount another expropriation. To prepare, Levasseur and Gros moved a second time, to an apartment in Manchester, New Hampshire. She found work as a waitress. He picked apples alongside Mexican migrant workers. He declines to identify the bank he and Manning robbed that fall, only saying that it was in Manchester. "I just walked into the place, by myself, with two guns, and I end up on the counter, covering the whole place myself," Levasseur recalls. "Talk about vulnerable." Manning drove the getaway car. They got away clean, with between $15,000 and $20,000.

The next step was to secure a new source of dynamite; the old sticks were starting to sweat, and Levasseur worried that they might be unstable. And so, shortly after midnight on November 10, 1976, the two men found themselves crawling on their bellies through a field outside the town of Bow, New Hampshire, wearing backpacks laden with pistols and hacksaw blades. Their target was McGoldrick Mine and Quarry Supply. They sawed through a fence and made off with a hundred pounds of dynamite sticks.

Levasseur then rented the first of a series of safe-house apartments the group would use, this one in Nashua, New Hampshire. They stored the dynamite there, and many of their guns, along with notes Levasseur had begun compiling on prospective bombing targets. They changed the locks and sprinkled talcum powder inside the door when they left, the better to see whether anyone had entered in their absence. Finally, on December 12, a month after the dynamite theft, they left a large, twenty-stick bomb outside a Union Carbide building in Needham, Massachusetts. Levasseur called in the warning, then a later claim of credit, but to his dismay the bomb failed to explode. Newspaper coverage the next day carried the first public identification of Levasseur and Tom and Carol Manning, who had been indicted on the 1975 bank jobs.

Fearing pursuit, Levasseur had everyone move yet again, this time to the Connecticut mill town of New Britain, southwest of Hartford. Gros and Levasseur rented an apartment above a Puerto Rican social club; the Mannings, one nearby. The men took construction jobs. Gros found work as a temp; Carol Manning babysat. Levasseur and Tom Manning began taking weekend trips to reconnoiter targets, driving their own cars and communicating via walkie-talkie. After several months Levasseur found the next target: a W. R. Grace chemical factory in Marlboro, Massachusetts. Grace had been accused of exploiting its Latin American workers, and the building was barely ten miles from the town of Clinton, where President Carter was holding a town hall meeting that March. Levasseur built the bomb, a large one, and left it outside the plant gate on the evening of March 12, 1977. It blew up at 8:24, shattering more than a hundred windows. Afterward they called in credit to United Press International, directing police to a communiqué slipped inside a Boston phone booth. Not till later that day, however, did they learn that while the W. R. Grace logo adorned the factory, Grace had sold it nine years before. They had inadvertently bombed the Ideal Roller and Graphics

Company, which made printing presses. "We screwed up there," Levasseur recalls. "That was pretty stupid."

Between actions, life for the couples began to slow in New Britain. Their various fake IDs held up; there was no sense that the authorities had their scent. Gros made friends at her office job, and for the first time she and Levasseur found themselves nervously attending the odd office party. She and Carol Manning did their best to construct the illusion of domesticity. Gros baked bread and made maple syrup. Carol refused to participate in any more actions; like Pat, she felt that raising her child—two-year-old Jeremy—was far more important than what they always euphemistically called their "political work."

The fear and chaos brought on by Joey Aceto's betrayal—he had, in fact, given the FBI chapter and verse—was slowly receding. Levasseur was still working at New Britain construction sites that May when, as he was sipping coffee at his boss's house one morning, the telephone rang. It was Gros. "Have you seen this morning's paper?" she asked.

"No."

"You need to see it right away."

Levasseur hung up, made an excuse, and walked to a convenience store to buy the New Britain newspaper. Deep on an inside page he was startled to see an old photo of himself. Beneath it was a news story: The FBI had just named him one of America's ten most wanted criminals. Fighting panic, he saw that it was a bad photo. Taking a deep breath, he returned to his boss's house, then did a full day's work. When he came home that night, he found Gros packing.

They moved to the neighboring city of Waterbury, the Mannings following close behind, where they rented another tiny apartment. The men found new construction jobs. Not long after arriving, Pat Gros discovered she was pregnant again. For reasons she only dimly understood, she was swept by waves of relief. "I was in denial a lot of the time, pretending that none of this was real," she recalls today. "I only figured out years later why I kept getting pregnant, and why it made me so happy. It was the only way I had to not get more involved. If I was pregnant, they couldn't ask me to rob a bank."

Pat seldom shared her doubts with Ray, but it was clear both she and Carol Manning were at best ambivalent about their lives underground. A rare airing of these feelings occurred in Waterbury. As Pat recalls, "Tommy came to me and said, 'Carol's been talking, she doesn't want to do this anymore.' He had a question about how effective we were being. I said, 'Well, yeah, look outside. There's not a lot of people wanting a revolution. There's nobody.' And he said, 'Do you think this is even worth doing?' I had to admit, I agreed with him."

They knew what Levasseur would say, but they talked to him anyway, and to their relief he kept his temper. He pointed out the obvious, that if they quit living underground, he and Manning faced years in prison.

Still, that lingering skepticism within the group, the sense that maybe their lives underground really were as futile as they sometimes seemed, contributed to a pause in their "political work." After the W. R. Grace bombing in Marlboro that March, Levasseur and Manning carried out no more bombings in 1977. Expropriations were too risky with only two of them, and by that fall the money again began to run low. Then, around Thanksgiving, Levasseur was laid off. He found a job installing security systems and enjoyed it, until he realized he was leaving his fingerprints at homes all over Waterbury; if even one was burglarized, detectives might find his prints and discover he was in the area. He quit the job, and by that winter both men were out of work. Their savings fell so low the Mannings reluctantly moved into Levasseur and Gros's apartment, four adults now, with two small children to raise. Gros was due in March.

Despite the long months of inactivity, Levasseur clung to his dream of reopening a revolutionary front in New England. His plans, in fact, were growing more ambitious. If they were to thrive as an underground cell and placate the women's concerns about endangering the children, they needed to physically separate their family and revolutionary lives. What they needed was a permanent safe house, a place he and Manning could store dynamite and guns and plan their actions; the Nashua flat had long since been vacated. Once a safe house was established, the couples could move far away, returning to it only to carry out actions. The plan, however, would take money, and everyone knew what that meant: another bank robbery. The women didn't want to hear it, but Levasseur was adamant. He'd had an epiphany, he said. It had come that fall while working construction.

Levasseur remembers the day clearly, almost forty years later. He had been digging a hole at a construction site, and with his foot still on the shovel, he had glanced up and seen a Brink's truck coasting to a stop at a bank across the street. Asking his boss for a moment, he had walked across to the bank and followed the two couriers as they lugged bags of cash inside. Standing in the lobby, he studied how the manager took the cash bags and slid them back toward the vault after a bit of chitchat with the couriers. The manager had finally strolled to the barred door outside the vault, unlocked it, and lugged the bags inside—but not, Levasseur could see, into the vault itself. The money just sat on the floor for a half hour, until a teller moved it inside. In that delay Ray saw an opportunity. If they could hit a bank as cash bags were being delivered but before they were stored in a vault, they could be in and out in under a minute. With hundreds of thousands of dollars. Even with only two of them, the idea seemed too enticing not to try.

All that winter Levasseur and Manning followed Purolator and Brink's trucks through the snow-clogged streets of Waterbury, studying and memorizing their routes. They settled on a target, a branch of the Banking Center on Piedmont Street, but by the time they were ready to move, it was already February. Gros was now eight months pregnant; the idea of her children's father staging an armed bank robbery on the eve of childbirth did not sit well with her. "There were several emotional discussions about that, whether to do the bank before or after the baby came," Levasseur recalls. As usual, he won the debate.

A massive blizzard, the largest to hit Waterbury in forty years, pushed the bank job back still further. Gros was entering her ninth month when the men finally made their move, on a snowy Thursday morning, March 2, 1978. Just before 10:00, minutes after they watched a Brink's truck deliver several large bags of cash, they burst into the bank. Both wore multicolored ski masks, Levasseur cradling a pistol, Manning a shotgun as he guarded the door. "Everybody down! Everybody down on the floor!" Levasseur hollered at the ten employees and customers. He hurdled the teller counter and strode to the open vault, where he easily scooped up several bags of cash lying on the floor.

Both men then ran back outside, circling into a rear parking lot, where their stolen getaway car, a green Ford station wagon, sat idling. They were in and out in less than two minutes. The next day's newspaper called it "a smooth operation done by professionals."*[1]

In fact, it was perfect. When they emptied the Purolator bags, Levasseur and Manning were stunned to realize they had made off with more than $55,000 in cash—and established the template for every robbery to come. Within days the two couples cleared out of their cramped apartment, decamping to new homes Gros found for them in Derby, a village near New Haven. Levasseur and Gros, now posing as Jack and Paula Horning, rented the second story of a duplex on Mount Pleasant Street. A month to the day after the robbery, Gros, with the help of a midwife, gave birth to her second child, Simone.

For the first time in two long years, the couples were truly able to relax. Levasseur and Gros bought a dog, a German shepherd they named Rocky, who would be with them until the end. Gros, who had injured her knee in a car accident years before, was finally able to go in for surgery; afterward she hobbled around on crutches. No longer needing to work, Levasseur took the summer to play househusband, spending long hours quieting little Simone, who was colicky. In his spare time he drove into New Haven and found a tattoo artist who, for a little extra cash, promised discretion. Levasseur sat for sixteen hours as she painstakingly covered his two large tattoos, a Panther on his left arm with the word LIBERATION and a dragon on his right arm.

Once settled in Derby, Levasseur was able to establish the long-planned operational headquarters for the Sam Melville Jonathan Jackson unit in an apartment back in New Britain, the first of a series of Connecticut safe houses he would maintain in the months to come. The location was ideal, midway between the target-rich suburbs of New York and Boston, where he was planning their next bombings. They bought a table and chairs from the Salvation

---

*This robbery was never publicly linked to Levasseur and Manning. However, in interviews for this book, Levasseur volunteered details of the robbery and its approximate date. These details clearly match the March 2, 1978, Waterbury robbery described in contemporary newspaper accounts, though Levasseur, concerned about legal ramifications, declined to confirm they were the same.

Army, plunked them down in the kitchen, and threw two mattresses in the bedroom. When they were done, Levasseur grinned, turned to Manning, and said, "Money changes everything. Ain't America grand?" Not long after, on the evening of October 27, 1978, the two carried out their first action in eighteen months, detonating two large bombs simultaneously outside Mobil Oil offices in Waltham and Wakefield, Massachusetts. Damage was minimal. The communiqué, which once again called for Puerto Rican independence, was left in a Cambridge phone booth.

Levasseur felt fulfilled: It was good to be back at work. Only one incident, in fact, marred their months in Derby. Gros and their teenaged babysitter—a new luxury, courtesy of the Waterbury bank—were driving to the grocery store when Gros took a turn too sharply and slid into a ditch. A tow truck extracted them, but a policeman appeared and took down Gros's registration and license. Worried about angering Levasseur, she didn't tell him. When he heard of the accident from the babysitter, he flew into a rage, insisting that Gros tell him again and again exactly what had happened. Neither could see any chance of exposure. He reminded her to change her license immediately.

Once her knee healed, they set in motion phase two of Levasseur's plan. To insulate their family lives from their "political" work, the couples decided to split up. Levasseur and Gros would move to Vermont, the Mannings to eastern Pennsylvania, where they had lived before moving to Maine. They established a new safe house, in a small apartment in New Haven, just off the Yale University campus. To stay in touch, Levasseur and Manning identified a series of pay phones and set a schedule of regular calls. When it was time to do underground work, they would meet in New Haven.

Once everything was set, Levasseur and Gros rented a house outside Rutland, Vermont, but after a few months they decided they wanted something more isolated. What they found, in the spring of 1979, was a remote farmhouse on a pond in far northeastern Vermont, adjacent to their new landlord's dairy pasture. The house was barely habitable, with no insulation and only a single woodstove for heat. During their first winter there Levasseur was forced to line the house's interior with bales of hay and cover the walls with plastic; it still took ten cords of wood to get them through to spring. Still, they loved it.

There was a swing set out back for the girls and, to Levasseur's delight, a concrete bomb shelter on the land where he could store his dynamite.

Even better, Vermont's "Northeast Kingdom" was teeming with counterculturists, many of them aging radicals like themselves, and for the first time since going underground, the couple, now posing as the Boulette family, were able to enjoy something like a social life. They made friends and cooked outdoors and went to county fairs. "I felt so comfortable there," Pat recalls. "Everyone was like us. All the people in communes, the bookstores, health stores. It was a beautiful place, and for the first time we could be ourselves, as much as possible. It wasn't like America, you know? And not a lot of cops."

Best of all, Levasseur agreed to take some time off from underground work after one final action. The bombing, on February 27, 1979, was their most ambitious to date. The target was a Mobil Oil regional headquarters in Eastchester, in New York's Westchester County. Ray built the bomb into an attaché case, then donned a business suit, walked into the building, and left the case in a third-floor bathroom. A receptionist took the warning call at 3:30 p.m., while the building was full of people. Ray warned that a bomb was set to go off in one hour.

"We are retaliating for the imprisonment and/or torture of Puerto Ricans by the Mobil Oil Company," he said.

"Who are you?" the receptionist asked.

Ray decided to throw the authorities a curve, posing as the FALN. "It doesn't matter," he said. "When we bombed Mobil Oil in New York there were people killed. Get the people out of the building."

The building was safely evacuated just as the bomb exploded, wrecking much of the third floor. No one was hurt. The communiqué, left in a Manhattan phone booth, said the attack commemorated the 1954 Puerto Rican nationalist attack on the U.S. House of Representatives.

Safely back in Vermont, Levasseur returned to his life as husband and father. He found a job as a housepainter, then as a lumberjack. "We wanted a little sabbatical, which can be the kiss of death for a *foco*," he recalls. "Marighella says the duty of every revolutionary is to create a revolution. But the duty of a revolutionary with two kids is to bring home a paycheck and support his family, too."

For a solid year, in fact, the men did no real underground work—no bomb-ings, no bank robberies. Instead, they intermittently rendezvoused in New Haven and from there embarked on long reconnaissance trips, scouting and mapping corporate headquarters, military installations, and courthouses across the Northeast, from Boston all the way south to Philadelphia, Levasseur sit-ting for hours outside a munitions factory or National Guard armory, tracing maps of the building, its highway approaches, and any guards in a notebook.

The women silently hoped their men would never return to underground work. There would be no revolution, they knew. A new decade was dawning, the 1980s; the very idea of a revolution seemed ridiculous now. Levasseur and Manning, however, would not be dissuaded. They had been through too much, sacrificed too much, to give up now. The time would come, Levasseur told Gros in bed at night, when they would recruit new members and launch attacks more daring than anything they had attempted before. She listened and nodded, hoping the day would never come.

Gros gave birth to their third child, a daughter they named Rosa, in March 1980. Down in Pennsylvania, Carol Manning soon was pregnant again as well. As each new day passed without a bombing or bank robbery, both women came to believe that their lives in anonymity might last forever.

But it was not to be. One morning that summer Gros drove into the Ver-mont village of St. Johnsbury to buy groceries. At one point as she walked the aisles, she felt eyes on her. She glanced up and noticed, to her amazement, just across the store, a familiar face. A tall woman, attractive, dark hair. It took a moment for the name to register: Sally Stoddard. She had worked in the prison-reform movement. Gros remembered her from a conference years before.

Her heart raced. She willed herself to finish the shopping, to appear nor-mal. As she finally headed for the checkout, she felt sure Stoddard was fol-lowing her. As the girl totaled up her groceries, Gros had the panicky thought that Stoddard would approach her. She must know they were underground. She wouldn't risk it. Would she?

She didn't. Gros hustled to her car, tossed in the groceries, and drove quickly home, where Levasseur was waiting. It was then that everything began to change.

Part Four

OUT WITH
A BANG

20

THE FAMILY

The Pan-Radical Alliance,
1977 to 1979

By 1977 the age of the urban guerrilla appeared all but over. The SLA was a dim memory, Patty Hearst now languishing in prison. The Weather Underground was no more. Only the FALN, the NWLF, and the little-noticed bombing groups in New England and Washington state soldiered on, not that anyone in Middle America much cared about the odd midnight explosion in Seattle or Boston or especially New York City. This was 1977. New York was a ruin. Things were always blowing up in New York.

What America wanted was to forget that all of this had ever happened—the sixties, the demonstrations, the riots, Vietnam, Nixon, Watergate, Hoover, the bombings, every bit of it. What Americans wanted most was to dance to the throbbing new beat of disco and, if so inclined, snort the occasional line of cocaine and have a good time. For ten years the news had all been very, very bad. A new president, Jimmy Carter, had taken office. A new day, a new America, was dawning.

How significant underground groups remained in this new America was the topic of a rare if brief debate prompted by Mark Rudd's surrender that

September. The author of the definitive SDS history, Kirkpatrick Sale, citing the FALN and the NWLF, asserted in a *New York Times* op-ed that the "armed struggle" movement was not only still vital but constituted "every bit as dedicated an underground as existed" in 1970. Sale estimated there were "several hundred" people still underground. "Not that they are exactly a dominant force," he argued, "but they are clearly the significant factors in creating social change in the 1970s and seem to be getting stronger every year."[1] This was a reach and drew scoffs from the *Times* critic Walter Goodman. Noting Sale's assertion that the "bulk" of Weatherman remained underground, he asked, "How many makes a bulk? Four? Seven? . . . Are there really hundreds of terrorists now operating in America or do they bulk only in Mr. Sale's wishful imagination?"

The truth, it turned out, was somewhere between the two estimates. Because despite it all, despite the Townhouse and the BLA's defeat and the SLA's immolation and the fact that no one anywhere in America seemed the slightest bit inclined to follow them into bloody revolution, there remained a ragged core of armed radicals who refused to surrender their dreams. Some had been with Weather, a few on the margins of the BLA. By 1977 the most committed had begun gathering in New York, deep amid the ruins of a bombed-out neighborhood in the South Bronx, at perhaps the most unlikely revolutionary incubator one could imagine: an acupuncture clinic. It was called Lincoln Detox.

The Bronx had been the middle-class "Jewish borough" of New York for decades until the 1950s, when its factories began closing and Jewish families fled en masse before a rushing tide of Puerto Ricans and African Americans. The population of the South Bronx, which slumps along the Harlem River across from the northern reaches of Manhattan, went from two-thirds white in 1950 to two-thirds black and Hispanic in 1960. Property values plummeted through the 1960s; landlords often couldn't find buyers, when they tried to sell, or even renters, forcing them toward bankruptcy. Scores resorted to stripping and then burning their properties for the insurance money. By the early 1970s arson had risen to epidemic proportions; by decade's end more than 40 percent of all the structures in the South Bronx had burned. Out-of-control fires blazed every night for years, creating a perpetual haze over much of the borough. Firefighters couldn't keep up. Entire blocks went up in smoke. Watching flames spread near Yankee Stadium during the 1977 World Series, Howard Cosell famously quipped, "The Bronx is burning."

Into the ruins of the South Bronx crept predators of every stripe. Drugs were epidemic; gangs ruled the streets. Those who remained endured un-imaginable poverty and anger. "Rage," the *Times* noted in a 1973 series, "per-meates all facts of life in [the] South Bronx." In 1970, when the worst was still to come, much of that rage was directed at the area's only public hospital, Lincoln Hospital, on Concord Avenue at East 141st Street. Built in 1898, Lincoln had been condemned in 1949, but plans for its replacement had bogged down over legal challenges from owners of a factory on the proposed new site who refused to relocate. By 1970 Lincoln was a filthy, squalid place, dangerous to doctors and patients alike. The quality of its care was so notori-ously poor that locals called it "the butcher shop." Beyond its walls, venereal disease and infant mortality were rampant.

These were the days when just about any community dispute in the streets of New York drew protesters, many of them angry radicals, and outrage over Lincoln Hospital attracted more than its share. Eighty percent of Lincoln's patients were Puerto Rican, and it was an upstart Puerto Rican version of the Black Panthers, the Young Lords, that led demands for change at the hospital. The Lords, a onetime youth gang whose signature action involved burning trash to protest the lack of garbage trucks serving the area, announced their intervention in Lincoln's affairs in July 1970, when dozens of its purple-bereted members burst into the hospital at dawn, barricaded themselves inside the old nursing building, and unfurled a Puerto Rican flag atop it. They pre-sented a list of demands to the hospital's administrators: resumption of house calls (doctors were too frightened to go out alone), a day-care center, a twenty-four-hour "grievance table" manned by community volunteers, takeover of the hospital by a coalition of local leaders and hospital staffers, and completion of the new facility.

When hospital leaders announced that many of the proposals were "valid," the Young Lords left peacefully—for the moment. In following days, however, its members were a constant and angry presence in hospital corridors. White doctors and nurses had long avoided Lincoln, and the Lords' main targets were the foreign-born staff members who had taken their place, many of them Korean and Filipino, who now found themselves being cursed as they scurried to tend patients. The Lords demanded more Puerto Rican staff members. In response, doctors and nurses resigned in droves. A series of sit-ins and demonstrations stretched on for weeks. The hospital descended into bedlam.

Near the height of chaos that November, the Young Lords returned in force, this time with a crowd of twenty-five or so drug addicts and others. They took over a sixth-floor auditorium and demanded that administrators let them establish a drug-treatment center. Lincoln operated its own small methadone clinic, one of the few in the area, but it was a garden hose spraying the forest fire of Bronx drug addiction. Once again the weary administration gave in, admitting the need. "We should be treating thousands of addicts," its administrator, Antero Lacot, told reporters, "but we are only treating a hundred. Every day we have to turn away 15 to 20 addicts who come here seeking help." The Lords simply remained in place, opening a makeshift clinic in the auditorium. Later they gained office space and nearly $1 million in state and city funding. Thus was born what soon became the South Bronx's largest drug-treatment center. Everyone called it Lincoln Detox.

From the beginning it was like no other clinic in New York. Run by radicals who established a socialist collective to administer it, Lincoln Detox drew many of its volunteers and paid staffers from the ranks of New York's militant leftists. They adorned its walls with photos of Che Guevara, Malcolm X, and, in time, Joanne Chesimard. Its volunteers included Michael "Cetawayo" Tabor and Afeni Shakur of the Panther 21, Brian Flanagan from Weather, as well as Bernardine Dohrn's sister, Jennifer, who fell for a Young Lords leader, Mickey Melendez, with whom she had three children. Practically overnight Lincoln Detox became a kind of clubhouse for New York's radical elite. According to Dhoruba Moore, when the Black Liberation Army needed medical supplies in 1971, the radicals at Lincoln turned them over by the truckload.

But it was the treatment Lincoln Detox offered that was truly radical, in every sense of the word. It was an article of faith among many militants that the plague of drugs was a scheme concocted by a white government to oppress blacks. This theory had been popularized by Malcolm X, who preached that drug addiction could be cured by freeing blacks of the self-hatred indoctrinated by whites. At Lincoln this meant augmenting methadone with a regimen of political education classes that included Marxist literature and lectures, all paid for with city funding. Every addict was given an eighty-six-page pamphlet called "The Opium Trail: Heroin and Imperialism," which claimed, among other eye-opening assertions, that a commitment to armed revolution could cure heroin addiction better than methadone alone. "By providing an alternative explanation and another focus for anger," its authors wrote, "as well as collective support and some sense of direction, the movement can be the best form of therapy."

The directors of traditional clinics rolled their eyes. "They got the biggest hunk of garbage put together that a million dollars could buy," one scoffed.[2] Still, Lincoln administrators, many of whom appeared intimidated by Detox staffers, tolerated most of it, only occasionally attempting to rein in the radicals, as when one acting director, new to the job, switched off the power when a group of 150 staffers and junkies commandeered the chapel to screen a documentary about a Mozambican revolutionary group. When the Detox crowd refused to leave, police and security guards were called, leading to the predictable melee. Twenty-three people were arrested.

Among the eager volunteers attracted to Lincoln Detox in those early days was a sharp young black radical named Jeral Williams, who would later gain infamy under his adopted Muslim name, Mutulu Shakur. Born in Baltimore to a housepainter father and a devout Christian mother—she was also blind—Shakur as a teenager had joined one of the edgiest of early black-power movements, the Republic of New Afrika (RNA). In 1968, the year Shakur signed up, the RNA held a convention in Detroit and proposed carving out a new black homeland from the states of Georgia, Alabama, Louisiana, Mississippi, and South Carolina; the group even elected a provisional government that included Malcolm X's widow. A weaker cousin to the larger and more significant Black Panthers, the RNA eventually crumbled under the onslaught of gunfights and FBI raids.

Shakur, only twenty the year Lincoln Detox opened, found a new home at the clinic; starting as a volunteer, he proved so energetic that he earned a $9,000-a-year job as an assistant drug counselor. Staffers remembered him as self-assured, cocky, and arrogant, a streetwise general in search of troops to follow his lead. He seemed to know everyone in radical circles, from Silvia Baraldini to Bernardine Dohrn. He steadily gained status at Lincoln, especially after marrying one of the Panther 21, Afeni Shakur, making him stepfather to her son, the future rapper Tupac Shakur. Mutulu Shakur rose further when he became an early convert to a new treatment that debuted at the clinic in 1974: acupuncture.

The problem, not that anyone at Detox cared to admit it, was that revolutionary politics as a cure for heroin addiction didn't actually work very well. Methadone was still used, but it too had its limits, and after four years many in the clinic were searching for new remedies. Acupuncture was introduced by a young doctor named Richard Taft, a stringy-haired graduate of the Baylor University Medical School in Houston, whose uncle, Robert A. Taft, Jr., was a Republican senator from Ohio; his great uncle was the twenty-seventh president, William Howard Taft. Dr. Taft taught the ancient Chinese art to Shakur and others until, as luck would have it, his dead body was found in a clinic closet in October 1974. No one at Detox publicly acknowledged the ironic fact that the founder of its newest heroin-treatment program had died of a heroin overdose himself, a syringe jammed into his arm. Counselors told patients Taft had been killed by the CIA.[3]

Still, acupuncture caught on. A practitioner named Mario Wexu arrived to train the staff after Taft's death, demonstrating how acupuncture could be used alongside traditional Western medicine, of which Shakur, for one, was contemptuous. Shakur and three other counselors began taking courses under Wexu through the Acupuncture Association of Quebec, and after a yearlong review and a month of clinical training, they earned doctor of acupuncture degrees. Shakur came to believe in the full range of acupuncture treatments, arguing that in his hands precisely placed needles could cure everything from hay fever to diarrhea. Wexu even took him to China to observe the work of traditional acupuncturists. By 1977, when Shakur assumed leadership of Lincoln Detox's acupuncture programs, his sway within the clinic had risen to the point where many staffers referred to him as its deputy director, though he wasn't.

Exactly why twenty-six-year-old Mutulu Shakur, budding doctor of acupuncture, turned to armed robbery would never be precisely explained. But he and his wife had a child on the way, and a $9,000 salary didn't buy much in New York, even in 1977. Though years removed from his teenaged sojourn in the Republic of New Afrika, Shakur still saw himself as an ardent black nationalist and revolutionary, and revolutionary ideas filled much of the conversation each day at Lincoln Detox. In 1976, when he began discussing the possibility of some kind of armed action with potential partners in crime, he said he wanted to raise money to give back to the poor blacks of the Bronx. What he didn't say, because this wasn't an effective way to recruit a revolutionary army, was that one reason he wanted more money was to fuel his growing appetite for the drug whose popularity was sweeping the nation: cocaine. The drug counselor was developing a taste for drugs, and $9,000 a year didn't buy much cocaine, then or ever.

Whatever his motivation, Shakur's transformation coincided with the arrival in his life of a true revolutionary, a cool, stoic figure all but worshiped by would-be white and black revolutionaries alike. It was time for Sekou Odinga to come in from the cold.

When Eldridge Cleaver was thrown out of Algeria in 1972, the Panthers with him scattered. Like Cleaver, Donald Cox found refuge in France. Michael Tabor ended up in Zambia. Only Sekou Odinga, the one Panther whose reputation actually grew despite the Algerian debacle, wanted to continue the struggle where it had begun, in the United States. Tall, quiet, and dark-skinned, with a pistol usually jammed into his belt in his role as Cleaver's principal bodyguard, "Sekou," one visitor to Algiers was quoted years later as saying, "is the most amazing of all the Panthers." Odinga drew comparisons to "Shaft" and other blaxploitation heroes of the day. The word used most often was "badass."

Odinga had long talks with the others before leaving Algiers; they knew what he wanted to do. He was still a wanted fugitive, indicted in the Panther 21 case; they thought returning to the States was suicidal. But Odinga remained dedicated to Malcolm's words. He still believed in the revolution. He left Algiers in the fall of 1972, drifting through Lebanon, Tanzania, and other African countries. Eventually, in the spring of 1973, he returned to the United States. "I flew back," he recalls. "It was easy. Security wasn't like it is now. You could use any small airport, go through Mexico or Canada."

As luck would have it, he reached New York just a few weeks before the May 1973 shootout in which Assata Shakur, still known as Joanne Chesimard, was captured on the New Jersey Turnpike. He had met with her just weeks before. "Everybody was having a tough time," he recalls. "But we were underground in a tough time. We were up against the strongest military power in the world; they were hell-bent on destroying us. Assata and them, they were being hunted. [She] and Zayd [Shakur], they were not expropriators. They had been pushed into doing things they didn't know how to do. At the time we worked up some plans to do things together. It was very rough. But it was still doable."

In fact, it wasn't. From the moment Odinga returned to the United States, it seemed another group of BLA soldiers was killed or captured every month. When the final BLA member, Twymon Meyers, was killed, in November 1973, Odinga realized he was on his own. "I had organized my immediate future with them in mind, but Zayd and them got killed before we were able to do much," he recalls. "That really stopped a lot of stuff."

Years later the FBI would allege that Odinga and Mutulu Shakur carried out a series of armed robberies during the late 1970s. What they never learned, Odinga says, was that his revolutionary expropriations actually began much earlier, after the BLA's collapse, in 1974. Odinga worked with his old friend Larry Mack and another black radical he declines to identify. "I couldn't even tell you how many there were," he says of the banks this group robbed. "At least ten before 1976. Connecticut, New Jersey, mostly New York. I remember 'expros' in Midtown [Manhattan], Long Island, Queens. I went back in twice to one in Queens. When the guard looked up and saw me for a second time, he just made this face and went, 'Oh no, not again.'"

This group "fell apart" in 1976, Odinga says, after his main partner decided to retire. It was then that he renewed his acquaintance with Mutulu Shakur. Odinga, several years older, had known him since Shakur was "thirteen or fourteen," Odinga says. "He would always come around. He liked my weed." When Shakur approached him about forming an underground group in 1976, Odinga had all but retired from robbing banks. He had apartments in Pittsburgh and New York and had opened a legitimate business, selling African jewelry with Zayd and Lumumba Shakur's father, who purchased their goods on trips to Africa. Odinga and Aba Shakur would drive south from New York, selling to shopkeepers, until reaching New Orleans, where they unfolded card tables on a street corner and sold what remained to tourists.

At first, Odinga recalls, he was skeptical about helping Mutulu Shakur rob anything. "Mutulu is a very good speaker, a good organizer," he recalls, "and I think that was what he was cut out to do. The military stuff, that wouldn't work out." So Odinga sat out Shakur's first robbery attempt, in late 1976. The target was in Pittsburgh, and while Odinga agreed to let Shakur use his apartment there as a staging area, he declined to take part. Instead Shakur recruited two friends from the Lincoln Detox crowd, Raymond Oliver and Chui Ferguson, an army veteran who had volunteered at Lincoln and now helped run a drug-rehabilitation clinic in Brooklyn. Ferguson, who suffered from back spasms, also happened to be one of Shakur's acupuncture patients.

So it was, on the cold morning of December 6, 1976, that a new underground group came into being. It didn't yet have a name, only a mission. After spending the night at Odinga's apartment, Shakur and his two partners drove their rental car into downtown Pittsburgh and parked a half block from the Mellon Bank. Pistols jammed inside their coats, Shakur and Ferguson took positions outside while Oliver lingered down the block. After ten minutes a truck from the Cauley Armored Car Service coasted to a stop in front of the bank. Inside the truck was $1.44 million in cash, proceeds from a Kaufmann's department store. When the two guards climbed out, Shakur and Ferguson drew their pistols.

At that point the robbery degenerated into black comedy. One of the guards fainted. The other followed orders and spread himself against the outer wall of the bank. They were just about to handcuff the two and rifle the truck when Ferguson, who had been suffering from back spasms all morning, was hit by another. For a moment he lost control of his arms and his gun went off. Before Shakur could do anything, a police car appeared. All three men panicked and ran. Ferguson made it only a few hundred feet before being felled by yet another back spasm. Oliver was tackled by a pair of detectives. Only Shakur escaped.*

This was hardly the auspicious debut Shakur had hoped for. Afterward he pestered Odinga to help him, and in time Odinga relented—to a point. "The idea was, we would each recruit four to nine or whatever crew members, who would help do things, and from time to time we would do things together," Odinga recalls. Each began with a single recruit. Odinga brought in Larry Mack, his old bank-robbing pal. Shakur recruited thirty-year-old Tyrone Rison, a onetime member of the Republic of New Afrika. A Vietnam vet who never lost his zeal for gunplay, Rison was a small man, five foot nine, earning him the nickname "Little Brother," sometimes shortened to "L.B."

Rison led an unremarkable life. He had a wife and children, lived in Queens's Rockaway neighborhood, and worked as a physical therapist. Still, hungry for action and wholly in agreement with Shakur's revolutionary patter, he eagerly signed up for the group's first expropriation. It came, of all places, at a meatpacking plant called the House o' Weenies on East 138th Street in the Bronx, three blocks south of Lincoln Hospital. On May 26, 1977, Odinga and Rison barged into the plant's business office, fired a few shots in the air, demanded and received an armload of cash, then dashed away, spilling bills behind them. Shakur, at Odinga's insistence, waited in the getaway car.

It was a start. For their next "action" Odinga identified a Citibank branch in the Westchester County suburb of Mount Vernon, just across the Bronx border. They cased the bank in detail. On October 19, Odinga and Mack burst inside, guns drawn, loudly announcing their intentions and ordering customers onto the floor. Running behind the teller cages, they relieved the cash drawers

---

*Both Ferguson and Oliver served brief prison sentences for their role in the aborted robbery. Neither gave Shakur's name to police.

of $13,800. Then Rison, who had been waiting outside in a gray getaway van with Shakur, scrambled inside and yelled, "Let's go!" It was their smoothest job yet.

At that point not much about their crimes was revolutionary. There were no communiqués, no money given to the poor, no rhetoric whatsoever, in fact, except what they uttered among themselves. The FBI didn't even know they existed. They were just stick-up men.

What transformed Mutulu Shakur's motley crew of mock revolutionaries from a collection of armed robbers happy to hold up a House o' Weenies into hard-core felons destined to commit the most outlandish crimes of the era was its incorporation of a small band of white radicals—all fleeing the wreckage of Weatherman and affiliated groups, all still ferociously committed to carrying out "the struggle," and all but a handful, as it happened, women.

This unlikely alliance began with Silvia Baraldini, the squat, prematurely gray radical who had risen from the Panther 21 defense committee to spearhead the Assata Shakur defense committee, assume a leadership position in the Prairie Fire Organizing Committee, and, after forcing its split in late 1976, co-found a new group, the May 19 Communist Organization.* May 19 began as a handful of women, no more than fifteen by Baraldini's estimate, most of them living in Brooklyn. Several, including the ex-Weathermen Judy Clark and Susan Rosenberg, had lingered on the fringes of the underground for years before joining the PFOC. After the split, "we went back to New York and we were kind of lost," Baraldini recalls. "We had never led organizations before. We were the rank and file. We had never done this. It took time to regroup."

Like Clayton Van Lydegraf and his Bay Area acolytes, a number of the May 19 women felt the seductive lure of the underground. It was Mutulu Shakur who made them see what a willing white woman could do for a black militant who couldn't afford to draw attention to himself. Baraldini and Shakur had known each other for years, but in 1977 their relationship began

---

*May 19 is the birthday of both Ho Chi Minh and Malcolm X.

to change. Shakur began dropping by her apartment late at night, talking revolutionary politics, sometimes taking her for drives; their discussion always turned to the need to lend a hand to oppressed African Americans.

"It started out with him asking me for small favors," Baraldini recalls. "I rented cars for him, I gave him money. They were little things, nothing really illegal. I perceived it as helping a friend."

Everything began to change one night in December 1977. Until that point Baraldini and the women of the May 19 Communist Organization, while committed to fighting racism and police brutality, hadn't done much of anything. That evening was ostensibly a Kwanzaa party, in someone's cramped Brooklyn apartment. But the true agenda revolved around a renowned radical the May 19 women had until recently known only by reputation: Marilyn Buck, famous in underground circles as the only white member of the BLA. It wasn't entirely accurate—the BLA didn't have any membership rolls—but in 1973 Buck had been convicted in a California federal court of illegally purchasing ammunition for the BLA, purportedly at the behest of Donald Cox, Eldridge Cleaver's aide-de-camp. An attractive brunette, Buck was a Texas minister's daughter who had emerged from SDS's University of Texas chapter. While like-minded peers joined Weatherman, she headed instead to San Francisco, where she fell in with the Black Panthers and, later, the BLA. To hard-core militants who snickered at "toilet bombers" like Bernardine Dohrn, Buck was the genuine item, brave, resourceful, and utterly committed to the cause. One FBI agent called her "the white Joanne Chesimard." "Marilyn was the queen," recalls Elizabeth Fink, who was at the Kwanzaa party that night. "She was the white girl—the white girl of the BLA."

The California court sentenced Buck to ten years and sent her to the federal women's prison in Alderson, West Virginia. In 1977, having served four years, she was granted a furlough and headed to New York, where she bunked with her lawyer, Susan Tipograph, and befriended Baraldini. By the night of the Kwanzaa party, word had spread through the radical women of May 19 that Buck had no intention of returning to prison.

"I remember the discussion that night: Should Marilyn go back?" Baraldini recalls. "Marilyn was firm: She wasn't going back. She needed protection. So some of us went along. We agreed to protect her. This was the first time any of us supported someone underground. That meant money, apartments, ID; we did all that for Marilyn. This was a very big deal. It was taking the step into the unknown, the point of no return. And it was one of the biggest mistakes we made. It eventually put the FBI onto us. She only had eighteen months [left in her sentence]. But we couldn't say no. This was Marilyn Buck. We couldn't say no."

Baraldini and her friends found Buck an apartment, the first of several she would use in the slums of East Orange, New Jersey. But Buck wanted more: She wanted to rejoin the underground. So Baraldini and Shakur arranged an introduction to the one man they all idolized, Sekou Odinga. "After Marilyn walked away from the joint," Odinga recalls, "she told people she wanted to get involved with the struggle again. They reached out to people, who reached out to me." They met at a hotel in the Washington, D.C., area. "We talked for about two or three hours," Odinga continues. "She wanted to plug in. She made that clear. She gave me her history, the things she had done for the BLA, her understanding of the struggle, especially the African struggle. I kind of grilled her. I probably treated her unfairly. Her thing was, 'Use me as you see fit.' I was pleased with her answers. She passed."

With the emergence of Baraldini and Buck, Odinga and Mutulu Shakur saw the potential for bigger and better things. They now had something the BLA hadn't had: an aboveground support network. They called it "the white edge." The group had no official name. Unofficially some began calling it "the Family."

As Mutulu Shakur's band of armed robbers in the Bronx grew in confidence through the early months of 1978, the investigations into the FALN were going nowhere. None of the jailed suspects would say a word. Worse, on January 23 a judge freed Maria Cueto and her assistant, Raisa Nemikin. In May several other suspects, including the Chicano activist Pedro Archuleta and the Rosado brothers, were released; they posed on the steps of the Federal Courthouse, clenched fists raised.

The FALN bombings, meanwhile, continued. On January 31, eight days after Cueto and Nemikin went free, two pipe bombs exploded in New York, one in a trash bin outside the Consolidated Edison building, the second beneath a police car five blocks north. No one was hurt; a caller took credit on behalf of the FALN. In the following days three more unexploded bombs were found, presumably intended to detonate along with the others. One was found by a group of boys in Harlem, who handed it to a passerby, who handed it to a construction worker, who helpfully disassembled it before handing it to a police officer.

Three months later came a more ambitious set of attacks: simultaneous actions in New York, Chicago, and Washington. The date was May 22. At 9:40 a.m. a pipe bomb exploded in a trash can in front of the Justice Department in Washington; no one was hurt. Twenty minutes later tiny Ping-Pong-ball incendiaries burst into flames at shops inside all three major New York–area airports, Newark, LaGuardia, and JFK. An hour later, in Chicago, a caller from the FALN phoned in bomb threats at O'Hare Airport and an adjacent hotel; no bombs were found.

FBI agents in all three cities scrambled to gather evidence and leads, but there was nothing to be learned. The FALN seemed able to strike anywhere, at any time, without interference. At the FBI offices on East Sixty-ninth Street, morale plunged to new lows. Then, after months without progress of any kind, things suddenly changed. It was a hot summer day, July 12, 1978. The call came from Queens.

Late that afternoon, in a fetid second-floor apartment on Ninety-sixth Street in the East Elmhurst section of Queens, the FALN's main bomb maker, Willie Morales, hunched over a workbench building his fourth device of the day, a pipe bomb. It consisted of a single stick of dynamite, wrapped in its original red paper, which Morales carefully slid into a sixteen-inch length of pipe, finishing the bomb by screwing on a metal cap. He worked alone, drops of sweat rolling down his sides in the heat, the only sounds the salsa music blaring from cars outside.

Morales was twenty-eight that day, a small, wiry man with unruly black curls. He liked to be called Guillermo. It had been eighteen months since his interview with FBI agents, who had dismissed him as a quiet, passive nobody. Like all his FALN brethren, he was an unlikely revolutionary. Morales had grown up in East Harlem and gone to college, earning a degree in film from the School of Visual Arts in Manhattan. He had worked a smattering of jobs: lab technician at the Department of Health, reading instructor at Public School 96, counselor for the Police Athletic League, lifeguard, even drug counselor in charge of referring addicts to drug treatment centers. Unlike the others, he wasn't sought by police and thus had never gone underground. For several years, until he'd recently been laid off, he was a ticket agent for Trans World Airlines, usually working at its 2 Penn Plaza office.

He had been working in this apartment for three months. Carlos Torres rented it for him. His only furniture was a thin cot by the front window, where he slept. It was a Hispanic neighborhood, where the pulsing rhythms of salsa and mariachi blared from car radios on those humid summer days. He fit in easily here; no one bothered him. In a rear closet he kept his materials: sixty-six sticks of dynamite, containers of black and smokeless gunpowder, plus sixty pounds of potassium chlorate, a chemical used in making explosives. Morales was especially adept at crafting the Ping-Pong-ball incendiaries the FALN liked to leave in Macy's and Gimbels. He had hundreds of balls. The closet also held two M1 carbines, a .45-caliber semiautomatic rifle, and a sawed-off shotgun.

As he worked Morales kept a homemade bomb-making manual beside him; its cover was adorned with the words IN THIS WE TRUST. Every bomb he made was exactly like its counterpart in the manual. Every single one detonated when the big hand on a wristwatch struck "9," just like the bombs Ron Fliegelman built for the Weather Underground. All three of the bombs he had built that day were set to explode, presumably intended to be taken to their locations that evening.

No one would ever figure out exactly what went wrong that sweltering day in the apartment on Ninety-sixth Street. What the FBI ultimately heard but could never confirm was that Torres had prepared the timer on that final pipe bomb and had made a mistake. The hour hand on the wristwatches had to be shaved smooth to insure proper detonation, and Torres, it was said, had whittled the wrong hand: not the hour hand but the minute hand. Thus when Morales set the bomb to go off in a matter of hours, he actually had only a matter of minutes.

At 5:20, as Morales was screwing the metal cap onto that last bomb, it exploded in his hands. The boom could be heard up and down the street. The blast blew off most of Morales's hands, sending his severed fingers zinging madly through the apartment. The metal cap he was holding rocketed into his chin, fracturing his jaw in at least five places, knocking out a number of teeth, ripping off his lips, and destroying his left eye; his face was a bloody mess. He must have been unconscious for a time, but if so, he quickly came to.

It was at that point, after realizing he was still alive, that Willie Morales did several amazing things. Despite having nine of his fingers blown off— only his left thumb remained intact—and despite having dreadful burns across his face, he still had the strength and presence of mind to gather an armload of FALN documents, which he somehow lugged into the bathroom and began trying to flush down the toilet. He left a trail of blood the whole way. When the bathroom door closed behind him, he had to fight to reopen it, as evidenced by the bloody stump marks he left on it.

Once the papers were flushed, Morales limped to the apartment door, locked it, then closed and locked each of the windows. Finally he went to the gas stove, blew out its pilot lights, and cranked the gas up to high—apparently twisting the knob with what remained of his mouth. Police sirens were already filling the air at that point. What Morales wanted, the FBI later surmised, was for the police to force their way into the apartment. Maybe an axe or a gun would do it, maybe the light switch. Whatever it was, he would need only the tiniest spark to ignite the gas spreading through the apartment. He was going to die, Morales suspected, but if so, he would take a dozen cops with him.

Firefighters were the first to arrive, stomping up the stairs in their heavy boots. They used an axe to crash through the door. Luckily, nothing produced the spark Morales had hoped it would. Immediately the firemen smelled the gas and saw the blood—blood everywhere. Waving their arms to dissipate the gas, they entered the apartment and stepped to the front windows to release it, which is when they found Morales sprawled, barely alive, on his cot. This was no ordinary explosion, the firefighters saw. This was a matter for the police.

Detectives from the NYPD's bomb squad were among the next to arrive, walking in as attendants carried Morales on a stretcher to a waiting ambulance. As yet no one had a clue who he was, nor could they tell at a glance. By the time paramedics began swathing his arms and upper body in bandages, Morales's head had swollen to the size of a basketball.

Don Wofford took the call a half hour after the blast; anytime anything blew up in New York City, the FBI agent got a call. He sent a half dozen agents to Queens, and one, Danny Scott, joined the NYPD's William Valentine at Elmhurst General Hospital, where they found Morales lying on a gurney wrapped in bandages, a bloody mummy. Valentine had been working FALN bombings for years. Studying the man's size and shape, he grabbed a tape measure and took his measurements. It was only a hunch, Valentine said, but he thought this might be Willie Morales.

After a bit Morales was able to mumble a few words. He told doctors his name was "William" and gave an address for his next of kin. Agent Scott drove to the address in East Harlem, the same building, he realized, to which he had tailed Puerto Rican activist Dylcia Pagan several times. Inside, he climbed the stairs and knocked on an apartment door. Pagan answered. Scott asked whether William was home.

"He's out visiting a relative," Pagan said. "Why?"

"Are you sure?"

"Yes, I'm sure, why? Is something wrong?"[4]

Scott explained about the man in the hospital. "We just wanted to be sure it wasn't your William," he said. Pagan turned pale. She said it couldn't be her William, but Scott could see that it was. Later that evening she appeared at the hospital. Morales was considerably more pleasant to her than he had been to Detective Valentine. Alluding to the bombed-out apartment, Valentine asked, "What happened in there?"

From beneath his bandages Morales managed a mumbled reply: "Fuck you. Fuck yourself."

Valentine just smiled. "Fuck me?"

"Fuck yourself."

"It's you that are fucked, pal," Valentine said. "You'll be wiping your ass with your elbows."[5]

Back at the apartment detectives and FBI agents busied themselves snapping photographs and combing through the debris. The bomb squad gingerly wrapped the three remaining pipe bombs in bomb blankets, then drove to a police range in the Bronx and detonated them in a pit. FBI agents fanned out to interview neighbors. All four of the wanted FALN members—Carlos and Haydee Torres, Oscar López and his companion, Lucy Rodriguez—were identified as visitors to the apartment.

Late that night, as agents and detectives continued studying the apartment on Ninety-sixth Street, Ping-Pong balls burst into flames at Macy's and a Korvette's store in Manhattan. The next day an FALN communiqué was delivered to the United Press office; it was identical to one found in the apartment. In the following days, as Morales was arraigned and indicted on explosives charges, the apartment began to yield an abundance of clues. One of the rifles had been reported stolen by a Chicano activist the FBI had been investigating in Denver. Best of all, the wreckage of Morales's workbench revealed a small Gestetner copier. It turned out to be the same machine Maria Cueto had purchased for the NCHA in September 1974, four months before the Fraunces Tavern bombing, and an FBI analysis indicated that it had been used to produce the five-star FALN logo atop the Fraunces communiqués.

At their desks on Sixty-ninth Street, Don Wofford and Lou Vizi felt that the pieces were finally coming together. They searched Pagan's apartment, found some FALN literature, and had her brought before the grand jury to provide fingerprints and voice samples. Pagan got the subpoena suspended after claiming she was pregnant with Morales's child, as in fact she was. She would give birth the following spring.

As the investigation progressed, Morales was shuttled among Kings County Hospital, the Rikers Island jail, and Bellevue Hospital. Claiming he was a prisoner of war, he refused to say much more than "fuck you" to detectives. Three radical lawyers took his case, and they peppered a judge with all manner of motions, including a request that Morales be treated according to the Geneva Convention, then "turned over to military authorities" and "removed to a neutral country." They complained incessantly about the quality of his care, saying he had been denied the right to artificial limbs. Hospital officials insisted they planned to make them once he was healthy. Finally, in January 1979, Morales's attorneys filed their most unusual challenge. In a lawsuit they alleged that police had "illegally confiscated" his severed fingers. The police had taken the fingers as evidence. Morales complained that they should have been sewed back on.

All through 1978, as Mutulu Shakur's band of revolutionary bank robbers added new members and ambitions, Shakur's base at Lincoln Detox in the South Bronx came under increasing pressure from city regulators. The trouble had been building for years. The city's Addiction Services Agency (ASA), which nominally ran the clinic, had cut off all funding in 1973 when Detox refused to provide census data or treatment records to justify it. But the clinic still received money from a separate city agency, the Health and Hospitals Corporation (HHC). Thus one agency, ASA, had oversight but no leverage to enforce it, and a second, HHC, handed over money with little supervision. Neither had the power to rein in the clinic's director, Luis Surita, who found it easy to strong-arm both agencies even when improprieties surfaced.

And surface they did. A 1973 ASA audit found that Detox was treating barely half the number of drug addicts its contract specified. Another noted that its treatments were four times more expensive than those at other city clinics. An HHC review in 1976 found nearly $1 million in unsubstantiated payroll, along with phenomenal absentee rates among staff members, as high as 71 percent in some cases; only half of forty-five paid staffers were on duty one day when HHS auditors arrived. The staff, meanwhile, charged the clinics for thousands of dollars of personal phone calls. In 1977, when HHC demanded the clinic's personnel records, it simply refused, claiming the records were private. That December, when a federal grand jury investigating kickback schemes subpoenaed records on thirty-six patients, one of the clinic's doctors refused and moved to quash the subpoena.

As New York City sagged into the worst fiscal crisis in its history, neither its beleaguered mayor, Abe Beame, nor any of his subordinates could summon the will to do battle with the clinic's angry radicals, who increasingly operated as an independent entity unanswerable to any authority. Every year or two either ASA or HHC would make noises about evicting Detox from the hospital. Time and again the staff organized angry protests in response. In the worst, in 1975, a group of Detox staffers stormed HHC's downtown Manhattan offices and barricaded themselves inside while they smashed furniture and windows in the president's anteroom. After that HHC officials appeared notably reluctant to confront the clinic.

That attitude disappeared abruptly in January 1978, when New York welcomed a new mayor, the feisty Ed Koch, who was sick and tired of radicals abusing city resources. Teamed with a media-friendly assemblyman named Charles Schumer (later the New York senator), Koch was unafraid of the denizens of Lincoln Detox and determined to put them out of business. "Hospitals are for sick people, not thugs," he groused in the *Times*. Detox officials, the mayor recalled years later, "ran it like Che Guevara was their patron saint, with his pictures all over the wall. It wasn't a hospital. It was a radical cell." The clinic's leaders, including Shakur, were determined to fight. When city officials called a meeting to discuss closing the clinic, one staffer declared, "I don't work for you. I work for the people of the South Bronx." When HHS officials told Surita that it intended to evict Detox from Lincoln Hospital, Surita retorted, "War is declared—cold war for now."[6]

For all the bravado, Koch smashed Lincoln Detox like a clove of garlic. As night fell on November 28, 1978, he had HHC's president, Joseph Lynaugh, summon Surita, Shakur, and ten other staffers to his downtown office at 125 Worth Street. When Shakur attempted to explain that the clinic was run by a socialist collective, Lynaugh cut him off. Almost everyone in attendance was being reassigned, Lynaugh announced, except for Surita; Lynaugh fired him on the spot. As the president spoke, the second part of Koch's plan was unfurling in the Bronx. A large group of uniformed police officers surrounded Lincoln Hospital and blocked every exit but that of the emergency room. Determined to physically evict the staff, they came armed with wire cutters, sledgehammers, and crowbars.

At 8:00 p.m., his meeting completed, Lynaugh appeared among the officers. Flanked by the mayor's press secretary and sundry other city officials, he ordered the two dozen Detox staffers on duty that night to leave immediately. Outnumbered, they complied. The Young Lord leader Mickey Melendez trudged out carrying a basket of personal items. Mutulu Shakur drove up at one point and, seeing that resistance was futile, boiled in anger. The clinic was closed, then reopened under a new name and under strict city control several blocks away. Shakur quit. A number of staffers sued, to no effect. Lincoln Detox's days as a radical haven were over.

Shakur found himself without a job, but where his fellow staffers lined up outside unemployment offices, he turned to area banks. The gang he had formed with Sekou Odinga had carried out only one armed robbery in the previous year, at a Chase Manhattan branch in Greenwich Village, but in the wake of Lincoln Detox's closing both the frequency and ambition of these "actions" would rise sharply. It was then that Shakur's "white edge"—Marilyn Buck and Silvia Baraldini—began to play significant roles in the group's bank robberies.

"There was an acceleration, yes," remembers Baraldini. "You know, when you showed you were willing to go to the next level, the requests never stop. What help you could give, you give it. It was hard to say no. For me, the eureka moment was one day [Mutulu] said, you need to be at a certain corner, you open the trunk and put us in and drive away. I don't remember the corner, the car, or even the year. I was scared shitless. But I did it. That was when I realized this was not just renting cars. This was when I realized what he was doing." It was around that point, Baraldini says, that she asked her May 19 comrades, Judy Clark and Susan Rosenberg, to help out. Both agreed.

"First we did very precise things that were useful, and we did them because we were white," Baraldini continues. "Cars, research. The most important thing was ID. We could buy the special cameras necessary to make it. We could do that with ease, and we did. A white girl like me does that, and no one looks twice. But a black man?"

Thirty-five years later, asked why she joined Shakur and Odinga in their bank robberies, Baraldini folds her hands and heaves a deep sigh. "We had developed a whole political vision of the U.S., how change would come to the U.S., that this involved the blacks getting their own nation. We thought we were helping people to promote that vision. It's unrealistic, yes, but we believed it. Also, I felt we were rectifying a long history of white people using black people in the U.S., going back to the Civil War. We really thought we were redressing that in some way. That was very important to us, too. There was also a question of resources. They were going to use the money to help the black community, and they did. Or at least I thought they did."

"Sounds crazy, right?" asks Elizabeth Fink. "Let me tell you, it was crazy then, too. These people, Judy and Silvia, they were driven crazy by their commitment to the blacks. It was like a cult. The question was, how crazy could you be?"

At first only Buck took part in the actual robberies. The first took place at the Livingston Mall in suburban New Jersey, a half hour west of the Holland Tunnel. On December 19, 1978, three weeks after Lincoln Detox's closing, Shakur and the gang's three other gunmen drove into the mall parking lot in a stolen Chevrolet Caprice station wagon. Buck followed in a gray van she had rented in the adjacent town of Millburn. Around 10:00 a.m. Odinga and Shakur wandered into the Bamberger's department store; Shakur was wearing a long black leather coat that concealed a walkie-talkie. A saleswoman noticed him strolling through boys' wear, seemingly talking to himself. Odinga, meanwhile, nosed through infant apparel. At one point he approached a saleslady and pleasantly asked, "What size does a seven-year-old wear?"

At about 10:15 a Coin Deposit Corporation armored car pulled up outside the store. Two armed guards emerged, one rolling a hand truck. Inside the store, Shakur, Odinga, and Larry Mack followed as the guards ascended an escalator toward the second-floor business office. Once the guards disappeared into the office, however, Mack became nervous and began edging away. Shakur was trying to lure him back when the guards reemerged, a brown duffel bag piled onto the hand truck. Odinga pulled his pistol and shouted, "This is a holdup! Nobody moves!"

One guard went for his gun but stopped when Shakur ran toward him, waving a pistol of his own. "On the floor! On the floor!" Shakur shouted. Both guards complied. At that point Larry Mack began walking toward the escalator. "Come back here!" Shakur shouted at Mack. "Come back here now!" Mack stepped back for a moment, then ran down the escalator all the way to the getaway car, where Tyrone Rison was waiting. When their two comrades didn't reappear after several minutes, Rison forced Mack to scramble back inside to see what was wrong. He found Shakur and Odinga hunched over the two prone guards, trying in vain to get handcuffs around their ankles. The cuffs were too small.

They left the guards as they were, then pushed the hand truck down the escalator and out to the car. In the duffel bag was $200,000 in cash. Rison drove to a rendezvous point, abandoning the stolen car, and the four men climbed into Marilyn Buck's waiting van, which had been legitimately rented and thus was unlikely to draw the attention of pursuing police. Buck drove them back across the George Washington Bridge to a safe-house apartment they had rented just over the Bronx border in the suburb of Mount Vernon. It was their smoothest and by far most lucrative robbery to date, and Buck had acquitted herself with aplomb.

The Family was ready for bigger things. Marilyn Buck, having spent time in prison herself, had a special affinity for those behind bars. That fall she drew up a list of underground figures they might help escape. At the top of the list was none other than Willie Morales, who went on trial in a Queens courtroom in early 1979. Found guilty, he appeared for sentencing April 20. An unruly crowd, packed with policemen, FBI agents, and dozens of Puerto Rican, black, and white radicals, jammed the courtroom. Shoving matches broke out. The NYPD's William Valentine escorted Morales out of the courtroom. At one point Morales looked Valentine in the eye and said, "You're a dead man."

Morales was taken to Bellevue, where he was given a cell in the third-floor prison ward as he waited for doctors to finally install the artificial hands he had been demanding. Ahead stretched years, maybe decades, behind bars. To all appearances, Willie Morales's career as a Puerto Rican revolutionary tilting against the imperialist *yanquis* was over. In fact, it was only beginning.

21

JAILBREAKS AND CAPTURES

The Family and the FALN, 1979–80

Even today, more than thirty-five years later, no one outside the FALN or the Family knows precisely how they did it or even who took part. But the planning, it was clear, had taken weeks, and few of the policemen and FBI agents who later investigated the plot to rescue Willie Morales had any doubt that it was spearheaded by Marilyn Buck, Sekou Odinga, and the FALN. Silvia Baraldini, while declining to discuss details, confirms that she received a "formal" request for aid from the FALN. "We were asked to do this one aspect, to bring in the tools," she says. "We were white, and women, so of course we could do this on our own. And we did."

Another key participant, it's been suggested, was the radical attorney Susan Tipograph, who represented not only Marilyn Buck but Willie Morales. Tipograph, it should be emphasized, was never charged in the case and has always denied any involvement. But prosecutors would later file affidavits that would strongly imply that it was she who smuggled the wire cutters to Morales.

At the time, May 1979, Morales was being held in the third-floor prison ward at Bellevue Hospital in Manhattan. Tipograph visited regularly. All visitors were required to be searched, but as federal prosecutors noted in a court filing four years later, "Tipograph became increasingly vehement that the attorney-client privilege protected her from a search by correction officers. On one occasion, when correction officers denied her request to be exempted from a search, she surrendered a knife only after repeated questioning."

According to prosecutors, on the evening of Friday, May 18, Tipograph arrived on the third floor and again objected when officers asked to search her. This time, for whatever reason, they relented. She was not searched, nor was her bag, nor was she made to walk through a metal detector. Somehow, at some point after this visit, Morales came into possession of a fourteen-inch pair of wire cutters. He hid them with the assistance of another prisoner, who helped him tie a series of shoelaces around his waist. To this he attached a small hook. When Morales placed the wire cutters on the hook, they dangled between his legs, unnoticeable under his bathrobe.

Over the next two nights Morales, working only with the stumps of his hands, used the wire cutters to clip through the wire of the metal grate that covered his cell window. None of the six guards saw or heard a thing as he worked. Then, at 2:30 a.m. on May 21, a Monday, Morales asked to go to the bathroom. The officer responsible for him, Thomas Ryan, led him to the toilet and back. At some point after that, Morales finished cutting a one-foot-square hole in his window grate. Then he raised the window and punched out its screen.

Forty feet below, stationed at positions up and down a courtyard that stretched along the building, stood several members of the Family, perhaps as many as a dozen. The only one who ever confirmed his involvement, in a later interview with the FBI, was Tyrone Rison, the Vietnam veteran known as "L.B.," who said he guarded one end of the alley with an assault rifle. Marilyn Buck was almost certainly there. They had a ladder and placed it against the redbrick wall beneath Morales's window.

By that point Morales had unfurled a ten-foot-long, flesh-colored bandage, tied one end to his bed, and tossed the other end out into the cool night air. It wouldn't reach down to the ladder, but it was the best Morales could muster. Somehow he wriggled through the hole he had cut. Then—and this was the part that flummoxed everyone afterward—the man with no fingers used the bandage as a rope to lower himself down the side of the building. He had wet the bandage to strengthen it, but in a matter of moments it snapped. FBI agents later surmised that he fell twenty feet onto a window-mounted air-conditioning unit below, which showed a sizable dent afterward; Morales would later blame the fall for minor kidney damage he suffered. He landed on the dewy grass below, leaving two deep footprints in the turf.

No one had heard or seen a thing; Officer Ryan, his supervisors later alleged, slept through the entire escape. One imagines that Morales exchanged a series of quick, elated hugs with his rescuers, who quickly slid him into a waiting car. By the time guards finally noticed his disappearance, an hour after dawn, Willie Morales was safely tucked away inside Marilyn Buck's small safe-house apartment in East Orange, New Jersey, an hour's drive west, eager to rejoin his comrades in the FALN.*

From the FBI's Sixty-ninth Street offices to City Hall to the Department of Correction, official New York was thunderstruck by the brazen escape. HANDLESS TERRORIST ESCAPES, proclaimed the *Post* headline. How on earth had a one-eyed man with no hands managed to cut his way out of a cell and shimmy down the side of a building? How had he gotten the wire cutters? Above all, why hadn't anyone noticed? Below Morales's window police found a broken stretch of bandage, a pair of hospital slippers, and Morales's glasses. The wire cutters had been left on the floor of the cell. As officers fanned out across the city in a fruitless manhunt, the city's corrections commissioner, William J. Ciuros Jr., stepped before the microphones at City Hall, admitted "there was sloppiness on our part," and announced that Officer Ryan was

---

*Officer Ryan would later claim that he looked in on Morales at 7:00 a.m. and saw "a form" in his bed. The disappearance would be discovered a half hour later, leading police to speculate that Morales had escaped during that half-hour window of time. This is highly unlikely.

being suspended for "negligence in permitting the escape." Three months later Ciuros himself and several of his aides were fired.

All day the escape was the talk of New York. Pete Hamill of the *Daily News* interviewed a dozen Puerto Ricans attending a prizefight at Madison Square Garden that night. "The guy had no hands, and he gets out of the third floor? Hey, if I had no hands, I couldn't even get breakfast, and Morales got out of the third floor at Bellevue?" a man named Pablo Miranda said. "He oughta get a medal, man. [You know] someone was downstairs with a car, man. The guy's in a bathrobe, he can't get on the IRT." A buddy chimed in, "Yeah, imagine a P.R. tryin' to get in a cab at 3 o'clock in the morning—in a bathrobe?"

"He'd have no legs, man," Miranda yelped. "Cabby'd run him right over, man."[1]

Even before Morales was whisked to safety, the Family had begun planning its next jailbreak. Their target this time was a woman they all admired, who personified the black struggle and had been behind bars now for six long years: Assata Shakur, better known as the "heart and soul" of the Black Liberation Army, Joanne Chesimard.

Her fame had only grown since the night she was captured on the New Jersey Turnpike. Most of the May 19 women, from Judy Clark to Susan Rosenberg, had demonstrated outside her trials. Between 1973 and 1977 there had been an amazing seven of them in all, from bank and bar robberies to an attempted-murder charge for one of the BLA's police shootings. With so few witnesses, six ended in dismissal or acquittal. Throughout, Chesimard proved a passionate defendant, shouting at judges and frequently being dragged from courtrooms. And it was her passion, in a way, that allowed her to stave off convictions. In the first proceeding, her trial for murdering New Jersey trooper Werner Foerster during her 1973 capture, she was granted a mistrial after becoming pregnant. The father was another BLA member, Fred Hilton, and it was said the child was conceived in a holding cell during one of the trials; for years afterward retired officers would tell fanciful tales of having watched the two having sex. She later gave birth to a baby girl. Chesimard was tried for Foerster's murder a second time, in New Brunswick, New Jersey, in 1977, in a trial marked by protests for which Silvia Baraldini served as spokesperson. She was found guilty on March 25, and given a life sentence.

In early 1979, when the Family began planning her escape, Chesimard was being held at a women's prison in New Jersey. To free her, and to raise money they hoped to give her to escape the country, they decided on another robbery, their first since the heist at the Livingston Mall nine months earlier. The robbery they staged at New Jersey's Paramus Mall on September 11, in fact, was a carbon copy of the earlier raid: another Bamberger's store, another pair of armored-car guards, another getaway van driven by Marilyn Buck. The car they used, a Ford Fairmont, was provided by the onetime Weatherman Kathy Boudin, who was working at a rental agency in midtown Manhattan; it was Boudin's first known work with the group. The robbery went smoothly enough, save for a guard they had to punch and a pistol that misfired, and in a matter of minutes they were safely inside a van Buck was driving toward the safety of Manhattan. The take came to $105,000.

They were ready.

From the beginning this was Sekou Odinga's job. He and Chesimard were close; he doesn't deny a suggestion that they had once been lovers. "I loved her, let's put it that way," he says quietly. "She was one of our heroes." The escape idea, he says, came from Chesimard herself, who sent a message through friends. Odinga drove to the prison and, though a wanted man himself, boldly walked in and visited her.

The setting, Odinga could see at a glimpse, was ideal. The Clinton Correctional Facility for Women sprawled across a rise among the green hills of rural western New Jersey, fifteen miles from the Pennsylvania border. The prison might be taken for a forlorn community college; there were no outer walls or fencing. Only one dormitory, the squat, yellow-brick South Hall, housed maximum-security prisoners, and only seventeen of those. It alone was surrounded by a fifteen-foot chain-link fence, topped by two feet of barbed wire.

"They took their security for granted," Odinga recalls. "They didn't even search people. They had metal detectors, but they never turned 'em on or used 'em. I just walked in and signed my [false] name. I saw her and said, 'Baby sis, so good to see you, when you coming home?'" In whispered conversations they discussed the possibility of an escape attempt. "Marighella used to say a good revolutionary has to be audacious: 'If you think it can be done, given the right circumstances, you can probably do it,'" Odinga says. "She thought it could be done. I thought so, too, for the simple reason that it was clear [the authorities] weren't thinking of it at all."

The autumn sky was a bright and cloudless blue as Odinga stepped out of his car at the front gate the morning of November 2, 1979. The reception area was a trailer at the entrance. Inside, Odinga signed the register. A guard checked his name against a list of visitors Chesimard had approved; he was waved through. There were no metal detectors. No one searched him. No one noticed the .357 Magnum nestled against the small of his back. Standing behind the trailer, Odinga waited a few minutes before a van arrived to ferry him to South Hall. Behind the wheel was thirty-one-year-old Stephen Ravettina. With a nod, Odinga slid into the passenger seat, and Ravettina drove him through the grounds.

At South Hall the only guard on duty, sitting in a glass booth inside the door, was an elderly matron named Helen Anderson. A kindly woman with a heart condition, she was known to inmates as "Mama A." She buzzed Odinga through a metal door into the visiting room. Inside Odinga hugged Chesimard and slid her the pistol.

After leaving Odinga, Stephen Ravettina climbed back into his van. His radio squawked. "Rav, there's more visitors at the gate for South Hall," a guard reported. Ravettina drove back to the trailer, where he saw two young black men standing outside, waiting. He stepped out and talked to one of the guards as the two men slid into the van, one taking the passenger seat, the other a seat behind. After a moment Ravettina hopped behind the wheel and began the return drive to South Hall. As they reached its fence, the man in the passenger seat, one of Mutulu Shakur's men, Mtayari Sundiata, produced a pistol and pressed it against Ravettina's head. When Ravettina glanced at his radio, Sundiata said coolly, "You don't wanna do that."

The two groups—Odinga and Chesimard inside, the others outside—approached a bewildered Helen Anderson at about the same time. "She wouldn't open the door," Odinga recalls. "I had a .357 Magnum, which would've shot right through that glass, or most of it. I had armor-piercing bullets, too. But what I did was just put a stick of dynamite on the window where she was sitting. Then it was just a matter of convincing her it was to her benefit to open these doors and live through the day, which is how I put it. She did, after talking with Assata a moment. Assata told her, 'We will do nothing to hurt you.' Once she was convinced, she let us out."

When Stephen Ravettina stepped inside, two guns at his back, he came face-to-face with Chesimard, brandishing a .357 Magnum, and Odinga behind her. Someone produced a set of handcuffs and cuffed Ravettina and Anderson together. "Come on, move it," one of the men said, and the little group, now numbering four black militants and their two hostages, walked outside and climbed into the van.

A new face, Winston Patterson, took the wheel. He had been hastily recruited the night before. The hostages later said Patterson was by far the most nervous of the group. As he drove away from South Hall, Patterson took a wrong turn into a dead end beside a prison building, forcing Chesimard to show him the way. The van backed up, then circled through a parking lot and bumped straight onto a grassy knoll, hitting the grass so hard "Mama A" hopped in her seat. When she shot a look at Ravettina, he whispered, "Shut up and be cool." Driving down the far side of the knoll, the van met a service road.

"Watch out for state police cars," Ravettina volunteered. "If the state police see this van, they'll blow it to smithereens."

Not a soul noticed the hurried escape. A minute later Patterson turned the van into a parking lot for the adjacent Hunterdon State School for the developmentally challenged. Odinga had two cars waiting, a blue compact and a white Lincoln Continental. Marilyn Buck emerged from one car, and the group began furiously opening trunks and changing license plates. As they did, Mutulu Shakur drove up in a blue van. Ravettina managed to see three digits on one license plate. He stopped looking when one of the black men pointed a gun his way. "Get down," he said. After a moment everyone leaped into the cars and sped off, leaving "Mama A" and Ravettina cuffed in the van.

"The waiting part was scary enough," recalls Silvia Baraldini, who was driving the Lincoln. "The thing I remember—like it was a film, like pictures— was the white van approaching. Driving over, they took a wrong turn and had to turn around. Then it all went very quickly. They came, they got out, we opened trunks and changed cars and drove off. It all went very quickly. It had to. What I remember is looking back at the white van and seeing what the FBI later called 'the two hostages' poking up their heads and peering out at us as we drove off. I'll never forget the looks on their faces."

Chesimard and Odinga curled inside the Lincoln's trunk. As Baraldini drove east toward Manhattan, she was startled to see state police cruisers screaming past, lights rolling. "I had a gun between my legs, a pistol, an automatic," she recalls. "I saw police everywhere. I watched one take a U-turn and drive back to the prison. And you know, what I thought was 'God, give me the strength to shoot if I have to.' Because I had never shot anybody. But if they stopped us and went for the trunk, I would have to shoot. I said I would. I kept thinking, 'I have to do this, I have to.'"

Back at the prison, Ravettina and "Mama A" had spread the alarm. Phone calls went out to State Police Headquarters in Trenton. Across the state, troopers stopped what they were doing and sped toward the prison. Within an hour roadblocks began going up. But it was too late. Baraldini says she dropped off Odinga and Chesimard at a parking garage in suburban New Jersey, and by the time the roadblocks went up, Chesimard had been deposited inside a dingy safe-house apartment in East Orange. The three vehicles were last seen speeding east, and by nightfall they had vanished. They had done it: In barely ten minutes, without attracting the notice of a single outside guard, the Family had rescued the most notorious female revolutionary of the decade.

The mood inside the apartment was jubilant. Buck took Chesimard's photo and dummied up a new driver's license. They gave her $50,000, half the proceeds of the Paramus Mall robbery, and offered the choice of fleeing to

Libya, China, Angola, or Cuba or remaining in the United States. Two nights later, with the state police canvassing the state in search of them, Chesimard folded herself into a car trunk. Buck and Shakur drove her west into Pennsylvania, where that night they reached an apartment building in the run-down East Liberty section of Pittsburgh. Chesimard would live there for the next nine months, until August 1980, when, according to later court testimony, she boarded a plane that landed in the Bahamas, from where she eventually made her way to the safety of Fidel Castro's Cuba. Today Odinga denies this. "There were lots of ways to get her out," he muses. "Mexico was always good."

The escape was front-page news across the country. Caught unawares, the FBI had no idea who might be involved. Sketches were drawn up of four suspects, a series of apartments were raided in Brooklyn and the Bronx, but the FBI found nothing.

After lying fallow for much of the previous year—a bid to avoid inflaming the Willie Morales proceedings, authorities speculated—the FALN sprang back to life that fall of 1979, initiating what proved to be the most harrowing period in its history. Much later authorities would gain the cooperation of one of its newer members, Freddie Mendez, who would provide a unique glimpse into the FALN's shadowy world during this time. Mendez was a twenty-seven-year-old Chicagoan who had belonged to several aboveground Puerto Rican independence groups. He would eventually enter the federal witness protection program, where retired agents say he remains to this day.

By the time the FALN's leader, Oscar López, recruited Mendez in 1979, the group's dozen or so members were scattered through at least six safe houses, including three flats in Chicago. Its East Coast headquarters was apartment 4D in a grim building at 2685 Kennedy Boulevard in Jersey City, New Jersey. There López's number two man, Carlos Torres, now atop the FBI's Most Wanted Fugitives list, lived with his wife, Haydee, and their toddler. López himself, along with his companion, Lucy Rodriguez, and the disfigured Morales, was living in a shambling house in a black neighborhood north of downtown Milwaukee.

The Milwaukee house served as the FALN's nerve center. López had dozens of ideas for actions, and the arrival of Morales seems to have inspired him to enact them all at once. A Patty Hearst–style kidnapping had long been under consideration; López compiled dossiers on myriad American millionaires and their families, including the oil-rich Hunts of Dallas and the Rockefellers. The 1980 presidential campaign was under way, and he was examining not only raids on various campaign offices but bombings at the Republican National Convention in Detroit that summer and the Democratic convention at Madison Square Garden; Torres had scouted the Garden, drawing maps of where bombs could be placed. López had more prosaic plans as well. There was always a need for money and guns.

The portrait Freddie Mendez later painted of the FALN was of a tightly knit, disciplined guerrilla cell, notably more professional than its 1970s-era peers. Its five fugitive members appeared to live off donations from the militant Chicago Puerto Rican community, plus the odd robbery; the others held jobs. Among themselves they used code names, dead drops, and explosives manuals. During planning sessions everyone wore pillowcases with eye slits, giving the gatherings an eerie, Klanlike feel. In the dirt-floor basement of the Milwaukee house they devised a firing range, hung a chalkboard to diagram actions, and built an elaborate explosives workshop, where Mendez learned to assemble bombs using the same design Ron Fliegelman had pioneered for Weatherman nine years earlier: a screw in the face of an alarm clock, detonated when the minute hand struck the screw at "9."

Professional methods, however, didn't ensure success, as Mendez discovered on his first mission, on October 17, 1979. He and onetime Tuley High student Dickie Jimenez were tasked with planting a bomb in the Democratic Party offices at the Bismarck Hotel in downtown Chicago. Carrying the bomb in a leather valise, they entered wearing suits and false mustaches—an FALN trademark. Posing as college students, they asked the receptionist for campaign literature, and Jimenez asked to use the washroom. The receptionist refused, saying it was only for staff, and that was that. They left, declaring the mission a failure.

Their first successful attack that fall came a month later: the bombing of three military offices in Chicago on the night of November 23. Explosions damaged washrooms at two recruiting stations, for the army and the marines, and blew off a metal door at the Illinois Naval Reserve armory. No one was hurt; a caller cited the U.S. Navy's use of its base on the Puerto Rican island of Vieques as a test-bombing site.

López was just getting warmed up. A month later he engineered a robbery that kept the FALN in funds for months. That morning a twenty-eight-year-old Purolator armored-car driver named Michael Arnold was walking out of the Pick 'n Save Warehouse Foods store on Milwaukee's Forest Home Avenue, having just retrieved the store's deposits, when a Hispanic man dressed as a mailman approached him in the lobby and jabbed a gun into his ribs. Arnold was guided into a restroom, where four other men were waiting, then handcuffed to a stall door. The robbers made off with the Pick 'n Save deposits, described only as "in five figures"; afterward police had no sense that the FALN was involved, though an article in the *Milwaukee Journal* described it as "the largest and best-planned robbery of the year."[*2]

López struck again three weeks later. Everyone gathered at the Milwaukee house on January 13, 1980, as Carlos Torres stood before the basement chalkboard and named their target: the Wisconsin National Guard Armory in Oak Creek, south of Milwaukee. The armory contained automatic weapons and bazookas that would keep the FALN in guns and ammunition for months, if not years. It also held explosives, allowing López to replace the old, sweating dynamite they had only belatedly realized was unstable; at one point, when Mendez was shown a bomb, one of the women pushed him away, telling him it might go off. They were expecting the raid to be child's play; Torres, who had scouted the building, said there was rarely more than one officer on duty. Six FALN members dressed in battle fatigues drove up outside the armory the next morning. The three women rushed inside first, only to find the lobby empty. Whether by accident or an effort to announce their presence, someone fired a shot. An officer on duty, Lieutenant Lawrence

---

*Police did say they suspected that the man in the mailman disguise was probably the same "mailman" seen loitering outside a neighborhood bank the week before. The man had been reported to police, bizarrely, after a woman noticed he was wearing high-heeled shoes.

Gonzales, emerged from his office just as López and the others charged inside.

Torres put a gun to Gonzales's head and demanded he show them the weapons room and turn over the combination. Gonzales led them to the room but said he didn't know the lock's combination; none of his keys fit. As they struggled with the lock, López circled outside the building, where he was startled to see a janitor hanging out a bathroom window, trying to call for help. "Get your ass back in there or I'll blow your head off," López shouted, waving a gun.

Inside, the door still would not budge. Gonzales tried to tell them the guns didn't have firing mechanisms anyway, as a safety measure; those were stored at a nearby police station. Torres wouldn't listen. In desperation he and López took a fire axe and hacked at the door for the better part of an hour. It wouldn't break. Finally, incensed, López took a rifle and some explosives manuals and stalked out.

No one knew that the FALN was behind the botched raid. Its failure did nothing to dissuade Oscar López. His next move, in fact, turned out to be the group's most ambitious to date. It happened on the morning of Saturday, March 15, 1980, two months after the Oak Creek raid. A few minutes after 9:00 three men and a woman dressed in ski parkas—their identities were never revealed—walked into an office building on Fifty-ninth Street in Midtown Manhattan, just off Park Avenue. Ignored by security guards, they headed to the elevators, pressed "9," and a few moments later emerged outside offices housing the New York City campaign headquarters of the Republican presidential candidate George Bush, who was locked in a primary duel with Ronald Reagan. Bush had just won Puerto Rico's first-ever primary, a development that radicals believed brought it one step closer to statehood.

The doors were locked. All four whipped pistols from their parkas, then slid pillowcases with eye slits over their heads. When the first worker arrived, a few minutes later, they pointed a pistol at him and demanded a key. He didn't have one. They bound his hands with tape. One by one, six more workers strode off the elevators, none with a key, and were tied up. "When I got off the elevator, there were two people standing with masks over their heads and pointing guns at me," one volunteer said later. "'Don't say anything, nobody will get hurt,' they said. I asked if this was some kind of joke. They said, 'This is a political action.'"

When a senior staffer finally arrived with a key, the raiders split into pairs, one remaining by the elevators while the second shoved the volunteers into the office. Inside, one of the masked men demanded a set of voter-registration lists. He was told they weren't available. Irked, the two raiders then spent ten minutes spray-painting FALN slogans on the office walls. One read simply, FALN. Another read, STATEHOOD MEANS DEATH. Afterward they fled.

Meanwhile, in Chicago, Oscar López and a three-person team wearing ski masks burst into the two-story Illinois headquarters of the Carter-Mondale campaign. "This is an armed takeover!" he shouted, brandishing a shotgun. They herded three volunteers into a corner, bound them with tape, then ransacked the office, ripping out telephones and spray-painting slogans on the walls. They repeated the process on the floor above before running out. No one was hurt. This time they found the voter lists. A few days later letters were mailed to 150 delegates; each contained veiled threats should Puerto Rico be made a state. Other delegates reported threatening phone calls. In one, the caller hung up after muttering, "Watch out for the bomb."

The raids were front-page news. The FBI did all the things it was supposed to do but once again found little to pursue. Its investigation to date, just about everyone admitted, had been a dismal failure: the defeats at every conceivable grand jury, interviewing and failing to arrest Carlos Torres and Willie Morales, Morales's escape. In New York supervisors came and went; none made any real difference. Lou Vizi, who had been at Fraunces Tavern, gave up, accepting a transfer to a robbery squad. Eventually his partner, Don Wofford, gave up, too.

The FALN was a ghost. "I can remember very clearly the feeling at that point," a retired FBI man recalls. "There was a sense that these guys might go on doing this, the bombings, literally forever."

On Thursday, April 3, 1980, Oscar López gathered his people in front of the basement chalkboard at the Milwaukee house. Everyone was there, including the New Yorkers, Carlos and Haydee Torres, even Dylcia Pagan, the activist dating Willie Morales. Their target was an armored car, and López went over the robbery and the escape plans in detail. It was the beginning of Easter weekend. The cops, he said, would be half-asleep.

The next morning Freddie Mendez joined the others donning their disguises. Most dressed in jogging suits, intending to masquerade as runners and college students. On the way out López opened a large box packed with weapons: rifles, handguns, knives, smoke grenades. Everyone took something. Mendez joined a group filing into a stolen van. López and the others jumped into waiting cars. Everyone headed south toward Chicago.

The action began a few minutes after one. A man and a woman stormed into a Budget rental-car office in Evanston, the leafy city where the campus of Northwestern University stretches along Lake Michigan. "Everybody down!" the man shouted. A dozen agents and customers, including a man with his nine-year-old son, were inside, and it took several minutes to tie them up. "Don't cry," the father told his son. "Just pray." Within minutes the robbers were gone, driving off in a Budget panel truck.

At 1:40, after one of the agents struggled free and called the police, descriptions of the pair and the stolen truck were broadcast across the area. At Northwestern, where the campus police were accustomed to helping out local officers, a dispatcher quickly rebroadcast the alert. Much to his surprise, a Northwestern officer radioed in fifteen minutes later. The truck was sitting in a campus parking lot just off its main thoroughfare, Sheridan Road.

As it happened, a team of five Evanston plainclothes officers was working surveillance nearby. They responded within minutes, quickly spying the stolen truck. The senior officer that afternoon, Sergeant Jerry Brandt, parked his unmarked car a few rows away, then popped the hood and, along with the others, pretended to be inspecting its engine. Shooting furtive glances toward the truck, they couldn't see anyone in or near it. Then, at 2:15, they watched as a small Hispanic man in a jogging suit appeared and walked toward it.

An hour or so later a white van drove up, and a Hispanic woman in a raincoat hopped out and began talking with the man. Together they opened the back of the Budget truck. Peering through binoculars now, Sergeant Brandt spotted rifle butts peeking out from beneath a carpet of some kind. He glanced at his men. "Let's go," he said.

The two suspects were still standing behind the truck, their backs turned, as Brandt and his men jogged through the parking lot, weapons low. Brandt took the woman. At the last minute she turned, shoving her hand into her raincoat, where Brandt was certain she held a gun. She began to struggle, slapping him with her left hand.

Three other officers slammed the man against the van, hitting him so hard that he lifted off the ground. He reached for a pistol jammed in his waistband, but an officer named Mike Gresham placed a .357 Magnum to his forehead first. "It's all right, it's all right," Gresham purred. "Take your time going for that gun. I can wait."

Sergeant Brandt, meanwhile, was still struggling with the woman.

"Hey, somebody, give me a hand over here!" he barked.

"Whatsa matter, Sarge?" one responded. "Can't handle ninety-nine pounds of pissed-off female?"

With the others' help, the woman was subdued. They found a revolver in her pocket, a .38 in the man's waistband, and three more guns in the van. Neither prisoner would talk, but the officers noticed something strange: The man was wearing a fake mustache. The pair were taken to Evanston police headquarters. Detectives from Chicago were called to begin questioning them.[3]

And that was that—or so it seemed. Except minutes before all this happened, the Evanston police switchboard had taken a call from a housewife who lived several blocks south of the campus. A group of young people in jogging suits were standing around a parked van, she said, smoking what she suspected might be marijuana. Two officers—Pat Lenart and Bill "Red" Lamerdin—responded within minutes. There they found not one but two vans, parked a block apart, and agreed to take one each. Lenart walked toward the first van. He could see a woman in the driver's seat. Approaching her window, he was about to say something when the engine revved.

Inside were nine members of the FALN, waiting for an armored car they expected at Northwestern. They had guns.

———

What happened next was described in court testimony years later by Freddie Mendez, who was in the rear of the van with Carlos Torres and seven others. The driver was Oscar López's companion, twenty-nine-year-old Lucy Rodriguez. "Cops," she said. "What do I do?"

"Brush him off," Torres said, suggesting she be as courteous as possible. As Officer Lenart approached, Torres whispered with his men. Two wanted to jump out shooting. Torres told them to be cool—he had "brushed off" police before. Rodriguez saw Lenart place a hand on his pistol. Torres said, "Start the engine."

Reaching the van, Lenart ordered Rodriguez to stop the engine and roll down her window. After a whispered exchange with the men behind her, she complied with a weak smile. Lenart said he was investigating a report of "kids" running into the van.

"No, officer," she said. "There are no kids in this van."

Lenart asked for her license. She fumbled in her purse, then rolled up the window and once again started the engine, apparently so Lenart couldn't hear her talking with the men in the back. Lenart again told her to turn off the engine. Again she complied. Lenart noticed she kept glancing at his gun. He sensed that something wasn't right. Just then the second officer, Red Lamerdin, having determined that the second van was empty, coasted to a stop on his motorcycle behind the van. Lenart motioned for him to watch the far side.

"Another cop," Rodriguez whispered.

Torres pushed through the curtain and sank into the passenger seat. Outside, two more officers arrived. Lenart stepped around the front of the van and told Torres to roll down his window.

"Officer, what's the problem?" he asked.

Lenart explained as Rodriguez disappeared into the back. Another man took her place behind the wheel. Lenart thought this was getting ridiculous. "I want everybody to get out," he said. A moment later one of the officers jerked open the van's rear doors. To their surprise, seven people emerged, four men and three women, followed by the two men up front. "You see, there's nothing going on," Torres said. "It doesn't smell like reefer, does it?"

As everyone stood behind the van, Freddie Mendez started to edge away. An officer told him to freeze. Suddenly Mendez placed a hand to his mustache. One of the officers noticed something strange: It moved. Just then another officer noticed what appeared to be a gun butt protruding from one of the women's purses. "Gun!" he shouted.

Officer Lenart ordered the men to lie on the ground. The suspects slowly stretched out facedown on the pavement. It was then the officers noticed how oddly everyone was dressed, wearing what appeared to be layers of clothing beneath their jogging suits. At least two more, like Mendez, were wearing fake facial hair. This was just too weird. Lenart decided to take them all in for questioning.

The nine of them said little as they were taken to headquarters. Scattered into interview rooms, not one would say a word, not even after being asked about the four pistols and the shotgun found in the van. One or two indicated that they spoke Spanish. Finally Mendez opened his mouth, saying he hadn't done anything.

The Evanston police had no clue who these silent people were—one or two officers thought they might be Middle Eastern—but everyone realized this was something more than a hold-up crew. They phoned the FBI. By nightfall three agents had arrived, including, as luck would have it, Greg Rodriguez, a Spanish speaker who had worked the West Haddon episode in 1976. He recognized Lucy Rodriguez and Carlos and Haydee Torres. When he called them by name, Haydee Torres spit at him. "You're a pig," her husband said, "and every pig has his Saturday, and yours will come soon."

Though the other eight suspects could not be identified, and though Oscar López and Willie Morales were clearly not among them, the FBI men agreed: This must be the FALN. By midnight Evanston headquarters was swarming with FBI agents and SWAT teams, the latter brought in to ring the building in the event López staged a rescue attempt. Because the prisoners wouldn't speak, it took days to identify them. All, it turned out, had been active in Puerto Rican independence groups. Carmen Valentín, the fiery counselor from Tuley High, was one. Elizam Escobar was an artist living in New York, Dickie Jimenez a student at the Illinois Institute of Technology.

Adolfo Matos worked at a Manhattan parking garage. None had been suspected of belonging to the FALN.

In the meantime agents, hoping to grab López and Morales, gathered the suspects' wallets, sorted through all the identification they could find, then spread across Chicago checking addresses. They found nothing for three long days, until they finally checked the address on Lucy Rodriguez's driver's license, which turned out to be the Milwaukee safe house. López and Morales were long gone, but inside agents found their files and weapons and FALN communiqués. That search led, in turn, to the Torres apartment in Jersey City, where agents found blasting caps and other bomb paraphernalia.

By then the FALN's supporters, including Carlos Torres's father, Reverend José Torres, had appeared in Evanston. That Sunday, two days after the arrests, they demonstrated outside police headquarters, waving Puerto Rican flags and chanting, "The fight continues." Someone called a New York newspaper and said the FALN would kill one police officer every day until Torres was released. Nothing came of it.

The next day, Monday, April 7, all eleven prisoners had to be dragged into an Evanston courtroom. Outside, fifty supporters chanted, "Drive the Yankees to the sea, Puerto Rico will be free!" The group's attorney, the noted radical Michael Deutsch, refused to recognize the court's authority, insisting his clients were captured combatants. "I am a prisoner of war!" Torres shouted as he was dragged from the courtroom. "Viva Puerto Rico Libre!"

Every arraignment, every court appearance, meant more of the same: shouting, spitting, demonstrators. The wheels of justice, however, ground forward. Haydee Torres, wanted for the Mobil bombing, went to trial first, that May in New York. She drew life. That summer the rest were tried on various state charges, including conspiracy to commit armed robbery. All, like Torres, refused to mount a defense. All were found guilty, drawing sentences from eight to thirty years each.

Federal prosecutors in Chicago, however, weren't satisfied. One, Jeremy Margolis, argued that the defendants should be tried under a "seditious conspiracy" law so obscure it had been used only twice—against the Puerto Rican nationalists in the 1950s-era attacks in Washington. As luck would have it, President Carter had just granted clemency to those same defendants the year before, suggesting that the Justice Department wouldn't look fondly on an identical prosecution. But Margolis was tenacious, and after winning Washington's approval, he won indictments against all ten FALN defendants that December.

The trial commenced in Chicago in February 1981. The courtroom was patrolled by bomb-sniffing dogs. The defendants, sitting in shackles, regularly interrupted the proceedings, shouting insults at the judge. At one point they began a hunger strike. None of it mattered. After barely a week of testimony, the jury found them all guilty. The judge handed down stiff sentences. Carlos Torres got seventy more years. The others drew sentences of between thirty and ninety years apiece. As the judge read their sentences, the prisoners hurled insults and threats. "If I weren't chained, I'd take care of you right now!" Carmen Valentín shouted. "There will soon be judges, marshals, members of the jury, prosecutors, agents, all of you—some of you will be walking on canes and in wheelchairs!"

No one was satisfied: None of the defendants had been charged with the FALN's deadliest bombing, at Fraunces Tavern. The prisoners themselves were unrepentant. Their supporters, especially those in Chicago, were alive with rumors and fanciful plans to somehow rescue them. Freddie Mendez, who struck a deal with prosecutors before the trial, claimed that one involved kidnapping the son of the new president, Ronald Reagan, and exchanging him for the prisoners.

And the violence, more than a few FBI men guessed, was far from over. Oscar López and Willie Morales were still at large, still able to recruit militants to the cause, still able to build bombs. Police suspected they were behind the explosion of two powerful pipe bombs in a locker room at New York's Pennsylvania Station at the height of rush hour a few days before Christmas. No one was hurt, but the station had to be evacuated, forcing thousands out into the cold and snarling rail service throughout the region. A caller directed police to a communiqué in a trash can, which took responsibility on behalf of the "Puerto Rican Armed Resistance," a previously unknown group. "It would appear that, if they are not connected, they have the same aims as the FALN," the NYPD operations chief, Patrick Murphy, told reporters.[4]

The incident was all but forgotten for five months. Then, on the morning of Saturday, May 16, 1981, someone calling on behalf of the same group phoned the Port Authority of New York and New Jersey, claiming that three bombs, including one aboard a Pan American flight leaving for Guatemala, would go off at JFK airport in fifteen minutes. The flight, which was already taxiing, was recalled and evacuated. As passengers spilled out, a twenty-year-old Pan Am handyman named Alex McMillan walked into a nearby men's room and noticed a bag on the floor. A ticket agent entered a moment later, and when McMillan pointed out the bag, the agent went for security. McMillan lingered in the bathroom, however, and when the bomb exploded, he absorbed what police called the "full force" of the explosion. He was dead by nightfall.

Alex McMillan became the FALN's sixth innocent victim. That evening police found a second bomb, unexploded, inside a vinyl bag outside Gate 18. A third was found before dawn in a women's restroom. Later that day an anonymous caller to the *Daily News* tied the incident directly to the FALN trials, saying it was "to protest the imprisoned people being held in Chicago." The next action, he promised before hanging up, "will be to eliminate President Reagan."

Monday brought a wave of bomb threats across the New York area, at the Chrysler and Empire State buildings, Grand Central Terminal, and Newark Airport, among many targets; more than a few New Yorkers were reminded of the mass evacuations following the 1977 FALN bombings. Two bombs turned up, mailed to the Honduran consulate and the U.S. mission to the United Nations; upon examination, they proved identical to the JFK bombs, all the same design as those built by the FALN and Ron Fliegelman. The next day someone claiming to be an FALN spokesman called the *New York Post* and said the bombs were the work of Willie Morales. The caller promised "a lot of bloodshed" should anything happen to the FALN prisoners in Chicago.

Ten days later, in the Chicago suburb of Glenview, a patrolman named Brian Bocca noticed a green Buick meandering through a residential neighborhood. It would stop, duck into a driveway, then slowly drive on. When the car made an illegal turn, Bocca pulled it over. Two men were inside. The driver, a Hispanic man in his thirties, produced an Oregon driver's license bearing the name José Ortiz. Bocca thought it looked fake. When a second officer arrived, they glanced inside the car and saw a pair of long-nosed pliers and an alligator clip, common burglary tools. Ordering the men from the car, they searched it and found a pistol with the serial number removed.

Both men were handcuffed and taken to the Glenview police station. Running their descriptions through computers at the National Crime Identification Center, officers were startled to discover that the driver's description exactly matched that of Oscar López. By nightfall FBI agents were on the scene, and a fingerprint check confirmed it: López, the man behind the deadliest bombing campaign of the era, had been captured in a routine traffic check. Presumably, like Carlos Torres, he had believed that his false identity would hold. His passenger turned out to be a new FALN recruit.

López had been living in an apartment on West Ainslie Street in Chicago since the Evanston arrests a year before. A search the next day uncovered guns, FALN communiqués, and, hidden behind a fake wall, six pounds of dynamite. Prosecutors scrambled to make a case, but despite a widespread belief that it was López who had masterminded the Fraunces Tavern attack, the FBI was unable to gather anything but circumstantial evidence. Instead, seven weeks later, he, too, was brought to trial on sedition charges, in a Chicago court filled with FALN supporters. The proceedings proved anticlimactic, ending in three days. López made an opening statement claiming to be a prisoner of war, with a "deep respect for human life," then sat in silence, refusing to participate. There was an audible gasp when Freddie Mendez took the stand. He admitted everything. In a closing statement López denounced the trial as a "lie and a farce." The jury took five hours to find him guilty.

"You are an unrehabilitated revolutionary," the judge said. "There's no point in giving you anything less than a heavy sentence." And with that he sentenced López to fifty-five years in prison. Still the FALN refused to die.

22

THE SCALES OF JUSTICE

Trials, Surrenders, and the Family,
1980–81

Six weeks after Joanne Chesimard's jailbreak, a new decade dawned: the 1980s. The era of the underground radical seemed an increasingly dim memory. There were still stragglers who had yet to turn themselves in, most notably Bernardine Dohrn and the remains of Weather's old leadership. Ray Levasseur was still out there robbing banks, but as far as the public was concerned, they were a lunatic fringe. What remained of the "armed struggle" movement was so obscure no one suspected that Mutulu Shakur and the Family even existed. They had managed to free Chesimard and Willie Morales without leaving a clue, at least none the FBI could find.

But the Family had a problem, a serious one. When something pollutes a radical cell's intellectual purity, whether it is allegations of sexism or racism, as happened with Weather, leftists call it a "corruption." The Family had been deeply corrupted from the outset by a familiar scourge: illegal drugs, mainly cocaine. Shakur was a heavy user, as were a dozen or more of the hangers-on who lounged about the acupuncture clinic he opened in a four-story brownstone on West 139th Street in Harlem in the summer of 1980. Shakur, who lived on the upper floors with several others, including his wife, two former stewardesses, and his assistants, called it the Black Acupuncture Advisory Association of North America (BAAANA). Later, when the FBI caught wind of things, a telephone wiretap recorded eighty-three separate drug purchases during a single four-week period.

Cocaine corrupted the Family at every turn. Because Sekou Odinga considered drug use counterrevolutionary, Shakur tried to keep his habit a secret, but it was no use; relations between the two steadily deteriorated. Money and guns were forever going missing from BAAANA's safe, all swapped for cocaine. To buy more—and without telling Odinga or the white women, who wouldn't approve—Shakur and his acolytes began robbing drug dealers and UPS trucks on their own. But it was never enough. Part of the problem was that BAAANA's acupuncturists, schooled in Shakur's revolutionary rhetoric, considered their work a public service; if customers couldn't pay, and in Harlem they often couldn't, they were treated for free. With little cash coming in, and much of it going for cocaine, the clinic lost money from its first day.

By 1980 Mutulu Shakur had become a classic coke fiend, a big talker with white powder on his upper lip, always desperate to make his next big score. The irony was that the white women, the true revolutionaries, knew nothing of his drug problem—not Marilyn Buck, Silvia Baraldini, Judy Clark, Susan Rosenberg, or the latest to join the group, the onetime Weatherman and Townhouse survivor Kathy Boudin, who worked odd jobs while raising a newborn with her partner, David Gilbert. To a woman, they believed they were supporting the second coming of the Black Liberation Army. "I knew nothing about drugs, nothing," Baraldini recalls. "I just thought Mutulu and those guys were hyper, you know, energetic, and they never slept. And I kept thinking, 'Why are they so pumped up and excited all the time?' I thought they were just on like a high metabolism. I didn't know."

The robberies that followed the Chesimard jailbreak illustrated the degradation of the Family's capabilities. The first, another armored car, came at lunchtime on February 20, 1980, outside a Korvettes department store in Greenburgh, a northern New York suburb. While Shakur and the women watched from getaway cars, Odinga, Tyrone Rison, and another Family member jumped the courier, handcuffed him, and forced him to lie on the pavement beside his vehicle. Unfortunately, the back door was locked, and another guard was inside. The trio punched, kicked, and threatened to shoot the hapless courier, but nothing would persuade the second guard to open the armored car. "Go ahead, kill him," he shouted. "I don't give a damn."[1]

Crestfallen, the Family withdrew without incident to the safety of a new safe-house apartment, in the suburb of Mount Vernon. Only then did Odinga realize the courier's keys could have opened the car's doors. They had surrendered too soon.

Two months later, on April 22, they did much better. The target was once again an armored car, this time a Purolator truck outside a bank branch in Inwood, New York, on Long Island. They rammed it with a rented van, then disarmed the driver when he emerged. As Tyrone Rison stood in the road, warning off traffic with an M16, the others rifled the truck, making off with $529,000, by far their biggest haul to date.

It was also the last successful robbery the Family was able to stage for more than a year. During the second half of 1980 much of its focus was directed toward a Brink's armored truck that serviced a Chemical Bank branch in Nanuet, New York, just across the Hudson River from the northern reaches of Manhattan. The job was laboriously scouted by a onetime BLA fighter named Jamal Joseph, who as a teenager had been a protégé of Dhoruba Moore's; after serving time for his role in the Sam Napier murder in April 1971, Joseph was back on the street, working intermittently with Shakur. But both times Shakur and his men set a trap for the Brink's truck, it inexplicably failed to appear.

It was during these scouting expeditions that some in the group first noticed the route of a second Brink's truck. Shakur began spending time in the area, studying the habits of its three couriers. But the more he discussed a possible robbery, the more Sekou Odinga resisted. Any robbery in the Nanuet area, he argued, would entail a getaway along one of the area's highways, many of which fed into the closest route back to Manhattan, the mighty Tappan Zee Bridge. There was no way to predict the traffic, and no way to escape it once it was encountered. Tyrone Rison termed the Nyack job "nothing but sure danger." No, Odinga warned. It "was nothing but sure death."[2]

On September 15, 1980, a full two and a half years after their indictment, W. Mark Felt and Edward S. Miller were finally brought to trial in a Washington federal court. The date had been delayed at least eight times; some in the capital, the few who cared, doubted that the two aging FBI men would ever face justice. Their onetime boss, L. Patrick Gray, the man who succeeded J. Edgar Hoover, was processed separately; the charges against him would later be dismissed altogether.

The proceedings, a kind of old-home week for the Nixon administration, were thick with the air of anticlimax. Nixon himself, in a rare public appearance, led a string of onetime White House and FBI officials who spoke in Felt and Miller's defense. But there was no denying that, however dangerous the Weather Underground had been, the two FBI men had approved illegal activities in their efforts to apprehend its leadership. They were swiftly convicted. The men faced up to ten years in prison. Two months later the judge handed down their sentences: a $5,000 fine for Felt, $3,500 for Miller. Neither would serve jail time. The light-as-air sentences suggested the court's skepticism of the whole affair. America yawned.

Among the few Americans with a keen personal interest in the Felt-Miller trial was an attractive young couple living in a fifth-floor apartment at 520 West 123rd Street in Manhattan, a few blocks from Columbia University. The woman, in her mid-thirties, was named Christine L. Douglas. Until giving birth to her second son that February—a midwife handled everything right there in the apartment—she had held down two jobs, as a manager at Broadway Baby, an infant-clothing store at Eighty-second and Broadway, and waitressing at Teacher's, a restaurant and bar a block away. The man, later described as an "aging hippie," was named Anthony J. Lee. He worked as a teacher at B.J.'s Kids, a day-care center on West Eighty-fourth Street. The couple lived quietly. Neighbors remembered them kindly.

Bernardine Dohrn and Bill Ayers had been underground for ten long years. Neither has ever said much about that odd three-year interregnum following Weather's breakup, a period in which they gave up making bombs and started a family. It appears they quickly left San Francisco, probably in 1977, and soon arrived in Manhattan, where they reestablished contact with their old underground friends, from Kathy Boudin to Brian Flanagan. Jeff Jones and Eleanor Stein had reunited and were living seven miles north, in the Bronx. For a time Dohrn and Ayers lived in a studio apartment on West Forty-sixth Street, where Ayers took a job at a health-food bakery. They moved uptown in 1979, taking a flat near Columbia.

Though they never quite believed it, no one was looking for them anymore. The FBI had all but stopped after the Squad 47 scandal. They had given up altogether once the fugitive warrant on Dohrn was dropped in 1979, after state prosecutors in Chicago, where she was still wanted on Days of Rage charges, indicated they wouldn't extradite her if she was captured. All charges against Ayers had been dropped years before. The couple had been discussing surrender for months when Cathy Wilkerson turned herself in that summer. Wilkerson had been living alone with her infant daughter on Chicago's South Side; she would end up serving a year in prison on charges related to her role at the Townhouse.

In mid-November, a week after Felt and Miller were found guilty, the couple piled into a blue station wagon and drove off. A week later their attorney, Michael Kennedy, telephoned a Chicago prosecutor and said Dohrn and Ayers were ready to surrender. On December 3 a crowd of reporters greeted them as they entered a Chicago courthouse. Forced to wait a half hour, they chatted amiably with the press. Inside Kennedy argued that Dohrn's $300,000 bond be reduced, and the judge agreed, cutting it to $25,000. Afterward Dohrn read a statement suggesting that she had never abandoned her radical beliefs. "This was a time when the unspeakable crimes of the American government were exposed and resisted by unprecedented numbers of its own people," she said. "Resistance by any means necessary is happening and will continue within the U.S. as well as around the world."

Afterward Dohrn and Ayers moved into an apartment in a house in Chicago owned by Ayers's younger brother. A month later they reappeared in court, where a judge gave Dohrn three years' probation and ordered her to pay a $1,500 fine. "I remember the night before they left to turn themselves in, my girlfriend and I had a dinner for them. We called it 'The Last Supper for Joe and Rose,'" recalls Brian Flanagan, using a set of early code names. "It was gourmet food, fine wines, first-growth Bordeaux. And then they go off to Chicago, and the feds were desperate for them to turn themselves in. Bernardine had to pay the fine, and she paid it with a check. Priceless!"

The excruciating irony that Bernardine Dohrn, the most-wanted underground figure of the era, could walk away virtually scot-free just weeks after two of her top FBI pursuers had been convicted of crimes against her was not lost on anyone involved. "The Weather Underground had done like a hundred bombings, and she was never prosecuted for one of them," recalls Lou Vizi, the FALN investigator. "That's amazing. I mean, absolutely amazing. You know who got prosecuted? Us. The FBI."

"What really galls me," says Don Strickland of Squad 47, "is we did all this stuff, risking our lives every day, putting our lives on the line. And we end up being the villains! And these Weatherman scumbags end up being the fucking Robin Hoods!"

For FBI partisans, the only welcome news in the episode came the following April, when President Reagan announced he had signed full pardons for both Felt and Miller. Both men swiftly vanished from the public eye. Not for twenty-five years, in fact, would the world learn that Felt had been keeping a far bigger secret than anything to do with the Weather Underground. In 2005 he admitted he had been "Deep Throat," the confidential source used by two *Washington Post* reporters, Bob Woodward and Carl Bernstein, to break the Watergate story.

One reaction to discussion of radical violence during the 1970s and early 1980s is that much of it was harmless; save for Fraunces Tavern, the policemen assassinated by the BLA, and the immolation of the SLA, not that many people died. But as the underground dwindled, its remaining members grew increasingly desperate, and dangerous. The single deadliest year for radical violence was in fact 1981, eleven years after the Townhouse. Seven people died, including young Alex McMillan in the FALN attack at JFK airport.

Most met their fate at the hands of the Family, which, as 1981 dawned, was riven with internal disputes and, at least where Mutulu Shakur and his cocaine-addled acolytes were concerned, sloppier and more violent by the day. Cocaine use was so out of hand that Shakur had a friend draw up official anti-drug guidelines, which were ignored. Sekou Odinga repeatedly confronted Shakur about his drug use; Shakur denied it. Worse, Odinga had invested money in the Harlem acupuncture center, and he suspected that that money too was going for cocaine. "Any kind of drug use bothered me," he recalls. "There was scuttlebutt that certain people were involved in heavy drugs, that they were losing control. Everyone involved denied it. I will say a lot of money [I invested] disappeared. I kept wondering, what is really going on?"

The May 19 women, especially Silvia Baraldini, brought tensions of their own. Baraldini and Marilyn Buck had grown to detest each other; both were immensely proud of their anointed positions alongside the black militants they revered, and each saw the other as a primary rival. Baraldini also despised Tyrone Rison, whom she thought insufficiently "political"—and rude. "Tyrone Rison was creepy," she says. "He was so into guns. We avoided him at all costs."

In an effort to organize themselves, Shakur and Odinga formally split the Family into two teams. The first, which they dubbed the "Primary Team," consisted of their best five soldiers—themselves, Tyrone Rison, and two of Shakur's men, Donald Weems (aka Kuwasi Balagoon) and Mtayara Sundiata. The Primary Team handled all the gunplay and made all the decisions in private meetings. The second group, dubbed the "Secondary Team," consisted of all the white women and anyone else they chose to rope into a robbery. Despite their strident feminism, the women largely did as they were told.

Tensions within the group grew after another pair of failed robbery attempts that winter, both in Danbury, Connecticut. One, on March 23, was one of Shakur's side jobs; Odinga and Rison weren't even told of it—they were on vacations, in fact—much less invited along. A Purolator truck, flush with cash from a Read's department store, had just pulled up outside a brokerage office that afternoon when Shakur and his deputies Balagoon and Sundiata rushed it, guns drawn. The courier, Daniel Archambault, was intercepted in the parking lot and made to lie flat. The man behind the wheel, Joseph W. Dombrowskas, a Purolator veteran, looked up from his clipboard to see a black man pointing a shotgun at him. When he refused to open the door, the shotgun went off, blasting a hole in a side window and showering him with glass. When Dombrowskas pulled his pistol and returned fire, Shakur and the others ran. Afterward Odinga and Rison were incensed—at being excluded, at the lack of professionalism, at the unnecessary violence. Odinga prided himself on smooth jobs without gunfire; he couldn't understand why Shakur's people were growing trigger happy.

It was inevitable that the Family's increasing appetite for violence would turn deadly. It happened on the drizzly morning of Tuesday, June 2, 1981, outside a Chase Manhattan branch in the northern reaches of the Bronx. It was another armored-car job, one the group had canceled twice before at the last second, fearing, apparently incorrectly, that they had been spotted by police. Judy Clark was the lookout, alerting the Primary Team, all jammed into a yellow Plymouth station wagon, when the Brink's truck was approaching the bank. When it appeared, Shakur pulled to a screeching halt beside and just behind it. Odinga jumped from the front seat, cradling a shotgun, and told the two couriers, William Moroney and Michael Schlachter, to freeze. They did so and followed his orders to lie on the pavement.

Back in the car, Rison, carrying an M16, was momentarily unable to open his door; a parked car blocked it. By the time Shakur inched the car forward, allowing Rison to exit, he was screaming and cursing. Emerging into the parking lot, Rison glanced at the two prone Brink's couriers and inexplicably opened fire, raking both men with bullets. Schlachter was hit three times; he would survive. Moroney, who was fifty-nine that day, a thirty-eight-year Brink's veteran, would not. He was shot four times, twice in the head. Odinga and the others gathered their wits long enough to grab several money bags, then drove off, at one point firing a burst of gunfire at a bakery truck whose driver was blocking their exit from the parking lot.

The murder of William Moroney was a turning point for the Family. For the first time they drew the attention of the NYPD, which launched a full-scale investigation, assigning fifty officers from the Major Case Squad, the Central Robbery Division, and the Bronx Detective Division to pursue the robbers full-time. A nearby security guard, Willie Lee, sat with police sketch artists, and the resulting drawings of three of the robbers were published in the *Daily News*; they closely resembled Shakur, Balagoon, and Sundiata. Shakur was shaken; he had his hair braided in an effort to change his appearance. Both Rison and Odinga began talking about retirement. After the robbery the two hid out in rural Georgia, where Rison had purchased a house. Shakur gave him money to buy more land so all of them could build homes nearby.

It wasn't just the Primary Team that was running scared. Moroney's murder also provoked an unprecedented revolt among the white women. "June 2, 1981, I'll never forget that day: the day Tyrone Rison shot the guard," says Silvia Baraldini, who was not involved in the robbery. "Everybody was very upset about that. Until then we had done everything possible to avoid violence. That had been our agreement. . . . I told [Shakur], 'This cannot be ignored.' We, the white women, decided a pause had to be taken. We said we would participate in nothing else until a meeting was held to confront these issues. But that didn't happen, because people were scared. They scattered to the four winds."

Not until it was far too late would Baraldini realize that no one, least of all Mutulu Shakur, was listening to a word she said.

All this—the string of botched robberies, the murder of William Moroney, the accelerating spiral into rampant violence and drug use—played out against the backdrop of a year-long debate within the Primary Team over the wisdom of the ambitious armored-car robbery Mutulu Shakur was planning outside a Chemical Bank branch in the suburb of Nanuet, across the Hudson River in Rockland County, New York. Shakur had studied the job for months and was certain it could be their biggest haul ever, easily more than $1 million in free cash. Shakur was so excited he gave the robbery a nickname: the Big Dance.

Money from the Big Dance, he assured a skeptical Odinga, would fulfill all their dreams. Odinga and Rison could retire in comfort if they wanted. Or they could join Shakur and Sundiata, who swore they planned to use their share of the proceeds to launch a true revolutionary assault, the planned bombing of a string of New York police precincts. Odinga had studied Shakur's plans for the Big Dance in detail, however, and he believed it was a suicide mission. If they got caught in traffic, they would be sitting ducks. Worse, Shakur planned to stage the robbery in the late afternoon, when the Brink's truck was ending its route laden with a full day's cash; for Odinga, this was far too close to rush hour. "The plan actually made sense," he recalls. "But it had to go perfectly. If just one thing went wrong, they were dead, and they had no backup plan. There was only one way in and out of that town, the highways, and they were going to use the highways. It was stupid."

For a time Odinga agreed to go along, though he and Rison secretly agreed to abort at the slightest hint of danger. They had actually attempted the Nanuet robbery no fewer than four times, once the previous fall and three times that May. Each time the truck either failed to show, or Odinga or Shakur bailed at the last minute; after the last attempt, Odinga said he would try no more. Each time Shakur urged him to reconsider, Odinga argued in favor of another bank, in the Bronx. The publicity and internal arguments that erupted in the wake of William Moroney's murder did nothing to curb Shakur's zeal for the job. By that fall he had decided once again to attempt the Big Dance, this time without Odinga and Rison. He and the other members of the Primary Team, Balagoon and Sundiata, thought the payoff was worth the risk. The white women, as usual, would do as they were told.

All that August and September Shakur made his preparations. He brought in several other of his BAAANA acolytes to help out. Marilyn Buck and Judy Clark agreed to drive trailing cars. "I was in Rome October 10 when I heard all this," Silvia Baraldini recalls. "Susan Rosenberg called me. [She said,] 'You have to come back. Things are bad.' So I return and the situation is this thing has been planned, and there's no going back. I couldn't stop it."

That Tuesday, October 20, 1981, was a special day for the three guards in the silver Brink's truck, the last they would enjoy after fifteen years working together. Peter Paige, a forty-nine-year-old father of three, was being transferred to a new route; all three men were feeling a bit nostalgic. That morning at 7:30, as a crisp north wind whipped leaves in the armored truck's wake, they headed down to a bank in Newark, the first stop in their daily run. At each stop Paige and his partner, Joe Trombino, hauled out the pushcart, rolled it inside, then returned to the truck laden with white canvas bags of cash as their driver, an easygoing forty-eight-year-old named James Kelly, filled out the paperwork on a clipboard in the front seat. Hopscotching their way up the west side of the Hudson, they had made seventeen stops when Kelly pulled the truck up in front of the Chemical Bank in Nanuet.

Sitting across the street in a red Chevrolet van, Shakur cursed as he glimpsed only a single bag on the pushcart Paige and Trombino wheeled out of the bank. Once again he decided to hold off. As the Brink's truck eased away from the curb, heading to its final stop, a bank inside the Nanuet Mall, Shakur fell in behind, furious, hoping they would hit pay dirt at the final stop. Everything was in place, maybe for the last time. A mile away, the ex-Weathermen David Gilbert and Kathy Boudin were waiting behind a department store in the switch vehicle, a U-Haul trailer. Marilyn Buck and Judy Clark were trailing the van in a tan Honda. This was not to mention the four cocaine-fueled armed robbers hunched behind Shakur in the van.

Five minutes later the Brink's truck coasted to a stop beside a rear entrance of the mall. It was 3:35. All across Nanuet and its adjoining suburbs, schoolchildren were piling into buses for the ride home. Fifteen miles away, traffic on the Tappan Zee Bridge was thickening. As Paige and Trombino rolled the pushcart inside for what would be their last stop together, Shakur idled the van in the parking lot, watching. On his nod, Kuwasi Balagoon jumped out and strode to a bench at a bus stop across from the armored truck.

"If you're waiting for the bus, we just missed it," a woman named Barbara Bowles volunteered. "We have an hour to wait."

Balagoon sat beside her. Keeping one eye trained on the mall entrance, he remarked what a beautiful autumn day it was, how striking the multicolored leaves were. Just the other morning, he said, he had seen a tree so red it reminded him of the burning bush.

"Oh, like in the Bible," Bowles said with a chuckle.

Balagoon fell silent as he studied the setup. There was scaffolding over the mall entrance. Two workers stood atop it. When Bowles asked if he knew what they were doing, he said, "No."

Balagoon was still staring at the mall when the Brink's men reappeared, the pushcart before them, three bulging bags draped down its length. Making a split-second decision, Shakur floored the accelerator, and the red van surged forward, racing between rows of parked cars. As it did, the two Brink's guards reached the back of the armored truck, Kelly mashed a button unlocking the rear door, and Trombino lifted one of the three bags and tossed it inside.

The van screeched to a halt beside the truck. Bedlam ensued. Three men in ski masks leaped out the back. Maybe it was the cocaine coursing through their veins, maybe the frustration of waiting all these months, but this time the Family shouted no warnings and took no prisoners. They just opened fire. Two men from the van hoisted automatic weapons and raked the truck with gunfire. As they did, Balagoon pulled a pistol and ran toward it, firing at the two guards. Trombino managed to yank out his pistol and fire a shot before a bullet tore into his shoulder, nearly ripping his arm off. Inside the truck, Kelly first thought he was hearing firecrackers. Spying the four men with guns, he yelled to Trombino, "Grab the shotgun!" Grasping his wound, Trombino hollered back, "I got no arm!"

Gunfire exploded across the mall parking lot. Peter Paige, shot in the throat, fell to an adjacent sidewalk and was dead within minutes. One of the attackers fired two blasts into the windshield, showering Kelly with glass and blowing him against the seat, where he fell unconscious. One of Shakur's men, Sundiata, jumped from the van and, along with the others, stepped over the fallen guards and snatched up six blood-smeared money sacks; all told, they contained nearly $1.6 million in cash. The sacks were so heavy Sundiata broke three fingernails lifting them. The attackers were in such a rush they failed to notice more money sacks inside. They left behind $1.3 million.

It was over in forty seconds. The red Chevy van and its occupants, all uninjured, roared off across the parking lot. Inside, Shakur and his men were jubilant, shouting, "We did it! We did it!" As they disappeared into afternoon traffic, Kelly came to. He staggered into the back of the Brink's truck, where blood lay so thick on the floor he later compared it to chocolate pudding. Stepping out the back, he cradled Trombino's head as a group of bystanders ran up, asking what they could do. Over and over and over, Kelly kept saying, "They shot my friends. They shot my friends. They shot my friends."*

While Mutulu Shakur readied for the robbery by cleaning guns and studying escape routes, David Gilbert and Kathy Boudin had been preoccupied with a more prosaic concern: finding a babysitter. Leaving Gilbert's green Toyota outside the sitter's building on West 108th Street that morning, Boudin had taken fourteen-month-old Chesa upstairs and dropped him off, promising to be back by five o'clock, even though the robbery was set for four, on the eve of rush hour. On the sidewalk she ran into a friend who volunteered to take Chesa on a play date in Central Park later. Boudin said that would be nice.

The couple had been underground for eleven years. Like almost all the Weathermen, they hadn't actually done much for ten of those years, not since their narrow escape from San Francisco FBI agents—"the Encirclement"— back in the spring of 1971. Gilbert had spent much of his time idling in Denver, though he later took credit for the bombing of a Puerto Rican bank branch in New York in 1975. He had actually gone aboveground for a time after Weather's demise, eventually joining Boudin in New York when she decided to begin helping Baraldini and the other May 19 women. After surviving both the Townhouse and the Encirclement, Boudin seems to have split her time between San Francisco, New York, and Boston, where she is believed to have helped out in several minor bombings. By 1980 she and Gilbert were squabbling new parents, living separately in New York, keeping their revolutionary dreams alive by helping Shakur and Odinga rob banks.

---

*James Kelly suffered a concussion but soon returned to work. Joe Trombino too recovered from his wounds, though he never fully regained the use of his left hand. He remained a Brink's guard for twenty years. Trombino died while making a pickup in the basement of the World Trade Center when it was attacked by terrorists on September 11, 2001. He was sixty-eight.

This was the first robbery they had joined—though Boudin, who took a job at a car-rental agency, had secured cars for several jobs—and she was nervous as Gilbert drove into the Bronx. They parked outside the offices of Kingsbridge Moving and Storage on 230th Street and rented an orange-and-silver U-Haul truck. From a burlap knapsack Gilbert lifted out several rolls of contact paper, which they hung inside the rear windows so no one could see inside. They then drove up the Hudson, crossing the river at the Tappan Zee Bridge, and were at the rendezvous point, the rear loading dock of an abandoned Korvettes department store, three hours before the robbery.

Boudin was deeply frightened. Guns scared her. As they waited, she couldn't sit still. Gilbert assured her everything would be fine. Finally, just before four o'clock, he suggested she walk around to the back of the truck and make sure everything was in place.

Just then Mutulu Shakur's red Chevy van swerved around the back of the store. Inexplicably, Shakur stopped the vehicle a hundred feet short of the truck. Gilbert, his rearview mirror obstructed for about thirty seconds by Boudin, didn't see the van. When he finally did, Boudin hopped back inside, and Gilbert—despite having been strictly admonished never to move from his designated position—drove over to the waiting van. By all accounts, this was the group's fatal error. The spot where Gilbert had parked could not be seen from nearby homes. But the spot Shakur chose could. Afterward more than one observer remarked that it was just the kind of sloppy error Sekou Odinga would never have made.

A single, unpaved lane, Main Drive, ran into the back of the Korvettes parking lot. A single house, separated from the lot by a chain-link fence, afforded a view of not only Shakur's van but Gilbert's U-Haul truck—and now a third car, the tan Honda driven by Judy Clark. And, as fate would have it, at that very moment a college student named Sandra Torgersen glanced up from an economics paper she was writing and peered through the living room of the house on Main Drive. Out in the parking lot she saw a black man with a rifle standing beside the van. A half-dozen other people, blacks and whites, men and women, were scurrying about, transferring what appeared to be heavy burlap bags between cars.

"Mom, there's a man with a gun outside," Sandra yelled to her mother,

Roxanne, who was busy in the basement. As Roxanne scurried up the stairs, Sandra grabbed a pen and paper and hustled out into the yard, hoping to scribble down license plate numbers. By the time she reached the fence, only the red van remained. It appeared abandoned. Sandra ran back inside and called the police. "I just saw something strange happen behind Korvettes," she told the dispatcher. Quickly she described the black men with guns and, crucially, all three vehicles: the van, the U-Haul, and the Honda. Police from all over Rockland County were already converging on the robbery site. Within minutes descriptions of the three vehicles were broadcast widely.

Police in the scenic village of Nyack, splayed atop high cliffs lining the Hudson River at the western end of the vast Tappan Zee Bridge, knew what to do when there was a robbery in Rockland County: block all routes to the bridge. When word of the Nanuet Mall gunfight was broadcast at 3:56 p.m., a young officer named Brian Lennon was sipping coffee in the Village Donut Shop on Main Street. Lennon's radio burbled, and a superior ordered him to block the entrance to the New York Thruway at Route 59, a mile west of the bridge. Lennon leaped into his patrol car and made it to the highway entrance in three minutes. The police band was exploding with orders and information, and by the time Lennon pulled his cruiser across the single-lane entrance to the Thruway, he had heard a description of the getaway cars.

The moment he stepped into the road, a shotgun in one hand, three vehicles were lined up in front of him. As luck would have it, the first was the gang's tan Honda. Judy Clark was behind the wheel, Marilyn Buck at her side. The second car was a BMW driven by a woman named Norma Hill, who, with her elderly mother beside her, needed to get to the dry cleaner's in time to dress for a dinner she and her husband were hosting that night at the Rainbow Room atop Rockefeller Center. Officer Lennon barely noticed either car. His eyes were trained on the orange-and-silver U-Haul truck directly beyond them. As he pointed his shotgun toward the truck, a pair of Nyack police cars pulled up behind it.

Officers emerged from both. One was Waverly Brown, an air force vet-

eran who was the only black man on the Nyack force; everyone called him
"Chipper." The second was a tall, thin sergeant named Edward O'Grady, a
red-haired Vietnam veteran. Both stepped onto the road behind the U-Haul,
guns drawn. A detective named Arthur Keenan followed.

Ahead, Officer Lennon waved Clark's Honda through. Glancing into her
rearview mirror, acutely aware of the drama unfolding behind her, she pulled
to the side of the road fifty feet beyond Lennon's cruiser, stepped out, and
peered back at the roadblock. Norma Hill slowed her BMW to ask what was
going on, but Officer Lennon dismissed her with a wave of his hand. "Move
on," he said.

Staring at the U-Haul as it inched forward, Lennon raised his shotgun
and pointed it directly at the dark-haired woman sitting in the passenger seat.
It was Kathy Boudin. At the wheel sat David Gilbert. Behind them, hidden
under a blanket, crouched Mutulu Shakur and four very excitable armed robbers carrying M16s and shotguns. As he drove, relaying reports on the traffic
to Shakur, Gilbert had been doing yoga-inspired breathing exercises to stay
calm. Beside him Boudin was coming unglued. The guns, the blood, the
machismo—it was all too much for her. She desperately wanted to get back to
the babysitter's.

When Officer Lennon motioned with his shotgun, Boudin opened the
passenger door and stepped out, hands held high. Almost immediately she
doubled over, as if in pain, shying away from Lennon's weapon. Gilbert
calmly stepped out of the van as well, hands over his head. He walked around
the vehicle and joined Kathy on the grassy roadside, where the three officers
and Detective Keenan trained their guns on them.

The three officers exchanged glances. No one spoke the obvious. The
Nanuet Mall attackers had been black men. This couple was white. The difference lay at the heart of Mutulu Shakur's plans and always had. David
Gilbert and Kathy Boudin believed they were aiding a black revolutionary
army. They were risking their lives for that one simple, foolish belief. To
Shakur, who cared far more for cocaine and cash than for some imaginary
black revolution, they were simply white faces, "crackers," whose sole use was
in distracting the police.

As they now proceeded to do.

Hunched on the roadside, Boudin noticed Sergeant O'Grady. "Tell him to put the gun back," she shouted over the din of traffic, alluding to Officer Lennon. O'Grady thought a moment. The radio had already carried a report of a U-Haul truck, driven by black men, heading south toward New Jersey. O'Grady slid his pistol into its holster, then turned to Officer Brown and said, "I don't think it's them." When Lennon shot him a glance, O'Grady said, "Put the shotgun back. I don't think it's them." Lennon walked back up the ramp to his cruiser, opened the door, and slid inside.

Detective Keenan, however, wasn't so sanguine. He stepped to the back of the U-Haul and yanked the rear door; it was locked. "I want to know what's in there," he said aloud.

A moment later the door burst open. The entrance ramp erupted in gunfire as five black men, all armed, leaped out and opened fire. Detective Keenan, struck in the thigh, dived to the roadside and rolled behind a pine tree. Two M16 rounds struck Waverly Brown in the chest and shoulder; when he fell to the pavement, screaming for help, another gunman walked up and fired into his chest. Sergeant O'Grady managed to pull his pistol and fire off one or two shots before being hit by three M16 rounds. He crumbled to the pavement in a spreading pool of blood.

It was over in seconds. The only officer left unhurt was Brian Lennon, sitting in his patrol car thirty feet up the ramp. When the gunfire stopped, he glanced back and saw several men standing around the U-Haul. He poked his shotgun out the window and fired a single blast, then ducked down. The next time he looked up, he was startled to see the U-Haul surging up the ramp toward him. A moment later it struck the patrol car, bumping it aside. Lennon peered up, saw the driver, pointed the shotgun, and pulled the trigger. Nothing happened. It was empty. The truck sped up the ramp, heading onto the Thruway. As it disappeared, Lennon drew his service revolver and fired two shots in vain.

Not all the attackers, however, made it back into the U-Haul. Two pointed a gun at a local doctor driving a silver Oldsmobile who tried to drive around the scene; he leaped out of his car as they stole it and drove off. David Gilbert, meanwhile, ran up the entrance ramp and joined Judy Clark in her tan Honda; it too drove off. Out on the Thruway, rubbernecking drivers were slowing their cars, staring at the scene. One, an off-duty corrections officer named Michael Koch, noticed a white woman running down the exit ramp after the fleeing U-Haul. Sensing something was amiss, he pulled his camper to one side of the highway, leaped out, and sprinted across eight lanes of traffic, hurdling the median divider like a track star. The woman was jogging alongside the highway when Koch, waving his badge and a gun, grabbed her from behind. She appeared panic-stricken, babbling, "He shot him, I didn't shoot him, he shot him, I didn't shoot him." Koch had no idea what was going on. He had no idea who Kathy Boudin was. But he pushed her back toward the entrance ramp, where the two fallen officers, Waverly Brown and Ed O'Grady, were dying.

Within minutes every police car in the county was racing toward the Thruway ramp. Among the first to appear was Alan Colsey, the twenty-nine-year-old police chief in South Nyack, who came upon the scene moments later. His radio reported that some of the attackers were fleeing in a U-Haul truck, some in a tan Honda, and some in a white 1980 Oldsmobile. Colsey could see there was no way to flee via the Thruway; it was fast turning into a parking lot. A lifelong area resident, he knew which way anyone heading for the city would need to go.

Colsey floored the accelerator and shot north toward Christian Herald Road, which winds east through a wooded area. He reached the road just as a tan Honda whizzed across his vision going at least fifty miles an hour. On its heels sped a white Olds. He wheeled in pursuit, watching as the two fleeing cars passed a line of others waiting at a red light. Colsey called for help, again and again, but the police band was as clogged as the Thruway; no one responded to his increasingly urgent pleas. Like it or not, he was on his own.

Colsey followed the cars into Nyack, past the volunteer-ambulance building, then down a hill toward a T-intersection. The Olds veered and made the turn, but the Honda's driver lost control, skidding through the intersection and crashing sideways into a concrete wall in front of a white Victorian home. Colsey stopped his car across the street and jumped out, drawing his pistol. Traffic kept streaming through the intersection, blocking his line of sight. He could hear the Honda's engine racing and see what appeared to be three people in the car. As he watched, a white man with a heavy black beard stepped out of the right side: It was David Gilbert. To Colsey's surprise, Gilbert began walking toward him, shouting something he couldn't hear over the din of passing cars. Colsey yelled for him to raise his hands. After a moment, he did.

The driver, a petite white woman in a tweed jacket and slacks, eased out next. She also raised her hands. By then two more policemen arrived. There was a third man in the backseat of the Honda, a black man who had been wounded. Colsey took them all into custody.

Everyone else got away. Behind them, Mutulu Shakur's cocaine-fueled gunmen had left three men dead and three others wounded.

"I was told to stay home all day that day," Silvia Baraldini recalls. "Then I got the call: Judy had been busted, with David." Baraldini hurried to the Mount Vernon apartment where the survivors were gathering. In their scramble to escape, Marilyn Buck's gun had gone off, wounding her in the knee. "I just remember everything was crazy, and we had to clean everything, get rid of all the fingerprints. We cleaned for hours. Cleaning, cleaning. Then the effort became to get Marilyn safe. That took like a whole month. [After a doctor friend treated the wound,] we got her out of the country. To Mexico."

Sekou Odinga was driving in Brooklyn when he heard the news on the radio: "An armored car robbery? In Rockland County? Right away I knew. My first reaction? Damn fools. I told you. Second reaction? What can I do to help? Another guy wanted to take me up there [to the Mount Vernon safe house]. I refused to go. It was just way too crazy."

Within hours, the hunt for the Brink's robbers became the top priority of every police officer and FBI agent in the New York area. For the moment, no one had a clue who any of the others were. A search of the captured vehicles, however, quickly led to Buck's apartment in East Orange, New Jersey. Buck was the Family's logistics expert and kept detailed records, all of which fell into police hands by the next day. By nightfall on Wednesday, barely twenty-four hours after the robbery, the NYPD had identified a string of the Family's safe houses, including the Mount Vernon apartment, which had been abandoned just hours before. As it happened, the building superintendent had grown suspicious and jotted down license plate numbers of several of the gang's cars.

One was the gray Chrysler LeBaron Sekou Odinga was driving through the South Ozone Park section of Queens two mornings later with Mtayari Sundiata slouched in the passenger seat. In an amazing bit of luck, an NYPD detective named Daniel Kelly noticed the plate while driving down Foche Boulevard. Kelly called for backup. After a minute Odinga noticed the pursuit and floored the accelerator, veering first onto the Van Wyck Expressway, then onto busy Northern Boulevard. "I knew I was in trouble when I saw them switch lanes on me," Odinga recalls. "That was my fault. I was rushing."

When the police cars hit their sirens and rolling lights, Odinga crashed across a concrete median and slammed into a violent U-turn, racing west toward Shea Stadium. Detectives in an unmarked car and an emergency-services truck gave chase, at one point sideswiping the Chrysler as Odinga struggled to retain control of the car. Sundiata rolled down his window and, producing a 9mm pistol, fired several shots. The police truck fell back. One of the Chrysler's tires blew out, forcing Odinga to veer into an adjoining ware-house district.

"I didn't know the area; it was stupid, a tactical error I made," Odinga recalls. "That's how I ended up on a dead-end street."

The two men jumped out of the car and ran into the rear yard of the Tully-DiNapoli Construction Company, where they split up. Sundiata leaped atop a stack of sewer pipes to make it over a fence. Jumping down on the far side, he confronted a pair of detectives. In the ensuing exchange of gunfire, Sundiata was shot in the head and killed.

Police poured into the area. A few minutes later four of them glimpsed Odinga hiding under a van. As they approached, Odinga aimed a pistol at them—and then dropped it. "I give up," he said.

After an underground journey that had taken him from New York to

Cuba, Algeria, and as far afield as Angola, Sekou Odinga's odyssey was at an end. The NYPD, from all appearances, did not welcome his return. When he was escorted from the 112th Precinct that evening, Odinga's body was covered with bruises and cigarette burns. Taken to the prison ward at Kings County Hospital, he was found to have sustained damage to his pancreas.

Bit by bit, police managed to assemble a picture of the Family. Kuwasi Balagoon was arrested peacefully in January 1982. Silvia Baraldini was arrested in November outside her Manhattan apartment. The rest would not be captured for years.

23

THE LAST REVOLUTIONARIES

The United Freedom Front,
1981 to 1984

On October 4, 1981, sixteen days before the Brink's robbery, the *Maine Sunday-Telegram* published an article on Ray Levasseur's underground group headlined WHERE ARE THE TERRORIST BOMBERS NOW? It was a good question. Levasseur and his group hadn't made a public statement in almost three years, since their last action, the bombing of a Mobil Oil office outside New York in early 1979.

In fact, the Sam Melville Jonathan Jackson unit was poised to reemerge, in a new form, bigger and more committed than ever. That summer of 1981 Levasseur and Pat Gros and their three girls had sold their extra belongings in a yard sale and left their farmhouse in northern Vermont for a larger home they rented outside the village of Cambridge, New York, across the border from the college town of Bennington; they enrolled their oldest daughter, Carmen, now five, in a Bennington Montessori school. Tom and Carol Manning, meanwhile, had moved to a sixty-acre farm outside Marshall's Creek, Pennsylvania, in the Pocono Mountains, an hour west of New York

City, where they lived as Barry and Diane Easterly. They had enrolled their son, eight-year-old Jeremy, at a nearby Montessori school. Carol was pregnant with a third child, due that December.

Everything had begun to change after Gros spied her old acquaintance Sally Stoddard at the grocery store in the summer of 1980. Gros had been frightened that Stoddard might turn them in. But Levasseur was thrilled. His greatest frustration remained his inability to recruit new members, and Stoddard, who had a long record of working with many of the same prison activists he had known in Maine and Massachusetts, was a possible conduit to any revolutionaries remaining among them. The women, Gros and Carol Manning, were less enthusiastic.

"Ray was really anxious to get people he could work with," Gros recalls. "He needed that connection to the outside political world. Carol and I, we were very unhappy about it. We were paranoid things would start popping again, the actions, the banks. We had two and three kids each, remember. Carol was really sick of it."

Levasseur was still debating how to approach Stoddard when, in August 1980, he spotted her at the Caledonia County Fair in Lyndonville. When he approached, Stoddard scrunched up her features and said, "Ray?" Levasseur smiled. No one had called him by his given name in almost five years. "Ray?" he answered. "Why would I want to be Ray?" They took a walk. Years later, what Stoddard remembered most vividly was Levasseur's admission that he sometimes pronounced his full name in the shower, alone, just to remind himself who he really was.

As Levasseur had surmised, Stoddard was still in touch with a number of Boston-area activists, most notably the father of her two children, a convicted armed robber named Richard Williams. Williams, in turn, was friends with a man Levasseur badly wanted to meet, an Estonian-born onetime SDS radical named Jaan Laaman. Dark, intense, and argumentative, Laaman had done prison time after bombing a New Hampshire police department in 1972. Afterward, like Levasseur and Williams, he had become involved in the New England prison-reform movement. Together with another radical friend, a tall, rail-thin African American named Kazi Toure, Laaman took several meetings with Levasseur that winter. The three of them were willing to help rob banks, Laaman said, but they wouldn't go underground. They could help the group more by remaining in place.

And so, as 1981 dawned, Levasseur could see his dream taking shape. Who would have imagined it? A full ten years after the Weathermen had gone underground, at least five years since any serious new radical cell had been formed anywhere in the United States, at a time when talk of an armed revolution seemed not only improbable but downright anachronistic, here were people prepared to rejoin the underground cause. "[I was] pretty excited," Levasseur recalls. "Three strong recruits and the potential for more, plus the real potential for having a network in the Boston area."

The now five-man group hit its first bank, in New Britain, Connecticut, on June 25, 1981. It went so smoothly that Levasseur realized the new recruits were ready for full-time revolutionary work. The long sabbatical in Vermont was over. He and Gros and the girls moved south, to the farmhouse in New York, to be closer to the others in Boston and to the corporate headquarters and military installations they planned to start bombing again.

That Monday morning Levasseur walked into the town clerk's office in Brattleboro, Vermont, to secure a birth certificate he needed for a new identity. It was that of a long-dead baby girl; Gros had been in the same office two weeks earlier and had arranged for it to be ready. What she hadn't noticed was that Brattleboro's police were headquartered in the same building. When a clerk retrieved the document for Levasseur, he noticed it was for a dead infant and became suspicious. He phoned the police.

An officer named Richard Guthrie strolled through a hallway into the clerk's office. When he asked for identification, Levasseur coolly pulled a 9mm automatic from beneath his jacket and ordered Guthrie and a clerk onto the floor. He stepped around the counter, yanked Guthrie's service revolver from its holster, and ordered a trio of clerks into a rear office. Without another word, he jogged from the office into his Chevy Malibu and drove away.[1]

An areawide alert immediately went out; roadblocks were set up all across southern Vermont. Speeding south from Brattleboro on Interstate 91, Levasseur passed a pair of state troopers parked on the median; they didn't notice him. Listening to the police scanner bolted beneath his dashboard, he realized he now had police behind him and ahead of him, at a roadblock being thrown up at the Massachusetts–Vermont state line. He would never make it through. A moment later he spied a rest stop, the last one in Vermont before the border. He veered into it, parked the car out of sight, and sprinted into the woods.

It was as desperate a moment as he had faced since going underground six years before. Thrashing through the underbrush, he had only the dimmest idea where he was heading. He tried to bear south, toward Massachusetts, aware that if the state police found his car at the rest area, they would soon be after him with dogs and helicopters. He ran through the woods for two hours, seeing no one. Several times he thought he heard dogs. At one point he spotted an airplane above the trees. After about ten miles he came upon a road. Keeping to the trees alongside it, he reached a general store—and a pay phone.

Gros took the call in the kitchen. Her car was in for repairs. Thinking quickly, she phoned a neighbor, borrowed his battered pickup, and, with her three daughters in tow, drove into Massachusetts, where an hour later she spied Levasseur loitering nervously at the general store. The neighbor's truck was so old that the horn blew whenever she hit the turn signal; Levasseur was apoplectic when she pulled up with the horn madly honking. "What the fuck are you doing?" he demanded.

They made it back to the farmhouse safely, and by the next evening they were gone. Jaan Laaman helped them pile some of their things into Gros's car; later, when they were sure the police hadn't found the house, they returned and took the rest. Laaman took two dozen boxes of Levasseur's magazines and books and stowed them in a self-storage unit outside Binghamton, New York. Piling the kids into the car, the couple headed for the Mannings' farmhouse in Pennsylvania and, within days, rented a place of their own in the town of Germansville.

Once they were settled, Levasseur drove to New Haven with Tom

Manning to caucus with Laaman and Richard Williams. It had been a close call. There was much to discuss, but to Levasseur's surprise, the new recruits seemed more interested in asking for more money; they had already run through their share of the New Britain proceeds. He couldn't understand how this could be but agreed to hand over cash at the next meeting. There was something else, though, something he couldn't put his finger on. It was something about Williams. "Richard was always late, always antsy, always wanting to leave early," Levasseur recalls. "I got irked. Afterward I remember telling Tom, 'He doesn't seem right. What's going on with him?'"

They knew Williams had once had some kind of drug problem and sometimes drank too much. Levasseur laid down strict rules about chemical use. Alcohol and marijuana were tolerated in moderation; anything harder was strictly forbidden. It made people sloppy, and sloppiness was something he wouldn't tolerate. Once, after Williams had gotten drunk at a group gathering, Levasseur had ordered him to do five hundred push-ups as punishment. According to Gros, it was Tom Manning who unraveled the mystery of Williams's behavior when he visited his Cambridge apartment and glimpsed drug paraphernalia in his bathroom.

Levasseur got in touch with Laaman, told him to meet him in New Haven, and confronted him there. Yes, Laaman admitted, Williams was a heroin addict. Worse, Laaman had known and hadn't told the others. Levasseur and Manning returned to Pennsylvania deeply shaken. They didn't dare tell the women. "Ray and Tom knew the girls would go nuts," says one intimate. "So they held off telling them awhile. Eventually, you know, they had to try and explain it, so they said Richard had come out of the prison struggle, that it was a symptom of his struggle against the system."

Discovery of a junkie in their midst prompted a series of soul-searching discussions among the Levasseurs and Mannings. They couldn't simply expel Williams; he knew too much, and they needed men. "Ray didn't know what to do," Gros recalls. "We couldn't just kill him. Because we didn't do that. What [were we going to do], bury him in the woods?"

After much discussion, Levasseur and Manning agreed that Williams would be taken into the Manning home, where he would undergo an impromptu course of revolutionary rehabilitation. Manning asked his land-lord for permission to have a friend stay with the family a few weeks, and in early December Williams arrived in a moving van, forlorn and repentant. He was still there on December 14, when Manning took his wife to a doctor's office in Kingston and helped her give birth to a boy they named Jonathan.

Things were just settling down for the Levasseurs and Mannings as Christmas approached. On the morning of December 21, Levasseur rose early, threw on a pair of overalls, and drove to Philadelphia, where he planned to scout banks. At the Manning home, Tom stepped out into the cold morning air and walked through new snow to his blue Chevy Nova with Williams, who had overcome the worst of his withdrawal symptoms. They drove east on Interstate 80, passing into northwest New Jersey, where they shopped for Christmas presents. They were heading home on the interstate around 4:15 p.m. when a state trooper's car pulled behind them, lights rolling. Inside was a thirty-two-year-old officer named Philip Lamonaco, New Jersey's 1979 trooper of the year. Manning pulled over on a stretch of highway lined with trees and brush.

What happened next has never been proven. But Levasseur and those close to him would always believe it was Williams who fired the eight bullets into Trooper Lamonaco, killing him. Williams's motivation, they say, was panic, mixed with a need to prove himself after the discovery of his heroin use diminished his status within the group. Years later Tom Manning would claim it was he, not Williams, who killed Lamonaco in self-defense—Lamonaco fired six shots, emptying his gun—but Manning's friends always believed he was just trying to protect Williams.

Whatever happened, it was over in less than a minute; the blue Nova streaked west down the interstate, leaving Trooper Lamonaco bleeding in the snow on the shoulder of the road. A motorist stopped and used Lamonaco's car radio to call for help. Ambulances appeared and took the trooper to Pocono Hospital in East Stroudsburg, Pennsylvania, where he was pronounced dead at 5:28. Manning and Williams, meanwhile, struggled to get away. Behind the wheel, Manning took the first exit he could, driving northwest on snowy roads. He turned onto one country lane, then another, trying to find a short-cut to Pennsylvania, but the last one he took, Polkville Road, was still clogged with unplowed snow. The car got stuck in five inches of slush. In desperation, the two men got out and ran into the woods. Later, police with bloodhounds would follow their tracks three miles to a truck stop back on the interstate.

Gros was in her kitchen, watching the girls, when the phone rang. Manning's voice was even, as usual, but she instantly knew something was wrong. He kept saying someone was "down." It took a moment for her to realize he was saying someone had been shot. "What-what-what do you expect me to do?" she stammered. "I'm here with the kids."

"We gotta get outta here!" he blurted. "You gotta come get us."

"I can't," she pleaded, but by the time she hung up, she had promised to rescue them. It was Brattleboro all over again. She began dressing the girls, only dimly realizing the absurdity of what she was doing: preparing three children to pick up a pair of cop killers. Then, just as she began hunting for her keys, Levasseur telephoned. Later that day he managed to find Manning and Williams and bring them home.

Their fingerprints were all over Manning's car: Levasseur knew they had a matter of days, maybe hours, before police tracked them down. And so, for the second time in two months, the Levasseurs, and now the Mannings, frantically cleared their homes of belongings; the Mannings left their Great Dane behind and a radio blaring. They piled everything and everyone into Gros's car, five adults and six children, including the Mannings' seven-day-old son. "Tom's car, Tom's house, our house, was gone," Levasseur remembers. "All our ID was gone. We had nothing at that point but our car, which we thought was still safe."

They drove east into New Jersey, watching for state troopers, and by the next evening managed to rent a roach-infested apartment in Yonkers, New York, just north of the Bronx. For the next week Levasseur and Manning couldn't risk leaving the apartment. Ironically, it was Williams, the man who had probably killed Trooper Lamonaco, who had to act as their liaison to the outside world, buying groceries and making phone calls. At night Levasseur stood at the window, brooding. This changed everything. It was one thing to be wanted for protest bombings that hurt no one. It was quite another to be sought for murdering a cop. The FBI and the New Jersey State Police, he knew, would throw every available resource toward their capture.

And they did. The morning after Trooper Lamonaco's murder, officers found Manning's abandoned car, riddled with bullet holes, and by nightfall had identified Manning's fingerprints inside. The next day photos of Levasseur and Manning peered from the front pages of newspapers across the Northeast. Hundreds of police poured into rural northwest New Jersey, going from house to house in what the *New York Times* called the most intensive manhunt in the state since the kidnapping of the Lindbergh baby in 1932. Three days later, with no clue as yet to the fugitives' whereabouts, more than two thousand police attended Trooper Lamonaco's funeral in Washington, New Jersey, the largest of its kind in state history. Shortly after, the FBI announced formation of a new Boston-based task force, dubbed "Bosluc," consisting of several dozen agents, along with troopers from six northeastern states, all working together in an effort to apprehend Levasseur, Manning, and the others.

Their first success came two weeks after Trooper Lamonaco's murder, in early January, when they found the Manning home in Marshall's Creek; the landlord called in the tip when he found it abandoned. Inside they found a drawing of Joanne Chesimard. The Mannings had been thorough—nothing police found gave any clue where they might be hiding—but they made one crucial mistake: Among the personal effects they left behind was a single photo of the Levasseurs and their children, the first inkling anyone in law enforcement had that they now had three daughters. In time, all their pictures, including the children's, would grace wanted posters.* The first, a photo of nine-year-old Jeremy Manning, was issued to the press on January 9, immediately after the farmhouse was located.

"When they started targeting the kids, that changed everything," recalls Levasseur, who remained moored in the Yonkers apartment all that January. "Every article emphasized the kids. That began to weigh on us a lot more. I

---

*Police located the Levasseur home in rural Germantown a week later. It yielded no further useful information.

told Pat, 'We shouldn't have the kids. This is just too much.'" They discussed trying to leave the girls with their grandparents, but Gros couldn't do it. Instead, they changed the girls' names and cut their hair. Carmen, who had long dark hair, had hers cut short. Simone, who had curls, allowed her hair to grow out.

But it wasn't just the girls who put them at risk. In time, Levasseur knew, the FBI would focus on the New England prison-activist community. Laaman, Kazi Toure, and their friends would be called in for questioning, and maybe worse. Once Laaman made it to Yonkers, Levasseur told him he would have to join them underground; he had no choice. When Laaman resisted, insisting there was nothing to link him to the group, Levasseur lashed out: "They'll have grand juries! You won't testify, so you're going to jail! Come on!" After heated discussion Laaman finally capitulated. He would go underground, he said, under one condition: His family had to come, too.

"Are you insane?" Levasseur asked.

Laaman's girlfriend, a flighty brunette named Barbara Curzi, had three children, the youngest fathered by Laaman.

"Three kids with the kind of heat we've got?" Levasseur asked. "No way. This is crazy! Absolutely fucking crazy!"

But Laaman would not budge. He wouldn't come underground without Barbara and the kids. "You guys got families," he said. "Why can't I have mine?" Levasseur gave in.

It took days for everything to come together. Curzi, as one might imagine, was not thrilled with the notion of going underground with three children. Levasseur and Manning, who were now both on the FBI's Most Wanted list, sat in the Yonkers apartment, brooding and pacing, until the end of January, when Laaman finally sent word that they were ready. It took another week to gather their belongings into a U-Haul trailer. Finally, on February 7, seven weeks after the Lamonaco killing, everything was set. Laaman and Toure agreed to rendezvous with Curzi and her children in a rest area on Interstate 95 in North Attleboro, Massachusetts, near the Rhode Island border, just after midnight.

When the men drove up, however, she wasn't there. They waited, Laaman behind the wheel, Toure trying to stay awake beside him. By 1:00 a.m., there was no sign of her. At 2:00, still nothing. A few minutes later a Massachusetts state trooper named Paul Landry drove his cruiser into the rest area and shone his headlights on Laaman's green Plymouth station wagon. When Landry approached the car, he noticed that the engine was on. Laaman rolled down the window with a smile and, answering Landry's questions, told him everything was fine. They were just two guys from New Hampshire driving down to New York and had stopped a moment to rest. When Laaman turned over their fake driver's licenses and a registration, Landry noticed Laaman's license had its photo clipped onto it. Toure's had no photo at all. Training his flashlight inside the car, Landry saw Toure reach his right hand inside his jacket.

Uneasy, especially about what might be in the jacket, Landry returned to his cruiser and called in the license and registration; everything came back clean. Still, something bothered him. He called for backup. A few moments later a second trooper, Michael Crosby, pulled his cruiser alongside. In a whispered conversation Landry said he thought the black passenger might be holding a gun or drugs.

The troopers approached the passenger-side door, tapped on the window with a flashlight, and motioned for Toure to get out. When Landry asked what was in his jacket and reached for it, Toure blocked his hand, but not before Landry realized that he was wearing a bulletproof vest. Landry immediately told Toure to put his hands on his head. "This guy has something," Landry barked to Crosby. "Watch the driver."

Just then Laaman reached his hand inside his jacket, where he hid a 9mm pistol. Landry drew his service revolver. Laaman leaped from the car, crouched down, and fired several shots across the car toward the troopers. Officer Landry grabbed Toure and dropped to the pavement. Officer Crosby ran for the protection of a Dumpster. Laaman fired several shots at Crosby, then sprinted for the dark woods at the edge of the rest area. Crosby raced to his car and radioed for help.

Toure was taken into custody and, under questioning at the police barracks in Foxboro, identified Laaman. An all-points bulletin was issued; dozens of police plunged into the area, shining searchlights into the woods up and down the interstate in an effort to find Laaman. Somehow he managed to elude them. Once again it was Pat Gros, asleep back in Yonkers, who took the call. Because she was the only one of the group not being sought by police, Levasseur let her retrieve Laaman. Barbara Curzi, meanwhile, drove toward the North Attleboro rest stop around 4:15 that morning and, seeing it swarming with police, continued driving south. By the next day everyone, including Laaman, Curzi, and all three of their children, was safe in the Yonkers apartment.

For the third time in four months, they had somehow survived a run-in with the authorities. But Levasseur, worried that Kazi Toure would talk, quickly realized they couldn't stay long. He sent Gros to Albany, where she found them two apartments. Laaman and his family initially bunked with the Levasseurs, all six of them packed into a dingy basement apartment on an alley. The Mannings found a place nearby. No one was especially happy with the arrangements, which were a far cry from the spacious farmhouses they had enjoyed before the Lamonaco killing.

Once they were settled in Albany, the top priority became money. All four men were now far too hot to work normal jobs, which meant that money for the expenses of three entire families, seven adults and nine children— everything from beer and food to diapers and baby formula and lunch boxes— would need to come from bank robberies, a situation Levasseur dreaded. Worse, the Mannings had lost everything in fleeing, the Levasseurs almost everything; everyone needed furniture and cars. Levasseur also wanted to raise cash for Toure's bail. So they moved quickly, finding the first bank, a branch of Chittenden Trust in South Burlington, Vermont. They hit it on April 2, four of them now, in a stolen getaway car—ski masks, body armor, guns waving, shouting, scooping up cash bags. The take was $61,000.

But it wasn't enough, not if they were to escape their run-down apartments in Albany and establish a new base of operations. They began scouting the next bank immediately, a branch of the Syracuse Savings Bank. As in Vermont, they rented a safe-house apartment nearby, along with a garage where they could keep the stolen cars they began using for reconnaissance. Once everything was set, on June 25, they rushed the bank lobby just after 11:00 a.m. Everything was going smoothly until Richard Williams went to grab the cash bags, which were lying on the floor inside the barred door to the vault. Somehow the door swung shut behind him—and locked. Williams grabbed the bars.

"I'm locked in!" he yelped.

Tom Manning grabbed an assistant manager by the collar and shoved her toward the locked door. "Open the door, bitch!" he ordered.

It was as tense a moment as the group had experienced inside a bank. The manager fumbled with her key ring as Manning hovered, his pistol at the ready. "Anybody moves, they're dead!" Levasseur shouted.

It took interminable seconds before a key was produced. After a moment Williams was freed. They sprinted from the bank, never noticing a police car sitting at a McDonald's across the street. As he sped away Ray thought they were being tailed. They had just taken up their guns, preparing to open fire, when the suspicious car disappeared. They made it back to Albany safely but noticed a neighbor watching them as they strode into the Levasseurs' basement apartment. Worried, they hovered over a scanner all that night and the next, until they were certain the police weren't onto them. The haul, however, more than made up for the anxiety. It came to $195,000, by far their largest to date.

It was a close call, too close for Gros and the other women. Levasseur didn't need to be reminded that they were robbing banks too close to home. They needed to move, and soon; the children had to be enrolled in classes by the time school started in August. After several scouting expeditions, they decided on their farthest relocation yet, to Ohio, a manageable eight-hour drive from the Interstate 90 corridor where Levasseur was most comfortable finding new banks. Flush with $250,000 in cash—a portion was sent to Boston for Toure's bail—Gros rented all three families houses within blocks of each other in a blue-collar neighborhood in Cleveland. The Levasseurs would now be the Petersons, the Laamans the Owens family, the Mannings the Carrs. Williams, however, decided not to join them. He remained part of the group, but for the time being he moved to a house he rented in North Carolina. After a few months Levasseur decided to move his family away from the others, renting a house in rural Deerfield, east of Akron. He felt comfortable in the countryside; the nearest neighbors were a quarter mile away.

By the fall of 1982 everyone was settled into new homes, and the group's focus shifted once again, to a renewed bombing campaign. It had been almost four years since their last action, and Levasseur was determined that the United Freedom Front (UFF), as they decided to rename the group, would stage a memorable return. Over the next two years they would go on to detonate ten more bombs, almost all in suburban New York: at an IBM office in Harrison in December 1982; an army reserve center on Long Island in May 1983; an army recruiting office in the Bronx in August 1983; a Motorola office in Queens in January 1984, and other offices of IBM, General Electric, and Union Carbide. All the bombs detonated when the buildings were empty; no one was seriously hurt. There were newspaper articles after each but no great hubbub. Levasseur's communiqués attacking corporate wrongdoing were largely ignored.

It was exhausting work. By 1983 Levasseur and Gros had been underground for seven years, and the cumulative strains were beginning to show. Gros's, in fact, increased as her three girls grew. Carmen was turning seven; the youngest, Rosa, was three. They had been forced to explain to the girls that they were fugitives. Without explaining the details of bank robberies and bombings, they said they were being sought for their political beliefs. Still, Gros felt that Carmen was beginning to understand what they had done. "They heard everything," Gros recalls. "When we were in meetings, in the basement. They knew."

Just before Christmas that year Gros was walking up the stairs at Laaman and Curzi's house when she suddenly suffered a panic attack, her first. Her heart racing, she allowed Curzi to drive her to an emergency room, where a polite young doctor, addressing her by her latest alias, leaned forward and said, "Mrs. Peterson, this is all about stress. You need to find a way to relax."

Levasseur wasn't in a position to comfort her. He was rarely home. In the fall of 1982, after their fifth successful expropriation along the I-90 corridor, he had decided it was time to change their area of operations. A Syracuse television station had broadcast a series of features on the UFF and its robberies, and thousands of new wanted posters were flooding upstate New York. He scouted Pittsburgh, Baltimore, and Washington but worried that the thick traffic in all three areas would make getaways uncertain. Eventually they settled on two Virginia cities, Norfolk and Richmond, which were large enough to hide in but small enough to navigate. They rented safe houses in both, then closed the New Haven apartment and opened one in Yonkers. Levasseur left the house in Ohio early most Monday mornings, driving the eleven hours to Virginia via Pennsylvania and Maryland to avoid New Jersey and typically wouldn't return until the weekend. When they weren't scouting banks in Virginia—they managed to rob two of them without event, both in Norfolk—they were studying new bombing targets in New York. Before long the constant travel began to wear him down.

"I was beginning to feel like a long-haul trucker," he recalls. "We were on the road *all* the time. All we did was recon trips, take a bank and then run back to New York to ram a bomb up IBM's ass."

He knew they couldn't do this forever. Then, on January 2, 1984, a slow news day, he was startled to switch on the *CBS Evening News* and see Dan Rather lead the broadcast with a story about the UFF, the bombings, the robberies, the kids, everything. There they were, he and Gros and the kids, the Mannings, everyone, right there on television. Deeply shaken, he sat down with Pat. Maybe, he said, it was time she turned herself in. They could leave the girls with her mother in Maryland. No doubt she would get a short sentence, maybe a year, then she and the girls could be free. "I said, 'You know, we're wearing down,'" Levasseur recalls. "'The kids are making us vulnerable.' But Pat wouldn't do it. She didn't want to break up the family."

By 1984, despite eight years of intensive investigation and the combined efforts of the FBI and police from six states, the authorities had no clue where Levasseur and his people were hiding, and no serious leads to pursue. The fact was, the two-year-old Bosluc task force had run out of energy. The prevailing view among its fifty or so members appeared to be that the UFF, like the FALN, would eventually make a mistake and get arrested, probably by some lucky sheriff.

That February, in a bid to revitalize the task force, the FBI brought in Leonard Cross, a clerkish, easygoing ex-marine who had earned accolades for breaking up a Croatian terrorist group believed to be responsible for bombings in New York. After several weeks debriefing task-force investigators and thumbing through the twenty-two thick volumes of reports they had amassed, Cross could see they were getting nowhere. About the only fresh idea he heard was in Maine, where an ex-con was scheduled to go on trial for helping the group in its very first bank job, all the way back in 1975. The Portland office planned to stake out the trial, on the remote chance Levasseur might stage a rescue attempt.

Probably the most innovative analysis, Cross saw, was being done by John Markey, an agent in Burlington, Vermont, who had been tracking the UFF's bank robberies since the South Burlington job in April 1982. At the time the UFF's involvement was only a hunch; with no "chatter" among Vermont criminals following a very professional job, Markey suspected that only Levasseur had the talent to pull it off. After four similar robberies along Interstate 90 in upstate New York, Markey issued a flier to every bank in the Northeast warning about the UFF. Indexing the dollar amounts of its hauls with the robbery dates, he estimated the group was living on $733 a day. At that rate, Markey warned, Levasseur would strike next between May 1 and June 12, 1984—and not, given the publicity lavished on Markey's flier by a Syracuse television station—in New York or New England. When the UFF robbed a bank in Norfolk, Virginia, on June 5, Markey telephoned the case agent and quipped, "It's your lucky day. I'm gonna tell you who just robbed your bank."

Back in Boston, Len Cross's first order of business was a reorganization. He had Bosluc redesignated a "domestic terrorism" task force, which streamlined its organization and upgraded its importance. He had a clerk break up the twenty-two volumes of reports into files for each bombing and bank job. Then he covered an entire wall of the Boston office with a map of New England, handed several boxes of color-coded pushpins to three agents, and had them mark the map with the UFF's every bank job, bombing, and address. When they finished, Cross stood before the map, hands on hips, and saw the pattern he hoped to find. The pushpins blanketed the Northeast, with the exception of a circular area centered on western Massachusetts, lapping into southern Vermont, northwestern Connecticut, and New York east of the Hudson.

"You know," he mused, "a pig never shits where it eats." The UFF, he was willing to bet, was hiding inside that circle.

To find out where, Cross devised what became the largest and most intricate manhunt in FBI history. He divided the target area into more than one hundred grids, most about ten miles square, and assigned an FBI agent and a state trooper to each. What made the UFF vulnerable, he thought, was their children. Computers were used to compile an exhaustive list of the four kinds of facilities Levasseur and the UFF families were known to haunt: Montessori and similar schools, pediatricians, pharmacies, and health food stores. The goal of "Operation Western Sweep," as it was called, was to display photos of the UFF fugitives at every such facility in southern Vermont, western Massachusetts, northwestern Connecticut, and most of eastern New York; they also planned to show photos of the remaining Brink's fugitives, including Marilyn Buck and Mutulu Shakur. By the time the operation was set to begin, in the first week of June, nearly two hundred agencies, from the FBI to local sheriffs, had agreed to contribute to the canvass.

Cross set up his war room in the middle of the target area, at a state police barracks in Westfield, Massachusetts. After a press conference on June 4— the day before the UFF struck in Norfolk—police and federal agents flooded into their zones; they checked schools, pharmacies, and pediatricians in 101 towns in western Massachusetts alone. Every evening someone from each grid square would bring reports to troopers stationed at the state border, who drove the reports to Westfield, where Cross had them entered into his computers.

For two solid weeks FBI agents and troopers visited every target in the zone. By June 19 they had finished, and Cross could finally, after weeks of preparation, see what they had achieved: nothing. Not a single hard lead.

"There were several hundred possible sightings which we are in the process of tracking down," Cross's FBI boss, James Greenleaf, told reporters, "but as yet we haven't come up with anything that sounds really exciting." And they wouldn't.

Cross couldn't believe it. He studied the data for weeks, hoping something would emerge. It never did. He realized they needed to go back to the drawing board. To begin, he convened a mass meeting of fifty state troopers and FBI and ATF agents at a Salem, New Hampshire, hotel in the middle of August. They had just settled in when the call came.

In early August, eight weeks after Operation Western Sweep, an auctioneer in Binghamton, New York, named Andy Walker was summoned to a U-Haul self-storage facility to cart out the contents of thirty compartments whose renters had failed to pay their upkeep. He loaded everything into his truck and hauled it back to his warehouse. It took days to inventory it all. At one point he was forced to break the lock off a battered foot locker. When he opened it, the first things he saw were parts of a shotgun. Delving further, he found wiring, alarm clocks, and literature—dozens of books and pamphlets, almost all devoted to radical politics. Walker walked to his telephone and called the FBI.

An agent from the Binghamton office was on his doorstep fifteen minutes later. Everything was carted to the FBI office, where the agent in charge, after leafing through the literature, had a hunch it might be Ray Levasseur's. A fingerprint analysis confirmed it. No one, however, could get too excited about going through things that had been sitting in a storage locker for two years. The boxes were sent to the FBI's Albany office, where they languished until Len Cross sent for them.

Inside the task force, Cross was among the few agents excited about the boxes from Binghamton. What on earth, more than one of his men said, could they learn from six-year-old gun parts and some musty old magazines? Cross had the boxes shipped to Boston anyway. When they arrived, he stacked them in a second-floor conference room and called in a trio of state troopers to help go through them all.

"Len, we're wasting time here," one remarked.

"We've got to," Cross said with a sigh. "These are leads."

They slid on rubber gloves and began lifting out the pamphlets and magazines. After barely a half hour a New Jersey trooper, Richie Barrett, said, "Oh, my God, Len, look at this." There, in a 1975 issue of *Dragon* magazine, was a diagram detailing how to build a bomb. As Cross peered at the article, Barrett said, "Look what it says about a brass screw." The diagram, Cross realized, was an exact match for Levasseur's bombs, down to the brass screw drilled into the faceplate. In a later *Dragon* they found an article explaining the best ways to write communiqués. Among the suggestions was mailing a copy of a copy of a copy. Cross had to smile. This was why they could never get any useful information off Levasseur's communiqués.

A little later Mike Nockunas, a Connecticut trooper, said, "Len, look at this." It was a catalogue for outdoor furniture. According to the postmark, it had been mailed in 1978 to someone named Jack Horning at 122 Mount Pleasant Street in Derby, Connecticut, just west of New Haven. "That's gotta be a safe house," Cross said.

Nockunas, a thirty-three-year-old trooper, volunteered to check the address. The next day he drove into Connecticut on the remote chance he could pick up Levasseur's six-year-old trail. In Derby he found the house, an aging two-bedroom in a blue-collar neighborhood, but the occupants knew no one named Horning. Neither did anyone else on Mount Pleasant Street. Nockunas began reinterviewing the neighbors, piecing together a picture of the area circa 1978. Finally he found a man who remembered two teenaged sisters who babysat for a family who might be the Hornings. Nockunas tracked down one of the girls, Jennifer Browne, now seventeen.* Yes, she remembered the Hornings and their two girls. In fact, she had photos of them. When the girl brought out a photo, Nockunas was startled to find himself staring into the faces of Ray Levasseur and Pat Gros.

For an hour he gently drew from Jennifer every memory of the Hornings. When she mentioned a car accident, Nockunas thought, "Bingo." An accident meant an accident report. By nightfall he was standing in the Derby Police Department, describing every detail of the long-ago wreck. The sergeant on duty said the records from 1977 and 1978 were in the basement, but he would look. Nockunas headed to Boston to brief Len Cross, and

---

*The name Jennifer Browne is a pseudonym.

as they were talking that night, the Derby sergeant called. In his hands he had a report of a one-car accident from September 2, 1978, at the foot of Mount Pleasant Street. "Paula Horning" was the driver, Jennifer Browne and an infant girl the passengers. The weird thing, the sergeant said, was that the name on Paula Horning's license wasn't Paula Horning. It was Judy Hymes.

This was a name they had never heard. Nockunas headed straight for his office in Meriden and all but ran to a computer terminal. He entered the "Judy Hymes" license in an FBI database. It was expired. But, he saw, it had been turned in for a new license in New York. A few more keystrokes and Nockunas saw the license had again been turned in, this time in Ohio. Then he saw it: the Judy Hymes in Ohio had just purchased a red-and-white Chevrolet van that August, two months before. The computer listed an address, 5318 North High Street, Box 65, in Columbus. Within minutes Nockunas had identified the address as that of a business called Mail Services Etcetera. It was a mail drop. It was, he realized with a start, an active UFF mail drop.

This was by far the best lead anyone had fielded in eight years. In Boston Len Cross got on the phone with the Cincinnati field office and explained the situation. An agent arrived at Mail Services Etcetera's office in a Columbus strip mall the next day. After working things out with the owner, agents installed a camera trained on Box 65, along with a buzzer that would sound in the manager's office if the box was opened from the outside. Agents rented a house across the street. If the buzzer sounded, the manager was to immediately call them.

On Monday, October 15, 1984, Cross had a four-man team in place to begin the surveillance; a new team would rotate in from Boston every week if necessary. The first day nothing happened. And the second. And the third. Apparently, Cross could see, this mail drop wasn't used much. At the end of that first week he sent out another team.

A second week passed with no sign of the Levasseurs, the Mannings, or the Laamans. In Washington supervisors began to grow restless. Multiagent stakeouts were expensive. How long was this going to take? Cross urged patience. This was the best lead they'd ever had, he emphasized. One of the Bureau's assistant directors, Oliver "Buck" Revell, gave him one final week. If the UFF hadn't checked its mail by Saturday, November 3, he was putting an end to the stakeout.

As it happened, Mike Nockunas was one of the four men manning the stakeout that week. There was little to do but drink coffee. Then, on that final Saturday morning, as the agents prepared to pack up, the phone rang. Box 65 had just been opened. Nockunas and the others stared at the monitor. There, standing in front of Box 65 across the street, was a face Nockunas knew well. "That's Patty Gros," he breathed.

A lookout said she was driving a white Chevy van with a red stripe down one side. Everyone scrambled into cars and wheeled toward the strip mall. In minutes they spotted the van as it left the parking lot. And then, amazingly, they saw a second, identical white Chevy van, a red stripe down the side. In the ensuing confusion, all but one of the pursuit cars elected to follow one van. The second van drew only a single car, driven by a Rhode Island trooper named Louis Reale.

The two processions headed in different directions through the streets of Columbus. Alone behind his van, Reale checked its license plate. After a few moments its registration came back: Judy Hymes. He had the right van. He got on the radio and tried to alert the rest of the pursuing agents, but in the heat of the chase, no one was willing to listen. It took several more minutes for the rest of the pursuing FBI agents and state troopers to let the other van go.

Reale kept his van in sight until the pilot of an FBI airplane, scrambled from a nearby airstrip, radioed that he was on it. Falling back now, relying on the aircraft, Reale followed its instructions as the van headed toward Interstate 71. By the time it reached the highway, he could see the other pursuit cars falling in behind him.

It was a gray, drizzly morning as the van, now with a half-dozen cars in loose pursuit, turned onto I-71, heading northeast toward Akron. In Boston Len Cross notified the FBI field offices in Cleveland, Detroit, and Pittsburgh. All were put on alert. High above central Ohio, meanwhile, FBI agents in the airplane watched as Gros repeatedly stopped at the roadside, stepped out and stretched, then drove the wrong way down an exit or two, common tactics used to identify pursuers. Clearly she knew what she was doing. Finally, one hundred miles north, they watched as she left the interstate at Exit 209, turning onto Route 224, heading east toward Akron. The trailing agents stayed well back for forty more miles, passing south of the city, until the van again left the highway, this time heading into a rural area between Akron and Youngstown. Barely a mile later agents in the airplane watched it turn into the driveway of a small house.

For the next hour, as agents on the ground stayed well away from the house, supervisors in Boston, Cleveland, and Washington debated whether to move in. As they did, two things happened. At one point a man emerged from the house and took a German shepherd for a walk in the yard. As the dog urinated, an agent was able to snap a long-distance photo. It was Ray Levasseur, they were certain. Then, a bit later, the airborne agents saw a second man emerge from the house, slide into a car, and drive out onto Route 225. As he headed north, two pairs of agents scrambled in pursuit.

For a half hour the agents followed as the car headed toward Cleveland. At one point it stopped in a rest area and the driver stepped out and used a pay phone. A minute later he returned to the car and continued north. The pursuing agents split up, one set following the car, the second heading for the pay phone. One of these agents quickly called the telephone company and asked for the number just dialed. Meanwhile, up ahead, the unidentified man in the car headed into the Cleveland suburbs. Within minutes his pursuers, a pair of New England troopers unfamiliar with Ohio roads, lost him.

It didn't matter. By dusk the number called from the pay phone had led the FBI, now augmented by the Cleveland police, to a two-story white frame house on West Twenty-second Street. In the windows agents could see jack-o-lanterns and Halloween decorations. Inside they were able to identify the man in the car, who turned out to be Richard Williams, as well as Jaan Laaman, Barbara Curzi, and their three children. As night fell, police took up positions all around the house. Down in Deerfield, meanwhile, the FBI brought in one of its Nightstalker aircraft, armed with infrared cameras and sensors, to watch the Levasseur home.

Throughout that Saturday night and into the morning of Sunday, November 4, FBI supervisors debated when and how to move in. They hadn't seen Tom and Carol Manning yet, and Len Cross argued persuasively that they should wait until they did. The Cleveland SAC, nominally in charge of the operation, agreed to hold off for now. But in the event that any of the suspects left their homes in the morning, all bets were off.

It was rainy and cold the next morning as Pat Gros tried to herd her squabbling daughters outside and into the van. Carmen, who was eight, and Simone, six, were arguing over who got to wear what. Rosa, still a toddler, was wobbling around the dining room, begging for attention. The German shepherd, now named Buck, was barking to be let out, and when he darted into the yard, Levasseur had to drag him back. Finally Gros got everyone out the door, then loaded desserts and gifts into the back with the girls. As she strapped them into their seats, Carmen popped a tape of Michael Jackson's *Thriller* into her boom box. Gros tied her hair back and slid behind the wheel. Levasseur sagged into the passenger seat and opened his newspaper.

It was Richard Williams's birthday, and they were having a party at the Laamans' house. As they swung out the driveway, Gros noticed that Levasseur seemed unusually relaxed. He normally had a nervous habit of glancing in the mirrors, but this morning he seemed interested only in the newspaper. He looked like another Ohio farmer, except for the 9mm pistol jammed into his waistband.

Out on the blacktop, she turned north toward Cleveland. Ten minutes later, as the windshield wipers kept a beat to Michael Jackson's yips and yelps, a Bronco with blackened windows suddenly roared by on the left. Then, as she watched, the Bronco's driver slammed on his brakes directly in front of them. As the Bronco slid to a stop on the wet pavement, Gros was forced to brake hard, pitching everyone in the van forward in their seatbelts.

"What the fuck are you doing, Pat?" Levasseur growled, crumpling his newspaper.

Before she could reply, the back of the Bronco opened and a man in body armor leaped out and aimed a pump shotgun at Levasseur's head.

"Oh, my God, Ray!" Gros cried.

Levasseur's first impulse was to run. But then he glanced through the rear window and saw a fleet of cars skidding to a halt all around. Within seconds more than fifty uniformed officers spilled out into the rain, training M16s and shotguns at the van. He made a face, glanced at Gros, then slowly rolled down his window and tossed out his pistol. In a flash an FBI agent ripped open his door, pulled him from his seat, and shoved him off the road onto the soggy lawn of a farmhouse. The home's owners stood in their bathrobes on the porch, arms crossed, as agents stripped off Levasseur's pants, yanked off his shoes, and slammed him facedown onto the wet grass. One agent nuzzled the barrel of an M16 into his ear and said, "That's it, Jack."

After a moment they rolled him onto his back. His eyes were ablaze. "Do you know who you're looking at?" he snarled.

No one said a thing.

"You're looking at a fucking revolutionary!"

The FBI men just stared. It was November 4, 1984. In two days Ronald Reagan and George Bush would be reelected to the White House. The word "revolutionary" no longer had any meaning in America, if it ever truly had. Lying there on a cold Ohio lawn, Ray Luc Levasseur was a spitting, snarling anachronism, a radical equivalent of the aging Japanese infantrymen found in Pacific caves well into the 1970s, men still fighting a war everyone else knew only from history books.

After a minute the agents flopped Gros down beside him. One wrapped the three girls in bulletproof vests and walked them over to say good-bye to their parents. "Where will you go?" Carmen asked her mother, tears welling in her eyes. Rosa and Simone stared at their feet.

"We'll probably be close by you," Gros said from the ground. "Give the men Grandma's number. You remember it, don't you? Don't let your sisters out of your sight. Stay together. And be brave."

The agents hustled the three little girls into the back of a squad car. Carmen rolled down the window, pushed back her long brown hair, and, as the car moved away, yelled, "I'll be brave, Mommy."

They arrested Laaman and Curzi and Williams later that day. The Manning family hadn't arrived yet, and quickly disappeared. They would remain at large for nearly six more months, eventually captured at their new home in Norfolk in April 1985.

EPILOGUE

On a cool evening in November 2010, two hundred people gathered at the Malcolm X and Dr. Betty Shabazz Center in Harlem for a memorial service celebrating the life of Marilyn Buck, who had died of cancer that summer, just a month after being released from federal prison. She had served twenty-five years.

The audience was a Who's Who of the old underground movement. Weather's Cathy Wilkerson sat in a rear corner beside her attorney, Elizabeth Fink. Beside them stood chiseled Ray Levasseur, looking fierce in a black knit cap. Kathy Boudin stood alone at the back. A BLA attorney, Robert Boyle, wandered among the crowd, shaking hands. Up front sat a tall African American man, Levasseur's old comrade Kazi Toure. One after another old friends rose to praise Buck—as a poet, as a friend, as a comrade. Someone read aloud a letter from Sekou Odinga. Amazingly, in more than an hour, no one said the words "bombing" or "bank robbery" or "murder" once. Buck's attorney was the only one who even came close, joking about what Buck would have thought of the Chase Manhattan branch that sat on a street corner outside.

A string of special guests was introduced. Linda Evans, the onetime Weatherman who was arrested with Buck in 1985, jogged down the aisle, smiling and waving her hands, as did two of the FALN women, friends from prison.

After about an hour Wilkerson and Fink rose to leave. "This is just too much," Wilkerson muttered. "This is ridiculous."

"This movement is dying, and no one here seems to know it," Fink agreed. "These people are just deluded. This is crazy."

No one that evening was in the mood to provide an honest assessment of what, if anything, the 1970s-era underground had achieved. But in terms of tangible successes, of hard-won political or moral victories, the short answer has to be: not much. They had launched a kind of war on America, and they had lost. Talk to the underground's veterans today—many of them in their sixties, most mellowed, some not—and almost all are hard pressed to point to any lasting impact the underground had on American society, short of metal detectors and bomb-sniffing dogs. While it drew the attention of law enforcement for more than a decade, the underground did little to force changes in the way America acted or was governed. Looking back across a chasm of forty years, those who pursued "armed struggle" might best be compared to the German "Werewolf" guerrillas who briefly attempted to resist Allied forces after the end of World War II, or to those Japanese infantrymen who emerged dazed from Pacific island caves decades after the war's end, not realizing that the fighting had stopped years before.

"It was all a mistake," Sekou Odinga admits today. "People weren't ready. People weren't ready for armed struggle. One of the things we now know, and should've known then, is we were way out in front of the people. A little more study would've made that clear. You can be a vanguard in the struggle, but you have to have the people behind you, and they weren't."

Asked what she and her peers achieved, Silvia Baraldini closes her eyes. "These things we did, they were in service of our politics." She looks down. "Sometimes I ask myself, was armed struggle necessary? Not necessarily. That's all I can say. But we thought so at the time. We thought so at the time. What matters is what we thought at the time."

"You have to understand, the underground, it became a cult," says Fink. "Weather, it was a cult. The SLA. The sixties drove them all crazy, all of us. All they did was listen to their own people, their own opinions. By '74, '75, when the war is over, you should have said, you know, 'What the fuck? The revolution isn't happening.' But they were crazy. I was part of that craziness. I know this to be true. It's just like the Middle East today, Al Qaeda, a lot of crazy people doing all this very bad shit."

One of the few positive legacies of the underground struggle, some of its adherents argue, is the example its leading figures set for young radical activists today, such as those in the "Occupy" movement. Young radicals today may not agree with, or be able to make sense of, the idea of protest bombings, but many clearly admire the passion and extreme commitment people like Bill Ayers devoted to trying to change America for the better. Ayers, who remains perhaps the most visible veteran of the underground struggle, is today an active author and lecturer; at bookstores and shopping malls young activists line up to get him to sign their books. The irony is lost on few of his peers. Ray Levasseur, who has completed his own memoir, wryly notes that articles he publishes on the Internet receive exponentially more exposure than any of the communiqués he issued after his many bombings.

What matters most about the underground, people like Cathy Wilkerson insist, is simply that it existed, that it demonstrated the lengths to which passionate Americans would go to confront what are now viewed, correctly, as Richard Nixon's corrupt government, an unjust war, and rampant racism at large in America. Three years after talking with her in that Brooklyn diner with her grandson, I asked Wilkerson what the underground had achieved. In an e-mail she replied:

> For the hundreds if not thousands of whites who engaged in some form of armed resistance, it mattered that we *chose* to step out of the encasing, protective cover of privilege—class and/or race—and take equal risk with those who had no choice but to fight for a better future. That our strategic choices were corrupted by the inherited arrogance of privilege is of secondary importance—both to me, looking back at it now, and to the many young people who continue to revisit our choices as a way to center themselves for the present. Few if any would argue we had some advanced insight into the mechanisms of political change, but many still take strength from the fact that we chose to identify with the victims of oppression and in that

commonness to wrestle with questions of social change, of some more beneficial course in relation to each other and to our planet.

She went on:

> The "Good German" metaphor hung over us, what happens if one doesn't pay attention. How easy, almost inevitable, it was to be complicit with the death and poisoning and starvation that resulted from exploitation. That is still true. To be complicit made us feel desperately unclean, rotting from within. While in retrospect our strategic choices were rooted in arrogance and ignorance, there are no regrets about the choice to do our best to acknowledge that rot and to rid ourselves of it. With age, we recognize that the struggle against the exterior forces—be they the laws of corporate profit, the advantages of racism, the inequality of resources—is co-joined with our inner struggles to live up to the best of human capacity both individual and social, our yearning for roses as well as bread, and our need to celebrate together. We didn't get this at all back then.
>
> Those with privilege really do not hear or see. The oppressed ask, what does it take to be listened to? The youth ask, what does it take to change things tomorrow—not in ten years or twenty. Does that ever really change? The issues we grappled with seem relevant today even if our solutions were lacking. We at least brought some of these issues to a larger public and since then a great many young people have thought about them as well.

This is perhaps the kindest way to view the underground struggle, as a well-meaning if misguided attempt to right America's wrongs. There are other observers, however, who argue persuasively that the crimes the underground committed overwhelm any altruistic motivations. The most insistent advocate of this view is a forty-nine-year-old New Jersey banker and writer named Joseph Connor, whose father, Frank, was one of those killed at Fraunces Tavern in 1975. In recent years Connor has launched what amounts to a one-man crusade to counter those who might applaud any aspect of the underground's legacy. He has testified against Oscar López's parole, appeared on Fox News to call Bill Ayers a "punk," and pressured the City College of New York to back off student-generated plans to name a building after Assata Shakur and Willie Morales.

Connor's campaign began that afternoon in January 1975 when, having just turned nine years old, he was waiting for his father to come home early to celebrate his birthday. "I remember my mom was making a meal," he says today. "It ended up being served to mourners at the funeral." Ever since, Connor has marveled at efforts to portray certain underground figures as anything other than murderers. "These people—the Weathermen, the FALN—they were deluded, self-motivated, egotistical, what's the word I'm looking for, people who just think of themselves and nobody else. It was all about them. They knew better than everybody else. You think of them as kids, and they were young for the most part, misguided youth. But they were murderers. Murderers first, revolutionaries second. They appointed themselves my father's judge, jury, and executioner. He represented something they didn't like, so they decided they had the right to kill him. Him and others."

But what truly drives him "mental," Connor goes on, is the notion that modern terrorism on U.S. soil dates only as far back as the first attack on the World Trade Center in 1993. "That gets me every time," he says. "To think that America thinks none of this ever happened, that it's not even remembered, it's astounding to me. You know, I blame the media. The media was more than happy to let all this go. These were not the kinds of terrorists the liberal media wanted us to remember, because they share a lot of the same values. They were terrorists. They were just the wrong brand. My father was murdered by the wrong politics. By leftists. So they were let off the hook. That's what we're left with today, a soft view of these people, when they were as hardened as anybody. They were just terrorists. Flat-out terrorists."

The men and women who peopled the '70s-era underground have gone on to lives as disparate as their backgrounds. Many who escaped prosecution reentered conventional society, embarking on belated careers as doctors, lawyers, and especially educators. Of those who were prosecuted, a dozen or so remain in prison, some more than forty years after their crimes; these include Mutulu

Shakur and his comrades Judy Clark and David Gilbert; Oscar López, the last of the FALN behind bars; Ray Levasseur's partners Tom Manning and Jaan Laaman; and Herman Bell and Anthony Bottom, now known as Jalil Muntaquim, convicted in the murders of Waverly Brown and Joseph Piagentini. Sekou Odinga was paroled in November 2014.

A number of deaths linked to underground groups, most notably the murders of Sergeant Brian McDonnell of the San Francisco police and the NYPD's Rocco Laurie and Greg Foster, remain unsolved. A handful of cases have been reopened in recent years, to mixed results. In 2003 the onetime BLA member Fred Hilton, now known as Kamau Sadiki, was successfully prosecuted for the 1971 murder of Atlanta police officer James Greene. Hilton had been living in Brooklyn, working as a Verizon repairman. Less successful was the prosecution of a group of onetime Black Panthers, including Herman Bell and Anthony Bottom, who came to be known as the "San Francisco Eight." They were indicted in January 2007 for the 1971 murder of Officer John V. Young at the city's Ingleside police station. Bell and Bottom pleaded guilty to voluntary manslaughter, while charges against the rest were eventually dropped.

Most veterans of the BLA melted into obscurity. Among the few to attract publicity in later years was Dhoruba bin-Wahad. After his first two trials ended in a hung jury and a mistrial, he was sentenced to twenty-five years to life for his alleged involvement in the shootings of patrolmen Curry and Binetti in 1971. In 1975 he sued to overturn his conviction, arguing that the government hadn't shared all it knew about his case. His litigation forced the FBI to divulge thousands of pages of documents about its notorious COINTELPRO harassment campaign, enough evidence that a judge finally freed bin-Wahad in 1990. After living for a time in West Africa, he resides today outside Atlanta. He turned seventy in 2015. Eldridge Cleaver died in 1998. Donald Cox died in 2013.

Thirty-seven years after her escape from a New Jersey prison, Assata Shakur still lives in Cuba. She operates a Web site, assatashakur.org, devoted to her revolutionary views. Despite periodic sightings around the world, there is no sense that the U.S. government has ever come close to apprehending her. In 2013 the FBI added her to its list of Most Wanted Terrorists, which produced a good deal of scoffing in some quarters. She remains a polarizing figure among those who knew her in her heyday. Silvia Baraldini, for one, believes that Shakur never did enough to help Sekou Odinga and others imprisoned for helping her escape. "Assata owes Sekou, she really does," says Baraldini. "In all their years in prison, I've never heard her once say, you know, there are people who really helped me, and they need your help. I've never heard her say that. And she needs to."

Baraldini was convicted of charges related to the prison break. Her forty-three-year sentence drew protests from leftists in her native Italy. Under an agreement with the Italian government, she was transferred to a prison outside Rome in 1999, freed on work release in 2001, and paroled in 2006. Today she lives with her partner, a chef, in Rome, where she sat for a series of interviews in 2013.

Several of her peers have not been so fortunate. Mutulu Shakur was captured in Los Angeles in 1986. Convicted of his role in the Brink's robbery, he drew a sixty-year sentence. He remains incarcerated today at a federal prison in Adelanto, California. Donald Weems, better known as Kuwasi Balagoon, died of AIDS in prison in 1986. After testifying against several of his comrades, Tyrone Rison is believed to have entered a witness protection program. Baraldini, for one, says his betrayal will never be forgotten. "Tyrone Rison, mark my words, he will be killed," she says today. "You think some things are over. That will never be over. Tyrone Rison will never be over."

Of the white activists who aided the Family, only Judy Clark and David Gilbert remain in New York prisons. Clark is at the Bedford Hills Correctional Facility for Women in Westchester County, where she trains guide dogs; she met with the author but declined to be interviewed on the record. Gilbert remains at the Auburn Correctional Facility in northern New York. An avid writer, he published a memoir in 2012. The other white women are now free. Susan Rosenberg received a fifty-eight-year sentence related to possession of explosives. She was granted clemency by President Clinton in 2001. Kathy Boudin was paroled from Bedford Hills in 2003. Today, after an appointment that drew criticism from the New York tabloids, she is an adjunct professor at the Columbia University School of Social Work.

After recovering from her self-inflicted gunshot wound following the

Brink's robbery, Marilyn Buck initiated one final chapter in her struggle against the U.S. government. Together with five other longtime underground figures, including Susan Rosenberg and the onetime Weatherman Laura Whitehorn, she formed the "Armed Resistance Unit," which took credit for eight bombings between 1983 and 1985, including a November 7, 1983, bombing of the U.S. Senate. That bomb, left under a bench, demolished a corridor, blowing off Senate Minority Leader Robert Byrd's office door. Buck was arrested in Dobbs Ferry, New York, in May 1985; the others were all rounded up as well. All drew lengthy sentences. All those still alive have been freed.

Six members of Ray Levasseur's United Freedom Front were convicted on conspiracy charges at a federal trial in Brooklyn in 1986. The highlight came when Levasseur, acting as his own attorney, cross-examined Edmund Narine, the would-be cabbie who lost his leg in the group's first bombing, at the Suffolk County Courthouse in 1976. (The group was later put on trial in Massachusetts, on charges of seditious conspiracy; this time all were acquitted or had charges dropped, in 1989.) Richard Williams, who also drew a life sentence for the murder of Trooper Philip Lamonaco, died of complications from hepatitis in a federal prison hospital in 2005. Tom Manning and Jaan Laaman remain in federal facilities today. Carol Manning, friends say, works in a factory in Maine. Pat Gros, who left Levasseur in the 1990s, is now a grandmother and works as a paralegal in Brooklyn.

Levasseur himself drew a forty-five-year sentence. He served his time at the federal prison in Atlanta and at the Colorado "Supermax" prison. After twenty years, a full thirteen of which were spent in solitary confinement, he was paroled in 2004. Today he lives with his second wife in a farmhouse they built in a field outside Belfast, Maine. Active in efforts to free underground figures who remain in prison, he turns seventy in 2016.

A second contingent of FALN fighters launched a brief second series of bombings, mostly in New York, in the early 1980s. Surveillance of a number of FALN supporters in the Chicago area eventually led the FBI to Willie Morales. In early 1983 the Bureau alerted Mexican authorities that Morales was hiding in the city of Puebla, southeast of Mexico City. When police went to arrest him, however, they found that Morales had five bodyguards. A shoot-out ensued. One policeman was killed, and all of the bodyguards. Morales was captured, but a U.S. extradition requests was denied, and he was eventually released and allowed to immigrate to Cuba, where he lives to this day.

Eighteen members of the FALN served lengthy prison sentences for their roles in the group's two campaigns. In the mid-1990s a clemency campaign drew the support of former president Jimmy Carter and ten Nobel Laureates. In 1999, with his wife, Hillary, seeking the support of Hispanic voters for a senatorial campaign in New York, President Bill Clinton offered clemency to sixteen of those imprisoned; all but two accepted. Both the House and the Senate passed measures condemning Clinton's action, which remains controversial in conservative circles to this day. Marie Haydee Torres, who (along with her husband) was not offered clemency, was released after serving almost thirty years, in 2009; today a friend says she lives in Miami. Carlos Torres was released from an Illinois prison in 2010. A crowd of five hundred supporters held a celebration in Chicago; an even larger crowd welcomed him on his return to Puerto Rico. Oscar López remains in a federal prison in Terre Haute, Indiana. He comes up for parole every few years. His supporters—and there are many in the Puerto Rican and radical communities—campaign for his release. In 2014 the Puerto Rican Day Parade in New York honored him as a "Puerto Rican patriot" who "was not convicted of a violent crime."

Of all those who went underground during the 1970s, few have gone on to more productive lives than alumni of the Weather Underground. Other than those who became involved with Mutulu Shakur, only Cathy Wilkerson served prison time, all of eleven months, on explosives charges related to the Townhouse. Most resumed more or less normal lives. Wilkerson remains a math instructor in the New York schools; she lives in Brooklyn with her long-time partner, the radical attorney Susan Tipograph. Ron Fliegelman worked as a special-education teacher in the New York schools for twenty-five years, retiring in 2007; today he and his wife live in Park Slope, Brooklyn, and are raising a son. Mark Rudd is a retired community college teacher in Albuquerque and gives talks about the sixties. Howard Machtinger lives in Durham, North Carolina, where he has worked as a high school teacher and at the University of North Carolina; he remains active in education reform efforts.

Jonathan Lerner is a writer in New York. Russell Neufeld practices law in Manhattan. Robbie Roth taught social studies at Mission High School in San Francisco. Clayton Van Lydegraf died in 1992. Annie Stein died in 1981. Mona Mellis died in 1993.

Several Weather alumni have risen to respected positions in their professions with very few knowing what they did in the 1970s. After attending law school, Paul Bradley, the pseudonym for one of Dohrn's right-hand men, went on to a twenty-five-year career at one of the nation's most prominent law firms. Today he lives in the Bay Area, where he advises a small start-up company or two; no one outside his family and other alumni has any clue that he spent years placing bombs in San Francisco–area buildings. Leonard Handelsman, a Weatherman in the Cleveland collective, went on to a distinguished career in psychiatry, becoming a full professor at Duke University, where he was medical director of the Duke Addictions Program. According to his longtime friend Howard Machtinger, who gave a eulogy when Handelsman died in 2005, no one outside his family knew of his life in the underground. Obituaries celebrated him only as a noted psychiatrist. Another Weatherman mentioned in this book became an accountant at a Big Four accounting firm in Vancouver. Today he is retired and active in local charities; he is not named here because of legal concerns. Another alumnus heads a children's charity in Ohio, where an Internet biography indicates he has been appointed by three governors to sit on state task forces.

Bernardine Dohrn has been a clinical associate professor of law at Northwestern University for more than twenty years. She has been active in efforts to reform the Chicago public schools and in international human rights activities. She has never disavowed her years as a Weatherman. Jeff Jones and Eleanor Stein were finally arrested in Yonkers, New York, in 1981 after the FBI received a tip on their whereabouts during the Brink's investigations. Jones received probation on old explosives charges and became an environmental writer and activist in upstate New York, where he and Stein live today. Stein received a law degree from Queens College in 1986 and is today an administrative law judge with the New York State Public Service Commission. Michael Kennedy, who represented certain of Weather's leaders, is today one of the most prominent attorneys in New York. Kennedy, who has served as a special adviser to the president of the United Nations General Assembly, lives with his wife, Eleanore, in a sumptuous apartment overlooking Central Park. Thanks to one of his old marijuana clients, he also happens to own *High Times* magazine.

All these people, from Mark Rudd to Bernardine Dohrn, had been living upright lives for more than twenty years when the final underground fugitives, those of the SLA, were arrested. The most celebrated of these cases was that of Kathy Soliah, who had avoided capture for almost twenty-five years when, in 1999, she was twice profiled on the television show *America's Most Wanted*. Following a viewer's tip, the FBI arrested her in St. Paul, Minnesota, where she was living as Sara Jane Olson; she had married a doctor, briefly lived in Zimbabwe, and given birth to three children. Taken back to California in handcuffs, Soliah initially pled guilty to a pair of old explosives charges, then withdrew her plea, after which she was sentenced to two consecutive ten-years-to-life terms.

The case generated a flurry of new interest in the SLA's murder of Myrna Opsahl at the Crocker National Bank robbery in 1975, which had never been prosecuted. In 2002 charges of first-degree murder were filed against Soliah, as well as Michael Bortin and Bill and Emily Harris, all of whom had been living quietly since brief jail sentences in the 1970s. Later that year police in South Africa arrested the last of the SLA fugitives, Jim Kilgore, who had been working under an assumed name as a history professor, married an American woman, and fathered two children. All five ended up pleading guilty; Emily Harris, now Emily Montague, admitted she had fired the fatal shot but insisted that the gun had gone off accidentally. The heaviest of the sentences was hers, eight years. By May 2009, when Kilgore was released, all had served their time. Today, of all those who joined the SLA, only Joseph Remiro remains behind bars, for the murder of Marcus Foster in 1973.

After her pardon and release from prison in 1979, Patty Hearst, now known as Patricia Campbell Hearst Shaw, married one of her bodyguards, Bernard Shaw, and settled down to a quiet life as a socialite and heiress. Today she is perhaps best known for occasional acting jobs, most notably in a series of cameos and small roles in movies by the independent filmmaker John Waters. Her husband, with whom she raised two children, died in 2013.

Hearst, like many of those who lived underground all those years ago, rarely speaks of her experiences today. Few do. Many have moved on; others will talk openly only with fellow radicals. When I put the question of legacy to Sekou Odinga, he heaved a heavy sigh and crossed his hands in his lap. He was sixty-eight the day we spoke. "Will I be remembered?" he asked. "I don't really care. Let's be real. What I care about are my children, and your children, and the children of tomorrow. I want them to study the past, and learn about it and carry on. Because America has only gotten worse. It has. At some point it's gonna fall, because all empires fall. It's on its way right now. There's not going to be any America in fifty years. There's not. And the youth of today has to be ready to pick up the pieces when that happens."

ACKNOWLEDGMENTS

This book, like so many others, is built on the kindnesses extended by so many people, from friends and family to research assistants to my fellow writers and historians. I have been very fortunate to work for and with some of the most talented people in media and publishing. Graydon Carter, the editor of *Vanity Fair* magazine, where I have had the privilege to write for twenty-three years, remains the very best in the business, probably one of the best ever. For twenty-one of those years I have worked with the same amazing editor, Doug Stumpf, whose patience I have probably tested more during this book than all my other books combined. His assistant, Jaime Lalinde, has been invaluable, and is surely on his way to a long career in this business. Andrew Wylie, my agent now for a startling twenty-six years, is unsurpassed; it is a rare gift to work with an agent this prominent and this capable, yet who rarely fails to return a message inside ten minutes. Andrew's colleague Jeff Posternak has overseen my daily hand-holding for years. I could not do this without Jeff. In Los Angeles, Brian Siberell at the Creative Artists Agency has been *Days of Rage*'s biggest proponent. Thanks to you all.

At Penguin Press, Scott Moyers edited this book with his typical sure hand. Mally Anderson orchestrated the prepublishing process with aplomb. Karen Mayer provided valuable guidance. My friend Kurt Eichenwald read the first two chapters and made useful suggestions. Daisy Prince and Ben Kalin tracked down hard-to-find news clippings. Melissa Goldstein gathered the photos. Joyce Pendola handled the fact-checking, a grueling six-month process that saved me severe professional embarrassment.

And then there is Liz Fink. I should pause here to offer a special word of thanks to the estimable Ms. Fink, who is probably best known in New York as one of the lead attorneys on the long-running litigation springing from the Attica riots in 1971. There is a word journalists use for a person who knows everything about his or her subject matter, and who offers unlimited help: the "rabbi." Over time, Liz became the rabbi for this book. Her knowledge of the 1970s-era underground is encyclopedic, and her memory is superb. It was Liz who introduced me to many of the important figures of the era, people like Ray Levasseur, Dhoruba bin-Wahad, and Silvia Baraldini, none of whom had ever publicly discussed details of their underground careers. I am deeply grateful to Liz and to the other radical attorneys, especially Dennis Cunningham and Robert Boyle, who gave me guidance along the way.

A number of people lent a hand gathering documents used in *Days of Rage*. These include Claude Marks at the Freedom Archives in San Francisco, who did so despite the fact that he clearly never trusted me; and James Mathis and the wonderful archivists at the Library of Congress and also at New York University's Tamiment Library, an incredible repository of left-wing history.

A far-flung network of retired FBI agents was indispensable, especially Don Wofford and Lou Vizi, who pursued the FALN; Stockton Buck, who pursued the New World Liberation Front; Leonard Cross, who pursued Ray Levasseur's group; Max Noel, William Reagan, and Donald Shackleford, the Weather Underground; and Danny Coulson, Jim Murphy, and Bob McCartin, the BLA. Perhaps the most generous of these men was Richard Hahn of Southern California, who laid out the entire story of the FALN, directing me to many of the sources he had made researching his own as-yet-unpublished book. A huge thanks to Rick, and to all those who took the time to offer guidance.

This book was produced during a challenging period in my life, a time when I have leaned on family and close friends as never before. My deepest thanks go to Winnie O'Kelley, who always gave wise counsel; to Brett Haire, who has looked after me like a member of his own family; to Ed and Mary-beth Leithead, who always had steaks and a bottle of red at the ready; and especially to the two young men I am proud to call my sons: Griffin Burrough, today a freshman and budding writer at Kenyon College; and Dane Burrough, a rising scholar of Russian history at Rice University. Thanks also to my parents, John M. and Mary Burrough of Temple, Texas, who were never too busy to listen, no matter the hour, and to Margaret Walsh.

Bryan Burrough
Austin, Texas
Winter 2015

A NOTE ON SOURCES

I produced *Days of Rage* much the way I wrote and researched my previous books. Much of the information in these pages comes from one of three main kinds of sources: previously published books, contemporary newspaper and magazine articles, and personal interviews. Documents generated by the FBI and the NYPD, along with an oral history or two, were also used.

Like many history writers, I have made books written by other authors the foundation of my research. They're the first items I collect, and are often the most authoritative version of public events. Some sections of *Days of Rage*, especially those dealing with Sam Melville, the SLA, and the Family, rely heavily on books written in the 1970s and 1980s. Other sections, especially chapters dealing with the Weather Underground, the BLA, the FALN, and Ray Levasseur's group, rely much more on personal interviews augmented by contemporary news coverage. Below I've sketched out the principal sources of information for each chapter. Full details on the books I mention can be found in the bibliography.

Chapter 1: The main sources for the story of Sam Melville and Jane Alpert are Alpert's excellent 1981 memoir, *Growing Up Underground*, and Albert A. Seedman and Peter Hellman's uproarious 1974 book, *Chief!* I also used information from the three major New York newspapers and Melville's FBI file, obtained via the Freedom of Information Act. Jane Alpert declined an invitation to be interviewed.

Chapter 2: To chart the rise of the Black Power movement, I relied on dozens of books. Probably the best single source of information was Peniel E. Joseph's 2007 *Waiting 'til the Midnight Hour*, a history of Black Power.

Chapter 3: The story of Weatherman's birth has been told in a number of books and memoirs, but perhaps the best account is one that few of them reference, Peter Collier and David Horowitz's trailblazing 1981 article in *Rolling Stone*, from which I drew liberally. The best of the SDS books by far is Kirkpatrick Sale's *SDS*. I've augmented these sources with contemporary news coverage and interviews of more than a dozen Weathermen.

Chapter 4: The story of Weatherman's initial ninety days underground is the first chapter derived largely from personal interviews, as are the following seven chapters. Among the most helpful interview subjects for this chapter were Howard Machtinger, Joanna Zilsel, Cathy Wilkerson, Jon Lerner, Paul Bradley, Mark Rudd, Ron Fliegelman, Brian Flanagan, Rick Ayers, Robert Roth, and Elizabeth Fink. Thai Jones's book, *A Radical Line*, gives information on Jeff Jones's introduction to the underground. Wilkerson's memoir, *Flying Too Close to the Sun*, gives the best account of Terry Robbins and the Townhouse. The late Larry Grathwohl's memoir, *Bringing Down America*, is an important source for the Midwest collective's exploits.

Chapters 5, 6, and 7: These three chapters, which constitute the story of Weatherman's rebirth and most significant political actions, draw on many of the same sources as chapter 4, including personal interviews with those mentioned above. William Dyson's story is told in an oral history given for the Society of Retired Special Agents of the FBI. The story of Squad 47 is told in contemporary news accounts, by onetime federal prosecutors, and by retired agents. Marvin Doyle's story is told in an unpublished monograph that Doyle shared with the author. Robert Greenfield's biography of Timothy Leary provides details of Leary's escape. Wesley Swearingen's story is told in his memoir, *FBI Secrets*. The story of the FBI investigations leading to the Encirclement is told with the help of newly released FBI documents on file at the National Archives, along with interviews of Dennis Cunningham, Max Noel, and William Reagan, among others.

Chapters 8, 9, and 11: The story of the BLA was pieced together from a variety of sources, including FBI documents on file at the National Archives; copies of wiretapped conversations between BLA operatives and Algeria provided by Robert Boyle; NYPD reports shared by a retired New York detective; parts of several histories of the Black Panther Party; contemporary news accounts, especially those in the *New York Daily News* and *New York Times*; as well as personal interviews with Sekou Odinga, Cyril Innis, Dhoruba bin-Wahad, Oscar Washington, Thomas McCreary, Danny Coulson, Jim Murphy, and Bob McCartin. A New York–area detective still investigating old BLA cases was also interviewed extensively. Also helpful were copies of the BLA organ, *Right On!*, on file at New York University's Tamiment Library. Assata Shakur's background is related in her memoir, *Assata*.

Chapter 10: This chapter draws on many of the same sources noted above. The story of the Cunningham-Mellis family's involvement was provided by Dennis Cunningham; his daughter, Delia Mellis; Elizabeth Fink; Cathy Wilkerson; Paul Bradley; Marvin Doyle; and William Reagan.

Chapters 12 and 13: The story of the SLA was principally derived from three histories of the group, especially Patty Hearst's memoir, told to Alvin Moscow, *Every Secret Thing*, and *The Voices of Guns* by Vin McClellan and Paul Avery. Also helpful were contemporary news accounts and several long articles in *Rolling Stone*. The story of George Jackson and the radicalization of California prisons is told in several books, especially the superb *The Rise and Fall of California's Radical Prison Movement* by Eric Cummins.

Chapter 14: The sections on the SLA were derived from the sources cited above, and those on the Weather Underground from internal Weather documents as well as the author's interviews. The opening section of the FALN story was first outlined to me by the retired FBI agent Richard Hahn. The FALN section in this chapter is largely derived from contemporary news accounts and extensive personal interviews with Don Wofford and Lou Vizi.

Chapter 15: The story of the New World Liberation Front was pieced together from contemporary news accounts and the author's interviews, especially those with Tony Serra, Stockton Buck, and three retired federal and local prosecutors. A 1978 master's thesis by Baron Lee Buck (no relation) contains the most detailed list of NWLF bombings.

Chapter 16: The story of the Weather Underground's demise was told largely via the author's interviews with alumni of Weather and the Prairie Fire Operating Committee, especially Russell Neufeld, Jonathan Lerner, Howie Machtinger, Silvia Baraldini, Elizabeth Fink, Cathy Wilkerson, Paul Bradley, and Ron Fliegelman. The story of Squad 47's demise and subsequent prosecution was assembled from contemporary accounts and personal interviews, especially those with Bill Gardner, Stephen Horn, and Donald Strickland.

Chapter 17: The story of the FALN's middle years was derived from contemporary news coverage and the author's interviews, especially those with Don Wofford, Lou Vizi, Roger Young, Richard Hahn, and Elizabeth Fink. The story of José and Oscar López's upbringing was adapted from a long essay written by José López and posted on the Internet.

Chapters 18, 19, and 23: The story of Ray Levasseur's group is derived largely from the author's extensive interviews with Levasseur and Pat Gros Levasseur, augmented by contemporary news articles and voluminous court records kept at the National Archives branch outside Boston (since closed).

Chapters 20, 21, and 22: The story of the Family is told in John Castelluci's definitive book *The Big Dance* and augmented here by information contained in news accounts, court records, and the author's exclusive interviews with Sekou Odinga and Silvia Baraldini.

NOTES

PROLOGUE

1. Joseph P. Fried, "Eleven Hurt by Bombs in 2 Movie Houses," *New York Times*, May 2, 1970.

CHAPTER 1: "THE REVOLUTION AIN'T TOMORROW. IT'S NOW. YOU DIG?"

1. Jane Alpert, *Growing Up Underground*, p. 179.
2. *New York Times*, Nov. 16, 1969.

CHAPTER 2: "NEGROES WITH GUNS"

1. Peniel Joseph, *Waiting 'til the Midnight Hour*, p. 17.
2. Eldridge Cleaver, *Target Zero*, p. xiv.
3. Curtis J. Austin, *Up Against the Wall*, p. 95.
4. Nikki Giovanni, "The True Import of Present Dialogue, Black vs. Negro (For Peppe, Who Will Ultimately Judge Our Efforts)," *The Collected Poetry of Nikki Giovanni: 1968–1998*.

CHAPTER 3: "YOU SAY YOU WANT A REVOLUTION"

1. Kirkpatrick Sale, *SDS*, p. 335.
2. Peter Collier and David Horowitz, "Doing It: The Inside Story of the Rise and Fall of the Weather Underground," *Rolling Stone*, Sept. 30, 1982, p. 87.

3. Cited in Tim Weiner, *Enemies*, p. 284.
4. Collier and Horowitz, p. 87.
5. Ibid., p. 88.
6. Ibid.
7. Sale, p. 603.
8. Collier and Horowitz, p. 91.
9. Mark Rudd, *Underground*, p. 181.
10. Collier and Horowitz, p. 91.
11. Cathy Wilkerson, *Flying Close to the Sun*, p. 303.
12. Bill Ayers, *Fugitive Days*, p. 179.

CHAPTER 4: "AS TO KILLING PEOPLE, WE WERE PREPARED TO DO THAT"

1. Collier and Horowitz, p. 98.
2. Larry Grathwohl, *Bringing Down America*, pp. 138–39.
3. *New York Times*, Feb. 22, 1970.
4. Wilkerson, p. 336.
5. Ibid., pp. 338–40.
6. Rudd, p. 194.
7. Wilkerson, p. 343.
8. Ibid., p. 344.
9. Thomas Powers, *Diana*, p. 142.

CHAPTER 5: THE TOWNHOUSE

1. Susan Braudy, *Family Circle*, p. 205.

2. *New York Times*, Mar. 12, 1970.

3. This version of the first minutes after the explosion has not previously been told. It results from a close reading of two sources. In his 1974 memoir, *Chief!*, Albert A. Seedman described the actions of Officers Waite and Calderone and included Calderone's description of someone calling for "Adam." However, Seedman believed that the two survivors, Wilkerson and Boudin, had already left the site; writing four years after the incident, when many details remained unknown, Seedman mistakenly assumed that the person calling for Adam must have been another, unidentified survivor. There were no other survivors. In her 2007 memoir, Wilkerson remembers calling for Adam. The Wilkerson and Seedman accounts agree that this happened immediately before a third and final explosion. The only conclusion to be drawn is that Wilkerson and Boudin were still in the wreckage when Calderone came to the back door. When they crawled free, no officers were present; Calderone was in the rear, and Waite had run for help. By the time officers returned to the front of the house, the women were gone. How differently events might have unfolded had the NYPD arrested Boudin and Wilkerson when, in those first few minutes, they had their opportunity.

4. Seedman, p. 257.

5. Ibid., p. 269.

6. Ayers, p. 201.

7. Thai Jones, *A Radical Line*, p. 219.

8. Rudd, pp. 214–15.

9. David Gilbert, *No Surrender*, e-book.

10. *New York Times*, June 14, 1970.

CHAPTER 6: "RESPONSIBLE TERRORISM"

1. *New York* magazine, Feb. 18, 1991.

2. Rudd, p. 226.

3. Robert Greenfield, *Timothy Leary*, p. 386.

4. Thai Jones, p. 223.

5. Greenfield, p. 394.

6. Terry H. Anderson, *The Movement and the Sixties*, p. 353.

7. *New York Times*, Oct. 13, 1970.

8. *New York Times*, Aug. 16, 1970.

CHAPTER 7: THE WRONG SIDE OF HISTORY

1. Wesley Swearingen, *FBI Secrets*, p. 72.

2. *Washington Post*, Jan. 6, 2008.

3. *New York Times*, Feb. 7, 1971.

4. Cited in Rick Perlstein, *Nixonland*, p. 542.

5. Anderson, p. 357.

6. Collier and Horowitz, p. 109.

CHAPTER 8: "AN ARMY OF ANGRY NIGGAS"

1. *New York Times*, Nov. 7, 1972; Daley, *Target Blue*, pp. 75–76.

2. Frank J. Rafalko, *MH/CHAOS*, p. 110.

CHAPTER 10: "WE GOT PRETTY SMALL"

1. *New York Times*, Aug. 19, 1976.

CHAPTER 11: BLOOD IN THE STREETS OF BABYLON

1. *New York Times*, Jan. 26, 1973.

2. *New York Daily News*, Jan. 9, 1974.

3. Danny Coulson and Elaine Shannon, *No Heroes*, pp. 73–77.

CHAPTER 12: THE DRAGON UNLEASHED

1. Eric Cummins, *The Rise and Fall of California's Radical Prison Movement*, p. 159.

2. Ibid., p. 164.

3. Ibid., pp. 240–41.

4. Les Payne and Tim Findley, *The Life and Death of the SLA*, p. 7.

CHAPTER 13: "PATTY HAS BEEN KIDNAPPED"

1. Payne and Findley, p. 267.

CHAPTER 14: WHAT PATTY HEARST WROUGHT

1. "FALN Terrorists Tied to 10 Bombings in Region," *New York Times*, Feb. 7, 1975.

CHAPTER 15: "THE BELFAST OF NORTH AMERICA"

1. Patty Hearst, *Every Secret Thing*, p. 370.
2. Ibid., p. 385.
3. *San Francisco Chronicle*, Jan. 14, 1976.
4. *San Francisco Chronicle*, Sept. 4, 1977.

CHAPTER 16: HARD TIMES

1. Dan Berger, *Outlaws of America*, pp. 216–17.

CHAPTER 17: "WELCOME TO FEAR CITY"

1. "Episcopal Leaders Badly Split over Hispanic Issue," *New York Times*, Mar. 22, 1977.
2. "Sifting Through Rubble and Rage of Blasts," *New York Daily News*, Aug. 4, 1977.
3. Molly Ivins, "100,000 Leave New York Offices as Bomb Threats Disrupt City," *New York Times*, Aug. 4, 1977, pp. 1, 26.

CHAPTER 19: BOMBS AND DIAPERS

1. *Waterbury Republican*, Mar. 3–4, 1978.

CHAPTER 20: THE FAMILY

1. *New York Times*, Sept. 17, 1977.
2. *New York Times*, Jan. 17, 1973.

3. John Castellucci, *The Big Dance*, p. 73.
4. Richard Hahn, unpublished FALN manuscript, p. 185.
5. Richard Esposito and Ted Gerstein, *Bomb Squad*, p. 82.
6. Castellucci, p. 74.

CHAPTER 21: JAILBREAKS AND CAPTURES

1. *New York Daily News*, May 23, 1979.
2. *Milwaukee Journal*, Dec. 26, 1979.
3. *New York Times*, Dec. 22, 1979.

CHAPTER 22: THE SCALES OF JUSTICE

1. Castellucci, p. 153.
2. Ibid., p. 197.

CHAPTER 23: THE LAST REVOLUTIONARIES

1. *Brattleboro Examiner*, Oct. 5, 1981.

BIBLIOGRAPHY

BOOKS

A collection of biographies and Safiya Bukhari. *Can't Jail the Spirit: Political Prisoners in the U.S.* Chicago: Editorial El Coqui, 1988.

Ahmad, Muhammad. *We Will Return in the Whirlwind: Black Radical Organizations 1960–1975.* Chicago: Charles H. Kerr Publishing Company, 2007.

Alexander, Shana. *Anyone's Daughter: The Times and Trials of Patty Hearst.* New York: Viking, 1979.

Alpert, Jane. *Growing Up Underground.* Secaucus, N.J.: Citadel, 1990.

Anderson, Terry H. *The Movement and the Sixties: Protest in America from Greensboro to Wounded Knee.* New York: Oxford University Press, 1995.

Anthony, Earl. *Spitting in the Wind: The True Story Behind the Violent Legacy of the Black Panther Party.* Malibu: Roundtable Publishing, 1990.

Armstrong, Gregory. *The Dragon Has Come.* New York: Harper & Row, 1970.

Austin, Curtis J. *Up Against the Wall: Violence in the Making and Unmaking of the Black Panther Party.* Little Rock: University of Arkansas Press, 2008.

Ayala, César J., and Rafael Bernabe. *Puerto Rico in the American Century: A History Since 1898.* Chapel Hill: University of North Carolina Press, 2007.

Ayers, Bill. *Fugitive Days: A Memoir by Bill Ayers.* New York: Penguin, 2001.

Ayers, Bill, and Bernardine Dohrn. *Race Course: Against White Supremacy.* Chicago: Third World Press, 2009.

Barber, David. *A Hard Rain Fell: SDS and Why It Failed.* Jackson: University of Mississippi Press, 2008.

Bates, Tom. *Rads: A True Story of the End of the Sixties.* New York: HarperCollins, 1992.

Berger, Dan. *Outlaws of America: The Weather Underground and the Politics of Solidarity.* Oakland: AK Press, 2006.

Bin Wahad, Dhoruba, Mumia Abu-Jamal, and Assata Shakur. *Still Black, Still Strong: Survivors of the U.S. War Against Black Revolutionaries.* Brooklyn: Semiotext, 1993.

Block, Diana. *Arm the Spirit: A Woman's Journey Underground and Back.* Oakland: AK Press, 2009.

Blunk, Tim, and Raymond Luc Levasseur, eds. *Hauling Up the Morning.* Trenton, N.J.: The Red Sea Press, 1990.

Braudy, Susan. *Family Circle: The Boudins and the Aristocracy of the Left.* New York: Alfred A. Knopf, 2003.

Brisbane, Robert H. *Black Activism: Racial Revolution in the United States, 1954–1970.* Valley Forge: Judson Press, 1974.

Bryan, John. *This Soldier Still at War.* New York: Harcourt Brace Jovanovich, 1975.

Bukhari, Safiya. *The War Before: The True Life Story of Becoming a Black Panther, Keeping the Faith, and Fighting for Those Left Behind.* New York: Feminist Press, 2010.

Cannato, Vincent J. *The Ungovernable City: John Lindsay and His Struggle to Save New York.* New York: Basic Books, 2001.

Carroll, Peter N. *It Seemed Like Nothing Happened: America in the 1970s.* New Brunswick: Rutgers University Press, 1982.

Castellucci, John. *The Big Dance: The Untold Story of Weatherman Kathy Boudin and the Terrorist Family That Committed the Brink's Robbery Murders.* New York: Dodd Mead, 1986.

Churchill, Ward, and Jim Vander Wall. *The Cointelpro Papers: Documents from the FBI's Secret Wars Against Dissent in the United States.* Cambridge: South End Press, 1990, 2002.

Cleaver, Eldridge. Ed. Kathleen Cleaver. *Target Zero: A Life in Writing.* New York: Palgrave Macmillan, 2006.

Cleaver, Kathleen, and George Katsiaficas. *Liberation, Imagination and the Black Panther Party: A New Look at the Panthers and Their Legacy.* New York: Routledge, 2001.

Cohen, Robert Carl. *Black Crusader: A Biography of Robert Franklin Williams.* Radical Books, 2008.

Collier, Peter, and David Horowitz. *Destructive Generation: Second Thoughts About the Sixties.* New York: Simon & Schuster, 1989.

Coulson, Danny, and Elaine Shannon. *No Heroes: Inside the FBI's Secret Counter-Terror Force.* New York: Pocket Books, 1999.

Craven, Carolyn, Tim Findley, and Les Payne. *The Life and Death of the SLA (Symbionese Liberation Army): A True Story of Revolutionary Terror.* New York: Ballantine, 1976.

Cummins, Eric. *The Rise and Fall of California's Radical Prison Movement.* Palo Alto: Stanford University Press, 1994.

Daley, Robert. *Prince of the City: The True Story of a Cop Who Knew Too Much.* Boston: Houghton Mifflin, 1978.

———. *Target Blue: An Insider's View of the NYPD.* New York: Delacorte, 1973.

Davis, James Kirkpatrick. *Spying on America: The FBI's Domestic Counterintelligence Program.* Westport, Conn.: Praeger Publishers, 1992.

DeBray, Régis. *Revolution in the Revolution?* New York: Grove Press, 2000.

————. *Praised Be Our Lords: The Autobiography.* London: Verso, 2007.

De Toledano, Ralph. *J. Edgar Hoover: The Man in His Time.* New Rochelle: Arlington House, 1973.

Dohrn, Bernardine, Bill Ayers, and Jeff Jones. *Sing a Battle Song: The Revolutionary Poetry, Statements, and Communiqués of the Weather Underground, 1970–1974.* New York: Seven Stories, 2006.

Donner, Frank. *Protectors of Privilege: Red Squads and Police Repression in Urban America.* Berkeley: University of California Press, 1990.

Dunbar-Ortiz, Roxanne. *Outlaw Woman: A Memoir of the War Years, 1960–1975.* San Francisco: City Lights, 2001.

Echols, Alice. *Daring to Be Bad: Radical Feminism in America, 1967–1975.* Minneapolis: University of Minnesota Press, 1989.

Esposito, Richard, and Ted Gerstein. *Bomb Squad: A Year Inside the Nation's Most Exclusive Police Unit.* New York: Hyperion, 2007.

Fanon, Frantz. *The Wretched of the Earth.* New York: Grove Press, 1963.

Farber, David. *The Age of Great Dreams: America in the 1960s.* New York: Hill and Wang, 1994.

Felt, Mark. *The FBI Pyramid: From the Inside.* New York: G. P. Putnam's Sons, 1979

Felt, Mark, and John O'Connor. *A G-Man's Life: The FBI, Being "Deep Throat," and the Struggle for Honor in Washington.* New York: Public Affairs, 2006.

Frankfort, Ellen. *Kathy Boudin and the Dance of Death.* New York: Stein & Day, 1983.

Frum, David. *How We Got Here: The 70s: The Decade That Brought You Modern Life (for Better or Worse).* New York: Basic Books, 2000.

Gilbert, David. *No Surrender: Writings from an Anti-Imperialist Political Prisoner.* Montreal: Abraham Guillen Press, 2004.

Giovanni, Nikki. "The True Import of Present Dialogue, Black vs. Negro (For Peppe, Who Will Ultimately Judge Our Efforts)," *The Collected Poetry of Nikki Giovanni: 1968–1998.* New York: Harper Perennial, 2007.

Gitlin, Todd. *The Whole World Is Watching: Mass Media in the Making and Unmaking of the New Left.* Berkeley: University of California Press, 2003.

Graebner, William. *Patty's Got a Gun: Patricia Hearst in 1970s America.* Chicago: University of Chicago Press, 2008.

Grathwohl, Larry. *Bringing Down America: An FBI Informer with the Weathermen.* New Rochelle: Arlington House, 1976.

Gray, L. Patrick, with Ed Gray. *In Nixon's Web: A Year in the Crosshairs of Watergate.* New York: Times Books, 2008.

Greenfield, Robert. *Timothy Leary: A Biography.* New York: Harcourt, 2006.

Guy, Jasmine. *Afeni Shakur: Evolution of a Revolutionary.* New York: Atria Books, 2004.

Hearst, Patricia Campbell, with Alvin Moscow. *Every Secret Thing.* New York: Pinnacle Books, 1982.

Hendry, Sharon Darby. *Soliah: The Sara Jane Olson Story.* Bloomington, Minn: Cable Publishing, 2002.

Hewitt, Christopher. *Political Violence and Terrorism in Modern America: A Chronology.* Westport, Conn.: Praeger Security International, 2005.

Hilliard, David, with Keith and Kent Zimmerman. *Huey: Spirit of the Panther.* New York: Thunder's Mouth Press, 2006.

Jackson, George. *Soledad Brother: The Prison Letters of George Jackson.* Chicago: Lawrence Hill Books, 1994.

Jackson, George L. *Blood In My Eye.* Baltimore: Black Classic Press, 1990.

Jacobs, Ron. *The Way the Wind Blew: A History of the Weather Underground.* London: Verso, 1997.

Jeffreys-Jones, Rhodri. *The FBI: A History.* New Haven: Yale University Press, 2008.

Jenkins, Philip. *Decade of Nightmares: The End of the Sixties and the Making of Eighties America.* New York: Oxford University Press, 2006.

Jones, Charles E. *The Black Panther Party [Reconsidered].* Baltimore: Black Classic Press, 1998.

Jones, Thai. *A Radical Line: From the Labor Movement to the Weather Underground, One Family's Century of Conscience.* New York: Free Press, 2004.

Jonnes, Jill. *South Bronx Rising: The Rise, Fall, and Resurrection of an American City.* New York: Fordham University Press, 2002.

Joseph, Peniel E. *Waiting 'til the Midnight Hour: A Narrative History of Black Power in America.* New York: Henry Holt & Co., 2006.

Jurgensen, Randy, and Robert Cea. *Circle of Six: The True Story of New York's Most Notorious Cop Killer and the Cop Who Risked Everything to Catch Him.* New York: Disinformation, 2007.

Kayton, Bruce. *Radical Walking Tours of New York City.* New York: Seven Stories Press, 1999, 2003.

Kempton, Murray. *The Briar Patch: The Trial of the Panther 21.* New York: Da Capo Press, 1973.

Kessler, Ronald. *The FBI: Inside the World's Most Powerful Law Enforcement Agency.* New York: Pocket Books, 1993.

———. *The Bureau: The Secret History of the FBI.* New York: St. Martin's Press, 2002.

Killen, Andreas. *1973 Nervous Breakdown: Watergate, Warhol, and the Birth of Post-Sixties America.* New York: Bloomsbury, 2006.

Kirkpatrick, Rob. *1969: The Year Everything Changed.* New York: Skyhorse, 2009.

Klehr, Harvey. *Far Left of Center: The American Radical Left Today.* New York: Transaction, 1988.

Kunstler, William M., with Sheila Isenberg. *My Life as a Radical Lawyer.* New York: Citadel Press, 1994.

Langum, David J. *William M. Kunstler: The Most Hated Lawyer in America.* New York: New York University Press, 1999.

Lardner, James, and Thomas Reppetto. *NYPD: A City and Its Police.* New York: Henry Holt, 2000.

Leary, Timothy. *Confessions of a Hope Fiend.* New York: Bantam, 1973.

———. *The Fugitive Philosopher.* Berkeley: Ronin, 2007.

Lerner, Jonathan. *Alex Underground.* Penpowerpublishing, 2009.

Leuci, Robert. *All the Centurions: A New York City Cop Remembers His Years on the Street, 1961–1981.* New York: HarperCollins, 2004.

Levy, Peter B. *Civil War on Race Street: The Civil Rights Movement in Cambridge, Maryland.* Gainesville: University Press of Florida, 2003.

Liberatore, Paul. *The Road to Hell: The True Story of George Jackson, Stephen Bingham, and the San Quentin Massacre.* New York: The Atlantic Monthly Press, 1996.

Lockwood, Lee. *Conversation with Eldridge Cleaver; Algiers.* New York: Dell, 1970.

Maas, Peter. *Serpico.* New York: Viking, 1973.

Mahler, Jonathan. *Ladies and Gentlemen, the Bronx Is Burning: 1977, Baseball, Politics, and the Battle for the Soul of the City.* New York: Farrar, Straus and Giroux, 2005.

Marable, Manning. *Race, Reform, and Rebellion: The Second Reconstruction and Beyond in Black America, 1945–2006.* Jackson: University Press of Mississippi, 2007.

Marighella, Carlos. *MiniManual of the Urban Guerrilla.* Montreal: Abraham Guillen Press, 2002.

McGuckin, Frank, ed. *Terrorism in the United States.* New York: H. W. Wilson, 1997.

McLellan, Vin. *The Voices of Guns.* New York: G. P. Putnam's Sons, 1977.

McWhorter, Diane. *Carry Me Home: Birmingham, Alabama, the Climactic Battle of the Civil Rights Revolution.* New York: Simon & Schuster, 2001.

Miller, Chris, and Jerry Roberts. *Hermosa Beach.* Charleston, S.C: Arcadia, 2005.

Newton, Huey P. *Revolutionary Suicide.* New York: Penguin, 2009.

Newton, Michael. *Bitter Grain: Huey Newton and the Black Panther Party.* Los Angeles: Holloway House, 1980.

O'Neill, William L. *The New Left: A History.* Wheeling, Ill.: Harlan Davidson, 2001.

O'Reilly, Kenneth. *Racial Matters: The FBI's Secret File on Black America, 1960–1972.* New York: Free Press, 1989.

Payne, Les, and Tim Findley with Carolyn Craven. *The Life and Death of the SLA.* New York: Ballantine Books, 1976.

Perlstein, Rick. *Nixonland: The Rise of a President and the Fracturing of America.* New York: Simon and Schuster, 2008.

Pickering, Leslie James. *Mad Bomber Melville.* Portland: Arissa Media Group, 2007.

Piercy, Marge. *Vida.* New York: Summit Books, 1979.

Powers, Richard Gid. *Broken: The Troubled Past and Uncertain Future of the FBI.* New York: Free Press, 2004.

Powers, Thomas. *Diana: The Making of a Terrorist.* Boston: Houghton Mifflin, 1971.

Rafalko, Frank J. *MH/CHAOS: The CIA's Campaign Against the Radical New Left and the Black Panthers.* Bethesda, Md.: Naval Institute Press, 2011.

Raskin, Jonah. *Out of the Whale: Growing Up in the American Left.* New York: Links, 1974.

Raskin, Jonah, ed. *The Weather Eye: Communiqués from the Weather Underground.* New York: Union Square Press, 1974.

Rhodes, Jane. *Framing the Black Panthers: The Spectacular Rise of a Black Power Icon.* New York: New Press, 2007.

Rorabaugh, W. J. *Berkeley at War: The 1960s.* New York: Oxford University Press, 1989.

Rosen, James. *The Strong Man: John Mitchell and the Secrets of Watergate.* New York: Doubleday, 2008.

Rosenberg, Susan. *An American Radical: Political Prisoner in My Own Country.* New York: Kensington, 2011.

Rudd, Mark. *Underground: My Life with SDS and the Weathermen.* New York: HarperCollins, 2009.

Sale, Kirkpatrick. *SDS: The Rise and Development of the Students for a Democratic Society.* New York: Random House, 1973.

Scheutz, Janice. *The Logic of Women on Trial: Case Studies of Popular American Trials.* Carbondale: Southern Illinois University Press, 1994.

Schulman, Bruce J. *The Seventies: The Great Shift in American Culture, Society, and Politics.* New York: Da Capo, 2001.

Seedman, Albert A., and Peter Hellman. *Chief!: Classic Cases from the Files of the Chief of Detectives.* New York: Avon, 1974.

Shakur, Assata. *Assata: An Autobiography.* Chicago: Lawrence Hill Books, 2001.

Silverman, Al. *Foster and Laurie.* Boston: Little, Brown, 1974.

Smith, Brent L. *Terrorism in America: Pipe Bombs and Pipe Dreams.* Albany: State University of New York Press, 1994.

Sobel, Lester A., ed. *Political Terrorism, Volume 2, 1974–78.* New York: Facts on File, 1978.

Stern, Susan. *With the Weathermen: The Personal Journal of a Revolutionary Woman.* New York: Doubleday, 1975.

Sullivan, William C., with Bill Brown. *The Bureau: My Thirty Years in Hoover's FBI.* New York: W. W. Norton, 1979.

Swearingen, Wesley M. *FBI Secrets: An Agent's Exposé.* Boston: South End Press, 1995.

Tanenbaum, Robert K., and Philip Rosenberg. *Badge of the Assassin.* New York: Dutton, 1979.

Thompson, Becky. *A Promise and a Way of Life: White Antiracist Activism.* Minneapolis: University of Minnesota Press, 2001.

Torres, Andrés, and Jose E. Velázquez, eds. *The Puerto Rican Movement: Voices from the Diaspora.* Philadelphia: Temple University Press, 1998.

Van Middeldyk, R. A. *The History of Puerto Rico.* Charleston, S.C.: BiblioBazaar, 2006.

Varon, Jeremy. *Bringing the War Home.* Berkeley: University of California Press, 2004.

Wagenheim, Kal, and Olga Jiménez de Wagenheim, eds. *The Puerto Ricans: A Documentary History.* Princeton, N.J.: Markus Wiener Publishers, 2008.

Wagner, James, with Patrick Picciarelli. *My Life in the NYPD: Jimmy the Wags.* New York: Onyx, 2002.

Washington, Nuh. *All Power to the People.* Toronto: Arm the Spirit, 2002.

Weiner, Tim. *Enemies: A History of the FBI.* New York: Random House, 2012.

Wilkerson, Cathy. *Flying Close to the Sun.* New York: Seven Stories, 2007.

Williams, Evelyn A. *Inadmissible Evidence: The Story of the African-American Trial Lawyer Who Defended the Black Liberation Army.* Lincoln, Neb.: iUniverse.com, 2000.

Wolfe, Tom. *Radical Chic & Mau-Mauing the Flak Catchers.* New York: Picador, 2009.

Woodward, Bob. *The Secret Man: The Story of Watergate's Deep Throat.* New York: Simon & Schuster, 2005.

Zimroth, Peter L. *Perversions of Justice: The Prosecution and Acquittal of the Panther 21*. New York: Viking, 1974.

PAMPHLETS

Bukhari, Safiya Asya. *Coming of Age: A New Afrikan Revolutionary*. Chicago: Spear & Shield Publications, undated.

Coordinating Committee, Black Liberation Army. *Message to the Black Movement: A Political Statement from the Black Underground*. Montreal: Abraham Guillen Press, undated.

In Her Spirit. Commemorative pamphlet celebrating the life of Marilyn Buck, 2010.

Muntaqim, Jalil. *On the Black Liberation Army*. Montreal: Abraham Guillen Press, undated.

Robert and Mabel Williams Resource Guide. San Francisco: Freedom Archives, 2005.

Williams, Robert F. *Self-Respect, Self-Defense, and Self-Determination*. San Francisco: Freedom Archives, 2005.

FILMS

Alegria, Andres, Claude Marks, and Freedom Archives. *Legacy of Torture: The War Against the Black Liberation Movement*. 28-min. DVD, Freedom Archives.

Johnson, Anita, and Claude Marks. *Prisons on Fire: George Jackson, Attica & Black Liberation*. CD, Prison Radio Project and Freedom Archives.

Self-Respect, Self-Defense, & Self-Determination. 72-min. video, Freedom Archives.

Valadez, John, Peter Miller, and Susanne Rostock. *Passin' It On: The Black Panthers' Search for Justice*. DVD, Docurama, 2006.

Voices of Three Political Prisoners. Three 10-min. videos, Freedom Archives.

What We Want, What We Believe. The Black Panther Party Library, Roz Payne Archives and Newsreel Films.

INDEX

IMAGE CREDITS